THE ART OF PROGRAMMING

Computer Science with C

Steven C. Lawlor
Foothill College

PWS PUBLISHING COMPANY

I(T)P® *An International Thomson Publishing Company*

Boston • Albany • Bonn • Cincinnati • Detroit • London • Madrid • Melbourne • Mexico City
New York • Pacific Grove • Paris • San Francisco • Singapore • Tokyo • Toronto • Washington

PWS Publishing Company
20 Park Plaza
Boston, MA 02116-4324

I⊤P®

International Thomson Publishing
The trademark ITP is used under license.

Library of Congress Cataloging-in-Publication Data
Lawlor, Steven C.
     The art of programming: computer science with C
        p.   cm.
     Includes index.
     ISBN 0-314-06814-7 (soft: alk. paper)
   1. C (Computer program language)   2. Electronic
digital computers—Programming.   I. Title.
QA76.73.C15L39   1996
005.13'3—dc20
                                           95-38925
                                               CIP

Sponsoring Editor: *David Dietz*
Marketing Manager: *Nathan Wilbur*
Composition: *The Curtis Company*
Copyeditor: *Mark Woodworth*
Interior Design: *Linda M. Robertson*
Cover Image: *Comstock*
Printing & Binding: *West Publishing Company*

Printed and bound in the United States of America.
00 01 02 — 10 9 8 7 6

 *This text is printed on
recycled, acid-free paper.*

For more information, contact:
PWS Publishing Company
20 Park Plaza
Boston, MA 02116

International Thomson Publishing Europe
Berkshire House
168–173 High Holborn
London WC1V 7AA
England

Thomas Nelson Australia
102 Dodds Street
South Melbourne, 3205
Victoria, Australia

Nelson Canada
1120 Birchmont Road
Scarborough, Ontario
Canada M1K 5G4

International Thomson Editores
Campos Eliseos 385, Piso 7
Col. Polanco
11560 Mexico D.F., Mexico

International Thomson Publishing GmbH
Königswinterer Strasse 418
53227 Bonn, Germany

International Thomson Publishing Asia
221 Henderson Road
#05-10 Henderson Building
Singapore 0315

International Thomson Publishing Japan
Hirakawacho Kyowa Building, 31
2-2-1 Hirakawacho
Chiyoda-ku, Tokyo 102
Japan

CONTENTS

PREFACE   **xv**

Chapter 1   **COMPUTERS AND PROGRAMMING**   **1**

How We Got Here: A Brief History (Optional)   **2**
    Early Efforts   3
    Modern Computer Generations   6
        Your Turn 1–1   *7*

The Computer System   **7**

Hardware   **8**
    Access to Data   8
    The CPU   8
    Main Memory   10
    Secondary Storage   11
    Input and Output   11
    Following Instructions   11
    A Simple Addition Operation   12

Software   **13**
    Operating Systems   14
        Your Turn 1–2   *14*

The Nature of Data   **15**

Number Systems: Ours and the Computer's   **15**
    Binary Numbers   16
    Hexadecimal Numbers (Optional)   17

Characters in the Computer   **19**

Units of Data Storage   21

The Bit   21
Bytes   22
Words   22
    Your Turn 1–3   *23*

Computer Languages   23

Language Levels   23
From Source to Execution   24
Integrated Development Environments   25

Modular Design   25

The Programming Process   26

Programming Stages   27
    Your Turn 1–4   *33*

Summary   33

Key Terms (in order of appearance)   33
Concept Review   34
Heads Up: Points of Special Interest   36
Your Turn Answers   37

Exercises   39

Program   40

Chapter 2

THE C LANGUAGE   41

The Language   42

Forming a C Program   43

Outline Form   44
Comments   44
Directives   44
Statements   45
Functions   45
    ANSI C Extra: The Main Function   *47*
Declarations   47
    Your Turn 2–1   *47*

Values In C   48

Numeric Values   48
Character Values   48
    Nuts 'n' Bolts: Special Characters   *49*

Simple Output   49

    Your Turn 2–2   *50*

Variables   50

Variable Names   50

Data Types and Declarations   52

Declarations   52
Integral Data Types   53
Floating-Point Data Types   55
String Data   56
    Your Turn 2–3   *57*

Arithmetic Expressions   58

Integer Arithmetic   60
Mixed Arithmetic   61
    Nuts 'n' Bolts: Mixed Arithmetic   *61*

Assignment   62

Forced Conversions   64
    Your Turn 2–4   *64*

Putting It Together   64

Summary   68

Key Terms (in order of appearance)   68
Concept Review   68
Heads Up: Points of Special Interest   70
Traps: Common Programming Errors   71
Your Turn Answers   71

Exercises   73

Programs   74

Chapter 3

BUILDING A C PROGRAM   77

Developing a Style   78

Modularity   78
Documentation   79
Commenting   80
Readability   80
    Your Turn 3–1   *81*

Directives   81

Including Header Files   81
Character Replacements   82
    Nuts 'n' Bolts: Defined Constants Versus Variables   *83*
    Your Turn 3–2   *83*

Streams   83

Output   84
Conversion Codes   85
Size Modifiers   87
Width and Precision   88

Input   90
Conversion Codes   91
Prompts   92
Size Modifiers   93
Flushing the Input Stream   95
Your Turn 3–3   96

Putting It Together   96

Summary   101
Key Terms (in order of appearance)   101
New Functions (in order of appearance)   101
Concept Review   101
Heads Up: Points of Special Interest   102
Traps: Common Programming Errors   103
Your Turn Answers   104

Exercises   105

Programs   106

Chapter 4

THE SELECTION STRUCTURE   111

Structured Programming   112
The Sequence Structure   113

The Selection Structure   114
Your Turn 4–1   116

Conditions   117
Relational and Equality Operators   117
Logical Operators   118
Your Turn 4–2   119
Nuts 'n' Bolts: What's True and What's False?   120

Statement Blocks   120

The if Statement   120
The else Clause   124
Nuts 'n' Bolts: More About Truth   124
The else if Construct   127
Your Turn 4–3   129

The switch Statement   129
Your Turn 4–4   135

Putting It Together   135

Summary   140
Key Terms (in order of appearance)   140
New Statements (in order of appearance)   140
Concept Review   140
Heads Up: Points of Special Interest   141
Traps: Common Programming Errors   142
Your Turn Answers   142

Exercises   144

Programs   145

Chapter 5

THE ITERATION STRUCTURE   149

The Iteration Structure   150

Loops In C   152
Pretest Loops   153
Posttest Loops   155
Sentinel Values   156
    Your Turn 5–1   157

Accumulating and Counting   158
Accumulation Operators   159

Counter-Controlled Loops   162
Using Floating-Point Counters   164
    Nuts 'n' Bolts: More on for   164
Increment and Decrement Operators   165
    Nuts 'n' Bolts: Increment and Decrement   166
Increment and Decrement in Expressions (Optional)   167
    Your Turn 5–2   167

Nested Loops   168
Rows and Columns   169
    Your Turn 5–3   170

Putting It Together   171

Summary   175
Key Terms (in order of appearance)   175
New Statements (in order of appearance)   176
Concept Review   176
Heads Up: Points of Special Interest   177
Traps: Common Programming Errors   177
Your Turn Answers   178

Exercises   179

Programs   180

Chapter 6	**FUNCTIONS**	**187**

How Functions Work   188
The Function Definition   190
The Function Call   191
The Function Declaration   192
The Function Return   193
Local Variables   194
The Return Statement   196
Passing Values   198
The Function Prototype   198
Why Use Functions?   203

External Variables   203
Your Turn 6–1   205

Some Existing Functions   205
Header Files   205
printf() and scanf() Revisited   206
Terminating a Program   208
Some Mathematical Functions   210
Random Numbers   211
Casts   213
Your Turn 6–2   215

Recursion (Optional)   215
Recursion or Iteration?   217

Putting It Together   218

Summary   223
Key Terms (in order of appearance)   223
New Statements and Functions (in order of appearance)   223
Concept Review   224
Heads Up: Points of Special Interest   225
Traps: Common Programming Errors   225
Your Turn Answers   226

Exercises   227

Programs   229

Chapter 7	**ARRAYS**	**237**

Indexed Variable Names   238

Array Declarations   238

Initializations   239
    Non ANSI C: Initializations of Arrays   240

The Variably Defined Variable   240

    Nuts 'n' Bolts: How Many Elements Are in Your Array?   241
    Nuts 'n' Bolts: The Zero Element   242
    Your Turn 7–1   247

Arrays and Functions   247

    Your Turn 7–2   251

Array Applications   252

Sequential Search   252
Binary Search   254
Parallel Arrays   256
Inserting   258
Sorting   260
    Your Turn 7–3   265

Arrays with More than One Index   265

Initializing Multiple-Indexed Arrays   267
Accessing Multiple-Indexed Arrays   268
Passing Multiple-Indexed Arrays to Functions   269
    Your Turn 7–4   272

Putting It Together   272

Summary   276

Key Terms (in order of appearance)   276
Concept Review   278
Heads Up: Points of Special Interest   279
Traps: Common Programming Errors   279
Your Turn Answers   279

Exercises   281

Programs   283

Chapter 8

STRINGS   291

String Values   292

String Values Versus Character Values   292

String Variables   293

Declaration and Initialization   293

String Assignments   294

    Your Turn 8–1   295

String Input   295

String Output   300
    Your Turn 8–2   *302*

String Manipulations   302
    Your Turn 8–3   *307*

Arrays of Strings   307
    Your Turn 8–4   *309*

Converting Between Numbers and Strings   309
    Numbers to Strings   309
    Strings to Numbers   310
        ANSI C Extra: Other ANSI Conversion Functions   *311*

Character Classification   312

Character Conversions   314
    Your Turn 8–5   *315*

Pointers—A First Glance   315
    Your Turn 8–6   *319*

Taking Strings Apart   319
    Your Turn 8–7   *323*

Putting It Together   323

Summary   331
    Key Terms (in order of appearance)   331
    New Functions (in order of appearance)   331
    Concept Review   334
    Heads Up: Points of Special Interest   335
    Traps: Common Programming Errors   336
    Your Turn Answers   336

Exercises   338

Programs   340

Chapter 9

FILES   347

File Identifiers   348

Buffered Input and Output   349

Opening Files   350
    File Modes   351
    Binary Versus Text Files   351

Closing a file   352
Your Turn 9–1   353

Character Access to files   353
Formatted Access   353
Single-Character Access   357
String Access   357
Your Turn 9–2   360

Moving the File Position Indicator   360
ANSI C Extra: Other File Position Indicator Access   362

File Housekeeping   364

Finding the End of a File   367
Function Error Returns   367
The End-of-File Function   367
Your Turn 9–3   368

Byte Access to Files   368
Your Turn 9–4   371
Nuts 'n' Bolts: Byte Access and Portability   372

Putting It Together   372
Creating a File for Testing   374
The `main()` Function and Menu   376
Printing the File   379
Adding to the File   381
Deleting from the File   383
Changing a Title   386
Changing the Numbers   388

Summary   391
Key Terms (in order of appearance)   391
New Functions (in order of appearance)   391
Concept Review   392
Heads Up: Points of Special Interest   393
Traps: Common Programming Errors   394
Your Turn Answers   394

Exercises   396

Programs   397

Chapter 10	**POINTERS**	**403**

Addresses and Pointers   404
The Pointer Data Type   404
Pointer Variables   406
Dereferencing   407

Pointers and Functions   409
Returning More than One Value   410
Using Returns and Pointers   412
Your Turn 10–1   415

Putting It Together   415

Pointers and Arrays   420
Offsets from the Base Address   421
Pointer Notation   421
Pointer Arithmetic   422
Your Turn 10–2   423

Putting It Together   423

Pointers and Strings   427
Pointer Versus Array Notation   428
Ragged Arrays   429
Arguments to the `main()` Function   434
Your Turn 10–3   436

Putting It Together   436

Allocating Memory   439
Your Turn 10–4   441
ANSI C Extra: Other Memory-Allocation Functions   441

Summary   441
Key Terms (in order of appearance)   441
New Functions (in order of appearance)   442
Concept Review   442
Heads Up: Points of Special Interest   443
Traps: Common Programming Errors   443
Your Turn Answers   444

Exercises   445

Programs   449

Chapter 11

RECORD-BASED DATA   **455**

Structures   456
Definitions and Declarations   456
Initializations   458
The `sizeof` a Structure   459

Accessing Structures   460
Non ANSI C: Assigning Structures   463
Your Turn 11–1   463

Arrays of Structures   **463**

Pointers to Structures   **466**

Structures and Functions   **469**
    Non ANSI C: Passing Structures   *470*
    Your Turn 11–2   *474*

Linked Lists (Optional)   **475**
    Structures Pointing to Structures   476
    Inserting into a Linked List   477
    Deleting from a Linked List   481
    Your Turn 11–3   *484*

Files and Structures   **484**

Direct Access to Files   **487**
    Your Turn 11–4   *489*

Putting It Together   **489**

Summary   **495**
    Key Terms (in order of appearance)   495
    Concept Review   496
    Heads Up: Points of Special Interest   497
    Traps: Common Programming Errors   498
    Your Turn Answers   498

Exercises   **499**

Programs   **501**

Chapter 12

THE PREPROCESSOR AND OTHER FEATURES   507

The Preprocessor   **508**

File Inclusion   **509**

Macro Replacement   **510**
    Nuts 'n' Bolts: String Functions?   *510*
    Parameterized Macros   511
    Nuts 'n' Bolts: Rescanning Macros   *512*
    Stringizing and Token Pasting   514
    Nuts 'n' Bolts: Macro or Function?   *515*
    A Macro's Lifetime   515
    Your Turn 12–1   *516*

Conditional Compilation   **516**
    Nuts 'n' Bolts: Comment Out or Conditionally Compile?   *519*

Preprocessor Error Messages   519

Renaming Data Types   520
 Your Turn 12–2 *522*

Putting It Together (The Preprocessor and typedef)   522

The Enumeration Data Type   524
 Nuts 'n' Bolts: enum *Values* *527*

The Conditional Expression   527

Combining Expressions   529
 Your Turn 12–3 *531*

Nonstructured Program Flow   531
 Labels 532
 Unconditional Transfers 532
 Jumping to the End of a Loop 533
  Your Turn 12–4 *536*

Unions   537
 Your Turn 12–5 *541*

Summary   541
 Key Terms (in order of appearance) 541
 New Statements (in order of appearance) 541
 Concept Review 541
 Heads Up: Points of Special Interest 543
 Traps: Common Programming Errors 544
 Your Turn Answers 544

Exercises   546

Programs   548

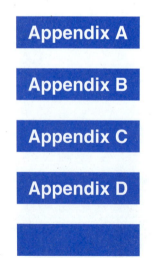

Appendix A **ASCII TABLE** **551**

Appendix B **OPERATORS IN PRECEDENCE** **553**

Appendix C **FUNCTION REFERENCE** **555**

Appendix D **printf() AND scanf() PARAMETERS** **561**

INDEX **563**

PREFACE

Is computer programming an art or is it a science? If done well, the answer is yes—to both questions. The scientific basis of computer programming is demonstrated in the constant application of the scientific method. We are faced with a problem; we formulate hypotheses—programs—to solve the problem; and we test the programs to prove their effectiveness in solving the problem.

Art, though, plays at least as important a part in the programming process. In almost any kind of situation that can be dealt with using computers, there is more than one possible solution—more than one program that will do the job. The programming artist will find the most effective solution, the one that not only satisfies the elements of the problem but also does so most efficiently and with greatest ease of use. Equally importantly, the artist will present the solution in a manner that is easily understood by the rest of the programming community.

With this book, Students can learn not only the science of programming—algorithm development and testing—but also the art of programming—proven techniques for program development and presentation.

THE OBJECTIVES OF THIS BOOK

Programming courses must combine two objectives that do not always overlap. One is to teach language syntax and usage—which words perform what actions on the computer. The second is to teach program development—how to efficiently and cleanly develop a computer solution for a problem. There must always be some tradeoffs between these objectives. The trick is to cover both objectives with the fewest tradeoffs, and to do so in a manageable and teachable unit.

The major objective of this book is the latter—program development—but in order to fulfill that objective, the student must have a working mastery of the former—language syntax and usage. The book combines these objectives by introducing programming concepts and immediately reinforcing them with the language concepts needed to implement them. The student learns a programming concept and is able to practice it immediately. By the end of the book, the student should be comfortable with good programming practice, and will have been exposed to most of ANSI C.

PROGRAMMING FUNDAMENTALS

The book is intended as an introduction to programming. No previous programming experience or knowledge of computers is required or expected. The student is introduced to proper and accepted techniques of structured program development—top-down design, modularity, encapsulation, and data abstraction. Examples throughout the book will show the entire development process clearly traced through the five major steps in program development:

1. **Task**. Identification of the problem to be solved.
2. **Analysis**. An in-depth analysis of the task including outputs and inputs, internal data requirements, and data relationships and formulas.
3. **Design**. The process for designing the solution including the statement of an overall algorithm and the stepwise refinement of that algorithm to a detailed solution.
4. **Implementation**. Translating the design into a computer program, clearly keyed to the design with comments and structure.
5. **Test**. Deciding on testing procedures and showing the results of the program, including execution charts for detailed analysis of the solution.

Structured, modular programming is always stressed. Too often it is tempting to forget structure in simple processes, but if good habits are not developed from the outset, the bad habits developed by default will be hard to break later.

THE PROGRAMMING LANGUAGE

Developing solutions which cannot be tested and implemented is no fun at all. It's like concocting a recipe for a delicious cake and not being able to bake it and taste it. In addition, it is an incomplete learning experience. The cake might be great or a disaster. How would you ever know?

The vast majority of our programming and computer science courses, then, use some computer language to practice the programming process. Increasingly, that language is C. C is a good choice for a number of reasons. The language is at a high enough level to allow implementation of proper structure and clear modularity, but it can access the computer at a low enough level to utilize some of the more basic features of the computer. C is also a commercially popular language. The student will not have to learn a language simply to demonstrate programming techniques and then never see it again in the real world. In addition, many C implementations have effective integrated development environments that make programming easier and less daunting for the beginner.

PEDAGOGICAL ELEMENTS

The book is meant to be accessible and nonthreatening for the student. To that end a number of pedagogical features are built into the book.

In-Chapter Features

▼ **Writing Style.** The writing style is purposely informal, designed to be open and friendly. Students will gain nothing from a book they won't read.

▼ **Chapter Previews.** Each chapter starts with a preview informing the students of the kinds of knowledge they should be expecting from the chapter.

▼ **Memory Diagrams.** A solid understanding of C requires a solid understanding of the interaction of the language with the computer's memory. These diagrams show sections of memory and the changes that take place as a result of a program's actions. There are examples throughout the book, but see the ones on pages 10 and 413.

▼ **Execution Charts.** These charts trace the execution of programs line by line, variable by variable. Students can look at the code presented, and be led carefully through its execution with all the features and pitfalls clearly outlined. They appear at the end of each chapter, and at key points within the chapters.

▼ **Margin Notes.** All important points are addressed within the flow of the text, but concepts of special note are referred to in short margin notes alongside the paragraphs that contain the full explanation. This allows a smooth text flow, sharp highlighting of key points, and efficient review.

Heads Up. These margin notes focus on key points of program design and implementation. There are good examples on almost every page.

Traps. Possible programming problems and common errors are addressed within the text flow, but highlighted by the *Traps* in the margin. Examples abound, but see the ones on pages 80, 192, or 410.

▼ **Your Turn.** At the end of each logical section—two to seven times per chapter—there are reading-reinforcement questions. The answers to these are collected at the end of each chapter.

▼ **Nuts 'n' Bolts Boxes.** These are optional boxes on the underpinnings of the C language.

▼ **ANSI C Extra and Non ANSI C Boxes.** These optional boxes show ANSI C features that complete the standard language but are not necessarily needed for demonstrating basic programming concepts. They also highlight differences between the ANSI standard and typical K&R implementations of C. *Nuts 'n' Bolts*, *ANSI C Extra*, and *Non ANSI C* boxes allow the student to delve into the language in more depth, and allow the instructor greater flexibility to adjust the depth of the course.

▼ **Putting It Together.** At least at the end of each chapter, but often at other key points in the chapter, a *Putting It Together* section appears following a more complete example of the materials just covered. These features follow a program through the full development process—task, analysis, design, implementation, and test—and always include detailed *Execution Charts* for the code produced.

End-of-Chapter Features

▼ **Key Terms.** These are collected in their order of appearance at the end of each chapter.

▼ **New Functions and Statements.** Brief descriptions of new functions and statements introduced in the chapter are collected here.

▼ **Concept Review.** Important concepts are summarized at the end of each chapter.

▼ **Traps and Heads Up Summaries.** All the *Traps* and *Heads Up* margin notes are gathered in this one place at the end of each chapter.

▼ **Exercises.** Student exercises at the end of each chapter require not just regurgitation of the material but the ability to effectively apply the chapter's concepts.

▼ **Problems.** Programming problems reinforce the chapter's materials. Most of the programs show expected outputs and give a list of suggested variables.

End-of-Text Features

▼ **Operators in Precedence.** Appendix B pulls together all the ANSI C operators, in precedence, and with examples of their usage. This one-page appendix may become the most dog-eared page of the student's textbook.

▼ **Function Reference.** Appendix C contains a reference to all the functions introduced in the book. For each function it shows the function prototype, outlines the purpose and parameters of the function, and gives the possible return values.

▼ **Quick Reference Card.** The last page of the book is a two-sided, card-stock, tear-out page containing one-line prototypes for all the functions introduced with the header file that contains the declaration for each function. This card can be used by the student during programming sessions, and some professors may allow the students to refer to it during tests.

MODULARITY AND FLEXIBILITY

Just as modularity is an important part of programming, it is an important part of this book. Courses vary considerably in the depth and in the order in which they cover language elements; therefore, the book has been organized with maximum flexibility. A course of instruction may be tailored to the individual needs and tastes of a professor or academic situation by assembling the modules of the book in a variety of forms. Almost any type of presentation can be accommodated in a smooth, orderly format.

Optional Features

Many of the sections of the book may be excluded from an individual course without loss of continuity. These sections fall within three categories:

1. **Boxes.** Any of the *Nuts 'n' Bolts*, *ANSI C Extra*, and *Non ANSI C* boxes may be included or excluded at the professor's discretion.

2. **Optional Modules.** Many of the modules within the chapters are marked as optional. Any or all of these may be excluded:

    How We Got Here: A Brief History (Chapter 1, page 2)
    Hexadecimal Numbers (Chapter 1, page 17)
    Incrementing and Decrementing in Expressions (Chapter 5, page 167)
    Recursion (Chapter 6, page 215)
    Linked Lists (Chapter 11, page 475)

3. **Modular Chapters.** See the description that follows.

Modular Chapters

Two of the chapters, Chapter 10, *Pointers*, and Chapter 12, *The Preprocessor and Other Features*, are entirely modular. Each module within these chapters is self-contained, with its own *Putting It Together* section and

Your Turn reading-reinforcement questions. There are *Exercises* and *Programs* at the end of each chapter to support these modules. In some cases, the modules include submodules, each of which may be required by the professor or not, according to the demands of the individual course. Below are the modules and submodules in each chapter:

Chapter 10, *Pointers*, page 403
    Basic Pointers, page 403
        Addresses and Pointers, page 404
        Pointers and Functions, page 409
    Pointers and Arrays, page 420
    Pointers and Strings, page 427
    Allocating Memory, page 439
Chapter 12, *The Preprocessor and Other Features*, page 507
    Basic Preprocessor Features, page 507
        The Preprocessor, page 508
        File Inclusion, page 509
        Macro Replacement, page 510
    Advanced Preprocessor Features, page 516
        Conditional Compilation, page 516
        Preprocessor Error Messages, page 519
        Renaming Data Types, page 520
    Other Language Features, page 524
        The Enumeration Data Type, page 524
        The Conditional Expression, page 527
        Combining Expressions (the comma operator), page 529
    Nonstructured Program Flow, page 531
    Unions, page 537

Order of Presentation

Many of us emphasize different things in our courses, and have different orders of presentation to support these emphases. To accommodate these differences, the topic modules within modular Chapters 10 and 12 may be treated in three different ways. Any one or a combination of these treatments will maintain a smooth flow of subject material.

1. The modules within Chapters 10 and 12 may be presented in their place in chapter order. In other words, the presentation would flow from Chapter 9 to Chapters 10, 11, and 12.

2. Any or all of the modules within Chapters 10 and 12 may be left out entirely without loss of continuity.

3. The modules within the two chapters may be assigned at earlier points in the course. Following is an order of presentation in which the individual modules are moved to the earliest appropriate places within the other chapters. Introducing the modules anytime at or after the suggested times below will ensure a smooth flow.

Chapter 1, *Computers and Programming*
Chapter 2, *The C Language*
    Data Types and Declarations
    Renaming Data Types (Chapter 12, page 520)
Chapter 3, *Building a C Program*
    Developing a Style
    Directives
    The Preprocessor (Chapter 12, page 508)
    File Inclusion (Chapter 12, page 509
    Macro Replacement (Chapter 12, page 510)
    Conditional Compilation (Chapter 12, page 516)
    Preprocessor Error Messages (Chapter 12, page 519)
    Input
    Addresses and Pointers (Chapter 10, page 404)
Chapter 4, *The Selection Structure*
    The `if` Statement
    The Conditional Expression (Chapter 12, page 527)
    The `switch` Statement
    The Enumeration Data Type (Chapter 12, page 524)
Chapter 5, *The Iteration Structure*
    Accumulating and Counting
    Combining Expressions (Chapter 12, page 529)
    Nonstructured Program Flow (Chapter 12, page 531)
Chapter 6, *Functions*
    How Functions Work
    Pointers and Functions (Chapter 10, page 409)
Chapter 7, *Arrays*
    The Variably Defined Variable
    Pointers and Arrays (Chapter 10, page 420)
Chapter 8, *Strings*
    Pointers—A First Glance
    Pointers and Strings (Chapter 10, page 427)
    Allocating Memory (Chapter 10, page 439)

THE PACKAGE

The Art of Programming: Computer Science with C includes a wealth of ancillary materials so that the instructor can tailor the teaching and learning environments to the particular situation. Included with the supplements are:

Resource Manual

The *Resource Manual*—Prepared by Steven C. Lawlor, Stephen Caird, Symantec Corporation, and Stephen J. Allan, Utah State University—is a unique concept. It contains introductions to a number of different C programming environments (Borland, Quick, Symantec, Visual, and UNIX) as well as a number of demonstration programs. The demonstration programs may be used as a supplement to class lectures, for extra examples for the students, or assigned to the students for analysis. The *Resource Manual* is packaged so that individual pages may be easily photocopied for student handouts, or copied in its entirety for distribution to the students.

Program Listings on Disk

All the program examples in the text are available on a disk packaged with the book. This allows the students to read about a concept and immediately reinforce the reading by running and experimenting with the example. In addition, listings for any programs in the *Exercises* sections are included on the same disk. Since many of these are debugging exercises, this allows the students to quickly see the results of their changes.

Also on this disk are source code files for all the demonstration programs in the *Resource Manual*. Whether or not the students receive the *Resource Manual* materials, the program examples should provide more breadth for them.

Solutions Manual/Test Bank

The *Solutions Manual/Test Bank*—Prepared by Rhoda Baggs Koss and Ian Koss—contains for each chapter:

1. Answers to the end-of-chapter Review Questions and Exercises.
2. Listings for suggested solutions for each of the programming problems at the end of the chapter.
3. Test questions (60–75 per chapter). These questions include a mixture of different testing formats: multiple choice, true/false, fill-in-the-blank, short answer, program tracing, code debugging, and code segment writing.

The test bank is available on disk.

Transparency Masters

These are copies of diagrams, illustrations, and examples from the text in easily reproducible form.

ACKNOWLEDGMENTS

A package such as *The Art of Programming: Computer Science with C* cannot be the product of only one mind. In this case it is the product of literally hundreds. All the folks at West, who are normally paid to do wonderful things, certainly earned more than their paychecks. I would especially like to thank Richard W. Mixter, the Sponsoring Editor, for his insight, encouragement, and perseverance; Keith Dodson, Developmental Editor, the guy who makes things happen and pulled together so many parts of the project; Lauren Fogel, who was instrumental in pulling together the ancillaries; Rita Jaramillo for keeping the office together; and Debra Meyer and Stefanie Reardon, Production Editors, who guided the book through the production process and into final form.

The Art of Programming: Computer Science with C was extensively reviewed. I felt that I was constantly on the hot seat, but the process was fruitful and made a much more useful final product. For their thoughtful reading and insightful comments, I wish to thank, in alphabetical order, professors:

Stephen J. Allan, *Utah State University*
Ernest Carey, *Utah Valley State College*
John S. DaPonte, *Southern Connecticut State University*
Edward Ferguson, *University of Maine*
Rhonda Ficek, *Moorhead State University*
Robert Gann, *Hartwick College*
James Gips, *Boston College*
Rick Graziani, *Cabrillo College*
Joseph Konstan, *University of Minnesota*
Nonna Lehmkuhl, *Northeastern University*
Paul Lou, *Diablo Valley College*
Mike Michaelson, *Palomar College*
William C. Meullner, *Elmhurst College*
Robert E. Norton, *San Diego Mesa Community College*
Joan Ramuta, *College of St. Francis*
Jim Roberts, *Carnegie-Mellon University*
Michael Rothstein, *Kent State University*
Ali Salehnia, *South Dakota State University*
Paul Schnare, *Eastern Kentucky University*
Shashi Shekhar, *University of Minnesota*
Robert P. Signorile, *Boston College*
Brenda R. Sonderegger, *Montana State University*
Deborah Sturm, *College of Staten Island*
Vaidy Suderam, *Emory University*
Mark Thomas, *California State University at Bakersfield*
John A. Trono, *St. Michaels College*
Donald Yee, *Mesa Community College*
Winnie Yu, *Southern Connecticut State University*

Janet Hare's job was to proofread the final manuscript to see if all the editing changes were actually made. She radically overstepped her bounds, offering numerous, substantive suggestions on style and presentation. She progressed from ex-student, to proofreader, to valuable reviewer, lending her intelligence and insight to the project.

One of the most important elements in the development of this book was extensive class testing, of both the current book and its predecessor *ANSI C Programming*, by the author and by many of his colleagues. I would like to thank professors John Berry, Elaine Haight, and Roberta Harvey for using it in their classes and providing invaluable feedback. Perhaps most of all, I would like to acknowledge my debt of gratitude to the hundreds of students who suffered, with amazing tolerance and good humor, through the early test editions, and provided the most important commentary.

Steven C. Lawlor
Cupertino, California

Chapter 1

COMPUTERS AND PROGRAMMING

PREVIEW

The computer is an undeniable part of daily life today. Those who will read this book have decided not just to accept the computer, but to take an active role in how the computer is used—not just to use it, but to direct its use. This chapter takes you on your first steps down that road. It gives you a basic understanding of the computer system and how it operates. After reading this chapter, you will know:

▼ The historical background of today's computers.

▼ What a computer system is and how its functional components work together.

▼ The overall types of instructions that direct the computer.

▼ How data appears within the computer.

▼ How computer instruction sets are designed.

Almost all of us are involved, in some fashion, with computers on a daily basis. They are in the cars we drive, the televisions we watch, the clocks that tell us the time, the microwave ovens that heat up our leftovers, and, of course, in the machines that populate many of our desktops. Computers typically write our paychecks . . . and send us our bills.

Without computers, life would certainly be a lot different. Computers, however, are relatively new on the human scene. We can measure civilization in thousands of years and the industrial revolution in hundreds. Yet computers have only been around for tens of years. This relative newcomer has been quick to take hold, dig in, and proliferate.

What is this machine, anyway? A simple definition of a computer is a machine that, given instructions, can manipulate data by itself. Calculators and typewriters can manipulate data, but they need a constant stream of instructions—someone constantly pushing the keys—to get any work done. With a computer, give it the data and a set of instructions, a program, and you can leave it alone to do its job.

Let us spend a little time looking back to see how these machines developed.

HOW WE GOT HERE: A BRIEF HISTORY (Optional)

Three basic needs drove humankind to develop the computer: the need to perform calculations faster and more accurately, the need to control processes consistently, and the need to handle larger and larger amounts of data.

❑ **FIGURE 1–1** Abacus. *Photo Courtesy of IBM Corporation.*

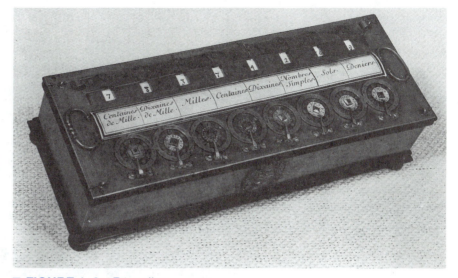

❏ **FIGURE 1–2** Pascaline. *Photo Courtesy of IBM Corporation.*

Early Efforts

We have been using mechanical aids for calculations for thousands of years. Evidence indicates that the Asians have been using the abacus (shown in ❏Figure 1–1), relatively unchanged, for almost 3,000 years.

Taxes played an important part in the development of one of the first mechanical calculators. Blaise Pascal, a French mathematician and child prodigy, wanted to help his father in his tax work. In 1642 he designed a box full of gears, ratchets, and wheels, eventually called the Pascaline, shown in ❏Figure 1–2. It would add, subtract, multiply, and divide. In all, about fifty of them were built, yet the venture was never a commercial success; the calculators had an unfortunate tendency to break down and make mistakes.

Over the next two centuries, a number of people attempted to go into the calculator business. A principal stumbling block was not the design of the gadgets, but the ability to make the parts with enough precision to perform accurately. It was not until 1820, when Thomas de Colmar introduced his Arithmometer, that calculating machines became commercially viable.

Some of the first attempts at process controls were based on the spiked drums that are the heart of the music box. From the early 1600s there were mechanically controlled organs that would play various selections and even move figurines in dancing patterns. In the early 1700s, various people experimented with mechanically controlled weaving looms to produce consistent patterns in cloth. In the early 1800s, Joseph Marie Jacquard was using punched cards to successfully control looms. The Jacquard loom became the standard of the weaving industry.

These two paths, calculation and process control, were brought together by Charles Babbage in the 1830s and '40s. Charles was a brilliant

❏ **FIGURE 1–3** Analytical Engine. *Photo Courtesy of IBM Corporation.*

and imaginative thinker, although not much of a doer. His first mental creation, the Difference Engine, was more a sophisticated calculator than a computer. It was designed to calculate mathematical tables and directly create the printing plates for them. He made some unsuccessful attempts at actually building one (with financial support from the British government), but finally lost interest and moved on. His ideas proved sound, however. A few years later, based on those ideas, George and Edward Scheutz actually built a Difference Engine.

Babbage moved on to an even more ambitious project, the Analytical Engine, shown in ❏Figure 1–3. This was to be an automatically sequenced (essentially a programmed) machine that could perform various calculations. Its sequencing would be controlled by punched cards, similar to Jacquard's. He spent years planning, designing, and developing solutions for various programming problems, but never actually built the machine. Much of what we know about Babbage's work was through the diligence and keen interest of Augusta Ada Byron, Countess of Lovelace and daughter of the poet Lord Byron. Having a sharp intellect herself, she appreciated the possibilities of Babbage's ideas and both translated and significantly added to his notes. In cooperation with him, she developed a number of sophisticated sequences for the Analytical Engine, and is

❏ **FIGURE 1–4** Tabulating Machine. *Photo Courtesy of IBM Corporation.*

often given credit for being the first computer programmer. It is truly unfortunate that, within her lifetime, her programs never had a machine on which to run.

The third path, handling large amounts of data, was the next to be explored. Every 10 years, the United States takes a census—a count of its people and their various characteristics. Today's census consists of an absolute mountain of data. The mountain is reduced to a figurative mole-hill, however, by computers. In 1880, the data mountain was not as high, but it took 12 years to compile the census results. This meant that the 1880 census information came out two years *after* the next census was taken. In 1890, Herman Hollerith adapted the Jacquard card idea by punching the raw data into cards. Using a machine (such as the one in ❏Figure 1–4) to sense the holes in the cards, he could tabulate the data in various ways. The census results were produced in about three years. In fact, the complete 1890 census information came out just shortly after the 1880 information.

Hollerith's data-handling ideas were used in a number of successful tabulating and accounting machines over the next half century. Hollerith's company eventually formed part of what is now IBM.

The truly programmable computer, combining rapid and accurate calculation, program control, and large data-handling characteristics, did not start to become a reality until the 1940s. There is a lot of argument over which was really the first actual "computer," but we could probably pick from among the Atanasoff-Berry machine (by John Atanasoff and

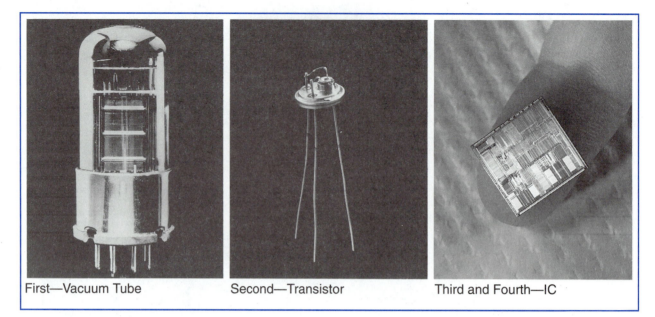

| First—Vacuum Tube | Second—Transistor | Third and Fourth—IC |

❏ **FIGURE 1–5** Generations of Computer Components. *Photos of vacuum tube and transistor courtesy of IBM Corporation.*
Photo of Pentium Processor courtesy of Intel Corporation.

Clifford Berry of Iowa State University) and the Z3 program-controlled calculator (by Konrad Zuse in Germany), both introduced in 1941, or ENIAC. The latter was a 30-ton monster containing almost 19,000 vacuum tubes and occupying a 1,500-square-foot room. ENIAC was built by the University of Pennsylvania and first operated in 1945. Zuse's machine, unfortunately, did not survive World War II.

Modern Computer Generations

Since the 1940s, advances in computers have come rapidly. The general trends have been faster processing, smaller size, more storage capacity, and lower cost. We typically look at modern computer development in terms of generations elements of which are shown in ❏Figure 1–5.

▼ *First Generation.* The first generation of computers used vacuum tubes as their principal components. The three just mentioned were first-generation machines.

▼ *Second Generation.* In the second generation, vacuum tubes were replaced by transistors, making computers smaller, faster, more reliable, and cheaper. The transistor was invented in 1947, but it was not until the introduction of the IBM 709TX in 1958 that second-generation computers became commercially viable.

▼ *Third Generation.* The individual transistor is tiny compared to a vacuum tube, but when we put many transistors as well as other components on a single chip of silicon, size decreases dramatically again. This integrated circuit, or IC, forms the basis for the third generation of computers. The IBM 360, introduced in 1964, was one of the first of this generation.

▼ *Fourth Generation.* The line marking the fourth generation of computers is a bit fuzzy. It is characterized by large-scale integration—putting thousands, or currently millions, of components on a single chip. Digital Equipment Corporation's minicomputer, the PDP-11, and IBM's 370 mainframe, introduced in 1970 and 1971, respectively, were among the first fourth-generation machines. Today's personal computers, from desktop size down to palm size, are the latest flowering of the fourth generation.

▼ *Fifth Generation.* Whatever it is, we are anxiously awaiting it.

Advances in computers are still coming rapidly. As soon as a new product is released, its replacement is in the design or testing phase. If the auto industry had experienced the same technology explosion, a Volkswagen would be able to carry 100 passengers, go 500 miles per hour, be the size of an ant, and cost 29¢.

YOUR TURN 1–1

1. What is a computer?
2. What is a program?
3. What three needs provided the incentives to develop the computer?
4. Name three important early calculators.
5. What do music boxes, weaving looms, and computers have in common?
6. Name some early uses for punched cards.
7. When were the first electronic computers developed?
8. What four general trends accompanied the development of the modern generations of computers?
9. What differentiated the four generations of modern computers?

THE COMPUTER SYSTEM

The word "system" is very important when we talk about computers. An effective computer system is an interconnected set of components working toward a common end. The system consists of two main categories—hardware and software. Hardware consists of the actual pieces of equipment—keyboards, screens, the components inside the boxes, printers, and so forth. To use a noncomputer example, a car, your Ferrari, is hardware.

Software is the instructions that direct the hardware—telling it how to perform tasks for us. One is not much good without the other. Take your Ferrari, for example. To use it for its intended purpose, getting from here to there, you must drive it—instruct it by pushing the pedals,

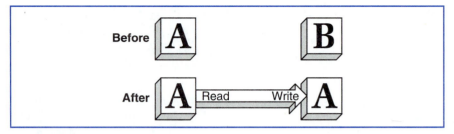

❏ FIGURE 1–6 Moving Data

A data move consists of a read and a write. The read copies the data from the location being read and the write replaces the data at the location being written.

turning the wheel, working the shift lever, and pressing the buttons. Without those instructions, your Ferrari is nothing but an expensive driveway ornament. Similarly, without software the computer is nothing but an expensive paperweight.

HARDWARE

Computers come in all sizes from pocket-sized to building-sized. While the larger systems can process more data at a faster rate, all computers are functionally quite similar. They have roughly the same categories of components that operate in about the same way.

Access to Data

Almost any operation in the computer involves accessing data. There are two, and only two, types of data access: read and write. A computer read operation is similar to reading a book. You look at the words on the page and copy them to your mind, but they are not removed from the page. Playing back an audio or video tape is a read operation. You may play it back as many times as you want; the data is not destroyed. A read access, then, simply makes a copy of the data while leaving the original intact.

A computer write operation is similar to writing on a sheet of paper, except that a computer write operation actually erases what was there before. Recording an audio or video tape is a more complete example of a write operation. The previous data is erased, and new data is recorded. A write access, then, replaces data where the write occurs.

As shown in ❏Figure 1–6, any movement of data in the computer involves a read and a write. Data is read from here and written there.

 **HEADS UP!**

Any movement of data is a combination of a read and a write.

The CPU

The heart of any computer system is its **central processing unit** (**CPU**). The CPU has three main functions: control, arithmetic operations, and

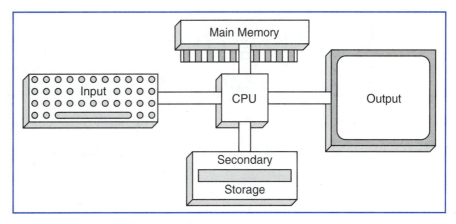

□ **FIGURE 1–7** A Computer System

A computer system consists of a number of functional components, all controlled by the CPU, which, in turn, follows program instructions.

logical operations. In its control function the CPU takes your instructions, one at a time, and following each, directs the rest of the computer system. It is your supervisor inside the system. You are the ultimate boss. You either write the instructions or load some other prewritten ones, but you give those instructions to the CPU and have it carry them out.

Once you give a set of instructions to the CPU and direct it to follow those instructions, you are no longer in control of the computer; the CPU is. Control will be returned to you only after those instructions are finished or some error condition forces the CPU to halt them. It is important to remember that the CPU is not some intelligent being but a brainless machine. It handles one instruction at a time, looking neither forward nor back, and never evaluating the propriety or outcome of the instruction. *You* would know to subtract deductions from an employee's paycheck; the CPU would just as happily add them if it was so directed. It would throw itself off a cliff if that was one of the instructions.

Analyzing the computer's output and making sure it has the proper instructions is, of course, up to you. You cannot expect any intelligent help from the CPU.

Many of the operations done by the computer are actually performed within the CPU. For these operations, it directs itself. For example, **Arithmetic operations**—addition, subtraction, multiplication, and division—are performed within the CPU. Obviously, a computer must perform arithmetic. Calculating a paycheck by multiplying the employee's hours by that employee's pay rate and subtracting various deductions is a typical example.

Logical operations—comparisons—are also performed within the CPU. Is this larger than that? Are these two items equal? You would probably also use logical operations in producing a paycheck. To determine whether to pay overtime, you would compare the employee's hours to 40.

Figure 1-8 Main Memory

			.			&		A				M					
5000	5001	5002	5003	5004	5005	5006	5007	5008	5009	5010	5011	5012	5013	5014	5015	5016	5

Locations

Q						*							5				
6000	6001	6002	6003	6004	6005	6006	6007	6008	6009	6010	6011	6012	6013	6014	6015	6016	6

Addresses

		H	e	l	l	o		W	o	r	l	d	!				
7000	7001	7002	7003	7004	7005	7006	7007	7008	7009	7010	7011	7012	7013	7014	7015	7016	7

		6				f										z	
8000	8001	8002	8003	8004	8005	8006	8007	8008	8009	8010	8011	8012	8013	8014	8015	8016	8

			2								@						
9000	9001	9002	9003	9004	9005	9006	9007	9008	9009	9010	9011	9012	9013	9014	9015	9016	9

❑ **FIGURE 1–8** Main Memory

Main memory consists of individual locations, each of which has an address. In this example, the character *A* is stored in location 5008, *2* in 9003 and *Hello World!* in locations 7002 through 7013.

To find the data on the employee's deductions, you would compare the employee's name to the names in your file of employees.

Main Memory

Having a CPU is a start, but you still need other components in your computer system as well. For example, where do the instructions come from that the CPU is following? Where does the CPU put the data that it is processing or the results of its efforts? As shown in ❑Figure 1–7, the CPU is connected to a **main memory**—a temporary, working storage area. Main memory stores two types of things: the current set of instructions that the CPU is following, and the data that these instructions manipulate.

Physically, main memory is made up of thousands or millions of **locations**—sets of components that store these individual pieces of data. As illustrated in ❑Figure 1–8, each location has an **address**—a unique number that the CPU can use to refer to the location. This address is similar in concept to our street addresses. There is only one 45 Oak Street in our town and there is only one location 721365 in the main memory. This construction allows **random access** to main memory; the CPU can reach any single location in memory—one letter, one number, or one instruction. That sounds reasonable and, in fact, it is necessary that the CPU be able to do that to get anything done. Yet some other storage systems, as we shall see, will not allow this individual access. Main memory is all electronic, no moving parts, so it is very fast; a piece of data might be accessed in a twentieth of a millionth of a second. This makes it hundreds or even thousands of times faster than other storage systems.

Main memory has its limitations, however. It is relatively expensive and it is volatile, meaning that when the power is turned off, it forgets. Therefore you use main memory only for active, current storage—the program with which you are currently working, and data associated with

HEADS UP!

Main memory is temporary, working storage.

it. (This may be a few programs with multitasking computers—meaning those that can run more than one program concurrently.) When you finish with a program, you replace it in main memory with a new one.

Secondary Storage

Disks, both hard and floppy, are the most common examples of **secondary storage**. Unlike main memory, secondary storage is permanent. You can change the data there anytime you want, but unless you do, the data will remain forever. Secondary storage is also relatively cheap; therefore you typically have lots of it connected to the system, often hundreds of times the main memory capacity.

This sounds so good that perhaps you should forget main memory and work only with secondary storage. Secondary storage, however, is slow—hundreds of times slower than main memory. More importantly, secondary storage is only accessible in chunks called physical records, or sectors or blocks depending on the device. These physical records may be from about eighty to thousands of characters long. In order to work with data effectively you must be able to access individual characters, or numbers or instructions, which you can only do in main memory.

You use both storage systems, then, in the computer. You do your work using main memory. The data or instructions you need are loaded into main memory and processed. If you wish to save these things permanently, you read them from main memory and write them to secondary storage, typically hard or floppy disks. This then allows you to write the instructions and data for the next project into main memory and process them.

For example, if you had data in secondary storage that you wished to change, a payroll record perhaps, your instructions to the CPU would direct it to read the physical record or records containing that payroll record into main memory, write the change to the individual characters in the record (the copy in main memory, of course), and then write the physical record back to its original space in secondary storage, replacing the original physical record. Your change would then be made permanent.

Input and Output

Even with all this, the system still lacks some essential items—ways for us humans to communicate with it. The most common type of input device is the keyboard, although there are others such as the mouse, the optical scanner, and so forth. Screens and printers are the most common types of output devices.

Following Instructions

The instructions controlling the CPU and the data that the CPU works with must be stored in main memory. If we have them in secondary

HEADS UP!

Secondary storage is permanent storage.

HEADS UP!

To work on data in secondary storage, it must first be moved to main memory.

storage, they must be read from there and written to main memory. The CPU has a number of small storage circuits called **registers**. One of these registers, the **instruction register**, is capable of holding a single computer instruction—only one. The instruction currently being followed must be there so that the CPU can react to it.

The CPU has a few (perhaps 4 to 16, depending on the CPU) other registers called **data registers**. These store the data that the CPU uses in arithmetic or logical operations. There are only a few of these registers, so data must continuously be moved in and out of them.

To perform a single instruction, the CPU must fetch the instruction from main memory, put it in its instruction register, interpret it, and perform it. That instruction will then be replaced in the instruction register by the next instruction. Since only a copy of each instruction is written to the instruction register, the original is not destroyed—it is still in main memory—but it is no longer visible to the CPU. The CPU can "see" only one instruction at a time.

That fact, or limitation, will be very important to you as you program. Humans can see the "big picture"—what led up to this action and what actions will follow. Computers cannot. They can see only the present, which to them is about a fifty-millionth of a second. If you could instruct your computer to take a step forward, it could not see that the result of that action might be to plunge off a thousand-foot cliff; it would simply step forward. Directing the hardware to perform some useful, reasonable task is up to you. The computer cannot help you.

A Simple Addition Operation

To us, adding two numbers together, such as 12 and 25, is a simple operation. To the computer, it involves at least three instructions, and a number of operations. The added complication, though, is more than made up for in speed and accuracy.

Let us take a graphical look at how the computer might do it. This is only part of a program; somehow the numbers must have been placed in main memory, and something must be done with the result after it is calculated.

1. Fetch the second instruction and put it in the CPU's instruction register.

2. That instruction directs the CPU to fetch the value from location 6016 and put it in a data register.

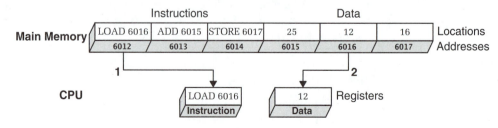

3. Fetch the second instruction and put it in the CPU's instruction register, replacing the first one.

4. That instruction directs the CPU to add the contents of location 6016 to the contents of the data register.

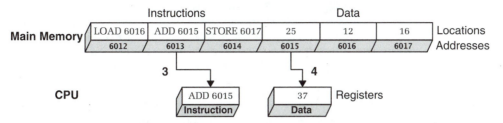

5. Fetch the third instruction and put it in the CPU's instruction register, replacing the second one.

6. That instruction directs the CPU to move the contents of the data register to location 6017, replacing the value there.

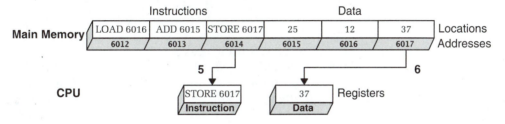

SOFTWARE

Hardware you can touch; software you can't. Software may be stored on various media, disks or paper perhaps, but software is simply ideas—instructions to make the hardware perform for you. A set of instructions is called a program. Some programs figure out the payroll, others fly aircraft, still others assist you in writing reports or books. Software is divided into two categories: system and application. You are probably most familiar with **application software**—that written to perform specific tasks for individual users of the computer system. Some examples are accounting, spreadsheet, word processing, and game programs. Most of the programs you write (and all that you will write from this text) will be applications.

System software provides services for all the users of the computer system. It has two main objectives. The first is to deliver the hardware's resources to you in a relatively simple manner. For example, to print some characters at the printer, the CPU must know to which wires the printer is connected, in what fashion and at what speed it should send the characters, whether the printer is currently busy printing characters previously sent to it (and if so, to wait until it is free), and how to react to

□ **FIGURE 1–9** The Operating System

To make programming easier and to make systems more compatible, an application program sends general instructions to system-program routines in the operating system. These routines translate and expand the general instructions into the specific ones needed to drive the hardware.

HEADS UP!

Your application software sends instructions to the operating system.

error conditions in the printer channel. All these details must be considered for each character printed, and doing so involves many computer instructions.

Since printing is such a common activity, you do not want to have to write those instructions into every program that uses the printer. Instead, the system designers have written printing routines into the system software that we all use. Our application program designates a set of characters and passes them along to the system-software printing routine. When that routine is finished, it passes control back to our application program, which continues on with its task.

The second main objective of system software is to provide compatibility between different hardware configurations. Computers within the same family often have different printers or screens, for example. A single configuration of the system software will allow the same set of application program instructions to accommodate the different hardware. This facilitates **portability** of application software—the ability to run the same application software on different hardware configurations.

Operating Systems

An **operating system**, described in □Figure 1–9, is a set of system-software programs. Your application program will have to make use of, and be compatible with, the operating system in use on your computer. Unfortunately, there is not just one operating system. Life would be too simple if you could write application software that would run on any machine. Some of the popular operating systems are MS-DOS, OS/2, Macintosh, Windows, and XENIX on microcomputers; and UNIX on micros, workstations, and midrange computers. Many manufacturers of midrange and mainframe computers supply their own operating systems. IBM, for example, has OS/400 for its AS/400 line of midrange computers, and Digital Equipment Corporation (DEC) has VMS on its VAX machines.

YOUR TURN 1–2

1. What are hardware and software and how do they differ? Why is one useless without the other?

2. Explain how data is moved from here to there using reads and writes. What data is erased and what is duplicated?

3. What is the CPU? What are its three main functions?

4. How does main memory differ from secondary storage?

5. What is the significance of individual locations and addresses in main memory?

6. Where does data or a program have to reside to be worked on? To be stored permanently?

7. Why is it important that a CPU has only a single instruction register?

8. How does application software differ from system software?

9. What is an operating system?

THE NATURE OF DATA

Humans and computers are different. One look at a representative sampling of each group will tell you that. We and they also process and store data differently. We do not fully understand how the human brain works, but we know exactly how the computer operates, and the way the computer stores and works with data is significantly different from the human way.

In many cases we are shielded from those differences because data is automatically translated to computer form on its way into the computer, and translated back on its way out to us. We never really see data in its pure computer form. We do, however, have to understand something about that form in order to appreciate what happens to our data inside the computer, as well as to ensure that we can make the most efficient use of the computer.

NUMBER SYSTEMS: OURS AND THE COMPUTER'S

Our **decimal number system** is based on 10 number symbols, 0 through 9. (*Decem* means 10 in Latin.) We have all grown up with numbers like 6 or 49 or 3,017, which are combinations of our 10 basic symbols. It would be hard for us to imagine those values expressed in any other way. Our 10-symbol system developed quite naturally because our earliest counting machinery had only 10 different elements, the ten fingers on a human's hands.

Each of the values 0 through 9 can be expressed with one symbol. To express numbers greater than 9 in the decimal system, we use combinations of symbols and positional notation. As shown in ❑Figure 1–10, a symbol's position determines its magnitude. In decimal, the first (rightmost) position tells how many ones, the second (to the left) tells how many tens, and so forth. The value 24 is two tens and four ones. Similarly, 4,680 means four thousands, six hundreds, eight tens, and no ones.

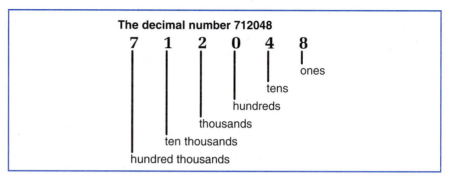

The decimal number 712048

7　1　2　0　4　8
|　|　|　|　|　|
　　　　　　　ones
　　　　　tens
　　　　hundreds
　　　thousands
　　ten thousands
　hundred thousands

□ **FIGURE 1–10**　*Decimal Positional Notation*
Positional notation determines a number's magnitude. Notice that in a decimal number system each higher position is 10 times the position before it: 1 times 10 is 10, 10 times 10 is 100, 100 times 10 is 1,000, and so forth.

Binary Numbers

HEADS UP!

All data must be translated to offs and ons to be processed by the computer.

The computer's basic counting machinery consists mainly of large sets or arrays of transistors acting as switches. These switches have only two possible states: off and on. Therefore, the computer is capable of working only with those states. We symbolize them with the digits zero and one. This means that instead of using the decimal system with 10 digits, the computer must express numbers in a **binary number system**—one with only two symbols, 0 and 1. Though humans express the value nine as 9, the computer must express it with a series of zeros and ones, 1001.

In decimal notation, the highest numeric value we can express with a single digit is nine (9). If we want to express the value 10, we have to start the current position over at zero (0), move to the next position, begin that

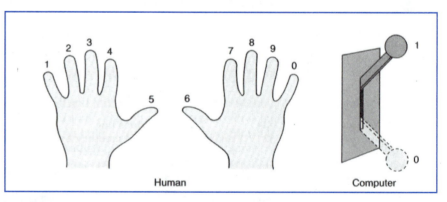

□ **FIGURE 1–11**　*The Human's Versus the Computer's Counting Machinery*
The computer's number system differs from the human's because of a fundamental difference in natural counting machinery. The human's has 10 positions while the computer's has only 2.

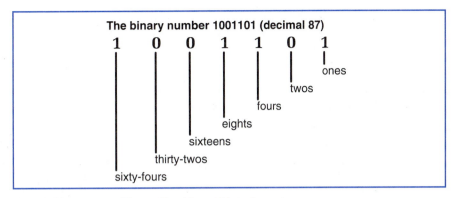

The binary number 1001101 (decimal 87)

1 0 0 1 1 0 1

ones
twos
fours
eights
sixteens
thirty-twos
sixty-fours

❏ **FIGURE 1–12** Binary Positional Notation
Positional notation works the same in binary as it does in decimal, except that each succeeding position is 2 times the position before it, rather than 10 times as in decimal.

with one (1), and write the value as 10. If we want to count beyond 99, we must start those two positions over and begin a third, to give us 100.

In binary notation, shown in ❏Figure 1–12, the highest numeric value we can express with a single symbol is 1. To express values greater than 1, we also use positional notation, but we must use more number positions because we can express fewer numbers, only one of two, in each position. To express the value one, we would use the symbol 1, the same as in decimal, meaning one one. But since 1 is as high as we can go in binary notation, to express the decimal value two we would have to use the next binary position. Binary 10 (pronounced *one oh* or *one zero*, never *ten*) means one decimal two and no ones, the equivalent of decimal 2. Following this logic, we would express decimal three as binary 11, one two and one one. Decimal four would require yet another binary position, 100, meaning one four, no twos, and no ones. Decimal 9 would be 1001 (one eight, no fours, no twos, one one) and decimal 77 would be binary 1001101. In the decimal system, each position is 10 times the position to the right of it because there are 10 symbols to use in each position. By contrast, there are only two symbols in the binary system; therefore, each position is only two times the position to the right of it.

To work with large numbers, computers use large combinations of zeros and ones. This takes a lot of transistor switching, but what the computer loses in numerical efficiency, it more than makes up for in speed. A human can add 9 to 19 in perhaps half a second. The computer would have to add 1001 to 10011, but it can do it in about a millionth of a second.

Hexadecimal Numbers (Optional)

Binary numbers tend to be long and cumbersome. The two-digit decimal number 99, for example, is binary 1100011. Still, in many applications,

To convert a decimal number to binary, divide the decimal number by 2; the remainder becomes the rightmost binary digit. Repeat the process using the quotient, the next remainder becoming the next binary digit to the left. Keep this up until the quotient is zero.

For example, 77 divided by 2 is 38 with a remainder of 1, so our rightmost binary digit is 1. The quotient 38 divided by 2 is 19 with a remainder of 0 so our next binary digit to the left is 0. (Our binary number is now 01.) Dividing 19 by 2 gives us 9 with a remainder of 1 (101). Dividing 9 by 2 gives us 4 with a remainder of 1 (1101). Our 4 divided by 2 gives us 2 with a remainder of 0 (01101). The 2 divided by 2 gives us 1 with a remainder of 0 (001101). Finally, 1 divided by 2 gives us 0 with a remainder of 1 (1001101). The process stops here because the quotient is 0. Decimal 77, then, is binary 1001101.

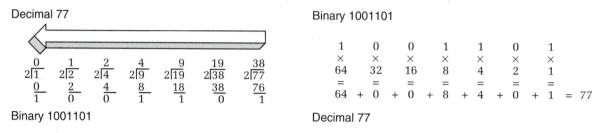

Going the other way, from binary to decimal, we add up the decimal values of the positions in the binary number that contain 1 digits. For example, from the right, 1001101 has a 1, no 2, a 4, an 8, no 16, no 32, and a 64. Adding this up, 1 + 4 + 8 + 64, we end up with 77 again.

❏ **FIGURE 1–13** Conversion Between Decimal and Binary

we must refer to the individual switch settings stored in the computer—in other words, to the individual binary digits. To do so, we typically use **hexadecimal** numbers, numbers with the base 16, because one hexadecimal digit represents exactly 4 binary digits.

A base-16 number requires 16 number symbols, so we borrow 0 through 9 from the decimal system and add A, B, C, D, E, and F for the values above 9 (see ❏Figure 1–14). Decimal 10 is A in hexadecimal ("hex" for short), and hex F is decimal 15. Decimal 16 would be hex 10.

To convert from binary to hex, group the binary digits in fours beginning from the right and convert each group to the appropriate hex digit. For example, we would separate binary 1101100 as 110 1100. The first

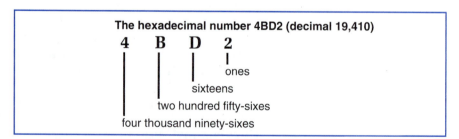

❏ **FIGURE 1–14** Hexadecimal Positional Notation

In hexadecimal notation, each succeeding position is sixteen times the position before it, rather than ten times as in decimal or two times as in binary.

Going from decimal to hex uses the same process as going from decimal to binary except that we divide by 16 and keep track of our remainder in hex digits. Hex to decimal follows the same pattern as binary to decimal except that the positions are powers of 16—1, 16, 256, 4,096, 65,536, and so forth.

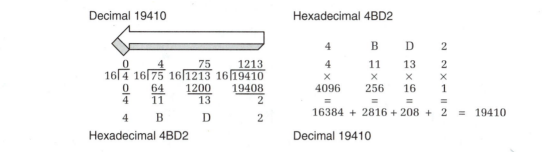

Decimal 19410

Hexadecimal 4BD2

$$\begin{array}{cccc} 0 & 4 & 75 & 1213 \\ 16\overline{)4} & 16\overline{)75} & 16\overline{)1213} & 16\overline{)19410} \\ 0 & 64 & 1200 & 19408 \\ \hline 4 & 11 & 13 & 2 \\ 4 & B & D & 2 \end{array}$$

$$\begin{array}{cccc} 4 & B & D & 2 \\ 4 & 11 & 13 & 2 \\ \times & \times & \times & \times \\ 4096 & 256 & 16 & 1 \\ = & = & = & = \\ 16384 + & 2816 + & 208 + & 2 = 19410 \end{array}$$

Hexadecimal 4BD2

Decimal 19410

In the decimal to hex conversion, as in the decimal to binary conversion, the rightmost number is determined first, moving to the left with each subsequent calculation.

❑ **FIGURE 1–15**   Conversion Between Decimal and Hex

group is decimal 6 or hex 6, and the second is decimal 12 or hex C. The complete hex number is 6C. See ❑Figure 1–15 for another conversion.

Table 1–1 shows the decimal numbers 1 through 20 along with their binary and hex equivalents.

CHARACTERS IN THE COMPUTER

A numeric value remains the same no matter which symbols we use to express it. A typical car has four wheels whether we call it 4 (decimal),

TABLE 1–1 Number System Conversion Table						
Decimal	**Binary**	**Hex**		**Decimal**	**Binary**	**Hex**
1	1	1		11	1011	B
2	10	2		12	1100	C
3	11	3		13	1101	D
4	100	4		14	1110	E
5	101	5		15	1111	F
6	110	6		16	10000	10
7	111	7		17	10001	11
8	1000	8		18	10010	12
9	1001	9		19	10011	13
10	1010	A		20	10100	14
Notice the extra digits it takes to express a number using only the two symbols available in the binary system.						

TABLE 1–2 Some ASCII Codes

Char	Decimal	Binary		Char	Decimal	Binary		Char	Decimal	Binary
Blank	32	0100000		A	65	1000001		a	97	1100001
,	44	0101100		B	66	1000010		b	98	1100010
.	46	0101110		C	67	1000011		c	99	1100011
;	59	0111011		D	68	1000100		d	100	1100100
?	63	0111111		E	69	1000101		e	101	1100101
				F	70	1000110		f	102	1100110
0	48	0110000		G	71	1000111		g	103	1100111
1	49	0110001		H	72	1001000		h	104	1101000
2	50	0110010		I	73	1001001		i	105	1101001
3	51	0110011		J	74	1001010		j	106	1101010
4	52	0110100		K	75	1001011		k	107	1101011
5	53	0110101		L	76	1001100		l	108	1101100
6	54	0110110		M	77	1001101		m	109	1101101
7	55	0110111		N	78	1001110		n	110	1101110
8	56	0111000		O	79	1001111		o	111	1101111
9	57	0111001		P	80	1010000		p	112	1110000

ASCII is a 7-bit coding scheme used by most micros, as well as many midrange and large computers. See Appendix A for a complete table.

HEADS UP!

Characters are represented in the computer by coding schemes composed of sets of offs and ons.

100 (binary), or IV (Roman). We saw that computers can handle numeric values easily with their two-symbol binary system. However, we know that computers work with more than just numbers. We have seen bills, advertising letters, and grade reports with As, Bs, and Cs on them. In fact, most computers can work with a set of at least 96 different printable characters.

How can computers work with 96 different character symbols when they can only store and understand 2? They do so by using various **coding schemes** that combine binary digits in definite patterns to represent different characters. One such scheme is the **American Standard Code for Information Interchange** (**ASCII**, pronounced *ask'-key*), shown in Table 1–2. A single ASCII code requires seven binary digits (zeros or ones), allowing for 2^7 or 128 different combinations. The ASCII system is used in almost all personal and desktop computers, as well as most midrange and large computers. An A in the ASCII coding scheme is 1000001; an N is 1001110.

The **extended binary-coded-decimal interchange code** (**EBCDIC**, pronounced *eb'-see-dick*) uses eight bits, which allows 2^8 or 256 possible code combinations, about half of which are actually used. EBCDIC is used on many minicomputers and mainframes. Most computers could use either coding scheme; the choice really depends on the scheme for which the software was written. Since both schemes represent essentially the same group of characters, there is software available to translate one code to the other so that ASCII computers can communicate with EBCDIC computers and vice versa.

The sets of binary digits that represent characters look to the computer just like binary numbers. For example, the characters *A* and *N* in ASCII are 1000001 and 1001110, which, if interpreted as binary numbers, would have the decimal values 65 and 78. If we could see inside the computer's memory, we would find only offs and ons and we could not tell whether they were supposed to represent numeric values or characters. To use a human analogy, holding up a hand could mean "5," "Hi," or "Stop."

How does the computer know whether a given set of binary digits is a number or a character? It really doesn't. Our program will tell the computer what to do with the set of digits, and that will determine whether they are used as characters or numbers. If we instructed the computer to perform a mathematical operation, it would use the digits as numbers rather than as characters. If we instructed it to print text, those binary digits would be interpreted as characters.

The ASCII (and EBCDIC) schemes were designed with this in mind. Notice that the alphabet is also in numerical order. The bits that represent the character *A* (in ASCII) has the numeric value 65 (in decimal), *B* is 66, *C* is 67, and so forth. Sorting characters alphabetically is just a matter of ordering the numeric values of their codes. Notice also that, in the ASCII code, all the lowercase letters have greater values than any of the uppercase letters. This causes a bit of a sorting problem, but we shall see that there are some easy ways to handle the problem.

UNITS OF DATA STORAGE

Humans store data in many different formats. In this book, for example, most of the data is stored in text form, with the character (a single letter, space, number, symbol, or punctuation mark) being the smallest unit. Characters are combined into words, which are combined into sentences, which are combined into paragraphs, which are combined into sections (under a heading), and so forth. Because the computer is not as flexible as the human brain, much more attention must be given to the machinery to have the data come out right. Let us examine the computer storage units that contain that data.

The Bit

We have called each symbol in a binary number a binary digit, or in computer terms, a bit. The number 11001110 (decimal 206) has eight bits (from right to left, no ones, 1 two, 1 four, 1 eight, no sixteens, no thirty-twos, 1 sixty-four, and 1 one hundred twenty-eight). To store this value, the computer would use eight switches. The right one would be off, the next three on, the next two off, and the left two on. The bit, the setting of one switch, is the smallest unit of computer storage. However, bits never sit alone in the computer but are grouped into larger units.

Bytes

Having the computer process data one bit at a time would be like putting sugar in your coffee one grain at a time; it is easier to use lumps. The computer processes bits in lumps called bytes, which saves computer instructions and time. Think about directing someone to put sugar in your coffee. It is much easier and faster to say, "Put in one lump," than "Put in one grain, another grain, another grain, another grain. . . ."

The **byte** is the smallest unit of data on which the computer can operate. If you instruct the computer to move data from here to there, it will move at least one byte at a time. If you instruct it to add, it will add at least one byte to another to make up a resultant byte. The addition may be done a bit at a time in the CPU, but the single instruction will direct the computer to add all the bits in each byte involved.

In virtually all modern digital computers the byte contains eight bits, not because of some mysterious electrical property, but for convenience. It makes sense to process data a character at a time, and a character, in either ASCII or EBCDIC, will fit within eight bits. (EBCDIC is an eight-bit code. ASCII is seven bits, but by adding an extra, meaningless bit it will fill an eight-bit space.)

If our computer uses binary notation for numeric values, these binary values will be forced to fit within whole bytes. It would take only one bit to express the binary value zero (0), but when we store it in the computer we use at least an entire byte in memory (00000000). Decimal 23 would be stored as 00010111. In fact, all our memory circuits are organized in bytes. Numbers with values above 255 (eight bits, 11111111) require two or more bytes of storage and, depending on the computer, might take two or more sets of instructions to process. (There are instructions in C that refer to individual bits. However, these instructions still force the CPU to take in full bytes even though the operations are bit-specific.)

Words

Even a small computer processes eight bits concurrently to save time and instructions. Larger machines process more bits concurrently (16, 32, or 64, for example) for the same reasons. We call the number of bits a computer can actually process simultaneously a **word**. Since each character occupies eight bits (one byte), words are often multiples of eight. Even though many word lengths are multiples of whole bytes, they are always expressed in bits. We refer to a 32-bit rather than a 4-byte word.

HEADS UP!

The byte is the smallest unit of data on which the computer operates.

HEADS UP!

The word is the actual unit of data that the computer can actually operate on.

1. Why is the computer limited to a binary number system?
2. Why is hexadecimal notation often used to represent binary numbers?
3. How are characters represented in the computer? Why?
4. What is the smallest unit of data storage?
5. What is the smallest unit of data the computer can operate on? How many bits has it?
6. What is the unit of data that a CPU actually operates on? How many bits has it?

COMPUTER LANGUAGES

Computers don't understand C—or Basic or Cobol or Pascal or any of the common programming languages. Each CPU has a set of instructions manufactured into it. The instructions differ for different brands and models of CPUs, yet they all have two things in common: they each consist of sequences of offs and ons (because that is the internal alphabet of the computer), and each one by itself doesn't do much. Displaying some characters on the screen is usually simple for you using a typical programming language, but it may require a dozen or more instructions to the CPU.

Language Levels

HEADS UP!

To execute, a program must be in machine language.

This manufactured-in language is referred to as the computer's **machine language**, a term also used to describe the entire category of built-in CPU languages. It is the lowest level of computer languages—easy for the computer but almost impossible for humans. When you write programs in high-level languages, like C, you can understand them, but they have to be translated to the computer's own machine language before the computer can execute them.

Writing a program in machine language might offer some advantages. Since it is the actual language of the computer, you could direct the computer to do anything it is capable of and in the most efficient manner. If a generalized language has to be translated into a specific machine language, compromises must be made. The job will get done but perhaps not with the greatest efficiency.

Nobody, however, programs in machine language. Trying to keep track of all those offs and ons (even if you use zero and one as symbols) would drive you nuts.

People can realize the advantages of machine-language programming by using **assembly languages**, the second level of languages. They are so called because a program called an assembler translates the assembly-language instructions into machine language to be executed. Simple

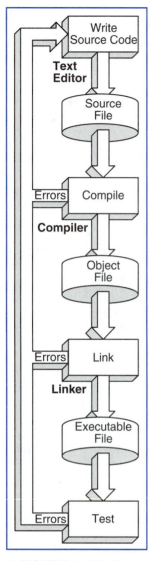

□ FIGURE 1–16 From Source to Execution

HEADS UP!

A program goes through many steps from source to execution.

assembly languages are merely symbolic machine languages. Instead of referring to an instruction as 0111010110110011, you use the word ADD, considerably easier on us humans. Programs must still be written in the same painstaking detail, though, because you are still dealing with the CPU's own instruction set. The trade-off between assembly and high-level languages is that a program in assembly executes as efficiently as possible, but takes a long time to write, whereas a program written in a high-level language may not execute as efficiently, but it will take less time to write.

High-level languages are meant to be easy for humans to work with. They are more similar to English (or some other human language), and one high-level-language instruction translates into many machine-language instructions, making high-level-language programs considerably shorter than machine-language programs. This does not mean that you can simply chat with the computer; strict vocabulary and syntax (construction of the instructions) are essential because the computer is nothing more than a machine and cannot understand our often relaxed and colorful way of speaking. Can you imagine what the very literal and precise computer would make of the expression "raining cats and dogs"?

From Source to Execution

A program written in C (or any other high-level language) is simply text—readable by humans but worthless to the computer. Let us follow the process of writing a C program and see how it turns into executable machine language.

You start by creating **source code**, the text program written in C. Since this is just text, you will use some kind of text-editing or word processing program to aid you in the writing. Once it is completed, you will save (copy) the source program to secondary storage.

The next step is to create **object code**, the program translated to machine language. A **compiler** program performs this operation. You execute the compiler, you tell it which source file you want translated, and the end result is an object program . . . or a batch of error messages. If there are errors at this stage, they must be corrected in the source code, so you must return to the previous stage—use the text editor, make the changes, and then compile again.

The compiled program is not ready to run yet. C, like most high-level languages, has libraries of prewritten routines that you as a programmer may use. You refer to them in the source code, and the references are embedded with the object code. You must now **link** your object code with the object code for the prewritten routines. Similar to the compiling stage, you execute a linker program, tell it the object files (yours and the libraries'), and it produces a file of **executable code**, the program that will actually run on the computer. Of course, if there are any errors at this stage, you must return to the source code for corrections and go through the process again.

The process is not finished yet. The computer only considers as errors things that it cannot execute. It has no understanding of what you want to do or whether an executing program will do it. You must test the program by running it and comparing it with known results. If there are errors here (referred to as logical errors), they must be corrected in the source code and the process repeated.

Integrated Development Environments

Many C compilers are available in **integrated development environments** (**IDE**s) that combine the processes we just described into one package. The packages from different vendors differ in their features, yet all of them allow you to work in one "desktop" environment that provides a source code editor in which to write the program, plus a one-command process that compiles, links, and runs the program (if it can get that far without serious errors), lists errors and warnings, and returns you to the source-code editing environment. All of these environments have some kind of "debugging" facilities that help you find the errors in your program.

MODULAR DESIGN

Attacking a huge, complicated task can be daunting and may seem as impossible as moving a mountain. The mountain, however, can be moved if we take it one shovelful at a time. Likewise, the huge project is easier if we break it down into small pieces, or **modules**, and attack each module separately. This process is known as **modular design.** Once the individual modules are completed, we can combine them together to complete the huge task.

HEADS UP!

Top-down, modular design makes the programming process easier.

But how do we break this huge task down into modules? By using **top-down design**. At the top layer is a single, concise statement (just a few words) of the overall objective of the project. In the second layer, the objective is broken down into a few major modules, perhaps two to five, which define the parts of the project needed to achieve the objective. Further layers break down each of these modules into the submodules needed to perform that module, and so forth until the whole system is described in detail. This process is called **stepwise refinement**.

For example, if we had a yard with nothing but weeds, our first-level, overall objective might be to "landscape the yard." This project can be broken down into a number of second-level modules: design the landscaping, grade the yard, install the sprinklers, plant the foliage, and plant the lawn. Each of those second-level modules can be refined further. Planting the foliage, for instance, can be broken down further into planting the hedge, trees, lawn-edge flowers, and accent bushes. And each of these submodules can in turn be broken down into sub-submodules. The

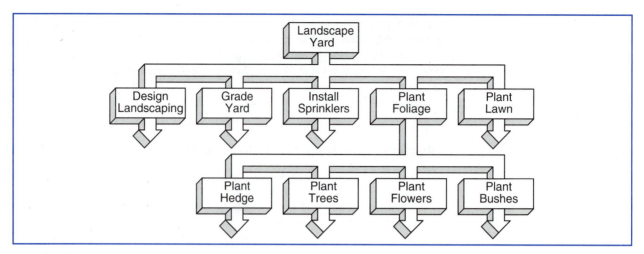

□ **FIGURE 1–17** Modular Design
Almost any process can benefit from modular design. Here we show part of the stepwise refinement used in designing a landscaping project.

process continues until each module and submodule is broken down to a point where it is an elemental process—"Plop the rose bush into this hole."

Top-down, modular design has some not-so-coincidental side benefits. Since the submodules are all described as separate tasks, they can be split among a number of people. For your yard, you may hire different experts to design the landscaping, install the sprinklers, and plant the bushes. Modules are often reusable. A submodule designed for one project maybe useful in another. Since it was fully developed for the first project, it can simply be lifted and inserted in the second. For example, grading the front yard for a lawn would be the same as grading the back yard for a patio.

THE PROGRAMMING PROCESS

The purpose of a program is to instruct the computer to perform some task. In writing the program you must, of course, give the proper instructions so that the task is completed as required. But there are many ways to write a program and things to consider other than just completing the task. In your programming you should always keep these objectives in mind:

▼ *Execution efficiency.* Will the program execute in a reasonable amount of time?

▼ *Programming efficiency.* Can you write, test, and complete the program in a reasonable amount of time?

▼ *Maintainability.* After the program is written and operating, can you or some other programmer easily make changes in it?

▼ *Source for future programs.* Code lifted from previous programs forms 93.86 percent (or thereabouts) of any new program. Is the code from this program written in such a way that it can be easily used in the future?

Often these objectives involve trade-offs. For example, it usually requires more programming effort to make a program that executes more efficiently. Since human time is much more expensive than computer time today, it might be economical to sacrifice some computational efficiency for ease of programming (except in time-critical applications such as screen updates, when waiting for the screen to fill would be frustrating). You will have to take extra care to ensure that your program is maintainable. Conditions and situations constantly change, and your program will have to change to keep up. If your routines are to be suitable for future use, you will have to consider applications for them other than just the current one.

In any case, all these factors indicate the need for planning.

Writing computer programs can be fun. Certainly, seeing the result of your correctly written program is fun. The tendency for new programmers is to try to reach this pinnacle of fun too quickly. When faced with a programming situation, they immediately sit down at the computer and start banging out computer code—computer instructions—without laying the proper groundwork. The result is 30 minutes of typing in this ill-conceived program, and 30 hours of debugging—cleaning out the mistakes and get it working. That is *not* fun. Nor is it time-efficient for you or, if you work as a programmer, cost-efficient for anyone employing you.

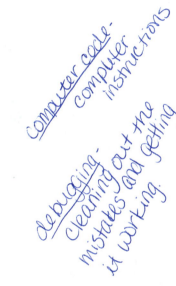

Computer code - computer instructions

debugging - cleaning out the mistakes and getting it working

Programming Stages

HEADS UP!

Plan before you start writing code.

In this section, we will examine a process for writing successful computer programs. At first, it may seem cumbersome and overly formal, but it is effective, it works, and it is the process that virtually all good programmers follow either formally or informally. The process can be divided into five distinct stages, each of which should be completed before moving on to the next.

1. **Task**. Investigate the situation to find out what solution the situation requires. Symptoms of the problem won't do. "It's taking too long to tabulate these chemical analyses" is insufficient. "Create a system to accept chemical sample readings, tabulate them, and print the results" is more to the point. The result of this step is to have a short, but clear, definition of the task to be performed.

2. **Analysis**. Look at the task from the user's point of view. What information or action do we need from the system? How should that information be presented or action taken? What data will have to be fed into the system to produce the information or action? Are there

additional factors or constraints affecting the task? The result of the analysis should be a **logical plan**—how the completed system should appear to the person using it.

3. **Design**. Develop the procedures—the **algorithm**—to execute the logical plan. How do we give the data to the system? What steps are required to turn the data into the required information or action? The result of the design should be a detailed process for the task—not in computer terms yet, but in terms that people, the most important person being yourself, can understand.

4. **Implementation**. The completed design can now be coded, translated to a computer language. The result of this stage is a computer program.

5. **Test**. Make sure your coded program works. Before actually testing, you should develop a **test plan** that verifies the program results in various possible situations.

Let us follow a simple task through to completion. Our company, MegaTurbo, Incorporated, provides computer systems consulting services as well as computer products to our clients. Since we spend all of our time on clients' projects, we haven't computerized our billing processes. Our hand-created bills are not only time-consuming, they are often wrong. We need to fix this situation.

TASK

The fact that our billing process takes too long and is error prone does not define our task. It is just symptom of the problem. What we must do is create a computer program to take billing data and, in a timely fashion, turn it into a final, correct bill.

ANALYSIS

Now that we have a simple statement of the task, we must develop a logical plan—look at the situation from the user's view. In the analysis phase, we should work very closely with the users, the people who are actually responsible for the billing in this example. We start with the output. Seems backward? Not really. We must look at what the system is supposed to accomplish, its outputs, and then work backward to see how we get there. We should be quite specific at this point, showing actual samples of how the outputs should appear. The output for our example should be a bill showing the total amount of services, product sales, sales tax, and a grand total. At this point, we should design the actual output format. In consultation with the users, the people who actually do the billing, we decide it should look like the following:

```
                 MEGATURBO, INCORPORATED
    To: Customer
    -----------------------------------------------
    Services                              $12345.67
    Product                                12345.67
    Sales tax                                617.28
                                          ---------
    Total                                 $25308.62
                                          =========
```

(In a real-world situation, the outputs would probably consist of a more itemized bill as well as outputting data to various files such as one that keeps track of each customer's billings.)

From the output we can determine our data requirements. From the user the system will require the name of the customer, the amount for services, and the amount for product. The system can calculate the sales tax from the amount of the product (services are not taxed in this state) and add everything together to determine the total bill.

Here again, we want to design the actual input in consultation with the user. We decide that it should look like the following (the data the user types is shown in boldfaced type):

```
Customer name: Customer
Amount for services: 12345.67
Amount for product: 12345.67
```

DESIGN

Our next step is to design the process for the computer. Here we will follow the top-down method using stepwise refinement to build a modular program. The overall process consists of three major steps:

1. Input customer, services, product
2. Calculate sales tax and total
3. Print bill

The first step is concise enough as it stands. The second and third steps can use some refinement. We can divide the second step into two parts:

2.1 Sales tax is 5% of product only
2.2 Total includes services, product, and sales tax

We can also divide the third step into two parts:

3.1 Print heading
3.2 Print body

In fact, we could even divide step 3.1 into two parts:

3.1.1 Print company information
3.1.2 Print customer information

For the total project, then, the process would be

1.   Input customer, services, product
2.   Calculate sales tax and total
2.1   Sales tax is 5% of product only
2.2   Total includes services, product, and sales tax
3.   Print bill
3.1   Print heading
3.1.1   Print company information
3.1.2   Print customer information
3.2   Print body

We have shown the design in a **pseudocode**, literally "false code," which is basically plain English in **outline form** with the minor modules indented within the major modules of which they are a part. Step numbers such as 3.1.2 are often used to make discussion of the steps easier. It is much easier to refer to step 6.2.9.3 than the step 26 lines down on the second page.

For this simple project, it may seem that we are carrying stepwise refinement too far, but it does serve to illustrate the process.

Once the design is completed, it should be tested. Step through it, or, better yet, have somebody else step through it to see if it really works. Time spent in the design stage is invariably well compensated for in time *not* spent in the coding and especially the testing stage. If problems occur later on, you will have a solid design to fall back on. If one could pick the most important step in the programming process, it would probably be the design step.

IMPLEMENTATION

In the implementation step, we simply translate the pseudocoded design into instructions that the computer will understand. Here we will use the C language, although the design could be translated into any other programming language. The actual C code for this task is shown in ⇨Program 1–1. Don't worry about the particulars of the language at this point; we will be spending the rest of the book learning the language. Do, however, notice how the modular design was translated into C code, and shown using blank lines and indenting.

Program 1-1

```c
#include <stdio.h>

#define SALES_TAX .05

void main(void)
{  float services, product, sales_tax, total;
   char customer[30];

   /******************************** Input customer, services, product */
      printf("Customer name: ");
      gets(customer);
      printf("Amount for services: ");
      scanf("%f", &services);
      printf("Amount for product: ");
      scanf("%f", &product);

   /************************************* Calculate sales tax and total */
      sales_tax = product * SALES_TAX;      /* Sales tax on product only */
      total = services + product + sales_tax;   /* Total includes services,
                                                    product, and sales tax */

   /*********************************************************** Print bill */

      /****************************************************** Print heading */

         /******************************** Print company information */
            printf("\n\n            MEGATURBO, INCORPORATED\n\n");

         /******************************** Print customer information */
            printf("To: %s\n\n", customer);

         printf("------------------------------------------\n\n");

      /****************************************************** Print body */
         printf("Services                    $%8.2f\n\n", services);
         printf("Product                     %8.2f\n\n", product);
         printf("Sales tax                   %8.2f\n", sales_tax);
         printf("                            ---------\n\n");
         printf("Total                       $%8.2f\n", total);
         printf("                            =========\n");
}
```

Output

```
Customer name: TechnoMagnum Company
Amount for services: 42304.8
Amount for product: 5612.45


        MEGATURBO, INCORPORATED

To: TechnoMagnum Company

----------------------------------------------

Services                        $42304.80

Product                          5612.45

Sales tax                         280.62
                                ---------

Total                           $48197.87
                                =========
```

Even without knowing C or any other computer language, you should be able to make out much of what the program is doing because of the programmer's choice of words and the program's layout. We will be discussing program style and readability constantly throughout the book. A wise programmer once said, "You should write your program so that a four-year-old can read it." We are not quite sure which four-year-old she was referring to, but if your program is easily readable, not only will others be able to understand it. You also, after not looking at it for a time, will be able to remember and see clearly what you did.

TEST

At this point, if we have done our job correctly, the programming process should be finished. No matter how confident we are, though, we will still have to prove it to others. We must have a test plan for the program. The plan should exercise the program in the situations likely to be encountered in actual use. One method for developing test data is to take data being used by the current system, manual or computerized, and see if it works in the new one.

Be sure to use data that stretches the situation to its limits—the largest purchase likely to be made, or billing for services but no product, or the longest customer name we deal with. A test using "International Amalgamated Hypercircuits, Incorporated" or a total that exceeded

$99,999.99 would turn up shortcomings in this program. You will see why as we examine the C language in more detail.

A program may fail for any number of reasons. In correcting the errors and retesting, we should be careful to stick to our design. Too often, the tendency is to experiment with code, neglecting the original design. If we finally get something working, it probably won't do the right thing. Always check your program against the design when trying to dig out errors.

YOUR TURN 1–4

1. Of the three language levels, which is required by the computer? Which is easiest for humans?

2. Trace the process of going from a program that you write, to a program capable of controlling the computer. Identify both the files produced along the way and the programs needed to produce them.

3. What is modular design, and how does it interact with top-down design and stepwise refinement?

4. What are the five stages of the programming process, and what is the end result of each stage?

SUMMARY

▲**KEY TERMS** (in order of appearance)

Computer	Application software
Program	System software
Hardware	Portability
Software	Operating system
Read	Decimal number system
Write	Binary number system
Central processing unit (CPU)	Hexadecimal number system
Control	Coding scheme
Arithmetic operation	American Standard Code for
Logical operation	Information Interchange (ASCII)
Main memory	Extended binary-coded-decimal
Location	interchange code (EBCDIC)
Address	Analysis
Random access	Logical plan
Secondary storage	Design
Register	Algorithm
Instruction register	Implementation
Data register	Test

Test plan	Compiler
Pseudocode	Link
Outline form	Executable code
Bit	Integrated development
Byte	environment (IDE)
Word	Module
Machine language	Modular design
Assembly language	Top-down design
High-level language	Stepwise refinement
Source code	Task
Object code	

▲CONCEPT REVIEW

▼ A **computer** is a machine that, given a **program**, can manipulate data by itself.

▼ Driving the development of the computer were needs to calculate faster, control processes more consistently, and handle large amounts of data.

▼ Calculation aids have been in use for almost 3,000 years—since the introduction of the abacus. Pascal introduced the Pascaline in 1642, and others experimented with mechanical calculators, but it was not until de Colmar's Arithmometer, in 1820, that such devices were commercially successful.

▼ Process controls of musical instruments and animated figurines have existed since the early 1600s, but Jacquard's successful punched-card-controlled loom marked a turning point in that field. Babbage in the 1830s and '40s combined the two paths with the design of the Analytical Engine.

▼ Hollerith, in 1890, applied the punched card to the task of handling the massive amounts of data for the U.S. census. Electronic computers, the forerunners of today's machines, did not appear until the 1940s with equipment like the Atanasoff-Berry computer, Zuse's Z3, and the ENIAC.

▼ Modern computers are divided into four generations: the first generation principally used vacuum tubes; the second, transistors; the third, integrated circuits; and the fourth, large-scale integrated circuits. The fifth generation lies in the future.

▼ Computer systems contain **hardware**, the equipment, and **software**, the instructions that direct the equipment.

▼ Much of what a computer does involves moving data from here to there. A move requires **reading**, copying, data from here, and **writing**, replacing, data there.

▼ The **central processing unit** (**CPU**) **controls** the rest of the system in accordance with our instructions. It also performs **arithmetic** and **logical operations**. **Main memory** consists of thousands or millions of data **locations**, each with a unique **address**. Main memory allows **random access**, and it is here that we store the programs and data with which we are currently working. **Secondary storage** is accessible only in chunks and is used for permanent storage.

▼ The CPU makes use of **registers** in executing instructions. It has only one **instruction register**, so it can see only one instruction at a time, and very few **data registers**, so it must continually move data in and out of them.

▼ **Software** is divided into **application software**, for tasks for individual users of the system, and **system software**, to provide common services for users and application software. Common system software facilitates **portability** of application software. An **operating system** is a collection of system-software programs.

▼ Computers do not store data the way we humans do. Since the computer uses off-on switches as its main data-storage method, it cannot directly use the **decimal** number system; instead it must store everything in the **binary** system. Although hex numbers cannot be directly stored, we often use the **hexadecimal** number system to refer to numeric values.

▼ Characters must also be stored using only offs and ons (or zeros and ones, as we usually refer to them). Various **coding schemes** are used, the most popular of which are the **American Standard Code for Information Interchange** (**ASCII**) and the **extended binary-coded-decimal interchange code** (**EBCDIC**).

▼ The units of data storage in the computer are based on its construction. The smallest unit of storage, the **bit**, is a single binary digit—the setting of one switch. To actually process data, bits are combined into larger units. The **byte**, eight bits, is the smallest unit that the computer can operate on, and the **word**, possibly consisting of many bytes, is what the computer actually processes.

▼ A programming language is one we use to communicate our instructions to the computer. The lowest level of computer language is **machine language**, the one actually used and understood by the CPU. Since it is extremely difficult for humans to use, we have developed other languages more suitable for us, but they still must be translated into machine language to control the computer. **Assembly language** is the next level, using human symbols but still quite detailed instructions. **High-level languages** were meant to be easier for humans to use.

▼ To create a usable computer program in a high-level language, you must first write **source code** in the high-level language, use a **compiler** to translate it to **object code**, and then **link** that object code to other preexisting object code to form an **executable program**.

Integrated development environments (**IDE**s) wrap these processes in one package.

▼ It is easier to design and write programs in smaller **modules** rather than in one big piece. This is the principle behind **modular design**, which is usually implemented by using **top-down design** and **stepwise refinement** to break the task into manageable modules.

▼ The overall programming process is usually thought of in five different stages. The **task** definition is a short statement of the job to be performed. The **analysis** develops a **logical plan** from the users' point of view. The end result of the **design** is the **algorithm**, showing the program's design in **pseudocode** in **outline form**, to execute the logical plan. The programmer will then **implement** the algorithm by coding it into a computer program. The final stage is to **test** the program using a predetermined **test plan**.

▲HEADS UP: POINTS OF SPECIAL INTEREST

▼ Any movement of data is a combination of a read and a write.

▼ The CPU directs the resto of the computer system.

▼ Main memory is temporary, working storage.

▼ Secondary storage is for permanent storage.

▼ To work on data in secondary storage, it must first be moved to main memory.

▼ The CPU has only one instruction register and can see only one instruction at a time.

▼ Your application software sends instructions to the operating system.

▼ All data must be translated to offs and ons to be processed by the computer.

▼ Characters are represented in the computer by coding schemes comprised of sets of offs and ons.

▼ The bit is the smallest unit of data.

▼ The byte is the smallest unit of data on which the computer operates.

▼ The word is the actual unit of data that the computer can actually operate on.

▼ To execute, a program must be in machine language.

▼ A program goes through many steps from source to execution.

▼ Top-down, modular design makes the programming process easier.

▼ Plan before you start writing code.

▲YOUR TURN ANSWERS

▼1–1

1. A computer is a machine that, given instructions, can manipulate data by itself.

2. A program is a set of instructions.

3. The need to perform calculations faster and more accurately, the need to control processes consistently, and the need to handle large amounts of data.

4. The abacus, the Pascaline, and the Arithmometer.

5. A method to consistently control their processes—programs in various forms.

6. Weaving looms, such as Jacquard's, and Babbage's Analytical Engine were controlled (or intended to be controlled) by punched cards. Hollerith's tabulating machines stored data on punched cards.

7. In the early to mid-1940s.

8. Faster processing, smaller size, more storage capacity, and lower cost.

9. The principal component shifted from the vacuum tube, to the transistor, to the integrated circuit, and finally to the large-scale integrated circuit.

▼1–2

1. Hardware is the equipment and software is the instructions to direct the equipment. Equipment that doesn't know how to operate is useless, as are instructions with nothing to instruct.

2. When data is moved, it is read (copied) from one location, and written to another, replacing what was there.

3. The central processing unit, in response to our instructions, controls the computer system, and performs arithmetic and logical operations.

4. Man memory allows random, fast access, but is volatile and relatively expensive. Secondary storage is slower and can access data only in blocks, but it is permanent and cheaper.

5. Individual pieces of data are stored in locations in main memory. Since each location has a unique address, the CPU can access any of these locations.

6. Both data and programs must be in main memory to be worked on, but they must be in secondary storage to be stored permanently.

7. It means that a computer can only look at a single instruction at a time. It cannot look forward or backward.

8. Application software performs specific tasks for individual users of the computer system. System software provides services for all the users of the computer system.

9. An operating system is a set of system-software programs.

▼1–3

1. Its basic counting machinery, the switch, has only two states, off and on, which we usually represent with the symbols *0* and *1*.

2. A single hexadecimal digit represents exactly four binary digits. A byte is two hex digits.

3. Characters must also be represented with offs and ons—zeros and ones. We use various character coding schemes, the most popular being ASCII, to represent the characters.

4. The bit, the setting of one switch, is the smallest unit of data storage.

5. The byte, eight bits, is the smallest unit we actually operate on.

6. The word is the actual unit of operation. Its number of bits depends on the computer.

▼1–4

1. The computer can run programs only in machine language, which is almost impossible for humans to understand. High-level languages are easier for people, but must be translated to machine language for the computer.

2. Source code, the program in C, is written using a text editor and producing a source file. The source file is compiled into an object file, which is linked with other object code to produce an executable file.

3. Modular design refers to designing a large project in small pieces or modules. The project is broken down, from the top down, by stepwise refinement—taking each module and expanding it into submodules, and then doing the same for each submodule until each submodule is an elemental process.

4. The first step produces a clear definition of the task to be performed. The analysis results in the system stated in logical, human terms. The design produces the algorithm to execute the logical plan using the computer. Implementation translates that design into a computer program. Testing verifies that the code works as it should.

EXERCISES

1. What *was* the first electronic computer? Research the topic, make your choice, and defend it.

2. Compare a third-generation computer, such as an IBM 360, to a typical desktop computer of today. How do they match up in calculation speed, as well as main memory and secondary storage capacity, size, and cost? Your library should contain data on historical computers, and the local computer store will provide data on the current ones.

3. What will herald the arrival of the fifth generation of computers? Is it here yet?

4. Examine a computer somewhere. (Please don't disassemble your school's mainframe.) See if you can identify the CPU, main memory, secondary storage devices, and various input and output devices.

5. Identify the operating system and the version of the C language available on your computer.

6. What is the binary equivalent of these decimal numbers?
   a. 5   101
   b. 21   10101
   c. 42   0101010
   d. 227   11000011

7. What is the decimal equivalent of these binary numbers?
   a. 1101   13
   b. 10110   22
   c. 100011   35
   d. 1101101   109

8. What is the hexadecimal equivalent of these decimal numbers?
   a. 10
   b. 51
   c. 147
   d. 688

9. What are the decimal and binary equivalents of these hexadecimal numbers?
   a. B
   b. 2C
   c. E84D
   d. 143F

10. Write your name in the ASCII code. (Use Appendix A for reference.)

11. What is the relationship between uppercase and lowercase letters in the ASCII code?

12. What is the word size of the computer you will be using in this course? Is it the same as the assumed word size of the implementation of C you will be using?

13. All other things being equal, a CPU with a 32-bit word usually will not execute a typical program twice as fast as a 16-bit CPU. Why not?

14. Was there ever a program written in machine language?

15. Make a top-down-design chart similar to the one in the text for your preparations to go to school or to work in the morning. Show the design in outline form.

16. Make a top-down-design chart similar to the one in the text for reconciling and balancing your checkbook. Show that design in outline form.

17. Make a top-down-design chart similar to the one in the text for a program that plays poker with the person at the keyboard. Show that design in outline form.

PROGRAM

1. Familiarize yourself with your own C environment by typing in and executing the following program:

Program

```
#include <stdio.h>

void main(void)
{
    printf("Hello world!\n");
}
```

Output

```
Hello world!
```

Chapter 2

THE C LANGUAGE

PREVIEW

In the previous chapter we examined the computer system and the process of programming it. Now we will concentrate on our chosen programming language, C. From this chapter, you should learn:

▼ The advantages and background of the C language.

▼ How a C program is formed.

▼ How values and variables are represented in C.

▼ The factors that differentiate data types.

▼ Declaration of both values and variables in those data types.

▼ The arithmetic operators and how arithmetic expressions are formed in C.

▼ The differences in operations with different or mixed data types.

▼ How to assign values to variables.

In many ways the C language is as simple as its name—yet that very simplicity gives it an elegance and efficiency available in few other programming languages. Many languages take great pains to shield the programmer from the inner workings of the computer. They are designed to be "intuitive" and "user friendly." Because of this isolation, however, the programmer cannot take advantage of all the computer's inner mechanisms. Compromises must be made. The job gets done, but perhaps not in the most efficient manner.

C sets up few such barriers. You can dive right into the heart of the computer and manipulate its pieces directly and efficiently. This does not mean that you must be a computer hardware expert; the description of the computer's functional components from Chapter 1 should be sufficient. With that understanding, you will find that C becomes intuitive at a more elementary level and it, too, becomes user friendly.

THE LANGUAGE

The C programming language has exploded in popularity in the last few years. It seems to be the "fad" language of the day. But unlike other fads that have emerged, blossomed, and then withered, C seems destined to be in flower for a long time. It has a number of advantages. A major one is the ability to use it to write programs that execute quite efficiently. Many system programs are written in C, as are many programs that depend on screen graphics such as computer-aided design. Execution speed is extremely critical in these areas.

Another advantage is its portability, in large part the result of C programmers themselves enforcing and demanding consistency in various implementations of the language. Yet another advantage is that C continues to grow with the advent of new techniques and greater demands on languages. A recent trend toward object-oriented programming, for example, has led to an extension of C called C++.

How did C get its name? Was there a B? An A?

There was no A. The seed language was the Basic Combined Programming Language (BCPL), developed in 1967. It was refined into a language called, simply, B, which Dennis Ritchie enhanced to form the original C language in 1972. In 1983, a group got together to set some official standards for C. They formed the X3J11 committee under the **American National Standards Institute** (**ANSI**), and by 1988 they had completed the standards for the C language. Before this standard, the de facto standards were contained in Appendix A of a book by Brian Kernighan and Dennis Ritchie called *The C Programming Language*. Their version is often referred to as **K&R** C.

ANSI C is based on K&R C, and so most current compilers will accommodate both versions. It is important to learn the ANSI version, however, because most C implementations (and virtually all new ones) adhere to the standards, and, at some point, the few things that K&R did differently will disappear from the language.

It would be impossible for the ANSI standards to cover everything; there is too much that is nonstandard about the various hardware and system software-configurations in existence. ANSI provides standard methods of displaying characters on the screen, for instance, but graphic screen controls differ so widely on various systems that graphics are not covered by the standard. The standard does, however, provide the solid core. Each compiler will add extensions to it to take advantage of the special capabilities of the hardware and system software for which it is destined.

FORMING A C PROGRAM

HEADS UP!

Whitespace is used to enhance the readability of programs.

C was designed to be a modular language, and the format of the actual program supports these features. Actually, while the C compiler is not very picky about the physical appearance of the program, it allows you, through proper design and tradition, to make your programs neat, readable, and understandable. For example, **whitespace**—spaces, tabs, line endings, and blank lines—is, for the most part, irrelevant to the compiler, but you can, and should, add it in specific places to indicate the outline of your program.

Let us examine the listing in ⇨Program 2–1 to see some of the characteristics of a properly formed C program.

⇨Program 2–1

```
/* A Sample Program
   Meant to illustrate the format of a C listing */

#include <stdio.h>                               /* Compiler directive */

void main(void)                     /* Beginning of function definition */
{  int quiz;                            /* Declaration of a variable */

   quiz = 20;                             /* Assignment statement */
   printf("A perfect quiz is %i points.\n",    /* Displays on screen */
          quiz);
   printf("Will I get perfect scores?\n");
}
```

Output

```
A perfect quiz is 20 points.
Will I get perfect scores?
```

Outline Form

The finished program should end up looking like the design we developed in the previous chapter—in outline form with main topics to the left and subordinate topics indented within the main topic. Here we have a number of main topics including `void main(void)`, which has a number of subordinate topics within it, all of which are indented one level (three spaces in this example) to the right.

Since line endings are mostly irrelevant, the material inside the `printf` parentheses is continued on the next line. We clearly indicate that by starting the second line immediately below where the similar material was in the first line. Notice, however, that the line is not split within the quoted material. Line breaks are not allowed inside quotes. The C compiler would not look kindly on the following statement:

▶TRAP◀

Splitting a line inside quotes.

```
printf("A perfect quiz          /* Displays on screen */
        is %i points.\n", quiz);
```

Comments

Almost every language has a method of including **comments**—notations that appear in the program listing but do not become part of the final executable code. In C, everything between `/*` and `*/` is ignored by the compiler, and so becomes a place to put comments. Line endings, as we said before, are ignored, so you may form multiline comments as shown in the first two lines of the sample listing.

```
/* A Sample Program
   Meant to illustrate the format of a C listing */
```

Be careful to end your comments. If you should forget the final `*/` at the end of one, the compiler will keep searching for it, ignoring program elements until it finds it at the end of the *next* comment—or perhaps not at all, in which case the rest of the program is treated as a comment. All the underscored material in the code below will be ignored by the compiler.

```
quiz = 20;                        /* Assignment statement
printf("A perfect quiz "          /* Displays on screen */
        "is %i points.\n", quiz);
```

▶TRAP◀

Don't "nest" comments, put one comment inside another, unless your compiler specifically allows it.

Since comments are ignored by the compiler, you may include anything there except, of course, `*/`. There are no other restrictions.

Directives

The elements known as **directives** do not immediately become part of the compiled code; instead, they are instructions to the compiler (or, in many

C implementations, to a separate program called a *preprocessor*, run just before compiling). These instructions tell the compiler to temporarily change the source code in some way, or, in some cases, determine which part of the source code is to be compiled. The changes may become part of the compiled code, depending on the directive. The `#include` in the sample directs the compiler to insert the source code found in the file `stdio.h` at this point in the source code before compilation.

```
#include <stdio.h>                  /* Compiler directive */
```

Directives always start with a pound sign (#) and end at the end of the physical line in the source code. This is an exception to the "line endings are irrelevant" rule. Notice that the comment at the end of the first line is still ignored. Some non-ANSI compilers require that directives begin at the left margin; ANSI C has no such restriction, although in any C, the # must be the first nonwhitespace character on the line.

We will look at `#include` and a few other directives in more detail later.

Statements

A **statement**, when compiled, becomes an instruction or group of instructions that performs a specific operation. The line

```
quiz = 20;
```

in the sample program is an assignment statement. It places the value 20 in the memory location labeled `quiz`. All single statements end with a semicolon and may be contained within the same physical line or may extend over many lines as with the first `printf()` in the sample.

```
printf("A perfect quiz "        /* Displays on screen */
        "is %i points.\n", quiz);
```

Functions

Some people call C a simple language because of the limited number of statements available. Others call C a complicated language (they use the euphemism "rich") because of all the functions available in it. What C lacks in statements, it more than makes up for in functions. A **function** is a set of instructions that performs an operation—often a much more complicated operation than is performed with a single statement. A function may include statements, references to other functions, machine-language instructions, and a host of other things. It may have been written by someone else and included with your compiler; or you may make it up yourself. Many preexisting functions are ANSI standard (you will concentrate on them in this book), while others are peculiar to a given compiler.

When a function is used, it sets off a specific chain of events. Using the function should not require knowing the exact events that will take place, only the effects that those events produce. For example, in shifting your automatic transmission into drive, you don't know (nor do you even *want* to know) about all the gears, valves, and pumps that are operating—just that you may now go forward.

A function may be defined (the operations within it are specified) in some library file that came with the compiler (or was purchased separately), or you may have defined it by writing it in your source code. The definition will include a name for the function. Once it is defined, it may be used or **called** (the operations in it performed) by including the name in a statement.

```
printf("A perfect quiz is %i points.\n", quiz);
```

The name is always followed by parentheses that contain the function's **arguments** (data that the function is to work with). Even if the function has no arguments, the parentheses are included. Function arguments are separated by commas.

The function `printf()` displays something on the screen. The material to be displayed is contained in the arguments in parentheses. The first argument determines the overall layout of what is displayed. If, as in

```
printf("Will I get perfect scores?\n");
```

it contains only normal characters in quotes, then those characters will be displayed exactly as they appear. The `\n` is called the **newline** character. It indicates that the output should drop to the beginning of the next line at that point. The end of the `printf()` function does not end a displayed line. Newline is seen as a single character by C, but, because it does not show as a distinct character symbol on the screen, we represent it with two characters, backslash and *n*.

The `%i` in

```
printf("A perfect quiz "        /* Displays on screen */
    "is %i points.\n", quiz);
```

indicates that there is some value to be inserted in the line at this point. In this case, it is the value of `quiz`, the next argument. Note that the `quiz` argument is on the next line. Remember, line endings and spaces make no difference in C. It is the semicolon that ends a statement.

C is designed to be a modular language, and modules are typically implemented in most languages by functions or procedures. A C program is written almost entirely in functions—one or more depending on the complexity of the program. When you execute a C program, it starts by calling the `main()` function. In the sample program you see this function

HEADS UP!

Function calls always have parentheses.

Your code is more readable with a space after the comma.

HEADS UP!

Newline characters drop the display to the next line.

HEADS UP!

Remember, directives, unlike statements, end at the end of the physical line.

THE MAIN FUNCTION

By default, the `main()` function is an `int` function rather than a `void` function. We will see what all this means in Chapter 6, but your compiler may object to `void main(void)`. If it does, use `int main(void)` instead. It still may object—something about returning values. If this happens, make the last statement of your program `return 0;` like the following:

```
int main(void)
{

    return 0;
}
```

defined starting with `void main(void)` (more on the voids later). Note that there is no semicolon after this line—it is not a statement but the beginning of a function definition. The statements below it, between the opening brace ({) and closing brace (}), are the operations in the function.

Declarations

In C, as in many other languages, before you use almost anything you must declare it. The **declaration** tells the compiler that a variable or a function can be a valid part of your program and specifies how it may be used. Among other things, it allows the C compiler to check your source code for proper usage and to verify the spelling of variables and functions. In the sample program, the variable *quiz* is being declared as containing an integer (whole number).

```
int quiz;                  /* Declaration of a variable */
```

Although you do not see it in the source code, `printf()` is also declared. Its declaration is contained in the included file `stdio.h`. This is called a **header file**; it contains declarations and definitions that would normally be found at the beginning, or head, of a program. Except for `main()`, every function that you use *must* be declared, whether you make an explicit declaration in your source code or include a file with the declaration in it. All ANSI-standard functions (and functions that are supplied with the compiler) are declared in various header files.

YOUR TURN 2–1

1. What are the advantages of the C language?
2. What group established the common standards for C?
3. Of what significance is whitespace in a C program?

4. How do we put comments in a C program?

5. What is the difference between a directive and a statement?

6. What are functions?

7. What does a declaration tell the compiler?

VALUES IN C

In Chapter 1 we looked at various number systems and at characters as they are stored in the computer. Now we must look specifically at how we express those values in C.

Numeric Values

We can divide numeric values into two categories: **real** numbers, those that allow decimal points; and **integral**, or whole, numbers. In C, decimal numbers in either category can be expressed exactly as we do in normal math. The real number 47.3908 means exactly the same in C as it does anywhere else. The same applies to the integer 253.

Character Values

Besides decimal, there are other ways of expressing numbers in C; one is ASCII (or EBCDIC if we happen to be using that type of computer). By enclosing a character in single quotes (apostrophes), we are really referring to its ASCII code. The notation `'A'` is the same as 65. The notation `' '` (a space) is the same as 32. We could add, for instance, 32 + 65 or `' '` + `'A'` or `' '` + 65 or any combination of representations and, depending on how we wish to display the result, show 97 or the character *a* (whose ASCII code is 1100001 or decimal 97). Remember, once it's stored, it's just a set of bits.

Some characters in ASCII (as well as EBCDIC) are not on the keyboard and therefore would be difficult to show in character notation. An example might be the form-feed code sent to a printer to tell it to go to the next page. In C we represent these characters with **special characters**, each of which consists of a backslash (\) followed by a printable character. Even though two characters are shown within the quotes, it represents, and is stored as, just a single character. Here is the standard list:

\0	Null (absence of a character)	\t	Horizontal tab
\a	Audible alarm (bell)	\v	Vertical tab
\b	Backspace	\'	Apostrophe (single quote)
\f	Form feed	\"	Quote (double quote)
\n	New line	\?	Question mark
\r	Carriage return	\\	Backslash

SPECIAL CHARACTERS

The use of special characters is a case in which ANSI C offers compatibility among various hardware configurations. Take the form feed (\f) for example. This is typically the ASCII code with a decimal value of 12, so we should be able just to use the number 12. But "typically" is a key word here; not all computer systems use the same codes to represent things. ANSI C has a list of special characters that represent certain functions that may be implementation dependent. The compiler will translate these to the proper code for that implementation. Newline (\n), for instance, is the character that returns the printer or cursor to the beginning of the next line. In some systems it is ASCII 10, but in others it is ASCII 13 followed by ASCII 10—actually two characters. It is still stored as one character but, depending on the implementation, it may represent the output of two.

▶TRAP◀

Using only a single backslash in a string to represent a backslash.

Notice that we need special characters to represent both the backslash and the apostrophe since we use those characters to create other special characters.

SIMPLE OUTPUT

To write useful programs, we must have a way of printing out the results. In the beginning of this chapter we saw that, using the `printf()` function, we could print out strings and embed numbers—values of expressions—in those strings. We will discuss this much more fully in the next

⇨**Program 2–2**

```
#include <stdio.h>

void main(void)
{   printf("Here is the character %c,\n", 'X');
    printf("and the numbers %i and %g.\n", 46, 12.345);
    printf("Now we will print %i as a number.\n", 'X');
    printf("Things will really be messed up if we confuse\n"
            "data types, such as %g and %i.\n", 46, 12.345);
}
```

Output

```
Here is the character X,
and the numbers 46 and 12.345.
Now we will print 88 as a number.
Things will really be messed up if we confuse
data types, such as -2.19317e-74 and 16424.
```

chapter, but for now we will use the code %c in the string to embed a single character, %i to embed an integer, and %g to embed a real number. ⇨Program 2–2 shows all three codes and the results of their use.

Notice that each % code has a corresponding argument after the quoted argument in the printf(). In the first printf(), for example, the space reserved by the %c in the string is filled with the value 'X' when the program is run. The second printf() has both a %i and a %g, with an integer and a real number after the string. We said that a character value is actually an integer number, the value of its ASCII code, so in the third printf(), we used the %i code to print it as a number.

It is very important in the printf() to match the % code with the type of data in the corresponding argument. The last printf() expects a real number and then an integer, in that order, so it interprets the bits in 46 as it would a real number, producing the nonsense you see in the strange notation with the *e* in it, and the bits in 12.345 as it would an integer, producing more nonsense.

▶TRAP◀

Data types that don't match.

YOUR TURN 2–2

1. What is the difference between an integer and a real number? How are both types represented in C using decimal notation?

2. How are characters represented in the computer? How are they related to numbers?

3. In a C language using the ASCII code, how does storage of the values represented as 'A' and 65 differ?

4. Why do we have special characters such as \n or \a? How do we represent the backslash?

VARIABLES

In any language, a **variable** represents a location or set of locations in the computer's main memory. We put values in these spaces so that we may use the values elsewhere in the program. The space is "variable" because we may change the value stored there at any time. When we refer to that space, its current value is used.

Variable Names

📖 HEADS UP!

Use variable names that indicate the purpose of the variable.

To reasonably refer to that space in memory, we must give it a **variable name** (or in ANSI C terms, a *variable identifier*). We are relatively free in naming variables in C. This allows us to use names that might have some meaning for us. For example, if we are going to store someone's pay in a variable, we would probably call it *pay* rather than *x* or *fp* or *iq*. There are, however, a few basic rules that we must follow:

▼ We can use many characters in a variable name. How many depends on the compiler, but ANSI C specifies that at least 31 will be significant. (Non-ANSI Cs may revert to the original C specification, which made only eight characters significant. Under these rules, *locomotive* and *locomotion* would be the same variable.)

▼ We can use only alpha characters (*A* through *Z* or *a* through *z*), numeric characters (*0* through *9*), or the underscore (_) in variable names. Notice that a space in a variable name is not allowed. To specify a two-word variable name, for "gross pay" for example, we might use the underscore in place of the space—*gross_pay*—or capitalize the first letter of each word—*GrossPay*.

▼ Variable names must begin with an alpha character or an underscore, not a number. *Farley* and *_bluto* are valid names, *2bad* is not. Typically, application programmers do not start variable names with an underscore. These are traditionally reserved for variables or functions defined with the compiler or other libraries.

▼ C is case-sensitive; upper- and lowercase characters are not treated the same. *Total*, *total*, and *TOTAL* would be three different variables. It would not be considered good form to have in your program variables whose names differed only in case. By tradition, variable names in C are typically all lowercase, but this is not a requirement. For readability, many C programmers capitalize the first character of each word in the variable and limit use of the underscore. They might have variables *Pay*, *GrossPay*, and *NetPay*.

▼ The C compiler looks for certain key words, words with special meanings, when it compiles a program. They are treated as **reserved words**—set aside for use by the compiler. We will use them in program statements, but we may not use them as variable names. Following is the list of ANSI C's 32 reserved words:

auto	double	int	struct
break	else	long	switch
case	enum	register	typedef
char	extern	return	union
const	float	short	unsigned
continue	for	signed	void
default	goto	sizeof	volatile
do	if	static	while

Your compiler will probably add some capability to the ANSI standards, so there will likely be extra reserved words that you will have to avoid. Also, to prevent confusion, we should avoid naming variables with the same names as functions. For example, *printf* would be a poor choice for a variable name.

DATA TYPES AND DECLARATIONS

As in most other languages, data can be stored in various forms, or **data types**, in C. The major differences between C's data types are the size in bytes of each type, and whether or not it allows a decimal point. Which data type you choose depends on whether your value might have a fractional component, as well as the size of the values you might use. With regard to size, your choice is often a trade-off between the amount of memory used and execution speed. Smaller data types take up less of your main memory and secondary storage, but C often must convert small data types to larger ones to perform calculations, and the extra conversion slows execution.

A single program may have many data types within it, and your operations may combine values of different types—for example, you may add values of two different types together for a meaningful result. We shall see, however, that there is a penalty to be paid for mixing data types that must be weighed against the advantages of storage size.

Declarations

▶TRAP◀

Forgetting to declare a variable.

Whenever we use a value or a variable, we will declare it and its data type. Variables must be explicitly declared before they are used. Values (or *literals* or *constants*, as they are often called when they are written directly in a program) are implicitly declared wherever they appear in the program. C will know a value's data type by the manner in which we write it. A **declaration** performs a number of functions:

▼ It directs C as to how to store the value—whether it can have a fractional component or whether it is allowed to be negative as well as positive, for example.

▼ It automatically **defines** it—meaning that it allocates memory to the value or variable. The type of declaration tells the computer how much memory.

▼ It may also **initialize** a variable—assign a meaningful value to that space in memory. Memory is never empty; there is always something lying about in it, which we colorfully refer to as "garbage" because we can't predict its value. A value used in a program should, of course, replace this garbage. A variable definition allocates memory to the variable, but it may or may not replace the leftover value. As part of our declaration and definition, we can assign a specific initial value to the variable.

Variable declarations follow this general form (the material in brackets, [ ], is optional):

datatype variable[= initialization];

For example:

```
int frequency;
int StartValue = 14;
```

Notice the semicolons at the end of the declarations; they are statements and therefore must end in semicolons.

We can declare more than one variable of a single type in one declaration statement by separating the declarations with commas.

```
int total, counter, interval;
int BeginRange = 0, EndRange = 100;
```

We can mix initialized and noninitialized declarations in the same statement (as long as they are of one type), but many consider it improper form. Notice that in the following declaration, *EndRange* is initialized to 100, but *BeginRange* is not initialized at all; it contains garbage.

```
int BeginRange, EndRange = 100;
```

Integral Data Types

Integral data types allow only integral, or whole, numbers—no decimal points. The numeric values are stored in straight binary form, padded with leading zeros to fill the appropriate size defined by the data type. Decimal 65 would be stored as 1000001 with enough leading zero bits to make it the right size. There are two basic integral types: `char` for "character" and `int` for "integer."

The **char** data type is eight bits long. Some people pronounce it as in the first four letters of "charm," others as "care" like the beginning of "character." The basis for the name, "character," is somewhat misleading. Yes, we do store in it what we humans understand as characters, but we can also store numbers there. In fact, the computer can't tell the difference. Remember, a character is simply a set of bits just like a number.

In a single `char` space we can store the code for *A* or perhaps the number 65. Since the ASCII code for *A* consists of the same bits as the binary representation for decimal 65, exactly the same value, 01000001, will be stored. Note the leading zero bit to make up eight bits. Once that set of bits is established, we may instruct the computer to treat it as a character (print it out, for example) or as a number (add it to another, for example).

Either integral data type may have one of two modifiers, `signed` or `unsigned`. The **signed** modifier means that the value may be either positive or negative. This is the default under ANSI rules, so if there is no modifier, the `char` (or `int`) is assumed to be `signed`. The **unsigned** modifier means that the number may only be positive. An `unsigned` `char` may have values from 0 to 255 (the decimal equivalent of 11111111). `signed chars`, because the sign takes up one bit, may have

▶TRAP◀

Leaving a semicolon off the end of a declaration.

HEADS UP!

The `char` data type is numeric.

values ranging from −128 to 127. By convention, we do not use signs with hex, or character notation (such as `'A'`); they may only be positive.

Some valid `char` declarations are:

```
char letter;
unsigned char index;
char TopGrade = 'A', BottomGrade = 'F';
char TopGrade = 65, BottomGrade = 70;
```

All of these declarations allocate 8 bits per variable, but the second one treats the stored value as only positive. The third and fourth declarations have exactly the same effect because the ASCII codes for *A* and *F* are 65 and 70. The two declarations could not exist in the same section of the program, of course, because we may not duplicate variable names.

The **int** data type has more bits than the `char`, but its size is not precisely defined by ANSI. It is often the word size of the machine for which the compiler is designed; however, there are a number of exceptions to that guideline. For example, PC-compatible computers have either 16- or 32-bit word sizes, but many C compilers for PCs use a 16-bit `int`.

The `int` data types may have a `signed` or `unsigned` modifier, but they may also have **short** or **long** modifiers. ANSI tells us only that a `long int` will have at least as many bits as a `short int`, but in most implementations a `short int` is 16 bits whereas a `long int` is 32. Notice that the data type `int` is the same size as either a `short int` or a `long int`. It depends supposedly on the word size of the machine, but that guideline is so often violated that it could depend on the type of computer the compiler is designed for, the phase of the moon, whether Jupiter is in Capricorn. . . . Know your compiler!

To enhance portability (being able to recompile unchanged source code for use on another type of machine) it is a good idea to declare your `int`s as either `short` or `long`.

The data type `int` is the default. If a declaration has modifiers but no data type, it is assumed that it is an `int` of some kind. Just `short`, for example, means `short int`. Here are some valid `int` declarations:

```
int current_page, last_page;
short age;                         /* Equivalent to short int age */
unsigned volts = 110;             /* Equivalent to unsigned int volts = 110 */
unsigned volts = 'n';              /* Equivalent to declaration above */
unsigned long NationalDebt;            /* An unsigned long int */
signed short Variance;          /* Modifier signed not needed under ANSI */
```

As mentioned, values are also declared when they are included in a program. If a value has no decimal point, such as −386, it is integral. Character values such as `'A'` have no decimal points, so they are always integral. Unless otherwise stated, integral values, including values expressed as characters, default to type `int` (remember, that may be the same size as either `short` or `long`, depending on your machine).

Decimal-notation integers and character values are stored as `signed` (even though we would never state a character such as `'A'` with a negative sign). In any case, if the value exceeds the size of a `short int`, it will be stored as a `long int`. For example, if the default `int` on your machine is 16 bits (with a maximum decimal value of 32,767) and you put the number 145832 in your program code, the compiler will store it in a `long int`–32 bits.

Notice that character values, even though they fit within 8 bits (the size of data type `char`) are stored as `int`s.

We may also explicitly declare values by following the value with an L or a U (or l or u) or both. The postfix L forces the value to be stored as a `long` and U as `unsigned`. The value `56UL` would be stored as an `unsigned long`.

Floating-Point Data Types

Real numbers, those with decimal points, are stored as **floating-point data types**. They are stored not in simple binary notation but in a binary form of scientific notation (typically IEEE—Institute of Electrical and Electronics Engineers—floating-point notation). In scientific notation, we use a **mantissa** of significant digits multiplied by some power of 10. For example, 7,146 might be expressed as 7.146×10^3. The two values are the same; 10^3 is 1000, and 7.146×1000 is 7,146. In our C program we can write the number as `7146.0` or `7.146e3`, that is, a mantissa of 7.146 and a power-of-10 **exponent** of 3. The second form is referred to as **E notation**.

For floating-point values, then, the computer stores the mantissa and the exponent. (Actually, since the computer works exclusively in binary, it stores a binary mantissa and the exponent as a power of two, but we will look at it in decimal to keep it simple.) The memory space allocated to the number is fixed, depending on the data type we declare, and is divided between mantissa and exponent. This means that there are limits on the size of both the mantissa and the exponent. The data type we choose will take those limits into account.

There are three different floating-point data types: **float**, **double**, and **long double**. In terms of the size of each, all ANSI guarantees is that a `double` is greater than or equal to a `float`, and a `long double` is greater than or equal to a `double`. In many microcomputer Cs, a `float` is 32 bits, a `double` is 64, and a `long double` 80. Unlike integral data types, floating-point data types always allow positive or negative values, and so cannot have the modifiers `signed` or `unsigned`.

Following are some examples of floating-point-variable declarations:

```
float WageRate = 12.75;
double area, volume;
long double humongous;
```

❏ **FIGURE 2–1** Data-Type Designations
Here are the ANSI C data types (except enum) with their key words and examples of explicit declarations of values where such declarations are allowed.

▶**TRAP**◀

Declaring a long double as a long.

When declaring a long double, be sure to state long double, not just long, because that would default to a long int.

A value with a decimal point will normally be stored as a double. We may explicitly declare it as a float with F or f, or a long double with L or l. A number written as 3.806e-3F (or .003806F) would be stored as a float instead of a double. A value with a large number of significant digits or a large exponent will automatically be stored as a long double.

String Data

A **string** is a set of characters. We include string values in a program by enclosing the characters in quotes:

```
"This is a bunch of characters"
```

The quotes are not part of the string; they just serve to tell the C compiler where the string begins and ends. For example, the statement

```
printf("This is a bunch of characters");
```

displays

```
This is a bunch of characters
```

on the screen.

To include quotes as part of the string, we must use the special character \". We must use the backslash with any of the special characters except the apostrophe and question mark, although the backslashes also work there.

```
"He said \"I\'m drowning in a sea of C!\""      /* \' not necessary here */
```

would be stored as

```
He said "I'm drowning in a sea of C!"
```

(The \" must be used within double quotes, "\"", so that C can differentiate between the quotes that mark the beginning and end of the string, and those that are meant to be within the string. There is no such problem with the apostrophe. However, the \' is necessary when showing the single character value apostrophe, '\'', because single character values are enclosed in apostrophes.)

This statement:

```
printf("Her name\nis \"Henrietta.\"");
```

would produce

```
Her name
is "Henrietta."
```

The character \n starts a new line and \" is a quote.

The compiler will **concatenate** (connect together end to end) adjacent strings. For example

```
"This is just "  "one string."
```

will be stored as

```
This is just one string.
```

Remember, whitespace, such as spaces, tabs, and line endings, is ignored by the compiler (unless it is inside quotes), so this concatenation property is often used to write a single long string using two lines in C code.

```
"This is just "
"one string."
```

is stored the same.

Since we can't put line endings between quotes, the following wouldn't work.

```
"This is just
  one string."
```

There are no string variables in C.

So how do we store variable sets of characters? As sets of individual character variables. We shall cover this in Chapter 8.

1. Which characters can be used in C variable names? What can the name start with?

2. Are *books* and *BOOKS* the same variable?

3. What does the data type say about a value or variable?

4. What does a declaration do in a program?

5. Which data types are integral? Which are floating-point?

6. What characters do we use at the end of numbers to declare values as unsigned? long? unsigned long? float? long double?

7. How do we put a quote mark in a string value?

8. How does C interpret two string values separated only by whitespace?

ARITHMETIC EXPRESSIONS

An **expression** is anything that can be reduced to a single value. Under this definition, a single value, say 14, qualifies as an expression, as does a single variable, say *pounds*, which would have a value in memory. We are more interested in expressions that require some evaluation by the computer—that made up of more than one value or variable; for example, 26 + 17. We have all done arithmetic and so have evaluated arithmetic expressions, but we must examine the strict rules that C applies to arithmetic expressions.

An arithmetic expression consists of values and/or variables connected by **arithmetic operators**, which tell the computer how to combine the values. The expression 26 + 17, for example, uses an operator, +, indicating that the values on either side, 26 and 17, are to be added together. The resultant value of the expression is 43.

Many expressions, such as 12 + 9 / 3, have more than one operator. A simple "chain" calculator would evaluate the expression by taking each of those operations in turn: 12 + 9 is 21, 21 / 3 is 7. C (or, for that matter, almost any other computer language) is not so simple. There are strict rules about which operation is to be done first no matter where it occurs in the expression. The rules involve **precedence**, a hierarchy or ranked order of operations that dictates the types of operations that are to be performed before other types; and **associativity**, which dictates order if two operations have the same level of precedence. Table 2–1 shows the arithmetic operators in precedence, highest first, and their associativity. Appendix B shows all the operators.

The same calculation, 12 + 9 / 3, would have a different result in C. Since the division operation is higher in precedence than addition, it would be performed first—9 / 3 is 3, 3 + 12 is 15.

We can force calculations to be in any order we choose by enclosing some of them in parentheses. Inner parentheses will be evaluated before outer parentheses, and before no parentheses. The same expression can be forced to the order that the simple calculator would follow by putting the addition operation in parentheses—(12 + 9) / 3.

The associativity rule applies when two operations are on the same precedence level. In the expression 12 / 6 / 2, the two division operations

TABLE 2–1 Arithmetic Operators in Precedence

Level	Type	Associativity	Operator	Symbol	Example
1	Unary	Right to left	Negate	−	−4
			Plus	+	+4
3	Multiplicative	Left to right	Multiply	*	6 * 4
			Divide	/	6 / 4
			Remainder	%	6 % 4
3	Additive	Left to right	Add	+	6 + 4
			Subtract	−	6 − 4
4	Assignment	Right to left	Equals	=	x = 4

are on the same level, but they associate from left to right, so we have 12 / 6 is 2, then 2 / 2 is 1.

The easiest way to make a C expression from a handwritten arithmetic expression is to spread the handwritten expression out in a straight line with the proper operators and then, referring back to the original handwritten expression, add parentheses to ensure that the C expression will be evaluated in the same order as the handwritten one. Let us examine the following handwritten expression, translate it to C, and show how it will be evaluated by the computer. The first C expression was written without parentheses to illustrate precedence and to show that without parentheses many expressions will not evaluate as we had intended.

Handwritten Expression

$$\frac{\dfrac{6+4}{2}\times4}{4+\dfrac{3\times2}{2-1}}\quad [=2]$$

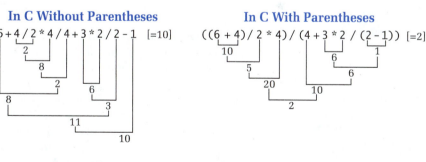

Note that in the second C expression (the one with parentheses), the inclusion of the parentheses around the top of the fraction

$$((6 + 4) / 2 * 4)$$

does not change the result. The parentheses are, indeed, unnecessary, but if they improve the readability or understandability of the program, they can certainly be included.

HEADS UP!

Parentheses can often improve the readability of an expression.

The code in ⇨Program 2–3 illustrates precedence and associativity.

⇨Program 2–3

```c
#include <stdio.h>

void main(void)
{
    printf("Without parentheses: %i, with: %i\n", 12 + 9 / 3, (12 + 9) / 3);
    printf("Without parentheses: %i, with: %i\n",
            6 + 4 / 2 * 4 / 4 + 3 * 2 / 2 - 1,
            ((6 + 4) / 2 * 4) / (4 + 3 * 2 / (2 - 1)));
}
```

Output

```
Without parentheses: 15, with: 7
Without parentheses: 10, with: 2
```

HEADS UP!

An operation on integers produces an integer result.

Exceeding the limits of the data type.

TRAP

Watch integer division.

HEADS UP!

The remainder operator works only with positive integers.

Integer Arithmetic

C performs its arithmetic according to the data types on which it is currently operating. If the data types in a particular operation are integer then the result will also be integer. This typically causes no problem except when the result exceeds the maximum capacity of an integer or when you are dividing. If you exceed the limits of an integer, you will get a meaningless result because many of the bits will not be stored—they will be thrown away. For example, 32000 * 10 (in a C implementation that defaults to a `short int`) yields the result –7680.

When dividing an integer by an integer the result will be an integer—a truncated version of what a floating-point division would yield. The result of the expression 3 / 2 is 1, not 1.5. Since both 3 and 2 are integers (they have no decimal points), an integer calculation will be done, producing an integer result. Note that this is not a round-off but a truncation; the result is not 2, but 1.

The **remainder** (or *modulo* or *modulus*) operator deserves special attention. It is valid only with positive integers, and the result is the remainder after dividing the value before the operator by the value after the operator. The result of the expression 5 % 3 is 2 because 5 divided by 3 is 1 with a remainder of 2. As the following long division shows, 762 % 35 is 27. Other examples are shown as C expressions at the right.

```
      21
  35)762
      70
      62
      35
      27
```

```
13 % 3 = 1

1 % 5 = 1

8 % 3 = 2

14 % 362 = 14
```

MIXED ARITHMETIC

Most C compilers don't do arithmetic on all the standard data types; this would require too many built-in routines and conversions. Typically, for integers the smallest size for calculations is type `int`. Remember, this might be equivalent to `short` or `long`, depending on your compiler. `Char`s are promoted to `int`s and, if the standard `int` is a `long`, `short`s are also promoted. `Long int` calculations on a `short int` compiler are naturally done using `long int` calculations. For floating points, nothing less than `double` is calculated. `Long double`s are, of course, calculated at `long double` size.

What does all this mean to you? Computing is a series of trade-offs. If you declare variables as type `float` rather than `double` (perhaps to save memory space), calculations on these `float`s will be done as `double`. In other words, the computer will have to go through extra conversions—`float`s to `double`s and then back to `float` for the result. The trade-off is storage space versus execution speed.

Be careful when using the remainder operator with negative numbers; the results vary with the particular implementation of C.

Each calculation is performed at the highest data type.

Mixed Arithmetic

In general, when data types are mixed in an expression, each operation will be performed at the highest data type involved in the expression— "highest" meaning the one that takes up the largest amount of memory. Since there is some overlap, floating-point types are considered higher than integral. It is important to recognize that the calculations are not all performed at the highest data type included in the expression; each operation is evaluated separately and performed at the highest data type involved in just that operation. Eventually the result will be of the highest data type in the entire expression, but it may take a while to get there. For example:

$$8.3 + \underbrace{5 / 2}_{2 \text{ (int)}} \quad [=10.3]$$
$$\underline{10.3 \text{ (double)}}$$

The expression 5 / 2 was performed first, and since both the 5 and the 2 are integers (they have no decimal points), 5 / 2 was performed as type `int` with a result of 2 (not 2.5). Compare that with this:

$$8.3 + \underbrace{5 / 2.0}_{2 \text{ (double)}} [=10.8]$$
$$\underline{10.8 \text{ (double)}}$$

In this case 2.0 (or even just 2.) is a floating-point value (actually a **double**; see the *Nuts 'n Bolts: Mixed Arithmetic* box) so 5 / 2. was

```
#include <stdio.h>

void main(void)
{  printf("Without the decimal point: %g, with: %g\n",
            8.3 + 5 / 2,
            8.3 + 5 / 2.0);
}
```

Output

```
Without the decimal point: 10.3, with: 10.8
```

calculated as a floating-point expression with a result of 2.5. ⇨Program 2–4 illustrates the differences in these calculations.

ASSIGNMENT

HEADS UP!

Fundamental rule of assignment.

As we said, variables identify spaces in main memory. These spaces are variable because they can contain various and changeable values. Putting a value into one of these spaces is known as **assignment**. We usually refer to "assigning a value to a variable," but technically, we are writing a value into the memory space identified *by* the variable.

We have seen how initial assignments can be included as part of declarations, but we must also make assignments as part of our program. For example, we may wish to store the results of a calculation in a variable, or change the value of a variable we had assigned previously. There are many ways of assigning values to variables, but all of them follow this fundamental rule:

A variable may have only one value at a time.

We may assign many different values to a variable, but each time we do, we write to the memory space reserved for that variable, and, as we saw in Chapter 1, a write operation replaces data. If the variable *checkers* had the value 137.93, and you assign 6.2 to it, the 6.2 would overwrite, or replace, the 137.93, and the value of *checkers* would then be 6.2. What happens to the 137.93? Unless you specifically copied it somewhere else in memory beforehand, it is lost.

The standard assignment operator is the equal sign (=). Referring to Appendix B or Table 2–1, we can see that in precedence it follows all the arithmetic operators, which means that after all the arithmetic is done, the assignment is made. The general form of an assignment is

variable = expression

where *variable* identifies a space in memory, and *expression* evaluates to a single value.

Following are valid assignment statements:

```
x = 14;
y = (x + 15) / 12.7;
interest = principal * rate * time;
```

Notice that in each case, there is a single variable to the left of the equal sign—something to assign the value to. (The variable is often referred to in references as a *modifiable lvalue*—an identifier that can properly be used at the left of the assignment operator.) The spaces in the statements are not actually necessary in C, but they tend to make the statements a little more readable. It is common practice to use spaces around most operators other than the unary ones. ⇨Program 2–5 shows assignment statements.

The resultant value of an assignment expression is the value of the assignment. Since the assignment operator's associativity is right to left, this allows more than one assignment to be made in a single statement. For example,

```
x = y = z = 17 + 9;
```

would calculate 17 + 9 first (the + is higher in precedence than =) and assign the value 26 to z. The value of the entire expression z = 17 + 9 is the assignment value 26, so that value would be assigned to *y*. The

HEADS UP!

For better readability, put spaces around all except unary operators.

⇨**Program 2–5**

```
#include <stdio.h>

void main(void)
{   float principal, rate, time, interest;

    principal = 1000;
    rate = .075;
    time = 3.5;
    interest = principal * rate * time;
    printf("The interest on $%g at %g%%\nfor %g years is $%g.\n",
            principal, rate * 100, time, interest);
}
```

Output

```
The interest on $1000 at 7.5%
for 3.5 years is $262.5.
```

value of $y = z = 17 + 9$ is now also 26, so that value would be assigned to x.

Forced Conversions

Any value may be assigned to any type of variable. Whether that value is actually stored in its original form is essentially up to you and how you write the assignment. A value assigned to a variable will always be of the type of that variable. It has to be; there is a specific memory space allocated and a specific form (integer or floating point) to be followed. If a floating-point value is assigned to an integer variable, the decimal part will be dropped. If a value is assigned to a data type that will not hold it, as many bits as possible will be stuffed in, but the result will be unrecognizable.

Many C programmers get into the habit of explicitly declaring their data types so that there are no forced conversions. Some variants of the language require this explicit typing and produce weird results if you depend on forced conversions.

YOUR TURN 2–4

1. How does precedence differ from associativity? Which is considered first?
2. Of the operators covered in this chapter, which are highest in precedence? Lowest?
3. How do we change the normal order of operations?
4. What happens if an arithmetic operation involving two integers yields what we would think of as a fractional result (such as dividing 3 / 2)?
5. What is the result of a remainder operation?
6. If dissimilar data types are involved in an arithmetic operation, of what data type is the result?
7. How many values may a simple variable have at one time?
8. Of what data type will an assignment be?

PUTTING IT TOGETHER

Let us look at an example to illustrate what we have learned to this point. We will develop this example just as we would any other program—going through the five steps of program development.

The people at Sticky Molasses Company need to know how much a trailer fully loaded with molasses weighs and would like us to write a program to tell them.

ANALYSIS

The total weight of the molasses trailer is an accumulation of various things. The weight of the trailer alone is 7,540 pounds. Molasses weighs 78.2 pounds per cubic foot. It is packaged in drums that are 2 feet high and a foot in diameter. The drums alone weigh 16 pounds. They are packed 8 to a pallet. The empty pallets each weigh 22 pounds. Lastly, the trailer holds 24 pallets. Our process must calculate the weight of each drum filled with molasses, then calculate the weight of a full pallet, multiply that by the number of pallets per trailer, and add the weight of the trailer.

For our calculations, the formula for the volume of a drum (a cylinder) is:

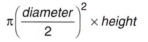

$$\pi \left(\frac{diameter}{2} \right)^2 \times height$$

We can round off the pallet weight to the nearest pound for our calculations.

We want the computer to show us the results of some of the interim calculations as well as the final total. The output should be similar to:

```
Each drum weighs:       ###.###### lbs.
(Pallet actual weight:  ####.###### lbs).
Pallet approx. weight:  #### lbs.
Total trailer weight:   ##### lbs.
```

DESIGN

This task is a relatively straightforward sequence of operations as follows:

    Calculate and display the weight of a full drum
    Calculate and display the weight of a full pallet
    Calculate and display the weight of the full trailer

Note: The line numbers shown with this program are there only for reference in the following execution chart; they are not part of the code. By looking at the Execution Chart, you can follow the process and changes in variable values as the program produces the output shown in the *Test* section.

```
   #include <stdio.h>

   void main(void)
 1 {  int diameter = 1, height = 2, pallet = 22, drums_pallet = 8,
         pallets_trailer = 24;
 2    long trailer = 7540;                        /* May be greater than 32767 */
 3    float drum = 16,                            /* Must store a real value */
            lbs_cu_ft = 98.5, pi = 3.1416;

      /************************* Calculate and display weight of full drum */
 4       drum = drum + pi * (diameter / 2.0) * (diameter / 2.0) * height
                  * lbs_cu_ft;
 5       printf("Each drum weighs:       %g lbs.\n", drum);

      /*********************** Calculate and display weight of full pallet */
        /********************* Calculate and display actual pallet weight */
 6         printf("(Pallet actual weight:  %g lbs).\n",
                   pallet + drum * drums_pallet);
        /********************* Calculate and display rounded pallet weight */
 7         pallet = pallet + drum * drums_pallet + .5;        /* Round off */
 8         printf("Pallet approx. weight:  %i lbs.\n", pallet);

      /*********************** Calculate and display weight of full trailer */
 9       trailer = trailer + 1L * pallet * pallets_trailer;   /* Force long */
10       printf("Total trailer weight:   %li lbs.\n", trailer);
   }
```

Output

```
Each drum weighs:       170.724 lbs.
(Pallet actual weight:  1387.79 lbs).
Pallet approx. weight:  1388 lbs.
Total trailer weight:   40852 lbs.
```

Since we must display the actual weight of a pallet as well as calculating and displaying the rounded weight of a pallet, let us expand the second module for the following result.

Calculate and display the weight of a full drum
[Calculate and display the weight of a full pallet]
  Calculate and display the actual pallet weight
  Calculate and display the rounded pallet weight
Calculate and display the weight of the full trailer

EXECUTION CHART

Line	Explanation	drum	pallet	trailer
1	Allocate space and initialize the variables in the statement. (Note that *drum* and *trailer* do not yet exist.)	---	22	---
2	Allocate space and initialize *trailer*. Although *trailer*'s initial value is only 7540, its eventual value will be larger than an `int` can hold in this C.	---	22	7450
3	Allocate and initialize *drum* and the others. Although *drum*'s initial value can be accommodated by an `int`, it must eventually hold a `float`.	16.000	22	7450
4	Since C has no exponentiation operator, diameter / 2 must be multiplied by itself to square it. The 2.0 in each division forces the calculation to `double`. Without the decimal points 1 / 2, an integer operation, would be 0 rather than 0.5.	170.724	22	7450
5	*drum*'s actual value should be 170.7238. The stored value is as much as this C can fit in a `float`.	170.724	22	7450
6	Since we don't have to store the value for future use, we calculated the actual pallet weight in the `printf()` function.	170.724	22	7450
7	Since *drum*, which is involved in the first calculation in the expression, is `float`, all the calculations will be done at type `double`. *pallet*, the variable to be assigned, is `int`, so the part of the result after the decimal point will be discarded and the integer component assigned to *pallet*. By adding .5 to the result before truncating, the value will be rounded.	170.724	1388	7450
8	*pallet* is displayed as an integer.	170.724	1388	7450
9	Both *pallet* and *pallets_trailer* are `int`. Multiplying them together might exceed an `int`'s capacity in this C (32767), so we forced the calculation to a `long` by multiplying *pallet* by 1L.	170.724	1388	40852
10	The total trailer weight must be displayed as a `long`. In the next chapter, we will see that &li is the code for a `long`.	170.724	1388	40852

IMPLEMENTATION

The design is implemented in ⇨Program 2–6.

TEST

We find that the values in the output match our hand calculations.

American National Standards Institute (ANSI)	Integral data type
	`char`
K&R	`signed`
Whitespace	`unsigned`
Comment	`int`
Directive	`short`
Statement	`long`
Function	Floating-point data type
Call	Mantissa
Argument	Exponent
Newline	E notation
Declaration	`float`
Header file	`double`
Real number	`long double`
Integral number	String
Special character	Concatenate
Variable	Expression
Variable name	Arithmetic operator
Reserved word	Precedence
Data type	Associativity
Declare	Remainder
Define	Assignment
Initialize	

▲CONCEPT REVIEW

▼ C was first developed in 1972 by Dennis Ritchie and its initial, de facto, standard was in a book by Kernighan and Ritchie (**K&R**). In 1988, the **American National Standards Institute** released the standard for **ANSI** C.

▼ C lends itself to modular design by allowing the use of **whitespace**, which is largely ignored by C. With it, you can make your program visually represent its organization in outline form. Elements of a C program include **comments**, which are ignored by the C compiler; **directives**, instructions to the compiler rather than the computer; **statements**, the instructions for the computer; **functions**, sets of statements that are **called** to perform a particular task with the **arguments** sent to them; and **declarations**, which inform C of your intent to use variables and functions. Declarations of functions provided with the compiler are contained in **header files**.

▼ Decimal numeric values, **real** or **integral**, are represented in C just as they are in handwritten math.

▼ Characters are stored in ASCII (or EBCDIC) form and, inside the computer, are indistinguishable from numbers. The character `'A'` is stored exactly like the decimal value 65 (the numeric value of its ASCII code). We can put characters in our C code that do not exist on the keyboard by using **special characters** such as \t for tab or \n for **newline**.

▼ Simple output is performed using the `printf()` function and the codes `%i` and `%g` to embed integral or real numeric values in the output.

▼ A **variable** is a space in the computer's memory. **Variable names** can be multicharacter combinations of alpha, numeric, or underscore characters, and are case-sensitive. None of ANSI C's 32 **reserved words** can be used as a variable name, nor can a variable name begin with a numeric character.

▼ When we use data, either as values or in variables, they must be declared as a specific **data type**. The **declaration** tells C whether the data is stored in straight binary fashion or IEEE floating-point notation; specifies how many bytes to allocate to the data; and **defines** the value or variable by allocating memory to it. A variable may also be **initialized** in a declaration.

▼ The **integral data types char** and **int** use straight binary notation and may be signed or unsigned. The int data type may be **short** or **long**. The **floating-point data types float**, **double**, and **long double** use IEEE **E notation**, storing a **mantissa** and an **exponent**. All floating-point data types are signed. **Strings**, sets of characters, are not really data types, but we may include string values in a program by putting the characters in quotes. Adjacent strings will be **concatenated** by C. There are no string variables in C.

▼ An **expression** is anything that reduces to a single value. Arithmetic expressions are made by combining values or variables together using **arithmetic operators**. The expressions must be carefully constructed because the order of operation is determined by the operators' **precedence** and **associativity**. The order of operations may be altered by enclosing operations in parentheses. Operators include not only the standard ones but also some special ones such as **remainder**.

▼ The results of arithmetic operations are dependent on the data types. An operation on two integers produces an integer result, truncating any decimal places. Operations mixing integers and floating-point values will produce floating-point results. Generally speaking, in mixed arithmetic lower data types are promoted to higher before the operation is performed.

▼ **Assignment** is the process of putting a value in a variable. A variable may have only one value at a time, so an assignment replaces any value that was there before. An assignment will always be of the data type of the assigned variable. C will perform conversions automatically if it needs to.

▲HEADS UP: POINTS OF SPECIAL INTEREST

▼ Whitespace is used to enhance the readability of programs. *Use tabs, spaces, and blank lines to give your program style and readability.*

▼ Directives end at the end of the line.

▼ Statements end with a semicolon.

▼ Function calls always have parentheses.

▼ Your code is more readable with a space after the comma.

▼ Newline characters drop the display to the next line.

▼ Remember, directives, unlike statements, end at the end of the physical line.

▼ A single character is actually a number. *It is the numeric value of the ASCII (or EBDIC) code.*

▼ The character value `'4'`, whose ASCII code is 52, is different from the numeric value 4.

▼ Use variable names that indicate the purpose of the variable.

▼ Variable names cannot contain spaces.

▼ You can't start a variable name with a number.

▼ Don't start normal variable names with an underscore. *These are usually used for special variables set up by the makers of the compiler.*

▼ The `char` data type is numeric.

▼ There is no such thing as an `unsigned float`. *All floating-point values are signed.*

▼ Parentheses can often improve the readability of an expression. *In some cases they are necessary; in others, they make the expression clearer.*

▼ An operation on integers produces an integer result. *Fractional parts are truncated.*

▼ The remainder operator works only with positive integers.

▼ Each calculation is performed at the highest data type. *That is, the higher of the data types on each side of the single operator. Floating-point is higher than integral, and within each category, The data type with the greatest number of bits is higher.*

▼ Fundamental rule of assignment. *"A variable may have only one value at a time."*

▼ For better readability, put spaces around all except unary operators.

▼ The assigned variable (or any other, for that matter) can never change data type.

▲TRAPS: COMMON PROGRAMMING ERRORS

▼ Splitting a line inside quotes. *Split a set of quoted characters with ending quotes on the first line and beginning quotes on the second.*

▼ Don't "nest" comments, put one comment inside another, unless your compiler specifically allows it.

▼ Using only a single backslash in a string to represent a backslash. *Use a double backslash.*

▼ Data types that don't match.

▼ Forgetting to declare a variable.

▼ Leaving a semicolon off the end of a declaration.

▼ Assigning a `long int` value to a `short int` variable will store garbage in the variable. *Half the bits will be thrown away.*

▼ Declaring a `long double` as a `long`. `long` *means* `long int`.

▼ Exceeding the limits of the data type.

▼ Watch integer division. *The results are truncated.*

▲YOUR TURN ANSWERS

▼2–1

1. Among the advantages of C are efficiently executing programs, portability, and its continued growth.

2. ANSI, the American National Standards Institute.

3. In most places, whitespace is ignored by the C compiler, so we can use it to make our programs more readable.

4. Characters between /* and */ are ignored by the compiler, so that becomes a place for comments.

5. Directives are instructions to the compiler or preprocessor. Statements directly become part of the executable code.

6. Functions are ways of modularizing a program. They perform sets of operations.

7. Declarations tell the compiler that the object declared can be a valid part of the program and specify how it can be used.

1. Real numbers allow decimal points; integers are whole numbers. The decimal notation for both types of numbers is the same in C as it is in math.

2. Characters are represented using coding schemes like ASCII. These schemes represent characters with sets of bits, which, as far as C is concerned, are numeric values.

3. They are stored exactly the same.

4. Special characters represent those that we cannot produce on the keyboard. The backslash is represented by two backslashes in a row, \\.

▼2–3

1. A–Z, upper- or lowercase, 0–9, and underscore (_). A name can start with anything but a number.

2. No, C is case-sensitive.

3. Whether it is represented by straight binary or exponential notation, and how many bits it occupies.

4. Directs C how to store values in the variable, allocates space in memory, and, possibly, initializes the variable.

5. `char` and `int` (with the possible modifiers `signed`, `unsigned`, `short`, and `long`) are integral; `float`, `double`, and `long double` are floating point.

6. U, L, UL, F, and L again for `long double`, but the decimal point differentiates it from a `long int`.

7. We must use the special character \".

8. As one continuous string value.

▼2–4

1. Precedence determines the order of operators of different levels; associativity of operators on the same level.

2. Unary operators are highest; assignment is lowest.

3. By enclosing operations within parentheses.

4. The result is truncated to the nearest integer.

5. The remainder when the first value is divided by the second.

6. The data type that takes the largest amount of memory, with floating-point being higher than integral.

7. One! Any new assignment will replace the old value.

8. It can only be the data type of the assigned variable. An expression result of another data type will be converted, perhaps creating a garbage result.

1. Compare C to either another high-level language, or to an assembly language. Which language will require less programming time to create the same program? Which program will operate more efficiently?

2. Rewrite this program in proper form. Compile and run both programs to see if they do the same thing.

```
#include <stdio.h>/* Here it comes */
void main(void){int number;number = 2;printf("We had
%i. ", number);number = number * 2;printf("Now we
have %i.\n", number);}
```

3. In an implementation of C using ASCII, to what character would the following expressions evaluate? (Refer to the complete table in Appendix A.)

   a. `'J' + ' '`   b. `'4' + '5'`
   c. `'p' - '?'`   d. `'~' # '<'`

4. Write `printf()` function calls to produce the following output. All numbers should be embedded in the output using the appropriate codes.

   ```
   2, 4, 6, 7.9,
   This program is definitely mine!
   ```

5. Of the following, which are invalid variable names? Why are they invalid?

   a. *Gnash*   b. *union*
   c. *9Times*   d. *too_many*

6. Of the following, which are invalid declarations? Why are they invalid?

   a. `unsigned float zip = 46;`
   b. `Double Dip;`
   c. `short stuff, pants = 12.6;`
   d. `long double disaster`

7. In the C that you use, in what data types would the following values be stored? In what data types could they actually fit?

   a. 91   b. 40265
   c. 45.   d. 1657.39854

8. What are the values and data types of the following expressions?

   a. `7 / 4`   b. `9 / 2. + 25 / 3`
   c. `6 + 4.8 / 2 * 3`   d. `25 % 5 + 12.5 * 2 / 5`

9. If $x = 5$ and $y = 2$ and both are integers, what are the values of the following expressions?

   a. `x % y + 14.6 / y`   b. `y = 1. * x / 2 + 3.5`
   c. `y = y * x`   d. `y = 16.2 * x / 3`

10. Fill out an execution chart for the following program. (*Note to future programmers:* Wouldn't this program be a lot easier to understand if it were well commented?)

Program

```
#include <stdio.h>

void main(void)
{  int bytes, code, dollars, pennies;
   float cost, per_byte = 1.42;

1      code = 3;
2      bytes = code * 17 * 2;
3      dollars = bytes * per_byte + .5;
4      printf("%i code segments cost %i dollars.\n", code, dollars);
5      code = code + 1;
6      bytes = code * 17 * 2;
7      cost = bytes * per_byte;
8      pennies = cost * 100 + .5;
9      printf("%i code segments cost %g dollars.\n", code, cost);
10     printf("   This time we count the %i pennies.\n", pennies % 100);
}
```

Output

```
3 code segments cost 145 dollars.
4 code segments cost 193.12 dollars.
   This time we count the 12 pennies.
```

█████   **PROGRAMS**

1. Enter and execute ⇨Program 2–1.

2. Enter and execute ⇨Program 2–5.

3. Write a program to give some information about yourself. It should produce something like the following:

```
NAME:  your name
MAJOR:
OTHER COMPUTER COURSES TAKEN:
OCCUPATION:
HOBBIES AND ACTIVITIES:
REASONS FOR TAKING THIS COURSE:
COMMENTS:
```

next week 9/20

4. Find the value of each of these expressions. Be sure to pay attention to data type. Write a program that confirms your answers.

    a. 3.5 + 8 / 3   b. 4 * 11.5 / 2 + 16
    c. 7.5 − 38 % 7 * 2 + 10   d. 25 / 2. + 13 / 3

5. Write a program that assigns $a = 4$, $f = 9$, $b = -6$, $x = 4$, and $h = 7$ and prints out the results of the following expressions. All the variables are integers but the results should be as shown. Your output should have the same form and the same values as shown. (The last digit may vary according to your C implementation)

    1. $a + f\dfrac{b^2 + h}{3}$ 2. $x + 6f\dfrac{h+9}{4-b}$

    3. $\dfrac{(a+b)^2}{f - \dfrac{x+1}{h-4}}$ 4. $\dfrac{\dfrac{(1+h)(1-f)}{3f}}{h^2 - x}$

Output

```
1 = 133
2 = 90.4
3 = 0.545455
4 = -106.667
```

6. There are 12 inches in a foot. Write a program in which you initialize the integer variable *inches* to a value, say 46, assign the number of feet to *feet*, and print the result.

next week 9/20

Variables

```
inches, feet
```

Output

```
46 inches is 3.83333 feet.
```

7. Write a program to find the average of the four values 4, 42, 16.7, and .0045.

due next week 10/4

Variables   **Output**

```
v1, v2, v3, v4            The four numbers are:
average                   4 42 16.7 0.0045
                          The average is:
                          15.676126
```

8. You are given a sphere with a radius of 25. Find the circumference, largest cross-sectional area, and the volume of the sphere. Remember, the fractional numbers you get may not exactly agree with those below.

Variables

pi	π (3.1416)
radius	25
circumference	$(2\pi r)$
area	largest cross-sectional area $(\pi r 2)$
volume	$\left(\dfrac{4}{3}\pi r^3\right)$

Output

```
Radius:               25
Circumference:        157.08
Cross-sectional area: 1963.499878
Volume:               65449.996094
```

9. Rewrite the program in the problem above to work with a radius of 14.

Output

```
Radius:               14
Circumference:        87.964798
Cross-sectional area: 615.753601
Volume:               11494.066406
```

10. Write a program that produces a bill and coin breakdown for an amount of money. Initialize the amount in the **float** variable *dollars* and use the *pennies* variable to keep track of the amount not yet converted to bills and coins. You will have to make use of integer arithmetic and the remainder operator in this program.

Variables

```
dollars   float
pennies   int
```

Output

```
The coin breakdown for 7.73 dollars is:
Dollar bills: 7
Half dollars: 1
Quarters:     0
Dimes:        2
Nickels:      0
Pennies:      3
```

Chapter 3

BUILDING A C PROGRAM

PREVIEW

Now that you have been introduced to the C language, you are ready to look at issues of style, usability, and readability. Here, we will examine:

▼ The elements that contribute to a program's style and readability.

▼ Using prewritten source code in a program.

▼ Defining constants for use in a program.

▼ The most basic output function.

▼ The most basic input function.

Programs don't just happen. They are very carefully crafted and, when completed, should not only do the job but also be a work of art. In Chapter 1 you looked at the steps in developing a program in any language, and in Chapter 2 you were introduced to the specific language, C. Here we will look at some of the elements that make your C program that work of art, including programming style and the basics of its human interface—input and output.

DEVELOPING A STYLE

A student asked the lecturer, "Should my program have a specific style?" "Yes," answered the lecturer, "most definitely!" and turned to the next question, leaving the student a bit baffled.

The lecturer's point was that a program must have a definite, cohesive, readable style, but not all styles will be the same. Your style will depend on a number of things, among them your own personality and, probably more significantly, the demands of the environment in which you find yourself. As a student, you will find that your school or professor may demand certain style elements. As an employee, you will be required by your employer to use the company's style. The reason for the style demands in either environment are the same: *communicability*. The people in each environment must deal with a number of programs from a number of programmers. If all the programmers use the same style, they will be much more able to read and understand each other's work.

It is very important that you develop an appreciation for style. Even though the style demands may change in the next environment you move to, the habit pattern you develop will make it easy for you to accommodate. The programs you see in this book follow a consistent style and, if there are no other style demands made on you, you might try following this style. There are certain style elements that are almost universal, and we will mention these in this chapter and in subsequent chapters as new concepts are introduced. Other elements differ from place to place. In Chapter 2, we mentioned our preference for lining up opening and closing braces in the same column. The "K&R" style opens the brace at the right end of the line preceding the statement block and closes it in the column under the left end of that line. As we see in ❑Figure 3–1, either style works, but if you mix them or have no consistent way of treating braces and blocks, your programs will be confusing.

Modularity

Top-down, modular design is a universally accepted program-design method, so your program should reflect its modularity. The beginning and the end of a program module should be obvious and clearly marked. The typical way of doing this is by using outline form as we saw in

HEADS UP!

You are probably not the only one who will have to read your programs.

HEADS UP!

Keep your style consistent.

❏ **FIGURE 3–1** Programming Styles

HEADS UP!

Outline form shows modularity.

Chapter 2. The beginning of the module should be a comment that identifies the module or, in appropriate cases, a statement (properly commented) that begins a module. Statements within the module should be indented one level underneath the beginning line. Submodules should be indented further within their containing modules, as shown below. Many programmers advocate including blank lines before program sections. Notice that the previous program has a blank line between the variable declarations (in this case only one declaration) and the rest of the statements—another common practice.

```
statement; /* Begins module */
{  statement;
   statement;
   /* Submodule starts here */
      statement;
      statement;
   statement; /* Back in the containing module */
   statement;
}
```

Documentation

HEADS UP!

Documentation is a constant process.

In Chapter 1 we looked at the five-step program development process. Many programmers add a sixth step, documentation—all those written things that describe the program and what it does. Documentation is not really a sixth step, to be done after the first five are completed; it is an ongoing process that begins with the first statement of the task. It includes the task statement, the logical design, the program design laid out in outline form, the program itself (including the proper comments), and manuals or written instructions on how to use the program.

As you can see, the documentation produced with each step of the development process is the basis for the next step. For example, coding a program is simply a translation of the program design produced in the analysis step.

Commenting

Just like handwriting styles, commenting styles differ. In the style in this book you will notice that the program code in its outline form is clearly identifiable from the left side of the program. Comments are always lined up at the right margin. This is one style; there are many others. Two general rules of commenting are always to comment those parts of the code that are not obvious from looking at the code itself, and never to comment on those that are obvious. The following comment is reasonable:

```
taxable = gross - retirement  /* Must occur before income tax calculated */
```

This comment only gets in the way:

```
printf("Total weight: %f\n", total_weight);  /* Display the total weight */
```

Readability

A program must, of course, do the job for which it was intended. Beyond that, the most important criterion for a program is **readability**. That should be the objective for your programming style. Two groups of people must be able to easily read and understand your program: other people, and you. You know that your program is not readable when, while you are working in one section of it and must refer to another section that you wrote last week, it takes you 20 minutes to figure out what you did in that section.

A number of factors contribute to readability:

▼ *Preliminary documentation.* Looking at the task statement, logical design, and program design will give the reader a quick overview of what the program does and how it does it. It forms an introduction to the program.

▼ *Modular outline form.* The outline form from the program design should be carried over into the program code itself. Modules and submodules should be easy to identify.

▼ *Variables.* Choose your variable names so that the name itself indicates the nature of the data in the variable. To store the beginning of a range of values, use *begin_range*, not *br*, or *x*.

▼ *Commenting.* Make your comments count.

▼ *Consistent style.* Whatever your style, keep it consistent.

YOUR TURN 3–1

1. What should be the objective of programming style?
2. How is modularity demonstrated in program statements?
3. When should the documentation be done?
4. How much commenting should be done in a program?
5. What five factors contribute to readability?

DIRECTIVES

HEADS UP!

Directives act before statements.

HEADS UP!

Directives end at the end of a line.

In a sample program in Chapter 2, we labeled one line as a **directive**, an instruction to the compiler rather than a statement to be translated directly to machine language. When we compile a program, the compiler typically invokes a **preprocessor**, which reacts to directives just before the actual compile operation. We shall look at the preprocessor more completely in Chapter 12, but two directives are used so frequently, even in the simplest programs, that they beg for at least partial attention now.

Notice that a directive does not end in a semicolon. For the simple directives given here, be sure that they are each contained on a single line.

Including Header Files

The `#include` directive instructs the compiler to temporarily, at the beginning of the compile process, insert the contents of a file at that point in the source code. We will look at the `#include` directive more fully in Chapter 12, but we will use it now to add some source code supplied by the compiler's publisher to the beginning of our programs. These files, called **header files** (of which `stdio.h` is an example), contain, among other things, declarations and definitions for standard ANSI C functions and constants.

The directive has this form:

```
#include <fileid>
```

where the *fileid* is the identification of the file to be placed in the source code.

For the first few chapters, all of our programs will have

```
#include <stdio.h>
```

near the beginning because we will be using functions, like `printf()` and `scanf()`, that are declared in `stdio.h`. As we add other functions to our repertoire, we will find many of them declared in other header files, so our programs will have a number of `#include` directives at the beginning.

Character Replacements

The **#define** directive, among other things, establishes a character replacement for a program.

```
#define pattern replacement
```

Following the directive, all occurrences of a specific **pattern** of characters in the source code are replaced by the characters in **replacement**. For example,

```
#define PI 3.14
```

will replace each PI in the source code with the characters 3.14. An instance of the specified pattern in quotes, of course, will not be replaced (as we see in the printf() below). We will not see the replacement; like the **#include** directive, it works only at the beginning of the compile process.

Source Code

```
#include <stdio.h>

#define PI 3.14

int main(void)
{  float radius = 25;
   float circ;

   printf("The circumference "
          "formula uses PI\n");
   circ = 2 * PI * radius
[and so forth]
```

Actual Code to Be Compiled

```
[The entire stdio.h file here]

int main(void)
{  float radius = 25;
   float circ;

   printf("The circumference "
          "formula uses PI\n");
   circ = 2 * 3.14 * radius
[and so forth]
```

By tradition, the **pattern** is all uppercase, as in PI. This makes the characters slated for replacement easy to spot in the source code, and reduces conflict with variables, which are traditionally in caps/lowercase or all lowercase. Remember, C is case-sensitive.

Why not just put 3.14 in the source code? We usually use the **patterns** as **defined constants**, symbols that represent specific values—PI representing the value 3.14, for example. One reason for putting them in the #define directive is to have them expressed at the beginning of the program where they may be easy to find if we want to change them. In our example, we may want our *circ* (circumference) or anything else based on π to be more accurate. All we have to do is to change the #define directive to, say,

```
#define PI 3.14159
```

DEFINED CONSTANTS VERSUS VARIABLES

Instead of using a defined constant, like

```
#define PI 3.14
```

why not use a variable, like

```
double pi = 3.14;
```

Either, of course, would do the job, but the defined constant is substituted at the beginning of the compile stage, not during the program's execution. It requires no more memory in the executable code than a `double` value, and no execution time. A variable requires space in the executable code for the same `double` value plus the `double` variable *pi*, and it requires the execution time to make the initial assignment of the value to the variable as well as the time to read the variable's value each time it is used.

Moral: If a variable isn't variable, either use the value directly or define it as a constant.

YOUR TURN 3–2

and every occurrence of `PI` will reflect the change.

Another reason for using the `#define` directive is to enhance program readability. For example, our process may have a high limit of 849.325 and a low limit of −35.769. We often refer to such numbers as "magic numbers." If someone reads those two numbers buried in the source code, it might require some research to find out what they mean. But seeing the words `HIGH` and `LOW` would provide an instant clue.

Remember, directives end at the end of a line. Do not put a semicolon at the end of them, especially the `#define`, which would include the semicolon as part of the replacement.

1. What is the difference between a directive and a program statement? At which point in the process does each one act?

2. What ends a directive?

3. Are the things in an include file source code or object code? Can you see the actual instructions put in your program by an `#include` directive?

4. What does the `#define` directive do?

5. Why would you use defined constants in your program?

STREAMS

Most computers have a number of input and output devices—keyboards, mouse devices, screens, printers, communication devices. Access to these pieces of equipment is different depending on the computer hardware, the operating system, and the device itself. In other words, it's enough to drive a person charged with maintaining standards crazy. Therefore, specific access to many of these devices is not covered in the ANSI standard; it is left to individual implementations of C and/or supplemental libraries of C routines.

The ANSI standard does, however, provide for generalized input and output through a standard mechanism called a **stream**. ANSI C allows us to establish any number of streams to be used within a program, but the standard itself provides three of the most used: `stdin`, `stdout`, and `stderr`. The **stdin** stream is normally associated with the keyboard, while **stdout** and **stderr** are associated with the screen. The `stderr` stream is where C directs its error messages. In this chapter we will concentrate on `stdin` and `stdout`, the two that allow us to send data to the program through the keyboard and that have the program print data on our screen.

HEADS UP!

The ANSI standard provides three standard streams.

OUTPUT

Working with the ANSI standard output stream is straightforward; we send characters to the stream, and the stream sends them to the device attached to it, usually a screen. Although there are a number of C functions that do this, we shall concentrate at this point on the most basic and versatile—**printf()**.

We have already seen that we can send character strings, characters enclosed in quotes, to the screen by putting the quoted string value within the parentheses. The statement

```
printf("This is an output line.\n");
```

when executed produces

```
This is an output line.
```

on the screen. The `\n` drops the cursor to the beginning of the next line.

The name of the function comes from the fact that `printf()` performs formatted printing. (The term "print" is something of a historical hangover, because virtually all `stdout` streams are associated with the screen, where we "display," not with a printer!) By formatting, we can specifically state how, in what format, we want the result to appear. We can display numbers rounded to two decimal places, start or end values at specific character positions on the line, use many `printf()`s to create columns lined up on the decimal point, and so forth.

Formatted printing in most languages, C included, is a two-step process. First we design the line—show where things go and reserve spaces for values of various data types to print. Second, we state what values should be placed in the spaces reserved for them. Both steps are specified as arguments to the function (the parameters between the parentheses).

HEADS UP!

Printing is a two-step process.

```
printf("control string", argument, argument, ..., argument)
```

The first step, and the first argument to the function, is the line design, called a format or **control string**. This is a set of characters that we use to tell C what we want to go where in our output. The control string can contain two types of characters: printable characters and conversion codes. Printable characters simply print at whatever position they happen to be in the format. Most characters are printable. In fact, as we have seen, it is possible to use the `printf()` function with only a single argument, the *control string*, in which all the characters in the format are output. (Remember, the special characters that were defined in Chapter 2, such as \" or \n, are used to represent single characters, and they are printable. Newline, of course, does not print anything visible, but it does move the cursor to the beginning of the next line.)

It is common to make the last output of any program a newline character. This ensures that the cursor will always be placed at the beginning of a new line for whatever program follows yours. To be doubly sure, many programmers make the first output a newline also.

Conversion Codes

In Chapter 2, we used the codes `%i` and `%g` in the `printf()` function. These are **conversion codes**. They are used to reserve space in the output for some other values to print—the value of a variable or expression, for example—and to show how those values should be converted to characters and printed. All conversion codes begin with a `%` and end with a **type specifier**, a character indicating the data type of the value that will be displayed at that location. For example, this program segment,

```
void main(void)
{   int dollars = 150;

    printf("I have %i dollars in my pocket.\n", dollars);
}
```

when executed displays

```
I have 150 dollars in my pocket.
```

All the characters in the format are printable except the conversion code `%i`, which reserves space for an integer value to print. The format requires a value to fill in that space, so C takes the value of the next argument, `dollars`, and puts it there. Given this format there must, of course, be a next argument. Notice that many of our first uses of `printf()` did not require any further arguments because there was nothing to fill in. In others, we were careful to have an argument of the matching data type for each code in the format string.

TABLE 3–1 Data Type Specifiers for `printf()`

Specifier	Data Type	Explanation	Sample	Output
c	char	A single character.	"%c",65	A
d	int	PreANSI version of i. Still valid in most ANSI implementations.	"%d",-4725 "%d",4725	-4725 4725
f	float or double	Standard signed decimal notation with six digits after the decimal point. Negative signs print, positive signs don't.	"%f",462.58 "%f",-1.7225	462.580000 -1.722500
g	float or double	Outputs in the numeric format that requires the fewest characters. Trailing zeros or trailing decimal points are not printed.	"%g",1.25 "%g",4.0	1.25 4
i	int	Signed integer with negative but not positive signs printing.	"%i",-4725 "%i",4725	-4725 4725
s	string	Prints an entire set of characters. We will look at strings later.		

 **HEADS UP!**

To print a %, use %%.

Since the % character is used as the beginning of a conversion instead of a printable character, to print a %, use %%.

```
void main(void)
{   float yours = 126.4, mine = 17.5628;

    printf("You have %g and I have %g, %g%% of that.\n",
           yours, mine, mine / yours * 100);
}
```

when executed will display

```
You have 126.4 and I have 17.5628, 13.8946% of that.
```

An argument for a conversion codes can, of course, be any valid expression, anything that can be reduced to a single numeric value—a number, variable, or, as in the last argument, a formula.

The most common type specifiers are listed in Table 3–1. Others that can also be used with `printf()` can be found in Appendix D.

In ⇨Program 3–1, we have used the %c code to print the value of *letter*, the character A. Remember, the conversion code not only leaves room for a value to print but also tells C how to convert the value into displayable characters. The %c code directs C to display the character whose ASCII code is the value of the argument. The %i code directs C to display the value of the argument in decimal characters; therefore, it printed *65* instead of *A*.

⇨**Program 3–1**

```c
#include <stdio.h>

#define FEET_METER 3.2808

void main(void)
{  char letter = 'A';
   int meters = 2;
   float feet = 25.8;

   printf("The character %c can also be interpreted as the number %i.\n",
          letter, letter);          /* %i can be used for char data types */
   printf("At %f feet per meter, %i meters is %g feet.\n",
          FEET_METER, meters, meters * FEET_METER);
   printf("%f feet is %g meters.\n", feet, feet / FEET_METER);
}
```

Output

```
The character A can also be interpreted as the number 65.
At 3.280800 feet per meter, 2 meters is 6.5616 feet.
25.799999 feet is 7.86394 meters.
```

In the second `printf()`, the %f code printed the value with six digits after the decimal point, adding extra digits where it needed them. The %g code printed the value without extra digits. In this case, both the %f and %g codes were used to print values of type `double`. The constant *FEET_METER*, because it is the real number 3.2808, is `double`, as is the result of the expression containing it.

In the third `printf()`, why isn't the value of *feet* the way we initialized it? Remember, the computer stores the numbers in binary E notation. The %f format prints with six decimal digits, so when C made the conversion, that was the closest approximation it could come up with.

HEADS UP!

Printing floating-point values often results in slight approximations.

Size Modifiers

Some data types optionally have **size modifiers** that further define the type. As shown in ⇨Program 3–2, the size-modifier character appears just before the type specifier; remember, the conversion code must end with the type specifier. The size modifiers h, for `short`, and l, for `long`, may modify any of the integral types, d or i in Table 3–1. The conversion code %li, then, indicates that a `long int` value will print here.

The L modifier may modify any of the floating-point type specifiers to indicate a `long double` value. Notice that the uppercase L is used for floating-point data types, whereas the lowercase l is used for integral data types.

HEADS UP!

Use l for long `int`s and L for `long double`s.

⇨Program 3–2

```
#include <stdio.h>

void main(void)
{   short cake = 12;
    long face = 987654321L;         /* The 'L' suppresses a warning message */
    float cork = -36.2;
    double trouble = 12345678.90123;
    long double big = 0.0;

    printf("%hi is a short and %li is a long\n", cake, face);
    printf("Floats like %f and doubles like %f\n"
            "use the same conversion code,\n", cork, trouble);
    printf("but long doubles, like %Lf, have their own.\n", big);
}
```

Output

```
12 is a short and 987654321 is a long
Floats like -36.200001 and doubles like 12345678.901230
use the same conversion code,
but long doubles, like 0.000000, have their own.
```

Width and Precision

HEADS UP!

The width parameter refers to the minimum width.

Right justification is the default.

Again as an option, we may set the minimum **width** of a print field by putting a number before the type specifier or size modifier, if one exists. This is useful in printing values in columns; each **printf()** function used to print in the columns should start the conversion code at the same character position, and then use conversion codes with the same width. Beware: The width parameter is the *minimum* width. If the value to be printed has more characters (including signs and so forth) than the minimum, the entire value will print, ruining the neat column. By default, fields with specified widths will be right-justified, that is, lined up on the right side. In other words, they will be padded with leading spaces. ⇨Program 3–3 shows the effects of the width parameter.

The value of *gotham* required seven characters, so when it printed in a field with a minimum of six characters it overflowed by one character.

HEADS UP!

Precision may be used without width.

In addition to the width of a field we may also, optionally again, state the **precision**. The precision parameter comes after the width if there is one, before the size modifier if there is one, and always starts with a decimal point. This parameter, shown in ⇨Program 3–4, means different things for different data types. For floating-point types other than the **g** type specifier, it specifies the number of digits after the decimal point; the value will be rounded to that number of digits.

⇨Program 3–3

```
#include <stdio.h>

void main(void)
{  long eastville = 322536, westport = 643, gotham = 6445821;

   printf("Eastville has %6li people.\n", eastville);
   printf("Westport has  %6li people.\n", westport);
   printf("Gotham has    %6li people.\n", gotham);
}
```

Output

```
Eastville has 322536 people.
Westport has     643 people.
Gotham has   6445821 people.
```

⇨Program 3–4

```
#include <stdio.h>

void main(void)
{  float yours = 126.4, mine = 17.5628;

   printf("You have %.2f and I have %.2f, %5.1f%% of that.\n",
          yours, mine, mine / yours * 100);
}
```

Output

```
You have 126.40 and I have 17.56,  13.9% of that.
```

HEADS UP!

Count all characters in the width.

With the exception of the formats, this ⇨Program 3–4 is exactly the same as the one a few pages back, but here we have forced a roundoff to a specific number of decimal digits. There are two spaces in this output instead of one between the comma and the 13.9%. The format was %5.1f, a minimum width of five, and 13.9 has four characters, so a leading space shows as part of the output field. Remember that the width is the minimum width of the entire field. Don't forget to count signs, decimal points, and digits after the decimal point.

For the **g** type specifiers, the precision parameter defines the maximum number of significant digits to be output; leading zeros do not count. For integral data types the precision parameter defines the minimum number of digits. Leading zeros are added to fill in.

⇨Program 3–5 shows the precision parameter used with various data types.

```
#include <stdio.h>

void main(void)
{   float x = 1.2345;
    int y = 1;

    printf("Number positions: 123456\n");
    printf("The value of x is %6.2f\n", x);
    printf("The value of x is %6.2g\n", x);
    printf("The value of y is %6.2i\n", y);
}
```

Output

```
Number positions: 123456
The value of x is   1.23
The value of x is    1.2
The value of y is     01
```

The format of a conversion code, then, is as follows (the items in brackets are optional):

%[*width*][.*precision*][*size*]*type*

INPUT

The printf() function takes all data types, converts them to characters, and displays those characters in whatever format you specify. The scanf() function does the opposite. It takes a series of characters in a specific format, converts the characters to the data types you specify, and assigns the data to spaces in memory. In the case of the scanf(), the data comes from the input stream stdin, typically associated with the keyboard.

The form of the scanf() function is similar to printf(). The first argument is a control string with conversion codes. Subsequent arguments define the locations in the computer's memory where the results of the conversions will be stored.

```
scanf("control string", location, location, ..., location)
```

To design the control string, we must know how the input will look. The only thing we are sure of is that it will end in a newline (\n) because we have to press the *Enter* or *Return* key to complete the input. Before that, is there an integer number followed by space followed by a decimal

number and a space and another decimal number? Once we know the input format, we design the control string to take the input characters and then to divide them into sets of characters to convert to the appropriate data types for the locations. For example, given the keyboard input

```
45.87 12\n
```

the statement

```
scanf("%f %i", &x, &y);
```

will assign the value 45.87 to the variable *x* and the value 12 to the variable *y*, leaving the \n in the input stream.

Notice the ampersands (&) in front of the variables *x* and *y*. The scanf() function arguments after the control string are not variables, but locations in main memory—memory addresses. We will discuss addresses in more detail later on, but for now, we will use C's simple notation to refer to the address of a specific variable—preceding the variable name with an ampersand. The notation **&x** means the address of the variable *x*—where it is located in main memory.

Conversion Codes

The conversion codes for scanf() are similar to, but not exactly like, those for printf(). The most common ones are listed in ❑Table 3–2. Others that can also be used with scanf() can be found in Appendix D.

When the scanf() function executes, it matches the characters in the input stream with the characters in the control string. A single conversion code in the control string will match input characters following these steps:

1. Leading whitespace characters (spaces, tabs, and newlines) are skipped (except for type specifier **c**). A previous scanf() will leave a newline in the input stream. With the exception of the %c code, this will not affect us because leading whitespace, this newline included, will be skipped.

2. Subsequent characters will be taken for conversion and assignment up to the first character that is inappropriate for the data type.

For example, if the input characters are •••46.8\n (the • indicates a space), a %i conversion code would skip the three spaces and store the value 46 at the memory location of the variable, leaving the characters .8\n for the next match. The conversion stopped there because a decimal point is not an appropriate character for an integer conversion.

In ⇨Program 3–6 (and subsequent ones), keyboard inputs are shown in boldface.

TABLE 3-2   Data Type Specifiers for `scanf()`

Specifier	Data Type	Explanation	Code	Sample Input	Assignment
c	char	A single character. Whitespace characters (space, tab, or newline) will be assigned, not skipped.	%c	ABC	'A' [65]
d	int	Pre-ANSI version of i. Still valid in most ANSI implementations.	%d	21 pieces	21
f, g	float	Decimal value in either standard or E notation.	%f	···62.15· [· is a space]	62.15
i	int	Integer value in decimal, octal, or hex notation.	%i	21 pieces	21
s	string	More about those later.			

⇨**Program 3–6**

```
#include <stdio.h>

void main(void)
{  float food, drink, tip, total, tax, bill;

   printf("Food total: ");
   scanf("%f", &food);
   printf("Beverages:   ");
   scanf("%f", &drink);
   printf("Tip:         ");
   scanf("%f", &tip);
   total = food + drink + tip;
   tax = total * .06;
   printf("Tax:         %6.2f\n", tax);
   bill = total + tax;
   printf("Please pay: %6.2f\n", bill);
}
```

Output

```
Food total: 34.82
Beverages:  16.75
Tip:        6
Tax:           3.45
Please pay:  61.02
```

 **HEADS UP!**

Always precede an input by a prompt.

Prompts

The `printf()`s before each of the `scanf()`s in ⇨Program 3–6 are called **prompts**. They exist to display something on the screen to tell the person at the keyboard what to type in. Can you imagine the previous program running without those `printf()`s? In almost every conceivable case, a `scanf()` should be preceded by a prompt.

⇨**Program 3–7**

```
#include <stdio.h>

void main(void)
{   int i;
    long l;
    float f;
    double d;

    printf("Enter values for an int and a long: ");
    scanf("%i %li", &i, &l);
    printf("Your int is %i and long is %li.\n\n", i, l);

    printf("Now, enter values for a float and a double: ");
    scanf("%f %lf", &f, &d);                        /* Proper %lf for double */
    printf("Your float is %f and double is %f.\n\n", f, d);

    printf("Enter more values for a float and a double: ");
    scanf("%f %f", &f, &d);                         /* Try using %f for a double */
    printf("Your float is %g and double is %g.\n", f, d);
}
```

Output

```
Enter values for an int and a long: 524 79735
Your int is 524 and long is 79735.

Now, enter values for a float and a double: 12.345 12.34567890123
Your float is 12.345000 and double is 12.345679.

Enter more values for a float and a double: 98.765 98.7654321
Your float is 98.765 and double is 12.3457.
```

Size Modifiers

Like `printf()`, the `scanf()` conversion codes can have size modifiers to further define the data type of the assignment, as shown in ⇨Program 3–7. The size modifiers h, for **short**, and l, for **long**, may modify the integral types, d or i. The conversion code %li, then, indicates that a set of digits will be assigned as a **long int**.

Under `printf()`, **float**s and **double**s use the same conversion code, %f. When an assignment is made by `scanf()`, we must differentiate between the two, so the lowercase l modifier is pressed into double

HEADS UP!

When it comes to **double**s, `printf()` and `scanf()` differ.

duty. When it modifies a floating-point specifier, f, or g, it indicates a double. The uppercase L modifier still indicates a long double assignment. The conversion code %lf indicates that a double assignment will be made.

Notice the nonsense the last line produced. The problem was actually the scanf() before the last line. By specifying %f instead of %lf, C filled up only half the space allocated for the variable *d*—in this implementation of C, the last half to be converted by the %g in the printf(). As a consequence, we got what was left over in the first half—the value put there by the previous scanf() using %lf. The results vary with different implementations of C, but they have one thing in common: they are garbage!

We have used whitespace as a **delimiter**—a separator between the values being input. Whitespace is the logical choice for a delimiter because it is an inappropriate character for a numeric input, so it stops

TRAP

Trying to input a double using %f.

HEADS UP!

Whitespace is the most reasonable delimiter.]

⇨**Program 3–8**

```
    #include <stdio.h>

    void main(void)
    {  int i;
       float f;

       printf("Enter an integer: ");
1      scanf("%i", &i);
       printf("Enter a float: ");
2      scanf("%f", &f);
3      printf("Integer: %i. Float: %f\n", i, f);
    }
```

Outputs

```
    Enter an integer: 1
    Enter a float: 2.34
    Integer: 1. Float: 2.340000

    Enter an integer: 1.23
    Enter a float: Integer: 1. Float: 0.230000
```

EXECUTION CHART

Line	Explanation	Stream Before Statement	Stream After Input	Stream After Statement	i	f
1	Input value for *i*.	---	1.23\n	.23\n	1	---
2	Input value for *f*.	.23\n	No input	\n	1	.23
3	Print values of *i* and *f*.	\n		\n	1	.23

the conversion on the current code, and is skipped as the next code starts processing.

Flushing the Input Stream

If the person at the keyboard is not careful to give responses that fit the control string in the scanf(), there is a chance that extra characters will be left in the input stream waiting to be converted by the next scanf(). For example, the first output of ⇨Program 3–8 shows how it should operate. In the second output, 1.23 was typed in as the integer. The scanf() converted to the first inappropriate character, the decimal point, and assigned the value 1 to the variable *i*. At that point, the input stream contained .23. The next scanf() found characters in the stream. They were appropriate for a float, so without waiting for any further input, it converted them and assigned the value 0.23 to *f*.

⇨**Program 3–9**

```
#include <stdio.h>

void main(void)
{   int i;
    float f;

    printf("Enter an integer: ");
1   scanf("%i", &i);
2   while (getchar() != '\n');                    /* Flush stream */
    printf("Enter a float: ");
3   scanf("%f", &f);
4   printf("Integer: %i. Float: %f\n", i, f);
}
```

Output

```
Enter an integer: 1.23
Enter a float: 4.56
Integer: 1. Float: 4.560000
```

EXECUTION CHART						
Line	Explanation	Stream Before Statement	Stream After Input	Stream After Statement	*i*	*f*
1	Input value for *i*.	---	1.23\n	.23\n	1	?
2	Empty the stream.	.23\n	---	---	1	?
3	Input value for *f*.	---	4.56\n	\n	1	4.56
4	Print values of *i* and *f*.	\n		\n	1	4.56

To clean up some of the problems we may encounter from characters left in the input stream, we can **flush**, in other words, empty, the stream with the following statement:

```
while (getchar() != '\n');
```

We need this statement now, at this point in the learning process, so we have introduced it even though we won't cover the various elements of the statement until later chapters.

⇨Program 3–9 is the same as ⇨Program 3–8 with a stream-flushing statement added.

YOUR TURN 3–3

1. Why does ANSI C utilize streams for input and output rather than simply going directly to the input and output devices?

2. What three standard streams are provided for in ANSI C? What devices are they usually associated with? What are they used for?

3. What is the first argument to the `printf()` function? What are the subsequent arguments?

4. What is the purpose of a conversion code in either `printf()` or `scanf()`?

5. What character begins a conversion code? What character ends it?

6. What are the possible characters that end conversion codes for `printf()` and `scanf()` and what do they mean?

7. What is a size modifier in a conversion code, and what are the possible ones for `printf()` and `scanf()`?

8. What is a width parameter in a conversion `printf()` code?

9. What is the precision parameter in a `printf()` conversion code?

10. What are the conditions that stop a conversion in a `scanf()`?

11. What is a prompt, and how do we display one?

12. How can we empty the input stream?

PUTTING IT TOGETHER

Gleam and Glitter Jewelers makes jewelry out of gold and diamonds. Before its designers embark on a project, though, they must have an idea of the cost based on the materials and labor involved. This cost estimate is also used by the company's salespeople to wheel and deal with potential customers, so it must be encoded and printed on the price tags. Their current manual system of figuring cost is more guesswork than anything else.

We must build Gleam and Glitter a program to consistently figure cost. The important parameters in the cost calculation must be easy to change as the staff members gain experience or conditions change.

ANALYSIS

The most significant costs for G and G's jewelry are gold, diamonds, and the time it takes to design and create the piece. We want our program to input these factors like this:

```
Gold - weight (oz), carats: 1.864, 18.5
Diamonds - weight (carats), grade: 2.33, 4
Design and creation time (hours): 12.5
```

Gold's value is determined by its weight, the cost of pure gold, and its purity (in carats, with 24 being pure gold).

$$value = weight \times cost \times \frac{carats}{24}$$

Diamond value is estimated by weight (in carats), grade (1 through 5), and the cost for grade 5 diamonds according to this formula:

$$value = weight \times \frac{cost}{2} \times \frac{grade}{5}$$

Design time is charged at an hourly rate determined by previous experience.

The program should calculate the value of each component as well as the total, and print a value analysis:

```
Value Analysis
  Gold:      1.864 oz  @  312 (18   carats) $  436.18
  Diamonds:  2.330 cts @ 1640 (4    grade)     1476.00
  Creation:  12.500 hrs @   55                  687.50
    Total value:                            $ 2599.68
```

DESIGN

The process consists of three main operations, which we shall treat as modules:

Input materials
Calculate values of materials
Print value report

Inputting of the materials can be expanded into the inputs needed for each of the individual materials:

    Input materials
        Input weight and purity of gold
        Input weight and grade of diamonds
        Input estimated hours for design and creation

A similar expansion can be done for calculating the values of each of the individual materials:

    Calculate values of materials
        Calculate gold value
        Calculate diamond value
        Calculate creation value

With the expansions done, the pseudocode for the whole process looks like this:

    Input materials
        Input weight and purity of gold
        Input weight and grade of diamonds
        Input estimated hours for design and creation
    Calculate values of materials
        Calculate gold value
        Calculate diamond value
        Calculate creation value
    Print value report

IMPLEMENTATION

The cost of gold, diamonds, and labor should be put in defined constants because these change from time to time, and they want to make it easy to modify the program. ⇨Program 3–10 shows the final code.

TEST

The output matches the hand calculations for the figures. Our test plan should include runs that validate extreme values for all the factors in the jewelry's cost. Note that the test shown inputs a fractional value for *carats* even though it must be assigned to an `int` variable.

```c
    #include <stdio.h>

    #define GOLD_COST 312
    #define DIAMOND_COST 1640
    #define HOURLY_COST 55

    void main(void)
    {  float gold, gold_value, diamonds, diamond_value;
       float creation, creation_value;
       int carats, grade;

       /*************************************************** Input materials */
1      printf("Gold - weight (oz), carats: ");
2      scanf("%f %i", &gold, &carats);
3      fflush(stdin);                    /* In case someone enters decimal value */
                                         /* Or while (getchar() != '\n'); */
4      printf("Diamonds - weight (carats), grade: ");
5      scanf("%f %i", &diamonds, &grade);
6      printf("Design and creation time (hours): ");
7      scanf("%f", &creation);

       /************************************* Calculate values of materials */
8      gold_value = gold * GOLD_COST * carats / 24;
9      diamond_value = diamonds * DIAMOND_COST / 2
                      * (1 + grade / 5.0);                   /* Force double */
10     creation_value = creation * HOURLY_COST;

       /*************************************************** Print value report */
       printf("\nValue Analysis\n");
11     printf("  Gold:    %8.3f oz  @ %4i (%-3i carats) $%8.2f\n",
               gold, GOLD_COST, carats, gold_value);
12     printf("  Diamonds:%8.3f cts @ %4i (%-3i grade)   %8.2f\n",
               diamonds, DIAMOND_COST, grade, diamond_value);
13     printf("  Creation:%8.3f hrs @ %4i              %8.2f\n",
               creation, HOURLY_COST, creation_value);
14     printf("     Total value:                        $%8.2f\n",
               gold_value + diamond_value + creation_value);
    }
```

Line	Explanation	Input Stream	gold	carats	
1	Prompt for gold data.		?	?	
2	Enter line at keyboard.	1.864 18.5\n	?	?	
2	Skip any whitespace and convert to inappropriate float character (%f).	18.5\n	1.864	?	
2	Skip whitespace and convert to inappropriate integer character (%i).	.5\n	1.864	18	
3	Flush input stream.		1.864	18	
			diamonds	**grade**	
4	Prompt for diamond data.		?	?	
5	Enter line at keyboard.	2.33 4\n	?	?	
5	Convert to inappropriate float character (%f).	4\n	2.33	?	
5	Skip whitespace and convert to inappropriate integer character (%i).	\n	2.33	4	
			creation		
6	Prompt for design and creation time.		?		
7	Enter line at keyboard.	\n12.5\n	?		
7	Skip whitespace (\n) and convert to inappropriate float character (%f).	\n	12.5		
			gold_val	**diam_val**	**creat_val**
8	Calculate gold value.	\n	436.176	?	?
9	Calculate diamond value. Since *grade* is integer, must force division to float.	\n	436.176	3439.08	?
10	Calculate creation value.	\n	436.176	3439.08	687.5
11	Output gold information.	\n	436.176	3439.08	687.5
12	Output diamond information.	\n	436.176	3439.08	687.5
13	Output creation information.	\n	436.176	3439.08	687.5
14	Output total value.	\n	436.176	3439.08	687.5

Output

```
Gold - weight (oz), carats: 1.864 18.5
Diamonds - weight (carats), grade: 2.33 4
Design and creation time (hours): 12.5

Value Analysis
  Gold:       1.864 oz  @   312 (18   carats) $   436.18
  Diamonds:   2.330 cts @ 1640 (4     grade)      3439.08
  Creation:  12.500 hrs @    55                    687.50
    Total value:                        $ 4562.76
```

SUMMARY

▲**KEY TERMS** (in order of appearance)

Documentation	`printf()`
Readability	Control string
Directive	Conversion code
Preprocessor	Type specifier
`#include`	Size modifier
Header file	Width
`#define`	Precision
Defined constant	`scanf()`
Stream	Prompt
`stdin`	Delimiter
`stdout`	Flush
`stderr`	

▲**NEW FUNCTIONS** (in order of appearance)

```
printf("control string", argument, argument, ..., argument)

scanf("control string", location, location, ..., location)
```

▲**CONCEPT REVIEW**

▼ It is important to maintain a consistent programming style. Some elements of style are modularity, **documentation**, and commenting. The major objective in maintaining a style is **readability** and communicability.

▼ A number of instructions available to us in C are **directives** that are acted on by the **preprocessor** rather than instructions to be compiled as part of the executable program.

▼ The **`#include`** directive instructs the computer to insert a file of source code at the point of the directive. Typical files to include are the **header files** that come with the compiler.

▼ Another commonly used directive is **`#define`**, which allows us to specify a set of characters and a replacement string. At the beginning of the compile process, the compiler substitutes the replacement string for all occurrences of the defined characters. The specified characters are typically used as **defined constants**. Putting them at the beginning of the program makes them easy to find if we want to change them, while using words rather than numbers can make the program more readable.

▼ ANSI C provides for standardized input and output using **streams**. Three that are automatically established by C are **stdin**, **stdout**, and **stderr**.

▼ The **printf()** function directs characters to the standard output stream, stdout. This function's first argument is a **control string**, which defines the format for the output. In addition to printable characters, the control string contains **conversion codes** that specify the format for various values. The values for conversion must be supplied in additional arguments to the printf() function.

▼ Conversion codes begin with a % and end with a **type specifier**, which defines the data type of the conversion. An optional **size modifier** further defines the type.

▼ The optional **width** specification defines the minimum width of a field, and the optional **precision** specifier defines the number of decimal places for floating-point numbers or the minimum number of digits printed (with zero fill) for integral data types.

▼ The **scanf()** function gets values from the stdin stream in almost the opposite way that printf() puts characters in the stdout stream. A major difference is that the arguments to scanf() must be addresses rather than variables. The ampersand (&) in front of a variable name refers to the variable's address.

▼ Input stream values (except for single-character input) are converted by skipping any leading whitespace and converting characters up to the next character inappropriate for the data type. A keyboard input is typically preceded by a **prompt**, a screen output informing the user of the kind of data expected.

▼ The scanf() function uses size modifiers similar to printf(), the exception being the use of lf to represent a double.

▼ The statement while (getchar() != '\n'); will **flush** (empty) an input stream.

▲HEADS UP: POINTS OF SPECIAL INTEREST

▼ You are probably not the only one who will have to read your programs. *Make your programs readable.*

▼ Keep your style consistent.

▼ Outline form shows modularity.

▼ Documentation is a constant process. *It is done throughout all the stages of program development.*

▼ Comment things that aren't obvious.

▼ Directives act before statements. *File inclusions and defined substitutions are done at the beginning of the compile. Statements execute when the compiled program is executed.*

▼ Directives end at the end of a line.

▼ Define directives will not replace characters in quotes.

▼ Defined constants are traditionally in all caps.

▼ Magic numbers make code less readable. `#define` *such numbers and use the defined constants in the code.*

▼ The ANSI standard provides three standard streams *They are* `stdin` *for keyboard input,* `stdout` *for screen display, and* `stderr` *for display of errors on the screen.*

▼ Printing is a two-step process. *The first is designing the output line with the control string; the second is filling in the line with the values of the arguments.*

▼ Make the last, and perhaps the first, output a `\n`. *This ensures that both the current program's and the next program's output begin on a new line.*

▼ To print a %, use %%. *Using* `printf()`, *a % begins a conversion code, so two must be used to output a %.*

▼ Printing floating-point values often results in slight approximations.

▼ Use l for `long int`s and L for `long double`s.

▼ The width parameter refers to the minimum width.

▼ Right justification is the default.

▼ Precision may be used without width.

▼ Count all characters in the width.

▼ `scanf()` usually leaves a newline in the input stream.

▼ Always precede an input by a prompt.

▼ When it comes to `double`s, `printf()` and `scanf()` differ. `printf()` *uses the conversion code* %f *for both* `float`s *and* `double`s. `scanf()` *uses* %f *for* `float`s *and* %lf *for* `double`s.

▼ Whitespace is the most reasonable delimiter. It is the default delimiter for almost all `scanf()` conversions.

▲ **TRAPS: COMMON PROGRAMMING ERRORS**

▼ Writing a program that, after time, even you cannot read.

▼ Putting an equal sign between the characters and their replacement. *In a* `#define`, *whitespace separates the pattern and the replacement.*

▼ Putting a semicolon at the end of a `#define`.

▼ The actual input not matching the control string. *The* `scanf()` *control string must be carefully designed, and the design carefully followed in the keyboard input.*

▼ Leaving out the & in `scanf()`. `scanf()` *requires addresses as arguments.*

▼ The stream position in an unexpected place because of an incorrect input. *Flushing the stream may help.*

▼ Trying to input a `double` using `%f`. `scanf()` *requires* `%lf` *for a* `double` *conversion.*

▲YOUR TURN ANSWERS

▼3–1

1. Communicability—being able to communicate your ideas to others, and to yourself.

2. Modularity is shown using outline form with indenting to show modules and submodules.

3. Documentation should be done continuously as the program goes through the various stages of development.

4. Comments should be included when they are needed to explain something that is not obvious from the code.

5. Readability factors are: the preliminary documentation, the task statement, logical design, and program design; modular outline form; choosing meaningful variable names; and proper commenting.

▼3–2

1. A directive is an instruction to the compiler or preprocessor. A statement directly becomes part of the executable code. Directives act before statements.

2. A directive ends at the end of the physical line instead of a semicolon (as a statement does).

3. Things in an include file are source code. They will not be viewable within your program because they are added only temporarily at the beginning of the compile process.

4. In the usage in this chapter, the `#define` directive replaces one set of characters with another.

5. Among other things, defined constants are used to allow easy modification of the values and to improve readability.

▼3–3

1. Standard streams allow compatibility between different implementations of C and different hardware.

2. The `stdin` stream is usually associated with the keyboard and used for input to the program; `stdout` with the screen for output; and `stderr` with the screen for error messages.

3. The first argument to the `printf()` function is the control string that defines the format of the output line. Subsequent arguments provide values to fill in the spaces left in the format.

4. A conversion code tells C how to convert the bits in memory to readable characters or vice versa.

5. Conversion codes begin with a % and end with a type specifier.

6. The type specifiers are summarized in Table 3–1 and Appendix D.

7. Size modifiers further define the data type of the type specifier. The modifiers h and l preceding i specify `short` or `long int`s, and L preceding f specifies `long double`s. With `scanf()`, lf specifies a `double`.

8. The width parameter specifies a minimum width for the field for `printf()`.

9. Precision for `printf()` states the number of decimal places for a floating-point field (or significant digits for a **%g** field) and the minimum number of digits with leading zero fill for integral fields.

10. Except for **%c**, conversion stops with the first inappropriate character for the data type.

11. Prompts are reminders displayed on the screen before inputs. They are displayed using `printf()`.

12. `while (getchar() != '\n');` is used to flush the input stream of unexpected or unwanted characters.

EXERCISES

1. Write the proper directive to put the header file *goodies.h* in your program.   *# include <goodies.h>*

2. Write the proper directive to change each instance of FEET_MILE to 5280.   *# define FEET_MILE 5280*

3. Why does ANSI C use input and output streams? How does the stream's use of a particular computer's operating system facilitate compatibility between different types of computers?   *Stdin Stdout Stderr*

4. Write the `printf()` conversion codes to provide the proper output from the values given. The vertical bars (|) show the whole field including spaces (· denotes a space). If vertical bars are not given, no width should be specified.

   a. 46 |46·| *%.3f*   b. 8.046 |··8.05| *%6.2f*

   c. 73.28 |73.3·| *%5.2f*   d. 86425 |·086425| *%.7f*

   e. 214   214.00 *%6.2f*   f. 'C'   67 *%i*

   g. 67   C   *%C*   h. 35.6 |···35.600| *%9.3f*

5. Show the output of these values given the `printf()` conversion codes (use · to denote a space).

   a. 'A'   %3i · *65*   b. 'A'   %c *A*
   c. 4.26   %6.1f··*4.3*   d. 425   %g *425*
   e. 381.67 %3.1f *381.7*   f. 16   %4.3i··*16*
   g. 1.2345 %.2f *1.23*   h. 52   %5i···*52*

6. Show the assignments made from these keyboard inputs given the `scanf()` conversion codes (· denotes a space).

   a. ··A   %c *blank*   b. ·29.6   %i
   c. 14.62 %f   d. 65   %c
   e. 1234T3 %i   f. 214.587924 %f

7. Rewrite the following program in proper form and show the output, given an input of 37.

```c
#include <stdio.h>
#define FACTOR 5.287
void main(void){int initial;float result;printf("Start with> ");scanf("%i",
&initial);result = initial * FACTOR;printf("Given %5.3i and a factor of"
" %g, the result\nis approximately %6.2f\n", initial, FACTOR, result);}
```

PROGRAMS

1. Using `printf()` with control strings that contain only whitespace (including newline) and `%c` conversion codes, write a program that prints the following pattern. You need no variables; your arguments after the control strings will be specific values.

Output

```
    >
    >   >
    >       >
  >>>          >
    >       >
    >   >
    >
```

2. Write a program that accepts two numbers from the keyboard and prints the following information.

Variables

```
first
second
```

Output

```
First number?  7
Second number?  2
The second goes into the first 3 times
with a remainder of 1.
The quotient is 3.5.
```

3. Write a program to print out a customer bill for Ajax Auto Repair. The parts and labor charges are input and a 6 percent sales tax is charged on parts but not on labor. Be sure to line up the output as shown.

Variables

```
Parts
Labor
SalesTax
Total
```
floats one statement

Output

```
PARTS?  104.50
LABOR?  182.15
```
tax rate #define

```
        AJAX AUTO REPAIR
        SERVICE INVOICE
PARTS               $ 104.50
LABOR                 182.15
SALES TAX               6.27
TOTAL               $ 292.92
```

4. Ajax would like a program to compute an employee's pay check. The employee's gross pay is the hours worked times the hourly pay. Income tax withholding, FICA tax, payroll savings plan, retirement, and health insurance are subtracted from the gross pay. From time to time the various rates for these deductions change, so the values should be put in #define directives.

Constants

FIT_RATE	15% of gross pay
FICA_RATE	6.2% of gross pay
SAVINGS_RATE	3% of gross pay
RETIREMENT_RATE	8.5% of gross pay
HEALTH_INS	$3.75 per employee

Variables

```
Hours
HourlyPay
GrossPay
FIT          Federal income tax withholding
FICA         Social security tax withholding
Savings      Payroll savings
Retirement
NetPay       Gross pay less deductions
```

Output

```
HOURS? 40
HOURLY PAY? 7.50

GROSS PAY:             $ 300.00

FEDERAL INCOME TAX: $   45.00
FICA:               $   18.60
PAYROLL SAVINGS:    $    9.00
RETIREMENT:         $   25.50
HEALTH INSURANCE:   $    3.75

NET PAY:               $ 198.15
```

5. Write a program to calculate interest on a loan. It should allow input of principal, rate in percentage form, and time in days. Use the following variables. Don't add any variables, don't leave any out. Your output should look like the one below.

$$interest = principal \times \frac{rate}{100} \times \frac{time}{365}$$

Variables

```
principal
rate
time        Integer
interest
```

Output

```
PRINCIPAL? 1450
RATE, TIME? 14.5 250

INTEREST: $144.01
```

6. Write a program to figure out the circumference, cross-sectional area, and volume of a sphere given a radius. The radius should be input and the rest printed out as shown.

Formulas

$\pi = 3.1416$
circumference $= 2 \times \pi \times$ radius
cross-sectional area $= \pi \times$ radius^2
volume $= {}^4/_3 \times \pi \times$ radius^3

Variables

Choose variables appropriate for the problem

Output

```
RADIUS: 25

CIRCUMFERENCE:             157.080
CROSS-SECTIONAL AREA:   1963.500
VOLUME:                  65449.996
```

7. Write a program that will accept keyboard input of various coins and return the total value.

Variables

input   Value from keyboard
total   To accumulate the value of the inputs

Output

```
Half dollars? 3
Quarters?     3
Dimes?        2
Nickels?      3
Pennies?      7
Your total is $2.67.
```

8. Write a program that accepts a number of seconds from the keyboard and converts it into days, hours, minutes, and seconds. Use integer arithmetic and the remainder operator.

Variable

seconds

Output

```
How many seconds? 106478
Days:     1
Hours:    5
Minutes: 34
Seconds: 38
```

Chapter 4

THE SELECTION STRUCTURE

PREVIEW

As programs become more complicated, we must do all we can to keep them simple. One simplification method is a technique called structured programming. In this chapter we will examine that technique and concentrate on one of its facets. In particular, we will look at:

▼ The basic principles of structured programming.

▼ The simplest of the structures.

▼ A structure that allows a program to branch in one of two directions.

▼ Setting up conditions for choosing one branch or another.

▼ Types of operators used in these conditions.

▼ The principal statement used to create a selection.

▼ Extending a selection to more than two branches.

▼ C's special multibranch structure.

Even a well-designed program may be difficult to write and even more difficult to communicate to others. Top-down, modular design adds consistency to the design process and makes it easier. Yet many programs are thousands of lines long, and the number of different but interconnected processes in the program can be mind-boggling. Wouldn't it be nice if we could reduce the variety of different processes that can be required in a complicated program?

STRUCTURED PROGRAMMING

The technique of **structured programming** does just that. It simplifies the programming process by using only three different types of programming patterns, called control **structures**, to build programs. By using them in various combinations you can write any (yes, any!) program, no matter how sophisticated.

The individual structures are simple; they are the fundamental building blocks of programs. These building-block structures are combined to form useful, and sometimes quite complicated, programs. One structure may follow another; be put inside another; be put inside one that is inside another, following another, inside another; and so forth. These simple patterns can be combined in any way you have to in order to get the job done. While the end result may be a complicated program, it is nevertheless composed of simple pieces.

These three structures are:

▼ *Sequence.* One operation after another. This is the structure we have been using up to this point.

▼ *Selection.* A choice between sets of operations. We will discuss this structure in this chapter.

▼ *Iteration.* Repetition of a set of operations. We will discuss this in Chapter 5.

A good structured programmer will outline the various structures in the program first in simple, human language as we have been doing in the design stage of our program development. The outline is often done in a slightly more formalized **pseudocode**, literally false code, that uses a few key words to indicate structures, but still employs human instead of computer language. Typically, the programmer will create the pseudocode outline using the same text editor that will be used to write the actual program source code. In fact, the pseudocode will become part *of* the source code.

Like our designs up to this point, a good structured outline looks like a well-ordered set of class notes. Major topics, in this case structures, are at the left margin; subsidiary topics, the structures inside, are indented within the major ones, and so forth. It is easy to see which structures are within other structures because they are indented within them.

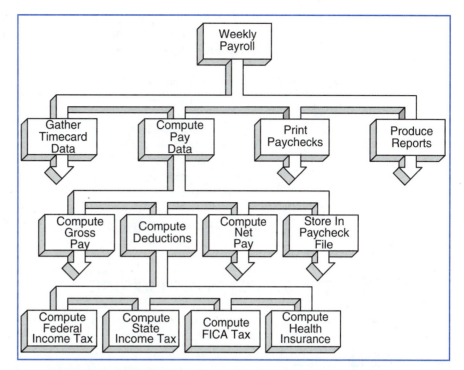

A top-down design for our weekly payroll starts with an overall statement of the task (Weekly Payroll), breaks that down into individual modules (such as Compute Pay Data), and keeps breaking modules down until they become self-contained program segments.

In the top-down design of a weekly payroll, illustrated in ❏Figure 4–1, there are numerous applications of each of these structures, and we shall use that to illustrate both the structures and a structured outline.

The Sequence Structure

Our **sequence structure** consists simply of one operation after another. In the payroll example we gather timecard data, compute pay data, print paychecks, and produce reports, in that order. Since the sequence is so simple, we have no special format or indenting for it, nor any special pseudocode key words. The sequence in our outline would be written like this:

> Gather timecard data
> Compute pay data
> Write paychecks
> Print reports

HEADS UP!

The sequence is the simplest structure.

In expanding this outline, we can put one sequence structure within another. **Compute pay data**, for example, can be expanded into four operations and inserted into the pseudocode,

Gather timecard data
Compute pay data
    Compute gross pay
    Compute deductions
    Compute net pay
    Store in paycheck file
Write paychecks
Print reports

giving us a sequence within a sequence.

THE SELECTION STRUCTURE

HEADS UP!

A program follows only one of the two branches.

HEADS UP!

Be sure your branching structures come back to the same path.

As you might have suspected, this outline will be expanded further and further—top-down modular design at work. **Compute gross pay**, for example, is more complicated because we may figure either regular plus overtime pay using an overtime formula, or simply regular pay. Each of these choices is a separate **branch** of the process—a particular path that the process may take. Notice that each time through the process, the program will follow only one of the two branches, overtime or regular pay, but no matter which branch is followed, the process will end up in the same place—gross pay will be calculated. This last property, ending up in the same place, is extremely important to the modular programming process. We must be able to replace **Compute gross pay**, a simple "operation," with an entire structure, but must always continue on to **Compute deductions**.

The second of the structures, the **selection structure**, shown in ❏Figure 4–2, sets up this branching situation. There must be some reason to take one branch or another—pay overtime or regular pay—so the selection begins with some condition. If the condition is true (the hours are greater than 40), we will perform one branch (Figure overtime pay); if they are not, we will perform the other (Figure regular pay).

If hours > 40   [Compute gross pay]
    Figure overtime pay
Else
    Figure regular pay
Rest of program

HEADS UP!

Indenting is extremely important.

Notice the key words and the indenting. The structure starts with *If* followed by the condition. The operations that are performed if the condition is true are indented under *If*. In this example it is only one operation, but it might be many, even including other structures. The false

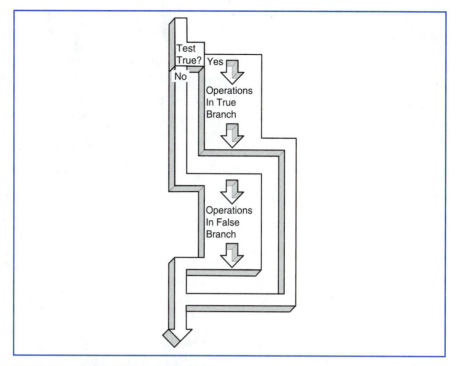

Depending on whether the condition established is true or false, a selection structure performs one branch or the other, and then moves on.

branch is indented under the key word *Else*. The entire selection structure ends when the indent level returns to the level of the *if*. This indicates the point at which the two branches come back together. Inserting this module in the outline, we end up with the following:

```
Gather timecard data
Compute pay data
    If hours > 40                          [Compute gross pay]
        Figure overtime pay
    Else
        Figure regular pay
    Compute deductions
    Compute net pay
    Store in paycheck file
Write paychecks
Print reports
```

Notice that the actual operations are at the left side of the outline while the comments, such as *Compute gross pay*, are at the right. The operations and their indenting should clearly show the various structures in the program; the comments explain what they do. Neither Congress

nor the International Association of Programming Gurus has passed a law mandating this style; it is the author's, and others may differ. But this works, and if you haven't already developed your own style, try this one.

Certain key principles are imperatives in top-down, modular, structured programming, without which the process breaks down.

▼ *One Entry, One Exit.* Each structure may have only one entry point and one exit point. This is important so that a single line can be replaced by an entire structure. Structures formed using the guidelines given above will follow this principle.

▼ *Proper Nesting.* To **nest** something is to enclose it entirely within something else. If, for example, a selection is put within a branch of another selection, the selection structure must begin and end within that branch. In the following examples, the left one is properly structured; the one on the right would be senseless:

If this is true	If this is true
Something	Something
If this is true	If this is true
Another thing	Another thing
Else	Else
Yet another	Still another
End of the if structure	Else
Else	Yet another
Still another	End of the if structure
End of the if structure	End of the if structure

Try following the one on the right through. It doesn't work!

Programming the paycheck process will not end here, of course. More lines in the outline will be considered as modules and expanded into submodules until each submodule is a small but complete programmable entity. By following this top-down procedure, the design stage will be simpler and more manageable. The programming stage will be equally simple and manageable because the final, complicated program may be built from simple, individual subprograms.

Now that we see how the selection structure works, let us apply it in the C language.

YOUR TURN 4-1

1. How does structured programming simplify the programming process? *simplifies the pattern*

sequence selection iteration (repitition)

2. How may structures be combined in a program?
3. What is pseudocode? *false code to represent the program*
4. Why is indenting important in pseudocode?
5. Which structure have our programs used before this chapter?
6. What is meant by "branches" in a program?

7. Which structure implements branching?

8. In a selection structure, where is the true branch and where is the false branch?

9. What are two imperative principles of top-down, modular, structured programming?

CONDITIONS

There must be some condition set up to tell the computer to take one branch or the other. This condition will evaluate to either true or false, and typically is some kind of comparison. For example, let us say that we are at a fork in the road. We have to get to the place beyond, but should we take the high road or the low road? If it's cold, the high road might be blocked with snow. If it's warm, the low road might be uncomfortably hot. It's decision time. If the temperature is over 60 degrees Fahrenheit, we'll take the high road. Otherwise, it's the low.

The condition in the example above is based on comparing the temperature with 60. It is either over 60 degrees—true; or it isn't—false.

A **condition** in C typically consists of one or more comparisons that relate one value to another. A comparison has the form

expression comparison_operator expression

For example:

```
x + 4 > 9
```

where we compare the value of the expression *x* + 4 with the value 9. An expression, remember, is anything that reduces to a single value; so, in essence, a comparison always compares two values. The *comparison_operator*, > in our example, tells the computer how the comparison should be made. If the value of *x* is 7, then 7 + 4 is 11, 11 is greater than 9, and the comparison is true.

Relational and Equality Operators

The *comparison_operator* comes from one of two categories: **relational operators** and **equality operators**. The operators differ, of course, in function, but the categories also differ in precedence, with the relational operators being higher than the equality operators. Both sets of operators are shown in Table 4–1. (The entire set of operators is shown in Appendix B.) Be sure to notice that the equal operator (==) is not the same as the assignment operator (=).

Operators of both categories have left-to-right associativity. In precedence, of the operators we have examined so far, all the arithmetic

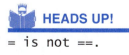

HEADS UP!

Conditions are either true or false; there are no maybes.

HEADS UP!

Comparisons compare values.

HEADS UP!

= is not ==.

TABLE 4–1 Relational, Equality, and Logical Operators

Operator	Symbol	Explanation	Example
Unary — Right-to-left associativity			
Logical NOT	!	Make false expression (0) true (1); make true (nonzero) false (0).	`!(time > present)`
Arithmetic — Discussed in Chapter 2			
Relational — Left-to-right associativity			
Greater	>	First greater than second?	`x + y > z - 19`
Less	<	First less than second?	`cost < maximum - 100`
Greater or equal	>=	First greater than or equal to second?	`load >= limit`
Less or equal	<=	First less than or equal to second?	`TestValue <= Norm`
Equality — Left-to-right associativity			
Equal	==	First equals second?	`Count + 1 == EndCount`
Not equal	!=	First not equal to second?	`CheckSum != NewSum`
Logical AND — Left-to-right associativity			
	&&	First and second true?	`val1 && val2`
Logical OR — Left-to-right associativity			
	||	First or second or both true?	`val1 || val2`
Assignment — Discussed in Chapter 2			

HEADS UP!

Parentheses can be added, and are encouraged, to increase readability.

operators come first, followed by the relational operators, followed by the equality operators, and ending with the assignment operators. This order of evaluation is convenient because the arithmetic expressions are reduced to values first, and then the values are compared according to the comparison operators.

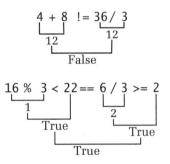

Logical Operators

Our conditions can consist of more than one comparison. We can tie multiple comparisons together with two of the **logical operators—and** (&&) and **or** (||). Using the *and* operator, if the comparisons on both sides are true, then the whole condition is true. If even one comparison is false, then the whole condition is false.

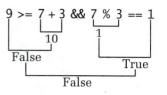

Using the *or* operator, if either or both of the comparisons are true, then the whole condition is true. Both comparisons would have to be false for the whole condition to be false.

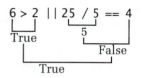

Many comparisons can be combined together using many *ands* and *ors*. The *and* operator is higher in precedence than *or*. Both of them are lower than the comparison operators, but higher than assignment, as you can see in Table 4–1. This means that comparisons are evaluated first and then combined by the logical operators. Order of evaluation can, of course, be adjusted any way we want by using parentheses.

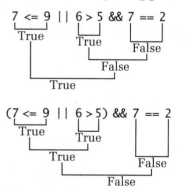

The **not operator** (!) is a logical operator, but it is also unary, acting on only one expression. In precedence and associativity, it falls in with the other unary operators. The logical *not* operator makes what was true false, and what was false true.

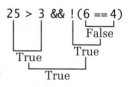

YOUR TURN 4–2

1. What is the typical, general form of a comparison?

2. Name the two classes of comparison operators and list the members of each class. Which class has a higher precedence?

3. What are the three logical operators and what is their precedence?

WHAT'S TRUE AND WHAT'S FALSE?

Could you lie to a computer? Easily. The computer, being a nonthinking machine, has no idea what is true or false, good or bad, or nice or nasty. Our human concepts of true and false are translated into strictly numeric terms for the computer. In C anything that evaluates to true is assigned the value one; false is assigned zero. The statement

```
printf("%i %i\n", 6 == 6, 3 > 9);
```

would produce

```
1 0
```

on the screen.

When trying to decide true versus false, C interprets any nonzero value as true and zero as false. The value of

```
7 > 3 && 14
```

is true, or one.

STATEMENT BLOCKS

▶TRAP◀

Leaving out the closing brace in a block.

Modularity is also enhanced by allowing statements to be grouped into blocks. Any time a statement is called for in a program, you can provide either a single statement or a block of statements. The block begins with an open brace ({) and ends with a close brace (}). Notice that the statements in any `main()` function, such as the one in ⇨Program 4–1, are within a block. The compiler doesn't care where it finds the braces, but you, being human and more visually oriented, will want to place them carefully. In this book, the open brace is at the same indent level as the statement or definition of which it is a part; the statements within the block are indented one level further; and the close brace is directly below (in the same column as) the open brace.

This format has three advantages: (1) the outline is easy to see because of the indentation; (2) it is hard to forget the close brace because of its alignment with the open brace; and (3) many other C programmers follow the same pattern.

THE if STATEMENT

In C, the selection structure is implemented by the **if** statement, which has this general form:

```
if (condition) statement;
```

We can, and usually do, substitute a block of statements for the single *statement* in the general form, giving us the more common form

```
if (condition)
{   statement;
    statement;
        . . .
}
```

The *condition* in the `if` statement is as we have described earlier and, of course, will evaluate to either true or false. If the condition is true, the statements within the block will be executed; otherwise, they won't. Notice that the condition is enclosed in parentheses, and there is no semicolon after the condition. To put a semicolon there would end the entire structure at that point.

In our pseudocode, the selection structure began with the *If* key word and ended when the indent level came back to that of the *If*. In C it begins with the same key word, `if`, and ends at the end of the single statement or at the closing brace at the end of the block of statements. Although C will not care, our indenting should match that which we set up for our pseudocode.

Let us look at a simple example, a guessing game. In ⇨Program 4–1 we will try to guess a value that was written into the program.

▶**TRAP**◀

Leaving the parentheses off the condition.

A semicolon after the condition in an `if`.

HEADS UP!

Indenting means something to us, but not to C.

⇨**Program 4–1**

```
#include <stdio.h>

#define SECRET 10

void main(void)
{   int guess;

    printf("What's your guess? ");
    scanf("%i", &guess);
    if (guess == SECRET)                           /* Secret value */
        printf("You guessed that ");
    printf("the secret number was %i.\n", SECRET);
}
```

Outputs

```
What's your guess? 10
You guessed that the secret number was 10.

What's your guess? 42
the secret number was 10.
```

In the first execution, the value of *guess* was equal to 10, so the statement inside the `if` structure was executed. In the second execution, *guess* was not 10, so the statement in the structure was skipped.

Be careful to notice that the symbol for equality is ==, two equal signs. A single equal sign is the assignment operator. See what happens when we change the `if` statement to:

```
if (guess = SECRET)
```

```
What's your guess? 8395
You guessed that the secret number was 10.
```

▶TRAP◀

Using = when you mean ==.

It did not work as we expected, because 10 (the value of *SECRET*) was assigned to *guess*, which became the value of the test expression `guess = SECRET`. C interprets anything nonzero as true (see the *Nuts 'n Bolts* box titled *What's True and What's False?*), so it executed the statement inside the structure.

While we are on the subject of the pesky equality operator, let us look at another strange possibility. In ⇨Program 4–2 we have changed the data type of *guess* to `float` and compared it to 0.1.

⇨**Program 4–2**

```
#include <stdio.h>

#define SECRET 0.1

void main(void)
{   float guess;

    printf("What's your guess? ");
    scanf("%f", &guess);
    if (guess == SECRET)
        printf("You guessed that ");
    printf("the secret number was %g.\n", SECRET);
}
```

Output

```
What's your guess? 0.1
the secret number was 0.1.
```

▶TRAP◀

Using equality or inequality operators with real numbers.

Why didn't it tell us we guessed it? Remember, real numbers are stored in a binary, E notation and often must be approximated to fit in that form. The approximations for *guess* and 0.1 were slightly different.

This most often occurs with fractional numbers and obviously can cause some unexpected results. One solution is to not use fractional numbers and use integral variables if possible. Another is to set an acceptable range and see if your number falls within that range. We could change ⇨Program 4–2 to ⇨Program 4–3.

⇨Program 4–3

```
#include <stdio.h>

#define SECRET 0.1
#define ACCEPT 0.01    /* Accept value within this amount of actual value */

void main(void)
{  float guess;

   printf("What's your guess? ");
   scanf("%f", &guess);
   if (guess >= SECRET - ACCEPT && guess <= SECRET + ACCEPT)
      printf("You guessed that ");
   printf("the secret number was %g.\n", SECRET);
}
```

Outputs

```
What's your guess? 0.1
You guessed that the secret number was 0.1.

What's your guess? 0.15
the secret number was 0.1.
```

Let us examine an example that does not involve equality. Assume that we have an automatic apple scale that weighs each apple and labels it accordingly. Unfortunately, the input interface is broken so an operator will have to type the weights into a keyboard. Apples are normally priced at 20¢ each, but if one weighs over 10 ounces, it is a premium apple and worth another 10¢. The program outline is as follows:

```
Establish base price
Enter weight
Print "Eve's"
If weight > 10
    Print "Premium"
    Add premium to price
Print "Apple" and price
```

⇨Program 4–4 translates this pseudocode into C.

MORE ABOUT TRUTH

Remembering that a zero value is interpreted as false, and that anything nonzero is true, we might have a program segment like this:

```
printf("How many extra? ");
scanf("%i", &extra);
if (extra)
    printf("There are %i extra.\n", extra);
[and so forth]
```

If *extra* is anything but zero, the condition will be true, and the `printf()` will be executed.

⇨**Program 4–4**

```
#include <stdio.h>

void main(void)
{   float weight, price = .2;

    printf("Enter weight of apple: ");
    scanf("%f", &weight);
    printf("Eve's ");
    if (weight > 10)
    {   printf("Premium ");
        price = price + .1;
    }
    printf("Apple. $%4.2f.\n", price);
}
```

Output

```
Enter weight of apple: 11.3
Eve's Premium Apple. $0.30.
```

Output

```
Enter weight of apple: 7.8
Eve's Apple. $0.20.
```

The else Clause

A more complete version of the **if** statement has statements in both the true and false branches. The false branch begins with an **else** statement:

if (*condition*) *statement*; else *statement*;

or more commonly

```
            if (condition)
            {  statement;
               statement;
                . . .
            }
            else
            {  statement;
               statement;
                . . .
            }
```

The Eve people don't want to call their apples just "Eve's Apples" even if they are only normal apples, so an apple weighing 10 ounces or less will be called an "Eve's Juicy Apple." Our change in design will be evident in ▷Program 4–5.

▷Program 4–5

```
#include <stdio.h>

void main(void)
{  float weight, price = .2;

   printf("Enter weight of apple: ");
   scanf("%f", &weight);
   printf("Eve's ");
   if (weight > 10)
   {  printf("Premium ");
      price = price + .1;
   }
   else
   {  printf("Juicy ");
   }
   printf("Apple. $%4.2f.\n", price);
}
```

Output

```
Enter weight of apple: 9.2
Eve's Juicy Apple. $0.20.
```

Output

```
Enter weight of apple: 10.1
Eve's Premium Apple. $0.30.
```

Bowing to market pressures, the Eve people now have set up four grades of apples. "Premium Apples" still weigh more than 10 ounces and cost an extra 10¢. "Juicy Apples" are the normal grade at a normal price, but they have to weigh more than 8 ounces. Those weighing more than 6 ounces but up to 8 are called "Snack Apples" and cost 5¢ less. All others are "Cooking Apples" selling for 10¢ less. This leaves us with four branches to deal with, but our selection structure only has two.

Weight	> 10	> 8 but <= 10	> 6 but <= 8	<= 6
Grade	Premium	Juicy	Snack	Cooking
Price	.30	.20	.15	.10

⇨**Program 4–6**

```
#include <stdio.h>

void main(void)
{  float weight, price = .2;

    printf("Enter weight of apple: ");
    scanf("%f", &weight);
    printf("Eve's ");
    if (weight > 10)
    {  printf("Premium ");
        price = price + .1;
    }
    else
    {  if (weight > 8)                          /* Brace necessary? */
        {  printf("Juicy ");
        }
        else
        {  if (weight > 6)                      /* Brace necessary? */
            {  printf("Snack ");
                price = price - .05;
            }
            else
            {  printf("Cooking ");
                price = price - .1;
            }
        }                                       /* Brace necessary? */
    }                                           /* Brace necessary? */
    printf("Apple. $%4.2f.\n", price);
}
```

Outputs

```
Enter weight of apple: 12
Eve's Premium Apple. $0.30.

Enter weight of apple: 9.2
Eve's Juicy Apple. $0.20.
```

Outputs

```
Enter weight of apple: 7.5
Eve's Snack Apple. $0.15.

Enter weight of apple: 5.9
Eve's Cooking Apple. $0.10.
```

The solution is to branch one of the branches. In the Eve case, if the weight is less than 10 ounces, our revised ⇨Program 4–6 will test to see if it is more than 8. The first **else** clause contains a complete selection structure with two branches and the condition `weight > 8`. The `else` clause within that selection structure will also contain a complete selection structure with two branches and the condition `weight > 6`.

To be in the "Juicy" category, apples had to weigh more than 8 ounces, but less than or equal to 10 ounces. Why didn't we write that `if` statement as in the following segment?

```
if (weight > 10)
{  printf("Premium ");
   price = price + .1;
}
else
{  if (weight > 8 && weight <= 10)
   {  printf("Juicy ");
   }
}
```

We could have, but the test for less than or equal to 10 would have been wasted. If the weight was not less than or equal to 10, the program would execute the statements in the true branch just below `if (weight > 10)`, jump to the end of that selection structure, and never reach the `else` branch and our test.

The `else if` Construct

If you examine the sets of braces in ⇨Program 4–6 with the comments `/* Brace necessary? */` beside them, you will see that these brace sets are really not necessary. Each of them encloses the material within an `else` clause, but that material in each case consists of only an `if` statement. Granted, the `if` statements contain statements within their clauses, but still they are single `if` statements. This section of the program could be rewritten:

HEADS UP!

An entire `if else` structure is considered as one statement.

```
if (weight > 10)
{  printf("Premium ");
   price = price + .1;
}
else
   if (weight > 8)                      /* No brace necessary before if */
   {  printf("Juicy ");
   }
   else
      if (weight > 6)                   /* No brace necessary before if */
      {  printf("Snack ");
         price = price - .05;
      }
      else
      {  printf("Cooking ");
         price = price - .1;
      }
```

HEADS UP!

else if, although not a key word, is a common construct.

Branching of `else` clauses with `if` statements is such a common occurrence that the `else` followed by the `if` is often written on one line almost as if it was one key word, **else if**. It is not, but the indenting that results outlines a very clear multibranch structure that is actually made of multiple two-branch `if else` statements. This section could be rewritten as:

```
if (weight > 10)
{  printf("Premium ");
   price = price + .1;
}
else if (weight > 8)
{  printf("Juicy ");                    /* Brace necessary? */
}                                        /* Brace necessary? */
else if (weight > 6)
{  printf("Snack ");
   price = price - .05;
}
else
{  printf("Cooking ");
   price = price - .1;
}
```

 HEADS UP!

Braces may make a program more readable.

You might have also noticed that the set of braces commented are not necessary either. There is only one statement, `printf("Juicy  ")`, within them. These braces could be eliminated, but to maintain consistency, we probably should retain them.

What if we had left out some of the other braces? For example, the ones after `else`?

```
else
    printf("Cooking ");
    price = price - .1;
```

It looks fine because of our nice, neat indenting. However, C will see it this way:

```
else
    printf("Cooking ");
price = price - .1;
```

TRAP

Program code that is indented properly but lacks proper punctuation.

Since there are no braces, the `else` branch ends with the semicolon at the end of `printf("Cooking ");`, and `price = price - .1;` will execute after the entire `if`, `else if`, `else` structure is finished, subtracting 10 cents from the price of *all* the apples.

Let us also compare our nested `if`s, using the `else if` construct, with sequential `if`s—one `if` after another. As an example, let us look at each with *weight* equal to 12.

Nested

```
if (weight > 10)
{  printf("Premium ");
}
else if (weight > 8)
{  printf("Juicy ");
}
else if (weight > 6)
{  printf("Snack ");
}
printf("Apple.\n");
```

Sequential

```
if (weight > 10)
{  printf("Premium ");
}
if (weight > 8)
{  printf("Juicy ");
}
if (weight > 6)
{  printf("Snack ");
}
printf("Apple.\n");
```

Outputs

```
Premium Apple.
```

```
Premium Juicy Snack Apple.
```

In both cases, the first test, `weight > 10`, was true. Using the nested `else if`s, the program printed *Premium*, and then jumped beyond the end of the structure and printed *Apple*. Using the sequential `if`s, the program did exactly the same thing, but the end of the structure, since there was no `else` came immediately after printing *Premium*, and the next statement to execute was `if (weight > 8)`. This test was also true, so it printed *Juicy*, and moved to `if (weight > 6)`, which was also true, so it printed *Snack*, and finally *Apple*.

▶**TRAP**◀

Using sequential `if`s when you need nested `if`s.

YOUR TURN 4–3

1. How do we put more than one statement inside an `if` branch? *braces*
2. Must a selection structure have an `else` branch? *no*
3. What is the difference between = and ==? *= -defines   == -equal to*
4. Why is it dangerous to compare two small real values?
5. Are braces required around the true and false branches? *only if more than one*
6. Is there an `else if` key word?
7. What is the difference between nested `if`s using the `else if` construct and sequential `if`s?

THE switch STATEMENT

The C language includes a multibranch alternative to the `if` statement called the **switch** statement. It has some severe limitations, but within these limitations, it can be very handy.

```
switch (integral_expression) {statement_block}
```

The *statement_block* is a number of statements within the various branches. The beginnings of the branches are distinguished by case identifiers, all beginning with the key word **case**.

```
case integral_value:
```

At the end of each of the branches is a **break** statement, which causes an immediate jump to the statement following a `switch` structure; in other words, to the statement beyond the closing `switch` structure brace.

```
switch (integral_expression)
{  case integral_value:
        statement;
        statement;
        . . .
        break;
   case integral_value:
        statement;
        statement;
        . . .
        break;
   case as many as are necessary:
        . . .
        break;
   default:
        statement;
        statement;
        . . .
}
```

A simple example is shown in ⇨Program 4–7.

The *integral_expression* following the `switch` key word must evaluate to some integral data type, `char` or `int`; floating-point results are not allowed. The value of the expression becomes a `case` value to be matched to the possible case identifiers within the statement block following the `switch`. For example, if the `integral_expression` evaluated to 6, the `switch` would look for `case 6:`.

Each of the `case`s within the block following `switch` has an *integral_value*, which, along with `case` and a following colon, becomes the identifier. For example, two of the cases might be `case 9:` and `case 6:`. The `switch` causes the program to jump directly to the matching identifier; in other words, the next code to be executed will be that immediately following the identifier. In the example, that would be the code following `case 6:`. If there are other `case`s in the execution path, they are ignored.

HEADS UP!

`switch`es can use only integral expressions.

HEADS UP!

A `case` must have an integral value; no expressions allowed.

⇨**Program 4–7**

```c
#include <stdio.h>

void main(void)
{   int number;

    printf("Enter a number and see if I am programmed"
            " to print out two times it: ");
    scanf("%i", &number);
    switch (number * 2)
    {   case 6:
            printf("Six.\n");
            break;
        case 4:
            printf("Four.\n");
            break;
        case 12:
            printf("Twelve.\n");
            break;
        case 8:
        case 10:
            printf("Either eight or ten.\n");
            break;
        default:
            printf("I don't know that one.\n");
    }
}
```

Output

```
Enter a number and see if I am programmed to print out two times it: 3
Six.

Enter a number and see if I am programmed to print out two times it: 5
Either eight or ten.

Enter a number and see if I am programmed to print out two times it: 1
I don't know that one.
```

HEADS UP!

Make default the last branch.

If there is no matching label, the jump is to the **default** label. The default label is not absolutely necessary and, if it appears, may be in any position within the block, but it may appear only once. In practice, there is usually a default label, and it is typically the last one. The last branch, default or otherwise, does not need a break statement, because execution would continue out of the switch structure anyway.

In ⇨Program 4–8, the Eve Company has modified its apple-labeling program so that the person at the keyboard inputs a character, *P, J, S,* or any other letter, indicating the grade, and the program prints the name and price.

⇨Program 4–8

```
        #include <stdio.h>

        void main(void)
        {   float price;
            char grade;

            printf("Enter grade of apple: ");
1           scanf(" %c", &grade);
2           printf("Eve's ");
3           switch (grade)
4           {   case 'P':
5               case 'p':
6                   price = .3;
7                   printf("Premium ");
8                   break;
9               case 'J':
10              case 'j':
11                  price = .2;
12                  printf("Juicy ");
13                  break;
14              case 'S':
15              case 's':
16                  price = .15;
17                  printf("Snack ");
18                  break;
19              default:
20                  price = .1;
21                  printf("Cooking ");
            }
22          printf("Apple. $%4.2f.\n", price);
        }
```

Outputs

```
Enter grade of apple: p
Eve's Premium Apple. $0.30.

Enter grade of apple: J
Eve's Juicy Apple. $0.20.
```

```
Enter grade of apple: s
Eve's Snack Apple. $0.15.

Enter grade of apple: Q
Eve's Cooking Apple. $0.10.
```

EXECUTION CHART

Line	Explanation	price	grade
1	Input apple grade.	??	J
2	Print first part of label.	??	J
3	Look for `case 'J':`.	??	J
9	Found identifier.	??	J
10	Ignore case identifier.	??	J
11	Assign *price*.	.2	J
12	Print "Juicy ".	.2	J
13	Continue execution beyond `switch` block.	.2	J
22	Print last part of label including *price*.	.2	J

HEADS UP!

Case identifiers in the normal flow of execution are ignored.

Using the wrong punctuation in a `switch` structure.

TRAP

Leaving out the `break`s.

A jump to a case identifier continues execution from that point on. Subsequent case identifiers in the code are ignored. The execution chart for an input of *J* (uppercase) shows the execution pattern. In our example, to allow for either capital or lowercase letters in the input, two cases are put together. If the value of *grade* is *j*, execution will continue from `case 'j':`. If *grade* is *J*, execution will continue from `case 'J':`, passing right by `case 'j':`.

As we stated in Chapter 2, character values such as `'P'` are integral numeric values—the ASCII codes for those characters. The program would have run the same had we substituted `case 80:`, using the ASCII value for *P*, instead of `case 'P':`, but we would have sacrificed readability.

A little review of punctuation is in order here. Notice that the *integral_expression* following `switch` is enclosed in parentheses and that there is no semicolon after the statement. All the statements within the following structure are contained within one set of braces. There need not be separate sets of braces in each branch, although there certainly could be if the structure warranted it. Each case identifier is followed by a colon, which tells C that it is a case identifier.

The `break` statements at the end of each `switch` branch are not necessary for C, but they are necessary for the use of `switch` as a multi-branch structure. If we left the `break`s out, execution would continue from whichever `case` matched through all the rest of the statements in the `switch` structure, as in ⇨Program 4–9. Again, we will follow the execution through with a *J* input.

All the apples are priced at 10 cents, even the "Eve's Premium Juicy Snack Cooking Apples."

```
      #include <stdio.h>

      void main(void)
      {  float price;
         char grade;

         printf("Enter grade of apple: ");
1        scanf(" %c", &grade);
2        printf("Eve's ");
3        switch (grade)
4        {  case 'P':
5           case 'p':
6              price = .3;
7              printf("Premium ");
8           case 'J':
9           case 'j':
10             price = .2;
11             printf("Juicy ");
12          case 'S':
13          case 's':
14             price = .15;
15             printf("Snack ");
16          default:
17             price = .1;
18             printf("Cooking ");
         }
19       printf("Apple. $%4.2f.\n", price);
      }
```

Outputs

```
      Enter grade of apple: p
      Eve's Premium Juicy Snack Cooking Apple. $0.10.

      Enter grade of apple: P
      Eve's Premium Juicy Snack Cooking Apple. $0.10.

      Enter grade of apple: J
      Eve's Juicy Snack Cooking Apple. $0.10.

      Enter grade of apple: s
      Eve's Snack Cooking Apple. $0.10.

      Enter grade of apple: F
      Eve's Cooking Apple. $0.10.
```

EXECUTION CHART

Line	Explanation	price	grade
1	Input apple grade.	??	J
2	Print first part of label.	??	J
3	Look for case 'J':.	??	J
8	Found identifier.	??	J
9	Ignore case identifier.	??	J
10	Assign *price*.	.2	J
11	Print "Juicy ".	.2	J
12	Ignore case identifier.	.2	J
13	Ignore case identifier.	.2	J
14	Assign *price*.	.15	J
15	Print "Snack ".	.15	J
16	Ignore default identifier.	.15	J
17	Assign *price*.	.1	J
18	Print "Cooking ".	.1	J
19	Print last part of label including *price*.	.1	J

YOUR TURN 4–4

1. What are the major limitations of the `switch` statement? *int or char*
2. After the `switch` jumps to a particular `case`, what happens if the program encounters another `case`? *ignores it*
3. What is the purpose of a `break` statement in a multibranch structure using `switch`? *to tell it to ignore all false statements*
4. Is a `default` statement necessary?

   not necessary but should have one

PUTTING IT TOGETHER

To tie together what we have learned here, let us consider a problem for a warehouse for computer products. Each computer that comes into the warehouse has a product code that tells something about that particular machine—where it was made, the type of CPU, and the capacity of the hard and floppy disks. Deciphering these product codes is cumbersome for the warehouse people. They would like us to use the computer to make their job easier.

TASK

Our task is to develop a program that allows a warehouse employee to

TABLE 4–2	Product Code Characters		
Character Positions	**Meaning**	**Characters**	**Translation**
1	Country of manufacture	U or A	United States
		J	Japan
		S	Singapore
		K	Korea
2	Type of CPU	3	386
		4	486
		5	Pentium
3–5	Capacity of hard disk	Number	Capacity in GB for Pentiums, MB for others
Remaining	Capacity of floppy	720	720 KB
		12	1.2 MB
		144	1.44 MB
		288	2.88 MB

type in a code, and have the computer print out the product characteristics.

ANALYSIS

The program should accept input of a product code and display the product's characteristics in a format similar to the following:

```
Enter product code: J4540144
Made in Japan
Processor: 486
Hard disk: 540 MB
Floppy: 1.44 MB
```

If the product code does not make sense, an error in input perhaps, the program should reject either the entire product code, or, when possible, decipher anything it can while printing error indications for anything it cannot decipher. A valid product code starts with an uppercase alpha character. If that is not present, the program should print an error message and quit.

The character positions in the product code and the meanings of the characters in those positions are in Table 4–2.

DESIGN

The overall structure of the process is:

```
Input product code
if code doesn't start uppercase alpha
    Print error message
else
    Decipher code
```

Deciphering the code is a bit more complicated, so we can expand that part of the pseudocode.

```
Input product code
if code not in range
    Print error message
else
    [Decipher code]
        Country of origin
        Type of CPU
        Capacity of hard disk
        Capacity of floppy disk
```

Deciphering each of the codes, except for the hard disk capacity, follows the same pattern. The character(s) in the position(s) are matched with valid possibilities and the appropriate translation is printed out. To decipher the hard disk capacity, we check the processor type and multiply the number by 1,000 if the processor is a Pentium.

```
if Pentium processor                              [Capacity of hard disk]
    Multiply hard disk capacity by 1000
```

IMPLEMENTATION

The characteristics in the product code are determined by the characters in the various positions of the code. We can use the `scanf()` function to separate these character sets and assign them to appropriate variables. Let us modify Table 4–2, making Table 4–3, to identify the data type of each characteristic, the variable to which we will assign the value, and the `scanf()` code that will perform the conversion for us.

The results are shown in ⇨Program 4–10.

TABLE 4–3 Product Code Characters in Program

Character Positions	Meaning	Data Type	Variable	Conversion Code
1	Country of manufacture	char	*country*	%c
2	Type of CPU	int	*processor*	%1i (one i, not el i)
3–5	Capacity of hard disk	float	*hard_drive*	%3f
Remaining	Capacity of floppy	int	*floppy*	%i

```
        #include <stdio.h>

        void main(void)
        {  char country;
           int processor, floppy;
           float hard_drive;

           /************************************************** Input product code */
           printf("Enter product code: ");
1          scanf("%c%1i%3f%i", &country, &processor, &hard_drive, &floppy);
2          if (country < 'A' || country > 'Z')                 /* Not alpha start */
3             printf("   Invalid product code.\n");
           else                                        /* Decipher good product code */
           {                                                /* Country of origin */
              printf("Made in ");
4             switch (country)
5             {  case 'U':                        /* Both U and A (America) mean U.S. */
6                case 'A':
7                   printf("United States\n");
8                   break;
9                case 'J':
10                  printf("Japan\n");
11                  break;
12               case 'S':
13                  printf("Singapore\n");
14                  break;
15               case 'K':
16                  printf("Korea\n");
17                  break;
18               default:
19                  printf("<Country invalid>\n");
              }
              /****************************************************** Type of CPU */
              printf("Processor: ");
20            switch (processor)
21            {  case 3:
22                  printf("386\n");
23                  break;
24               case 4:
25                  printf("486\n");
26                  break;
27               case 5:
28                  printf("Pentium\n");
29                  break;
30               default:
31                  printf("<Invalid processor>\n");
              }
```

(continued)

```c
       /*********************************************** Capacity of hard disk */
              /* Hard drives for Pentium computers stated in gigabytes in */
           /* product code and must be converted; all others in megabytes */
32     if (processor == 5)
33         hard_drive = hard_drive * 1000;
34     printf("Hard disk: %g MB\n", hard_drive);

       /********************************************* Capacity of floppy disk */
       printf("Floppy: ");
35     if (floppy == 720)              /* This could also be done using switch */
36         printf("720 KB\n");
37     else if (floppy == 12)
38         printf("1.2 MB\n");
39     else if (floppy == 144)
40         printf("1.44 MB\n");
41     else if (floppy == 288)
42         printf("2.88 MB\n");
       else
43         printf("<Invalid floppy>\n");
   }
}
```

EXECUTION CHART

Line	Explanation	Input Stream	country	processor	hard_drive	floppy
1	Enter line at keyboard.	S53.6188\n	?	?	?	?
	Assign first character.	53.6188\n	S	?	?	?
	Convert one character to int.	3.6188\n	S	5	?	?
	Convert three characters to float.	188\n	S	5	3.6	?
	Convert to inappropriate int character.	\n	S	5	3.6	188
2	See if *country* out of range A – Z. It isn't.	\n	S	5	3.6	188
4	Look for case S:. Find it in line 12.	\n	S	5	3.6	188
13	Print *Singapore*.	\n	S	5	3.6	188
14	Jump beyond end of switch structure.	\n	S	5	3.6	188
20	Look for case 5:. Find it in line 27.	\n	S	5	3.6	188
28	Print *Pentium*.	\n	S	5	3.6	188
29	Jump beyond end of switch structure.	\n	S	5	3.6	188
32	*processor* equals 5.	\n	S	5	3.6	188
33	Adjust *hard_drive*.	\n	S	5	3600	188
34	Print *hard_drive* specs.	\n	S	5	3600	188
35	See if *floppy* equals 720. It doesn't.	\n	S	5	3600	188
37	See if *floppy* equals 12. It doesn't.	\n	S	5	3600	188
39	See if *floppy* equals 144. It doesn't.	\n	S	5	3600	188
42	See if *floppy* equals 288. It doesn't.	\n	S	5	3600	188
43	Print *Invalid floppy*.	\n	S	5	3600	188

The test involves running many sample codes, being sure that we see that all valid codes work correctly and that all invalid ones are rejected. The single output shown here is one of the tests, the one shown in the execution chart.

Output

```
Enter product code: S53.6188
Made in Singapore
Processor: Pentium
Hard disk: 3600 MB
Floppy: <Invalid floppy>
```

SUMMARY

▲**KEY TERMS** (in order of appearance)

Structured programming	Relational operator
Structure	Equality operator
Pseudocode	Logical operator
Sequence structure	And operator
Branch	Or operator
Selection structure	Not operator
Nest	Block
Condition	`else if`

▲**NEW STATEMENTS** (in order of appearance)

```
if (condition) statement;
if (condition) statement; else statement;
switch (integral_expression) {statement_block}
case integral_value:
break
default:
```

▲**CONCEPT REVIEW**

▼ **Structured programming** simplifies the programming process by limiting programs to combinations of only three control **structures**. Structured programs are often designed using a slightly more formalized **pseudocode**

- ▼ The **sequence structure**, one operation after another, is the simplest of the structures.

- ▼ The **selection structure** contains two **branches**. Which branch the execution will take depends on a **condition** consisting of one or more comparisons. Comparisons are made of expressions connected by **relational operators** or **equality operators**.

- ▼ Branches may contain any statement or **block** of statements, including other structures, in which case, the structures are said to be **nested**.

- ▼ Comparisons can be tied together with the **logical operators** *and* and *or*. The *not* **operator** is a unary operator that makes what was true false, and vice versa.

- ▼ The `if` statement implements the selection structure. It may contain only one true branch, in which case the false branch is to do nothing; or it may have an `else` clause where the false branch is stated.

- ▼ The equality operator, when used with real numbers, especially small fractions, sometimes yields unexpected results due to approximation in storing the numbers.

- ▼ To form a multibranch structure, one branch of an `if else` statement may contain another complete `if else` statement. It is so common to branch the `else` branch of the selection structure that most programmers treat the `else if` construct as a single multibranch structure.

- ▼ The `switch` statement sets up a more limited multibranch structure by allowing the program to jump to any of a number of case identifiers. The integral expression following `switch` is evaluated, and C searches for a corresponding value following any number of **case** statements. If it finds no match, it looks for a **default** label. Execution resumes at the appropriate `case` or `default`. Subsequent `case`s are ignored.

- ▼ A **break** statement causes the execution to transfer to the statement following the end of the `switch` structure. These `break`s are typically used to separate the `switch` structure into individual branches.

▲HEADS UP: POINTS OF SPECIAL INTEREST

- ▼ Any program may be built from only three basic structures.
- ▼ Design your program carefully before writing the code.
- ▼ To make pseudocode useful, keep it simple.
- ▼ The sequence is the simplest structure.
- ▼ A program follows only one of the two branches.
- ▼ Be sure your branching structures come back to the same path. *Each structure may have only one entry point and one exit point.*

▼ Indenting is extremely important. *It makes structure obvious.*

▼ Style is just as important in pseudocode as in the actual program. *Both should be readable and clearly show structure.*

▼ Conditions are either true or false; there are no maybes.

▼ Comparisons compare values. *Any expressions should be evaluated before the comparison.*

▼ = is not ==. *Don't confuse the assignment operator with the equal operator.*

▼ Parentheses can be added, and are encouraged, to increase readability.

▼ Indenting means something to us, but not to C.

▼ An entire `if else` structure is considered as one statement.

▼ `else if`, although not a key word, is a common construct.

▼ Braces may make a program more readable. *They may not be necessary, but can certainly be added for readability.*

▼ `switch`es can use only integral expressions.

▼ A `case` must have an integral value; no expressions allowed.

▼ Make `default` the last branch.

▼ Case identifiers in the normal flow of execution are ignored.

▲TRAPS: COMMON PROGRAMMING ERRORS

▼ Leaving out the closing brace in a block.

▼ Leaving the parentheses off the condition.

▼ A semicolon after the condition in an `if`.

▼ Using = when you mean ==.

▼ Using equality or inequality operators with real numbers.

▼ Program code that is indented properly but lacks proper punctuation.

▼ Using sequential `if`s when you need nested `if`s.

▼ Using the wrong punctuation in a `switch` structure.

▼ Leaving out the `break`s.

▲YOUR TURN ANSWERS

▼4–1

1. By building even complicated programs of combinations of three simple patterns.

2. Structures may be combined in any way needed to do the job.

3. Pseudocode is a language only slightly more formal than a plain-English outline that is used to represent a structured program.

4. Indenting shows the structure of a program by clearly outlining which structures are within which, and which follow which.

5. Our previous programs have all followed the sequence structure.

6. Branches are different paths a program might take according to some conditions.

7. The selection structure implements branching.

8. The true branch begins at the line following (and indented within) the *If* key word and condition; it ends before the *Else* key word or at the end of the structure if there is no *Else*. The false branch begins at the line following (and is indented within) the *Else* key word and ends at the end of the structure. The end of the structure is shown when the indent level returns to that of the *If* and *Else* key words.

9. A structure should have only one entry point and one exit point, and structures must be properly and completely nested.

▼4–2

1. A comparison is usually two expressions separated by some comparison operator.

2. Relational operators, >, <, >=, and <=, are higher in precedence than equality operators, == and !=.

3. Logical operators, in order of precedence, are *not* (!), *and* (&&), and *or* (| |).

▼4–3

1. By enclosing the statements within braces.

2. No, if the false branch is to take no action.

3. The = operator makes an assignment; the == operator makes a comparison.

4. Because of the approximations made in storing such values in binary E notation.

5. Only if there is more than one statement in the branch.

6. There is no `else if` key word, but the two key words are often used together in multibranch structures.

7. The entire set of nested `if`s is one structure; if it is set up using `else if`, only one branch will execute. Sequential `if`s are separate structures, and many may execute.

▼4–4

1. The `switch` can only compare the value of an integral expression to a number of integral values.

2. `case` statements encountered in normal execution are ignored.

3. The **break** statement used at the end of branches effectively separates the branches by sending execution to the end of the **switch** structure.

4. A **default** statement is not necessary if the **default** branch is to take no action.

EXERCISES

1. In mathematics, we might state a range for x as $1 < x < 5$. Show how we should write the following range expressions in C.

   a. $1 < x < 5$ b. $16 \geq x \geq -7$

   c. $22.6 \geq x > 12.03$ d. $36 < x \leq y < 115$

2. Correct the errors in this program segment:
```
if(y > 25)
  { x = 2;
    printf("x is %i\n", x);
  }
else
    y = 19;
```

3. Write the condition that is true if $6 \leq x \leq 25$ or $x > 100$.

4. If $a = 1$, $b = 2$, and $c = 3$, are the following conditions true or false?

   a. a >= c - b   *true*

   b. b / 2 == a || c < 3

   c. b < c -2 || a * 3 >= c && b > a

   d. 5 || !b && c

   next week

5. The following code segment compiles without error, but it prints *that's it* no matter what the value of x is. What's wrong?
```
if (x ==4)
    printf("That's it\n");
else
    printf("Wrong number\n");
```

6. Put the following program segment in proper structured format using nested **if**s.
```
if (p >= 6) {x = 25; printf("High p value\n");} else
if (p >= 2) {x = 50; printf("Minimal p value\n");}
else {x = 100; printf("p below minimum\n");}
```

7. Do the same for the program segment above but use the **else if** construct.

8. With traffic lights, R (for red) means "Stop," Y means "Caution," and G means "Go." Any other color letter means "Weird." Given the statements below, write the program segment that prints what the color letter means. Use the **else if** construct.

```
        printf("Color letter: ");
        scanf("%c", &color);
```

9. Do the same for the problem segment above using the `switch` statement.

10. What is wrong with the following program segment?

```
float p, x, y;

Switch p + 14 / y
    case 12.6
        printf("1\n");
    case x
        printf("2\n");
    else
        printf("0\n");
```

11. What is the difference in these two program segments? What value of *x* is produced if its initial value is 2?

```
if (x > 0)                  if (x > 0)
    x = x + 2;                  x = x + 2;
else if (x > 2)             if (x > 2)
    x = x + 4;                  x = x + 4;
```

PROGRAMS

1. Write a program to compare two numbers with executions similar to the following.

Variables

```
number1, number2
```

Outputs

```
Enter two numbers 37.589 24
37.589 is greater than 24.

Enter two numbers 26.3354 47.2
47.2 is greater than 26.3354.

Enter two numbers 84 84
They are equal.
```

2. Adams County (county code *A*) has a 7 percent sales tax rate; the rest of the state has a 6 percent rate. Write a program to print out the amount owed on a purchase including sales tax, given the amount of the purchase and the county.

Variables

```
Purchase    Amount of purchase
County
TaxRate     Determine using selection
```

Outputs

```
AMOUNT OF PURCHASE? 15      AMOUNT OF PURCHASE? 26
COUNTY? B                   COUNTY? A
TOTAL BILL: $ 15.90         TOTAL BILL: $ 27.82
```

3. Write a program that changes 12-hour, a.m.-p.m. time into 24-hour time. It should execute like the samples. (*Hint:* Scan for a dummy `char` variable to move the input stream past the colon.)

Variables

```
hours
minutes;
suffix     a - a.m.; p - p.m.; n - noon; m - midnight
dummy      To pass by the :
```

Outputs

```
Enter time (H:Mx): 6:42p
1842 hours

Enter time (H:Mx): 9:5a
0905 hours

Enter time (H:Mx): 12:00m
2400 hours

Enter time (H:Mx): 12:0n
1200 hours
```

4. A truth table shows the results of values when combined in certain ways. Write a program to show truth tables for combining true and false values using the *and* operator and *or* operator. Print out the results as the values of the *and* or *or* expressions (0 or 1).

Variables

```
T    Variable with true value
F    Variable with false value
```

Output

```
AND Truth Table        OR Truth Table
      T   F                  T   F
  T   1   0              T   1   1
  F   0   0              F   1   0
```

5. The Ace Courier Service charges $10 for the first pound or fraction thereof and $6 per pound for anything over one pound. Write a program that figures the charges.

Variable

```
weight
```

Outputs

```
WEIGHT? .7      WEIGHT? 2.5      WEIGHT? 4.2
CHARGE: 10      CHARGE: 19       CHARGE: 29.2
```

6. Social Security (FICA) tax is currently 7.65 percent of earnings up to $50,400 for the year. Write a program that accepts earnings for the current week and previous cumulative earnings up to the current week, and returns the amount of FICA tax to be withheld.

Variables

```
CurrentEarnings
PrevEarnings
```

Outputs

```
This week's pay? 700        This week's pay? 1850
Previous pay? 12600         Previous pay? 50200
FICA to withhold: $ 53.55   FICA to withhold: $ 15.30
```

7. Write a program to assign grade points according to a letter score. An *A* is 4 grade points; *B* is 3; *C*, 2; *D*, 1; and *F*, 0. Use the `else if` construct.

[handwritten: rewrite the with switch program]

Variables

```
grade
grade_points
```

Outputs

```
Letter grade: B    Letter grade: F
Grade points: 3    Grade points: 0

Letter grade: a    Letter grade: Q
Grade points: 4    Grade points: Invalid letter grade.
```

8. Rewrite the previous program using the **switch** statement.

9. The HiRisq Insurance Company determines auto insurance rates based on a driver's age, the number of tickets in the last three years, and the value of the car. The base rate is 5 percent of the value of the car. Drivers under 25 years of age pay 15 percent over the base, and drivers from 25 through 29 pay 10 percent over. A driver with one ticket pays 10 percent over the rates already figured. Two tickets draws a 25 percent extra charge; three tickets adds 50 percent; and drivers with more than three tickets are refused. Write a program to show a driver's insurance premium.

Variables

Choose appropriate variables

Outputs

```
DRIVER'S AGE? 35              DRIVER'S AGE? 19
NUMBER OF TICKETS? 1          NUMBER OF TICKETS? 3
VALUE OF CAR? 10000          VALUE OF CAR? 850
PREMIUM: $ 550               PREMIUM: $ 73.3125


DRIVER'S AGE? 29              DRIVER'S AGE? 81
NUMBER OF TICKETS? 2          NUMBER OF TICKETS? 4
VALUE OF CAR? 15000          VALUE OF CAR? 12500
PREMIUM: $ 1031.25           COVERAGE DENIED
```

Chapter 5

THE ITERATION STRUCTURE

PREVIEW

Iteration is the last of the three structures and completes our knowledge of the control patterns. In this chapter we will see:

▼ How to set up the basic iteration structure.

▼ Two different places in the loop to put conditions for staying in the iteration structure.

▼ Some common concepts usually applied within the iteration structure.

▼ The special case of controlling the iteration structure with a counter.

▼ Putting iterations within iterations.

149

One major reason for using a computer rather than doing things by hand is that many of our tasks are repetitive. With only the two structures we have covered so far, the sequence and selection, to repeat a set of operations we would have to either execute the program a number of times or rewrite the same code over and over in the same program. Neither solution sounds entirely satisfactory, so in this chapter we will introduce the mechanism for directing the computer to repeat a set of operations.

THE ITERATION STRUCTURE

HEADS UP!

Loops must have conditions.

This repetitive pattern is called an **iteration structure** or a **loop**. Under the structured-programming guidelines, there must always be an end to the repetition—some condition set up that will tell the computer whether it should perform the operations in the loop again or go beyond the loop to the rest of the program. This condition may be tested either before the loop operations are performed (at the beginning of the loop) or after (at the end of the loop).

In our payroll example (shown in ❑Figure 4–1 in the previous chapter), computing the pay must be done for each employee; the same operation must be done many times. The overall structure of the payroll process was:

Gather timecard data
Compute pay data
Write paychecks
Print reports

Following the top-down modular procedure, we can expand the Compute pay data module with an iteration structure:

Begin loop   [Compute pay data]
   Compute employee pay
End loop

HEADS UP!

True conditions continue the loop.

This would not be good programming practice, however, because we have stated no conditions for continuing the loop or exiting it. The program would compute pay forever. In C, the test condition is always for continuing the loop—when the condition is true, the operations are repeated. If we choose to test at the beginning of the loop, we might write the outline this way:

While more employees
   Compute employee pay

Alternatively, we may wish to test at the end of the loop as follows:

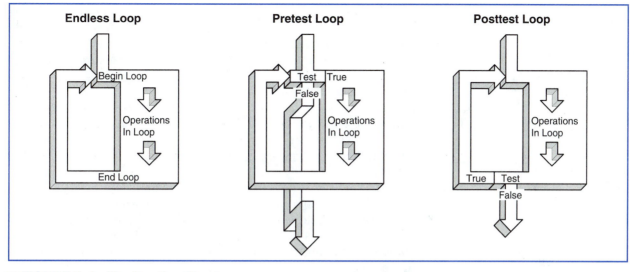

❏ FIGURE 5–1 The Iteration Structure

The Iteration structure, or loop, repeats a process. The endless loop repeats forever; obviously it is not good programming practice because it allows no way to end the process. In a pretest loop the conditions are tested at the beginning of the loop. A posttest loop tests for the conditions at the end of the loop.

Do
    Compute employee pay
While more employees

We have used the word *While* to state our test and, if the test was at the end of the iteration structure, the word *Do* to begin the loop. These are the same key words you will use later when you actually program the loop in C, so we might as well use them for our informal outline here.

Notice the difference between testing at the beginning of the loop (a **pretest** loop) and testing at the end (a **posttest** loop). The difference isn't much except for the first time through. In a pretest loop, if the conditions are not true when the program reaches the loop, the operations within the loop are never performed. Perhaps this section figures the pay for temporary employees and there might not be any in a particular week.

In a posttest loop, the operations are performed at least once no matter what the conditions are, because the test is not made until the program reaches the end of the structure. Perhaps, whether we have any temporary employees or not, we still must produce a check, even if it is void, to keep the bank happy.

Most of the time it doesn't make any difference whether you choose a pre- or posttest loop, but you still must examine each situation carefully. If there is a possibility that you may not want the program to execute the operations within the loop, you should choose a pretest loop. If the operations must be performed at least once no matter what, choose a posttest loop.

HEADS UP!

Choose pretest or posttest according to the situation.

The top-down design is progressing. We will replace the single line **Compute pay data** with the structure above. The *Do* form was chosen because we must produce at least one check, even if it is void. We have kept the original line at the side to explain what the structure does.

```
Gather timecard data
Do                                              [Compute pay data]
   Compute employee pay
While more employees
Write paychecks
Print reports
```

We now have an iteration structure within our sequence.

As we saw in Chapter 4, though, computing the pay for a single employee consists of a number of tasks, so we will use our expansion from Chapter 4 to substitute for **Compute employee pay**, and include it within the iteration.

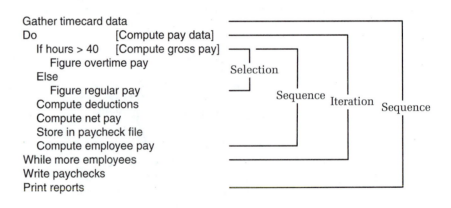

Structurally speaking, the overall program is a sequence. Within the sequence, the steps from **Do** to **While** form an iteration; within the iteration is another sequence; and within that sequence is a selection with the two methods for figuring pay as its branches.

LOOPS IN C

In Chapter 4 we looked at conditions in C—those expressions that evaluate to either true or false. The conditions we use for the iteration structure will be formed in the same way. In C, the iteration structure condition is always that for continuing rather than exiting the loop. When the condition is true, C will repeat the statements in the loop.

Pretest Loops

A pretest loop begins with the keyword **while**. The general form of this configuration of the iteration structure is:

```
while (condition) statement;
```

For the *statement* referred to above, we can substitute a block of statements—a group of statements enclosed in braces—which leads us to the most common form of the structure:

```
while (condition)
{  statement;
   statement;
       . . .
}
```

Notice the punctuation and indenting. The *condition* is enclosed in parentheses; each statement in the block is indented one level and ends with a semicolon; and there is no semicolon after the condition or after the block's closing brace. The punctuation is required by the C compiler. The indenting and line endings are for us; they make the program more readable.

➪Program 5–1 allows a customer to type in the price of an item and the quantity being purchased, and get the total amount for that item. The customer can do this over and over again until there are no more items. Notice the initial input of the *answer* before entering the loop. This is a pretest loop and must have something to test at the loop's beginning.

▶TRAP◀

Putting a semicolon after the condition in a pretest loop.

▶TRAP◀

Testing a variable containing garbage at the beginning of a loop.

➪**Program 5–1**

```
#include <stdio.h>

void main(void)
{  float price;
   short quantity;
   char answer;

1     printf("Do you wish to enter a purchase (Y/N)? ");
2     scanf(" %c", &answer);
3     while (answer == 'Y' || answer == 'y')        /* Upper or lowercase Y */
4     {  printf("Enter 'price quantity': ");
5        scanf("%f %hi", &price, &quantity);
6        printf("The total for this item is $%6.2f.\n", price * quantity);
7        printf("Another (Y/N)? ");
8        scanf(" %c", &answer);
9     }
10    printf("Thank you for your patronage.\n");
}
```

EXECUTION CHART

Line	Explanation	price	quantity	answer
1	Prompt for input. Notice that the values for the variables at this time are undetermined.	?	?	?
2	The %c will take one character from the input stream. The space before the conversion code will match any whitespace that might have been left in the input stream. This is not terribly important here, for the first input, but it will be important in the similar statement in line 8.	?	?	y
3	The beginning of the loop and also the test. Since this is a pretest, there must be something to test; this was provided by line 2. As with all pretest loops, the condition might be such that we would never execute the loop at all but go directly beyond the closing brace to line 10. In this case, however, the value of *answer* is *y*. Because of the *or* operator (| |), the condition will be true with either upper- or lowercase *Y*.	?	?	y
4	Another input prompt.	?	?	y
5	Input *price* and *quantity* separated by a space.	1.98	6	y
6	Prints out the result in dollars and cents.	1.98	6	y
7	Yet another input prompt.	1.98	6	y
8	This input gives the program something to test when it goes back to the beginning of the loop. The space in front of the conversion code will match the newline left at the end of the stream by the previous scanf() and request that the system wait for a new input. Without the space, the %c assigns the existing newline to *answer* and continues without waiting.	1.98	6	Y
9	End of the block that makes up the body of the while loop. The program will go back to the test in line 3.	1.98	6	Y
3	Condition true, continue with loop.	1.98	6	Y
4, 5	Input new values.	4.29	15	Y
6	Print result.	4.29	15	Y
7, 8	Ask the question.	4.29	15	n
3	Neither relation is true, so the condition is false.	4.29	15	n
10	The program is now beyond the loop and, since this is the last statement, it finishes.	4.29	15	n

Output

```
Do you wish to enter a purchase (Y/N)? y
Enter 'price quantity': 1.98 6
The total for this item is $ 11.88.
Another (Y/N)? Y
Enter 'price quantity': 4.29 15
The total for this item is $ 64.35.
Another (Y/N)? n
Thank you for your patronage.
```

Posttest Loops

We could have set this up as a posttest loop if we assumed that a person who did not wish to make a purchase would not have run the program. In other words, the body of the loop would be executed once no matter what. The posttest loop begins with a **do** statement and has this general form:

```
do statement; while (condition);
```

with our usual implementation of it looking like this:

```
do
{   statement;
    statement;
    .
    .
    .
}while (condition);
```

There was no semicolon after the closing brace in the pretest loop but there is, and must be, one at the end of the *condition* in the posttest loop. ⇨Program 5–2 is a rewrite of ⇨Program 5–1 using a posttest loop.

⇨**Program 5–2**

```
#include <stdio.h>

void main(void)
{   float price;
    short quantity;
    char answer;

    do
    {   printf("Enter 'price quantity': ");
        scanf("%f %hi", &price, &quantity);
        printf("The total for this item is $%6.2f.\n", price * quantity);
        printf("Another (Y/N)? ");
        scanf(" %c", &answer);
    }while (answer == 'Y' || answer == 'y');
    printf("Thank you for your patronage.\n");
}
```

```
Enter 'price quantity': 2.45 12
The total for this item is $ 29.40.
Another (Y/N)? y
Enter 'price quantity': .99 4
The total for this item is $  3.96.
Another (Y/N)? n
Thank you for your patronage.
```

Sentinel Values

 **HEADS UP!**

A sentinel value should be something weird.

▶TRAP◀

Not testing for the sentinel value until after it is used in a normal situation.

In ⇨Program 5–2 we ask the person at the keyboard a separate question about whether to continue or not. We could eliminate that question by interpreting special responses to the other question about price and quantity as not normal data but a signal to the program to do something different. We call the value of this special response a **sentinel value**. The sentinel value must be something that would not occur in the normal course of operations—for example, a price and quantity of zero.

Simply removing the *answer* input and testing for a *price* not equal to zero, as in ⇨Program 5–3, is insufficient. The sentinel value, zero, is assigned to the sentinel variable, *price* in the `scanf()` function, then used to calculate the total for the item (which should not really be an item), and then tested in the `while` statement. Notice that the output is a little silly.

The sentinel value must be tested for immediately. One structured solution is shown in ⇨Program 5–4.

⇨Program 5–3

```c
#include <stdio.h>

void main(void)
{   float price;
    short quantity;

    printf("Enter 0 0 to quit.\n");
    do
    {   printf("Enter 'price quantity': ");
        scanf("%f %hi", &price, &quantity);
        printf("The total for this item is $%6.2f.\n", price * quantity);
    }while (price != 0);
    printf("Thank you for your patronage.\n");
}
```

Output

```
Enter 0 0 to quit.
Enter 'price quantity': 2.45 12
The total for this item is $ 29.40.
Enter 'price quantity': 0 0
The total for this item is $  0.00.
Thank you for your patronage.
```

⇨**Program 5–4**

```c
#include <stdio.h>

void main(void)
{   float price;
    short quantity;

    printf("Enter 0 0 to quit.\n");
    printf("Enter 'price quantity': ");
    scanf("%f %hi", &price, &quantity);
    while (price != 0)
    {   printf("The total for this item is $%6.2f.\n", price * quantity);
        printf("Enter 'price quantity': ");
        scanf("%f %hi", &price, &quantity);
    }
    printf("Thank you for your patronage.\n");
}
```

Output

```
Enter 0 0 to quit.
Enter 'price quantity': 3.75 2
The total for this item is $  7.50.
Enter 'price quantity': 10.59 6
The total for this item is $ 63.54.
Enter 'price quantity': 0 0
Thank you for your patronage.
```

The `printf()` and `scanf()` functions are repeated, but that is necessary so that the `while` has something to test and we don't print a meaningless result.

YOUR TURN 5–1

1. What is the purpose of an iteration structure?
2. When the condition in a C iteration structure is true, does the execution of the loop continue or stop?
3. What is the difference between a pretest and a posttest loop? How is each implemented in C?

4. How are sentinel values used to control loops?

ACCUMULATING AND COUNTING

Accumulation, adding (or multiplying, or whatever) values to a variable to keep a running result, is a common operation in loops. The accumulation process is to take the value of the variable in which we are accumulating, add another value to it, and store the result in the accumulator variable. Using *total* as our accumulator variable and *new* as a value we want to add to the accumulator, an accumulation statement would look like this:

```
total = total + new;
```

HEADS UP!

An assignment statement is not an equation.

As an algebraic equation, that makes no sense at all—but this is a statement representing a sequence of instructions to the computer, not an equation. Remember also, from our discussion in Chapter 4, that = does not mean equality, it means assignment. Let us suppose that the value of *total* is 100 and *new* is 5. Since addition (+) is higher in precedence than assignment (=), the addition expression is evaluated first. The computer will add the value of *total* (100) to the value of *new* (5), giving the result 105. The assignment operator is next, so the value 105 is assigned to *total*, replacing the 100.

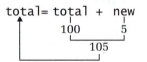

We can use any arithmetic operator. In the previous example we accumulated by adding to the *total* variable. Below, starting with the same values, we will use the multiplication operator. The new value of *total*, of course, will be 500.

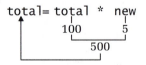

To work effectively, the accumulator variable, *total* in this example, must have a reasonable value before an accumulation operation is performed. If we had declared *total* as follows:

```
int total;
```

TRAP

Not initializing an accumulator.

without any other assignments to *total*, garbage times anything will still be garbage. Variables to be used as accumulators must be **initialized**, given a first value, somehow, whether it is in the declaration:

HEADS UP!

Initialization can be by any kind of assignment.

HEADS UP!

Any of the arithmetic operators can be part of an accumulation.

```
int total = 100;
```

or in some other assignment operation:

```
printf("What do you want to start with?");
scanf("&i", &total);
```

Accumulation Operators

Since accumulation is such a common operation, the designers of C gave us some shorthand notation for it: a set of **accumulation operators** formed by the arithmetic operator for the type of accumulation we are doing, followed by an equal sign. For example, the statement

```
total = total * new;
```

could be rewritten

```
total *= new;
```

This operator does not represent some new kind of mathematical operation; it simply indicates two separate operations. When evaluating an expression, C takes the variable before the operator (*total* in the example), copies both it and the arithmetic operator following it to the other side of the equal sign, and then compiles the result. There is no execution advantage to the accumulation operator; it just saves a little typing in the source code.

```
total *= new;
```
Becomes
```
total = total * new;
```

The precedence and associativity of the accumulation operators are the same as the assignment operator—last on our list and right to left. If *total* is 100, *new* is 5, and *old* is 3, *total* will become 108.

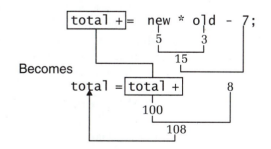

HEADS UP!

Like any other assignment, accumulation is low in precedence.

Notice that the whole effect of the accumulation operator comes after the multiplication and subtraction. The copy of the *total* variable is not made before the expression is evaluated, but during the evaluation when the accumulation operator is reached.

Let us put an accumulation operation to use in ⇨Program 5–5 to keep track of the total bill and print out its value after finishing the loop.

⇨**Program 5–5**

```
#include <stdio.h>

void main(void)
{   float price;
    float total = 0;
    short quantity;

    printf("Enter 0 0 to quit.\n");
    printf("Enter 'price quantity': ");
    scanf("%f %hi", &price, &quantity);
    while (price != 0)
    {   printf("The total for this item is $%6.2f.\n", price * quantity);
        total += price * quantity;
        printf("Enter 'price quantity': ");
        scanf("%f %hi", &price, &quantity);
    }
    printf("Your total is $%6.2f.\n", total);
}
```

Output

```
Enter 0 0 to quit.
Enter 'price quantity': 6.35 8
The total for this item is $ 50.80.
Enter 'price quantity': 2.50 10
The total for this item is $ 25.00.
Enter 'price quantity': 0 0
Your total is $ 75.80.
```

To work correctly, the accumulator variable, *total*, was initialized to zero at the time of its declaration. Without that initial assignment the first value of *total* would have been whatever was lying around in memory. Accumulating on top of that would not have been very productive.

The accumulation statement,

```
total += price * quantity
```

is exactly equivalent to

```
total = total + price * quantity
```

so *price* and *quantity* are multiplied and that result is added to *total*, replacing the previous value of *total*.

    Counting is specialized, simplified accumulation. Instead of adding a different value to the accumulation variable each time the statement is executed, the counting process adds the same value—1 or 9 or 2.8 or whatever we are counting by. The statement

```
count += 5;
```

would count by fives.

    If we wanted to know how many purchases were made, we could count by one at each purchase and, after exiting the loop, print out that total, as we have done in ⇨Program 5–6.

HEADS UP!

Counting is accumulating the same value each time.

⇨Program 5–6

```
#include <stdio.h>

void main(void)
{  float price;
   float total = 0;
   short quantity, items = 0;

   printf("Enter 0 0 to quit.\n");
   printf("Enter 'price quantity': ");
   scanf("%f %hi", &price, &quantity);
   while (price != 0)
   {  printf("The total for this item is $%6.2f.\n", price * quantity);
      total += price * quantity;
      items += 1;
      printf("Enter 'price quantity': ");
      scanf("%f %hi", &price, &quantity);
   }
   printf("Your total is $%6.2f for %hi different items.\n", total, items);
}
```

Output

```
Enter 0 0 to quit.
Enter 'price quantity': 22.95 3
The total for this item is $ 68.85.
Enter 'price quantity': 7.29 8
The total for this item is $ 58.32.
Enter 'price quantity': 15 4
The total for this item is $ 60.00.
Enter 'price quantity': 0 0
Your total is $187.17 for 3 different items.
```

COUNTER-CONTROLLED LOOPS

In some cases we want to execute a set of statements a certain number of times—10, 100, 416, or whatever—or we want to look at, for example, every fifth instance of an event. We will use a counter to control our loop. ⇨Program 5–7 prints out the numbers 1 through 3. We will use it to illustrate the elements needed for a **counter-controlled loop**

⇨Program 5–7

```
#include <stdio.h>

void main(void)
{  int count;

   count = 1;                                    /* Initialization */
   while (count <= 3)                                    /* Test */
   {  printf("%i\n", count);                             /* Body */
      count += 1;                                      /* Counter */
   }                                                      /* End */
   printf("Finished, but why is the count %i?\n", count);
}
```

Output

```
1
2
3
Finished, but why is the count 4?
```

The following elements are necessary for a successful counter-controlled loop:

▼ **Initialization**. A counter, like any accumulator, must start with some initial value.

▼ **Test**. This is a pretest. The loop will continue until the counter is greater than 3.

▼ **Body**. The statement(s) that the loop was set up to repeat.

▼ **Counter**. Adds one to the counter variable each time through the loop.

▼ **End**. Sends the program back to the test at the beginning.

Since counting and counter-controlled loops are so common in programming, C, like many other languages, has a special form for them, the **for** statement:

```
for (initialization; test; counter) statement;
```

or more commonly

```
for (initialization; test; counter)
{   statement 1;
    statement 2;
        . . .
}
```

⮡Program 5–8 will execute exactly as did ⮡Program 5–7.

HEADS UP!

These two programs are equivalent.

⮡**Program 5–8**

```
#include <stdio.h>

void main(void)
{   int count;

    for (count = 1; count <= 3; count += 1)
    {   printf("%i\n", count);                      /* Braces not required */
    }
    printf("Finished, but why is the count %i?\n", count);
}
```

Output

```
1
2
3
Finished, but why is the count 4?
```

HEADS UP!

For readability, use the **for** loop only for loops controlled by counters.

To answer the question at the end of the program, when the count was less than or equal to 3, the loop continued. The counter had to go beyond 3 (to 4) to make the loop condition false and exit the loop.

For the most part, the actions caused by a statement occur at the location of the statement within the program. The **for** statement is the

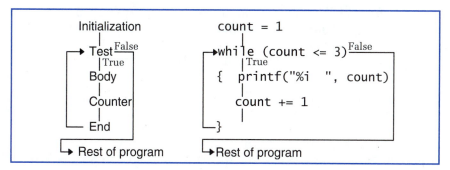

□ **FIGURE 5–2**   Counter-Controlled Loops

NUTS'N BOLTS

MORE ON for

We have identified the parameters of the `for` statement as an initialization, a test, and a counter. Internally, C makes no such distinctions. Any statements can be used in the position we have identified for the initialization and counter, and any expression can be used in the test position. C will simply execute whatever statement is in the initialization position, test whatever expression is in the test position, perform any statements in the body, execute whatever statement is in the counter position, and then go back to the test position.

C is very loose about what we put in these various positions, but *we* probably should not be. If we are not specifically writing a counting loop—with initialization, test, and counter—we should probably use a `while` or do loop.

HEADS UP!

Counting occurs at the end of the `for` loop.

exception; its actions are spread around the loop. As shown in ⊔Figure 5–2, the first action, the initialization, occurs only once before the repeating parts of the loop. The second, the test, is the first repeated action in the loop. The third, the counter, actually occurs at the end of the body of the loop—in some cases, hundreds of statements away from the `for` statement.

Using Floating-Point Counters

C will accept any simple data type as a counter, but floating-point counters can sometimes lead to unexpected results. Remember from Chapter 2 that floating-point values are stored in binary E notation and that conversion to this notation involves approximating the decimal value. Consider ⇨Program 5–9.

⇨**Program 5–9**

```
#include <stdio.h>

void main(void)
{  float count;

   printf("Values from 0 to 1 in steps of 0.1\n  ");
   for (count = 0; count <= 1; count += 0.1)
      printf("%.2f  ", count);
   printf("\nFinal count: %.2f\n", count);
}
```

Output

```
Values from 0 to 1 in steps of 0.1
   0.00  0.10  0.20  0.30  0.40  0.50  0.60  0.70  0.80  0.90
Final count: 1.00
```

This loop should have printed 1.00 within the loop, with the final count being 1.10—greater than 1. From the output we can see no evidence of the problem, but it involves the conversion to binary E notation. In the approximations made in the counting process, the accumulated number that we see as 1.00 is actually slightly larger than 1.00 in its binary form, forcing the loop to exit at that point.

The moral here is to avoid floating-point loop counters if at all possible. ⇨Program 5–9 could be written as ⇨Program 5–10, and the correct results obtained.

⇨Program 5–10

```c
#include <stdio.h>

void main(void)
{   int count;                                      /* Use an integer as a counter */

    printf("Values from 0 to 1 in steps of 0.1\n  ");
    for (count = 0; count <= 10; count += 1)
       printf("%.2f  ", count / 10.0);          /* Force double calculation */
    printf("\nFinal count: %.2f\n", count / 10.0);
}
```

Output

```
Values from 0 to 1 in steps of 0.1
  0.00  0.10  0.20  0.30  0.40  0.50  0.60  0.70  0.80  0.90  1.00
Final count: 1.10
```

Increment and Decrement Operators

Counting, especially by 1, is a common computer operation. We can add 1 to a variable by the process of accumulation as used above. For example,

```
whatever = whatever + 1;    or    whatever += 1;
```

adds 1 to the value of *whatever*.

C provides us with the ++ operator to add 1 to, **increment**, a variable as well as the -- operator to subtract 1 from, **decrement**, a variable. These are classed in precedence and associativity with the unary operators, but they actually perform assignments—change the values of variables. They can only be used with variables (it wouldn't make sense to change a constant value or the value of an expression) and they can only add 1 to or subtract 1 from the variable—not 2, 9, or 46. If *rabbit* is 17, it will be 18 after this statement:

```
++rabbit;
```

⇨Program 5–11 shows increment and decrement in action.

⇨**Program 5–11**

```
#include <stdio.h>

void main(void)
{   int rabbit = 17;

    printf("Rabbit is %i.\n", rabbit);
    ++rabbit;
    printf("Now, rabbit is %i.\n", rabbit);
    --rabbit;
    printf("Rabbit is back to %i.\n", rabbit);
}
```

Output

```
Rabbit is 17.
Now, rabbit is 18.
Rabbit is back to 17.
```

HEADS UP!

Increment and decrement operators are commonly used in **for** loops.

One common place to find increment and decrement operators is in counter-controlled loops, incrementing or decrementing the loop counter variable. In our previous loop example in ⇨Program 5–8, our **for** statement looked like this:

```
for (count = 1; count <= 3; count += 1)
```

It could have just as easily been written like this:

```
for (count = 1; count <= 3; ++count)
```

Or, for that matter, like this:

```
for (count = 1; count <= 3; count++)
```

In this case, it doesn't matter whether we increment *count* before we use it in the expression or after, because we are not using its value in the expression—only changing it.

Increment and Decrement in Expressions (Optional)

The increment and decrement operators become more interesting because they can be used in arithmetic expressions, changing the values of the variables they are attached to as the expression is being evaluated. The operator may appear as a prefix, before the variable that it changes, or as a postfix, after the variable. If it appears before, then the variable is changed before its value is used in the expression. If it appears after, the value of the variable is used in the expression, and then the variable is changed.

In this example, if *Quantity* is 2 and *Price* is 3.5, after the following statement is performed, *TotalSales* will be 7.0 and *Quantity* will be 3.

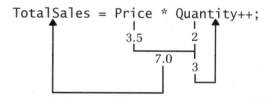

If the increment operator is put in front of the variable, *Quantity* will still end up being 3, but *TotalSales* will be 10.5.

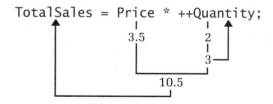

YOUR TURN 5–2

1. How does accumulation work?
2. Why is initialization of an accumulator variable important?
3. How does counting differ from accumulation? How are they the same?
4. What five elements are necessary in a counter-controlled loop? What does each do?

5. At what point in the loop does each parameter of a `for` statement execute?

6. Why is using a floating-point loop counter not advised?

7. What is the difference between `++x` and `x++` when used in an arithmetic expression?

NESTED LOOPS

Any valid statement or set of statements may be included within a loop. For example, the following program segment is a loop that prints the numbers 1 to 4.

Program Segment   **Output**

```
for (x = 1; x <= 4; ++x)                1  2  3  4
{  printf("%i  ", x);
}
```

There is no reason why this could not be part of another loop:

Program Segment   **Output**

```
for (y = 1; y <= 3; ++y)                Line 1:  1  2  3  4
{  printf("Line %i:  ",y);             Line 2:  1  2  3  4
   for (x = 1; x <= 4; ++x)             Line 3:  1  2  3  4
   {  printf("%i  ", x);
   }
   printf("\n");
}
```

A loop within another loop is referred to as a **nested loop**. Nesting may be as deep as needed—a loop within a loop within a loop within . . . as long as you make sure of two things:

▼ An inner loop must be entirely contained within an outer one. This simply follows our rules of combining structures. With proper indenting, as in the example above, violation of this rule will be obvious.

▼ If the loops are counter controlled, each loop that is operating simultaneously (nested within another) must have a different loop counter variable, such as x and y above. If you violate this rule, one loop will be modifying the other loop's counter, yielding a mess!

⇨Program 5–12 allows the user to enter a positive integer and prints a table of all integers from the one entered back to 1. The second column of the table is the product of all integers from 1 to the integer in the first column—mathematically, the factorial of the value in the first column.

HEADS UP!

Properly nest loops.

HEADS UP!

Have separate loop counters.

⇨Program 5–12

```
#include <stdio.h>

void main(void)
{  int n, count, factorial;

   printf("Enter a positive integer: ");
   scanf("%i", &n);
   printf("Integer  Factorial\n");
   for ( ; n >= 1; --n)                         /* n initialized by scanf() */
   {  printf("   %3i   ", n);
      factorial = 1;
      for (count = 1; count <= n; ++count)
         factorial *= count;        /* Only 1 statement, no braces needed */
      printf("%i\n", factorial);
   }
}
```

Output

```
Enter a positive integer: 5
Integer  Factorial
      5  120
      4  24
      3  6
      2  2
      1  1
```

HEADS UP!

Typically, the outer loop controls the row, and the inner loop the column.

Rows and Columns

One common use for nested loops is row and column applications. We use the outer loop to set the row, and then use the inner loop to vary across the columns. Returning to the outer loop sets up the next row, and the inner loop varies across the columns, and so forth.

For example, we might use a program like ⇨Program 5–13 to set up a table showing the decimal equivalent of fractions with numerators and denominators varying from 1 to 10.

The numerators make up the columns in the table and the denominators the rows. Accordingly we have used the variable *num* to control the columns, across the table, and *den* to control the rows, down the table. Let us follow a row through. The denominator is set to 1 in the outer loop, and the value of the denominator is printed. Then, still within the denominator loop, the numerator is varied from 1 to 10 and the fraction printed in an inner loop. At the end of the numerator loop, after all 10 fractions have been printed, we drop down to the beginning of the next row to get ready for the next denominator.

⇨**Program 5–13**

```
#include <stdio.h>

void main(void)
{   int num, den;

    /********************************************** Print numerator heading */
    printf("                 Numerator\n                ");
    for (num = 1; num <= 10; ++num)
       printf("  %2i  ", num);
    printf("\nDenominator\n");

    /***************************************************** Print table */
    for (den = 1; den <= 10; ++den)                /* Establish denominator */
    {   printf("           %2i ", den);            /* Print denominator heading */
        for (num = 1; num <= 10; ++num)            /* Numerators from 1 to 10 */
           printf("%5.2f ", 1.0 * num / den);             /* Force double */
        printf("\n");                              /* Drop down to next row */
    }                                              /* Go to the next denominator */
}
```

Output

```
            Numerator
            1     2     3     4     5     6     7     8     9     10
Denominator
        1   1.00  2.00  3.00  4.00  5.00  6.00  7.00  8.00  9.00 10.00
        2   0.50  1.00  1.50  2.00  2.50  3.00  3.50  4.00  4.50  5.00
        3   0.33  0.67  1.00  1.33  1.67  2.00  2.33  2.67  3.00  3.33
        4   0.25  0.50  0.75  1.00  1.25  1.50  1.75  2.00  2.25  2.50
        5   0.20  0.40  0.60  0.80  1.00  1.20  1.40  1.60  1.80  2.00
        6   0.17  0.33  0.50  0.67  0.83  1.00  1.17  1.33  1.50  1.67
        7   0.14  0.29  0.43  0.57  0.71  0.86  1.00  1.14  1.29  1.43
        8   0.12  0.25  0.38  0.50  0.62  0.75  0.88  1.00  1.12  1.25
        9   0.11  0.22  0.33  0.44  0.56  0.67  0.78  0.89  1.00  1.11
       10   0.10  0.20  0.30  0.40  0.50  0.60  0.70  0.80  0.90  1.00
```

YOUR TURN 5–3

1. What is a nested loop?
2. What two rules must be followed for the correct formation of a nested loop?
3. Why, in a table situation, does the outer loop typically control the row and the inner loop the column?

PUTTING IT TOGETHER

T. Farthington Gotbucks, IV, is looking into alternative interest-bearing investments for all the money he has inherited. The investments he is considering are all interest bearing and compounded quarterly (the interest calculated and added back to the balance four times a year), and all extend for three years.

TASK

Write a program for T. Farthy that will allow him to input the rate for a prospective investment, and show him how that investment would progress over three years.

ANALYSIS

The output should be a chart showing the investment's history—starting amount, interest, and ending amount—for each quarter of each year. It should also show the total interest earned in each year as well as over the three years. So that any investment possibility can be compared on equal grounds, the program should start with $1,000 for each. The form should be similar to the following:

```
           Start Interest       End
Year 1
     1   ####.##     ##.##   ####.##
     2   ####.##     ##.##   ####.##
     3   ####.##     ##.##   ####.##
     4   ####.##     ##.##   ####.##
    Total interest for the year: $###.##
[Same for years 2 and 3.]

Ending balance: $####.##.  Interest earned: $###.##.
```

The input will consist of an interest rate to be analyzed. Anything less than 5 percent or greater than 20 percent will be deemed an unreasonable rate and should be rejected.

The interest is calculated by multiplying the current balance by the rate by the time period, one quarter of a year in this case. A new balance is calculated by adding that interest to the current balance.

DESIGN

Overall his program shoulddo the following:

Enter interest rate
Produce chart

Since he wants to perform many analyses, the program should be in a loop.

While new analysis desired
    Enter interest rate
    Produce chart

If the interest input is outside the reasonable range, the program should ask for another input.

While new analysis desired
    Enter interest rate
    If input out of range
        Print error message
    Else
        Produce chart

To make the chart show each quarter's activity with a yearly summary of the balance and total interest, we can expand the **Produce chart** section:

[Produce chart]

Initialize balance and total interest
Yearly for three years
    Initialize yearly interest
    Quarterly for four quarters
        Print quarter and beginning balance
        Figure interest and add to yearly interest and balance
        Print interest and new balance
    Add year's interest to total
Print final totals

IMPLEMENTATION

The Gotbucks investment program is shown in ⇨Program 5–14.

TEST

HEADS UP!

Be sure your test data is correct.

The tests should include representative rates within the acceptable range as well as tests to reject rates outside the range. The tests should be compared with results obtained by hand. The following test did not actually agree with the hand-calculated results. It was found that there was a mistake in the interest calculation for quarter two of year three in the hand calculation.

```
    #include <stdio.h>

    void main(void)
    {  float rate, balance;
       float interest;                              /* Interest for the quarter */
       float yearly_interest;              /* Accumulated interest within year */
       float total_interest;                       /* Total accumulated interest */
       int year, quarter;

       printf("Enter interest rate (zero to quit): ");
1      scanf("%f", &rate);
2      while (rate != 0.0)
3      {  if (rate < 5.0 || rate > 20.0)              /* If input out of range */
4             printf("   Out of the reasonable range.\n");
          else
5          {  printf("\n              Start Interest       End\n");
6             balance = 1000;
7             total_interest = 0;                    /* Initialize for new chart */
8             for (year = 1; year <= 3; ++year)
9             {  printf("Year %i\n", year);
10               yearly_interest = 0;             /* Initialize yearly interest */
11               for (quarter = 1; quarter <= 4; ++quarter)
12               {  printf("      %i   %7.2f", quarter, balance);
13                  interest = balance * rate / 100 * .25;
14                  yearly_interest += interest;
15                  balance += interest;
16                  printf("  %7.2f  %7.2f\n", interest, balance);
17               }
18               printf("    Total interest for the year: $%.2f\n",
                         yearly_interest);
19               total_interest += yearly_interest;              /* Accumulate */
20            }
21            printf("\nEnding balance: $%.2f.  Interest earned: $%.2f.\n\n",
                      balance, total_interest);
          }
          printf("Enter interest rate (zero to quit): ");
22        scanf("%f", &rate);
23     }
    }
```

EXECUTION CHART

Line	Explanation	rate	year	quarter	balance	interest	yearly_ interest	total_ interest
1	Enter interest rate.	.125	?	?	?	?	?	?
2	*rate* not the sentinel value, perform loop.	.125	?	?	?	?	?	?
3	*rate* less than 5, condition true.	.125	?	?	?	?	?	?
4	Print out of range message.	.125	?	?	?	?	?	?
22	Enter new *rate*.	12.5	?	?	?	?	?	?
2	Still not sentinel value, perform loop.	12.5	?	?	?	?	?	?
3	*rate* neither <5 nor >20, condition false.	12.5	?	?	?	?	?	?
5	Print table heading.	12.5	?	?	?	?	?	?
6, 7	Initialize *balance* and *total_interest*.	12.5	?	?	1000.00	?	?	0
8	Initialize *year*, test *year*, enter loop.	12.5	1	?	1000.00	?	?	0
9	Print *year*.	12.5	1	?	1000.00	?	?	0
10	Initialize *yearly_interest*.	12.5	1	?	1000.00	?	0	0
11	Initialize and test *quarter*, enter loop.	12.5	1	1	1000.00	?	0	0
12	Print *quarter* and *balance* at start.	12.5	1	1	1000.00	?	0	0
13	Calculate *interest* for quarter.	12.5	1	1	1000.00	31.25	0	0
14	Accumulate *yearly_interest*.	12.5	1	1	1000.00	31.25	31.25	0
15	Accumulate *balance*.	12.5	1	1	1031.25	31.25	31.25	0
16	Print *interest* and ending *balance*.	12.5	1	1	1031.25	31.25	31.25	0
17	Increment *quarter*.	12.5	1	2	1031.25	31.25	31.25	0
11	Test, *quarter*<= 4, continue loop.	12.5	1	2	1031.25	31.25	31.25	0
11–17	After 4 times through the loop.	12.5	1	4	1130.98	34.27	130.98	0
17	Increment *quarter*.	12.5	1	5	1130.98	34.27	130.98	0
11	Test, *quarter* not <= 4, exit loop.	12.5	1	5	1130.98	34.27	130.98	0
18	Print *yearly_interest*.	12.5	1	5	1130.98	34.27	130.98	0
19	Accumulate *total_interest*.	12.5	1	5	1130.98	34.27	130.98	130.98
20	Increment *year*.	12.5	2	5	1130.98	34.27	130.98	130.98
8	Test, *year* <= 3, continue loop.	12.5	2	5	1130.98	34.27	130.98	130.98
9, 10	Print *year*, initialize *yearly_interest*.	12.5	2	5	1130.98	34.27	0	130.98
11	Initialize and test *quarter*, enter loop.	12.5	2	1	1130.98	34.27	0	130.98
8–20	After 3 times through *year* loop (and 4 times through the *quarter* loop for each time through the *year* loop).	12.5	3	5	1446.66	43.84	167.54	446.66
20	Increment *year*.	12.5	4	5	1446.66	43.84	167.54	446.66
8	Test, *year* not <= 3, exit loop.	12.5	4	5	1446.66	43.84	167.54	446.66
21	Print *balance* and *total_interest*.	12.5	4	5	1446.66	43.84	167.54	446.66
22	Enter interest rate.	0	4	5	1446.66	43.84	167.54	446.66
23	Go back to top of while loop.	0	4	5	1446.66	43.84	167.54	446.66
2	*rate* is sentinel value, exit loop.	0	4	5	1446.66	43.84	167.54	446.66

Output

```
Enter interest rate (zero to quit): .125
   Out of the reasonable range.
Enter interest rate (zero to quit): 12.5

          Start Interest      End
Year 1
     1  1000.00     31.25  1031.25
     2  1031.25     32.23  1063.48
     3  1063.48     33.23  1096.71
     4  1096.71     34.27  1130.98
   Total interest for the year: $130.98
Year 2
     1  1130.98     35.34  1166.33
     2  1166.33     36.45  1202.77
     3  1202.77     37.59  1240.36
     4  1240.36     38.76  1279.12
   Total interest for the year: $148.14
Year 3
     1  1279.12     39.97  1319.09
     2  1319.09     41.22  1360.32
     3  1360.32     42.51  1402.83
     4  1402.83     43.84  1446.66
   Total interest for the year: $167.54

Ending balance: $1446.66.  Interest earned: $446.66.
Enter interest rate (zero to quit): 0
```

SUMMARY

▲**KEY TERMS** (in order of appearance)

Iteration structure	Counter-controlled loop
Loop	Test
Pretest	Body
Posttest	Counter
Sentinel value	End
Accumulation	Increment
Initialization	Decrement
Accumulation operator	Nested loop
Counting	

```
while (condition) statement;
do statement; while (condition);
for (initialization; test; counter) statement;
```

▲CONCEPT REVIEW

▼ The **iteration structure**, or **loop**, repeats a set of statements. The condition for repeating the statements is given in a **while** statement. If it is a **pretest** loop, the while appears at the beginning of the loop. If it is a **posttest**, the loop starts with a **do** statement and the while appears at the end of the loop.

▼ Often, the condition for a loop involves a **sentinel value**, a special value for a variable that is being used in the loop that is tested for each time through the loop. When the sentinel value of the variable is found, the loop is exited.

▼ Two other concepts that are commonly used with loops are **accumulating**, keeping a running total, and **counting**, adding some fixed value to a variable each time through the loop.

▼ Accumulation is so common in programming that C has a number of accumulation operators that provide us with a simpler notation.

▼ In the case of a **counter-controlled loop**, a counter is the determining factor for exiting the loop. This loop has five important ingredients: an **initialization** of the counter; a **test** to determine if the loop should repeat; a **body** of statements to repeat; a **counter** statement that adds to the counter; and an **end** of the loop that sends the execution back to the test. The parameters for these various elements can all be stated in a **for** statement.

▼ Floating-point counters sometimes give us unexpected results because of the rounding in storing floating-point numbers.

▼ **Increment** and **decrement** operators, which also make assignments, are often used in counting loops.

▼ Since any valid statement or structure can be included within any other, we often encounter **nested loops**, one loop within another. We can nest loops (and other structures) as deep as we need to as long as the nesting is complete, and as long as each loop has a different counter variable.

▼ Row and column formations are common applications of nested loops. Typically, the outer loop controls the row and the inner loop, the column.

▲HEADS UP: POINTS OF SPECIAL INTEREST

▼ Loops must have conditions. *Infinite loops are not considered proper structured programming.*

▼ True conditions continue the loop.

▼ Choose pretest or posttest according to the situation. *Pretest loops may never execute; postest test execute at least once.*

▼ A sentinel value should be something weird. *Don't make the sentinel value a possibility for normal use.*

▼ An assignment statement is not an equation.

▼ Initialization can be by any kind of assignment.

▼ Any of the arithmetic operators can be part of an accumulation.

▼ Like any other assignment, accumulation is low in precedence.

▼ Counting is accumulating the same value each time.

▼ These two programs are equivalent. *Any* `for` *loop can be rewritten with a* `while` *loop.*

▼ For readability, use the `for` loop only for loops controlled by counters.

▼ Counting occurs at the end of the `for` loop.

▼ Increment and decrement perform assignments.

▼ Increment and decrement operators are commonly used in `for` loops.

▼ Properly nest loops.

▼ Have separate loop counters. *Each loop in a nested set must have its own unique loop counter.*

▼ Typically, the outer loop controls the row, and the inner loop the column.

▼ Be sure your test data is correct. *When checking your program's results against hand calculations and they don't agree, suspect your hand calculations as well as the program.*

▲TRAPS: COMMON PROGRAMMING ERRORS

▼ Putting a semicolon after the condition in a pretest loop.

▼ Testing a variable containing garbage at the beginning of a loop.

▼ Not putting a semicolon after the condition in a posttest loop.

▼ Not testing for the sentinel value until after it is used in a normal situation.

▼ Not initializing an accumulator.

▼ Expecting a floating-point counter to behave. *Remember, floating-point values are approximations.*

▼5–1

1. An iteration structure repeats a set of operations.

2. A true condition continues execution of a loop.

3. A pretest loop tests for continuation of the loop at the beginning of the loop. In C, it begins with a `while` keyword followed by the condition in parentheses. It ends at the end of the statement or block of statements following the condition. A posttest loop tests at the end of the loop. In C, it begins with the key word **do**, followed by a statement or block, and ends with `while` and a condition terminated with a semicolon.

4. A variable used in the normal course of operations is tested each time through the loop. If it contains the sentinel value, then the loop quits.

▼5–2

1. An accumulation process adds (or multiplies, or whatever) the value of a variable to some other value and stores the result in the original variable.

2. If the accumulator variable contains garbage before the accumulation, it will contain garbage after.

3. Counting is accumulation, but with the difference that it adds the same value each time instead of different values.

4. Any counter-controlled loop must contain an initialization, a test, a body, a counter, and an end.

5. The initialization occurs before the loop; the test at the beginning of the loop; and the counter at the end of the loop.

6. Floating-point numbers are approximated when they are calculated and stored. Successive approximations may lead to erroneous results.

7. If the operator falls before the variable, the variable is incremented before it is used in the expression. If the operator falls after, the variable is incremented after being used.

▼5–3

1. A nested loop is one loop contained with another loop.

2. The inner loop must be entirely contained in the outer, and, if they are both counter controlled, the counter variables must be different.

3. The typical output machinery, whether screen or printer, moves across the columns in a row, then down to the next row, across the columns, then down, and so forth. The columns are generated within the rows, hence the column loop within the row loop.

EXERCISES

1. Rewrite the following program statements using acceptable, readable form.

```
printf("Input a number ");scanf("%f", &numb);while (numb != 0){
printf("That's not zero. Another ");scanf("%f", &numb);}
printf("Finally a zero.\n");
```

2. Fill in an execution chart for the following program segment with the given execution.

```
int quiz, total = 0, quizzes = 0;

printf("Quiz score? ");
scanf("%i", &quiz);
do
{   total += quiz;
    ++quizzes;
    printf("Quiz score? ");
    scanf("%i", &quiz);
}while (quiz > 0);
printf("Average quiz: %.1f\n", 1.0 * total / quizzes);
```

```
Quiz score? 16
Quiz score? 19
Quiz Score? -1
Average quiz: 17.5
```

3. Rewrite these **while** loops using the **for** statement.

```
x = 14;                          y = 65;
while (x >= 3)                   while (y <= 85)
{   printf("%i\n", x);           {   printf("%i\n", y);
    x -= 5;                          y += 5;
}                                }
```

4. Rewrite these **for** statements using **while** loops.

```
for (x = 250; x >= 100; x -= 50)
    printf("%i\n", x);


for (y = 1226; y <= 1426; y += 2)
    printf("%i\n", y);
```

5. What will the output be from the following program segment?

```
for (x = 16; x >= 4; --x);
    printf("Hello\n");
for (x = 16; x >= 4; --x)
    printf("Hello\n");
    printf("How are you\n");
```

6. What will the output be from this program segment?

```
for (a = 1; a <= 5; ++a)
{  printf("%i", a);
   for (b = a; b >= 1; --b)
      printf(" %i", b);
   printf("\n");
}
printf("%i %i\n", a, b);
```

PROGRAMS

1. Write a program that prints the smallest of five numbers input. Use an
   if statement to see if the new number input should replace the current minimum.

Variables

input	Number input at keyboard
min	To keep track of smallest
count	Loop counter

Output

```
Enter number 1: 59.2
Enter number 2: -3.789
Enter number 3: 42.5
Enter number 4: -28
Enter number 5: 12.6
The smallest is -28
```

2. You have found some cockroaches in your apartment. Rather than call
   the exterminator, you decide to perform an experiment. You count the
   number of roaches and then wait a week and count them again to
   determine their breeding rate. Print out the estimated roach population from that point on, assuming that the breeding rate remains constant. Stop at the week that shows over a million roaches. You need
   not actually continue the experiment to validate your computer
   results—call the exterminator.

Variables

```
initial_roaches
roaches
breeding_rate
week
```

Output

```
Roaches at beginning of week: 6
Roaches at end of week: 38

Week      Roaches
  2            38
  3           240
  4          1520
  5          9626
  6         60964
  7        386105
  8       2445331
```

3. A Pythagorean triple is three integers that make up the sides of a right triangle; for example, 3, 4, and 5. The sides may be calculated according to the formulas given as long as a is greater than b. Write a program that shows possible triples for a and b varying from 1 to 5.

Formulas

$side1 = a^2 - b^2$
$side2 = 2ab$
$hypotenuse = a^2 + b^2$

Variables

```
a, b
side1, side2, hypotenuse
```

Output

Side1	Side2	Hypotenuse
3	4	5
8	6	10
5	12	13
15	8	17
12	16	20
7	24	25
24	10	26
21	20	29
16	30	34
9	40	41

4. The game Totals can be played by any number of people. It starts with a total of 100 and each player in turn makes an integer adjustment between −20 and 20 to that total. The winner is the player whose adjustment makes the total equal to 5. Use only the three variables given.

Suggested Variables

```
total
adjustment
counter        Number of adjustments
decimal        Test for decimal point in input
```

Output

```
WE START WITH 100. WHAT IS
YOUR ADJUSTMENT? -20
   THE TOTAL IS 80
YOUR ADJUSTMENT? 4.6
    NOT AN INTEGER BETWEEN -20 AND 20
YOUR ADJUSTMENT? -35
    NOT AN INTEGER BETWEEN -20 AND 20
YOUR ADJUSTMENT? -20
   THE TOTAL IS 60
YOUR ADJUSTMENT? -15
   THE TOTAL IS 45
        .
        .
        .
YOUR ADJUSTMENT? -6
   THE TOTAL IS 5
THE GAME IS WON IN 14 STEPS
```

5. Write a program to assign a letter grade given a numeric score: 90 or above is an A; 80, B; 70, C; 60, D; and below 60, F. The program should continue to accept values until a negative number is input. The program should print how many of each letter grade were assigned after the input is completed. Use the `else if` construct in your program.

Variables

```
score                    Score input
a_s, b_s, c_s, d_s, f_s  Counters for letter grades
```

Output

```
SCORE? 92
  THE GRADE IS A
SCORE? 70
  THE GRADE IS C
   .
   .
   .
SCORE? -1
```

(continued)

```
2 A'S
2 B'S
4 C'S
0 D'S
1 F'S
```

6. Modify the program above to use the `switch` statement.

7. Specific points on a compass may be expressed in general directions. For example, 130° is in an easterly direction. Write a program that will take directions in degrees and give them one of four general-direction titles: 315° up to but not including 45° is north, 45°–135° is east, 135°–225° is south, and 225°–315° is west. The program should reject invalid readings and end when a negative compass reading is input.

Variable

degrees   Direction in degrees input at keyboard

Output

```
COMPASS READING? 104
  EAST
COMPASS READING? 370
INVALID, ENTER ANOTHER COMPASS READING? 242
  WEST
COMPASS READING? -1
```

8. Write a program that converts feet to meters. Use a `for` loop. It should go from 1 to 10 feet in half-foot steps. One meter equals 3.28083 feet. To avoid approximation problems in fractional counting, use an integral loop counter and calculate the proper figures on output.

Variable

feet   Integral loop counter

Output

```
FEET TO METERS CONVERSION TABLE
FEET     METERS
 1.0     0.30480
 1.5     0.45720
 2.0     0.60960
       .
       .
       .

 9.0     2.74321
 9.5     2.89561
10.0     3.04801
```

9. Write a program to show the area of a circle (πr^2) and the volume of a sphere ($^4/_3\pi r^3$) for all radii between 100 and 150 cm in increments of 5 cm ($\pi = 3.1416$).

Variable

```
radius
```

Output

RADIUS	AREA	VOLUME
100	31416.0	4.18880E+06
105	34636.1	4.84906E+06
110	38013.4	5.57530E+06
115	41547.7	6.37064E+06
120	45239.0	7.23825E+06
125	49087.5	8.18125E+06
130	53093.1	9.20280E+06
135	57255.7	1.03060E+07
140	61575.4	1.14941E+07
145	66052.1	1.27701E+07
150	70686.0	1.41372E+07

10. Write a program to create a multiplication table for all combinations of two numbers from 1 to 8.

Variables

```
multiplier
multiplicand
```

Output

	1	2	3	4	5	6	7	8
1	1	2	3	4	5	6	7	8
2	2	4	6	8	10	12	14	16
3	3	6	9	12	15	18	21	24
4	4	8	12	16	20	24	28	32
5	5	10	15	20	25	30	35	40
6	6	12	18	24	30	36	42	48
7	7	14	21	28	35	42	49	56
8	8	16	24	32	40	48	56	64

11. Write a program that allows you to input a desired total, after which it prints all the possible combinations of three nonnegative integers that add up to that total. Set up nested loops to generate the three numbers and then test each combination to see whether its total equals the

input total. The individual numbers never have to be greater than the desired total.

Variables

```
total        The desired total
c1, c2, c3   Counters to generate the three numbers
count        To count the number of valid combinations
```

Output

```
Desired total: 4
  0  0  4
  0  1  3
    . . .
  3  1  0
  4  0  0
15 number combinations total 4.
```

12. Write a program to produce the following output. Use nested `for` loops.

Output

```
1
1  2
1  2  3
1  2  3  4
1  2  3  4  5
1  2  3  4  5  6
1  2  3  4  5  6  7
1  2  3  4  5  6  7  8
1  2  3  4  5  6  7  8  9
1  2  3  4  5  6  7  8
1  2  3  4  5  6  7
1  2  3  4  5  6
1  2  3  4  5
1  2  3  4
1  2  3
1  2
1
```

13. The value of e^x can be calculated by expansion of the Taylor's series,

$$1 + x + \frac{x^2}{2}! + \frac{x^3}{3}! + \ldots + \frac{x^n}{n}!\ .$$

The expansion stops when the final term,

$$\frac{x^n}{n}!$$

is less than some value *epsilon*. Write a program that defines *epsilon* as an appropriately small value and allows input of the value for x. Remember, C does not have an exponentiation or a factorial operator, so you will have to calculate x^n and the various factorials in loops. Use appropriate variables and an effective output form.

Chapter 6

FUNCTIONS

PREVIEW

Modular programming is both a technique and an objective in today's programming environment. In C modularity is implemented through a structure based on functions. In this chapter we will closely examine the principles of function use, and learn how we can create functions for our own purposes. Here you will learn:

▼ How functions are set up and included in programs.

▼ How to send values to functions to be processed.

▼ How to get processed values back from functions.

▼ Reasons for using functions in programs.

▼ Some of the functions that exist in ANSI C.

The elegance and sophistication of the C language is largely due to its free use of functions, and indeed its virtual dependence on them. The language itself has very few statements, but along with your C compiler you will undoubtedly receive a wealth of different functions—not only the standard ANSI set but also others, many of which address the unique capabilities of your particular hardware. If the language still doesn't do what you want it to, you can make up your own functions.

In fact, making up your own functions is a desired objective. Top-down, modular designs are easily implemented by translating each module into a separate function. If you set up these modules carefully, making sure they are totally self-contained and do not affect processes outside of them, you can use the modules you have designed for one program as modules in another.

We have already used two of the standard ANSI functions, `printf()` and `scanf()`. When we included the name of the function, `printf`, for example, in a program statement and gave it something to work with, such as (`"The number is %i\n", value`), it performed its intended operation at that point in the program. Here we will look at the mechanisms by which these functions operate.

HOW FUNCTIONS WORK

Let us look at an example process and see how we might use functions to modularize it. A company figures and writes its employees' paychecks by hand, a process its accounting personnel are finding cumbersome. They have called on us to help them.

TASK

Provide a program to calculate the data for employees' paychecks.

ANALYSIS

Each paycheck and check stub must contain the following information:

    Employee number
    Employee department
    Number of other dependents claimed by the employee
    Hours worked
    Pay rate
    Gross pay
    Total deductions
    Net pay

The employee number and department is derived from the employee identification code. The last digit is a department code, and the preceding digits are the employee number. The department codes are:

1   Information Systems

2   Accounting

3   Manufacturing and others

The employee's gross pay is the number of hours worked times the pay rate.

Taxes consist of federal income tax and state income tax. Both taxes are the gross pay times the appropriate tax rate. The federal income tax rate is reduced by 1 percent for every dependent, including the employee personally.

Net pay is the gross pay minus the taxes minus a deduction for health insurance for each dependent beyond the employee.

To operate, then, the program must be given the employee ID, total number of dependents claimed, hours worked, pay rate, federal and state tax rates, and health insurance deduction. The tax rates and health insurance deduction change infrequently enough that they can be defined in the program.

DESIGN

To reach the desired output from the inputs listed, the program must:

Input dependents
Decode employee ID
Calculate gross pay
Calculate taxes
Calculate net pay

IMPLEMENTATION AND TEST

Let us use each of these steps as different modules and show various methods of handling the modules. The first module, Input dependents, we will handle as we have done with our other programs to this point—as inline code in the main() function.

```
void main(void)
{  int dependents;

   printf("Dependents (including employee)? ");
   scanf("%i", &dependents);
}
```

The second module will require some expansion:

[Decode employee ID]
    Input employee ID
    Separate employee number
    Print employee number
    Separate department code
    Decode and print department code

Instead of putting it in the `main()` function, let us put it in its own function, *info()*.

```
void info(void) /********************************** Decode employee info */
{  int emp_id, emp_num, dept;

    printf("Employee ID? ");
    scanf("%i", &emp_id);
    emp_num = emp_id / 10;        /* Separate emp num by deleting last digit */
    printf("Employee #%i in the ", emp_num);
    dept = emp_id % 10;     /* Dept num - remainder is last digit of emp_id */
    switch (dept)
    {  case 1:
            printf("Information Systems");
            break;
        case 2:
            printf("Accounting");
            break;
        default:
            printf("Manufacturing or other");
    }
    printf(" department.\n");
}
```

HEADS UP!

The function definition is all
the statements in the function.

The Function Definition

This code is referred to as a **function definition**. It defines the function's operation—tells C what actions to take in the function.

If this were the `main()` function and we ran the program, a sample test would produce:

```
Employee ID? 8471
Employee #847 in the Information Systems department.
```

In other words, this section of code could operate by itself.

The Function Call

Since we want this mini-program, the *info()* function, to be part of a larger program, let us have our `main()` function **call** it—set it in operation as part of the `main()` function code. ⇨Program 6–1 adds the call to the `main()` function.

⇨**Program 6–1**

```
    #include <stdio.h>

    void info(void);                                    /* Function declaration */

    void main(void)
 1  {   double gross, tax;
 2      int dependents;

        printf("Dependents (including employee)? ");
 3      scanf("%i", &dependents);
 4      info();                                         /* Function call */
 8      printf("Write the check!\n");
 9  }

                                                        /* Function definition */
    void info(void) /******************************** Decode employee info */
i1  {   int emp_id, emp_num, dept;

        printf("Employee ID? ");
i2      scanf("%i", &emp_id);
i3      emp_num = emp_id / 10;       /* Separate emp num by deleting last digit */
i4      printf("Employee #%i in the ", emp_num);
i5      dept = emp_id % 10;    /* Dept num - remainder is last digit of emp_id */
i6      switch (dept)
i7      {   case 1:
i8              printf("Information Systems");
i9              break;
i10         case 2:
i11             printf("Accounting");
i12             break;
i13         default:
i14             printf("Manufacturing or other");
        }
i15     printf(" department.\n");
i16 }                                                   /* End of function definition */
```

Line	Explanation	main() function variables:	gross	tax	depend
1, 2	Declare variables in `main()`.		?	?	?
3	Input *dependents*.		?	?	5
4	Call *info()*.		?	?	5
		info() function variables:	emp_id	emp_num	dept
i1	Declare variables in *info()*.		?	?	?
i2	Input *emp_ia*.		8471	?	?
i3	An integer division by 10 deletes last digit.		8471	847	?
i4	Print the employee number.		8471	847	?
i5	The remainder of a division by 10 will be the last digit.		8471	847	1
i6	`switch` on *dept*.		8471	847	1
i7	Matching `case`.		8471	847	1
i8	Print department name.		8471	847	1
i9	Go beyond end of `switch`.		8471	847	1
i15	Print "department."		8471	847	1
i16	End of function, return to call point in `main()`.		8471	847	1
		main() function variables:	gross	tax	depend
4	Statement completed, go to next statement.		?	?	5
8	Final printout.		?	?	5

Output

```
Dependents (including employee)? 5
Employee ID? 8471
Employee #847 in the Information Systems department.
Write the check!
```

TRAP

Not declaring a function.

Leaving the semicolon off a function declaration.

The Function Declaration

The **function declaration**, before the `main()` function, tells C that the *info()* function can be called from some subsequent point in the program. The declaration is nothing more than the first line of the function definition copied to a point near the top of the program with a semicolon added to the end. The semicolon is important here. The function declaration, like any other declaration, is a statement and must end in a semicolon.

A function declaration must appear before the function is called. We have put it near the top of the program so that we can call the function from anywhere in the program—from within `main()`, or perhaps from within some other function. The function definition also acts as a declaration, and, in fact, if we had put the definition before `main()`, we would not have needed the separate declaration. It is common in structured programming, however, to put the controlling module, `main()` in C, first, and all the submodules, other C functions, after it. This allows the overall process to be described in relatively simple terms near the beginning of the code. The detail is expanded after it.

The Function Return

The function call transfers execution to the function. In our example, we will input *dependents*, and the next statement to execute will be the declarations in the *info()* function. Execution continues with the statements in the function until the function runs out of statements—the program reaches the closing brace in the function. At that point execution will **return**, go back to where it left off at the call. The next statement to execute, then, will be `printf("Write the check!\n");` in the `main()` function. When the program reaches the closing brace of the `main()` function, there is nowhere to return, so the program quits.

Let us add the next module, Calculate gross pay, to our program in a *gross_pay()* function. With this module, we will make more sophisticated use of the function return. We will need the value of the gross pay later in the program, so we will design the *gross_pay()* function with a **return value**—a value that will substitute for the function call after the function finishes execution. We will call the *gross_pay()* function from the `main()` function as follows:

```
void main(void)
{   double gross;
    int dependents;

    printf("Dependents (including employee)? ");
    scanf("%i", &dependents);
    info();                                 /* Decode employee info */
    gross = gross_pay();              /* Function call and assignment */
    printf("Write the check for $%.2f!\n", gross);
}
```

We have declared *gross* as a **double** variable, therefore we want the return value of *gross_pay()* to be of data type **double**, because it will be assigned to *gross*. Following is the declaration of the *gross_pay()* function:

```
double gross_pay(void); /***************************** Calculate gross pay */
```

The declaration of *gross_pay()* function, and the first line of its definition (without the semicolon), begins with the key word **double**. This first element of a function declaration is the data type of the return value of the function. We refer to *gross_pay()* as a **double** function, the type of its return value, because we can call the function anywhere in the program that we can use a **double** expression. The function's value will be a **double** after it has executed. For example, we might have included the *gross_pay()* function call within the **printf()**:

```
printf("Write the check for $%.2f!\n", gross_pay());
```

Or we might add a bonus to an employee's pay like this:

```
printf("Write the check for $%.2f!\n", gross_pay() + bonus);
```

HEADS UP!

The return value will always be the data type declared for the function.

Because of our declaration, we can be assured that *gross_pay()* will be a **double** value.

The key word **void** at the beginning of a function declaration, such as that in the **main()** and *info()* functions, means that the function returns no value. No value is substituted for the function call after the function executes.

HEADS UP!

A function can have only one return value.

A function may have only one return value, because the value substitutes for the call. If a function could return two values (which it can't), where would the extra value go?

Let us see how we will generate this **double** return value. Following is the function definition:

```
double gross_pay(void) /***************************** Calculate gross pay */
{  double hours, rate, gross;                    /* Local variables */

   printf("Hours? ");
   scanf("%lf", &hours);
   printf("Rate? ");
   scanf("%lf", &rate);
   gross = hours * rate;
   printf("Gross pay:  %7.2f\n", gross);
   return gross;
}
```

Local Variables

The second line of the *gross_pay()* function definition declares three **double** variables, *hours*, *rate*, and *gross*. Because these variables were declared within this function, they are **local** to the function. Their **lifetime**, the part of the program in which C has allocated memory for them, begins when they are declared and ends when the function execution ends. When C finishes executing the *gross_pay()* function, the memory space for these three variables will be deallocated—made available for C to use for some other purpose.

All the variables we have used in the **main()** function have been local to **main()**. Of course, since that has been the only function, the variables have "lived" throughout the program's execution. The variable

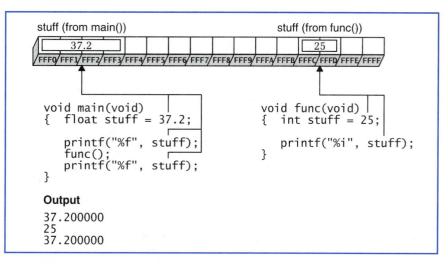

□ FIGURE 6–1 Local Variables

Two local *stuff* variables are declared in this program. The lifetime of the one at memory address FFF0 extends to the end of the main() function, but its visibility is only during execution of statements from main(). The one at FFFC exists and is visible only during execution of the *func()* function. When execution returns to main(), it ceases to exist and the *stuff* at FFF0 is once again visible.

hours will exist from execution of its declaration, at the entry to the *gross_pay()* function, until the function is finished executing. If the function is called again, an entirely new *hours* will be created, with an entirely new garbage value, and it will be destroyed again at the function's end.

But what about the variable *gross*? It has been declared in both the main() and *gross_pay()* functions. They are actually two different variables with two different places in memory. They might as well have been named *apples* and *petunias*, for all C cares. The *gross* declared in main() exists from its declaration to the closing brace at the end of the main() function, essentially throughout the program. However, its **visibility** (or *scope*), the part of the program in which we can access the variable by name, is also local to the main() function. That means that when C is not executing statements from main(), it cannot "see," or access, the *gross* declared in main(). Therefore, when it is executing statements from *gross_pay()*, the only *gross* it can see is the one declared in *gross_pay()*.

As shown in □Figure 6–1, local variables make it possible for us to write a function without having to worry about the function's variables having the same name as the variables in some other function. This property is especially handy if we make use of the function in some other program. We can simply copy the function without having to check inside it for conflicts.

The Return Statement

The statements in *gross_pay()* execute until C encounters a **return** statement,

return *expression*;

where the value of ***expression*** is the return value of the function and substitutes for the call. In our example, the value of *gross* is returned to substitute for the `gross_pay()` call in `main()`.

The **return** need not be physically the last statement in the function, nor need it assign a return value to the function. In fact, there can be more than one **return** in a function, or, as in the case of the *info()* function, none at all. When a **return** is encountered, execution leaves the function and returns back to the calling point. The *info()* function does not return a value, but it could possibly have a number of **return** statements. The following segments will execute equivalently:

No Return

```
switch (dept)
{  case 1:
       printf("Info Systems");
       break;
   case 2:
       printf("Accounting");
       break;
   default:
       printf("Manufacturing");
}
printf(" dept.\n");
```

Many Returns

```
switch (dept)
{  case 1:
       printf("Info Systems dept.\n");
       return;
   case 2:
       printf("Accounting dept.\n");
       return;
   default:
       printf("Manufacturing dept.\n");
       return;
}
```

HEADS UP!

A strictly structured function has only one return.

Many structured programmers would balk at the program segment on the right because the **switch** structure has many, not one, exit points. To be universally accepted, you should have no more than one **return**, and it should be at the end of the function.

In ⇨Program 6–2, let us examine our program with the new function added. We won't repeat the *info()* function in the code, but assume it is there.

⇨**Program 6–2**

```
#include <stdio.h>

void info(void);                  /* Decode employee info */
double gross_pay(void);           /* Calculate gross pay */
```
(continued)

```
    void main(void)
1   {   double gross, tax;
2       int dependents;

        printf("Dependents (including employee)? ");
3       scanf("%i", &dependents);
4       info();                                          /* Decode employee info */
5       gross = gross_pay();                             /* Calculate gross pay */
8       printf("Write the check!\n");
9   }
    double gross_pay(void) /**************************** Calculate gross pay */
g1  {   double hours, rate, gross;                       /* Local variables */

        printf("Hours? ");
g2      scanf("%lf", &hours);
        printf("Rate? ");
g3      scanf("%lf", &rate);
g4      gross = hours * rate;
g5      printf("Gross pay:  %7.2f\n", gross);
g6      return gross;
    }
```

can run by itself

Output

```
Dependents (including employee)? 5
Employee ID? 8471
Employee #847 in the Information Systems department.
Hours? 40
Rate? 15
Gross pay:    600.00
Write the check!
```

EXECUTION CHART				
Line	**Explanation**	**main() function variables:** *gross*	*tax*	*depend*
5	Call *gross_pay()*.	?	?	5
		gross_pay() function variables: *hours*	*rate*	*gross*
g1	Declare local variables in *gross_pay()*.	?	?	?
g2	Input *hours*.	40	?	?
g3	Input *rate*.	40	15	?
g4	Assign *gross*. This has no effect on the *gross* in main(); it is still garbage.	40	15	600
g5	Print *gross*.	40	15	600
g6	Set return value of *gross_pay()* to *gross*, end execution in the function, and return to main().	40	15	600
		main() function variables: *gross*	*tax*	*depend*
5	Assign return value of *gross_pay()* to *gross*.	600	?	5
8	Final printout.	600	?	5

Passing Values

We have seen how a function can return the results of its labors, but we can also, as part of the call, **pass** it values—give it values to work with. Here we are not limited to a single value; we may pass it as many values as we need. In our paycheck example, to calculate the taxes, the module needs the gross pay and the number of dependents. Let us set up the call to a *taxes()* function so that the call passes that data to the function, returns the value of the taxes, and assigns that to the variable *tax*.

```
tax = taxes(gross, dependents);     /* Calculate taxes */
```

To generalize, a function call consists of the following:

function_name(argument, argument, . . . argument)

where an *argument* is any expression (anything that reduces to a single value), and there can be any number of arguments.

If we are to send these values to the function, there must be something in the function to receive them. We must declare variables in the function to be initialized with these values. The first line of the *taxes()* function definition will be

```
double taxes(double g_pay, int dependents) /************ Calculate taxes */
```

and the generalized form of a definition first line is

return_type function_name(declaration, declaration, . . . declaration)

The function call not agreeing with the parameter declarations in the function.

where each *declaration*, or **parameter declaration**, is the declaration of a local variable to be initialized with a value passed to the function.

There must be a match between the function call and the function definition. The definition declares a fixed number of variables in a certain order, each with its own particular data type. In the *taxes()* example, there are two variables declared, the first a **double** and the second an **int**. The call must provide two values of those data types in that order, and it does—the type of *gross* is **double** and the type of *dependents* is **int**.

The Function Prototype

The ANSI committee has set some definite standards, referred to as a function **prototype**, for a function declaration. It must state the *return_type*, the *function_name*, and the data types of the variables to be declared and initialized with the values passed. It need not include the variable names. This would be an acceptable prototype for the *taxes()* function we showed earlier:

```
double taxes(double, int);                          /* Calculate taxes */
```

As we noted before, the declaration of the function can be the first line of its definition copied before `main()`, with a semicolon added to it. This makes a perfectly acceptable prototype:

```
double taxes(double g_pay, int dependents);        /* Calculate taxes */
```

HEADS UP!

Prototypes are more readable with variable names.

Most programmers leave the variable names in the prototype for two reasons: (1) with most text editors, it is easy to copy a complete line from one place to another; and (2) the declaration is more easily understood with descriptive variable names in it. The C compiler will ignore the variable names here in any case.

The function prototype allows the compiler to catch possible errors in the program. Because it knows what to expect, it can match the function call's return type with that of the function, as well as the number and types of passed values.

HEADS UP!

Make sure your data types match when calling functions.

Under the ANSI rules, a function's return value is converted to the prototyped data type, and values passed to the function are converted to match the declarations. A good programmer, however, should not depend on these automatic conversions. For one thing, there may be some loss of value, for example if a `long` is converted to a `short`. For another, popular extensions to the C language, C++ for example, will not make such conversions in many cases.

Let us add the *taxes()* function to ⇨Program 6–3.

⇨**Program 6–3**

```
#include <stdio.h>

#define FED_RATE 0.2                          /* Federal income tax rate */
#define STATE_RATE 0.1                          /* State income tax rate */

void info(void);                               /* Decode employee info */
double gross_pay(void);                         /* Calculate gross pay */
double taxes(double g_pay, int dependents);        /* Calculate taxes */

   void main(void)
1  {  double gross, tax;
2     int dependents;

      printf("Dependents (including employee)? ");
3     scanf("%i", &dependents);
4     info();                                  /* Decode employee info */
5     gross = gross_pay();                      /* Calculate gross pay */
6     tax = taxes(gross, dependents);              /* Calculate taxes */
8     printf("Write the check!\n");
9  }
```

(Continued)

```
t1  double taxes(double g_pay, int dependents) /************ Calculate taxes */
t2  {  double fed_tax, state_tax;

t3      fed_tax = g_pay * (FED_RATE - .01 * dependents);
t4      state_tax = g_pay * STATE_RATE;
t5      printf("Taxes:      %7.2f\n", fed_tax + state_tax);
t6      return fed_tax + state_tax;
    }
```

Output

```
Dependents (including employee)? 5
Employee ID? 8471
Employee #847 in the Information Systems department.
Hours? 40
Rate? 15
Gross pay:    600.00
Taxes:        150.00
Write the check!
```

EXECUTION CHART

Line	Explanation	main() function variables:	gross	tax	depend
6	Call *taxes()*, passing values of *gross* and *dependents*.		600	?	5
		taxes() function variables:	g_pay	depend	fed_tax	state_tax
t1	Declare and initialize local variables *g_pay* and *dependents*.		600	5	---	---
t2	Declare local variables *fed_tax* and *state_tax*.		600	5	?	?
t3	Calculate federal tax.		600	5	90	?
t4	Calculate state tax.		600	5	90	60
t5	Print total taxes.		600	5	90	60
t6	Set return value of *taxes()* to *fed_tax* + *state_tax*, end execution in the function, and return to main().		600	5	90	60
		main() function variables:	gross	tax	depend
6	Assign return value of *taxes()* to *tax*.		600	150	5
8	Final printout.		600	150	5

In the `return` statement, t6, the return value was calculated from an expression, rather than given the value of a single variable. Remember, the `return` statement can contain any expression.

Let us finish the program by adding a function that calculates and prints the net pay. In the calculation of net pay, the health insurance deduction is based on the number of dependents, not including the employee personally. In the function call, then, we will pass one less than the total number of dependents claimed.

```
net_pay(gross, tax, dependents - 1);                    /* Calculate net pay */
```

These values will be assigned to the variables declared in the first line of the *net_pay()* definition:

```
void net_pay(double g_pay, double tax, int dependents) /******** Net pay */
```

The variable *dependents* in the *net_pay()* function is a totally different variable than *dependents* in main(), so the fact that they have different values is no problem.

Since *net_pay()* will print out the final result, it need not return anything to the main() function. Therefore its return value is declared as void. ⇨Program 6–4 shows the revised code.

⇨**Program 6–4**

```
   #include <stdio.h>

   #define FED_RATE 0.2                            /* Federal income tax rate */
   #define STATE_RATE 0.1                          /* State income tax rate */
   #define HEALTH 10   /* Health insurance deducted for each extra dependent */

   void info(void);                               /* Decode employee info */
   double gross_pay(void);                         /* Calculate gross pay */
   double taxes(double g_pay, int dependents);       /* Calculate taxes */
   void net_pay(double g_pay, double tax, int dependents);        /* Net pay */

   void main(void)
 1 {  double gross, tax;
 2    int dependents;

      printf("Dependents (including employee)? ");
 3    scanf("%i", &dependents);
 4    info();                                     /* Decode employee info */
 5    gross = gross_pay();                          /* Calculate gross pay */
 6    tax = taxes(gross, dependents);                /* Calculate taxes */
 7    net_pay(gross, tax, dependents - 1);          /* Calculate net pay */
 8    printf("Write the check!\n");
 9 }

n1 void net_pay(double g_pay, double tax, int dependents) /******** Net pay */
n2 {  double net;

n3    net = g_pay - tax - (HEALTH * dependents);
n4    printf("Net pay:    %7.2f\n", net);
n5 }
```

EXECUTION CHART

Line	Explanation	main() function variables:	gross	tax	depend	
7	Call *net_pay()*, passing values of *gross*, *tax*, and *dependents* − 1.			600	150	5
		net_pay() function variables:	g_pay	tax	depend	net
n1	Declare and initialize local variables *g_pay*, *tax*, and *dependents*.		600	150	4	---
n2	Declare local variable *net*.		600	150	4	?
n3	Calculate net pay.		600	150	4	410
n4	Print net pay.		600	150	4	410
n5	End of function, return to call point in `main()`.		600	150	4	410
		main() function variables:	gross	tax	depend	
7	Statement completed, go to next statement.			600	150	5
8	Final printout.			600	150	5

Output

```
Dependents (including employee)? 5
Employee id? 8471
Employee #847 in the Information Systems department.
Hours? 40
Rate? 15
Gross pay:    600.00
Taxes:        150.00
Net pay:      410.00
Write the check!
```

HEADS UP!

A function call is an expression of a declared data type.

Remember, functions may be called in any place the function's return value is appropriate. For example, we could rewrite our program to combine statements 6 and 7 together:

```
net_pay(gross, taxes(gross, dependents), dependents - 1);  /* Net pay */
```

In passing values to *net_pay()*, C will have to evaluate *taxes()* first. The output will be exactly the same.

We would not want to combine 5, 6, and 7:

```
net_pay(gross_pay(), taxes(gross_pay(), dependents), dependents - 1);
```

because that would call *gross_pay()* twice—and the operations within *gross_pay()* include inputting *hours* and *rate*, then printing the gross pay, all of which would occur twice. In addition, different implementations of

C evaluate the arguments in different orders, some from first to last, others from last to first. Our output might be either

```
Hours?  40                    or      Hours?  40
Rate?   15                            Rate?   15
Gross pay:      600.00                Gross pay:      600.00
Hours?  40                            Taxes:          150.00
Rate?   15                            Hours?  40
Gross pay:      600.00                Rate?   15
Taxes:          150.00                Gross pay:      600.00
Net pay:        410.00                Net pay:        410.00
```

Why Use Functions?

Now that we see how functions operate, we should recap a bit and list the reasons we use functions:

▼ *Modularity.* Functions are an excellent way of implementing modularity.

▼ *Readability.* In a modular program, as all of ours should be, the overall process is outlined in the `main()` function, with all the subprocesses detailed in functions that follow.

▼ *Debugability.* It is easier to debug, clean out the errors, in a small section of code than in a complicated program. As in our paycheck example, each function was tested and debugged as it was written.

▼ *Repeatability.* If a process is used more than once during a program (perhaps there are several points at which we must decode an employee ID), the code may be written only once, debugged, and then called any number of times.

▼ *Reusability.* Most new programs are written by reusing as much code as possible from old programs. For example, tax calculations may have to be done not only in the payroll program but also in the tax-reporting program. The *taxes()* function has already been written and debugged, so we can simply copy it into the tax-reporting program. In fact, we may make a file of the source code for common functions and `include` the file in a number of programs. By using local variables in the functions, we do not have to worry about the variables in a particular function conflicting with the variables in any other.

EXTERNAL VARIABLES

In the last example, all of the variables declarations were internal, within some function. The internally declared variables were local to the function. Their visibility was limited to code within the function, and their lifetime lasted only until execution of the function code finished—at a return or the closing brace of the function.

When we prototyped the functions, the declarations were **external**, outside of any function. These declarations gave the functions **global** visibility—they could be used anywhere in the program.

We can also declare variables externally, giving them global lifetime (lifetime extending from the declaration to the end of the program) and global visibility (accessibility from within any function in the program). Why bother with all these local variables, passing values, and returns? Why not simply declare our variables externally so that any function can access them? We could rewrite part of our previous example as ⇨Program 6–5.

⇨Program 6–5

```
    #include <stdio.h>

    void info(void);                              /* Decode employee info */
    void gross_pay(void);                         /* Don't need return value */

    double gross;                                 /* Global variable */

    void main(void)
1   {   double tax;                               /* gross not declared here */
2       int dependents;

        printf("Dependents (including employee)? ");
3       scanf("%i", &dependents);
4       info();                                   /* Decode employee info */
5       gross_pay();                              /* Function changes gross */
8       printf("Write the check!\n");
9   }

    void gross_pay(void) /****************************  Calculate gross pay */
g1  {   double hours, rate;                       /* gross not declared here */

        printf("Hours? ");
g2      scanf("%lf", &hours);
        printf("Rate? ");
g3      scanf("%lf", &rate);
g4      gross = hours * rate;                     /* Same gross as main() uses */
g5      printf("Gross pay:  %7.2f\n", gross);
    }                                             /* Don't need return value */
```

The execution would be the same, but most programmers would shy away from such construction. The *gross_pay()* function is no longer an

independent module; it depends not only on data from another function but also on specific variable names. Making a change in one part of your program may lead to unexpected changes in other parts, and modifications and debugging become difficult. The price in execution for using local variables is small compared to the benefits in programming and maintainability. Do yourself and other C programmers (who might have to look at your program) a favor and keep your code as clean and independent as possible.

YOUR TURN 6–1

1. What is a function definition?
2. What does a function call do?
3. What is the relationship between the arguments in a function call and the declarations in parentheses after the function name in the definition?
4. Describe the actions of the `return` statement.
5. What does the return type or declaration `void` mean?
6. Differentiate between the terms "lifetime" and "visibility".
7. Differentiate between the terms "local" and "global".
8. Differentiate between the terms "internal" and "external".
9. Why is ANSI prototyping advantageous?
10. How do local variables lead to better modularity within programs?
11. List five reasons for using functions.

SOME EXISTING FUNCTIONS

An ANSI C compiler will come with a complete stock of functions—certainly all those defined in the ANSI standard do, and usually others that work with the specific target computer. To this group you may add an unlimited number of functions that you can buy from third-party vendors and that you write yourself.

Header Files

Under ANSI, all functions should be prototyped—explicitly and completely declared—typically near the beginning of the program. When we use the ANSI functions and usually all the functions provided by third-party vendors, we don't have to write the declarations; they are already written in separate files called **header files**. These files, by convention, have the extension *.h* and are usually kept in some specific directory on the system. The file `stdio.h` is one such file; its name stands for "standard input and output headers." These files are source code, readable by

you and me, and we put them in our source code using the `#include` directive.

```
#include <stdio.h>
```

We never see the source code because the compiler, when it reaches that directive in our source code, shifts to the header file and copies lines from it. When it runs out of lines from the header file, it returns to where it left off in our source file and continues on.

We can, however, see the code in the header file by using a text editor and calling up the header file. If you try this, be sure not to make any modifications! You would find that the header files contain prototyped function declarations (among other things) but not function definitions. The definitions are in **libraries** of object code waiting to be combined with your program, if they are needed, during the linking process (refer to the *From Source to Execution* section in Chapter 1).

HEADS UP!

The functions themselves are in compiled library files, not header files.

Header files also contain definitions of many constants that are used in ANSI C as well as other things that are system dependent. For example, a possible return value of the `scanf()` function is EOF, a constant defined in `stdio.h`. The value of this constant will be different for different implementations of C. We don't have to know the actual value of EOF because its value is defined for us in each implementation of ANSI C. We can just refer to EOF in our program.

When you use a library function, then, you must `#include` the proper header file for it; otherwise, C will not recognize the function name. When we introduce a library function in this book, we will always put the header-file name in angle brackets out to the right of the description.

TRAP

Not including the proper header file for a library function.

`printf()` and `scanf()` Revisited

We have used the `printf()` and `scanf()` functions since almost the beginning of the book. Now let us examine them more closely in light of what we know about functions. The declaration of the `printf()` function is as follows:

Function   **Library**

```
int printf(control_string, arguments)          <stdio.h>
```

This declaration (in slightly different form) is in the header file `stdio.h`, which is why

```
#include <stdio.h>
```

has been at the beginning of all our programs.

HEADS UP!

The control string in
`printf()` determines the
number and types of its
subsequent arguments.

The first function we chose to examine happens to contain exceptions to many of the standard traditions. The *control_string*, which we have already described, we will examine in more detail once we have tackled strings (Chapter 8). The `printf()` function has a variable number of arguments, the types and number of which are controlled by the conversion codes in the *control_string*. Each conversion code requires an argument of the same data type in the argument list.

Although we have not used its return value so far, `printf()` returns an integer value equal to the number of characters printed. In case of some error, it returns a negative value.

```
if (printf("Class: %5i\tMembers: %5i\n", class, members) == 28)
    success = 1;
else
    success = 0;
```

If everything works right, the return value of the `printf()` above should be 28 (note that the tab and the newline each count as one character, and each `int` should occupy five character positions). If the return value is not 28, either there has been an error (setting the return value to negative) or perhaps one of the values exceeds the minimum width of five characters set in the conversion codes. The function still executes, of course, even though it is part of a condition in an `if` statement; the line will be printed.

The `scanf()` declaration is also in `stdio.h`. We will represent it by

```
int scanf(control_string, arguments)          <stdio.h>
```

Again, we will discuss the *control_string* more fully when we discuss strings (in Chapter 8), but, like the `printf()`, the types and number of arguments are determined by the *control_string*.

The return value of `scanf()` is the number of items that have been successfully converted and assigned. Usually, that is the number of conversion codes in the control string, with two possible exceptions. If there is an error in the input—something that the `scanf()` cannot handle—the return value will be different. If the `scanf()` encounters an end-of-file condition, it will return the value of the defined (in `stdio.h`) constant EOF. This should not occur if we use the `scanf()` for normal keyboard input.

The return value of `scanf()` can be used for a number of purposes. In ⇨Program 6–6, it is the test value in a `while` loop.

The condition for our `while` loop compares the return value of the `scanf()` to 3, the value we expect to get if three integers are input. When the relation is evaluated, the `scanf()` is called (and, of course, executed) and its return value compared to 3. Any character inappropriate for an `int` (except for whitespace) in the input stream will halt the `scanf()`, and the return value will be the number of assignments to that point. A *q*, or any other nonnumeric character, is invalid; so in our example, an input of *q* stops the function and returns zero—a value not equal to 3.

▷**Program 6–6**

```c
#include <stdio.h>

void main(void)
{  int i1, i2, i3, subtotal, total=0;

   printf("Enter three integers or 'q' to quit: ");
   while (scanf("%i %i %i", &i1, &i2, &i3) == 3)
   {  subtotal = i1 + i2 + i3;
      printf("These three total   %4i\n", subtotal);
      total += subtotal;
      printf("Enter three integers or 'q' to quit: ");
   }
   printf("The grand total is %5i\n", total);
}
```

Output

```
Enter three integers or 'q' to quit: 1 2 3
These three total      6
Enter three integers or 'q' to quit: 4 5 6
These three total     15
Enter three integers or 'q' to quit: q
The grand total is     21
```

▶TRAP◀

Forgetting to flush the input stream.

Be aware that the *q* remains in the input stream. If there was another `scanf()` later in the program, it would not wait for more keyboard input, but instead would use the characters currently in the stream. A `while(getchar() != '\n');` statement would take care of the problem.

Terminating a Program

When C runs out of statements in the `main()` function, the program quits; this is the normal way of terminating a program. But what if something unexpected happens? The program might receive erroneous or meaningless data; it could get stuck in a loop; the programmer in the office next to yours could stick her finger in a light socket, causing your computer to cough; or whatever. You may want to build other exit points into your program to give the program a "normal" termination instead of printing 147 pages of gibberish and then dying.

Most operating systems are capable of reacting to a termination of a program that has run successfully versus one that has run unsuccessfully.

To do that, however, the operating system must receive a signal from the program as it terminates, indicating success or failure. The **exit()** function provides both the termination and the indicator to the operating system.

```
void exit(int status)                                    <stdlib.h>
```

The *status* can be any value or expression, but for the operating system to recognize it, we should use the constants EXIT_SUCCESS or EXIT_FAILURE, also defined in stdlib.h, to send the proper signal to the operating system.

```
if (result < 0)
    exit(EXIT_FAILURE);
else
    exit(EXIT_SUCCESS);
```

> **HEADS UP!**
>
> If you can foresee a possible error condition, either handle it in the program or provide an orderly exit().

The return value is **void** because there is no program left to which to return a value! The **exit()** function is demonstrated in ⇨Program 6–7.

⇨Program 6–7

```
#include <stdio.h>
#include <stdlib.h>

void main(void)
{   int asc;

    printf("Enter an ASCII code and I will show\n"
           "you the character it represents: ");
    scanf("%i", &asc);
    if (asc < 32 || asc > 126)
    {   printf("Not a printable ASCII code.\n");
        exit(EXIT_FAILURE);
    }
    printf("The character is '%c'.\n", asc);
}
```

Outputs

```
Enter an ASCII code and I will show
you the character it represents: 65
The character is 'A'.

Enter an ASCII code and I will show
you the character it represents: 312
Not a printable ASCII code.
[Program ends]
```

ANSI C has a number of other functions dealing with program termination, cleaning up loose ends, and communicating with the operating system. They are beyond the scope of this book, but as you become more sophisticated in your C programming, you will want to look them up.

Some Mathematical Functions

ANSI C contains over two dozen mathematical functions, and most ANSI C implementations feature even more. While we will not discuss all of them, a few examples should give you enough to tackle most tasks—and the understanding to research other available functions.

The absolute value of a number is the magnitude of the number irrespective of sign; in other words, expressed without a sign. The absolute value of 5 is 5. The absolute value of −5 is also 5. Three functions, **abs()**, **labs()**, and **fabs()**, return absolute value. The choice of function depends on the data type you are working with.

Function	Library
int abs(int *expression*)	<stdlib.h>
long labs(long *expression*)	<stdlib.h>
double fabs(double *expression*)	<math.h>

C has no exponentiation operator, no way of directly raising a number to a power. Raising values to integer powers can be accomplished by successive multiplication—2^3 is $2 \times 2 \times 2$—but that is certainly insufficient for general exponentiation. C's **pow()** function handles the task for us.

```
double pow(double expression, double exponent)   <math.h>
```

The *exponent* can, of course, be any expression. The return value will be the *expression* raised to the power of the *exponent*, that is, $expression^{exponent}$.

The pow() function follows the usual rules of exponentiation. The *expression* and *exponent* cannot both be zero. If the *exponent* is zero, then pow() returns 1. If the *expression* is negative, the *exponent* must be a whole number.

⇨Program 6–8, on the next page, prints the volume of a sphere of any radius.

If you want a square root, you can either raise something to the 0.5 power or use the **sqrt()** function:

```
double sqrt(double expression)                   <math.h>
```

which returns the square root of the *expression*.

In addition to pow() and sqrt(), there is a full set of logarithmic functions.

```
#include <stdio.h>
#include <math.h>

#define PI 3.1416

void main(void)
{  double radius;

   printf("Enter the radius: ");
   scanf("%lf", &radius);
   printf("Volume: %12.2f\n", 4 / 3. * PI * pow(radius, 3));
}
```

Output

```
Enter the radius: 6.28
Volume:         1037.45
```

The **trigonometric functions** are straightforward in C. For example, to get the sine of an angle,

```
double sin(double angle)                              <math.h>
```

The *angle* in C is represented in radians, not degrees. The following function call would return the sine of *degrees* expressed in degrees.

```
sin(degrees * 3.1416 / 180)
```

There are also functions for the arc sine and hyperbolic sine as well as those for cosine and tangent. All require double arguments and return double values, and all are declared in `math.h`.

sin	asin	sinh
cos	acos	cosh
tan	atan	tanh

For a summary of all the ANSI C mathematical functions, see Appendix C.

▶TRAP◀

Expressing angles in degrees.

Random Numbers

C has three functions that, when used together, generate random numbers (or more properly, pseudorandom numbers—mathematically generated random numbers). The first, **rand()**, mathematically generates a pseudorandom number by taking a number, referred to as the **seed**, and applying some monstrous algorithm to it so that the result looks nothing *like* the seed:

```
int rand(void)                                      <stdlib.h>
```

There is no argument; not even a seed. C maintains the seed number within the system. We don't know where it is but C does. The value of the pseudorandom number is always positive and between zero and RAND_MAX, a constant defined in stdlib.h. To illustrate random numbers, let us run ⇨Program 6–9 three times.

⇨**Program 6–9**

```
#include <stdio.h>
#include <stdlib.h>

void main(void)
{
    printf("Three random numbers:\n %i %i %i\n",
           rand(), rand(), rand());
}
```

Outputs

```
Three random numbers:        Three random numbers:        Three random numbers:
 10982 130 346                10982 130 346                10982 130 346
```

All three series of random numbers are exactly the same!

If you start with the same seed (the default seed is 1) and apply the same formula to it, you are bound to get the same results. We must use the **srand()** function to set another seed.

▶TRAP◀

Not setting a seed.

```
void srand(unsigned seed)                           <stdlib.h>
```

Modifying ⇨Program 6–9 we get ⇨Program 6–10.

⇨**Program 6–10**

```
#include <stdio.h>
#include <stdlib.h>

void main(void)
{
    srand(10);
    printf("Three random numbers:\n %i %i %i\n",
           rand(), rand(), rand());
}
```

Outputs

```
Three random numbers:        Three random numbers:        Three random numbers:
  10345 30957 3463             10345 30957 3463             10345 30957 3463
```

At least the series is different from the earlier one, but we still get the same thing each time we run the program. It's the same problem: same seed, same series. We must have a way of changing the seed with each execution. One way is through the computer system's clock. The **time()** function gives us the computer clock's current time and date. The form of the time and date varies from system to system but at least its value will be different each time we run the program.

```
time_t time(NULL)                                              <time.h>
```

The data type **time_t** is defined in the header file **time.h**, but it is compatible with the unsigned integer required for **srand()**. As well as returning the time and date, **time()** will also store it in a memory location of our choosing. The **NULL** argument directs the function to just return the value and not store it anywhere else in the system.

Casts

A careful programmer will not depend on ANSI C's automatic data-type conversions, however, so we will **cast**, convert the data type, of the return of the **time()** function to **unsigned**. The **cast operator** is simply the desired data type in parentheses. The expression

```
(unsigned)time(NULL)
```

will evaluate to an **unsigned** data type. The cast operator is very high in precedence (see Appendix B for all the operators) so it operates before almost anything else.

Let's try our program again in ⇨Program 6–11.

⇨Program 6–11

```c
#include <stdio.h>
#include <stdlib.h>
#include <time.h>

void main(void)
{
    srand((unsigned)time(NULL));
    printf("Three random numbers:\n %i %i %i\n",
            rand(), rand(), rand());
}
```

Outputs

```
Three random numbers:        Three random numbers:        Three random numbers:
 3288 27551 25218             12653 22807 69               527 19141 5956
```

HEADS UP!

You only need one call to srand() in a program.

Success! Because each call to rand() returns the next in a series of random numbers, srand() needs to be called only once. Be sure, though, to set the seed—that is, call srand()—before calling rand().

Typically, we want random numbers in a predetermined range, 1 to 100, or –5 to +5, for example. Numbers between 0 and RAND_MAX, whatever that is, are rarely valuable, so we must convert that range into one that satisfies our requirements.

Take the case of radio station WHEN that plays only music from the late sixties. At 10 A.M. each day, they randomly pick a year between 1965 and 1969, and play records only from that year. Their songs might not be modern, but their station is, so they want their computer to pick the random year. To generate an integer in a specific range, as in ⇨Program 6–12, we must first know the number of integers in the range. We can determine that by subtracting the bottom of the range from the top and adding 1. There are five integers in the range 1965 through 1969. We can generate integers in a range of 0 through 4, five integers, by dividing the return from rand() by 5 and taking the remainder; it must be 0 through 4.

⇨Program 6–12

```c
#include <stdio.h>
#include <stdlib.h>
#include <time.h>

void main(void)
{   int count;

    srand((unsigned)time(NULL));
    printf("Ten random numbers:\n");
    for (count = 1; count <= 10; ++count)
        printf("  %i", rand() % 5);
    printf("\n");
}
```

Output

```
Ten random numbers:
  3  2  4  2  0  3  1  2  4  0
```

If we then add the starting value for the range to that expression, we get exactly the range we want. With this replacement printf(), we would get the following output:

```c
printf("  %i", rand() % 5 + 1965);
```

Output

```
Ten random numbers:
   1965   1967   1966   1965   1969   1969   1968   1967   1966   1967
```

YOUR TURN 6–2

1. What is the purpose of a header file?
2. What is the return value of `printf()`? `scanf()`?
3. How is the `exit()` function used?
4. How do `abs()`, `labs()`, and `fabs()` differ?
5. What is the unit of measure of the angles in trigonometric functions?
6. How are random numbers generated in C?
7. What does a cast do?

RECURSION (Optional)

One function may call another function by including the function name in its code. In an earlier example, the `main()` function called the *pay()* function. Control passed to the *pay()* function, which returned a value that substituted for the function call in the `main()` function. C places no limits on which functions can call which other functions, as long as the called function is visible from the calling function. In fact, a function may call itself—a situation known as **recursion**. For purposes of analysis, a recursive call can be treated the same as one function calling another—as if there were two separate functions. In a recursive situation, though, the "two" functions do exactly the same thing.

Many processes lend themselves to recursive solutions, especially those that repeat an operation as some factor moves toward an ending condition. The classic example, and probably the best, is calculating the factorial of a number. The factorial of a number is the number times the number minus 1, times that number minus 1, and so forth until the multiplier becomes 1. For example, 4 factorial (4!) is

$$4 \times 3 \times 2 \times 1 \text{ or } 24$$

We could also say that 4! was $4 \times 3!$

$$4 \times (3 \times 2 \times 1) \text{ or } 4 \times 6 \text{ or } 24$$

and 3! was $3 \times 2!$ and 2! was $2 \times 1!$. The sequence ends when the number gets back to 1, which has a defined factorial of 1.

Summing up:

$$4! = 4 \times 3! = 4 \times 3 \times 2! = 4 \times 3 \times 2 \times 1!$$

A number factorial, then, is that number times the factorial of the number minus 1. It sounds as if we are defining the term in terms of itself—and we are. If we had the proper, preexisting *factorial()* function, we could say that

$$4! = 4 * \text{factorial}(3) \quad \text{or} \quad n! = n * \text{factorial}(n - 1)$$

Let us set up that function, then.

```
int factorial(int n)
{
    return = n * factorial(n - 1);
}
```

This, of course, would be infinite; the function would continue to call itself. We need some ending condition. The mathematical definition of the factorial provides us with one: 1! is defined as 1. Therefore, if we send the *factorial()* function a value of 1, we will have it return 1 instead of calling itself again.

```
    int factorial(int n)
    {
f1      if (n <= 1 )           /* <= to account for zero and negative arguments */
f2          return 1;
        else
f3          return n * factorial(n - 1);
    }
```

To analyze the execution of this function, it is convenient to treat each call as a call to a separate instance of the function—as if there were many, many functions with the name *factorial*. In essence, that is what C does. Let us look at the values passed by each call and each return. In the execution chart we show which instance of the function is being examined.

EXECUTION CHART					
Line	Instance	Explanation	n	pass	return
f1	1	*n* not <= 1.	4		
f3	1	Call *factorial()*.	4	3	
f1	2	*n* not <= 1.	3		
f3	2	Call *factorial()*.	3	2	
f1	3	*n* not <= 1.	2		
f3	3	Call *factorial()*.	2	1	
f1	4	*n* is <= 1.	1		
f2	4	Return 1.	1		1
f3	3	Return 2 * 1.	2		2
f3	2	Return 3 * 2.	3		6
f3	1	Return 4 * 6.	4		24

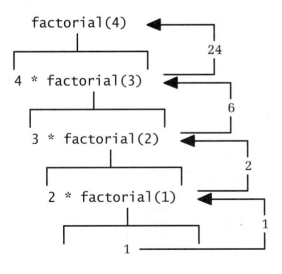

Recursion or Iteration?

Any situation that could be described recursively could also be described iteratively, that is, using a loop. For example, the *factorial()* function could be rewritten as

```
       int factorial(int n)
 f1   {  int fact = n;     /* An accumulator to build up the factorial value */

f2, f3, f4      for (--n; n > 1; --n)
     f5             fact *= n;
     f6        return fact;
       }
```

If we pass the function a value of 4, it executes as follows:

Line	Explanation	n	fact
EXECUTION CHART			
f1	Declare and initialize the factorial accumulator.	4	4
f2	Decrement *n*.	3	4
f3	*n* is > 1, execute loop.	3	4
f5	Multiply *n* into the *fact* accumulator.	3	12
f4	Decrement *n*.	2	12
f3	*n* is > 1, execute loop.	2	12
f5	Multiply *n* into the *fact* accumulator.	2	24
f4	Decrement *n*.	1	24
f3	*n* not >1, exit loop.	1	24
f6	Return the value of the *fact* accumulator.	1	24

Which is better? Each could be said to describe the calculation of a factorial. The first follows the theoretical basis of a factorial; the second, the typical hand calculation of it. In general, though, recursive solutions tend to be less efficient. There is a great deal of overhead in a function call. Each call must assign the passed value somewhere in memory and then to the function variable to which it is passed. In addition, the call must store the memory address at which the program will resume when it returns. The return must perform similar operations with the return value as well as finding out where to return.

Use recursive algorithms with care. If it makes the program more understandable and the difference in efficiency is not too great, a recursive function may be worth using.

PUTTING IT TOGETHER

The Lucky 13 Car Wash and Casino washes your car while you gamble away the rest of your money on slot machines. They would like to install computers that play "21" (blackjack) with the customers, and would like us to write a computer program for them. We are a little busy now, but we said that we will give them a start.

TASK

Write an abbreviated program that will deal just the first hand for the house (the dealer) and the player. It should be set up the way a casino would like it—with an infinite number of decks of cards, making it possible to deal more than one card of the same number and suit.

ANALYSIS

In the game of blackjack, the initial deal for the house consists of one card face up, so that its value and suit can be seen, and one face down. The player's hand consists of two cards face up. Each card has a suit, a face (2, 5, jack, queen), and a value (face value except for jack, queen, and king, which count 10; and ace, which can count as either 1 or 11). The object of the game is to keep drawing cards to get as close to 21 as possible. If your hand totals over 21, you lose. In this program, we will be concerned with only the initial deal of two cards.

For each hand, we should print out the face and suit for the card or cards and, for the player, since we can see both cards, print the total for the hand. Since the house may take more cards later, we may as well also keep track of the house's hand total.

DESIGN

Overall, the program will be organized like this:

        Deal for house
        Deal for player

Expanding the modules above, then, we have:

    [Deal for house]
        Show first card face
        Add to hand total
        Show first card suit

[Deal for player]
   Show first card face
   Add to hand total
   Show first card suit
   Show second card face
   Add to hand total
   Show second card suit
   Print hand total

Three card faces and three suits are being shown, and three times the card value is being added to the hand total. Instead of writing this code three times, let's write one set of functions and call them three times. We can create one function, *Card()*, to print out a random card face and add its value to a hand total passed to it.

[Card]
   Pick random card
   Show face
   Add to hand total

Since aces can count as 11 or 1, we count them as 11 if the resultant total is not over 21, or as 1 otherwise.

Another function, *Suit()*, can print out a random suit.

[Suit]
   Pick random suit
   Show suit

The overall design, then, is:

[Deal for house]
  [Card]
  [Suit]
[Deal for player]
  [Card]
  [Suit]
  [Card]
  [Suit]
  Print hand total

IMPLEMENTATION

The individual functions are expanded in ⇨Program 6–13.

⇨Program 6–13

```
#include <stdio.h>
#include <stdlib.h>
#include <time.h>
```

(continued)

```
      int card(int total);            /* Prints random card and adjusts hand total */
      void suit(void);                              /* Prints a random suit */

      void main(void)
      {  int player, house;                   /* Hand totals for both sides */

1     srand((unsigned)time(NULL));            /* Set a varying seed */

      /**************************************************** Deal for house */
      printf("House has a ");
2     house = card(0);                  /* Start with zero total for hand */
      printf(" of ");
3     suit();
      printf(" and a down card\n");

      /**************************************************** Deal for player */
      printf("You have a ");
4     player = card(0);                 /* Start with zero total for hand */
      printf(" of ");
5     suit();
      printf(" and a ");
6     player = card(player);             /* Add to previous hand total */
      printf(" of ");
7     suit();
8     printf(" for %i\n", player);              /* Player's hand total */
      }

      int card(int total) /********* Prints random card and adjusts hand total */
      {  int value;

c1    value = rand() % 13 + 1;           /* Random number between 1 and 13 */
c2    switch (value)
c3    {  case 1:         /* Ace is 11 unless hand over 21, then it is 1 */
c4        printf("Ace");
c5        if (total + 11 <= 21)                   /* Ace as 11 within 21 */
c6          value = 11;                           /* Set ace value to 11 */
        else
c7          value = 1;                            /* Set ace value to 1 */
c8        break;
c9      case 11:
c10       printf("Jack");
c11       value = 10;
c12       break;
c13     case 12:
c14       printf("Queen");
c15       value = 10;
c16       break;                                              (continued)
```

```
c17        case 13:
c18            printf("King");
c19            value = 10;
c20            break;
c21        default:                                    /* 2 through 10 */
c22            printf("%i", value);
        }
c23    return total + value;
    }

    void suit(void) /********************************* Prints a random suit */
    {
s1     switch (rand() % 4 + 1)                /* Random number between 1 and 4 */
s2     {  case 1:
s3            printf("Spades");
s4            break;
s5        case 2:
s6            printf("Hearts");
s7            break;
s8        case 3:
s9            printf("Diamonds");
s10           break;
s11       default:
s12           printf("Clubs");
        }
s13    return;
    }
```

TEST

Testing this program could be fun. In any case, a number of tests should be done including those that verify the handling of face cards (jack, queen, and king) and aces. One important test is a hand with two aces to make sure that the second ace is being added as 1 instead of 11. An easy way to do that is to temporarily change the statement that generates a random card value between 1 and 13 to

```
value =  1; /* rand() % 13 + 1; */  /* Random number between 1 and 13 */
```

to ensure that you get two aces.

This program is, of course, only the start of a complete blackjack game, which, with your current knowledge of C, you could finish.

The following Execution Chart shows values of variables that exist but are not visible in parentheses.

Outputs

```
House has a 5 of Spades and a down card
You have a King of Hearts and a Ace of Diamonds for 21
```
                                                                        (continued)

```
House has a Queen of Diamonds and a down card
You have a Jack of Hearts and a 3 of Spades for 13

House has a Jack of Spades and a down card
You have a 8 of Spades and a 4 of Diamonds for 12
```

EXECUTION CHART

Line	Explanation	player	house	total	value
1	Set seed for later random numbers. The variables *player* and *house* have garbage values; *total* and *value* do not exist.	?	?	---	---
2	Call *card()*, pass 0.	?	?	---	---
c1	Generate random number between 1 and 13. The variables *player* and *house* still exist but are not visible.	(?)	(?)	0	5
c2	Look for case 5:. Doesn't exist, so look for default: at c21.	(?)	(?)	0	5
c22	Print card face.	(?)	(?)	0	5
c23	Return previous *total* plus the new *value*.	(?)	(?)	0	5
2	Assign return value to *house*.	?	5	---	---
3	Call *suit()*.	?	5	---	---
s1	Expression evaluates to 1; look for case 1:. Find at s2.	(?)	(5)	---	---
s3	Print "Spades".	(?)	(5)	---	---
s4	Jump beyond end of structure.	(?)	(5)	---	---
s13	Return.	(?)	(5)	---	---
4	Call *card()*, pass 0.	?	5	---	---
c1	Generate random number between 1 and 13.	(?)	(5)	0	13
c2	Look for case 13:. Find at c17.	(?)	(5)	0	13
c18	Print "King".	(?)	(5)	0	13
c19	Set *value* to 10.	(?)	(5)	0	10
c20	Jump to end of structure.	(?)	(5)	0	10
c23	Return previous *total* plus the new *value*.	(?)	(5)	0	10
4	Assign return value to *player*.	10	5	---	---
5	Call *suit()*, print "Hearts".	10	5	---	---
6	Call *card()*, pass *player*.	10	5	---	---
c1	Generate random number between 1 and 13.	(10)	(5)	10	1
c2	Look for case 1:. Find at c3.	(10)	(5)	10	1
c4	Print "Ace".	(10)	(5)	10	1
c5	Test to see if 11 plus the previous *total* would be 21 or less. It would.	(10)	(5)	10	11
c6	Set *value* to 11.	(10)	(5)	10	11
c8	Jump to end of structure.	(10)	(5)	10	11
c23	Return previous *total* plus the new *value*.	(10)	(5)	10	11
6	Assign return value to *player*.	21	5	---	---
7	Call *suit*, print "Diamonds".	21	5	---	---
8	Print *player*.	21	5	---	---

SUMMARY

▲**KEY TERMS** (in order of appearance)

Function definition	Prototype
Call	Internal
Function declaration	External
Return	Global
Return value	Header file
Void	Library
Local	Trigonometric function
Lifetime	Seed
Visibility	Cast
Pass	Cast operator
Parameter declaration	Recursion

▲**NEW STATEMENTS AND FUNCTIONS** (in order of appearance)

```
return expression;
```

```
void exit(int status)                                            <stdlib.h>
```
Purpose: Terminate program in orderly fashion indicating *status* of termination.
Return: None.

```
int abs(int expression)                                          <stdlib.h>
```
Purpose: Obtain absolute value of int *expression*.
Return: Absolute value of int *expression*.

```
long labs(long expression)                                       <stdlib.h>
```
Purpose: Obtain absolute value of long *expression*.
Return: Absolute value of long *expression*.

```
double fabs(double expression)                                    <math.h>
```
Purpose: Obtain absolute value of double *expression*.
Return: Absolute value of double *expression*.

```
double pow(double expression, double exponent)                    <math.h>
```
Purpose: Raise *expression* to the power of *exponent*.
Return: Result of the exponentiation.

```
double sqrt(double expression)                                    <math.h>
```
Purpose: Obtain the square root of the *expression*.
Return: Square root of the *expression*.

```
int rand(void)                                                   <stdlib.h>
```
Purpose: Obtain next in a series of random numbers.
Return: Value between zero and RAND_MAX.

```
void srand(unsigned seed)                                          <stdlib.h>
```
    Purpose: Set the *seed* for generation of random numbers.
    Return: None.

```
time_t time(NULL)                                                  <time.h>
```
    Purpose: Used as shown to give a different seed for random-number generation.
    Return: Random-number seed.

▲CONCEPT REVIEW

▼ **Function definition** code is all the operations in the function. The **call** sets this code in operation. Like almost anything else in C, functions must have a **function declaration** before they are called.

▼ When a function finishes execution, it **returns** to the calling point, often with a **return value** that substitutes for the call. Functions without return values are declared with a **void** data type.

▼ Variables declared within a function, even in the parameter declarations, have both **local lifetime** and **visibility** within the function.

▼ If a function has a return value, that value must be assigned to the function call by a `return` statement. The `return` statement can also be used to terminate a function that does not return a value.

▼ Values may be **passed** to a function. These values initialize the variables in the **parameter declarations** of the function definition. The call must match the function's return type and the types of the parameter declarations.

▼ A function **prototype** is a formalized declaration that tells the compiler what it needs to know to properly error check (and type convert) function calls.

▼ There are a number of reasons to use functions. Among them are: modularity, readability, debugability, repeatability, and reusability.

▼ All the variables we have referred to have been declared **internally**, within a function. **External** declarations have **global** visibility and, in the case of variables, global lifetime. Global variables reduce the modularity of a program, however.

▼ Most existing functions are in object-code libraries with their declarations in source-code **header files**, which we must `#include` if we are to use them.

▼ The functions `printf()` and `scanf()` both have return values. The first is the number of characters printed and the second is the number of assignments made.

▼ Other functions reviewed were `exit()`, to terminate a program; `abs()`, `labs()`, and `fabs()`, to return absolute values; `pow()` to raise values to powers; `sqrt()`, to take the square root; various **trigonometric functions** with their arguments all stated in radians;

rand() and srand() to generate pseudorandom numbers; and time() to provide a constantly varying **seed** value.

▼ We saw that we could **cast** an expression using a **cast operator** to yield the same value with a different data type.

▼ A function can be called from anywhere in the program, including from a statement within that function—a process known as **recursion**.

▲HEADS UP: POINTS OF SPECIAL INTEREST

▼ The function definition is all the statements in the function.

▼ Most structured programmers put main() first.

▼ The return value substitutes for the call.

▼ The return value will always be the data type declared for the function.

▼ A function can have only one return value.

▼ Each call to a function sets up new local variables.

▼ Local variables make our functions more portable. *Variable names local to one function will not conflict with the same variable names in other functions.*

▼ A strictly structured function has only one return.

▼ Prototypes are more readable with variable names.

▼ Make sure your data types match when calling functions.

▼ A function call is an expression of a declared data type. *It reduces to a value of that type.*

▼ Use external variables sparingly, if at all.

▼ Header files are source code.

▼ The functions themselves are in compiled library files, not header files.

▼ The control string in printf() determines the number and types of its subsequent arguments.

▼ If you can foresee a possible error condition, either handle it in the program or provide an orderly exit().

▼ There are different absolute value functions for different data types.

▼ You only need one call to srand() in a program.

▲TRAPS: COMMON PROGRAMMING ERRORS

▼ Not declaring a function.

▼ Leaving the semicolon off a function declaration.

▼ The function call not agreeing with the parameter declarations in the function.

▼ Depending on a certain order of argument evaluation. *It is up to the compiler whether functions' arguments are evaluated left to right or right to left.*

▼ Not including the proper header file for a library function.

▼ Forgetting to flush the input stream.

▼ Expressing angles in degrees. *Trigonometric functions require angles in radians.*

▼ Not setting a seed. *A call to the* `rand()` *function will then use the default seed—the same one each time the program is run.*

▲YOUR TURN ANSWERS

▼6–1

1. The function definition starts with the declaration of its return type, its name, and initialized local variables, and it contains all of the code that makes the function operate.

2. The function call passes values to a function and sets the function in operation.

3. The variables declared in the first line of a function definition are initialized by the values of the expressions in the call.

4. The `return` statement ceases execution of the function, passes the value of the expression (if any) back to the calling point to substitute for the call, and continues program execution at the calling point.

5. A `void` return type means that no value is being returned by a function. A `void` declaration means that no variables are being declared to be initialized by passed values. In other words, the function call can have no arguments.

6. The lifetime of a variable is the part of the program in which memory is allocated for that variable. The visibility of a variable (or function) is the part of the program in which the variable can be accessed (or function called) by name.

7. Global lifetime or visibility is from declaration throughout the entire program. Local is within only a certain section, such as within one function.

8. Internal is within a function; external is outside of any function. Internal declarations are local; external ones are global.

9. A function prototype allows the compiler to check for mismatched arguments and data types, and to convert some values to the proper types.

10. By using local variables, we do not have to worry about variables in the function conflicting with variables in the rest of the program.

11. Modularity, readability, debugability, repeatability, reusability.

▼6–2

1. Header files contain standard definitions of constants and declarations of functions that exist in function libraries.

2. The `printf()` function returns the number of characters printed, or a negative value if there is an error; `scanf()` returns the number of assignments, or the defined constant `EOF` if there is an error.

3. The `exit()` function forces a normal termination of a program and returns a status code to the operating system.

4. They all return an absolute value, but of `int`s, `long`s, and `doubles`, respectively.

5. The angles sent to trig functions must be in radians.

6. The `rand()` function puts a seed number through a complicated algorithm to generate the next in a series of "random" numbers. To get a different series with each execution of the program, `srand()`, which changes the seed, should be sent the return from a `time()` function call.

7. The result of a cast operation is a different data type containing the same value (if the new data type can accommodate the value).

EXERCISES

1. Given the following `main()` segment, fill in the first line of the function definition. How would the prototyped declaration appear?

```
double t;                _____ func(_____ x, _____ y)
float a;
int f;

    . . .
t = func(f, a);
```

2. Given the following function, write a proper call statement to send it the value 16, as well as the values of *a* and *b* + *c*. The result of the function should be stored in *d*.

```
void main(void)                    double func(float x, double y, float z)
{  float a;                        {
   int b, c;                           return (x + y) / z;
   long double d;                  }
```

3. Modify the following program so that the marked code is executed in a *miles_per_gallon()* function. The `main()` function should have no *gallons*, or *miles_per_gallon* variables, and the function should be called directly from the last `printf()` function.

```
#include <stdio.h>

void main(void)
{  int beg_miles, end_miles;
   float odo_adjust, gallons, miles_per_gallon;

   beg_miles = 296;
   end_miles = 513;
   odo_adjust = 1.15;

                                  /* This stuff should be in a function */
   printf("How many gallons? ");
   scanf("%f", &gallons);
   miles_per_gallon = (end_miles - beg_miles) * odo_adjust / gallons;
                                  /* End of function stuff */

   printf("Miles per gallon: %.2f\n", miles_per_gallon);
}
```

4. Given the statement
   ```
   while (scanf(%f %f", &a, &b) == 2)
   ```
   Why wouldn't the loop exit with an input of just the Return or Enter key?

5. What is wrong with the function calls in the following `printf()`?
   ```
   int izzy;
   long lardo;
   float flakey;

   printf("%f %f %f\n", labs(izzy), abs(lardo),
   fabs(flakey));
   ```

6. Write a *sine()* function that returns the sine of an angle passed in degrees. Call the `sin()` function from your function.

7. Show an execution chart for the following program that prints a two-decimal-place random number in a given range.
   ```
   #include <stdio.h>
   #include <stdlib.h>
   #include <time.h>

   float two_place(float bottom, float top);
   ```

(continued)

```
void main(void)
{  float low, high;

   srand((unsigned) time(NULL));
   printf("Enter low high for range: ");
   scanf("%f%f", &low, &high);
   printf("Number: %.2f\n", two_place(low, high));
}

float two_place(float bottom, float top)
{  int range, begin, rnd_num;

   range = (int) ((top - bottom) * 100);
   begin = (int) (bottom * 100);
   rnd_num = rand() % range + begin;
   return rnd_num / 100.0;
}
```

8. Rewrite the *two_place()* function in the program above so that it has no variables other than those declared in the formal parameters, and it has only a **return** statement. (*Hint:* Remember external variables.)

PROGRAMS

1. Create a function whose job is to print a page heading. It should print the next page number passed to it. Use the following driver—**main()** function segment—to test your function.

Driver

```
void main(void)
{  int p;
   for (p = 1; p <= 5; ++p)
      page(p);
}
```

Function and Variable

```
page()
  page_no
```

Output

```
Major Document     Page 1

Major Document     Page 2
```

(continued)

```
Major Document      Page 3

Major Document      Page 4

Major Document      Page 5
```

2. Write a program that accepts any number from the keyboard and tells you whether it is a nonnegative integer. The number should be sent to the function *int_test()*, which returns either the integer value, or −1 if the number is negative, or zero if it is nonnegative but not an integer. Inputs should continue until a zero is input.

Functions and Variables

```
Main()
   input      From keyboard
   integer    Return from function
int_test()
   value      From main()
   result     Value to return
```

Output

```
Your number: 48
The number is 48.
Your number: -14.3
The number is negative.
Your number: 12.345
The number is not an integer.
Your number: 0
```

3. Write a program that will show the maturity value (principal plus accumulated interest) on a deposit at interest rates of 4, 5, 6, and 7 percent. The formula should be calculated in a separate function, but the output should be from `main()`.

$$maturity\ value = p\left(1 + \frac{r}{100}\right)^y$$

Functions and Variables

```
main()
   years      Number of years
   rate       Interest rate (percent)
   principal
mat_val()      Maturity value function
               Any local variables needed for function
```

Output

```
AMOUNT? 1000
NUMBER OF YEARS? 5

MATURITY VALUES AT VARIOUS INTEREST RATES
4% 1216.65    5% 1276.28    6% 1338.22    7% 1402.55
```

4. The formula for determining the number of possible combinations of N things taken K at a time is:

$$C = \frac{N!}{K!(N-K)!}$$

Write a program to use this formula. $N!$ means "N factorial." The factorial of a number is the number times the number minus 1, times that number minus 1, and so forth until the multiplier is 1. For 5! (five factorial) $= 5 \times 4 \times 3 \times 2 \times 1 = 120$. The factorial calculations should be done in a separate function. N and K must be positive integers with $N >= K$ for the formula to work.

Functions and Variables

```
main()
  c          Combinations
  n          Number of things
  k          Number taken at a time
factorial()
  counter
  fact       Accumulator for factorial
```

Output

```
HOW MANY THINGS? 7
HOW MANY AT A TIME? 4
NUMBER OF POSSIBLE COMBINATIONS IS 35
```

5. Write a program that allows input of two sides of a right triangle and calculates the hypotenuse according to the Pythagorean theorem (*Hypotenuse*^{2} = *side1*^{2} + *side2*^{2}). Use no multiplication; use the `pow()` and `sqrt()` functions instead. Use only the variables given.

Variables

```
side1, side2, hypotenuse
```

Output

```
Enter first second side: 3 4
Hypotenuse: 5
Enter first, second side: 24.75 38.2
Hypotenuse: 45.5171
```

6. Write a program to determine the sides and angles of a right triangle given one side and the adjacent angle. Remember that the angles in the trigonometric functions are expressed in radians.

Variables

		Formulas
`side`	Given side	Hypotenuse = side / cosine
`op_side`	Opposite side	Opposite side = side × tangent
`hypotenuse`		Other angle = 90 - given angle
`angle`	Given angle	Radians = degrees × π / 180
`op_angle`	Opposite angle	π = 3.1416

Output

```
ENTER ANGLE? 30
ENTER ADJACENT SIDE? 10
OPPOSITE SIDE= 5.77352
HYPOTENUSE= 11.547
OPPOSITE ANGLE= 60
```

7. The pseudorandom numbers generated by C should be pretty good, statistically. Write a program to see how good. Generate 1,000 integers between 1 and 5, and keep track of how many of each were produced. Try it with a million. (*Hint:* Don't forget to use `long`s for your accumulators.) Save as *RANDOM* for modification later.

Functions and Variables

```
main()
   ones, twos, threes, fours, fives   Accumulators
   count       Loop counter
rnd()          Integer between 1 and 5
```

Sample Output

Ones	Twos	Threes	Fours	Fives
220	211	197	204	168

8. Write a guessing game for the computer in which the computer generates a random whole number between 1 and 100 and the player tries to guess that number. The program should allow only ten guesses, and tell the player whether the guess is too low, too high, or right.

Functions and Variables

```
main()
   secret      The number to be guessed
   guess       The players guess
   guesses     The number of guesses
rnd()          Function for random number between 1 and 100
```

Output

```
THE SECRET NUMBER IS BETWEEN 1 AND 100.

WHAT IS YOUR GUESS? 5
TOO LOW, GUESS AGAIN? 45
TOO LOW, GUESS AGAIN? 92
TOO HIGH, GUESS AGAIN? 46

RIGHT! IT TOOK YOU 4 TRIES.
```

Output

```
THE SECRET NUMBER IS BETWEEN 1 AND 100.

WHAT IS YOUR GUESS? 7
TOO LOW, GUESS AGAIN? 46
  .
  .
  .
TOO HIGH, GUESS AGAIN? 71

YOU LOSE, THAT WAS YOUR LAST GUESS. THE NUMBER WAS 74.
```

9. Write a simple calculator so that you can input an expression with two values separated by an operator and the computer will print out the proper result. Your calculator should include the ^ operator for exponentiation. All calculations should be done in an appropriate function (the functions will be small) and the results printed in `main()`.

Functions and Variables

```
main()
  op              Operator
  x, y            Values for calculation
add()
subtract()
multiply()
divide()
exponentiate()
  a, b            Local variables for each function
```

Output

```
Enter expression (q to quit): 34.7+23.5
  58.2
Enter expression (q to quit): 5.27 * 32.6
  171.802
```

(continued)

```
Enter expression (q to quit): 1.41414 ^ 2
  1.99979
Enter expression (q to quit): 657.82 / 0
  Can't divide by  0
Enter expression (q to quit): 534 & 26
  Invalid operator
Enter expression (q to quit): q
```

10. Write a program to make change in coins. The `main()` function should accept input of the purchase and the amount tendered, and the *change()* function should print the number of quarters, dimes, and so on.

Functions and Variables

```
main()
  purchase
  tendered
change(amount)
  cents       Convert the float amount to the int cents
```

Output

```
Purchase: 3.08
Amount tendered: 4
Quarters: 3
Dimes    : 1
Nickels  : 1
Pennies  : 2
```

11. In the kids' game "Paper, Rock, Scissors" each player chooses one of the three and the winner is determined by the relationship between the two choices. "Paper covers rock," so paper wins; "rock breaks scissors," so rock wins; and "scissors cuts paper," so scissors wins. If both choose the same, it is a tie and no one wins. Write a program to play the game against the computer until the player enters *q* instead of a choice.

Functions and Variables

```
main()
  machine                      The machine's choice: p, r, or s
  player                       The player's choice
  result                       Win, lose, or tie
  score                        Accumulated score
char MachineChoice(void)       Prints paper, rock, or scissors
  choice                       Random choice
```

```
Choose (p)aper, (r)ock, (s)cissors or (q)uit: p
   The machine chooses scissors.    You lose!    Your score: -1
Choose (p)aper, (r)ock, (s)cissors or (q)uit: s
   The machine chooses scissors.    Its a tie!    Your score: -1
Choose (p)aper, (r)ock, (s)cissors or (q)uit: p
   The machine chooses rock.    You Win!    Your score: 0
Choose (p)aper, (r)ock, (s)cissors or (q)uit: r
   The machine chooses scissors.    You Win!    Your score: 1
Choose (p)aper, (r)ock, (s)cissors or (q)uit: q
```

Chapter 7

ARRAYS

PREVIEW

In this chapter we will look at data in groups called arrays, and learn how we can most easily manipulate these arrays in C. After reading this chapter you should understand:

▼ What arrays are and what they are composed of.

▼ How arrays are stored in memory.

▼ How we declare and initialize arrays.

▼ How we pass arrays to functions.

▼ Using arrays of arrays.

▼ Some common applications for arrays.

Data often does not come one piece at a time, but in collections—groups of tens, hundreds, or thousands of values to be processed. We could, possibly, think of tens, hundreds, or even thousands of different variable names, but keeping track of them and processing them one after another would require a lot of C code. Instead, let us designate a collection of variables with a name for the collection and use a number to designate individual elements of the collection. We will still have tens, hundreds, or thousands of variables with as many names, but the names will be easier to keep track of.

INDEXED VARIABLE NAMES

In algebraic notation, we use variables such as X and Y. We can also use subscripted variables such as X_1, X_2, and X_3 (the subscript is the little number following the letter). Subscript notation is typically used for grouping collections of variables. For example, the values of 10 samples in a chemical analysis might be stored in S_1, S_2, on up to S_{10}. Each of the variables is completely separate and has its own value, but we can see that they are all part of a collection because we have given them the same name, S. The different subscripts identify each separate variable in the collection.

We can apply this same concept in C, using an **array**, which is a collection of individual variables, referred to as **elements**. We give the array a name, such as *samples*, and identify each element of the array with an **index** in brackets—*name[index]*—for example, *samples[1]*, *samples[2]*, on up to *samples[10]*. As in algebra, we can refer to the collection of samples as *samples*, but we must remember that the collection is made up of individual variables or elements. Even though we may refer to the collection, we must access each of the individual elements.

In algebra, we can choose whatever subscripts we want. In C, we cannot. The first index value is always zero, and the rest go up from there.

An array element may be used like any other variable; remember, it is only a single one of a collection of variables. For example, if `samples[4]` is an `int`, it can be treated like any other `int`.

```
samples[4] = 25;
printf("The value is %i\n", samples[4]);
```

This program segment will print out the value 25.

HEADS UP!

C indices always start with zero.

ARRAY DECLARATIONS

Like everything else in C, arrays must be declared. The array can be composed of elements of any data type, but a single array must contain

elements of the same type. We can have an array of ints or doubles, but not an array that contains combinations of the two types. A single declaration defines the array and declares all the elements of the array.

Suppose that we were the proprietors of a muffin stand on the corner and wanted to keep track of the number of muffins sold each day of the week. We would need seven variables for the seven values. We can establish these in an array of seven elements. The statement

```
short sales[7];
```

declares the array *sales*. In the declaration, the number in brackets is not an index but the number of elements in the array. It must be a constant expression; variables are not allowed here. The elements of an array are always stored contiguously (right next to each other) in memory. This declaration, then, allocates contiguous space in memory for seven elements, *sales[0]*, *sales[1]*, *sales[2]*, on up to *sales[6]*.

Using a diagram of main memory similar to that in Chapter 1, we show memory for the *sales* array allocated as follows (we have used hexadecimal notation for memory addresses, a common practice):

??	??	??	??	??	??	??		
FFF0/FFF1	FFF2/FFF3	FFF4/FFF5	FFF6/FFF7	FFF8/FFF9	FFFA/FFFB	FFFC/FFFD	FFFE/FFFF

sales[0] sales[1] sales[2] sales[3] sales[4] sales[5] sales[6]

The array *sales* begins at memory address FFF0. The element *sales[0]* occupies two memory locations beginning at address FFF0; *sales[1]* begins at FFF2; and so forth. The question marks in the memory spaces indicates that the values of the elements are all garbage—they have no meaningful values yet.

The declaration said short sales[7]; but there is no space allocated for *sales[7]*. In some other languages the value in the declaration is the highest index, but not in C. Here it is the number of indices. The highest index value will be 1 less than the number of elements declared.

Initializations

Since array elements are like any other variables, we can assign them in statements such as

```
sales[5] = 47;
sales[0] = 3806;
```

Also, like other variables, we can initialize array elements at the time of their declaration. We can declare array elements explicitly by putting their values, separated by commas, in braces. Remember, an array

declaration establishes a number of elements, so we will have to have a number of values to assign to them.

```
short sales[7] = {3806, 28, 4522, 476, 1183, 47, 12};
```

HEADS UP!

Initializing at least one element sets all the uninitialized elements to zero.

We do not necessarily have to initialize the entire array. If we initialize any of the elements, the rest will automatically be set to zero by C. For example,

```
short sales[7] = {3806, 28, 4522};
```

assigns those values to *sales[0]*, *sales[1]*, and *sales[2]*, and C will initialize *sales[3]* through *sales[6]* to zero.

We can easily initialize an array to all zeros like this:

```
short sales[7] = {0};
```

TRAP

`short sales[7] = {1};` does not initialize all the elements to 1.

The element `sales[0]` will be explicitly set to zero, and all the rest will be set to zero by default.

If we initialize the array, we can even leave the space within the brackets blank. The C compiler will figure out the number of array elements to allocate. The declaration

```
short sales[] = {3806, 28, 4522, 476, 1183, 47, 12};
```

will allocate and initialize seven elements, `sales[0]` through `sales[6]`.

THE VARIABLY DEFINED VARIABLE

A major advantage of using arrays is that we can reference different elements, essentially different variables, by changing the index. To make

NUTS'N BOLTS

HOW MANY ELEMENTS ARE IN YOUR ARRAY?

You have declared your array as `float apples[3]`, and C has allocated space in memory for three floats, *apples[0]*, *apples[1]*, and *apples[2]*. Is that all the elements you have in your array? Yes and no. Yes, that is all the space allocated for the elements in this array, but no, you can access *apples[35]* if you want to. C does not keep track of the number of elements in your array, so you are free to use any indexes you want. You are also free to shoot yourself in the foot with your own gun!

When you refer to an array element, such as *apples[1]*, C uses the index to count element spaces away from the beginning of the array; *apples[1]*, is one `float` from the beginning of the *apples* array. The variable *apples[35]*, then, would be 35 `floats` away from the beginning of the *apples* array. You can actually assign a value there—C won't stop you—but the place in memory was not allocated for that element, and may have been allocated for some totally different purpose. What will happen? If you're lucky and the space was unallocated, the program might work. Or it may crash miserably, wiping out everything you've worked on all day.

The moral here is that it is up to you to keep your array indexes within the allocated bounds. C won't do it for you.

---

that easier, we can put any expression, anything that evaluates to a numeric value, within the brackets. For example, all of the following are valid:

```
sales[4]
sales[x]
sales[b + q * pow(d, f / 2)]
```

HEADS UP!

Avoid floating-point subscripts.

TRAP

Going out of the array's range.

The index will be determined by the value of the expression within the brackets. The index must be a nonnegative integer value, so if the expression evaluates to a floating-point value, it is truncated to an integer. The notation `sales[4.9]` refers to the variable *sales[4]*. Be careful of floating-point indices, however. Something that evaluates to what looks to be 4.0 may actually be stored in the binary version of 3.99999999, which would truncate to 3.

It is up to you to see that the indices are within the range allocated in the declaration of the array. The notations `sales[-1]` and `sales[10]` will lead to two values, the first located in the 2 bytes before the array, and the second 20 bytes after the beginning of the array, which is 6 bytes past the end of the array. What is there? Who knows? (See the Nuts 'N Bolts section *How Many Elements Are In Your Array?*)

▷Program 7–1 prints out the muffin sales for each day of the week—the values stored in each element of the *sales* array. The value of *day* determines the index. Notice that the index will be *day* – 1. Sinces indices always start with zero, sales for the first day will be found in *sales[0]* and sales for the seventh in *sales[6]*.

THE ZERO ELEMENT

Sometimes, having the array indexes start with zero is handy, such as when taking readings of a chemical reaction starting with the time the reaction was initiated—at time zero—and at one-minute intervals after that.

Other times it's a pain in the neck—Acme's trucks, for example. Humans would normally number things starting from 1, not from 0. Therefore, we must accommodate in our program by having the weight for truck 1 in *weights[0]* and using notation such as `weights[truck - 1]`.

There are other ways of accommodating for the zero index. One is to train everyone to count from 0 instead of 1—probably not practical! Another is to declare our array one larger than we need and simply not use the zero element. The weight for truck 1 is stored in *weights[1]* and so forth, and we can refer to `weights[truck]`. The element *weights[0]* may not be used, but memory for it will still be allocated. If memory is at a premium, this approach will be impractical.

Which approach you choose will depend on your particular situation.

(handwritten: two loops)

(handwritten, left margin: All in two weeks)

⇨**Program 7–1**

```
#include <stdio.h>

#define DAYS_IN_WEEK 7

void main(void)
{   short sales[DAYS_IN_WEEK] = {3806, 28, 4522, 476, 1183, 47, 12};
    short day;

    for (day = 1; day <= DAYS_IN_WEEK; ++day)
       printf("Sales for day %hi =%5hi\n", day, sales[day - 1]);
}
```

(handwritten: Enter a sale for day %i:", day);
(handwritten: scanf("%i", &sales(day-1));)

Output

```
Sales for day 1 = 3806
Sales for day 2 =   28
Sales for day 3 = 4522
Sales for day 4 =  476
Sales for day 5 = 1183
Sales for day 6 =   47
Sales for day 7 =   12
```

Let us see how we might use arrays in another example. The shipping clerk at the Acme Widget Company must keep track of each truck that has left the plant and how much weight it was carrying, and, at the end of the day, must produce a shipping report.

Create a program for Acme to keep track of and report on its trucks.

Acme has a fleet of five trucks, conveniently numbered 1 through 5, and any or all of them might be used in any order on a given day. As each truck leaves it is weighed and the truck number and weight recorded. This data could be input into the computer as follows:

```
Truck? 4
Weight? 312.5
```

At the end of the day, an input of zero for the truck number would end input. At that point, the clerk must produce a report showing the number of each truck that was used and the weight it was carrying, as well as the total number of trucks and total weight.

```
Shipping Report
      Truck  Weight
          1   702.5
          2   816.3
          4   312.5
          7  1124.7
      -----  ------
Total     4  2956.0
```

The principal data requirement is a list of truck weights. A weight of zero should indicate that a truck was not used.

The program consists of two main modules:

> Input weights
> Print report

We want to continue to input weights until the end of the day, when we input a zero truck number—a sentinel-value-controlled loop.

> [Input weights]
>   Initialize all weights to zero
>   Input truck number
>   While truck number not zero
>   Input weight
>   Input truck number

In "desk testing" this module, we see that there is nothing that prevents the shipping clerk from entering a truck number that is not within Acme's range of trucks. We can expand Input truck number to include such a test.

```
[Input truck number]
    Do
        Input truck number
    While truck number < 0 or > 5
```

To print the report we will have to look at each of the five trucks and, if it is not zero, print the weight, accumulate it into a total, and count the truck.

```
[Print report]
    For 5 trucks
        If weight not zero
            Print truck number and weight
            Accumulate weight
            Add to truck count
    Print truck count and accumulated weight
```

IMPLEMENTATION

To store the weight for each of the five trucks, we need five variables. We could make up five—*the_big_blue_Ford*, *the_Nissan_with_the_dented_fender*, and so forth—but instead, let us use an array with five elements. We can keep track of which truck's weight is in which element by using the index as the truck number. We will have to make a slight adjustment since the truck numbers start at 1 and C indices start at 0, but subtracting 1 from the truck's number should take care of it. The weight for truck 5, then, will be in element 4.

In ⇨Program 7–2, the weight of each of the trucks is kept in the array *weights[]*, and the truck number, *truck*, minus 1 is the index.

⇨**Program 7–2**

```
#include <stdio.h>

#define FLEET 5                        /* Number of trucks in the fleet */

int truck_in(void);                            /* Input Truck Number */

void main(void)
1 {   float weights[FLEET] = {0};      /* Initialize entire array to zero */
      int truck;                                    /* Truck number */
      int tot_trucks = 0;           /* Counter for total trucks for report */
      float tot_weight = 0;               /* Total weight for report */
```
                                                            (continued)

```
 2      truck = truck_in(); /********************************** Input Data */
 3      while (truck)                            /* Exit loop when zero entered */
        {  printf("Weight? ");
 4         scanf("%f", &weights[truck - 1]);
 5         truck = truck_in();
        }
        printf("\nShipping Report\n"); /************************ Print Report */
        printf("     Truck  Weight\n");
 6      for (truck = 1; truck <= FLEET; ++truck)
 7         if (weights[truck - 1])                        /* If weight nonzero */
 8         {  printf("     %5i  %6.1f\n", truck, weights[truck - 1]);
 9            ++tot_trucks;
10            tot_weight += weights[truck - 1];
           }
        printf("       -----  ------\n");
11      printf("Total %5i  %6.1f\n", tot_trucks, tot_weight);
     }

     int truck_in(void) /********************************* Input Truck Number */
     {  int truck;

        do
        {  printf("Truck (1 to %i, 0 to quit)? ", FLEET);
t1         scanf("%i", &truck);
t2      }while (truck < 0 || truck > FLEET);  /* Don't let invalid truck past */
t3      return truck;
     }
```

Output

```
Truck (1 to 5, 0 to quit)? 7
Truck (1 to 5, 0 to quit)? 4
Weight? 1825.8
Truck (1 to 5, 0 to quit)? 2
Weight? 883.5
Truck (1 to 5, 0 to quit)? 1
Weight? 829.4
Truck (1 to 5, 0 to quit)? 0

Shipping Report
     Truck  Weight
         1   829.4
         2   883.5
         4  1825.8
       -----  ------
Total    3  3538.7
```

EXECUTION CHART

Line	Explanation main():	weights[5]					truck	tot_trucks	tot_weight
1	Initialize entire array to zero.	0.0	0.0	0.0	0.0	0.0	---	---	---
2	Call *truck_in().*	0.0	0.0	0.0	0.0	0.0	?	0	0

					truck_in():	truck
t1	Input truck number.					7
t2	Out of range, condition true.					7
t1	Input another truck number.					4
t2	In range, condition false.					4
t3	Return truck number and go back to `main()`.					4

Line	Explanation main():	weights[5]					truck	tot_trucks	tot_weight
2	Assign return value to *truck.*	0.0	0.0	0.0	0.0	0.0	4	0	0
3	*truck* nonzero.	0.0	0.0	0.0	0.0	0.0	4	0	0
4	Input value for *weights[3].*	0.0	0.0	0.0	1825.8	0.0	4	0	0
5	Input another truck number.	0.0	0.0	0.0	1825.8	0.0	2	0	0
3	*truck* nonzero.	0.0	0.0	0.0	1825.8	0.0	2	0	0
4	Input value for *weights[1].*	0.0	883.5	0.0	1825.8	0.0	2	0	0
5	Input another truck number.	0.0	883.5	0.0	1825.8	0.0	1	0	0
3	*truck* nonzero.	0.0	883.5	0.0	1825.8	0.0	1	0	0
4	Input value for *weights[0].*	829.4	883.5	0.0	1825.8	0.0	1	0	0
5	Input another truck number.	829.4	883.5	0.0	1825.8	0.0	1	0	0
3	*truck* zero	829.4	883.5	0.0	1825.8	0.0	1	0	0
6	Initialize *truck* to 1, test for <= 5.	829.4	883.5	0.0	1825.8	0.0	1	0	0
7	Test for *weights[0]* nonzero. It is.	829.4	883.5	0.0	1825.8	0.0	1	0	0
8	Print truck data	829.4	883.5	0.0	1825.8	0.0	1	0	0
9	Count trucks.	829.4	883.5	0.0	1825.8	0.0	1	1	0
10	Accumulate weight.	829.4	883.5	0.0	1825.8	0.0	1	1	829.4
6–10	Repeat process for all trucks.	829.4	883.5	0.0	1825.8	0.0	6	3	3538.7
11	Print totals.	829.4	883.5	0.0	1825.8	0.0	6	3	3538.7

TEST

We should test various possibilities including entry of a wrong truck number. We also see that the shipping clerk can enter the same truck number twice, but this can be a way of correcting a mistaken entry.

1. How is an indexed variable similar to any other variable? *own name & space*
2. How does an indexed variable differ from a normal variable?
3. What is an array? *set of variables stored together*
4. Why do we use arrays? *must share the same datatype*
5. What is the first index value for any indexed variable in C? *0*
6. In the array declaration `float stuff[10];` how many elements are allocated and what is the index of the last allocated variable? *10, last is 9*
7. Given the declaration `float stuff[5] = {1.1, 2.2, 3.3};`, what will be the value of *stuff[1]*? Of *stuff[3]*? Of *stuff[5]*? *2.2 0*
8. Given the declaration above, does *stuff[what]* have a specific value? *Anything*
9. Of what data type is an index? *int*

ARRAYS AND FUNCTIONS

Let us write a function *sum_array()* that returns the sum of the values of all the elements in an array. Our call must pass the array to the function, and the function definition must declare variables to accept the array. Using our *sales* array as an example, one possible call would be

```
sum_array(sales[0], sales[1], sales[2],
        sales[3], sales[4], sales[5], sales[6])
```

meaning that the definition would have to have seven **short** variables to accept those values.

```
short sum_array(short value0, short value1,
            short value2, short value3,
            short value4, short value5,
            short value6)
```

Possible, but ugly!

Rather than passing all the values in the array, let us instead tell the function where the array begins in memory, and allow the function to access that memory. The array name without any index, *sales* in our example, references the address of the beginning of the array in memory. In our earlier memory diagram, the address *sales* was FFF0. Let us send that to the function. Using that concept, the call will be simpler,

```
sum_array(sales)
```

as will the first line of the definition,

```
short sum_array(short value[])
```

HEADS UP!

An array name references the address of an array.

The declaration in this function definition appears to allocate an array, a set of contiguous elements. But notice that there is no value in the brackets, nor should there be one. The declaration does not allocate an array, only an array name representing a memory location—the one passed in the function call. In this case, *value* is the same address as *sales*.

We can use *value* in the *sum_array()* function just as we used *sales* in the main() function. The index refers to an element that many elements away from the beginning. The element *value[2]* refers to the third element in the array—two away from the beginning.

In ⇨Program 7–3, we add the *sum_array()* function to our previous program to print out the total sales.

⇨**Program 7–3**

```
#include <stdio.h>

#define DAYS_IN_WEEK 7

short sum_array(short value[]);

void main(void)
{   short sales[DAYS_IN_WEEK] = {3806, 28, 4522, 476, 1183, 47, 12};
    short day, total;

    for (day = 1; day <= DAYS_IN_WEEK; ++day)              /* day from 1 to 7 */
        printf("Sales for day %hi =%5hi\n", day, sales[day - 1]);
    total = sum_array(sales);
    printf("Total sales =    %hi\n", total);
}

short sum_array(short value[])
{   short count, sum = 0;

    for (count = 0; count < DAYS_IN_WEEK; ++count)    /* count from 0 to 6 */
        sum += value[count];
    return sum;
}
```

Output

```
Sales for day 1 = 3806
Sales for day 2 =   28
Sales for day 3 = 4522
Sales for day 4 =  476
Sales for day 5 = 1183
Sales for day 6 =   47
Sales for day 7 =   12
Total sales =    10074
```

Since a function that returns a value can be used in any place that data type can be used, we could put the function call directly in the `printf()`, eliminating the need for the *total* variable:

```
printf("Total sales =      %hi\n", sum_array(sales));
```

Where does the *value* array in the *sum_array()* function end? Remember, C does not keep track of the end of allocated arrays, only where they start. We repeat: keeping track of the end of the array is up to *you*. In ➪Program 7–3, the function was written specifically for a seven-element array. To make it more general, in addition to the address of the array, we would also have to pass the number of elements,

```
sum_array(sales, DAYS_IN_WEEK)
```

and redefine our function to initialize a variable (*elements*) with that value, and then use it to control the summation loop.

```
short sum_array(short value[], int elements)
{   short count, sum = 0;

    for (count = 0; count < elements; ++count)
        sum += value[count];
    return sum;
}
```

Another way to handle the problem is to put a sentinel value at the end of the array, –1 for example. Any operations on the elements of the array would stop when we reached the element with the value –1. This solution is shown in ➪Program 7–4 on the next page.

The number of elements in the *sales* array is one larger than the number of *DAYS_IN_WEEK* to allow for the sentinel value at the end. We have shown this by explicitly stating the number of elements in the declaration `short sales[DAYS_IN_WEEK + 1]`. The number of initializing values alone would have had the same effect.

As we have said, *value* in the *sum_array()* function is the same address as *sales* in `main()`. Memory is allocated as follows.

The memory locations are accessed by *sales* in `main()` and by *value* in *sum_array()*, but they are the same memory locations with the same values. That means if we change the value of *value[2]*, we are also changing the value of *sales[2]*. When we return to the `main()` function, *sales[2]* will show the new value.

⇨**Program 7–4**

```
#include <stdio.h>

#define DAYS_IN_WEEK 7

short sum_array(short value[]);

void main(void)
{   short sales[DAYS_IN_WEEK + 1] = {3806, 28, 4522, 476, 1183, 47, 12, -1};
    short day;

    for (day = 1; day <= DAYS_IN_WEEK; ++day)              /* day from 1 to 7 */
        printf("Sales for day %hi =%5hi\n", day, sales[day - 1]);
    printf("Total sales =    %hi\n", sum_array(sales));
}

short sum_array(short value[])
{   short count = 0, sum = 0;

    while (value[count] != -1)                   /* Loop until sentinel reached */
    {   sum += value[count];
        ++count;
    }
    return sum;
}
```

To illustrate, let us say that the boss wants us to double our sales. We can create a function *double_array()*, which will double each value of the array passed to it, the *sales* array in this case.

In ⇨Program 7–5, on the following page, we have also added the *show_array()* function that prints out the array.

Notice that we have eliminated the constant *DAYS_IN_WEEK*. The number of initializing values in the declaration of *sales* sets the number of elements in the array, and the sentinel value in the last element tells any operation on the array where the last element is. We must be sure, of course, that there is no possibility of sales of −1.

```
#include <stdio.h>

void double_array(short value[]);
void show_array(short value[]);

void main(void)
{   short sales[] = {3806, 28, 4522, 476, 1183, 47, 12, -1};

    printf("Sales array before:");
    show_array(sales);

    double_array(sales);

    printf("Sales array after: ");
    show_array(sales);
}

void double_array(short value[])
{   short count = 0;

    while (value[count] != -1)
    {   value[count] *= 2;
        ++count;
    }
}

void show_array(short value[])
{   short count = 0;

    while (value[count] != -1)
    {   printf(" %5hi", value[count]);
        ++count;
    }
    printf("\n");
}
```

Output

```
Sales array before:    3806    28  4522   476  1183    47    12
Sales array after:     7612    56  9044   952  2366    94    24
```

YOUR TURN 7–2

1. In what two ways can we effectively "pass an array to a function"?

2. What does the declaration of an array in the formal parameters of a function actually declare?

3. If we pass an array by name and change some of the elements using the local name in the function, what will happen to the corresponding elements in the calling function?

ARRAY APPLICATIONS

Because we can variably define an array element by defining its index, we find there are many processes that lend themselves to array use that would be quite difficult without arrays. Following are a few examples.

Sequential Search

In a **sequential search** (or *linear search*) we start at the beginning of a list of items and look at each in turn until we either find the one we are looking for or reach the end of the list. Let us go back to the example of the Acme Widget Company and its five trucks. Each of Acme's five trucks has a license plate with a different number. Let us put these licenses in an array, and search through the array to identify which truck has a certain license. In ➪Program 7–6, we will start the search at the beginning of the array, and stop searching when we have found what we are looking for or we reach the end of the array.

The overall pattern for ➪Program 7–6 is:

```
Start at beginning of list
While Item not found and still in list
    Go to next item
If item found
    Acknowledge it
Else
    Indicate failure
```

➪ **Program 7–6**

```
#include <stdio.h>

#define FLEET 5                              /* Number of trucks in the fleet */

void main(void)
{   int licenses[FLEET] = {312, 47, 555, 100, 36};      /* Truck licenses */
    int license;                                     /* License to search for */
    int truck;                                          /* Truck number */
```
(continued)

```
        printf("License? ");
        scanf("%i", &license);
        truck = 1;                          /* Start at beginning of list of trucks */
        while (license != licenses[truck - 1]      /* Search while no match */
                && truck <= FLEET)                     /* and still in list */
            ++truck;
        if (truck <= FLEET)                 /* Truck number in list, found truck */
            printf("Truck number %i.\n", truck);
        else                                          /* Out of the list */
            printf("No such license.\n");
}
```

Outputs

```
License? 312
Truck number 1.

License? 534
No such license.

License? 36
Truck number 5.
```

As in the previous example, the trucks in ⇨Program 7–6 were numbered from 1 to 5, and their licenses stored in array elements 0 through 4. We knew that we had found the license in the list if the truck number was within the bounds of the list when we exited the loop. If the number was not within the bounds, we printed "No such license."

Let us use this concept in ⇨Program 7–7 to establish a function, *truck_in()*, that will either return the truck number with a particular license or zero if we want to end input. We will not be allowed to leave the function unless we have a successful search, a valid license, or input 0.

⇨Program 7–7

```
#include <stdio.h>

#define FLEET 5                             /* Number of trucks in the fleet */

int truck_in(int licenses[]);               /* Match license to truck */

void main(void)
{   int licenses[FLEET] = {312, 47, 555, 100, 36};    /* Truck licenses */
                                                      /* Truck number */
    printf("Truck %i.\n", truck_in(licenses));
}
```

(continued)

```
int truck_in(int licenses[]) /******************* Match License to Truck */
{  int license;                                    /* License to search for */
   int truck;

   do
   {  printf("License (0 to quit)? ");
      scanf("%i", &license);
      if (license)                                 /* License not zero */
      {  truck = 1;                    /* Start at beginning of list of trucks */
         while (license != licenses[truck - 1]  /* Search while no match */
                && truck <= FLEET)                 /* and still in list */
            ++truck;
      }
      else
         truck = 0;
   }while (truck > FLEET);                          /* Truck not 0 or in list */
   return truck;
}
```

Outputs

```
License (0 to quit)? 313
License (0 to quit)? 312
Truck 1.

License (0 to quit)? 36
Truck 5.
```

Binary Search

If the items through which we are searching are in order, we can significantly reduce the searching time by using a **binary search**. With such a search, each time we consider an item, we eliminate half the list of items rather than just the single item. If we are presented with a number from 1 to 10 and guess the one in the middle, 5, and are told that the number is too low, we know the number is between 6 and 10. We have eliminated half the possible range with one guess. We can then repeat the process with the remaining range and so forth until either we have found the correct value, or the range disappears.

To keep track of the range, we can set up two variables, *low* and *high*, as we have done in ❏Figure 7–1. The middle of the range, *mid*, will be (*low* + *high*) / 2. If the value at *mid* is too high, we set *high* to *mid* − 1, cutting the range in half, and repeat the process. The search stops when either the correct value is found, or the *low* is greater than the *high*, indicating that there are no more numbers in the range.

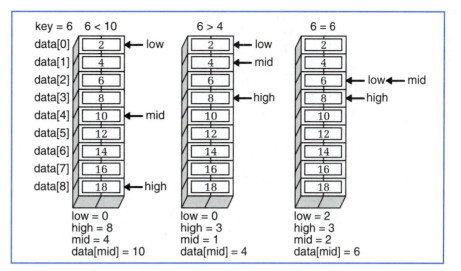

□ **FIGURE 7–1**   A Binary Search

Establish low, high, and initial midpoint
While range left and key value not found
    If key < mid value
        Limit search to lower end of range
    Else
        Limit search to upper end of range
    Establish new midpoint

Notice that *low*, *high*, and *mid* keep track of the indices in the array being searched, not the values in those elements. Since these indices are integers, the result of the midpoint division will also be an integer. For example, (0 + 3) / 2 is 1.5, but will be truncated to 1, making the midpoint 1.

Arrow-Matic Sanitary Construction uses odd lengths of sewer pipe in their work. Before they cut a new pipe, they would like to search their stock of pipe pieces for an appropriate length. ⇨ Program 7–8 uses a binary search to find a length of pipe in their stock.

⇨**Program 7–8**

```
#include <stdio.h>
#define PIPES 9

void main(void)
{   float length[PIPES] = {0.8, 1.2, 1.3, 1.9, 2.2, 2.6, 3.1, 3.7, 3.8};
    float key;                                  /* Length to search for */
    int low = 0,                        /* Bottom of the current search range */
        high = PIPES - 1,               /* Top of the current search range */
        mid;                                    /* Index at middle of range */
```
(continued)

```
        printf("What length pipe? ");
        scanf("%f", &key);
        mid = (low + high) / 2;                    /* Look at middle of range */
        while (low <= high && key != length[mid])
        {   if (key < length[mid])                      /* Search value too low */
                high = mid - 1;                   /* Limit range to lower half */
            else                                       /* Search value too high */
                low = mid + 1;                    /* Limit range to upper half */
            mid = (low + high) / 2;                  /* Look at middle of range */
        }
        if (key == length[mid])
            printf("Pipe %i is %.1f long.\n", mid + 1, key);
        else
            printf("Pipe length %.1f not found.\n", key);
    }
```

Output

```
What length pipe? 2.2
Pipe 5 is 2.2 long.

What length pipe? 3.8
Pipe 9 is 3.8 long.

What length pipe? 1.6
Pipe length 1.6 not found.

What length pipe? 4.1
Pipe length 4.1 not found.

What length pipe? 1.3
Pipe 3 is 1.3 long.
```

Parallel Arrays

Since Acme's trucks are constantly being replaced, rather than painting new numbers on the sides of the trucks, let us have Acme's shipping clerk refer to them by license number rather than truck number. We certainly don't want to set up thousands of *weights* elements to accommodate any possible truck number as an index. That would be a waste of valuable memory space.

Instead, let us use both the *licenses* array and the *weights* array side by side—as **parallel arrays**, as shown in Table 7–1.

The weight for the truck with license 100 is 1825.8. The index for the elements in each array ties them together.

Using this concept, plus the function from the previous example, we can rewrite ⇨Program 7–7 to allow the shipping clerk to input the license number and weight, as in ⇨Program 7–9.

TABLE 7–1 Parallel Arrays

	Licenses			Weights
licenses[0]	312		weights[0]	829.4
licenses[1]	47		weights[1]	883.5
licenses[2]	555		weights[2]	0.0
licenses[3]	100		weights[3]	1825.8
licenses[4]	36		weights[4]	0.0

⇨Program 7–9

```
#include <stdio.h>

#define FLEET 5                              /* Number of trucks in the fleet */

int truck_in(int licenses[]);                      /* Match License to Truck */

void main(void)
{   int licenses[FLEET] = {312, 47, 555, 100, 36};       /* Truck licenses */
    float weights[FLEET] = {0};               /* Initialize entire array to zero */
    int truck;                                              /* Truck number */
    int trucks = 0;                      /* Counter for total trucks for report */
    float tot_weight = 0;                         /* Total weight for report */

    truck = truck_in(licenses); /***************************** Input Data */
    while (truck)                              /* Exit loop when zero entered */
    {   printf("Weight? ");
        scanf("%f", &weights[truck - 1]);
        truck = truck_in(licenses);
    }
    printf("\nShipping Report\n"); /************************* Print Report */
    printf("      Truck  Weight\n");
    for (truck = 1; truck <= FLEET; ++truck)
        if (weights[truck - 1])                        /* If weight nonzero */
        {   printf("      %5i  %6.1f\n",
                   licenses[truck - 1], weights[truck - 1]);
            tot_weight += weights[truck - 1];
            ++trucks;
        }
    printf("      -----  ------\n");
    printf("Total %5i  %6.1f\n", trucks, tot_weight);
}
```

(continued)

```
int truck_in(int licenses[]) /******************* Match License to Truck */
{  int license;                                      /* License to search for */
   int truck;

   do
   {  printf("License (0 to quit)? ");
      scanf("%i", &license);
      if (license)                                     /* License not zero */
      {  truck = 1;                        /* Start at beginning of list of trucks */
         while (license != licenses[truck - 1]  /* Search while no match */
               && truck <= FLEET)                      /* and still in list */
            ++truck;
      }
      else
         truck = 0;
   }while (truck < 0 || truck > FLEET);           /* Truck not 0 or in list */
   return truck;
}
```

Output

```
License (0 to quit)? 442
License (0 to quit)? 100
Weight? 1825.8
License (0 to quit)? 47
Weight? 883.5
License (0 to quit)? 312
Weight? 829.4
License (0 to quit)? 0

Shipping Report
      Truck  Weight
        312   829.4
         47   883.5
        100  1825.8
      -----  ------
Total     3  3538.7
```

Inserting

An **insert** begins with a set of values in order, and adds one more value to the set. The new value is added so that the set remains in order after the addition. We will store the set of values in an array, which will have to be one element larger than the number of values in the original set, because we are going to add one more value. If we are going to insert a value into a set of 100 values, our array will have to consist of at least 101 elements.

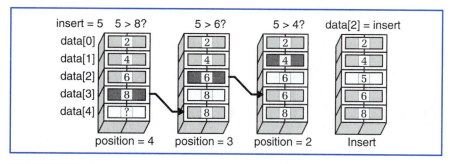

□ **FIGURE 7–2** An Insert

We know that the new value should be inserted in the set where it is greater than the number before and less than the number after. Now all we have to do is explain that to the computer. Let us consider a set of four values—2, 4, 6, and 8—to which we want to add one more—5. As shown in □Figure 7–2, we will declare an array of five variables *data[5]*, assign the values to the first four variables in the array, and assign the value we wish to insert to *insert*. We will consider each position in the array as a possible insert position and use the variable *position* to keep track of it. The element in that position would be *data[position]*. We will either assign our insert value (*insert*) to that element or go on to the next position.

There will already be a blank position at the end of the array, so let's use that as our first possible insert position. (In □Figure 7–2, the possible insert position is represented by a clear area.) If our insert value is greater than the value of the element before our possible insert position (*data[position – 1]*), then it must belong in this position (*data[position]*). (The darker shaded area is the element before the possible insert position.) If it is not greater, then it must belong somewhere above, so let's begin to make space for it by moving a value down one position—assigning the value of *data[position – 1]* to *data[position]*. Then we can move our possible insert position up one element by decrementing *position* and repeat the process.

The process will stop when we have either found the proper insert position or considered all the positions back to the second. If it doesn't belong in the second position, it must belong in the first. In either case, if we have decremented our *position* correctly, we can simply insert—assign *insert* to *data[position]*. ⇨Program 7–10 shows the code.

Try ⇨Program 7–10 with the *insert* values 1 and 9, which should insert at the beginning and the end of the array—the boundary conditions, in this case.

⊃Program 7–10

```c
#include <stdio.h>

#define LIST_SIZE 5                            /* Size of the list after insert */

void main(void)
{   int data[LIST_SIZE] = {2, 4, 6, 8};
    int insert = LIST_SIZE;
    int position;

    /************************************** Print set before insert */
    printf("Before: ");
    for (position = 0; position < LIST_SIZE - 1; ++position)
        printf("  %i", data[position]);
    printf("\nInsert:   %i\n", insert);

    /*********************************************************** Insert */
    position = LIST_SIZE - 1;  /* Start from empty variable at end of set */
    while (insert < data[position - 1] && position >= 1)
    {   data[position] = data[position - 1];       /* Move next value down */
        --position;                                /* Go up the set */
    }
    data[position] = insert;                    /* Add insert value to set */

    /************************************** Print set after insert */
    printf("After : ");
    for (position = 0; position < LIST_SIZE; ++position)
        printf("  %i", data[position]);
    printf("\n");
}
```

Output

```
Before:   2   4   6   8
Insert:   5
After :   2   4   5   6   8
```

Sorting

A sort arranges a set of values in order. Unlike those in an insert, the values in a set to be sorted do not have to start out in any particular order, and no new value is added to the set. There are a number of different sort routines—some more efficient at sorting certain types of data, some extremely complicated, some quite specialized. We will use one form of a **bubble sort** here, not because of its great efficiency, but because it is one of the least complicated.

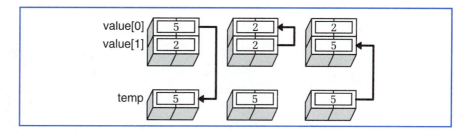

□ **FIGURE 7–3** A Swap

It is called a bubble sort because it makes a number of passes through the set and, with each pass, smaller numbers "float," like bubbles, to the top, while larger numbers "sink." Each pass starts at the beginning of the set and compares the values of the first and the second elements. If they are in order nothing is done, but if they are out of order, they are **swapped**, their values exchanged, so that at least those two values will be in order. The process continues with the second and third elements, the third and fourth, and so forth.

A more appropriate name for this process might be a "sinker sort." While smaller values are bubbling up, larger values are sinking to the bottom in a more ordered fashion. With a single pass through the set, we are assured that the largest value will be at the bottom of the set. We can now make another pass, but this time we will stop a position before the bottom of the set, because we know that the value at the bottom is already in its proper place. With each pass we will move the bottom of the set up one, stopping after the bottom of the set is in the second position. With all those values in their proper position, the first must be in place.

Overall, the sort follows this pattern:

Move bottom position from last to second by ones
   Make exchange pass through set

The exchange pass starts at the top of the set and compares adjacent values beginning with the first and ending one before the current bottom of the set—comparing the second to the bottom with the bottom.

Move bottom position from last to second by ones
   Move position from first to one before bottom   [Exchange pass]
     If adjacent element values not in order
      Swap them

The swap requires an extra, temporary variable. Graphically, it looks like □Figure 7–3

The whole process, using five `short` values, looks like □Figure 7–4. The lightly shaded areas are adjacent values being compared. The darker shaded values are those in their proper positions.

⇨Program 7–11 implements the sort diagrammed in □Figure 7–4.

 **HEADS UP!**

In a sort, declare the array for the number of values in the set.

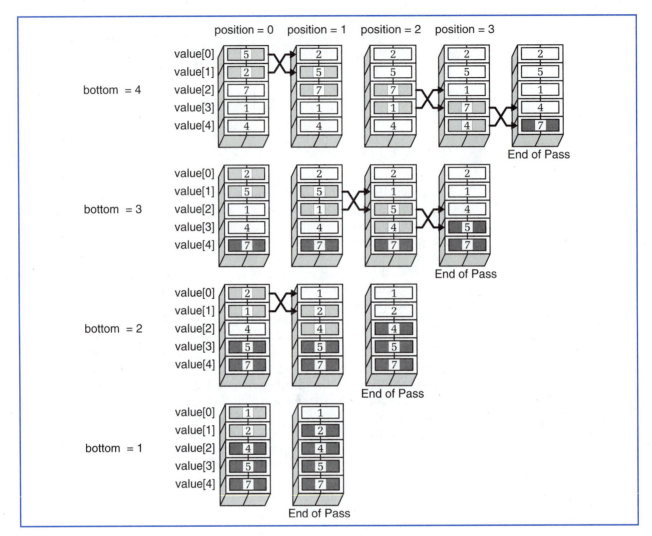

position = 0   position = 1   position = 2   position = 3

☐ FIGURE 7–4 A Bubble Sort

⇨**Program 7–11**

```
#include <stdio.h>

#define VALUES 5

void print_array(short arr[]);

void main(void)
{   short value[VALUES] = {5, 2, 7, 1, 4};
    short position, bottom, temp;
```

(continued)

```
      printf("Before sort: ");
      print_array(value);

      /*********************************************************** Sort */
                                /* Move bottom from last to second by ones */
      for (bottom = VALUES - 1; bottom > 0; --bottom)
                               /* Move position from first to one before bottom */
         for (position = 0; position < bottom; ++position)
                                 /* If adjacent element values not in order */
            if (value[position + 1] < value[position])
            {  temp = value[position];                            /* Swap them */
               value[position] = value[position + 1];
               value[position + 1] = temp;
            }

      printf("After sort:  ");
      print_array(value);
}

void print_array(short arr[])
{  short index;

   for (index = 0; index <= VALUES - 1; ++ index)
      printf("%hi ", arr[index]);
   printf("\n");
}
```

Output

```
Before sort: 5 2 7 1 4
After sort:  1 2 4 5 7
```

Notice that in the last pass, no swaps were made. If an entire pass is completed and no swaps are made, the entire set must be in order. This condition may occur well before the last pass, in which case there is no need to continue the process. We can modify our program to test for that condition also.

> Set bottom to last element
> While bottom > first position and swaps made in last pass
>   Move position from first to one before bottom   [Exchange pass]
>   If adjacent element values not in order
>   Swap them
>   Move bottom up one

To keep track of whether swaps were made we will use a **flag** variable, *swaps*, which we will set to true, +1, if a swap was made. At the beginning of each pass, it will be set to false, 0, so that if no swaps were made, it will be false after the pass. The following `main()` function shows this change:

```
void main(void)
{   short value[VALUES] = {5, 2, 7, 1, 4};
    short position, bottom, temp;
    int swap = 1;                                      /* Flag indicates swap made */
                                /* Set to 1 so that loop will execute first time */

    printf("Before sort: ");
    print_array(value);

    /***************************************************************** Sort */
    bottom = VALUES - 1;
    while (bottom > 0 && swap)
    {   swap = 0;                                        /* No swaps made yet */
        for (position = 0; position < bottom; ++position)
            if (value[position + 1] < value[position])
            {   temp = value[position];
                value[position] = value[position + 1];
                value[position + 1] = temp;
                swap = 1;                                /* Swap made */
            }
        --bottom;
    }
```

Returning to the Acme Widget Company, let us apply the sort to the parallel arrays we used to keep track of the truck licenses and weights in each truck. If we want to print out the shipping report in license order, we can sort the *licenses* array, and each time we swap the *licenses* elements, we will swap the corresponding *weights* elements. In other words, each change we make in the *licenses* array will also be made in the *weights* array.

If we add this call to the `main()` function just before printing the report,

```
sort(licenses, weights); /***************************** Sort by license */
```

the following function will sort the parallel arrays:

```
void sort(int licenses[], float weights[]) /************ Sort by license */
{   int position, bottom, ltemp;
    float wtemp;
    int swap = 1;                                      /* Flag indicates swap made */
```

(continued)

```
        bottom = FLEET - 1;
        while (bottom > 0 && swap)
        {   swap = 0;                                        /* No swaps made yet */
            for (position = 0; position < bottom; ++position)
                if (licenses[position + 1] < licenses[position])
                {   ltemp = licenses[position];              /* Swap licenses */
                    licenses[position] = licenses[position + 1];
                    licenses[position + 1] = ltemp;
                    wtemp = weights[position];               /* Swap weights */
                    weights[position] = weights[position + 1];
                    weights[position + 1] = wtemp;
                    swap = 1;                                /* Swap made */
                }
            --bottom;
        }
    }
```

With the same data input, the new report will be:

```
Shipping Report
        Truck   Weight
           47    883.5
          100   1825.8
          312    829.4
        -----   ------
Total       3   3538.7
```

YOUR TURN 7-3

1. What is a sequential search?
2. What conditions end a sequential search?
3. Why is a binary search more efficient than a sequential search?
4. What special conditions must exist for a binary search to work?
5. What are parallel arrays?
6. In an insert operation, how many elements must the array have?
7. Which is the first possible insert position in the set? The last?
8. In a sort operation, how many elements must the array have?
9. What is the greatest number of passes that might be made through an array of 10 elements in a bubble sort?

ARRAYS WITH MORE THAN ONE INDEX

Arrays may have more than one index. No matter how many indexes, however, we can still view them as separate elements with separate values, but with a more flexible way of referring to them. The following are possible declarations:

```
float axle[7][100], bearing[20][12][25];
int flexus[200][2][4][2];
```

As an example, let us say that our major product, the Finortna, comes in any combination of two models, standard and deluxe, and three colors, red, green, and puce. This gives us six possibilities, but two different criteria, model and color. If we allowed the first index to represent the model and the second the color, we could store the inventories of Finortnas in a double-indexed array *inventory[2][3]*.

```
short inventory[2][3];
```

The typical way of looking at a double-indexed array is as a two-dimensional table as in Table 7–2. The inventory of deluxe, red Finortnas would be stored in *inventory[1][0]*, while standard, puce ones would be in *inventory[0][2]*.

TABLE 7–2	The Finortna Table		
inventory	**[ ][0]**	**[ ][1]**	**[ ][2]**
[0][ ]	46	12	122	(Standard)
[1][ ]	62	20	88	(Deluxe)
	(Red)	(Green)	(Puce)	

A convenient way to view this is as an array of arrays. In fact, this gives us a good insight into how C actually allocates memory space for it. There are three elements in the *inventory[0]* array and three in the *inventory[1]* array. Since C guarantees us contiguous storage, if the address, *inventory*, is FFF0, then storage would be like this:

46	12	122	62	20	88			
FFF0/FFF1	FFF2/FFF3	FFF4/FFF5	FFF6/FFF7	FFF8/FFF9	FFFA/FFFB	FFFC/FFFD	FFFE/FFFF	

inv[0][0] inv[0][1] inv[0][2] inv[1][0] inv[1][1] inv[1][2]

We have contiguous storage of two arrays with contiguous storage of the variables in each array. In essence, the second index (or last index, if there are more than two) varies first.

We saw that the array name was a reference to the address of the array. This also holds true for arrays with more than one index. The name *inventory* references the address FFF0, the address of *inventory[0][0]*. But if this is an array of arrays, then *inventory[0]* must be the "name" of the first three-variable array and *inventory[1]* the "name" of the second. This

is indeed the case, with *inventory[0]* being a reference to the address of the first, FFF0 (the address of *inventory[0][0]*) and *inventory[1]* being a reference to the address of the second, FFF6 (the address of *inventory[1][0]*).

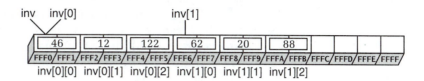

Initializing Multiple-Indexed Arrays

We could initialize the *inventory* array as we did our one-index ones—by putting enough values in braces in the declaration.

```
short inventory[2][3] = {46, 12, 122, 62, 20, 88};
```

Since we are dealing with an array of arrays, the values will be assigned to each major array in turn. If we view the array as a two-dimensional table, the assignments will be in *row-major order*. In other words, 46, 12, and 122 will be assigned to row zero—*inventory[0][0]*, *inventory[0][1]*, and *inventory[0][2]*—and 62, 20, and 88 will be assigned to row one—*inventory[1][0]*, *inventory[1][1]*, and *inventory[1][2]*.

C also allows us to separate the arrays-within-the-array by nesting braces,

```
short inventory[2][3] = {{46, 12, 122}, {62, 20, 88}};
```

which we would probably write more illustratively like this:

```
short inventory[2][3] = {{46, 12, 122},
                         {62, 20,  88}};
```

maintaining the tablelike view of the array.

If we do not supply enough values, the rest of the elements will be initialized to zero. But, if we use nested braces, this applies to each of the subarrays. For example,

```
short inventory[2][3] = {{46, 12},
                         {62     }};
```

is equivalent to

```
short inventory[2][3] = {{46, 12, 0},
                         {62,  0, 0}};
```

If we supply enough values, we can leave the rightmost index blank, and leave it to the compiler to fill it in. Thus,

```
short inventory[2][] = {46, 12, 0, 62, 0, 0};
```

is equivalent to the previous declaration.

The second to last example, showing the values of all the elements in tablelike fashion is certainly clearer than the ones before or after it. The one before it would be acceptable if each row had 50 columns and only the first 1 or 2 were to be explicitly initialized. The last example is just plain ugly!

Accessing Multiple-Indexed Arrays

We could print out the values in the *inventory* array by using nested for loops; the outer one controls the first index, the row, and the inner one controls the second index, the column. ⇨Program 7–12 shows how.

⇨**Program 7–12**

```
#include <stdio.h>

#define MODELS 2
#define COLORS 3

void main(void)
{   short inventory[MODELS][COLORS] = {{46, 12, 122},
                                        {62, 20,  88}};
    int model, color;

    printf("             RED   GREEN    PUCE\n");
    for (model = 0; model < MODELS; ++model)
    {   if (model == 0)
            printf("STANDARD ");
        else
            printf("DELUXE   ");
        for (color = 0; color < COLORS; ++color)
            printf("%6hi ", inventory[model][color]);
        printf("\n");
    }
}
```

Output

```
             RED   GREEN   PUCE
STANDARD      46      12    122
DELUXE        62      20     88
```

Passing Multiple-Indexed Arrays to Functions

As we know, passing the array name (the address of the array) to a function does not tell the function how many elements are in the array. Nor, of course, would it tell the function how many indexes the array can safely use or the organization of those indexes. In our declaration of the formal parameters of the array in the function, however, we can fill in some of that information by showing how many index positions there are, and stating the number of indexes in each position but the first. The function still will not know the overall size of the array, but its pattern, at least, is evident.

Using Finortnas as an example, and viewing the array within the array as the columns within a row, given our declaration of

```
short inventory[2][3];
```

in the `main()` function, this function will allocate space for the array that can be viewed as

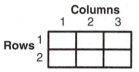

When we pass the array's address to a function,

```
func(inventory)
```

we are telling the function where the array starts in memory. In the formal parameters of the function, we can state how many elements there are in each array-within-the-array, but still not how large the entire array is.

To receive the call above, the *func()* function would be declared as

```
func(short inv[][3])
```

and in *func()*, the array is viewed as

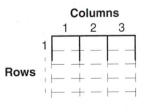

Program 7–13 is Program 7–12 rewritten to print out the inventory in a function. The output is exactly the same.

Program 7–13

```
#include <stdio.h>

#define MODELS 2
#define COLORS 3

void print_inv(short inventory[][COLORS]);

void main(void)
{   short inventory[MODELS][COLORS] = {{46, 12, 122},
                                       {62, 20,  88}};

    print_inv(inventory);
}

void print_inv(short inventory[][COLORS])
{   int model, color;

    printf("              RED  GREEN   PUCE\n");
    for (model = 0; model < MODELS; ++model)
    {   if (model == 0)
            printf("STANDARD ");
        else
            printf("DELUXE   ");
        for (color = 0; color < COLORS; ++color)
            printf("%6hi ", inventory[model][color]);
        printf("\n");
    }
}
```

We can send an array within the array to the function separately by passing its address—array notation without the second index. The formal parameters of the function, of course, will have to receive the address of a single-indexed array.

Let us write a program that shows the total inventory for Standard and for Deluxe Finortnas. In the program we will want the sum of each array-within-an-array. Earlier in this chapter, we developed the *sum_array()* function (in three versions) that returned the sum of the elements in an array. Let us simply use this function (the second version) to total each of the subarrays in Program 7–14.

```
#include <stdio.h>

#define MODELS 2
#define COLORS 3

short sum_array(short value[], short elements);

void main(void)
{   short inventory[MODELS][COLORS] = {{46, 12, 122},
                                       {62, 20,  88}};

    printf("Standard: %6hi\n",
           sum_array(inventory[0], COLORS));            /* First */
    printf("Deluxe  : %6hi\n",
           sum_array(inventory[1], COLORS));            /* Second */
}

short sum_array(short value[], short elements)
{   short count, sum = 0;

    for (count = 0; count <= elements - 1; ++count)
       sum += value[count];
    return sum;
}
```

Output

```
Standard:    180
Deluxe  :    170
```

Why not use a double-indexed array for the Acme Widget Company's trucks? We could view the truck data in a table with each truck represented with a column, and the license in the first row and the weight in the second:

	Truck				
License	312	47	555	100	36
Weight	829.4	883.5	0	1825.8	0

HEADS UP!

All elements of an array must be of the same data type.

The problem with this approach is that the data in the first row is of a different type than that in the second. Arrays must be of all one data type. We can still visualize the data as a table, but we will have to implement it using parallel arrays.

1. Can we set up an array of arrays?
2. Given the declaration `stuff[4][3];`, what does the notation `stuff[2]` signify?
3. How can we use the array-of-arrays concept in initializing arrays?
4. When we pass a multiple-indexed array to a function, how many indexes do we provide values for in the function's formal parameters?
5. How can we pass an array within an array to a function?

PUTTING IT TOGETHER

Professor Fassbinder maintains a strict seating chart in her class; her students are known only by their row and seat numbers. For some time, she has suspected that students in the window seats, that is, the first seat in each row, perform less well than those in the other seat positions, and she would like to confirm her suspicions.

TASK

Provide Professor Fassbinder with a program that will allow her to input scores by seat position and print out an analysis by seat position.

ANALYSIS

The program should allow input of scores by row and seat in any order, stopping when zero is entered for the row and seat, similar to the following:

```
Enter row seat: 1 3
Enter score: 17
Enter row seat: 4 2
Enter score: 19
Enter row seat: 0 0
```

The program should then print out a report grid with averages for each seat position, but only for those positions that actually have scores entered.

```
Seat         1     2     3
Row 1       xx          xx
    2       xx
    3       xx    xx    xx
    4             xx

Avgs        xx.x  xx.x  xx.x
```

The principal data requirements are the scores in the grid, and, to calculate the averages, the total score and count for each seat position.

DESIGN

The program has two overall modules:

    Enter scores
    Print report

Entering the scores is a typical sentinel-value-controlled loop, as discussed in Chapter 5. The row and seat should be entered before the scores so that they may be checked for validity. There is no row 6, seat 7, for example. Once a valid row and seat are entered, a score may be input.

    [Enter scores]
        Enter row and seat
        While row not zero
            If row and seat valid
                Enter score
            Else
                Print error message
            Enter row and seat

Printing the report also consists of two sections: printing the grid, and printing the averages.

    [Print report]
        Print grid
        Print averages

Filling in the grid will show each of the individual scores in their row and seat positions. This would be the time to count and accumulate the scores in each seat position. We only want to print, count, and accumulate positions where there are students; in other words, where the scores are not zero. (Students in Professor Fassbinder's class get at least one point for filling in their name.) If the score is zero, we simply print blanks to fill that position in the grid.

    [Print grid]
        For each row
            For each seat
                If score zero
                    Print blanks in seat grid
                Else
                    Print score in seat grid
                    Accumulate score in seat-position total
                    Count score in seat-position count

Once the seat positions are counted and accumulated, we can print out the averages—but only for those seat positions that have a count greater than zero. This also frees us from the possibility of divide-by-zero errors.

```
[Print averages]
    For each seat
        If count not zero
            Calculate and print average
        Else
            Print blanks
```

IMPLEMENTATION

The `main()` function in the resulting ⇨Program 7–15 follows the overall program modules with simply a call to an *input()* function followed by a call to an *output()* function. To keep track of the scores, we are using an array with two indexes, the first representing the row and the second, the seat. The address of the array is passed to each function so that the functions can work directly with the array. Two more arrays are needed in the *output()* function to keep track of the count and the accumulated total in each seat position. These arrays need only one index—to represent the seat position.

⇨**Program 7–15**

```
#include <stdio.h>

#define ROWS 4                                      /* Number of rows */
#define SEATS 3                              /* Number of seats per row */

void input(int scores[][SEATS]);                       /* Enter scores */
void output(int scores[][SEATS]);                       /* Print report */

void main(void)
{   int grades[ROWS][SEATS] = {{20},{18},{16}};
            /* Seat 1 for rows 1, 2, and 3 initialized for test purposes */
                            /* Also initializes everything else to zero */

1       input(grades);                                  /* Enter scores */
2       output(grades);                                 /* Print report */
}
```

(continued)

```
/*********************************************** Enter scores by row and seat */
     void input(int scores[][SEATS])
     {   int row, seat;

         printf("Enter row seat (0 0 to quit): ");
i1       scanf("%i %i", &row, &seat);
i2       while (row != 0)                                    /* Input til zero row */
i3       {   if (row > 0 && row <= ROWS &&                   /* Within valid ranges */
                 seat > 0 && seat <= SEATS)
             {   printf("Enter score: ");
i4               scanf(" %i", &scores[row - 1][seat - 1]);
             }
i5           else
i6               printf("Invalid row or seat.\n");
             printf("Enter row seat: ");
i7           scanf("%i %i", &row, &seat);
         }
     }
     /************************** Print report showing seat-position averages */
     void output(int scores[][SEATS])
     {   int row, seat;
         int total[SEATS] = {0};            /* Accumulator for each seat position */
         int count[SEATS] = {0};            /* Count scores in each seat position */

         /*********************************************** Print seat grid */
o1       printf("\nSeat      1     2     3\nRow");
o2       for (row = 0; row < ROWS; ++row)              /* Go through each row */
o3       {   printf(" %i ", row + 1);                  /* Zero index is row 1 */
o4           for (seat = 0; seat < SEATS; ++seat)          /* Seats in each row */
o5           {   if (scores[row][seat] == 0)              /* Don't print zeros */
o6                   printf("      ");
                 else
o7               {   printf("  %4i", scores[row][seat]);
o8                   total[seat] += scores[row][seat];           /* Total for seat */
o9                   ++count[seat];                              /* Count for seat */
                 }
             }
o10          printf("\n    ");
         }
         /*********************************************** Print averages */
o11      printf("\nAvgs    ");
o12      for (seat = 0; seat < SEATS; ++seat)              /* For each seat total */
o13          if (count[seat] != 0)              /* Don't print average if no scores */
o14              printf("  %4.1f", (float) total[seat] / count[seat]);
             else
o15              printf("      ");
o16      printf("\n");              /* End with cursor at the beginning of a new line */
     }
```

In designing the test, we have chosen simple values that are easy to validate by hand. We have made sure that each row position and seat position is represented, as well as having blanks in the grid. To make testing easier, we have initialized a few of the variables. After the tests are concluded, the declaration of the array in `main()` should be changed to

```
int grades[ROWS][SEATS] = {0};
```

The output below shows one of the tests. The one factor that this test does *not* show is inputs to validate that a blank average will be printed if no scores exist in that seat position. That test was made and the program passed.

Output

```
Enter row seat (0 0 to quit): 1 3
Enter score: 17
Enter row seat: 4 2
Enter score: 19
Enter row seat: 3 3
Enter score: 15
Enter row seat: 3 2
Enter score: 20
Enter row seat: 0 0

Seat         1     2     3
Row 1       20          17
    2       18
    3       16    20    15
    4             19

Avgs      18.0  19.5  16.0
```

SUMMARY

▲**KEY TERMS** (in order of appearance)

Array	Parallel array
Element	Insert
Index	Bubble sort
Sequential search	Swap
Binary search	Flag

EXECUTION CHART

Line	Explanation	main():		grades[4][3]		
1	Call *input()*, pass address of *grades* array.			20	0	0
				18	0	0
				16	0	0
				0	0	0

Line	Explanation	input():	row	seat	scores[][3]		
i1	Input *row* and *seat*.		1	3	20	0	0
					18	0	0
					16	0	0
					0	0	0
i2	Continue while *row* not equal to zero.		1	3	Same		
i3	Check for valid range.		1	3	Same		
i4	Input score into *scores[0][2]*.		1	3	20	0	17
					18	0	0
					16	0	0
					0	0	0
i7	Input *row* and *seat*.		4	2	Same		
i2	Continue while *row* not equal to zero.		4	2	Same		
i3	Check for valid range.		4	2	Same		
i4	Input score into *scores[3][1]*.		4	2	20	0	17
					18	0	0
					16	0	0
					0	19	0
i2–i7	Continue until 0, 0 input. Return.		0	0	20	0	17
					18	0	0
					16	20	15
					0	19	0

Line	Explanation	main():		grades[4][3]		
2	Call *output()*, pass address of *grades* array.			20	0	17
				18	0	0
				16	20	15
				0	19	0

Line	Explanation	output():	row	seat	total[3]			count[3]			scores[][3]		
o1	Print heading.		?	?	0	0	0	0	0	0	20	0	17
											18	0	0
											16	20	15
											0	19	0
o2	Loop through rows.		0	?	0	0	0	0	0	0	Same		
o3	Print side heading for each row.		0	?	0	0	0	0	0	0	Same		
o4	Loop through seats.		0	0	0	0	0	0	0	0	Same		
o5	Value of *scores[0][0]* not zero.		0	0	0	0	0	0	0	0	Same		
o7	Print score.		0	0	0	0	0	0	0	0	Same		
o8	Accumulate *scores[0][0]* in *total[0]*.		0	0	20	0	0	0	0	0	Same		
o9	Add 1 to *count[0]*.		0	0	20	0	0	1	0	0	Same		
o10	Drop to next line and indent.		0	0	20	0	0	1	0	0	Same		
o2–10	Continue through nested loop.		4	3	54	39	32	3	2	2	Same		
o11	Drop to next line, print side head.		4	3	54	39	32	3	2	2	Same		
o12	Loop through seats.		4	0	54	39	32	3	2	2	Same		
o13	*count[0]* not zero.		4	0	54	39	32	3	2	2	Same		
o14	Print average for seat 1.		4	0	54	39	32	3	2	2	Same		
o12–15	Continue through seat loop.		4	3	54	39	32	3	2	2	Same		
o16	Drop to next line, return, and end.												

▲CONCEPT REVIEW

▼ An **array** is a collection of **elements**, essentially variables, each of which has a different **index**. An indexed variable may be used anyplace an ordinary variable may be used, and in the same manner.

▼ Arrays are declared as a set by putting the name and the number of elements in a declaration statement. Initializations can accompany declarations by putting the values in braces. For example: float stuff[5] = {2.5, 3.1, 0.6};

▼ If any of the elements of an array are initialized, those that are not initialized become zero.

▼ An index may be any expression. The array element referred to is determined by the value of the expression, meaning that the element can be changed by changing the value of the expression.

▼ Values of array elements may be passed to functions just like values of normal variables, but more commonly we send functions the address of the array using the name so that the function can access any element of the array.

▼ A **sequential search** starts at the beginning of a set of values and continues until a specified value is found or the end of the set is reached.

▼ A **binary search** works on an ordered set of values and eliminates half the values with each comparison.

▼ **Parallel arrays** allow us to work with different characteristics of an item, typically with different data types. Any operation performed on one array is also performed on the other to keep them parallel.

▼ An **insert** adds a value to an ordered set.

▼ A sort, such as **bubble sort**, puts an unordered set in order. The operation involves **swapping** values of adjacent array elements. We can make a bubble sort more efficient by setting up a **flag** to till us if a swap has been made or not.

▼ Variables may have many indexes. They can be viewed as arrays of arrays, stored in an order that reflects the last index varying first.

▼ A notation that does not include all the indexes indicates the address of that subarray within the array.

▼ Arrays with more than one index are declared with sets of brackets containing the number of indexes in each position. They can be initialized by putting values in braces in the declaration. By using nested braces, we can tell the compiler specifically which values belong to which subarray.

▼ When multiple indexes are used in the formal parameters of a function declaration, all indexes except the first are explicitly stated.

▼ C indexes always start with zero.

▼ An array must be of a single data type.

▼ The last valid index is 1 less than the number in the declaration.

▼ Initializing at least one element sets all the uninitialized elements to zero.

▼ Avoid floating-point subscripts.

▼ An array name references the address of an array.

▼ An array passed by its name can be modified in a function.

▼ When inserting, declare an array one larger than the current set. *In an insert, the array must accommodate the number of values after the insert.*

▼ Test the boundary conditions when testing any code.

▼ In a sort, declare the array for the number of values in the set. *A sort adds no values to the list.*

▼ Each index must have its own set of brackets.

▼ A double-indexed array is an array of arrays.

▼ Array notation with the last index missing is an address.

▼ The last index varies first.

▼ Notice how this form makes the declaration clearer. *Initializing a double-indexed array in rows and columns maintains the table-like quality of such an array.*

▼ All elements of an array must be of the same data type. *This includes the arrays-within-the-array in a multiple-indexed array.*

▲TRAPS: COMMON PROGRAMMING ERRORS

▼ `short sales[7] = {1};` does not initialize all the elements to 1.

▼ Going out of the array's range.

▼ Using a plausible value for a sentinel.

▲YOUR TURN ANSWERS

▼7–1

1. An indexed variable, like any other variable, has its own name, its own value, and its own place in memory.

2. Changing the index, changes the element or variable referred to.

3. An array is a set of indexed elements of the same data type. In C all the elements will be contiguous in memory.

4. One reason for using arrays is to create a large number of variables. Another is so that we can change the variable name in our program by changing the value of the index.

5. Indexed variable sets in C always start with the index zero.

6. Ten variables are allocated with; the last index being 9, that is, *stuff[9]*.

7. *stuff[1]* will be 2.2. Since only *stuff[0]*, *stuff[1]*, and *stuff[2]* have initialization values, *stuff[3]* will be zero. *stuff[5]*, while we can actually access it, is beyond the end of the array, so its value is garbage.

8. It would have no specific value because the array element is not determined. If *what* was 2, for example, the value of *stuff[what]* would be 3.3.

9. An index will be an integral data type. If a floating-point value is given, it is truncated to an integer.

▼**7–2**

1. By passing all the values in the array as separate values, and by passing the array address using the array name.

2. It declares only an array prefix to hold the address passed to it by the function call.

3. Since both names are the same address, changes in the elements in the called function will also change the corresponding elements in the calling function. They are the same memory spaces.

▼**7–3**

1. In a sequential search, you step through a list of values, starting from the first, comparing each in turn with the desired value.

2. The sequential search ends when the value from the list matches the desired value or the end of the list is reached, indicating that the desired value is not in the list.

3. A binary search eliminates half the range of values with each test.

4. The values must be in order for a binary search to work.

5. Parallel arrays allow us to keep different types of data on the same group of items. We ensure that the arrays remain parallel by performing the same operations, such as swapping, on one as we do the other.

6. At least one more than the number of values in the list before inserting.

7. The first possible insert position will be the element one beyond the end of the assigned list. The last to be considered is the second position. If the insert isn't completed by that time, the value must belong in the first position.

8. A sort array must have at least as many elements as there are values to sort.

9. Nine. One less than the number of values in the list. At that point the first one must be in the right place.

1. Yes, by using more than one index.

2. *stuff[2]* is the address of the third array—*stuff[2][0]* through *stuff[2][2]*.

3. By enclosing the values for each subarray in its own set of braces.

4. All but the first index are filled in. The organization of the array is shown but not its size.

5. Leaving off the last index in the call will pass the address of the array within the array. The function's formal parameters will naturally have to declare the address of an array with one less index.

EXERCISES

1. Write appropriate array declarations for the following:
   a. The *prices* of products 1 through 10.
   b. A *customer_data* array that stores height, weight, and shoe size of 10 customers.
   c. A *scores* array for students by row and seat in three different classes.
   d. An array to store *sales* for 10 product numbers sold in 4 sales regions over a 5-year period.

2. Show the declaration for a *things* array of 10 `double` elements that also initializes the first element to 0, the second to 2.5, and all the rest to zero.

3. How many addressable elements has each of the arrays declared in the following?
   a. `int x[5][2];`
   b. `long double f[5][2][4][3];`
   c. `short a[] = {4, 2, 3, 8};`
   d. `float z[5] = {3.1, 2.8};`

4. What is wrong with the following declarations?
   a. `long double x[2][12] = {{25}, {0}};`
   b. `long x[2, 6];`
   c. `float q[2][3] = {2.1, 3.3};`
   c. `char c[3] = {'a', 'b', 'c', 'd'};`

5. Find the error in the following code segment and tell what error indication will be given.
   ```
   int count, array[5] = {1, 2, 3, 4, 5};
   for (count = 1; count <= 5; ++count)
       printf("%i\n", array[count]);
   ```

6. Given the following declarations, which statements are invalid and why?

```
double one[10], two[5][5], value = 1.0;
```
   a. `two[3][0] = 25;`   b. `value = two[3][5];`
   c. `printf("%f\n", two[1]);`   d. `one[2] = two[3][4];`

7. Would the following code segment run? If it did and you entered 46, what would the output be?

```
float x[3] = {0};

printf("Enter a number: ");
scanf("%f", x);
printf("%f, %f, %f\n", x[0], x[1], x[2]);
```

8. Why is the following search loop inadequate?

```
while (values[count] != search_value)
    ++count;
```

9. How would you set up variables for floating-point *pressure* values for each of your integrally numbered *tires* (1 through 5, don't forget the spare) on your car?

10. Rewrite the binary search program from the text so that it works with a list in descending (high to low) order rather than its current ascending order. Change the declaration of the array to

```
float length[PIPES] = {3.8, 3.7, 3.1, 2.6, 2.2, 1.9,
1.3, 1.2, 0.8};
```

11. What is the problem with this insert segment?

```
pos = 4;
while (insert_value < val[pos] && pos > 1)
```

12. Given the declaration `float  stuff[10];` correct this bubble sort segment.

```
        last = VALUES_TO_SORT;
        while (last >= 0 && swap)
        {   swap = 1;
            for (position = 0; position <= last; ++position)
                if (value[position] < value[position + 1])
                {   temp = value[position];
                    value[position + 1] = value[position];
                    value[position + 1] = temp;
                    swap = 0;
                }
            ++last;
        }
```

13. Rewrite the sort program from the text so that it sorts in descending (high to low) order rather than ascending.

14. You want to pass the array `double  array[10];` to the function *func()*, which uses the identifier *arr* to receive the array. Assuming no

return value, show the call to *func()* and the first line of the definition of *func()*.

15. Show the output from this program:

```c
#include <stdio.h>

void main(void)
{   int array[3][2] = {{6, 2},
                       {3, 5},
                       {1, 7}};
    int r, c;

    for (r = 0; r < 2; ++r)
    {   for (c = 0; c < 3; ++c)
            printf("%i   ", array[c][r]);
        printf("\n");
    }
}
```

16. Rewrite the previous program so that the printout (the nested `for` loops) is done in a separate function *print()*. Use the same variables in *print()* as were used in `main()`.

PROGRAMS

1. Modify ⇨Program 7–1 in the text to input the sales values and print out their total. You will no longer need the initialization of the *sales* array.

2. Write a program to input a set of five numbers and print them out in the reverse order of input. Put both the input and printing in loops.

Variables

```
numbers[]
counter
```

Output

```
Input five numbers:
1? 28.47
2? .0021
3? 7492
4? 12.5
5? 6
Here they are:  6   12.5   7492   0.0021   28.47
```

3. Write a program that accepts input of five values from the keyboard and prints out the values and their difference from the mean (average) value.

Variables

```
value[]
mean        Also use for the total
count
```

Output

```
Enter 5 values separated by whitespace.
46.2 12.6 32.654 6 25.44
Number     Value  Difference
     1     46.20       21.62
     2     12.60      -11.98
     3     32.65        8.08
     4      6.00      -18.58
     5     25.44        0.86
```

4. Modify ⇨Program 7–2 so that the `main()` function contains only declarations and calls to *input_data()* and *print_report()*. Write the appropriate functions.

5. Write a program that adds two four-element arrays together. The first array should be initialized with values 1, 2, 3, and 4; the second, with values 5, 6, 7, 8. Both arrays should be passed to the function *add_arrays()*, which adds corresponding variables of each array together and leaves the results in the second array. The second array should then be printed out by the `main()` function.

Functions and Variables

```
main()                add_arrays()
  array1[]              a1[], a2[]
  array2[]              counter
  counter
```

Output

```
Resultant array: 6 8 10 12
```

6. Modify the *RANDOM* program from Chapter 6 to replace the accumulators with an array of accumulators. The program should be much shorter, but the output should be similar.

Functions and Variables

```
numbers[]    Accumulators
count        Loop counter
rnd()        Integer between 1 and 5
```

7. Write a function that merges two ordered integer arrays into a third ordered array. The two arrays should be able to contain any number of nonnegative values. The last value in each array should be the sentinel value, −1. This value should also be placed at the end of the merged array. For test purposes, use `main()` driver below. Test again by swapping the array initialization values.

Functions and Variables

```
merge()
  array1[], array2[], merged[]
  sub1, sub2, sub_m        Subscripts for the three arrays
```

Driver

```
void main(void)
{   int array1[] = {1, 4, 6, -1};          /* 2nd test {2, 3, 5, 7, 8, -1} */
    int array2[] = {2, 3, 5, 7, 8, -1};          /* 2nd test {1, 4, 6, -1} */
    int sub = 0, merged[50];

    merge(array1, array2, merged);
    while (merged[sub] != -1)
        printf("%i ", merged[sub++]);        /* Increment sub after printing */
    printf("\n");
}
```

Output

```
1 2 3 4 5 6 7 8
```

8. Write a program that will initialize an array of characters to *ABCDE* and allow you to shift, in circular fashion, those characters to the right any number of places you specify. The shifting should be done in the function *shift()*, but all the printouts should be from `main()`.

Functions and Variables

main()	shift()	
chrs[]	chrs[]	
places	places	
count	count	
	temp[]	To store a copy of the array

Outputs

```
Before shifting: ABCDE
Shift how many places? 2
After shifting: DEABC
```

(continued)

```
Before shifting: ABCDE
Shift how many places? 8
After shifting: CDEAB

Before shifting: ABCDE
Shift how many places? 5
After shifting: ABCDE

Before shifting: ABCDE
Shift how many places? 41
After shifting: EABCD
```

9. Rewrite the sequential search example so that the search is a separate function. This function should work with an array of any number of `int` elements, but you will have to pass it the number of elements. It should return the index of the element found, or −1 if the value was not found.

10. Rewrite the binary search program example to allow you to identify the bin number, an integer, of a piece of pipe. Once the pipe is found, the bin number is printed out. Use parallel arrays to associate a bin number with a pipe length.

11. Bargain Benny's Used Car Emporium is having its fourth annual going-out-of-business sale and wants to gives its salespeople up-to-the-minute information on cars no longer in stock. To do this, a list of stock numbers, in numerical order, of sold cars is posted. Write a program for them that will allow a stock number to be input, inserted in the list, and a new list printed each time a car is sold. The program should handle up to 20 sales a day. Input stock number 0 to get out of the program.

Variables

`stock[]`	Array of stock numbers
`sold`	Input for stock number sold
`total_sold`	Number of cars sold (and end of *stock* array)
`position`	Insert loop counter variable

Output

```
What number sold? 71132
    Sold: 71132
What number sold? 38814
    Sold: 38814  71132
What number sold? 41825
    Sold: 38814  41825  71132
What number sold? 0
```

12. Write a program that accepts any number of values (up to 100) from the terminal and sorts them in descending order (highest number first). Use some alpha character, such as *q*, to end input.

Variables

Choose appropriate variables

Output

```
Input numbers, type 0 to end input
> 27
> 92
> -116
> 41
> .007
> -.007
> 0
HERE THEY ARE IN DESCENDING ORDER
 92  41  27  0.007 -0.007 -116
```

13. A sample of 11 packages from a day's run of a packing machine are weighed and the weights input into the computer. Write a program that figures the mean and median weight. The mean is the total weight divided by 11. The median is the middle (sixth) value of the ordered set of weights.

Variables

```
weight[]
bottom, position, temp, swap    Sort variables
total                           Total weight accumulator
```

Output

```
Enter 11 weights:
 1> 10.4
 2> 10.2
 3> 10.3
 4> 9.8
 5> 9.8
 6> 10.4
 7> 10.3
 8> 10.3
 9> 10.1
10> 9.9
11> 10.1
The mean is 10.14545
The median is 10.2
```

14. Modify the preceding program to show the mode (the value occurring most frequently). (*Hint:* After ordering the values, compare each with the next and add to a counter if the values are the same. When a different value is reached, start the counter over again.) Assume there is only one mode.

Additional Variables

```
mode
mode_occurrences    Number of times the mode occurs
value_occurrences   Number of occurrences of a particular value
```

Addition to Output

```
The mode is 10.3
```

15. Modify the preceding program so that it works with 12 weights. The median is now the mean of the two middle (sixth and seventh) values.

Output

```
Enter 12 weights:
 1> 10.4
 2> 10.2
 3> 10.3
 4> 9.8
 5> 9.8
 6> 10.4
 7> 10.3
 8> 10.3
 9> 10.1
10> 9.9
11> 10.1
12> 10.2
The mean is 10.15
The median is 10.2
The mode is 10.3
```

16. Write a function, *sort_float()*, that will sort any array of floats in either ascending or descending order. You will have to pass the function the address of the array, its size, and either the character *A* for ascending order or any other character for descending order. Show it tested with an appropriate `main()` driver that declares and initializes an array, prints the unsorted array, sorts it, and prints it after sorting.

17. Write a program that deals a hand of five cards. To make it accurate, you will have to start with a deck (an array) of 52 cards and shuffle the deck. In a *shuffle()* function, set up your deck numbered from 1 to 52 and another deck with numbers randomly assigned. Sort the random deck and, with each swap in the sort, also swap corresponding

cards in the real deck. When the random deck is in order, the real deck will be random. Use the function *show_card()* to print the suit and number of each card.

Functions and Variables

Choose appropriate variables

Sample Outputs

```
Your hand: Queen-Diamonds Queen-Hearts 8-Clubs 4-Clubs 7-Spades

Your hand: 5-Spades Ace-Hearts 10-Clubs King-Diamonds 4-Hearts
```

18. Skewed Opinion Research, Inc., sent out survey questionnaires with three questions. Each question was to be answered on a 1 to 5 scale, 1 meaning "awful" and 5 meaning "fantastic." Write a program that will allow input of the data, store it in a two-dimensional array, and print out the average response to each question. The program should handle any number of questionnaires (up to 20). Entry of the sentinel value zero should end the input loop.

Suggested Variables

response[ ][ ]	To store responses to the questionnaires
question	Question number (0, 1, or 2)
questionnaire	Questionnaire number
total[ ]	Accumulators for figuring question averages

Output

```
Input three responses for each:
Questionnaire 1? 4 2 5
Questionnaire 2? 1 4 1
Questionnaire 3? 3 5 2
Questionnaire 4? 3 1 2
Questionnaire 5? 3 3 4
Questionnaire 6? 2 2 3
Questionnaire 7? 5 2 1
Questionnaire 8? 3 2 4
Questionnaire 9? 0

Average response for question 1 is: 3.000
Average response for question 2 is: 2.625
Average response for question 3 is: 2.750
```

19. Channel 117's weatherman and cooking commentator has been keeping track of daily high temperatures for each day of the last four

weeks. Write a program that will initialize an array with this data, and allow him to put in a temperature range and print out all the days (week number and day number) that have high temperatures in this range.

20. The wackos in the lab, with unlimited government funding, have decided to experiment with growing green slime mold. They started with five samples, carefully identified with distinct sample IDs, all weighing 1.0 gram. They subjected these samples to various conditions over five days, measuring their weights at the end of each day. Write a program that initializes a double-subscripted array, *slime*, to their results. Use the first variable in each subarray as the sample ID. If the test results don't match their expectations, naturally they want to be able to change the test results.

Your program should print out a table of their results using the function *print_table()*, allow them to change any result using the function *change_table()*, and print a new table. The *change_table()* function will have to search the table for the correct ID. This search should be in a separate function, *sample_row()*, that returns the correct row or −1 if the ID could not be found. The *change_table()* function should print out "Invalid day" or "Invalid ID" if either is the case.

Variables, and Constants

Choose appropriate ones

Output

```
Sample Days: 1    2    3    4    5
       417    1.2  1.8  2.7  4.0  5.6
       244    1.0  1.0  1.0  3.8  8.2
       106    1.1  1.2  1.3  1.2  0.6
       333    0.9  0.7  0.5  0.2  0.0
       822    0.8  1.2  2.6  4.9  8.8
Change sample ID day: 333 5
Change 0.0 to what? .1
Sample Days: 1    2    3    4    5
       417    1.2  1.8  2.7  4.0  5.6
       244    1.0  1.0  1.0  3.8  8.2
       106    1.1  1.2  1.3  1.2  0.6
       333    0.9  0.7  0.5  0.2  0.1
       822    0.8  1.2  2.6  4.9  8.8
```

Chapter 8

STRINGS

PREVIEW

Most of our programming up to this point has been with numeric values. Here we will discuss character values and strings. After studying this chapter you should know:

▼ How C stores and interprets string values.

▼ How we accomplish variable storage of strings.

▼ Ways to input and output strings.

▼ Different ways of manipulating strings.

▼ How we store arrays of strings.

▼ How to convert between strings and numbers.

▼ How to classify characters and convert from one classification to another.

▼ How we use variables to store addresses.

▼ Methods of separating strings into component parts.

A string is a collection of characters—any characters, as long as they are part of the character coding scheme, such as ASCII, used on your computer. The computer itself attaches no special significance to the characters in the string; in fact, we saw in Chapter 2 that the computer can't even tell the difference between characters and numbers. It is only our instructions that tell it how to interpret a set of bits in storage.

STRING VALUES

We have used string values before in the control strings of both `scanf()` and `printf()`. They were collections of characters enclosed in quotes. Let us examine how these characters are actually stored in memory. We know that the characters are stored as sets of bits, and that each character takes up one byte (eight bits). Each character, then, is data type `char`. Putting a string value in our source code directs C to allocate memory for those characters—an array of `char`s. `"Algonquin"` in our source code will cause the C compiler to allocate memory like this:

Like any other array, the string is identified by its base address, the address of the first value (character, in this case). Also, like any other array, once the memory is allocated, we are left with the problem of how to tell where the string ends in memory. C solves the problem by putting a null character (`'\0'`) in the memory location immediately following the last character of the string. When we ask C to perform some process on a string, displaying it perhaps, it starts at the base address and reads characters until it reaches a null.

But where is this base address? As with variables, we will probably never know, nor do we care as long as C can keep track of it. In our diagram, we showed FFF0, but that was just a guess.

The notation for the address of a string value is the string value itself—the characters in double quotes. The string value `"Algonquin"` is the address where C has chosen to store the string—it is the address of a set of `char` values. In our diagram, it was FFF0.

String Values Versus Character Values

In Chapter 2 we were introduced to character values such as `'A'`, `'f'`, and `'\t'`. These, we saw, were simply numbers—the ASCII (or EBCDIC) values of the character codes. In fact, they were of type `int`, although we could certainly store them in `char` variables if we wanted.

There is a significant difference between the character `'A'` and the string `"A"`. The former is an integer with the value 65 (in ASCII) that takes up two or four bytes depending on the size of an integer in a particular C. The latter is the address of an array of two `char`s, the first with the value 65 (*A* in ASCII), and the second with the value zero (the null character, `\0`).

STRING VARIABLES

As we mentioned back in Chapter 2, there aren't any string variables. But we have seen that a string value is stored as an array of `char`s, that is, beginning at some address in memory, continuing in contiguous memory locations, and terminated by a null. Let us follow that pattern, then, and store our string in an array of `char` variables.

Declaration and Initialization

In deciding on a declaration of a `char` array, we must consider the largest string we might have to store in it, because C will allocate the space and then probably allocate something else right next to it. Also, C will not prevent us from overwriting what we consider the end of the string; in other words, writing into the space allocated for the next variable or whatever.

If we are declaring a `char` array for names and most of them are "John", "Maria", "Edna", and such, but one person might be named "Cadwallader", then we must allocate at least 12 characters of space for the string. Twelve? There are only 11 characters in "Cadwallader." Remember that C considers a string as starting at some memory address and ending in a null character. We must leave an extra space for the null character.

```
char name[12];
```

This allocates 12 variables, *name[0]* through *name[11]*. They have no meaningful values yet, but we can initialize them at the time of their declaration.

```
char name[12] = {'Z', 'e', 'l', 'd', 'a'};
```

We have assigned values to the first five variables of the array. The rest of the variables in the array, since we have initialized the first few, will be assigned the value zero, which, not entirely coincidentally, is the null character.

name[0]   name[2]   name[4]   name[6]   name[8]   name[10]
  name[1]   name[3]   name[5]   name[7]   name[9]   name[11]

Remember from Chapter 7 that the name of an array refers to its address in memory. We now have a string value in memory beginning at the address *name*, FFF0 in the example, and ending at the first null at FFF5. We can refer to it as the *name* array or, since we are using it to store a set of characters, the *name* string.

The same declaration could have been accomplished this way:

```
char name[12] = {90, 101, 108, 100, 97};
```

using the ASCII values for the characters, but it is a bit easier to understand using the former method.

The same declaration and initialization could also be accomplished this way:

```
char name[12] = "Zelda";
```

C would interpret the quoted string as five character values and store them in the first five variables of *name*, setting the rest to null.

We should mention that a declaration could also be made this way:

```
char name[] = "Zelda";
```

leaving out the number of variables in brackets. This would differ from the previous declaration of *name* because only six variables, *name[0]* through *name[5]*, would be allocated (remember the null; C does).

STRING ASSIGNMENTS

Since strings are sets of separate variables for each character, we can assign them one character at a time.

```
void main(void)
{  char name[12];

   name[0] = 'Z';
   name[1] = 'e';
   name[2] = 'l';
   name[3] = 'd';
   name[4] = 'a';
   name[5] = '\0';
}
```

We have been careful to explicitly assign the null character at the end of the string. Without it, a typical string operation would start with *Z* and continue until some garbage character in memory happened to be the null character.

We could not have done this:

```
name = "Zelda";
```

Even though the statement is similar to that in our earlier declaration, it is interpreted quite differently. In this case, `"Zelda"` refers to the address where the string is stored in memory, and not to the individual characters. The notation `name` also refers to an address—the address of the 12-variable `char` array—but `name` is not a variable; it cannot be assigned.

In essence, assigning a string must be done a character at a time. We will see, however, that there are a wealth of ANSI C functions that we can call on to do this for us.

TRAP

Attempting to assign a string value (address) to an array prefix.

HEADS UP!

An array name cannot be assigned.

YOUR TURN 8–1

1. Since there is no string data type in C, in what data type do we store strings?
2. Where does a string value stored in memory begin and end?
3. How does the string value "A" differ from the character value 'A'?
4. In what kind of variables do we store strings?
5. How does C ensure that we do not assign strings to unallocated locations?
6. What is the difference between these four declarations?

```
char name[12] = {'Z', 'e', 'l', 'd', 'a'};
char name[12] = {90, 101, 108, 100, 97};
char name[12] = "Zelda";
char name[] = "Zelda";
```

7. How are strings assigned in C?

STRING INPUT

TRAP

Putting a & in front of an array name in `scanf()`.

We have used the `scanf()` function to input numbers and individual characters. We can also use it to input strings using the `%s` conversion code. In its arguments, `scanf()` expects to find addresses. The name of a character array *is* an address, and it is typically used to provide an argument for `%s`, in which case there is no need for an `&` to convert it to an address.

```
scanf("%s", name);
```

The function will take a set of characters from the input stream (from the current position to the next whitespace) and write them beginning at the address *name*. It will also add a null at the end of the characters to maintain C's concept of a string. If our previous assignment to *name* had been *Zelda* and we typed in *Ed*, memory would look like this:

E	d	\0	d	a	\0	\0	\0	\0	\0	\0	\0				

FFF0 FFF1 FFF2 FFF3 FFF4 FFF5 FFF6 FFF7 FFF8 FFF9 FFFA FFFB FFFC FFFD FFFE FFFF

name[0] name[2] name[4] name[6] name[8] name[10]
  name[1] name[3] name[5] name[7] name[9] name[11]

Part of *Zelda* is still lying around, but it makes no difference because C's string ends at the first null, in FFF2.

In ⇨Program 8–1, `scanf()` is used to input both a number and a string. The *out_string()* function prints out the value of the string by moving through the elements in the **char** array until the character is a null.

⇨Program 8–1

```c
#include <stdio.h>

#define LENGTH 10

void out_string(char string[]);                          /* Prints string */

void main(void)
{   char product[LENGTH];
    float price;

    printf("Enter price and product: ");
    scanf("%f %s", &price, product);      /* & with price but not product */
    printf("The price of a ");
    out_string(product);
    printf(" is %.2f.\n", price);
}

void out_string(char string[]) /*************************** Prints string */
{   int index = 0;

    while (string[index] != '\0')         /* Null at the end of the string */
    {   printf("%c", string[index]);                    /* Print character */
        ++index;                              /* Move to the next character */
    }
}
```

Outputs

```
Enter price and product: 12.98 widget
The price of a widget is 12.98.

Enter price and product: 12.98, widget
The price of a , is 12.98.
```

HEADS UP!

Know how `scanf()` works.

TRAP

Assigning characters beyond the space allocated for the string.

In the second execution, we tried to use the comma as a delimiter between the two values input. Comma, an inappropriate character for a number, ended that conversion, but the comma was left in the input stream. Since comma is appropriate for a string, C started the string at the comma and went to the next whitespace, including only the comma in the string.

The *product* array has 10 elements, meaning that we can effectively store only 9 characters. What if we type in a 15-character product name? It will be assigned, overflowing the space allocated for the *product* array and messing up something else. We can limit the number of characters that will be converted by putting a width modifier in front of the *s* type code—**%ws**. For example,

```
scanf("%9s", product);
```

will stop conversion at the first whitespace or a maximum of 9 characters. If it reaches the maximum, characters left over remain in the stream. For the string *product*, 9 was appropriate because it is a 10-element array but one must contain the null.

Whitespace is the default delimiter for `scanf()`, which means that inputting a single string with whitespace in it is not possible. If there might be two-word product names, such as *red shoes*, we would have to use something other than `scanf()`, as presented here, to input the product.

Now that we know something about strings, we can better appreciate the `scanf()` function:

```
int scanf(char *control_string, arguments)        <stdio.h>
```

The notation `char *control_string` is new to us. The asterisk in front of the *control_string* indicates that the *control_string* is the address of a `char` variable. In this case, it is the address of the first in an array of `char` elements—in other words, a string.

We saw in Chapter 3 that we could input a single character using `scanf()`'s `%c` code. This code would assign the ASCII value of any character—whitespace or whatever—to its corresponding variable. The **getchar()** function is quite similar. It returns a single character from the input stream. It has the form

```
int getchar(void)                                 <stdio.h>
```

It has no value passed to it, but the value it returns is the next character from the input stream and, like `scanf("%c", . . .)` all characters are accepted by `getchar()`, even the newline. If an end-of-file condition is encountered (this will be more likely when we use a form of `scanf()` for files in Chapter 9), the return value is the constant EOF defined defined in `stdio.h`.

We used the `getchar()` function in Chapter 3 to flush the input stream:

```
while (getchar() != '\n');        /* Flush stdin stream */
```

Now would be a good time to discuss it.

We looked at `while` in Chapter 5. In the flushing loop, there is nothing in the body of the loop, but the condition calls the `getchar()` function. With each test of the condition, we get another character from the input stream until we get the newline at the end of the stream, making the condition false. At that point, the stream will be empty.

As we know, nothing in C will stop you from assigning characters to memory locations beyond the end of the allocated array. Let us use the `getchar()` function to write our own function, *in_line()*, that will assign an entire input line to an array, but ensure that we do not overflow the array. In ⇨Program 8–2, we will send the function the address of a string and its declared length. The function will take characters from the input stream and assign them to the string until either the newline in the stream is read or the string's index has reached the allocated length − 2. Since we must save room for the null at the end of the string, we can only assign length − 1 characters, and because the index starts at zero, its value will be length − 2 at that point.

⇨**Program 8–2**

```
#include <stdio.h>
#define LENGTH 10

void in_line(char line[], int max);              /* Inputs line */
void out_string(char string[]);                  /* Prints string */

void main(void)
{   char string[LENGTH];

    printf("Your input> ");
    in_line(string, LENGTH);
    while (string[0] != '\0')
    {   printf("    Stored: ");
        out_string(string);
        printf("\nYour input> ");
        in_line(string, LENGTH);
    }
}
```

(continued)

```
void in_line(char line[], int max) /**** Inputs line but does not exceed */
                                     /* the length of the allocated array */
{   int index = 0;

    line[index] = getchar();
    while (line[index] != '\n' && index < max - 1)
    {   ++index;
        line[index] = getchar();
    }
    if (line[index] != '\n')                     /* If not at end of stream */
        while (getchar() != '\n');                            /* Flush it */
    line[index] = '\0';                      /* Put null at end of string */
}

void out_string(char string[]) /************************* Prints string */
{   int index = 0;

    while (string[index] != '\0')            /* Null at the end of the string */
    {   printf("%c", string[index]);                       /* Print character */
        ++index;                              /* Move to the next character */
    }
}
```

Output

```
Your input> Hi there
    Stored: Hi there
Your input> Is virtual reality really real?
    Stored: Is virtua
Your input>
```

Note that the return value of getchar() is an int, but we are assigning it to an element of a char array. C will make that conversion for us, but that int data type will become important to us when we use a form of getchar() with files in Chapter 9.

The **gets()** function is quite similar to the *in_line()* function above except that it does not limit the number of characters assigned to the string.

```
char *gets(char *string)                              <stdio.h>
```

If the call to the function is successful, the return value is the address of the *string* that was passed to the function. If not, it returns the NULL address. **NULL** is an address defined in stdio.h. Notice that it is written in all capital letters and has no relation whatsoever with the null character, which we symbolize with '\0'.

With the gets() function—or *in_line()*—it is very important to know what is in the input stream before the call, especially after a call to

HEADS UP!

NULL is not null.

`scanf()`. Whitespace is the default delimiter in `scanf()`, and newline qualifies as whitespace. Typically, `scanf()` leaves the newline in the input stream after it finishes. When `gets()` executes and you are expecting the program to stop while you enter the secrets of life, `gets()` sees the newline, which it interprets as an empty string—perfectly acceptable to it—and it assigns the empty string to the secrets of life, and the program goes on without stopping. To be sure that the input buffer is empty before the call to `gets()`, you may want to flush the `stdin` stream.

The `gets()` function, like `scanf()`, does not know how many characters are allocated to a string. If you declare `char s[10]` and input 40 characters in a `gets(s)` call, C will happily write beyond the end of the allocated string space, gleefully messing up anything that was there before. Also, don't forget, `char s[10]` will only accommodate a nine-character string; the last character must be a null.

STRING OUTPUT

Like `scanf()`, we have used `printf()` to work with single characters using the `%c` conversion code. The `%s` conversion code outputs an entire string. Its argument must be an address of an array of `char`s and it will print all the values from that address to the end of the string—the first null character. ⇨Program 8–3 shortens ⇨Program 8–1 considerably by replacing the loop in which we printed out single characters with a single `printf()` conversion.

⇨**Program 8–3**

```
#include <stdio.h>

#define LENGTH 10

void main(void)
{   char product[LENGTH];
    float price;

    printf("Enter price and product: ");
    scanf("%f %s", &price, product);
    printf("The price of a %s is %.2f.\n", product, price);
}
```

Output

```
Enter price and product: 12.98 widget
The price of a widget is 12.98.
```

The string conversion code for `printf()` uses many of the same modifiers as those for numbers,

```
                    %flag width.precision s
```

with any of them being optional. If *precision* is used, it must always have the dot preceding it.

The *width* modifier states the minimum number of characters to be printed. If the string is too short, leading blanks are added—remember, right justification is the default. Too many characters will extend the length of the field, just as it does with numbers. The *precision* argument states the maximum number of characters. Long strings will be chopped off at the end.

By default, outputs are right-justified. We can change that to left justification by putting a **flag**, a dash, just after the %.

⇨Program 8–4 and its output are lined up so that you can see which line produced what.

⇨Program 8–4   **Output**

```
#include <stdio.h>

void main(void)
{  char item[20] = "Flange";

   printf("X%sX\n", item);           XFlangeX
   printf("X%8sX\n", item);          X  FlangeX
   printf("X%-8sX\n", item);         XFlange  X
   printf("X%4sX\n", item);          XFlangeX
   printf("X%4.4sX\n", item);        XFlanX
   printf("X%4.3sX\n", item);        X FlaX
}
```

The **putchar()** function is the output counterpart of `getchar()`.

```
int putchar(int character)                          <stdio.h>
```

Its return value is the value of the *character* passed to it if it is successful; otherwise, it is EOF. The function puts a single character on the screen much like `printf("%c", character)` would.

The **puts()** function is the output counterpart to `gets()`. While `gets()` gets a single line from the input stream and stores it as a single string, `puts()` takes a single string and sends it to the output stream—the screen. The null character is replaced with newline so that the cursor will drop down to the next line after the string is printed.

```
int puts(char *string)                              <stdio.h>
```

The return value is nonnegative if it is successful, EOF if not.

1. What two functions can we use to read strings typed in at the keyboard?

2. How can we ensure that we do not go beyond the space allocated for a string when the string is assigned using `scanf()`? What hazards does it involve?

3. How can we establish our own delimiters using `scanf()`?

4. In what two ways can we input a single character from the input stream? How do their actions differ?

5. What two functions can we use to display strings?

6. What does the *precision* parameter do in `printf()`?

7. What does the dash flag do in `printf()`?

8. How does the `puts()` function act differently from `printf("%s", . . .)`?

9. In what two ways can we display single characters? How do their actions differ?

STRING MANIPULATIONS

HEADS UP!

Most C functions will allow you to write beyond the space allocated for a string.

Now that we know how strings are stored, we can perform all kinds of operations on them—print them out, assign values to them, take them apart, reassemble them, and so forth. To make life easier for us, ANSI C includes a group of functions to do many of these manipulations for us. Common to all these functions is C's concept of a string—a group of contiguous characters starting at some address and ending with a null character. Also common to most of them is that C does nothing to stop you from assigning characters beyond the memory locations allocated for an individual string. You must take care of that yourself.

We could determine the length of a string, the number of characters in it, by starting at its base address and moving a character at a time until we found the null character. That is what the ANSI **strlen()** function does.

```
size_t strlen(char *string)                    <string.h>
```

Its return value is the number of characters in the *string*, not including the null at the end. The **size_t** data type is implementation dependent—typically, but not always, an **unsigned int**. It is established in the **string.h** header file (and usually other header files as well).

The **strcpy()** function copies a string from one location to another.

```
char *strcpy(char *destination, char *source) <string.h>
```

This function copies the *source* string, including the terminating null character, to the location of the *destination*. It is up to you to see that there is enough allocated room at the *destination* to accommodate the entire *source* string. The return value is the address of the *destination* string.

The strcpy() function has many uses, but one is to just assign a string value to an array. Remember, a string value is the address of a null-terminated string in memory, so, given the declaration, the following statement will assign *Algonquin* at the location *string*.

```
char string[20];

strcpy(string, "Algonquin");
```

A way to be sure that you do not overflow the space allocated at the *destination* is to use the **strncpy()** function, which copies up to a stated maximum of characters.

```
char *strncpy(char *destination, char *source, size_t max)        <string.h>
```

▶TRAP◀

Not copying a terminating null with strncpy().

This function can be tricky, though. If C encounters a null in the *source* string before it reaches *max* characters, it copies all the characters up to and including the null, leaving the *destination* string with an exact copy of the *source*. Otherwise, C copies the first *max* characters from the *source* string. If those characters include the terminating null, fine. If not, no null is added. ⇨Program 8–5 shows an example of the latter situation.

⇨**Program 8–5**

```
#include <stdio.h>
#include <string.h>

void main(void)
{   char name1[12] = "Albemarle", name2[12] = "Ferdy";

    strncpy(name1, name2, 4);
    printf("%s\n", name1);
}
```

Output

```
Ferdmarle
```

Before Function

A	l	b	e	m	a	r	l	e	\0	\0	\0				
FFE0	FFE1	FFE2	FFE3	FFE4	FFE5	FFE6	FFE7	FFE8	FFE9	FFEA	FFEB	FFEC	FFED	FFEE	FFEF

name1[0] name1[2] name1[4] name1[6] name1[8] name1[10]
　　name1[1] name1[3] name1[5] name1[7] name1[9] name1[11]

F	e	r	d	y	\0	\0	\0	\0	\0	\0	\0				
FFF0	FFF1	FFF2	FFF3	FFF4	FFF5	FFF6	FFF7	FFF8	FFF9	FFFA	FFFB	FFFC	FFFD	FFFE	FFFF

name2[0] name2[2] name2[4] name2[6] name2[8] name2[10]
　　name2[1] name2[3] name2[5] name2[7] name2[9] name2[11]

After Function

F	e	r	d	m	a	r	l	e	\0	\0	\0				
FFE0	FFE1	FFE2	FFE3	FFE4	FFE5	FFE6	FFE7	FFE8	FFE9	FFEA	FFEB	FFEC	FFED	FFEE	FFEF

name1[0] name1[2] name1[4] name1[6] name1[8] name1[10]
　　name1[1] name1[3] name1[5] name1[7] name1[9] name1[11]

F	e	r	d	y	\0	\0	\0	\0	\0	\0	\0				
FFF0	FFF1	FFF2	FFF3	FFF4	FFF5	FFF6	FFF7	FFF8	FFF9	FFFA	FFFB	FFFC	FFFD	FFFE	FFFF

name2[0] name2[2] name2[4] name2[6] name2[8] name2[10]
　　name2[1] name2[3] name2[5] name2[7] name2[9] name2[11]

You could ensure that your string was properly terminated by assigning a null character to the fifth character position of the first string (*name1[4]*).

```
strncpy(name1, name2, 4);
name1[4] = '\0';
printf("%s\n", name1);
```

The **strcat()** function concatenates strings—puts one string at the end of another.

```
char *strcat(char *string, char *add)          <string.h>
```

TRAP

Not enough allocated space at the end of the string to be lengthened.

This function copies the string at *add* to the location of the null in *string*. It overwrites the null in *string* and includes the terminating null at the end of *add*. Be sure there is enough allocated space at the location *string* for all the characters in both strings plus the terminating null. The return value is the address of the combination string, *string*.

```
char first[20] = "Arlo ", last[] = "Bilbao";

printf("%s\n", strcat(first, last));
```

will print

```
Arlo Bilbao
```

and *first* will contain the value *Arlo Bilbao* with a terminating null. The string *Bilbao* is still at the location *last*, of course. Since the return value of strcat() is the address of the concatenated string, it is used as the argument in the printf().

We can limit the number of characters copied from the **add** string with **strncat()**.

```
char *strncat(char *string, char *add, size_t max)                    <string.h>
```

The strncat() function does not have the problem associated with strncpy(); a terminating null is always added at the end of the concatenated string.

Often we must compare two strings to see which is greater. But how do we know whether *Murgatroyd* is greater than *Stella*? Let us examine how C makes the comparison. Each character value is nothing more than a number—the numeric value of its ASCII (or EBCDIC) code. C will compare these individual values character by character, beginning with the first character position (variable) in each string and moving toward the end. C makes the greater-than, less-than decision the first time it finds a difference in the character position it is currently comparing.

Murgatroyd and *Stella* are easy. C compares an *M* (ASCII 77) with an *S* (ASCII 83). The *S* is greater, so *Stella* is greater than *Murgatroyd*. Notice that the number of characters in each string is not significant. The first difference ends the comparison.

How about *Aaron* and *Aardvark*? The first three character positions in each string are the same, but in the fourth position are *o* and *d*. The *o* (111) is greater than the *d* (100) so *Aaron* is greater than *Aardvark*. But *aardvark* is greater than *Aaron* because, in the first character position, *a* (97) is greater than *A* (65). *Bytes* is greater than *Byte* because the *s* in *Bytes* is greater than the null at the end of *Byte*.

Again, ANSI C has saved us from the necessity of writing the string comparison ourselves by providing the **strcmp()** function.

```
int strcmp(char *string1, char *string2)                    <string.h>
```

The two strings are compared and the return value set to a positive value if **string1** is greater, zero if they are equal, or a negative value if **string1** is less.

```
if (strcmp(name, "Muleford") == 0) printf("We have found him!\n");
```

The following statement does us no good at all:

```
if (name == "Muleford") printf("We have found him!\n");
```

because we are simply comparing two addresses, both of which the C compiler assigned based on available space.

HEADS UP!

String comparisons are done one character position at a time.

HEADS UP!

In ASCII, all lowercase characters are greater than any uppercase character.

▶TRAP◀

Comparing two string addresses instead of using strcmp().

Like `strncpy()` and `strncat()`, the **`strncmp()`** function compares only up to *max* characters in each string.

```
int strncmp(char *string1, char *string2, size_t max)                <string.h>
```

⇨Program 8–6 uses a number of the functions just presented. Notice that the *combined* string has only 25 characters allocated to it, making its effective length 24 characters. To ensure that we do not overflow the allocated space, we have limited the number of characters we will concatenate to the end of the string to 24 less the number of characters already in the string. If the strings are equal, we will copy a message to the *combined* string. But again, we do not want to overflow the allocated space, so we used `strncpy()`. Since that function may not copy the terminating null, we specifically put one in the last byte of *combined*.

⇨**Program 8–6**

```c
#include <stdio.h>
#include <string.h>

#define LENGTH 20
#define COMBO 25                        /* Not enough room for 2 full strings */

void main(void)
{   char string1[LENGTH], string2[LENGTH], combined[COMBO];

    printf("Give me two strings and I will put them together\n"
           "with the greatest first and a space in between.\n"
           "Your first string? ");
    gets(string1);
    printf("Your next string? ");
    gets(string2);
    if (strcmp(string1, string2) > 0)               /* First string greater */
    {   strcpy(combined, string1);
        strcat(combined, " ");                               /* Add space */
        strncat(combined, string2, COMBO - 1 - strlen(combined));
                                                         /* Don't overflow */
    }
    else if (strcmp(string1, string2) < 0)        /* Second string greater */
    {   strcpy(combined, string2);
        strcat(combined, " ");                               /* Add space */
        strncat(combined, string1, COMBO - 1 - strlen(combined));
                                                         /* Don't overflow */
    }
    else
        strncpy(combined, "They're equal. Which is first?", COMBO);
    combined[COMBO - 1] = '\0';                    /* In case null not copied */
    printf("The result: ");                 /* Don't want newline following */
    puts(combined);
}
```

Output

```
Give me two strings and I will put them together
with the largest first and a space in between.
Your first string? Hi there, pal.
Your next string? What's cookin'?
The result: What's cookin'? Hi there
```

YOUR TURN 8–3

1. What function returns the number of characters in a string?

2. What two functions will copy characters from one location to another? How do they differ?

3. What two functions concatenate one string to another? How do they differ?

4. What two functions compare two strings? How do they differ? How are the comparisons made?

ARRAYS OF STRINGS

We said that a string is an array of characters and that a double-indexed array is an array of arrays, so we could store an array of strings in a double-indexed `char` array.

```
char words[4][6] = {"zero", "one", "two", "three"};
```

The braces around the string values are necessary because they enclose a block of values. We could also declare it as

```
char words[][6] = {"zero", "one", "two", "three"};
```

leaving the first index out. Because of the initialization values, C knows how many arrays to set up.

This array takes up 24 bytes of memory, organized like this:

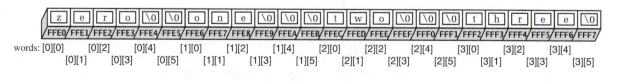

HEADS UP!

Index notation without the last index(es) becomes an address.

Remember, when we leave the last index off an array identifier, it becomes the address of that array-within-an-array. In other words, *words[2]* is the address of *words[2][0]*, or *two*. Using that concept, we can access the *words* array as in ⇨Program 8–7.

⇨**Program 8–7**

```
#include <stdio.h>

#define STRINGS 4
#define SIZE 6

void main(void)
{   char words[STRINGS][SIZE] = {"zero", "one", "two", "three"};
    int count;

    for (count = 0; count < STRINGS; ++count)
        printf("Digit: %i. Word: %s\n", count, words[count]);
}
```

Output

```
Digit: 0. Word: zero
Digit: 1. Word: one
Digit: 2. Word: two
Digit: 3. Word: three
```

▶TRAP◀

Exceeding the boundaries of your allocated array within the array.

As always, staying within the boundaries of the arrays is up to you. Let us see what happens if we change the value of *words[1]* to something greater than five characters.

New Program Segment

```
strcpy(words[1], "singular");
for (count = 0; count < STRINGS; ++count)
    printf("Digit: %i. Word: %s\n", count, words[count]);
```

Output

```
Digit: 0. Word: zero
Digit: 1. Word: singular
Digit: 2. Word: ar
Digit: 3. Word: three
```

The `strcpy()` function wrote *singular\0* beginning at the address *words[1]*. The `printf()` function printed the string beginning at *words[1]* and then the string beginning at *words[2]*—hence the strange, but explainable, output. In memory, it looks like this:

YOUR TURN 8–4

1. What is an array of strings?
2. Given the declaration char s[4][10], what is s[2]?
3. Given the declaration in the previous question, how would you print the third string in the array?

CONVERTING BETWEEN NUMBERS AND STRINGS

Something that looks like a number to us, 123.45 for example, can be stored in the computer in two very different ways—as a number (the binary IEEE notation equivalent to that value) or as a string (the seven characters *123.45\0*). Each form has its advantages. We can perform mathematics on numbers; we cannot on strings even if they look like numbers. We humans can easily understand the string; it is in familiar characters instead of weird binary notation. Also, if we store the individual characters, we have access to them. We can take the number-looking string apart and perhaps reassemble it some other way.

Because each method of storage has its unique set of advantages, it might be worthwhile to be able to convert from one notation to the other and vice versa. In fact, we have already been making conversions since Chapter 2. The printf() function converted numbers stored in memory to sets of characters and displayed them on the screen. In the other direction, scanf() converted the characters from the input stream to ASCII code values stored in numeric variables.

Numbers to Strings

We can use a variation of printf() called **sprintf()** to write characters directly into memory—typically to a space allocated for a string.

```
int sprintf(char *string, char *control_string, arguments)          <stdio.h>
```

HEADS UP!

sprintf() works just like printf() but adds a null.

What would normally be displayed on the screen by printf() will be written to memory at the address *string*. All the formatting properties that we used with printf() are available with sprintf(). Like other string functions, sprintf() puts the trailing null at the end of the string. The return value is the number of characters written to the string, not including the null.

⇨Program 8–8 stores the characters representing an amount of pay in the string array *paycheck[]*. We have used sprintf() to add other characters and round the numeric result to two decimal places.

⇨Program 8–8

```
#include <stdio.h>

void main(void)
{   char paycheck[40];
    double hours = 36.7, rate = 12.36;

    sprintf(paycheck, "Pay is $%.2f.", hours * rate);
    puts(paycheck);                         /* Display so we can see result */
}
```

Output

```
Pay is $453.61.
```

Strings to Numbers

There are several ways of converting strings to numbers. Like `printf()`, `scanf()` has its string-in-memory counterpart **sscanf()**.

int sscanf(char *_string_, char *_control_string_, arguments)   <stdio.h>

This function takes the characters stored at _string_ instead of the input buffer, converts them according to the _control_string_, and stores them at the addresses given in the arguments. The return values are also the same—the number of assignments successfully made, or EOF—but in this case, EOF is returned if the end of the string is reached rather than the end of the file.

The `sscanf()` function is especially useful if there are extraneous characters in the string to be ignored in the conversion, as in ⇨Program 8–9.

⇨Program 8–9

```
#include <stdio.h>

void main(void)
{   char paycheck[] = "Pay is $451.63.";
    float pay;

    sscanf(paycheck, "Pay is $%f.", &pay);
    printf("%f\n", pay);                    /* Display so we can see result */
}
```

Output

```
451.630000
```

OTHER ANSI CONVERSION FUNCTIONS

The ANSI functions `strtod()`, `strtol()`, and `strtoul()` allow you to do some extra things with string-to-number conversions including returning the address where the conversion stopped (the inappropriate character) and, in the latter two, allowing you to state the radix (base) of the string representation.

Three other functions will convert strings to numbers. The **atof()** function, pronounced "a to f" and standing for "alpha to floating-point," converts a *string* to type `double`. The **atoi()** function ("alpha to integer") converts a string to an `int`; and **atol()** ("alpha to long") to a `long`.

 **HEADS UP!**

Use the appropriate function for the data type.

```
double atof(char *string)                        <stdlib.h>
int atoi(char *string)                           <stdlib.h>
long atol(char *string)                          <stdlib.h>
```

In each case, the conversion begins at the address *string*, skips any leading whitespace, and ends at the first inappropriate character for that data type or the end of the string (the null). ⇨Program 8–10 illustrates these conversion functions.

⇨**Program 8–10**

```
#include <stdio.h>
#include <stdlib.h>

void main(void)
{   char string[] = "123.456 is a number.";
    int intvar;
    long longvar;
    double doublevar;

    intvar = atoi(string);
    longvar = atol(string);
    doublevar = atof(string);
    printf("The string: %s\n", string);
    printf("Int: %i, long: %li, double: %f\n", intvar, longvar, doublevar);
}
```

Output

```
The string: 123.456 is a number.
Int: 123, long: 123, double: 123.456000
```

▶**TRAP**◀

Exceeding the limits of your data type.

If the number represented by the characters in the string is larger than the data type can accommodate, the resulting assignment will be meaningless.

CHARACTER CLASSIFICATION

Often we are presented with a string of characters and must look inside it to interpret it. Is it a complete sentence? Does it present parameters for our program to work with? If so, what are the parameters? To examine it we must look at the individual characters. We can easily test to see if a particular character is an *A* or a comma, but usually we want to look at the type of character rather than its individual value. Is it an uppercase alpha character? Is it a punctuation character?

ANSI C provides us with a number of functions to classify individual characters. They all have the same format:

```
int function(int character)                          <ctype.h>
```

For example,

```
int isalpha(int character)                           <ctype.h>
```

returns a nonzero value if the **character** is a letter, that is, *A* through *Z* or *a* through *z*, or returns zero if it is not a letter.

⇨Program 8–11 asks for a letter from the keyboard and will loop until it gets one.

⇨**Program 8–11**

```
#include <stdio.h>
#include <ctype.h>

void main(void)
{   int in;              /* Declare as int to save conversions in execution */

    do
    {   printf("Type a letter and <enter>: ");
        in = getchar();                        /* Assign the character to in */
        getchar();                      /* Pass newline at end of input buffer */
    }while (!isalpha(in));                           /* Loop while not zero */
    puts("Finally, an alpha character!");
}
```

Output

```
Type a letter and <enter>: 4
Type a letter and <enter>: 8
Type a letter and <enter>: /
Type a letter and <enter>: g
Finally, an alpha character!
```

We can examine a string character by character by sending the character values to the isalpha() function as in ⇨Program 8–12.

⇨Program 8–12

```
#include <stdio.h>
#include <ctype.h>

void main(void)
{  char string[] = "23 skidoo.";
   int chr = 0;                            /* Character position in string */

   while(string[chr] != '\0')             /* Loop to the end of the string */
   {  if (isalpha(string[chr]))
         printf("'%c' is alpha\n", string[chr]);
      else
         printf("'%c' is not alpha\n", string[chr]);
      ++chr;                                     /* Go to next character */
   }
}
```

Output

```
'2' is not alpha
'3' is not alpha
' ' is not alpha
's' is alpha
'k' is alpha
'i' is alpha
'd' is alpha
'o' is alpha
'o' is alpha
'.' is not alpha
```

The complete list of ANSI classification functions follows. These functions are similar to isalpha() in that their declarations are found in ctype.h, and they return a nonzero int if their conditions are satisfied, or zero if they are not.

isalnum() Returns nonzero if the *character* is alphanumeric: 0–9, A–Z, or a–z.

isalpha() Returns nonzero if the *character* is alphabetic: A–Z or a–z.

iscntrl() Returns nonzero if the *character* is a control code: ASCII 1–31.

isdigit() Returns nonzero if the *character* is a decimal digit: 0–9.

isgraph() Returns nonzero if the *character* is printable, not including space.

islower() Returns nonzero if the *character* is lowercase: a–z.

isprint() Returns nonzero if the *character* is printable, including space.

ispunct() Returns nonzero if the *character* is punctuation.

isspace() Returns nonzero if the *character* is whitespace: space, form feed (\f), newline (\n), return (\r), horizontal tab (\t), or vertical tab (\v).

isupper() Returns nonzero if the *character* is uppercase: A–Z.

isxdigit() Returns nonzero if the *character* is a hexadecimal digit: 0–9, A–F.

CHARACTER CONVERSIONS

There are two simple functions, **toupper()** and **tolower()**, that convert lowercase characters to uppercase and vice versa. Their forms are:

```
int toupper(int character)                              <ctype.h>

int tolower(int character)                              <ctype.h>
```

If the *character* is not alpha, A–Z or a–z, it will be returned unchanged.

To illustrate both functions, in ⇨Program 8–13, let us take a sloppily written name and clean it up by putting it in caps/lowercase.

⇨**Program 8–13**

```
#include <stdio.h>
#include <ctype.h>

void main(void)
{   char string[] = "mYRnA H. bALthAZaR, III";
    int chr;                              /* Character position in string */

    printf("Before: %s\n", string);
    string[0] = toupper(string[0]);           /* First character uppercase */
        /* chr moves from the second character of the string to the end */
    for (chr = 1; string[chr] != '\0'; ++chr) /* 2nd chr to end of string */
        if (string[chr - 1] == ' ')          /* Chr after space, uppercase */
            string[chr] = toupper(string[chr]);
        else                              /* Not after space, lowercase */
            string[chr] = tolower(string[chr]);
    printf("After : %s\n", string);
}
```

Output

```
Before: mYRnA H. bALthAZaR, III
After : Myrna H. Balthazar, Iii
```

mYRnA H. bALthAZaR, III was a combination of upper- and lowercase letters as well as punctuation and spaces. All the characters were sent to one function or the other, but **toupper()** changed only the lowercase letters and **tolower()** changed only the uppercase letters. All the others were returned unchanged. Our trick did not work very well on *III.*

YOUR TURN 8–5

1. What function is often used to convert numbers to strings?
2. What four functions are commonly used to convert strings to numbers?
3. How does the method of conversion in **sscanf()** differ from the other three?
4. The text introduces 11 functions used to classify characters. Name them and tell what classifications they determine.
5. What is the return value for the classification functions if the character fits the classification? If it doesn't?
6. Which two functions convert a letter between upper- and lowercase?
7. What effect do these conversion functions have on characters that are nonletters or letters that are already in the proper case?

POINTERS—A FIRST GLANCE

We have seen function formats such as

```
int scanf(char *control_string, arguments)     <stdio.h>
```

containing the declaration

```
char *control_string
```

HEADS UP!

A pointer variable contains an address.

We said that the asterisk in front of the variable meant that the variable contained the address of a character rather than the character itself. This address variable is referred to as a **pointer**—it points to, contains the address of, some other value in memory. We have also seen that most of the formal parameters of the string functions we have examined contained such declarations. Since a string starts at a specific address and ends at the first null, the function needs only the beginning address to access the string, so we send such addresses to the functions.

We can declare pointer variables as part of our own programs. In fact, many of the string functions we will be examining return pointers, and we may want to store those pointers in variables. The declaration

```
char *ptr;
```

allocates memory for a pointer variable. It contains an address, which at this time (assuming an automatic storage class) is garbage—it doesn't point to anything in particular. We refer to the variable as a "pointer to char." Because of the data type specified in the declaration, C knows that it points to—contains the address of—a char data type.

We also said that the prefix of an array was an address, or a pointer, using that terminology. The prefix, remember, is constant. Its value may not be changed. In other words, we may not make it point to somewhere else in memory. We could, however, assign that address to a pointer variable, as ⇨Program 8–14 shows.

⇨**Program 8–14**

```
#include <stdio.h>

void main(void)
{   char string1[] = "Daisy";
    char string2[] = "Rose";
    char *any_string;

    printf("any_string is now  %s\n", any_string);     /* Compiler  warns */
    any_string = string1;
    printf("any_string is now  %s\n", any_string);
    any_string = string2;
    printf("any_string is now  %s\n", any_string);
}
```

Output

```
any_string is now  _@j!}`~t
any_string is now  Daisy
any_string is now  Rose
```

After the declarations, memory might have been organized something like the following. (We are assuming a pointer variable takes up three bytes. It probably doesn't in your C, but it makes illustration easier.)

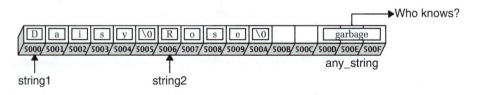

The pointer *any_string* does not have a valid value. When we printed it in the first `printf()`, it pointed to a place in memory that happened to have the characters shown followed by a zero byte—a null. That memory area, before it reached a zero byte, might have contained the Gettysburg Address, machine language for a picture of Donald Duck, or something that might have locked up the screen!

After assigning the value of *string1* to *any_string* memory would look like this:

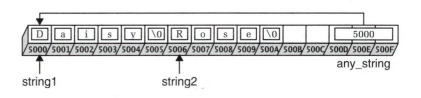

and *any_string* points to the same place as *string1*. The second `printf()` shows this.

Assigning the value of *string2* to *any_string* makes it point to *Rose*, as the last `printf()` shows.

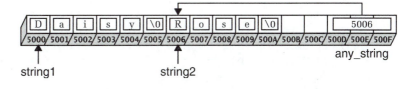

HEADS UP!

The asterisk means different things in different places.

In a declaration, the asterisk means that the variable following it is a pointer—in our case, a pointer to `char`. Anywhere else, the asterisk in front of a pointer variable means that we are referring to the data to which the pointer points—in our case, a `char`. In our example, *any_string* is the address of *R* in memory. The notation *any_string*, however, refers to the data at that address; in other words the `char` value *R*.

In fact, using that notation, we can change the data at that address. This statement,

```
*any_string = 'H';
```

puts the character *H* at the memory location to which *any_string* points—where the *R* used to be. Now if we printed the string starting at the address *any_string*, it would be *Hose*. Since *any_string* points to the same place as *string2*, printing *string2* would also produce *Hose*. The name *string2* is a constant; it cannot be changed; *any_string*, however, is a variable; it can be changed, as we have already done. Changing it, of course, makes it point to a different place in memory with different data in it.

We have added to ⇨Program 8–14 to show the asterisk notation and how it works. The `while` loop at the end of ⇨Program 8–15 starts with *any_string* pointing to *H* and adds to *any_string*, moving the pointer, until it points to a null—the end of the string. Printing character by character, it prints out *Hose*.

⇨**Program 8–15**

```
#include <stdio.h>

void main(void)
{   char string1[] = "Daisy";
    char string2[] = "Rose";
    char *any_string;

    printf("any_string is now  %s\n", any_string);        /* Compiler  warns */
    any_string = string1;
    printf("any_string is now  %s\n", any_string);
    any_string = string2;
    printf("any_string is now  %s\n", any_string);
    printf("The data at any_string is %c\n", *any_string);
    *any_string = 'H';                           /* Change the value at any_string */
    printf("any_string is now  %s\n", any_string);
    printf("and string2 is now %s\n", string2);          /* string2 is same */
    printf("Moving the pointer along to the first null, we get ");

    while (*any_string != '\0')                      /* Data at any_string not null */
    {   printf("%c", *any_string);     /* Print individual character values */
        ++any_string;                             /* Move any_string to next address */
    }
    printf("\n");
}
```

Output

```
any_string is now  _@j!}`~t
any_string is now  Daisy
any_string is now  Rose
The data at any_string is R
any_string is now  Hose
and string2 is now Hose
Moving the pointer along to the first null, we get Hose
```

1. What does an asterisk mean in a declaration such as `char *what;`?
2. What is the difference in the meaning of *what* and *that* in these two declarations: `char what[10];` and `char *that;`?
3. Given the declaration `char *that, what[] = "Flower";` and the statement `that = what + 1;`, what string does *that* point to?
4. Given the declaration and statement in the previous question, if we added the statement `*that = 'P'`, what string would *that* point to? What string would *what* point to?

TAKING STRINGS APART

Often we are faced with the task of disassembling a string into some component parts, a process referred to as **parsing** a string. Perhaps an input contains several parameters and we must separate them; or we are examining the individual words in a sentence; or a name must be divided into first, middle initial if one exists, and last. To do this we must look for clues that tell us where one part ends and another begins. The first part ends in a space; the second comes before a third, which is enclosed in parentheses; or whatever.

HEADS UP!

Make your routines as error-proof as possible.

To accomplish this disassembly, we must know what the clues are and have C find them for us. The more flexible our algorithm is, the more useful it will be. For example, making it immaterial how many spaces there are between parameters allows the program to handle some possibly sloppy parameters.

The **strstr()** function (usually referred to as "string string") returns the address of the beginning of a *search* string within a *reference* string.

```
char *strstr(char *reference, char *search)    <string.h>
```

HEADS UP!

`strstr()` searches for a specific set of characters.

If the *reference* string does not contain the *search* string, the function returns the `NULL` address constant. The code segment

```
char location[] = "Des Moines, Iowa";
```

```
printf("State: %s\n", strstr(location, ", ") + 2);
```

would print out *Iowa*. The `%s` conversion code requires an address, a pointer, which `strstr()` returns. In this case it will be the address of the beginning of the comma-space combination within *location*—the address of the comma. The name of the state begins two characters after the comma, so adding 2 to the return value of `strstr()` gives us the address of *I*. The `%s` conversion code, then, will print from there to the terminating null—*Iowa*.

Notice that if the comma were not in the *location[]* array, we would be asking `printf()` to print what was at the NULL address—probably nothing we would want to see displayed on our screen. We will test for this condition in ⇨Program 8–16.

⇨Program 8–16

```c
#include <stdio.h>
#include <string.h>

void main(void)
{   char location[] = "Des Moines, Iowa";

    if (strstr(location, ", ") == NULL)
        printf("There is no \", \" in %s.\n", location);
    else
        printf("State: %s\n", strstr(location, ", ") + 2);
}
```

Output

```
State: Iowa
```

Since we are calling the `strstr()` function twice in this program, in ⇨Program 8–17 we will assign its return value to a pointer variable with a single call, and use that pointer for the rest of the program.

⇨Program 8–17

```c
#include <stdio.h>
#include <string.h>

void main(void)
{   char *comma, location[] = "Des Moines, Iowa";

    comma = strstr(location, ", ");
    if (comma == NULL)
        printf("There is no \", \" in %s.\n", location);
    else
        printf("State: %s\n", comma + 2);
}
```

The `strstr()` function is probably the most basic of the functions that find specific characters within a string. The **strchr()** function is similar except that it finds the first occurrence of a single character instead of an entire string.

```
char *strchr(char *reference, int character)  <string.h>
```

If the *character* is not found in the *reference* string, the function
returns the NULL address constant. In the `strchr()` function, the null
character at the end of the string is a possible search character. A search
for it provides a pointer to the position one beyond the last character in
the string.

We could use this to find and display the dollar amount in the string
given:

Program Segment   **Output**

```
char string[] = "Widgets cost $49.95";      Cost: $49.95
printf("Cost: %s\n", strchr(string, '$'));
```

The `%s` conversion for `printf()` expects the address of a string of
the same data type as the return from the `strchr()`function. In this case
the return from `strchr()` is the address of the *$*, so the string printed by
`printf()` extends from the *$* to the first null—the end of the string.

The **strrchr()** function is similar to `strchr()` except that it
searches in reverse order, starting from the end of the *reference* string,
finding the last occurrence of the *character*.

Another similar function is **strpbrk()**, which finds the first occur-
rence of any one of the characters of the *search* string in the *reference*
string.

```
char *strpbrk(char *reference, char *search)  <string.h>
```

For example, if we were not quite sure whether two items in a *string*
were separated by a comma, a space, a dash, or a slash, we could find the
separator with:

```
separator = strpbrk(string, ", -/");
```

where *separator* is a pointer variable.

The **strtok()** function is particularly useful in extracting **tokens**,
sets of characters, from strings. It searches a reference string for any character from a string of *delimiters* (separating characters) and replaces
that delimiter with a null, effectively ending the string there. The return
value is the address of the reference string. The token, then, is the string
at the returned address.

```
char *strtok(char *reference, char *delimiters)              <string.h>
```

For example, ⟡Program 8–18 extracts the characters representing the
month from the date given. Notice it would not matter whether we
expressed the dates as *12/6/1492*, *12-6-1492*, or *12 6 1492*. Or, for that
matter, if we had a date like *9/17/92*.

⇨Program 8–18

```
#include <stdio.h>
#include <string.h>

void main(void)
{   char date[] = "12/6/1492";

    printf("Date: %s\n", date);
    strtok(date, "/- ");                    /* Null inserted at delimiter */
    printf("Month: %s\n", date);
}
```

Output

```
Date: 12/6/1492
Month: 12
```

After the call to strtok(), *date* still points to the same place, but the string is shortened because the null was inserted where the first slash was.

HEADS UP!

strtok() searches for any of a set of characters, and then moves its starting point.

The strtok() function, however, remembers where the null was inserted. A subsequent call to strtok() with NULL (the defined NULL pointer) as the *reference* string argument is a signal to the function to make the *reference* argument the address of the character after the inserted null from the previous call. In other words strtok() will start where it left off last time. The returned value will be the new *reference* address. We can illustrate this with ⇨Program 8–19, which divides a date into *month*, *day*, and *year* strings.

⇨Program 8–19

```
#include <stdio.h>
#include <string.h>

void main(void)
{   char date[] = "12/6/1492";
    char *month, *day, *year;

    printf("Date:  %s\n", date);
    month = strtok(date, "/- ");            /* Null inserted at delimiter */
    printf("Month: %s\n", month);
    day = strtok(NULL, "/- ");              /* Start where last left off */
    printf("Day:   %s\n", day);
    year = strtok(NULL, "\0");          /* Null will be replaced with null */
                                        /* in other words, no change */

    printf("Year:  %s\n", year);
}
```

Output

```
Date:   12/6/1492
Month:  12
Day:    6
Year:   1492
```

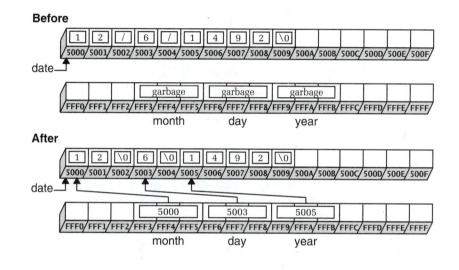

YOUR TURN 8–7

1. What does it mean to parse a string?

2. Which function searches for a particular set of characters in a string? A single character? The last occurrence of a single character? Any of a set of characters?

3. How does `strtok()` differ from `strpbrk()`?

PUTTING IT TOGETHER

The Flab to Fab Fitness Club keeps height and weight statistics on all its members. The people who type the data into the computer have been only directed to put in the full name, first name first, followed by a colon, the height, followed by a comma, and then the weight. The files are sloppy because everyone inputs the data differently. Some use feet and inches and pounds, others use meters and centimeters and kilograms, some use a combination of the two; some leave spaces, others don't . . . It's a mess.

Write a program that will take name, height, and weight in almost any form and translate it to a consistent style.

There are a few bright spots in this input debacle. The name is always first name first, and is always followed by a colon; the height is always followed by a comma; and the weight is always last. Other than that, our program must be able to handle different units of measure and almost anyone's guess as to spacing.

No matter what the input, the output should always be a 20-character name field, last name first, followed by the height in hundredths of meters, and the weight in hundredths of kilograms. Following are some samples of possible inputs and their reformatted results.

Sample Outputs

```
Enter listing: Abner Troy Brindle: 6 ft 2 in, 192 lbs
Brindle, Abner Troy  1.88 meters   87.27 kg.

Enter listing: Sheila Shirley Schildkin:1m46cm,115pds
Schildkin, Sheila Sh 1.46 meters   52.27 kg.

Enter listing: Rocky Q. Flowers: 161 cm, 85 kg
Flowers, Rocky Q.    1.61 meters   85.00 kg.
```

Our data consists of three elements to convert. We can view the overall process as:

```
Get input
Process name
Process height
Process weight
Present listing
```

The processing of the name, height, and weight will, of course, require more attention. In each case the element must be extracted from the listing, and then adjusted to the new configuration.

```
Get input
[Process name]
    Extract name                              [Look for the colon]
    Adjust name
```

```
        [Process height]
            Extract height                              [Look for the comma]
            Adjust height
        [Process weight]
            Extract weight                              [The last part of the listing]
            Process weight
        Present listing
```

To adjust the name we would have to:

```
[Adjust name]
    Divide name into first and last
    Build new name with last name first
```

To adjust the height we would have to:

```
[Adjust height]
    [Convert first part]
        Find digits
        Find units
        Convert digits according to units
    If any second part, convert it
        Find digits
        Find units
        Convert digits according to units
    End if
```

To adjust the weight we would have to:

```
[Adjust weight]
    Find digits
    Find units
    Convert digits according to units
```

The rest of the program is expanded in the code.

IMPLEMENTATION

In writing the program, we will follow the pattern in our design and put the Adjust name, Adjust height, and Adjust weight procedures in separate functions. Since these are the most complicated parts, that will allow us to write the code for each independently and test each one separately before combining it all. Eventually, we want to put our adjusted listing into data files, so we will create the fully formatted listing in memory before displaying it on the screen. ⇨Program 8–20 shows how.

```
#include <stdio.h>
#include <string.h>
#include <ctype.h>
#include <stdlib.h>

#define NAME_LEN 40
#define LINE_LEN 40

void adjust_name(char name[]);
float adjust_height(char *height_in);
float adjust_weight(char *weight_in);

void main(void)
{   char input[LINE_LEN], name[NAME_LEN], listing[LINE_LEN];
    char *height_in, *weight_in;
    float height, weight;

    /**************************************************** Enter listing */
    printf("Enter listing: ");  /* Can't use puts() and stay on same line */
1   gets(input);

    /***************************************************** Process name */
2   strcpy(name, strtok(input, ":"));              /* Extract name */
3   adjust_name(name);

    /**************************************************** Process height */
4   height_in = strtok(NULL, ",");                 /* Extract height */
5   height = adjust_height(height_in);

    /**************************************************** Process weight */
6   weight_in = strtok(NULL, "\0");                /* Weight is left over */
7   weight = adjust_weight(weight_in);

    /********************************************* Store and print listing */
8   sprintf(listing, "%-20.20s %4.2f meters %6.2f kg.",
            name, height, weight);
9   puts(listing);
}
```

The *adjust_name()* function finds the dividing point between the first and middle names, and the last. That point is the second space in the name. Replacing that space with a null effectively ends the first and middle names. We build a new name in a temporary string starting with the last name, beginning one location after the now null character. We concatenate a comma and space onto that, and then the characters at *name*, which now ends where the second space used to be.

EXECUTION CHART—`main()`

Line	Explanation	input[] name[]
1	Copy input stream to *input[]*, replace \n with \0.	`Abner Troy Brindle: 6 ft 2 in, 192 lbs` `?`
2	`strtok()` replaces : with \0; returns the address *input*. `strcpy()` copies string at *input* to *name*.	`Abner Troy Brindle\0 6 ft 2 in, 192 lbs` `Abner Troy Brindle\0`
3	Call *adjust_name* and pass the address *name* to *name* in *adjust_name()*.	`Abner Troy Brindle\0 6 ft 2 in, 192 lbs` `Brindle, Abner Troy\0` (after call)

Line	Explanation	input[] At address *height_in*
4	`strtok()` starts where it left off and replaces next comma with \0. Return assigned to *height_in*.	`Abner Troy Brindle\0 6 ft 2 in\0 192 lbs` `6 ft 2 in\0`
5	call *adjust_height*, pass *height_in*. Assign return (1.8796) to *height*.	`Abner Troy Brindle\0 6 ft 2 in\0 192 lbs` `in\0` (after call)

Line	Explanation	input[] At address *weight_in*
6	`strtok()` starts where it left off and replaces next \0 with \0. Return assigned to *weight_in*.	`Abner Troy Brindle\0 6 ft 2 in\0 192 lbs` `192 lbs\0`
7	Call *adjust_weight*, pass *weight_in*. Assign return (87.2727) to *weight*.	`Abner Troy Brindle\0 6 ft 2 in\0 192 lbs` `lbs\0` (after call)

Line	Explanation	input[] At address *listing*
8	Store results converted to appropriate form at *listing*.	`Abner Troy Brindle\0 6 ft 2 in\0 192 lbs` `Brindle, Abner Troy  1.88 meters  87.27 kg.\0`
9	Display string at *listing*, replacing \0 with \n.	`Abner Troy Brindle\0 6 ft 2 in\0 192 lbs` `Brindle, Abner Troy  1.88 meters  87.27 kg.\0`

```
     void adjust_name(char name[])
     /***************** Changes name from first name first to last name first */
     {  char temp_name[NAME_LEN], *last_name;

        /********************** Divide name into first (and middle) and last */
n1      last_name = strchr(strchr(name, ' ') + 1, ' ') + 1;      /* 2nd space */
n2      *(last_name - 1) = '\0';                        /* End first and middle name */

        /**************************** Build new name with last name first */
n3      strcpy(temp_name, last_name);                        /* Put in last name */
n4      strcat(temp_name, ", ");                             /* Add comma */
n5      strcat(temp_name, name);                             /* Add first name */
n6      strcpy(name, temp_name);                        /* Copy result back to name */
     }
```

EXECUTION CHART—*adjust_name()*

Line	Explanation	name[] temp_name[]	At address last_name
n1	Inner `strchr()` returns address of first space; outer `strchr()` starts there and finds address of second space. Last name starts after that.	Abner Troy Brindle\0 ?	Brindle
n2	Put \0 before last name to end first and middle names.	Abner Troy\0Brindle\0 ?	Brindle
n3	Copy characters at *last_name* up to \0 to *temp_name*.	Abner Troy\0Brindle\0 Brindle\0	Brindle
n4	Concatenate comma and space.	Abner Troy\0Brindle\0 Brindle, \0	Brindle
n5	Concatenate first name.	Abner Troy\0Brindle\0 Brindle, Abner Troy\0	Brindle
n6	Copy characters at *temp_name* to *name*. Address *last_name* still 10 bytes beyond beginning of *name*.	Brindle, Abner Troy\0 Brindle, Abner Troy\0	ner Troy

Converting the height, we must first get to the first digit, passing any spaces or whatever precedes it. We can send that address to the `atof()` function—the conversion will stop at the first inappropriate character for a floating-point number. Next we must find the first character of the units; that is all we need to determine what type of units they are. Depending on the units we make the proper conversion.

EXECUTION CHART—*adjust_height()*

Line	Explanation	At *height_in*	*height*	*height1*
h1	Increment *height_in* while it is not pointing at a digit.	6 ft 2 in\0 6 ft 2 in\0	?	?
h2	Convert to inappropriate character—the space.	6 ft 2 in\0	6	?
h3	Increment *height_in* while it is not pointing at an alpha character. This could have been done with `while`, like h1.	6 ft 2 in\0 ft 2 in\0 ft 2 in\0	6	?
h4	Convert what *height_in* points at to uppercase.	Ft 2 in\0	6	?
h5	Look for `case 'F':`, find in h6.	Ft 2 in\0	6	?
h7	Convert *height* in feet to meters.	Ft 2 in\0	1.8288	?
h8	Go past end of `switch` structure at h14.	Ft 2 in\0	1.8288	?
h15	`strpbrk()` returns address of next occurrence of any digit.	2 in\0	1.8288	?
h16	Return is not NULL.	2 in\0	1.8288	?
h17	Convert to inappropriate character—the space.	2 in\0	1.8288	2
h18	Increment *height_in* while it is not pointing at an alpha character.	in\0	1.8288	2
h19	Convert what *height_in* points at to uppercase.	In\0	1.8288	2
h20	Look for `case 'I':`, find in h21.	In\0	1.8288	2
h22	Convert *height1* in inches to meters; add to *height*.	In\0	1.8796	.0508
h23	Go past end of `switch` structure at h27.	In\0	1.8796	.0508
h28	Return value of *height*.	In\0	1.8796	.0508

From there, we search for another digit. If we find one, we go through a similar operation to convert it and add it to the height.

```
         float adjust_height(char *height_in)
         /************************* Changes height from almost any units to meters */
         { float height, height1;

              /****************************************** Convert first part of height */
                   /********************************************************* Find digits */
h1               while (!isdigit(*height_in)) ++height_in;      /* Get to first digit */
h2               height = atof(height_in);          /* Convert until inappropriate chr */

                   /*********************************************************** Find units */
h3               for ( ; !isalpha(*height_in); ++height_in);       /* Beg of units */
h4               *height_in = toupper(*height_in);        /* Only first chr necessary */

                   /******************************************** Convert according to units */
h5               switch (*height_in)                      /* Value at height_in */
h6               { case 'F':                                        /* Feet */
h7                    height *= .3048;
h8                    break;
h9                 case 'I':                                      /* Inches */
h10                   height /= 39.37;
h11                   break;
h12                case 'C':                                  /* Centimeters */
h13                   height /= 100;
h14              }

              /***************************** Convert second part of height, if any */
                   /********************************************************* Find digits */
h15              height_in = strpbrk(height_in, "0123456789");          /* Next digit */
h16              if (height_in != NULL)                 /* If there is a next digit */
h17              { height1 = atof(height_in);   /* Convert until inappropriate chr */

                   /*********************************************************** Find units */
h18              for ( ; !isalpha(*height_in); ++height_in);       /* Beg of units */
h19              *height_in = toupper(*height_in);        /* Only 1st chr necessary */

                   /******************************************** Convert according to units */
h20              switch (*height_in)                      /* Value at height_in */
h21              { case 'I':                                      /* Inches */
h22                   height += height1 / 39.37;
h23                   break;
h24                case 'C':                                  /* Centimeters */
h25                   height += height1 / 100;
h26              }
h27            }
h28          return height;
         }
```

In the *adjust_height()* function we have presented two different ways of finding the next digit. The first,

```
while (!isdigit(*height_in)) ++height_in;              /*Get to first digit */
```

moves the pointer along until `isdigit()` is not false; and the second,

```
height_in = strpbrk(height_in, "0123456789");          /* Next digit */
```

uses `strpbrk()` to find the next digit.

Adjusting the weight is similar to adjusting the height. We find the digits, find the units, and adjust accordingly.

```
     float adjust_weight(char *weight_in)
     /************************* Changes weight from almost any units to kg */
     { float weight;

         /***************************************************** Find digits */
w1       while (!isdigit(*weight_in)) ++weight_in;      /* Get to first digit */
w2       weight = atof(weight_in);             /* Convert until inappropriate chr */

         /****************************************************** Find units */
w3       for ( ; !isalpha(*weight_in); ++weight_in);    /* Beginning of units */
w4       *weight_in = toupper(*weight_in);          /* Only first chr necessary */

         /*************************************** Convert according to units */
w5       if (*weight_in == 'L' || *weight_in == 'P')     /* Convert if pounds */
w6           weight /= 2.2;

w7       return weight;
     }
```

EXECUTION CHART—*adjust_weight()*

Line	Explanation	At *weight_in*	*weight*
w1	Increment *weight_in* while it is not pointing at a digit.	192 lbs\0 192 lbs\0	?
w2	Convert to first inappropriate character (space) and assign to *weight*.	192 lbs\0	192
w3	Increment *weight_in* while it is not pointing at an alpha character.	192 lbs\0 92 lbs\0 2 lbs\0 lbs\0 lbs\0	192
w4	Convert character at *weight_in* to uppercase.	Lbs\0	192
w5	Content at *weight_in* is 'L'.	Lbs\0	192
w6	Convert *weight* to kg.	Lbs\0	87.2727
w7	Return *weight*.	Lbs\0	87.2727

Testing this program could begin with the sample output we presented in the analysis stage. We should try to think up all combinations of names, units, spaces, and whatever else someone might enter, and see if they work. In this program there are obviously lots of input possibilities we have not accounted for. For example, if someone has no middle name, the process blows up. As you can see, foolproofing inputs can be a programming nightmare!

SUMMARY

▲KEY TERMS (in order of appearance)

NULL	Pointer
Flag	Parse
size_t	Token

▲NEW FUNCTIONS (in order of appearance)

`int getchar(void)`   `<stdio.h>`
Purpose: Read one character form keyboard.
Return: Success: ASCII (or EBCDIC) value of character read. Error: EOF.

`char *gets(char *string)`   `<stdio.h>`
Purpose: Read a line from the keyboard into the *string*.
Return: Success: *string*. Error: NULL.

`int putchar(int character)`   `<stdio.h>`
Purpose: Display the *character* on the screen.
Return: Success: ASCII (or EBCDIC) value of *character* displayed. Error: EOF.

`int puts(char *string)`   `<stdio.h>`
Purpose: Display the *string* on the screen.
Return: Success: Nonnegative. Error: EOF.

`size_t strlen(char *string)`   `<string.h>`
Purpose: Find number of characters at *string*.
Return: Number of characters at *string*.

`char *strcpy(char *destination, char *source)`   `<string.h>`
Purpose: Copy *source* string to *destination*.
Return: *destination*.

```
char *strncpy(char *destination, char *source, size_t max)          <string.h>
    Purpose: Copy up to max characters of source string to destination.
    Return:  destination.

char *strcat(char *string, char *add)                               <string.h>
    Purpose: Put add string at the end of string.
    Return:  string.

char *strncat(char *string, char *add, size_t max)                  <string.h>
    Purpose: Put up to max characters of add string at the end of string.
    Return:  string.

int strcmp(char *string1, char *string2)                            <string.h>
    Purpose: Compare two strings.
    Return:  Positive value if string1 greater, negative if string2, zero if equal.

int strncmp(char *string1, char *string2, size_t max)               <string.h>
    Purpose: Compare up to max characters of two strings.
    Return:  Positive value if string1 greater, negative if string2, zero if equal.

int sprintf(char *string, char *control_string, arguments)          <stdio.h>
    Purpose: Store at string the values of arguments in format specified in control_string.
    Return:  Success: Number of characters printed. Error: negative value.

int sscanf(char *string, char *control_string, arguments)           <stdio.h>
    Purpose: Assign values from string to argument variables according to control_string.
    Return:  Success: Number of assignments made. Error: EOF if end of string.

double atof(char *string)                                           <stdlib.h>
    Purpose: Convert string to double.
    Return:  Success: Converted number. Error: Meaningless assignment.

int atoi(char *string)                                              <stdlib.h>
    Purpose: Convert string to int.
    Return:  Success: Converted number. Error: Meaningless assignment.

long atol(char *string)                                             <stdlib.h>
    Purpose: Convert string to long.
    Return:  Success: Converted number. Error: Meaningless assignment.

int isalnum(int character)                                          <ctype.h>
    Purpose: Test if character is alphanumeric: 0–9, A–Z, or a–z.
    Return:  True: Nonzero. False: Zero.

int isalpha(int character)                                          <ctype.h>
    Purpose: Test if character is alphabetic: A–Z or a–z.
    Return:  True: Nonzero. False: Zero.

int iscntrl(int character)                                          <ctype.h>
    Purpose: Test if character is a control code: ASCII 1–31.
    Return:  True: Nonzero. False: Zero.

int isdigit(int character)                                          <ctype.h>
    Purpose: Test if character is a decimal digit: 0–9.
    Return:  True: Nonzero. False: Zero.
```

```
int isgraph(int character)                                          <ctype.h>
    Purpose: Test if character is printable, not including space.
    Return:  True: Nonzero. False: Zero.

int islower(int character)                                          <ctype.h>
    Purpose: Test if character is lowercase: a–z.
    Return:  True: Nonzero. False: Zero.

int isprint(int character)                                          <ctype.h>
    Purpose: Test if character is printable, including space.
    Return:  True: Nonzero. False: Zero.

int ispunct(int character)                                          <ctype.h>
    Purpose: Test if character is punctuation.
    Return:  True: Nonzero. False: Zero.

int isspace(int character)                                          <ctype.h>
    Purpose: Test if character is whitespace: space, \f, \n, \r, \t, or \v.
    Return:  True: Nonzero. False: Zero.

int isupper(int character)                                          <ctype.h>
    Purpose: Test if character is uppercase: A–Z.
    Return:  True: Nonzero. False: Zero.

int isxdigit(int character)                                         <ctype.h>
    Purpose: Test if character is a hexadecimal digit: 0–9, A–F.
    Return:  True: Nonzero. False: Zero.

int toupper(int character)                                          <ctype.h>
    Purpose: Convert lowercase character to upper.
    Return:  If character lowercase letter, uppercase equivalent, otherwise no change.

int tolower(int character)                                          <ctype.h>
    Purpose: Convert uppercase character to lower.
    Return:  If character uppercase letter, lowercase equivalent, otherwise no change.

char *strstr(char *reference, char *search)                         <string.h>
    Purpose: Find a search string in a reference string.
    Return:  Success: Address of search string in reference string. Error: NULL.

char *strchr(char *reference, int character)                        <string.h>
    Purpose: Find the first occurrence of a character in a reference string.
    Return:  Success: Address of the character in the reference string. Error: NULL.

char *strrchr(char *reference, int character)                       <string.h>
    Purpose: Find the last occurrence of a character in a reference string.
    Return:  Success: Address of the character in the reference string. Error: NULL.

char *strpbrk(char *reference, char *characters)                    <string.h>
    Purpose: Find first occurrence of any of characters in reference.
    Return:  Success: Address of occurrence. Error: NULL.

char *strtok(char *reference, char *delimiters)                     <string.h>
    Purpose: Extract and mark end of tokens in reference string.
    Return:  Success: Address of beginning of reference string. Error: NULL.
```

▼ A string is an array of chars in memory. It begins at a particular address and extends to the first null character. A quoted string value represents the address where C has chosen to store those characters.

▼ A character values such as 'A' is a number. A string values such as "A" is a set of character values beginning at an address and stored with a trailing null.

▼ Strings may be declared and initialized in the same manner as other arrays, but we may also state the initializing characters in quotes, rather than stating them as separate values.

▼ Strings must be assigned one character at a time. There are ANSI C functions that help with this.

▼ The scanf() function using the %s conversion code reads a string from the standard input stream and writes it at a designated address. We can limit the number of characters read.

▼ The getchar() function returns a single character from the input stream. gets() assigns characters from the input stream up to the next newline to a single string. As with many functions that return a pointer value, gets() returns the NULL pointer if there is an error in the assignment.

▼ String output is accomplished with printf() and the %s conversion code. The dash flag left-justifies the output in the field. putchar() is for single characters, puts() for entire strings.

▼ ANSI C has a number of functions that aid us in manipulating strings. strlen() returns the number of characters in a string (as a size_t data type); strcpy() and strncpy() copy a string to another location; strcat() and strncat() copy one string to the end of another; and strcmp() and strncmp() compare one string to another.

▼ Arrays of strings may be set up by declaring an array of arrays—a double-indexed array. An array notation without the last index(es) is the address of an array within the array.

▼ The sprintf() function works similarly to printf() except that the characters are written to a designated address and a null terminator is added. It is often used to convert numbers to strings.

▼ The sscanf() function converts characters from a memory location rather than the input stream, and can be used to convert strings to numbers. The atof(), atoi(), and atol() functions convert strings to doubles, ints, and longs.

▼ The isalnum(), isalpha(), iscntrl(), isdigit(), isgraph(), islower(), isprint(), ispunct(), isspace(), isupper(), and isxdigit() functions test characters to see if they fit into various classifications.

▼ The **toupper()** function converts a lowercase alpha character to uppercase, and **tolower()** does the opposite.

▼ A **pointer** is an address. We may use pointer variables, declared with asterisk notation, to store addresses. In other parts of the program, the asterisk notation accesses the data being pointed to.

▼ There are a number of functions that help us in **parsing** strings. The **strstr()** function finds one string within another, while **strchr()** and **strrchr()** find a specific character within a string. The **strpbrk()** function finds the first occurrence of any of a number of characters in the string. The **strtok()** function helps us to extract series of **tokens** from strings.

▲HEADS UP: POINTS OF SPECIAL INTEREST

▼ In memory, characters and numbers look the same.

▼ Strings in C end in a null character.

▼ A string value is an address.

▼ A character in single quotes is a numeric value.

▼ Don't forget the null character when allocating strings.

▼ An array name cannot be assigned.

▼ Know how scanf() works.

▼ NULL is not null. *The* NULL *pointer is not the same as the* \n *character.*

▼ scanf() stops at whitespace, including newlines.

▼ Be careful using gets() and scanf() in the same program. scanf() *leaves the newline in the stream, while* gets() *does not skip leading whitespace and removes the newline from the stream.*

▼ Most C functions will allow you to write beyond the space allocated for a string.

▼ String comparisons are done one character position at a time.

▼ In ASCII, all lowercase characters are greater than any uppercase character.

▼ Index notation without the last index(es) becomes an address.

▼ sprintf() works just like printf() but adds a null.

▼ Use the appropriate function for the data type.

▼ A pointer variable contains an address.

▼ The asterisk means different things in different places.

▼ Make your routines as error-proof as possible.

▼ strstr() searches for a specific set of characters.

▼ strchr() searches for a specific single character.

▼ strrchr() searches backward for a specific single character.

▼ `strpbrk()` searches for any of a set of characters.

▼ `strtok()` searches for any of a set of characters, and then moves its starting point.

▲TRAPS: COMMON PROGRAMMING ERRORS

▼ Not allocating enough space for strings.

▼ Attempting to assign a string value (address) to an array prefix.

▼ Putting an & in front of an array name in `scanf()`.

▼ Assigning characters beyond the space allocated for the string.

▼ Not copying a terminating null with `strncpy()`.

▼ Not enough allocated space at the end of the string to be lengthened.

▼ Comparing two string addresses instead of using `strcmp()`.

▼ Exceeding the boundaries of your allocated array within the array.

▼ Exceeding the limits of your data type.

▼ Accessing or copying characters to a meaningless address.

▲YOUR TURN ANSWERS

▼8–1

1. Strings are stored as arrays of `char`s.

2. The string begins at some base address—wherever C has chosen to put it—and ends with a null.

3. The string "A" is stored as an array of two `char`s, the ASCII code for *A* followed by null. The notation in quotes refers to its base address in memory. 'A' is an `int` and simply the numeric value of its character code—65.

4. We store strings in arrays of `char` variables.

5. C doesn't! That is up to us.

6. The first three are identical. Each allocates 12 `char`s, sets the first 5 to *Zelda*, and makes the rest null. The fourth allocates only 6 `char`s, enough for *Zelda* and null.

7. Strings are assigned a single character at a time.

▼8–2

1. `scanf()` using the `%s` or `%[]` conversion codes, or `gets()`.

2. We can use a width parameter in the conversion code, but if the stated width is reached, the stream position is left wherever the conversion stopped—usually not where we wanted it.

3. By using the brackets and the caret indicating the characters that are not acceptable in the conversion.

4. By using the %c conversion code in scanf(), or the getchar() function. They both act equivalently.

5. printf(), using the %s conversion code, or puts().

6. It states the maximum number of character that will print in a field.

7. The dash flag in printf() left-justifies the output instead of the default right justification.

8. puts() always outputs a newline at the end of the string. printf() only outputs a newline if it is part of the string.

9. Using the %c conversion code in printf(), or the putchar() function. They both act equivalently.

▼8–3

1. The strlen() function returns the number of bytes from the address sent to it to the first null.

2. strcpy() copies a string from one address to another, including the terminating null. strncpy() does the same, but will not exceed a maximum number of bytes, even if the null is not copied.

3. strcat() copies a string from one address to the end of a string at another address. strncpy() does the same, but will not copy more than a maximum number of bytes.

4. strcmp() and strncmp() compare bytes a position at a time from each address given. The comparison is made according to the numeric value of the ASCII codes. The comparison stops at the first difference or, in the case of strncmp(), at a maximum number of bytes.

▼8–4

1. Since a string is an array of chars, an array of strings is an array of arrays of chars.

2. The address of the beginning of the third string–the address of *s[2][0]*.

3. printf("%s", s[2]); or puts(s[2]);.

▼8–5

1. The sprintf() function, which writes directly to memory, will convert numbers to their character representations.

2. The sscanf() function reads characters directly from memory and will convert them to numbers. Also, atof(), atoi(), and atol() functions convert strings to **double**, **int**, or **long** data types.

3. The conversions are made the same way, skipping whitespace and converting up to the first inappropriate character.

4. `isalnum()`, alphanumeric; `isalpha()`, alphabetic; `iscntrl()`, control code; `isdigit()`, decimal digit; `isgraph()`, printable, not including space; `islower()`, lowercase; `isprint()`, printable, including space; `ispunct()`, punctuation; `isspace()`, whitespace; `isupper()`, uppercase; `isxdigit()`, hexadecimal digit.

5. The return values are nonzero if the character fits the classification and zero if it doesn't.

6. The `toupper()` and `tolower()` functions.

7. They have no effect on such characters or letters.

▼8–6

1. It means that *what* is an address variable, a pointer, that can contain the address of a `char`.

2. Very little. Both are pointers to `char`, but *what* is constant and points to 10 bytes of allocated space, whereas *that* is a variable and points to no place in particular.

3. The statement makes *that* point to an address one beyond *what*, which makes it point to *lower*.

4. Since *that* points to the *l* in *lower*, changing the data at that address to *P* makes *that* point to *Power*. *what* points to *FPower*, whatever that means.

▼8–7

1. Parsing a string is separating it into its component parts—words or special codes, for example.

2. The `strstr()` function searches for a particular set of characters in a string, `strchr()` for a single character, `strrchr()` for the last occurrence of a single character, and `strpbrk()` and `strtok()` for any of a set of characters.

3. The `strtok()` function replaces the character with a null and remembers its address. Future calls with a NULL *reference* argument will start where it left off the last time.

EXERCISES

1. Which are correct declarations and initializations for strings?
   a. `char a[10] = "Alice";`
   b. `char a[] = "Alice";`
   c. `char a[10] = 'A', 'l', 'i', 'c', 'e';`
   d. `char a[10] = {0};`
   e. `char a[5] = "Alice";`

2. Given this declaration and statement, which will execute without error messages, and which will produce valid data?

```
char s1[16] = "Rita", *s2, s3[] = "Al";
s2 = s3;
```
   a. `scanf("%s", &s1);`
   b. `scanf("%s", s2);`
   c. `s2 = "Farley";`
   d. `s1 = "Fred";`
   e. `s1 = s2;`
   f. `s2 = s1;`
   g. `strcpy(s1, s2);`
   h. `strcat(s1, s2);`
   i. `strcat(s2, s1);`
   j. `*s2 = 'L';`
   k. `++s2;`

3. Given the following declarations, what will be assigned at *a* and *b* as a result of the following `scanf()` operations, all with the input "Happy New Year"?

```
char a[20], b[20], c[] = "Happy New Year";
```
   a. `scanf("%s %s", a, b);`
   b. `scanf("%9s %s", a, b);`
   c. `sscanf(c,"%4s %s", a, b);`
   d. `sscanf(c,"%[NHap] %s", a, b);`
   e. `sscanf(c,"%s, %s", a, b);`
   f. `sscanf(c,"%[^e]e %s", a, b);`

4. What will be the difference in output between these two statements?

```
printf("%s", "Hello");
puts("Hello");
```

5. What problem might be encountered with the following section of code, and how might we fix it?

```
scanf("%f%i", &a_float, &an_int);
gets(a_string);
```

6. What output will the following program produce?

```
#include <stdio.h>
#include <string.h>
#include <ctype.h>

void main(void)
{   char s[] = "Algernon";
```

(continued)

```
        printf("%c\n", s[2]);
        printf("%s\n", &s[2]);
        printf("%i\n", strcmp(s, "Farley"));
        printf("%i\n", strncmp(s, "Algeria", 5));
        printf("%c\n", *strchr(s, 'g'));
        printf("%i\n", strlen(s));
        printf("%i\n", islower(s[2]));
        printf("%s\n", strstr(s, "ger"));
        printf("%c\n", *strpbrk(s, "nle"));
    }
```

7. What output will the following program produce?

```
#include <stdio.h>
#include <stdlib.h>

void main(void)
{   char s[] = "123.456 and so forth";
    float f;

    printf("%i\n", atoi(s));
    printf("%f\n", atof(s));
    sscanf(s, "%f", &f);
    printf("%f\n", f);
    sprintf(s, "%i", (int) f);
    printf("%s\n", s);
}
```

8. What output will the following program produce?

```
#include <stdio.h>
#include <string.h>

void main(void)
{   char s[] = "Steven C. Lawlor: Author, Raconteur & Scholar";

    printf("%5.5s", strtok(s, " .:"));
    printf("%s\n", strtok(NULL, ":") + 2);
    printf("%s\n", strtok(NULL, "&") + 1);
}
```

PROGRAMS

1. After giving us functions like isalpha() and islower(), how could the ANSI C committee forget the *isvowel()* function? Redeem them by writing the function to work similarly to the others mentioned. It should return nonzero if the character is a vowel (*a, e, i, o,* or *u,* upper- or lowercase), or zero if it is not a vowel. Test the function in a

program that allows input of a string—gets()—and single character output—putchar()—of the characters in the string with the vowels highlighted as shown.

Variables and Functions

```
main()                                   isvowel()
  string                                   character
  pos     Character position in string     result
```

Output

```
Aloysius Washington
<A>l<O>ys<I><U>s W<A>sh<I>ngt<O>n
```

2. In the ASCII code, an uppercase letter has a value 32 less than the corresponding lowercase letter. Write a program that will allow you to input any string and print it in all uppercase. The function *caps()* should make the actual changes in the string. Do not use any string functions.

Functions and Variables

```
main()          caps()
  string[]        string[], sub
```

Output

```
Your input? What? It isn't I!
The output: WHAT? IT ISN'T I!
Your input? The cost: $2,345.67.
The output: THE COST: $2,345.67.
Your input?
```

3. The program above will work on either an ASCII or an EBCDIC machine, not on both. Rewrite it using string functions so that the same program will work on either machine.

4. Write a program to compare two strings without using any library functions. The program should print out which string is greater or that they are equal.

Variables:

```
string1
string2
```

Outputs

```
FIRST STRING ? ABNER          FIRST STRING ? ZELDA
SECOND STRING? CRUMP           SECOND STRING? BEULAH
CRUMP IS GREATER THAN ABNER    ZELDA IS GREATER THAN
                               BEULAH

FIRST STRING ? NORBERT         FIRST STRING ? ROSE
SECOND STRING? Nancy           SECOND STRING? ROSE
Nancy IS GREATER THAN NORBERT  ROSE EQUALS ROSE
```

5. Write a function, *stringcmp()*, that works like `strcmp()`, but is not case-sensitive. In other words, *NORBERT* would be greater than *Nancy*. Test it with an appropriate `main()` function driver.

6. Good people all have last names that begin with the letters *G* through *L*; all the others are bad. Write a program that differentiates the good people from the bad.

Variable:

name

Outputs

```
Name? Attila the Hun          NAME? G
Attila the Hun is a bad person. G is a good person.

Name? Farley                  NAME? [Your name]
Farley is a bad person.       ???? is a ???? person.

NAME? Lawlor                  Name? M
Lawlor is a good person.      M is a bad person.
```

7. Expand the first program in the *Arrays of Strings* section so that it sorts the strings and then prints out the sorted result. Of course, the digits and words will not match. The output should be as below:

Output

```
Digit: 0. Word: zero
Digit: 1. Word: one
Digit: 2. Word: two
Digit: 3. Word: three
```

(continued)

```
Digit: 0. Word: one
Digit: 1. Word: three
Digit: 2. Word: two
Digit: 3. Word: zero
```

8. Generate 10 random characters in the ASCII range (0 to 127). For each, if it is printable, print it and tell whether it is an upper- or lowercase character, a decimal digit, or punctuation. If it is not printable, print its ASCII code and whether or not it is a whitespace character.

Sample Output

```
Q us an uppercase character.
<SPACE> is whitespace.
ASCII 18 is not printable.
ASCII 13 is not printable but is whitespace.
6 is a decimal digit.
f is a lowercase character.
```
[and so forth]

9. How many 9s can you depend on in a **double** in your C? Write a program that keeps adding 9s to a string and, to see if they are accurately held in a **double**, converts the string to a **double** and then back to a string. You should have the program stop when the original string does not match the string after conversion.

Variables

digits	Original string
number	String converted to number
digits1	Number converted back to string

Output (in a typical C)

```
                 9  9
                99  99
               999  999
              9999  9999
             99999  99999
            999999  999999
           9999999  9999999
          99999999  99999999
         999999999  999999999
        9999999999  9999999999
       99999999999  99999999999
      999999999999  999999999999
     9999999999999  9999999999999
    99999999999999  99999999999999
   999999999999999  999999999999999
  9999999999999999  10000000000000000
```

10. The Farfel Corporation has made a list of its salespeople and their weekly sales. Write a program to print this list in either alphabetical or sales volume order depending on your input. (*Hint:* Use a parallel sort.)

Partial variable list:

```
names[ ]
sales[ ]
```

Data:

Jones	8604
Smith	3716
Brown	7071
Hill	12336
Green	5004

Outputs

Sort by? **name**

Brown	7071
Green	5004
Hill	12336
Jones	8604
Smith	3716

Sort by? **sales**

Hill	12336
Jones	8604
Brown	7071
Green	5004
Smith	3716

11. Write a program that accepts any double-precision number and returns the number as a string rounded to two decimal places with commas inserted in the correct places. Use an appropriate function to convert the number to a string.

Outputs

Input number? **123456.789**
Number with commas: 123,456.79

Input number? **12.345**
Number with commas: 12.35

12. A company is writing form letters to a list of people. Each listing has a last name, a first name, and sometimes a middle initial. Variations of the name will appear in three places. The envelope will have the first initial and last name; the heading in the letter will have the full name (first name first); and the greeting will have only the first name. Write a program to input a name—using gets()—and return it in each of three forms.

Partial Variable List:

`name`	Name input
`envelope`	Name for envelope
`heading`	Name for heading
`greeting`	Name for greeting
`ref1`	Location of the first space
`ref2`	Location of second reference point (second space or the end of the string plus one)

Sample Outputs

```
Name: Vanderklunk Ophelia T.
    O. Vanderklunk
    Ophelia T. Vanderklunk
    Ophelia

Name: Nisblinger Ted
    T. Nisblinger
    Ted Nisblinger
    Ted

Name: Phurd Agnes Q.
    A. Phurd
    Agnes Q. Phurd
    Agnes
```

Chapter 9

FILES

PREVIEW

Data that we wish to store permanently must be stored in files in secondary storage. After reading this chapter, you should have a working knowledge of

▼ How files are identified, and how we work with sections of them at a time.

▼ How C establishes its connection between a program and a file.

▼ Working with files using human-readable characters.

▼ Keeping track of the program's position in a file.

▼ Accessing a file in bytes by directly copying between memory and the file.

M ost of computing is manipulating data—often large volumes of data. This data must be stored permanently, be called up when needed, have changes made to it, be stored again, and so forth. We have, of course, used data in our previous programs. Typically we have entered it through the keyboard, processed it, and output it on the screen. Because of the nature of main memory, the data was temporary. Now we shall look at permanent retention of data in secondary storage.

Anything kept in secondary storage is considered by the operating system to be a **file**. We often separate files into two categories, program files and data files. To C it makes no difference; both are collections of bytes stored on disk. To us, though, it will probably determine how we organize and access them. The concentration here will be on data files, although the same rules and techniques apply to everything in secondary storage.

FILE IDENTIFIERS

Every block of data in secondary storage must have a unique identifier. We can't just ask the computer, "Remember that stuff I put on the disk last week?" Different operating systems have different rules for file identifiers. We will look at some general ones that will work with most systems, but you will have to get the particulars from the documentation for your own operating system.

In most operating systems, a file identifier can consist of a name and an extension. The **name** usually can be at least eight characters long, and if you stick with the alpha (*A* through *Z*) and numeric (*0* through *9*) characters, you should be safe. (Many operating systems now allow "long file names" that can even include spaces, but the rules given here will still work.) Some operating systems are case-sensitive; some are not. For example, UNIX treats an uppercase *A* as a different character from a lowercase *a*, while DOS and Windows do not. Your file might have a name like *PAYROLL* or *lt930412*.

An **extension** is typically up to three characters of the same kinds as those allowable in a name. Extensions are often used to group files together in categories. C program source files usually have the extension *C*, executable programs often *EXE* or *COM* (for "command"). All of a company's payroll files might have the extension *PAY* and its employee files *EMP*. Extensions are usually not required, but if they exist, they follow the name and are separated from it by a dot (**.**). Here are some typical file identifiers:

PROGRAM.C	0396Actg.Qtr
PROGRAM.EXE	X
a.out	Agnes.WHO

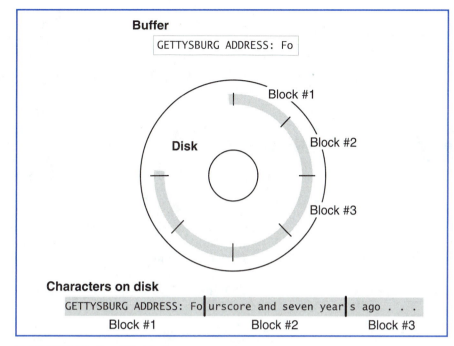

Buffer

GETTYSBURG ADDRESS: Fo

Block #1

Block #2

Disk

Block #3

Characters on disk

GETTYSBURG ADDRESS: Fo urscore and seven year s ago . . .

Block #1   Block #2   Block #3

❑ **FIGURE 9–1**   File Buffer

In addition to the identifier, most operating systems allow their secondary storage to be divided into logical storage areas called folders or directories and subdirectories. To work with such a system, we must give the system not only the identifier but also a path to follow to find its way to the proper directory or subdirectory. In our directions to C we can give not only the file identifiers but also path directions if they are required or allowed in the operating system.

BUFFERED INPUT AND OUTPUT

As we saw in Chapter 1, we cannot access secondary storage a single byte at a time, only in blocks of bytes—perhaps hundreds or thousands of bytes per block. Our program, however, will have to work with single bytes. The solution to this apparent contradiction is to bring a block of bytes into main memory where we can access each byte separately. We call the area in main memory where we temporarily store a block a **buffer** , as illustrated in ❑Figure 9–1.

To access the bytes in a disk block, that particular block must be copied into a buffer in main memory. If our next access takes us into another disk block, the first one is written back to secondary storage and the new one copied into the buffer. We may do the buffering process ourselves, but ANSI C has a number of functions that handle buffering so that it is

HEADS UP!

File buffering should be
transparent to us.

"transparent" to us—we don't even realize that it is happening. We can access the file as if we are calling for bytes from a continuous collection of them on the disk. C, with the help of the operating system, will keep track of the byte position in the disk file by maintaining a **file position indicator**, and will automatically move things in and out of buffers when it needs to.

OPENING FILES

We must inform C of our intention to use a particular file in a program. When we do, C sets up an area in memory with the data type **FILE**, a special data type, really a collection of data, defined in `stdio.h`. This data collection, referred to as the **file description**, contains information about the file such as our current position in the file, where the end of it is, where the associated buffer is located in memory, the size of the buffer, and a number of other things.

The **fopen()** function directs C to set up the file description and prepare the file for use.

```
FILE *fopen(char *file_id, char *mode)                <stdio.h>
```

The *file_id* is the path (if any), file name, and extension (if any) of the file we intend to use. The *mode* is how we intend to use it. The return value is the address of the area in memory that holds the file description that C sets up as a result of the function call. If the file cannot be opened, the return value will be the NULL pointer. For example,

```
FILE *payfile;
```

```
payfile = fopen("\\ACCTG\\PAYROLL.D5", "rb+");
```

Referring to the FILE data
type in lowercase.

HEADS UP!

The pointer to the file
decsription is worthless until
the file is opened.

Using a single backslash in a
string.

We briefly looked at pointers in Chapter 8. The first statement declares *payfile* as a pointer, not to a data type `char` as in the last chapter, but to a data type FILE. The second, through the call to `fopen()`, establishes a file description for the *PAYROLL.D5* file in the *ACCTG* directory, and assigns the pointer to this description to *payfile*. We usually refer to the pointer to the file description (*payfile*) as the "pointer to the file" or simply the "file pointer." From this point in the program, when we access the *PAYROLL.D5* file with an ANSI function, we will pass the function the file pointer (the address of the description that we stored in *payfile*), and it will find all the particulars of the file there.

Notice that for this operating system, the *file_id* in the `fopen()` function includes backslashes. The actual *file_id* above is really "\ACCTG\PAYROLL.D5". We used double backslashes in the string to represent a single backslash, because the single backslash is the beginning of a special character. The `'\a'`, for example, is the audible alarm—it makes the computer beep!

File Modes

The file *mode* is a text string containing certain key characters that tell C how we are going to use the file. There are three basic modes:

"**r**" Opens an existing file with the file position indicator at the beginning of the file. In the absence of further code characters, this file can only be *read* from. If the file does not exist, the NULL pointer will be returned.

"**w**" Creates a new, empty file with the file position indicator at the beginning (which, since it is empty, is also the end). If a file with the same identifier already exists, the new, empty one will replace it. In other words, any data in the previous file will be lost! In the absence of further code characters, this file can only be *written* to. If the file cannot be created (no disk space or an invalid path, perhaps), the NULL pointer is returned.

"**a**" Opens an existing file or, if none exists, creates a new one. The file position indicator is placed at the end (which would also be the beginning if a new file was created). In the absence of further code characters, this file can only be written to, but unlike "w", no data is lost because the writing takes place at the end of the file (the file is *appended* to). In most Cs, you cannot move the file position indicator to a place anywhere before the original end of the file. An error in the opening process returns the NULL pointer.

Any of these codes may be followed by a plus sign ("r+", "w+", or "a+") indicating that the file may be both read from and written to. However, before changing from reading to writing or vice versa, you must call one of four functions that access the file buffer—fseek(), rewind(), fflush(), or fsetpos(). We will look at those functions shortly.

Binary Versus Text Files

Programmed correctly, C will work with almost any type of file you can dream up. However, for its own workings it divides files into two types, binary and text, the principal differences being in the line endings in the file and the detection of the end of the file.

The file modes we referred to above have all been those of **text files**. Text files try to match the internal storage of data in C to the typical formatting of text for the operating system being used. The possible adjustments are in the line endings and end-of-file indications. Internally, C stores line endings with the single newline character (\n), typically referred to as a line feed (ASCII 10). A text file in UNIX uses the same character at the end of a line, so no change is made when going between main memory and secondary storage.

MS-DOS, Windows, and some other operating systems, however, consider a line ending to be the combination of a return (\r, ASCII 13) and a line feed—a two-character combination. Single-character newlines in main memory, then, are translated into two-character, return/line-feed

Opening a file for "**w**" that has needed data in it.

Changing between reading to writing without calling one of the file positioning functions.

Text files differ with different operating systems.

combinations when written to a file, and vice versa going from a file to main memory. (Whether this is really typical of MS-DOS and Windows text files might be questionable; a good many DOS and Windows text editors and most word processors use just the line-feed character. It is up to you to find out what is in your files and how to treat them in your programs.)

Some MS-DOS and Windows files use a control-Z character (ASCII 26) as an end-of-file indicator. If this character is encountered in a text file, the program will get an end-of-file indication. UNIX and many other systems, MS-DOS and Windows included, track the end of a file by knowing where the file position indicator is and the number of bytes in the entire file. The control Z will be treated like any other character by a UNIX C implementation, but it will be interpreted as the end of the file by an MS-DOS or Windows C.

Binary files are the most straightforward. They assume nothing about the operating system and don't make any special adjustments or translations. What is in the program or main memory will be written to the file verbatim, and vice versa. We can declare our file mode to be binary by including a *b* in the *mode* string in either the second or last position. (For example, "r+b" or "rb+", or "wb", and so forth.)

What all this really means is that you must know the makeup of the file you are trying to access and whether it fits the standard for your operating system. Many files won't have line endings in them at all, making the difference between the types moot. We will work with these files as binary. In fact, it is always safe to use binary. You can work with the return character (\r) as just another character if it exists at the end of the line.

HEADS UP!

When in doubt, use binary.

CLOSING A FILE

The act of closing a file writes the contents of the current buffer, if it has changed, into the appropriate place in secondary storage, making changes permanent, and deallocates the memory space for both the file buffer and the file description. The **fclose()** function closes a file.

int fclose(FILE *file)   <stdio.h>

The *file* is the pointer to the file description that was established when the file was opened. The function returns a zero if successful, EOF if not. We would close \ACCTG\PAYROLL.D5 by referring to its description pointed to by *payfile*.

HEADS UP!

A crash does not automatically close files.

fclose(payfile);

Files are automatically closed at a normal program termination, including the execution of an **exit()** function, but they are not closed when the program crashes. An abnormal ending to the program, then, leaves the buffers forgotten in main memory, not updating secondary storage, and possibly losing data.

Most programmers are careful to close any file they open as soon as the file is no longer required by the program. The practice saves memory space and prevents possible data loss if something unexpected should happen.

YOUR TURN 9–1

1. What are the rules for file identifiers on your system?
2. What is file buffering?
3. What is a file description?
4. What is the purpose of a pointer to FILE?
5. Which file modes work with existing files? Which create new files?
6. Which file modes allow read access and which allow write?
7. What is the difference between binary and text files?
8. What does closing a file do and what function does it serve?

CHARACTER ACCESS TO FILES

We will look at two different ways of accessing files. One, **character access** (or *formatted access*), reads and writes files much as we did with the keyboard and the screen—strictly in characters. If we printed a floating-point number, for example, we used printf() to convert the E-notation storage into the characters that represent its value. The second is **byte access** (or *unformatted* or *binary*), in which we store sets of bytes on the file without regard to what they represent. The E-notation floating-point number, for example, would be copied from its location in memory and written to the file in exactly the same form—virtually unreadable to humans using a text editor. We assume, however, that when we read it back from the file, our program will again store it in a floating-point variable so that it makes sense to C.

Formatted Access

We have used the printf() function to write characters to the screen, and we can use the **fprintf()** function in almost exactly the same way to write characters to a file.

```
int fprintf(FILE *file, const char *control_string, arguments)        <stdio.h>
```

For example,

```
fprintf(payfile, "Name: %s, Pay rate: %6.2f\n", name, pay)
```

The `fprintf()` arguments, except for the first, have the same meaning as they would for `printf()`. The difference is that instead of the characters appearing on the screen at the location of the cursor, they will be written to the file at the location of the file position indicator. The file, of course, is the one referred to in the first argument, the pointer to a file description established in an `fopen()` function.

The file must be opened in some mode that will allow writing to it—"w", "wb", "a", "ab", or anything with a plus sign in it such as "rb+".

⇨Program 9–1 will accept any number of inputs from the keyboard and write them to a file.

⇨**Program 9–1**

```c
#include <stdio.h>
#include <stdlib.h>

#define CHRS 40

void main(void)
{   FILE *employee;                              /* Pointer to file description */
    int dependents;
    float pay_rate;
    char name[CHRS];

    /******************************************* Go from keyboard to file */
    if ((employee = fopen("EMP.DAT", "w")) == NULL)    /* Check for error */
    {   printf("Cannot open file\n");
        exit(EXIT_FAILURE);
    }

    printf("Names should be Last, First or <Enter> key to quit.\n");
    printf("Enter name: ");
    gets(name);
    while (name[0] != '\0')                  /* Loop while name string not empty */
    {   printf("Enter pay rate, dependents: ");
        scanf("%f %i", &pay_rate, &dependents);
        fflush(stdin);                           /* Or while(getchar() != '\n') */
        fprintf(employee, "%-10.10s/%6.2f/%2i\n",          /* Write to file */
                name, pay_rate, dependents);
        printf("Enter name: ");
        gets(name);
    }

    fclose(employee);
}
```

Output

```
Names should be Last, First or <Enter> key to quit.
Enter name: Quibble, Marvin
Enter pay rate, dependents: 12.34 2
Enter name: Jones, Hatshepset
Enter pay rate, dependents: 9.38 8
Enter name: Montmorrissey, Clyde
Enter pay rate, dependents: 23.98 1
Enter name:
```

File Contents

```
Quibble, M/ 12.34/ 2
Jones, Hat/  9.38/ 8
Montmorris/ 23.98/ 1
```

We open the file in the `if` structure, which tests the return value stored in *employee*. If the return value is `NULL`, there must have been a problem so we print the error message and make an orderly exit from the program. In the `while` loop condition we flush the input stream to get rid of the newline left over from the last `scanf()` input, and then use `gets()` to input the string *name*. The test in the `while` loop checked the first character of `name`. If it is null, it means that we pressed only the Enter key and the string is empty. Therefore, we would exit the loop.

The input counterpart of `printf()` is `scanf()`. The input counterpart of `fprintf()` is **`fscanf()`**.

```
int fscanf(FILE *file, const char *control_string, arguments)        <stdio.h>
```

HEADS UP!

`fprintf()` and `fscanf()` work the same as their nonfile counterparts.

TRAP

It's `%s` or `%[]`, not `%[]s`.

Both `scanf()` and `fscanf()` have the same arguments, parameters, and return values, but `fscanf()` has an additional argument—the pointer to the file description.

Both `scanf()` and `fscanf()` have an additional conversion code that is of limited use in the keyboard input of `scanf()`, but is quite useful when inputting from files in `fscanf()`. In writing the *EMP.DAT* file, we have included specific delimiters, the slashes, to separate values in the file. We can use those delimiters to tell a `scanf()` string conversion when to stop reading characters. Instead of using `%s` for a string conversion, we will use the `%[]` code. Inside the brackets we will put a caret (∧) followed by any characters we want to be recognized as delimiters—those that end a string conversion. For example, `%[∧,-]` will end a string conversion at either comma or dash, whichever comes first. Whitespace, the usual default delimiter, becomes just another character when we use `%[]`.

Since the conversion stops at the delimiter, the position in the input stream will also be at that delimiter. Usually, we must move past it to get to the next set of characters to be read. We can do this by reading the single character, the delimiter, using `%*c`. The asterisk means to read the next character in the stream, but do not assign it anywhere. In other words, we do not provide the conversion code with a memory location in the argument list. For example, if our file, whose description was at *file*, contained an author and a book title, the two being separated by either a semicolon or a colon, the line

```
Presley, Elvis; The Joy of Classical Music
```

could be read into **char** arrays *author* and *title* with

```
fscanf(file, "%[^;:]%*c %[^\n]%*c", author, title);
```

Presley, Elvis would be assigned to *author*, the semicolon read but not assigned, *The Joy of Classical Music* assigned to *title*, and the ending newline read but not assigned, leaving the stream at the beginning of the next line.

Let us expand our program above, using the new conversion code, to read the data from the file after having put it there. Notice that the file was closed and reopened for reading ("r").

Additional Code

```
/*********************************************** Go from file to screen */
if ((employee = fopen("EMP.DAT", "r")) == NULL)
{  printf("Cannot open file\n");
   exit(EXIT_FAILURE);
}
printf("Name          Pay Rate  Dependents\n");
while (fscanf(employee, "%[^/]%*c %f%*c %i%*c",
       name, &pay_rate, &dependents) != EOF)
   printf("%s      %6.2f             %2i\n", name, pay_rate, dependents);
fclose(employee);
}
```

Additional Output

```
Name          Pay Rate  Dependents
Quibble, M      12.34         2
Jones, Hat       9.38         8
Montmorris      23.98         1
```

In the **fscanf()** function, we had to make sure that we anticipated the format of the characters in the file. When we wrote to the file, we set up a slash (/) as a delimiter between values. The default delimiter of whitespace would not have worked because some of the names were written with a space between the first and last names. It would have worked between the numbers, but we wanted to be consistent. The string, then, we specifically delimited with a slash ([^/]). That would stop the string conversion, but the slash would be left in the buffer. We passed it in the buffer by putting a %*c conversion code in the control string immediately following the brackets. A space was left before each number in the control string to pass any whitespace that might be in front of either number in the input stream. The second slash would have stopped the conversion of the floating-point number, so it had to be treated like the first slash. The final %*c conversion was for the newline at the end of each line of the file.

The `while` loop that reads from the file continued until `fscanf()` returned EOF, the defined constant indicating that the end of the file was reached.

Single-Character Access

Single-character access from the keyboard and to the screen is performed by `getchar()` and `putchar()`. Their counterparts with files are **getc()** and **putc()**.

```
int getc(FILE *file)                        <stdio.h>

int putc(int character, FILE *file)         <stdio.h>
```

Like their counterparts, `getc()` returns the next character from the file buffer, and `putc()` returns the character written. Both return EOF if an error occurs.

String Access

The **fgets()** and **fputs()** are the file counterparts of `gets()` and `puts()`.

```
char *fgets(char *string, int max, FILE *file) <stdio.h>

int fputs(const char *string, FILE *file)      <stdio.h>
```

The return values are the same as for their counterparts. For `fgets()` the return is the pointer to the *string* if it is successful, the NULL pointer if not. For `fputs()` the return is nonnegative if successful, EOF if not.

Although the intent is the same, there are some significant differences between `gets()` and `fgets()`. The latter has the *file* argument, of course, but while `gets()` stops reading characters only at the newline in the input stream, `fgets()` has three different criteria for stopping its read:

1. It reaches the end of the file.

HEADS UP!

Notice the differences between `gets()` and `fgets()`.

2. It encounters a newline. If this happens, unlike with the `gets()` function, the newline is retained as part of the string.

3. It takes *max* – 1 characters from the file buffer. The reason for one less character here is to save room for the null at the end of the string when it is written to the array in memory. If you declared an array as `string[40]`, you could safely say `fgets(string, 40, employee)` because it would only take a maximum of 39 characters from the file buffer. If `fgets()` reaches *max* – 1 characters, any leftover characters will still be in the buffer; the pointer will not move to the next newline or the end of the file or wherever.

In any case, like `gets()`, `fgets()` will always add a null at the end of the characters it writes in memory.

The `fputs()` function is very similar to its counterpart except that a newline is not added to the string on output. The two functions, `fputs()` and `fgets()`, are typically used on the same files. If a string was read by `fgets()`, it would usually have a newline at the end of it, which would be written to the string array. If the same string were written by `fputs()`, that newline would be put back in the file.

If you are writing to a file that should have newlines at significant points, such as would be read by `fgets()`, you will have to be sure that the newline is included in each string you write, whether it is from an `fputs()` or an `fprintf()`.

⇨Program 9–2 shows `fputs()` and `fgets()` in action. A teacher has a file of questions. When a student runs a program with the *give_test()* function in it, the program administers the test from whatever file is passed to it. The function stores both the questions and the answers in another file whose description is also passed to the function.

The teacher can then run a program with the *review_test()* function in it, which will print out the questions and the answers.

HEADS UP!

Notice the differences between `puts()` and `fputs()`.

QUIZ.QST File

```
What is C?
How big is a byte?
Who was Babe Ruth?
```

⇨Program 9–2

```
#include <stdio.h>
#include <stdlib.h>
#include <string.h>

#define LEN 80                                    /* Maximum string length */

void give_test(FILE *quest, FILE *ans);
void review_test(FILE *ans);
```
(continued)

358   9 / FILES

```
void main(void)
{  FILE *questions, *answers;

   if ((questions = fopen("QUIZ.QST", "r")) == NULL)
   {  puts("Can't open file of questions.");
      exit(EXIT_FAILURE);
   }
   if ((answers = fopen("QUIZ.ANS", "w")) == NULL)
   {  puts("Can't open file for answers.");
      exit(EXIT_FAILURE);
   }
   give_test(questions, answers);
   fclose(questions);
   fclose(answers);
   answers = fopen("QUIZ.ANS", "r");
   review_test(answers);
   fclose(answers);
}
void give_test(FILE *quest, FILE *ans)
{  char question[LEN], answer[LEN], *newline;

   puts("Answer each question carefully:");
   while (fgets(question, LEN, quest) != NULL)
   {  newline = strchr(question, '\n');           /* Find newline */
      *newline = '\0';                            /* and get rid of it */
      printf("%s ", question);
      gets(answer);                          /* Has no newline stored */
      strcat(answer, "\n");                       /* Add newline */
      fputs(question, ans);                /* Does not add newline */
      fputs(" ", ans);
      fputs(answer, ans);                  /* ans has newline at end */
   }
}
void review_test(FILE *ans)
{  char answer[LEN];

   puts("\nHere is this student's feeble attempt:");
   while (fgets(answer, LEN, ans) != NULL)
      printf("%s", answer);
}
```

Output

```
Answer each question carefully:
What is C? The third letter of the alphabet.
How big is a byte? No bigger than you can chew.
Who was Babe Ruth? The inventor of a candy bar.
```

(continued)

Here is this student's feeble attempt:
What is C? The third letter of the alphabet.
How big is a byte? No bigger than you can chew.
Who was Babe Ruth? The inventor of a candy bar.

YOUR TURN 9–2

1. What is the difference between character and byte access to files?
2. How do `fprintf()` and `fscanf()` differ from `printf()` and `scanf()`?
3. What are the file versions of `getchar()` and `putchar()`?
4. What are the differences between `fgets()` and `gets()`?
5. What are the differences between `fputs()` and `puts()`?

MOVING THE FILE POSITION INDICATOR

HEADS UP!

A file access always moves the file position indicator.

The data we want from a file is not always at the beginning. We may have to reach into the middle or go toward the end to get it. One method of moving the file position indicator is by accessing the file. Whenever we read or write, the file position indicator is moved to a position just beyond our last access. However, there are more efficient ways of moving the file position indicator.

The **rewind()** function moves the file position indicator to the beginning of the file, regardless of where it was before the `rewind()`.

```
void rewind(FILE *file)                              <stdio.h>
```

As usual, the *file* argument is the pointer to the description of the file whose file position indicator we want to move.

In ⇨Program 9–2, we moved the file position indicator back to the beginning of a file to which we just wrote by closing and opening the file.

```
fclose(answers);
answers = fopen("QUIZ.ANS", "r");
```

The same thing could have been accomplished by

```
rewind(answers);
```

with a lot more efficiency. In the original opening of the *answers* file we should have specified the mode as "w+" so that we could also read from the file. We said that we should not switch from writing to reading or vice versa without executing one of four functions. The `rewind()` function was one of them.

This function will only bring us to the beginning of the file, however. We may want to jump directly into the middle somewhere. In that case we should use the more general **fseek()** function.

```
int fseek(FILE *file, long offset, int origin) <stdio.h>
```

The return value is zero if the move was successful, or nonzero if there was a problem.

The *offset* argument is the number of bytes to move in the file. It may be positive for a forward move, or negative for a backward move. It may also be large enough to move the file position indicator beyond the end of the file or before the beginning; C will not check for that or stop it. Any data you read there would be meaningless, and writing there could be disastrous. Be sure you know where the end of the file is before moving the file position indicator.

The *offset* argument is a long integer, and some Cs will not convert what you have to that data type; so be sure you cast your argument as **(long)** if it is not already. For example, to move 10 bytes you should pass the value 10L.

The *origin* is where the move should start—the beginning, the current file position, or at the end. The *origin* argument can take one of three values, all defined constants from **stdio.h**.

▶TRAP◀

Moving the file position indicator out of the range of the file.

SEEK_SET   The *origin* is the beginning of the file. An *offset* from here, naturally, should not be negative, although C will not check it for you.

SEEK_CUR   The *origin* is at the current file position. The *offset* can be either positive or negative.

SEEK_END   The *origin* is the end of the file. The *offset* should not be positive, although C will not check it for you.

Like **rewind()**, this is one of the functions that will allow you to change from reading to writing or vice versa, if the opening mode allows it.

The **rewind()** function for the *QUIZ.ANS* file could be rewritten as

```
fseek(answer, 0L, SEEK_SET)
```

Either one would do the job, but the former is probably simpler and more straightforward.

If we had a file made up of records of exactly *rec_len* size, we could set the file position indicator at the *record* record as follows:

```
fseek(file, (long)((record - 1) * rec_len), SEEK_SET);
```

If *rec_len* was 10 and we were looking for the third record, the *offset* would evaluate to 20, moving the file position indicator 20 bytes. That would put it past the first two records to the 21st byte position, the first position in the third record.

OTHER FILE POSITION INDICATOR ACCESS

Two other ANSI functions can be used to access the file position indicator. fgetpos() stores the file *position* in a specified memory location, and fsetpos() sets the file position indicator to the *position* stored in a specified memory location.

```
int fgetpos(FILE *file, fpos_t *position)              <stdio.h>

int fsetpos(FILE *file, fpos_t *position)              <stdio.h>
```

The data type fpos_t is system dependent, but defined in stdio.h.

We can find out the current file position by using the **ftell()** function.

```
long ftell(FILE *file)                                 <stdio.h>
```

The return value is the current position of the indicator stated as an offset from the beginning of the file. It returns −1 if there is a problem. This function is particularly useful when we want to remember where we were in a file so that we may return there later. In our *review_test()* function we might have had use for the following statements.

```
previous_answer = ftell(ans);
```

saves our current position, and

```
fseek(ans, previous_answer, SEEK_SET);
```

will return us there later.

Let us write ⇨Program 9–3 to change the pay rate of one of the employees in our *EMP.DAT* file.

⇨**Program 9–3**

```
#include <stdio.h>
#include <stdlib.h>
#include <string.h>

#define CHRS 40

void main(void)
{  FILE *employee;                          /* Pointer to file description */
   int dependents;
   float pay_rate;
   char name[CHRS], change[CHRS];
   long current_position = 0;     /* To save position of record last read */
```
(continued)

```c
/************************************************** Open file */
if ((employee = fopen("EMP.DAT", "r+")) == NULL)    /* Check for error */
{  printf("Cannot open file\n");
   exit(EXIT_FAILURE);
}
/************************************************** Get new data */
printf("Whose pay rate do you want to change? ");
gets(change);
change[10] = '\0';              /* Shorten to 10 characters to match file */

/************************************************** Find position in file */
while (fscanf(employee, "%[^/]%*c %f%*c %i%*c",    /* Skip /'s in file */
            name, &pay_rate, &dependents) != EOF
        && strcmp(name, change))
    current_position = ftell(employee);

/************************************************** Make change in file */
if (strcmp(name, change))           /* Other than zero, they don't match */
    puts("Employee not on file.");
else
{  printf("New pay rate? ");
   scanf("%f", &pay_rate);
   fseek(employee, current_position, SEEK_SET);      /* Set position */
   fprintf(employee, "%-10.10s/%6.2f/%2i\n",  /* Write record to file */
           name, pay_rate, dependents);
}

/************************************************** Go from file to screen */
rewind(employee);
printf("Name           Pay Rate  Dependents\n");
while (fscanf(employee, "%[^/]%*c %f%*c %i%*c",
            name, &pay_rate, &dependents) != EOF)
    printf("%s      %6.2f              %2i\n", name, pay_rate, dependents);
fclose(employee);
}
```

Output

```
Whose pay rate do you want to change? Montmorrissey
New pay rate? 3.57
Name          Pay Rate  Dependents
Quibble, M     12.34        2
Jones, Hat      9.38        8
Montmorris      3.57        1
```

In the file *EMP.DAT* all the records have the same number of bytes. This makes changing the file easy. We can write the same number of bytes at the position of the record we want to replace without affecting any of the other records. In fact, we could have just written the *pay_rate* to the file because we know from the **fprintf()** format that the pay rate is 11 bytes from the beginning of the record.

```
fseek(employee, current_position + 11, SEEK_SET);
fprintf(employee, "%6.2f", pay_rate);                /* Write record to file */
```

Making changes in *QUIZ.QST* or *QUIZ.ANS* files would not be as easy because the records are of different lengths. Replacing a long one with a short one leaves garbage in the file. Replacing a short one with a long one overwrites the next record. The only way to change such a file is to set up two files and copy from one to the other, making changes along the way. We will look at an example of that after we look at some "File Housekeeping."

FILE HOUSEKEEPING

There are a number of little chores that we must perform to keep our files clean and up to date. One of these is deleting files from secondary storage, which we do with the **remove()** function.

```
int remove(const char *filename)                     <stdio.h>
```

The *filename* is the file identifier, including any path names necessary to find it in secondary storage. For example, in an MS-DOS system,

```
remove("C:\\RECORDS\\STUDENT.DAT")
```

deletes the file *STUDENT.DAT* from the *RECORDS* directory on the *C* disk.

UNIX does not typically use the **remove()** function, because a single file in that system can be referenced in several directories via links to the file. These UNIX systems use the related function, **unlink()**,

```
int unlink(const char *filename)                     <stdio.h>
```

which removes the file from the directory. For example,

```
unlink("/records/student.dat")
```

Attempting to remove a file that is open.

When there are no more surviving links to the file, then the file will actually be removed.

The file must exist to be deleted, and it must not be open. A successful deletion returns zero. The return is nonzero otherwise.

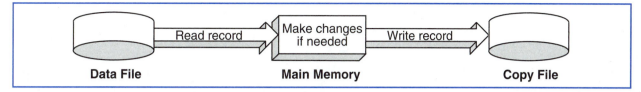

Data File   **Main Memory**   **Copy File**

❑ **FIGURE 9–2**   Changing Files

We can change the name of a file in secondary storage with the **rename()** function.

```
int rename(const char *oldname, const char *newname)              <stdio.h>
```

This function will change the *oldname* to the *newname*. The *oldname* file must exist and must not be open, and there may not already be a file in the current folder or directory with the *newname*.

```
rename("STUFF", "JUNK")
```

will rename the file *STUFF* in the default directory to *JUNK*.

As in `remove()`, full path names may be included, and a successful operation returns zero, whereas a nonzero indicates failure.

As promised, we will now write a function that makes changes in a file with unequal-length records. Since we cannot simply write over the record we want to change, we must copy the data from one file to another, making changes as we copy.

We will need two files, then—the original and another to which to copy the data. As shown in ❑Figure 9–2, copying involves reading the data, a record at a time, into variables in main memory, and then writing the values of those variables to the other file. While the data for a record is in main memory, we can examine it to see if we want to make a change.

In ⇨Program 9–4, we will set up a function *change_quiz()* and pass it the name of the file to change. It will set up a temporary file and make needed changes as it copies. Before it returns, the function will get rid of the original file and change the name of the temporary file to the original name.

HEADS UP!

Changing files with unequal-length records requires copying from one file to another.

⇨**Program 9–4**

```
#include <stdio.h>
#include <string.h>
#include <ctype.h>

#define LEN 80                                    /* Maximum string length */

void change_quiz(char qst_file[]);
```

(continued)

```
void main(void)
{
    change_quiz("QUIZ.QST");
}

void change_quiz(char qst_file[])
{   FILE *quest, *temp;                          /* Temporary file to copy to */
    char question[LEN], answer[LEN], *newline;

    if ((quest = fopen(qst_file, "r")) == NULL)     /* Open original file */
        puts("Could not open file, no changes made.");
    else
    {   temp = fopen("TEMP.$TM", "w");               /* Open temporary file */
        puts("Which question do you want to change?");
        while (fgets(question, LEN, quest) != NULL)  /* Read from original */
        {   newline = strchr(question, '\n');             /* Find newline */
            *newline = '\0';                         /* and get rid of it */
            printf("%s (Y/N)?", question);
            gets(answer);                         /* Has no newline stored */
            if (toupper(answer[0]) == 'Y')
            {   printf("New question: ");
                gets(question);
            }
            fputs(question, temp);    /* Write to temporary, changed or not */
            fputs("\n", temp);                        /* Add newline back */
        }
        fclose(quest);
        fclose(temp);
        remove(qst_file);             /* unlink(qst_file); in a UNIX system */
        rename("TEMP.$TM", qst_file);
    }
}
```

QUIZ.QST File Before

```
What is C?
How big is a byte?
Who was Babe Ruth?
```

Output

```
Which question do you want to change?
What is C? (Y/N)?n
How big is a byte? (Y/N)?y
New question: How many bits in a nybble?
Who was Babe Ruth? (Y/N)?n
```

```
What is C?
How many bits in a nybble?
Who was Babe Ruth?
```

FINDING THE END OF A FILE

If we know exactly what is in the file and how many bytes it occupies, then we can always determine where the end of the file is and ensure that we do not pass it unexpectedly. But often we add to or delete from files, changing their lengths and the location of their ends. There are a number of techniques in C that we can use to tell whether we are at the end of the file.

Function Error Returns

We can test the return value of a function we are using to access the file to see if it returns the expected value or not. The `fscanf()` function returns the defined constant `EOF` if it encounters the end of the file; `getc()` returns `EOF` on any error, including the end of the file; and `fgets()` returns the defined `NULL` pointer on any error. Each of these functions, except `fscanf()`, lumps all error conditions, including attempting a read at the end of the file, into the same category. Usually, the error condition truly is the end of the file, but we cannot be absolutely sure.

The End-of-File Function

The **feof()** function checks to see if the **end-of-file indicator** is set. In almost all cases, this indicator is set by an attempt to read at or beyond the end of the file.

```
int feof(FILE *file)                              <stdio.h>
```

This function returns a nonzero value if the end-of-file error is set, or zero if it is not. This is an after-the-fact function. It only returns nonzero if something else has set the indicator. We could not set up a program segment like this and expect it to work acceptably:

```
while (feof(file) == 0)              /* or, more simply, while ( !feof(file)) */
{   fgets(string, 50, file);
    and so forth
}
printf("Yup, we're at the end of the file.\n");
```

because just being at the end of the file will not make feof() return non-zero. It is the fgets() function that will eventually set the indicator, and we do not want to perform the "and so forth" with an invalid *string*. We should rewrite it this way:

```
while (fgets(string, 50, file) != NULL)
{   and so forth
}
if (feof(file))
    printf("Yup, we're at the end of the file.\n");
else
    printf("Something weird happened!\n");
```

or:

```
fgets(string, 50, file)
while ( !feof(file))
{   and so forth
    fgets(string, 50, file)
}
printf("Yup, we're at the end of the file.\n");
```

The end-of-file error indicator must be specifically cleared for it to go away. This can be accomplished by a call to rewind().

YOUR TURN 9–3

1. What two function calls would move the file pointer to the beginning of the file *data*?
2. Name the defined constants for the fseek() *origin* for the beginning, the current position, and the end of the file.
3. What function returns the current file position?
4. How can we delete a file from secondary storage?
5. What function changes the name of a file in secondary storage?
6. What condition makes the feof() function return nonzero?

BYTE ACCESS TO FILES

Many of our files are made up of combinations of character and numeric data. The *EMP.DAT* file is a good example. To store the employee data, we converted the numerics into characters with the fprintf() function and filled the file with characters. A distinct advantage of this approach is that we humans, using a text editor, can read both the character and the numeric data in the file.

If only our programs and not humans were going to read the file, we would probably want to store the data in the most efficient form in terms of both the amount of storage space and the processing required for reading and writing. Converting the numeric data to characters and vice versa takes processing time and usually requires more bytes for storage. For example, the value 12345 stored as characters takes five bytes. Stored as a short it takes only two.

Instead, let us take a direct copy of the bytes in memory and put it in the file—no translation, minimal storage.

The fwrite() function does just that. We tell it the space in memory, and it writes the contents in the file.

```
size_t fwrite(const void *location, size_t bytes,
              size_t items, FILE *file)         <stdio.h>
```

Starting at *location* in memory, fwrite() takes a number of *items* of *bytes* length, and writes them to the file described at *file*. The return value is the number of items or partial items written. It should be the same as *items* if everything goes right. For example, given the declaration,

```
float beans[10];
```

assuming a four-byte float,

```
fwrite(beans, 4, 10, beanfile);
```

will write the entire *beans* array on the file described at *beanfile*, and return 10. It does this because C guarantees contiguous allocation of arrays, and the prefix *beans* is the address of the beginning of the array.

The *location* argument was declared as a **pointer to void**. This is an ANSI pointer type that stores a memory address without regard to the data type to which it points. The fwrite() function must work with all data types. In fact, the function doesn't care which data type is stored at the address; it simply copies the prescribed number of bytes to the file.

The **fread()** function does exactly the opposite; it takes a number of bytes from a file and writes them at an address in main memory. You must be very sure that there is enough allocated space at that memory location; C gives you no help there.

```
size_t fread(const void *location, size_t bytes,
             size_t items, FILE *file)          <stdio.h>
```

The arguments are exactly the same.

Given the declaration

```
float beans[10];
```

this statement would read 10 floats, 40 bytes, from the file and assign them to the array *beans*.

HEADS UP!

A pointer to **void** can point to any data type.

```
fread(beans, 4, 10, beanfile);
```

Wouldn't it be embarrassing if those 40 bytes in the file did not represent floats? Only to you, though, not to C.

⮕Program 9–5 allows input of any number of days' production of axle grease in tons and stores the data in a file. Then it prints the data from the file on the screen.

⮕**Program 9–5**

```c
#include <stdio.h>
#include <stdlib.h>

#define INT_SIZE 2
#define FLOAT_SIZE 4
#define MAX_DAYS 60                                    /* No more than 60 days */

void main(void)
{   FILE *goo;
    float grease[MAX_DAYS];
    int count, day = 0;

    /**************************************************** Open file */
    if ((goo = fopen("PRODUCT", "wb+")) == NULL)
    {   printf("Can't open PRODUCT file.\n");
        exit(EXIT_FAILURE);
    }
    /*************************************************** Input values */
    do
    {   ++day;
        printf("Tons for day %2i (-1 to quit): ", day);
        scanf("%f", &grease[day - 1]);
    }while (grease[day - 1] != -1);
    --day;                                 /* Last input (-1) doesn't count */
    /********************************** Write number of values on file */
    if (fwrite(&day, INT_SIZE, 1, goo) != 1)
    {   printf("Error writing file.\n");
        exit(EXIT_FAILURE);
    }
    /********************************************* Write values on file */
    if (fwrite(grease, FLOAT_SIZE, day, goo) != day)
    {   printf("Error writing file.\n");
        exit(EXIT_FAILURE);
    }
    rewind(goo);       /* Reset pointer and allow change from write to read */
```

(continued)

```
/***************************** Read number of values from file */
if (fread(&day, INT_SIZE, 1, goo) != 1)
{  printf("Error reading file.\n");
   exit(EXIT_FAILURE);
}
/********************************************* Read values from file */
if (fread(grease, FLOAT_SIZE, day, goo) != day)
{  printf("Error reading file.\n");
   exit(EXIT_FAILURE);
}
/***************************************************** Print report */
printf("\nDay  Tons\n");
for (count = 1; count <= day; ++count)
    printf(" %2i %5.1f\n", count, grease[count - 1]);
fclose(goo);
}
```

Output

```
Tons for day  1 (-1 to quit): 36.4
Tons for day  2 (-1 to quit): 25
Tons for day  3 (-1 to quit): 42.38
Tons for day  4 (-1 to quit): -1

Day  Tons
  1  36.4
  2  25.0
  3  42.4
```

Each of the file operations above has an error check to see if everything is going according to plan. The file was opened in the "wb+" mode so that a new file would be created, it could be both written and read, and there would be no translations for line endings. In the input loop, the criterion tested for was whether the current input, *grease[day – 1]*, was –1.

The number of items to be written on the file, *day*, was put on the file first; then the items themselves by specifying the *FLOAT_SIZE* as the number of bytes and *day* as the number of items. Reading from the file was in exactly the same order—the integer *day* first and then *day* sets of bytes for the array *grease*. The principle of contiguous storage for arrays becomes very important in cases such as this.

HEADS UP!

If you **fwrite()** it to the file, you must **fread()** it from the file.

YOUR TURN 9–4

1. What are the advantages of byte access to files over character access?

2. What are the principal advantages of character access to files?

3. Describe the arguments to **fread()** and **fwrite()** and tell how they are used by the functions.

BYTE ACCESS AND PORTABILITY

Byte access to files may be fast, but it limits the portability of both the files and the programs. We have already mentioned the fact that most of the ANSI standard data types are not standard in the number of bytes in the data type. If an `int` were put on a file as two bytes, but then the program was recompiled on another system that used four-byte `int`s, the data coming back from the same file would be garbage. Systems also differ in the order in which they store bits. Some put the most significant bit on the left, others on the right. Be sure you know the system particulars before you try to move either programs or files from system to system.

PUTTING IT TOGETHER

Sheldon Diefendorfer has an immense collection of movies on videotape. Right now they are stored on shelves in no particular order, and whenever Shelly wants to watch a video, it takes him an hour to locate the tape. While Shelly's tastes in movies may be a little strange, he's basically a nice guy and has done some favors for us in the past, so we volunteered our computer expertise to help him out.

TASK

Develop a cataloging system to help Shelly keep track of his videos and find them on the shelves.

ANALYSIS

Shelly has some specific data requirements for his video collection. For each movie, he wants to keep track of the title, the year it was released, the length, and its position on his shelves. His shelf positions are labeled from 1 to 5,000. (He will have to add more soon.)

He needs total flexibility with the system to allow him to make any type of change to his video file. We propose that the program start off with a menu of choices like this:

```
Do you want to:        Change:
  [A]dd a video?         A [T]itle?
  [D]elete a video?      A [Y]ear?
  [P]rint the list?      A [L]ength?
  [Q]uit?                A [S]helf position?
Take your pick:
```

He would type in the bracketed letter, in caps or lowercase, to make his choice.

The [P]rint option would display the data on the file in the following form:

```
YEAR   LEN SHELF   TITLE
####   ## ####     The complete title
```

The length is in minutes, and the title was put last because its number of characters can vary greatly and the columns would look neater that way. The listing is alphabetically by title.

To add a video, he would type in the title, date, length, and shelf position, and the program would put it in its proper place in the file. The dialog would be as follows:

```
New title: Killer Tomatoes Strike Back
Year, length, shelf position: 1990 88 4180
```

To delete a video, he would type in a few of the first characters of the title; the computer would find the first match and ask for confirmation before deleting. If he responded that he did not want to delete, the computer would find each subsequent match until either he responded that he did want to delete or the computer ran out of matches, in which case no deletions would be made. That dialog might be as follows:

```
Delete title: Frank
Delete Frankenstein? n
Delete Frankenstein Meets the Space Monster? y
```

He should be able to change any part of any record. The change dialog will be similar. The computer asks for confirmation on the title, prints out the current value, and waits for the new value. For example, changing the shelf position of a video might look like this:

```
Change position of title: R
Change Rock'N'Roll High School Forever? y
Change 2615 to: 4403
```

DESIGN, IMPLEMENTATION, AND TEST

Normally, these steps would be taken in order—the entire design completed before coding and testing—but, since the program is designed with highly encapsulated, stand-alone modules, we will look at the three processes for each module. We hope this will save you, the reader, a lot of page flipping.

The one factor that will be consistent within all the modules will be the format of the file—all the modules will have to work with the same data file. In designing this file, two factors are of prime importance. First, the printouts should be in alphabetical order by title, so it was decided to maintain the file in the same order. Second, Sheldon has spent a fortune in videotape, and therefore cannot afford much in the way of floppy disks, so storage space must be kept to a minimum.

As we shall see when we look at record-based data in Chapter 11, having files with equal-length records offers many advantages. One disadvantage, however, is typically a lot of wasted space on the file to make the records even. For example, consider *Hud* and *Incredibly Strange Creatures Who Stopped Living and Became Mixed-Up Zombies, The.* (Yes, it's a real movie! In fact, it was later released as *Teenage Psycho Meets Bloody Mary*, maybe because the first name was too long.). Each title would have to be at least 81 characters, meaning that we would have to pad *Hud* with 78 trailing blanks or nulls—a tremendous waste of file space. Therefore, we will make our file with unequal length records. *Hud* would be stored with just 3 characters followed by a newline to show where the title ends.

The numbers—year, length, and shelf position—will not be converted to characters for the file. Instead, they will be stored in short variables in memory, and the contents of those variables copied directly to the file.

Creating a File for Testing

DESIGN

Before releasing this program to Shelly, we want to test it thoroughly. Our first process, then, will be to create a dummy file for testing and to give him a file to start with. It follows this pattern:

```
[New file]
    Open file
    Write records
    Close file
```

Writing each record can be done in a separate module, especially since we will have to do the same process in other parts of our program.

```
[Write record]
    Write title in characters
    Put newline at end of title
    Write year, length, shelf position in bytes
```

IMPLEMENTATION

We will implement these two modules in the ⇨Functions *new_file()*, and *write_record()*.

⇨**Functions *new_file()* and *write_record()***

```
      void new_file(void) /************* Creates new file for testing purposes */
n1  {   FILE *video;

n2        video = fopen("VIDEOS.DAT", "wb");
n3        write_record(video, "Blob, The", 1958, 95, 4265);
n4        write_record(video, "Cannibal Women in the Avocado Jungle of Death",
                      1988, 90, 3328);
n5        write_record(video, "Frankenstein Meets the Space Monster", 1965, 75,
                      1005);
n6        write_record(video, "Rock'N'Roll High School Forever", 1990, 94, 2615);
n7        fclose(video);
    }

w1  void write_record /********************** Writes a single record to file */
         (FILE *video, char title[], short year, short length, short shelf)
w2  {   fputs(title, video);
w3      fputs("\n", video);      /* Newline at end of title so that fgets works */
w4      fwrite(&year, SHORT_SIZE, 1, video);
w5      fwrite(&length, SHORT_SIZE, 1, video);
w6      fwrite(&shelf, SHORT_SIZE, 1, video);
    }
```

EXECUTION CHART—*new_file()* and *write_record()*

Line	Explanation	main():	video
n1	Declare a variable for the address of a file description.		???
n2	Open the file for write-only, assign description pointer. It will be different on different systems.		EF08
n3–n6	Call function, pass values.		EF08

	write_record():	video	At title	year	length	shelf
w1	Initialize variables from call.	EF08	Blob, ...	1958	95	4265
w2	Write title to file.	EF08	Blob, ...	1958	95	4265
w3	Put newline at end of title on file. Will need this so that future fgets() functions will work.	EF08	Blob, ...	1958	95	4265
w4	Copy 2 bytes from the address of *year* to file.	EF08	Blob, ...	1958	95	4265
w5, w6	Do the same for *length* and *shelf*.	EF08	Blob, ...	1958	95	4265

		main():	video
n7	Close the file, release memory.		???

TEST

The test for this section is to run it and see if it works. Seeing if it works, though, is difficult because the file is not directly readable. We see a printout below, but the numeric values are garbage as far as a human is concerned. Here, they are a word processor's interpretation of what the bytes look like when they are printed as characters. We will have a better test when we write the function that prints out the file.

VIDEOS.DAT File

```
Blob, The
¦Ð_²©»Cannibal Women in the Avocado Jungle of Death
ÄçZœ÷¥Frankenstein Meets the Space Monster
-µK¾íšRock'N'Roll High School Forever
Æ‰^§7¿
```

The main() Function and Menu

The main() function will contain all the includes for the header files and the function declarations. It also defines three constants, which will be used for subscripts of an array that will store the values of the year, length, and shelf position of the video.

The principal role of the main() function is to provide the menu of choices for maintaining the video file. Before the user is offered the menu, though, we check to see that the video file actually exists. The structure is:

> If file does not exist
>   quit
> Do as many operations as desired
>   Print menu
>   Input choice
>   React to choice
> While choice not to quit

The expansion of this can easily be done in the code.

The only data requirements here are the address of a file description that we will use to test to see if the video file exists, and a variable for the user's choice. The reaction to the choice will be to call a function to service that choice.

⇨Program 9–6 shows our coding of the main function. The entire program includes the code for the other functions to follow.

```
    #include <stdio.h>
    #include <stdlib.h>
    #include <string.h>
    #include <ctype.h>

    #define SHORT_SIZE 2              /* Number of bytes in short data type */
    #define MAX_CHRS 50        /* Maximum length for a title, less one for \0 */
    #define ITEMS 3                  /* Number of data items kept for each video */
                                /* Indices for data items array for each video */
      #define YEAR 0
      #define LENGTH 1                                        /* In minutes */
      #define SHELF 2                              /* Position on the shelves */

    void add(void);
    void del(void);
    void change_title(void);
    void change(int sub);
    void print_file(void);
    void write_record(FILE *video, char title[], short year,
                      short length, short shelf);
    void new_file(void);

    void main(void)
1   {   FILE *video;
        char choice;

    /*   new_file();                  Used only for the first run of the test */

        /*************************************** Test to see if file exists */
2       if ((video = fopen("VIDEOS.DAT", "rb")) == NULL)
        {   puts("Video file missing.");
            exit(EXIT_FAILURE);
        }
3       fclose(video);

4       do /*********************************************************** Menu */
5       {   puts("Do you want to:        Change:");
            puts("   [A]dd a video?       A [T]itle?");
            puts("   [D]elete a video?    A [Y]ear?");
            puts("   [P]rint the list?    A [L]ength?");
            puts("   [Q]uit?              A [S]helf position?");
            printf("Take your choice: ");
6           choice = toupper(getchar());
7           fflush(stdin);                   /* Or while (getchar() != '\n') */
```
                                                                   (continued)

```
8          switch (choice)
9          {  case 'A':
10               add();
11               break;
12             case 'D':
13               del();
14               break;
15             case 'T':
16               change_title();
17               break;
18             case 'Y':
19               change(YEAR);
20               break;
21             case 'L':
22               change(LENGTH);
23               break;
24             case 'S':
25               change(SHELF);
26               break;
27             case 'P':
28               print_file();
          }
29      }while (choice != 'Q');
    }
```

EXECUTION CHART—`main()`

Line	Explanation	video	choice
1	Declare a variable for the address of a file description.	???	???
2	Open the file for read-only because a missing file will cause an error, assign description pointer. It will probably be different from that assigned in *new_file()* function. If it is NULL, then file could not be opened, we would print the message, and exit the program.	ED92	???
3	Close the file. Each function will open it in a mode appropriate for the function.	???	???
5	Print menu.	???	???
6	Get a character from the input stream. The user will have to type the character and press Enter (or Return). Send character to the `toupper()` function, and assign the uppercase result to *choice*.	???	'P'
7	Flush the newline from the input stream.	???	'P'
8	Use *choice* to control `switch`.	???	'P'
27	Jump to `case 'P':`.	???	'P'
28	Call *print_file()* function.	???	'P'
29	*choice* not equal to 'Q', so loop back to 4.	???	'P'

The test for this section is to see if the menu is printed when the video file exists, and to see that the program is sent to the right function for the choice.

Output

```
Do you want to:          Change:
   [A]dd a video?           A [T]itle?
   [D]elete a video?        A [Y]ear?
   [P]rint the list?        A [L]ength?
   [Q]uit?                  A [S]helf position?
Take your pick: p
```

Printing the File

Printing the file involves reading the data from the file and displaying it on the screen. We must continue these operations until we get to the end of the file. To facilitate reading the numeric data from the file, we establish an array of shorts, *data*. One call to fread() will allow us to read the entire array—all three numeric values. The function follows this pattern:

```
Open file
Print heading
While not at the end of the file
    Read title
    Read numbers
    Print numbers
    Print title
Close file
```

The coding for the ⇨Function *print_file()* closely follows the design.

The test is for the proper appearance of the output. This will also test the *new_file()* function. If there are problems, we must do a little digging to ascertain which function is at fault.

```
     void print_file(void) /******************** Displays the data in the file */
p1  {  FILE *video;
        char title[MAX_CHRS];
        short data[ITEMS], sub;

p2      video = fopen("VIDEOS.DAT", "rb");
p3      puts("\n  YEAR    LEN SHELF    TITLE");
p4      while (fgets(title, MAX_CHRS, video) != NULL)
p5      {  fread(data, SHORT_SIZE, ITEMS, video);
p6          for (sub = 0; sub < ITEMS; ++sub)
p7             printf("%6i", data[sub]);
p8          printf("   %s", title);
p9      }
p10     puts("");
p11     fclose (video);
     }
```

Output

```
YEAR    LEN SHELF    TITLE
1958     95  4265    Blob, The
1988     90  3328    Cannibal Women in the Avocado Jungle of Death
1965     75  1005    Frankenstein Meets the Space Monster
1990     94  2615    Rock'N'Roll High School Forever
```

EXECUTION CHART—*print_file()*

Line	Explanation	video	At *title*		data[3]	
p1	Declare a variable for the address of a file description.	???	---			---
p2	Open the file for read only.	EE9C	???	???	???	???
p3	Print the report heading.	EE9C	???	???	???	???
p4	Get a string from the file. When the return from fgets() is the NULL pointer, we are at the end of the file.	EE9C	Blob, …	???	???	???
p5	Read the numbers. We send fread() the address of the array as well as the size of one element and the number of elements. It will get that many bytes, 6 in this case, and put them at *data*.	EE9C	Blob, …	1958	95	4265
p6–p7	Print each element in the array. The values will be the year, length, and shelf position, just as we wrote them on the file.	EE9C	Blob, …	1958	95	4265
p8	Print the title at the end of the numbers.	EE9C	Blob, …	1958	95	4265
p4–p9	Repeat the process until fgets() returns NULL.	EE9C	Rock …	1990	94	2615
p10	Print a blank line at the end of the report.	EE9C	Rock …	1990	94	2615
p11	Close the file, release memory.	???	Rock …	1990	94	2615

Adding to the File

Because of the unequal record lengths, we will copy the data from one file to another, making changes as we copy.

When adding a record, we must maintain the file in alphabetical order, so we will look for a record that is alphabetically greater than the one we wish to add and then insert the new record before it. Once we have made the insertion, we can change the value we have already inserted to something greater than the greatest possible record so that our insertion criteria will not be met again as we copy the rest of the records. In our case, we have chosen to make the *title* a tilde (~), the greatest printable character, ASCII 126.

The pattern of our function is as follows:

```
Open the original data file
Create the new file
Input new title, year, length, and shelf position
While not at the end of the original file
    Read next title
    Read numbers
    If new title < next title
        Write new title, year, length, shelf position
        Change new title so that it will not be found again
    Write title
    Write numbers
If record not added
    Add record to end
Close files
Delete original data file
Rename new file with original file name
```

⇨Function *add()* shows the coding for this section.

In testing the *add()* routine, we should be sure to test adding a record at both the beginning and the end of the file as well as the middle. In our testing, we notice that our titles are case-sensitive, which would make the title *Machine* . . . come after the title *MacTavish* . . . instead of the other way around. The usual solution to this is to make strings into all upper-case characters before any comparisons.

```
        void add(void) /******************************** Adds a record in order */
a1   {   FILE *video, *temp;
        char title[MAX_CHRS], new_title[MAX_CHRS];
        short data[ITEMS];
        short year, length, shelf;

a2      video = fopen("VIDEOS.DAT", "rb");
a3      temp = fopen("TEMP.$TM", "wb");

        printf("New title: ");
a4      gets(new_title);
        printf("Year, length, shelf position: ");
a5      scanf("%hi %hi %hi", &year, &length, &shelf);
a6      while (getchar() != '\n');                    /* Dump trailing newline */

a7      while (fgets(title, MAX_CHRS, video) != NULL)
a8      {   fread(data, SHORT_SIZE, ITEMS, video);
a9          if (strcmp(new_title, title) < 0)         /* Should use all ucase */
a10         {   write_record(temp, new_title, year, length, shelf);
a11             new_title[0] = '~';          /* Highest chr, won't find it again */
            }
a12         fputs(title, temp);
a13         fwrite(data, SHORT_SIZE, ITEMS, temp);
a14     }
a15     if (new_title[0] != '~')                          /* Add to end of file */
a16         write_record(temp, new_title, year, length, shelf);

a17     fclose(video);
a18     fclose(temp);
a19     remove("VIDEOS.DAT");
a20     rename("TEMP.$TM", "VIDEOS.DAT");
    }
```

Output

```
    New title: Buffy, the Vampire Slayer
    Year, length, shelf position: 1992 100 4180
    Take your choice: p

        YEAR   LEN SHELF   TITLE
        1958    95  4265   Blob, The
        1992   100  4180   Buffy, the Vampire Slayer
        1988    90  3328   Cannibal Women in the Avocado Jungle of Death
        1965    75  1005   Frankenstein Meets the Space Monster
        1990    94  2615   Rock'N'Roll High School Forever
```

EXECUTION CHART—*add()*

Line	Explanation	At *new_title*	At *title*	year	length	shelf	data[3]		
a1	Declare variables for the addresses of file descriptions.	---	---			---			---
a2	Open the original data file for read only.	???	???	???	???	???	???	???	???
a3	Create the new file.	???	???	???	???	???	???	???	???
a4	Input *new_title* to add.	Buffy …	???	???	???	???	???	???	???
a5	Input new year, length, and shelf position.	Buffy …	???	1992	100	4180	???	???	???
a6	Get rid of newline from input stream.	Buffy …	???	1992	100	4180	???	???	???
a7	Get a *title* from the data file. fgets() is not NULL.	Buffy …	Blob, …	1992	100	4180	???	???	???
a8	Read the numbers. Put 6 bytes at *data*.	Buffy …	Blob, …	1992	100	4180	1958	95	4265
a9	*new_title* not less than *title*.	Buffy …	Blob, …	1992	100	4180	1958	95	4265
a12–a13	Write the *title* and numbers to new file.	Buffy …	Blob, …	1992	100	4180	1958	95	4265
a7	Get a *title* from the original file. fgets() is not NULL.	Buffy …	Can …	1992	100	4180	1958	95	4265
a8	Read the numbers. put 6 bytes at *data*.	Buffy …	Can …	1992	100	4180	1988	90	3328
a9	*new_title* less than *title*.	Buffy …	Can …	1992	100	4180	1988	90	3328
a10	Write *new_title* record to new file.	Buffy …	Can …	1992	100	4180	1988	90	3328
a11	Change *new_title* so test at a9 will never be true.	~	Can …	1992	100	4180	1988	90	3328
a12–a13	Write the title and numbers to new file.	~	Can …	1992	100	4180	1988	90	3328
a7–a14	Repeat the process until fgets() returns NULL.	~	Rock …	1992	100	4180	1990	94	2615
a15	If *new_title* not ~, we would not have inserted, so a16 would have written the new record at the end of the copy file.	~	Rock …	1992	100	4180	1990	94	2615
a17–a18	Close both files.	~	Rock …	1992	100	4180	1990	94	2615
a19	Delete the original data file.	~	Rock …	1992	100	4180	1990	94	2615
a20	Put the original data file's name on the new file.	~	Rock …	1992	100	4180	1990	94	2615

Deleting from the File

DESIGN

Deleting from the file is similar to adding to the file, except that we will copy all the records except the one we wish to delete. To make it easier to use, we will allow Shelly to type in only a few characters of the title he wants to delete. We will print the full title and ask for confirmation before we delete. Once the program makes a deletion, we will set the delete title to a tilde (~) so that there will be no more matches.

Open the original data file
Create the new file
Input title to delete
While not at the end of the original file
    Read title
    Read numbers
    Default to not deleting unless changed later
    If delete title = title
       Print full title
       Input Y or N for delete
    If not delete
       Write title, year, length, shelf position to new file
    Else   [Have made deletion]
       Set delete title so it won't be found again
Close files
Delete original data file
Rename new file with original file name

⇨Function *del()* deletes a record.

⇨Function *del()*

```
    void del(void) /************************ Deletes a record from the file */
d1  {   FILE *video, *temp;
        char title[MAX_CHRS], del_title[MAX_CHRS], answer;
        short data[ITEMS];

d2      video = fopen("VIDEOS.DAT", "rb");
d3      temp = fopen("TEMP.$TM", "wb");

        printf("Delete title: ");
d4      gets(del_title);
d5      while (fgets(title, MAX_CHRS, video) != NULL)
d6      {   fread(data, SHORT_SIZE, ITEMS, video);
d7          answer = 'N';                           /* Default to don't delete */
d8          if (strncmp(del_title, title, strlen(del_title)) == 0)
                                    /* Test as many characters as typed in */
d9          {   printf("Delete %.*s? ",             /* Print without newline */
                    strlen(title) - 1, title);
d10             answer = toupper(getchar());
                while (getchar() != '\n');          /* Dump newline from stream */
            }
```

(continued)

```
d11          if (answer != 'Y')                          /* If not delete, write */
d12          {  fputs(title, temp);
d13             fwrite(data, SHORT_SIZE, ITEMS, temp);
             }
             else                                        /* Have made deletion */
d14             del_title[0] = '~';                       /* Don't find it again */
d15          }
d16       fclose(video);
d17       fclose(temp);
d18       remove("VIDEOS.DAT");
d19       rename("TEMP.$TM", "VIDEOS.DAT");
       }
```

EXECUTION CHART—del()

Line	Explanation	At del_title	At title	answer	data[3]		
d1	Declare variables for the addresses of file descriptions.	---	---	---			---
d2–d3	Open the original data and new files.	???	???	???	???	???	???
d4	Input del_title to delete.	Frank	???	???	???	???	???
d5	Get a title from the original file. fgets() is not NULL.	Frank	Blob, ...	???	???	???	???
d6	Read the numbers. Put at data.	Frank	Blob, ...	???	1958	95	4265
d7	Default delete answer to no.	Frank	Blob, ...	N	1958	95	4265
d8	del_title not equal to first 5 characters of title.	Frank	Blob, ...	N	1958	95	4265
d11	answer not equal to Y.	Frank	Blob, ...	N	1958	95	4265
d12–d13	Write the record to new file.	Frank ...	Blob, ...	N	1958	95	4265
d5–d15	Do the same for the next record.	Frank ...	Can ...	N	1988	90	3328
d5	Get a title from the original file. fgets() is not NULL.	Frank	Frank ...	N	1988	90	3328
d6	Read the numbers. Put at data.	Frank	Frank ...	N	1965	75	1005
d7	Default delete answer to no.	Frank	Frank ...	N	1965	75	1005
d8	del_title equal to first 5 characters of title.	Frank	Frank ...	N	1965	75	1005
d9	Print full title but stop before newline.	Frank	Frank ...	N	1965	75	1005
d10	Input answer and make uppercase.	Frank	Frank ...	Y	1965	75	1005
d11	answer equal to Y.	Frank	Frank ...	Y	1965	75	1005
d14	Skip writing the record and change del_title.	~	Frank ...	Y	1965	75	1005
d5–d15	Go through same process for any subsequent records. No matches will be found; all records will be written to new file.	~	Rock ...	Y	1990	94	2615
d16–d17	Close both files.	~	Rock ...	Y	1990	94	2615
d18	Delete the original data file.	~	Rock ...	Y	1990	94	2615
d19	Put the original data file's name on the new file.	~	Rock ...	Y	1990	94	2615

As in adding, it is important to test deletions at the beginning and the end as well as in the middle of the file.

Output

```
Delete title: Frank
Delete Frankenstein Meets the Space Monster? y
Take your choice: p

    YEAR   LEN  SHELF   TITLE
    1958    95   4265   Blob, The
    1992   100   4180   Buffy, the Vampire Slayer
    1988    90   3328   Cannibal Women in the Avocado Jungle of Death
    1990    94   2615   Rock'N'Roll High School Forever
```

Changing a Title

Changing a title is similar to the other two types of changes—the file must be copied and the title changed in the process. Again, we will allow Shelly to input only a few characters of the title to be changed.

⇨Function *change_title()* follows the file-copying pattern for changing file data.

Again, testing changes at the beginning and the end of the file is imperative. Our thorough testing of this routine has pointed up a flaw: the changed title is always placed in the same position in the file as the original title. That means the new title might not remain in alphabetical order. For example, if we changed *Incredibly Strange Creatures Who Stopped Living and Became Mixed-Up Zombies, The* to *Teenage Psycho Meets Bloody Mary*, it would undoubtedly not be in the right place. A way to correct the problem would be to make the change be a combination of a deletion and an addition.

⇨**Function *change_title()***

```
      void change_title(void)  /******************************** Changes a title */
t1  {  FILE *video, *temp;
       char title[MAX_CHRS], ch_title[MAX_CHRS], answer;
       short data[ITEMS];

t2     video = fopen("VIDEOS.DAT", "rb");
t3     temp = fopen("TEMP.$TM", "wb");

       printf("Change title: ");
t4     gets(ch_title);
t5     while (fgets(title, MAX_CHRS, video) != NULL)            /* Read record */
t6     {  fread(data, SHORT_SIZE, ITEMS, video);
t7        if (strncmp(ch_title, title, strlen(ch_title)) == 0)
                                      /* Test as many characters as typed in */
t8        {  printf("Change %.*s? ",                   /* Print without newline */
                   strlen(title) - 1, title);
t9           answer = getchar();
             while (getchar() != '\n');      /* Dump newline from input stream */
t10          if (toupper(answer) == 'Y')
             {  printf("To: ");
t11             gets(title);                 /* Change the title in the record */
t12             strcat(title, "\n");                    /* Add newline for file */
t13             ch_title[0] = '~';                     /* Don't find it again */
             }
          }
t14       fputs(title, temp);                               /* Write record */
t15       fwrite(data, SHORT_SIZE, ITEMS, temp);
       }
t16    fclose(video);
t17    fclose(temp);
t18    remove("VIDEOS.DAT");
t19    rename("TEMP.$TM", "VIDEOS.DAT");
    }
```

Output

```
    Change title: Bl
    Change Blob, The? y
    To: Blob the Sequel, Part VIII, The
    Take your choice: p

        YEAR   LEN SHELF    TITLE
        1958    95  4265    Blob the Sequel, Part VIII, The
        1992   100  4180    Buffy, the Vampire Slayer
        1988    90  3328    Cannibal Women in the Avocado Jungle of Death
        1990    94  2615    Rock'N'Roll High School Forever
```

EXECUTION CHART—*change_title()*

Line	Explanation	At *ch_title*	At *title*	*answer*		*data[3]*	
t1	Declare variables for the addresses of file descriptions.	---	---	---			---
t2–t3	Open the original data and new files.	???	???	???	???	???	???
t4	Input *ch_title* to change.	BI	???	???	???	???	???
t5	Get a *title* from the original file. `fgets()` is not NULL.	BI	Blob, …	???	???	???	???
t6	Read the numbers. Put at *data*.	BI	Blob, …	???	1958	95	4265
t7	*ch_title* equal to first 2 characters of *title*.	BI	Blob, …	???	1958	95	4265
t8	Print full title but stop before newline.	BI	Blob, …	???	1958	95	4265
t9	Input *answer*.	BI	Blob, …	y	1958	95	4265
t10	Uppercase *answer* equal to Y.	BI	Blob, …	y	1958	95	4265
t11	Input new *title*.	BI	Blob t …	y	1958	95	4265
t12	Add newline to *title*.	BI	Blob t …	y	1958	95	4265
t13	Change *ch_title* so we don't find it again.	~	Blob t …	y	1958	95	4265
t13–t15	Write the record to new file.	~	Blob t …	y	1958	95	4265
t6–t15	Go through same process for any subsequent records. No matches will be found; all records will be written to new file.	~	Rock …	y	1990	94	2615
t16–t17	Close both files.	~	Rock …	y	1990	94	2615
t18	Delete the original data file.	~	Rock …	y	1990	94	2615
t19	Put the original data file's name on the new file.	~	Rock …	y	1990	94	2615

Changing the Numbers

DESIGN

```
Receive choice from menu
Open the data file
Input title to change
While not at the end of the file
    Read title
    Read numbers
    If change title = title
        Print full title
        Input Y or N for change
        If change
            Print old data
            Input new data
            Set file position to proper place
            Write record to file
            Set position indicator to end of file to force loop exit
Close file
```

The numbers all occupy the same amount of space in the file. Changing them will be much easier because we can simply find them in the file and write over them. We don't need another file. After we have found what we are looking for, we can back up the file position indicator and write in the same spot. In this case, we will write the entire *data* array. The menu process will send the subscript of the array variable we want to change to the *change()* function, which will change that variable and rewrite the entire array.

IMPLEMENTATION

⇨Function *change()* follows the more direct method of changing file data.

⇨Function *change()*

```
c1   void change(int sub) /************** Changes one of the other parameters */
c2   {   FILE *video;
         char title[MAX_CHRS], ch_title[MAX_CHRS], answer;
         short data[ITEMS];

c3       video = fopen("VIDEOS.DAT", "rb+");                    /* Must read and write */


         printf("Change title: ");
c4       gets(ch_title);
c5       while (fgets(title, MAX_CHRS, video) != NULL)          /* Read record */
c6       {   fread(data, SHORT_SIZE, ITEMS, video);
c7           if (strncmp(ch_title, title, strlen(ch_title)) == 0)
                                    /* Test as many characters as typed in */
c8           {   printf("Change %.*s? ",                 /* Print without newline */
                     strlen(title) - 1, title);
c9               answer = getchar();
                 while (getchar() != '\n');              /* Dump end of input stream */
c10              if (toupper(answer) == 'Y')             /* Confirm if proper title */
c11              {   printf("Change %i to: ", data[sub]);
c12                  scanf("%i", &data[sub]);
                     fflush(stdin);                      /* Dump end of input stream */
c13                  fseek(video, -(long)(ITEMS * SHORT_SIZE), SEEK_CUR);/*Back up*/
c14                  fwrite(data, SHORT_SIZE, ITEMS, video);
c15                  fseek(video, 0L, SEEK_END);         /* Force loop exit */
                 }
             }
c16      }
c17      fclose(video);
     }
```

TEST

We must test this routine with year, length, and shelf position with a variety of titles.

Output

```
Change title: C
Change Cannibal Women in the Avocado Jungle of Death? y
Change 3328 to: 4403
Take your choice: p
```

```
YEAR  LEN SHELF   TITLE
1958   95  4265   Blob the Sequel, Part VIII, The
1992  100  4180   Buffy, the Vampire Slayer
1988   90  4403   Cannibal Women in the Avocado Jungle of Death
1990   94  2615   Rock'N'Roll High School Forever
```

EXECUTION CHART—change()

Line	Explanation	At ch_title	At title	answer	data[3]		
c1	Initialize *sub* with value from main().						
c2	Declare variable for address of file description.	---	---	---			---
c3	Open the data file.	???	???	???	???	???	???
c4	Input *ch_title* to change.	C	???	???	???	???	???
c5	Get a *title* from the data file. fgets() is not NULL.	C	Blob ...	???	???	???	???
c6	Read the numbers. Put at *data*.	C	Blob ...	???	1958	95	4265
c7	*ch_title* not equal to first character of *title*.	C	Blob ...	???	1958	95	4265
c5–c16	Do same for *Buffy* . . . record.	C	Buff ...	???	1992	100	4180
c5	Get a *title* from the data file. fgets() is not NULL.	C	Can ...	???	1992	100	4180
c6	Read the numbers. Put at *data*. File position now beyond numbers at beginning of *Franken* . . .	C	Can ...	???	1988	90	3328
c7	*ch_title* equal to first character of *title*.	C	Can ...	???	1988	90	3328
c8	Print full title but stop before newline.	C	Can ...	???	1988	90	3328
c9	Input *answer*.	C	Can ...	y	1988	90	3328
c10	Uppercase *answer* equal to Y.	C	Can ...	y	1988	90	3328
c11	Print original data for array variable.	C	Can ...	y	1988	90	3328
c12	Input new data.	C	Can ...	y	1988	90	4403
c13	Back up file position by the number of bytes in *data* array. It should now be at the beginning of the numbers in the *Cannibals* record.	C	Can ...	y	1988	90	4403
c14	Copy the 6 bytes in *data* array to file, overwriting the 6 bytes there.	C	Can ...	y	1988	90	4403
c15	Move file position to end of file.	C	Can ...	y	1988	90	4403
c5	Attempt to get a *title* from the data file. fgets() is NULL.	C	Can ...	y	1988	90	4403
c17	Close file.	C	Can ...	y	1988	90	4403

SUMMARY

File	Binary file
Name	Character access
Extension	Byte access
Buffer	SEEK_SET
File position indicator	SEEK_CUR
FILE	SEEK_END
File description	End-of-file indicator
Text file	Pointer to void

▲ **NEW FUNCTIONS** (in order of appearance)

`FILE *fopen(const char *file_id, const char *mode)`   `<stdio.h>`
   Purpose: Open a `file_id` file for `mode`, and establish a description and stream for it.
   Return: Success: Pointer to `file` description. Error: NULL.

`int fclose(FILE *file)`   `<stdio.h>`
   Purpose: Flush `file` stream (if open for write) and deallocate `file` description.
   Return: Success: Zero. Error: EOF.

`int fprintf(FILE *file, const char *control_string, arguments)`   `<stdio.h>`
   Purpose: Write on `file` values of arguments in format specified in `control_string`.
   Return: Success: number of characters written. Error: negative value.

`int fscanf(FILE *file, const char *control_string, arguments)`   `<stdio.h>`
   Purpose: Assign values from `file` to argument variables according to `control_string`.
   Return: Success: number of assignments made. Error: EOF if end of file.

`int getc(FILE *file)`   `<stdio.h>`
   Purpose: Read single character from the `file`.
   Return: Success: ASCII (or EBCDIC) value of character read. Error: EOF.

`int putc(int character, FILE *file)`   `<stdio.h>`
   Purpose: Write the `character` on the `file`.
   Return: Success: ASCII (or EBCDIC) value of `character` written. Error: EOF.

`char *fgets(char *string, int max, FILE *file)`   `<stdio.h>`
   Purpose: Read a line (up to `max` – 1 characters) from the `file` into the `string`.
   Return: Success: `string`. Error: NULL.

`int fputs(const char *string, FILE *file)`   `<stdio.h>`
   Purpose: Write the `string` onto the `file`.
   Return: Success: Nonnegative. Error: EOF.

`void rewind(FILE *file)`   `<stdio.h>`
   Purpose: Return the pointer to the beginning of `file`.
   Return: None.

```
int fseek(FILE *file, long offset, int origin)                              <stdio.h>
```
   Purpose: Set the *file* pointer at *offset* bytes from *origin*.
   Return: Success: Zero. Error: Nonzero.

```
long ftell(FILE *file)                                                      <stdio.h>
```
   Purpose: Obtain current position of *file* pointer.
   Return: Success: Bytes from beginning of *file*. Error: −1L.

```
int remove(const char *filename)                                           <stdio.h>
```
   Purpose: Delete the file *filename* from secondary storage.
   Return: Success: Zero. Error: Nonzero.

```
int unlink(const char *filename)                                           <stdio.h>
```
   Purpose: Remove link to the file *filename* from secondary storage, or remove file if last link.
   Return: Success: Zero. Error: Nonzero.

```
int rename(const char *oldname, const char *newname)                       <stdio.h>
```
   Purpose: Change the name of the file *oldname* in secondary storage to *newname*.
   Return: Success: Zero. Error: Nonzero.

```
int feof(FILE *file)                                                       <stdio.h>
```
   Purpose: Determine whether end-of-file indicator for *file* is set.
   Return: Nonzero if end-of-file indicator set.

```
size_t fwrite(const void *location, size_t bytes, size_t items, FILE *file) <stdio.h>
```
   Purpose: Write *bytes* * *items* bytes from *location* to *file*.
   Return: Success: *items*. Error: Something other than *items*.

```
size_t fread(const void *location, size_t bytes, size_t items, FILE *file) <stdio.h>
```
   Purpose: Read *bytes* * *items* bytes from *file* to *location*.
   Return: Success: *items*. Error: Something other than *items*.

▲CONCEPT REVIEW

▼ Any entity in secondary storage is referred to as a **file**. It must be identified by a combination of a **name**, an optional **extension**, and possibly a path.

▼ A program cannot work directly with individual bytes in a file, so a portion of the file is brought into main memory in a **buffer**. C will keep track of its byte position in a file by maintaining a **file position indicator**.

▼ The **fopen()** function establishes in main memory a **file description** of data type **FILE** that includes, among other things, the file identifier and its mode. The address of the description is returned by the function.

▼ The file's mode tells whether C should look for an existing file, or a new one should be created; whether the file can be read from, written to, or both; and whether it is a **binary file** or a **text file**.

▼ The **fclose()** function writes the contents of the current buffer, if it has changed, into the appropriate place in secondary storage, making changes permanent, and deallocates the memory space for both the file buffer and the file description.

▼ **Character access** to a file refers to storing all data on the file in readable characters (converting numbers to strings) and converting back to the proper data types when reading, whereas **byte access** copies bytes from main memory (storing numbers in binary numeric form) and reads them back the same way.

▼ Formatted character access is accomplished using **fprintf()** for writing and **fscanf()** for reading. Single-character access uses **getc()** and **putc()**, and string access uses **fgets()** and **fputs()**.

▼ The file position indicator may be reset to the beginning of the file using **rewind()**. The **fseek()** function moves the file position indicator a stated number of bytes from one of three origin positions: **SEEK_SET**, the beginning of the file; **SEEK_CUR**, the current position; and **SEEK_END**, the end of the file. The **ftell()** function returns the current byte position of the file position indicator.

▼ A file may be deleted from secondary storage by **remove()** (or the related **unlink()** for some UNIX systems), or have its name changed by **rename()**.

▼ A read attempted at the end of the file will cause an **end-of-file indicator** to be set. We can test for that with **feof()**. The error condition can be cleared using **rewind()**.

▼ The **fread()** and **fwrite()** functions perform byte access to files, shifting data between a file and a specific location in main memory. The memory location is stated as a **pointer to void**, meaning that a given number of bytes will be stored there regardless of the data type.

▲HEADS UP: POINTS OF SPECIAL INTEREST

▼ Is your operating system case-sensitive?

▼ File buffering should be transparent to us.

▼ The pointer to the file description is worthless until the file is opened. *The pointer has nothing to point to.*

▼ Text files differ with different operating systems. *Line endings and end-of-file indications differ.*

▼ When in doubt, use binary. *No translations are made with binary files.*

▼ A crash does not automatically close files. *Your file changes may not have been written to the disk.*

▼ It's good practice to explicitly close any file you open.

▼ Files written using character access are readable with ordinary text editors.

▼ fprintf() and fscanf() work the same as their nonfile counterparts.

▼ Notice the differences between gets() and fgets(). *Line endings are not stored with* gets().

▼ Notice the differences between puts() and fputs(). *Line endings are not output with* fputs().

▼ A file access always moves the file position indicator.

▼ Changing files with unequal-length records requires copying from one file to another.

▼ Don't forget to clear the end-of-file indicator. *If you have attempted access at the end of the file, the end-of-file condition will remain set until cleared.*

▼ A pointer to void can point to any data type.

▼ If you fwrite() it to the file, you must fread() it from the file.

▲TRAPS: COMMON PROGRAMMING ERRORS

▼ Referring to the FILE data type in lowercase.

▼ Using a single backslash in a string.

▼ Opening a file for "w" that has needed data in it. *This file mode starts you with a new, empty file.*

▼ Changing between reading to writing without calling one of the file positioning functions.

▼ It's %s or %[], not %[]s. *Don't get your string conversion codes in* printf() *or* fprintf() *mixed up.*

▼ Moving the file position indicator out of the range of the file.

▼ Attempting to remove a file that is open.

▼ Expecting feof() to return nonzero just because the file position is at the end. *You must attempt access at the end.*

▲YOUR TURN ANSWERS

▼9–1

1. A typical file identifier can consist of a path, a file name, and an extension, using at least the alpha and numeric characters.

2. Moving blocks of a file in and out of a buffer in main memory so as to be able to access the data a byte at a time.

3. An area in memory set up by an open() function that contains information about the file including the file position indicator.

4. To maintain the address of the file description so that if a function receives this address, it can find out anything it might need to know about the file.

5. The modes "r" and "a" work with existing files. Mode "w" will create a new file, as will "a" if one does not already exist.

6. Mode "r" allows read access whereas "w" and "a" allow write. Any mode will allow either access if followed by "+".

7. For text files, C may possibly translate line endings and look for special end-of-file indications, depending on the operating system. C makes no translations for binary files.

8. The `fclose()` function returns the buffered data to secondary storage and deallocates the buffer and file-description memory.

▼**9–2**

1. Character access treats the file as we have done with the screen and keyboard—translating everything to and from human-readable characters. Byte access simply copies bytes to and from the file.

2. The first argument for either function is the pointer to the file description, and the access is to the file rather than the screen and keyboard. Otherwise, they are the same.

3. `getc()` and `putc()`.

4. Unlike `gets()`, `fgets()` has a *max* characters argument and does not strip the newline from the end of the string.

5. `fputs()` does not add a newline to the end of the string; `puts()` does.

▼**9–3**

1. `rewind(data)` or `fseek(data, 0L, SEEK_SET)`.

2. `SEEK_SET, SEEK_CUR, SEEK_END`.

3. `ftell()`.

4. The `remove()` function deletes a file. (The `unlink()` function breaks a link to the file in UNIX systems, deleting the file if the last link has been broken.)

5. `rename()`.

6. An attempted read at the end of the file.

▼**9–4**

1. Byte access requires no conversion of data, and it typically results in shorter files.

2. The files produced are readable by humans using text editors and the programs are more portable.

3. The first argument is simply a memory address, the second and third arguments are multiplied together to determine a number of bytes, and that number of bytes is moved between memory and the file described in the fourth argument.

EXERCISES

1. Investigate the file identification rules for your operating system.
   a. How many characters are allowed in a file name?
   b. Are file identifiers case-sensitive?
   c. Are spaces allowed in file identifiers?
   d. Are extensions allowed, and if so, how many characters may they contain?
   e. What kinds of "paths" are allowed—disk designations, folders, directories, subdirectories, and so forth?

2. Show the proper file mode for opening a file in each case.
   a. Read from an existing text file but ensure that the program can make no changes.
   b. Create a new binary file for both read and write access.
   c. Read and write any part of an existing text file.
   d. If a file doesn't exist, create it; otherwise allow reads and writes anywhere beyond the end of the original binary file.

3. What are the differences between binary and text files in your operating system?

4. Write a generalized function, *openfile()*, that opens a file whose identifier is passed to it, in the mode passed to it. If it is opened successfully, the function should return the pointer to the file description. If not, the function should print an error indication and terminate the program.

5. Point out the problems in the following program segment.
```
char string[50];
FILE stuff;

if (fopen(stuff, +bw, MYFILE) == EOF)
{   puts("Can't open file.");
    exit(EXIT_FAILURE);
}
fscanf("%s", string, MYFILE);
fgets(string, MYFILE);
fclose(MYFILE);
```

6. The file pointer is positioned at the beginning of the following characters in a file. Show the `fscanf()` function control string needed to read the data into a string and two `float`s.
```
Farley, 46.5 / 7.1
```

7. Why won't this program segment work?
```
fgets(data, 50, file);
fputs(data, file);
```

8. Show the statement needed to move the file position indicator back to the position prior to the following read.

```
fread(mem, 25, 2, file);
```

9. Put statements before and after the following that will return the file position to where it was before the read.

```
fgets(string, 1000, file);
```

10. Why won't this stop at the end of the file?

```
while ( !feof(file))
{  fgets(data, 50, file);
   statements
}
```

11. Correct the following program segment.

```
file1 = fopen("FIRST", "rb);
file2 = fopen("SECOND", "wb");
    [Copy from one file to the other]
rename("SECOND", "FIRST");
```

12. What are the problems in the following program segment?

```
#define FLOAT_SIZE 4
FILE junk;
float arr[10];

fopen(junk, "JUNK", "wb+");
fread(junk, FLOAT_SIZE, 40, arr);
arr[4] = 487.2;
fwrite(junk, FLOAT_SIZE, 40, arr);
fclose("JUNK");
```

PROGRAMS

1. Modify ⇨Program 9–1 so that the entire name rather than the first 10 characters is put in the file, and the numbers take up only the room required for them. The file contents should end up as shown with the same inputs. Rewrite the *Additional Code* so that the report will print as shown.

File Contents

```
Quibble, Marvin/12.34/2
Jones, Hatshepset/9.38/8
Montmorrissey, Clyde/23.98/1
```

Additional Output

```
Name                 Pay Rate   Dependents
Quibble, Marvin        12.34         2
Jones, Hatshepset       9.38         8
Montmorrissey, Clyde   23.98         1
```

2. Write a program that allows input of names and ages from the keyboard and stores them, in characters, in the file *PEOPLE.DAT*. After the input is finished, the program should print out what is in the file as well as the average age. Enter the names in alphabetical order so that the file may be used in later programs.

Variables

```
people          Pointer to file description
name[]
age
total, count    To calculate average age
```

Output

```
Enter name/age: Freebisch, Lance/72
Enter name/age: Jones, Abner/45
Enter name/age: Smith, Melvin/26
Enter name/age:
Name        Age
Freebisch,  72
Jones, Abn  45
Smith, Mel  26
Average age: 47.67
```

3. Write a program that searches the file *PEOPLE.DAT* (from the problem above) sequentially for a name (last name only) input from the keyboard.

Variables

```
people      Pointer to file description
name_in[], last_name[], first_name[]
age
```

Output

```
Enter last name: Jones
Jones, Abner  45
Enter last name: Freebisch
Freebisch, Lance  72
Enter last name:
```

4. Write a program that will allow you to input a last name and change any last or first name or age in the file *PEOPLE.DAT* referred to in Program 2.

5. Write a program that will allow you to add a record, in alphabetical order, to the file *PEOPLE.DAT* referred to in Program 2.

6. Write a program that will allow you to input a last name and delete the record with that last name from the file *PEOPLE.DAT* referred to in the problem above.

7. Rewrite ⇨Program 9–2 so that the *QUIZ.ANS* file contains only the answer, not the question followed by the answer. The output should be the same.

8. A real estate firm uses a computer to keep track of houses available to sell. They regularly publish two sets of listings, one of smaller houses, less than 2,000 square feet, and one of houses 2,000 square feet and over. The individual listing contains the listing date, address, price, and square footage. The date should be in six-digit fashion with year, month, and day (for example, May 4, 1996, would be 960504). Write a program that will accept listings from the terminal and enter them in either of two files, *SMALL* or *LARGE*. After entry is complete, both sets of listings should be printed out.

Variables

```
small, large    File description pointers
date
address
price
sq_feet
```

Output

```
Date, address, price, sq. feet?
960122,14 Walnut,174550,2250
Date, address, price, sq. feet?
960128,345 Oak,143990,1450
Date, address, price, sq. feet?
960205,22 Elm,156450,1700
Date, address, price, sq. feet?
960213,988 Maple,204550,3300
Date, address, price, sq. feet?
960301,76 Apple,172500,1900
Date, address, price, sq. feet?
```

(continued)

```
HOUSES LESS THAN 2000 SQ. FT.
List date    Address      Price     Sq. Feet
960128       345 Oak      143990    1450
960205       22 Elm       156450    1700
960301       76 Apple     172500    1900

HOUSES 2000 SQ. FT. OR MORE.
List date    Address      Price     Sq. Feet
960122       14 Walnut    174550    2250
960213       988 Maple    204550    3300
```

9. Write a program that works with two files (*EMPLOY* and *WEEKLY*). *EMPLOY* should store the employee name, wage, retirement, and tax rate, and should be filled by input from the terminal. Input is stopped by pressing just the Enter key, at which time the user is asked for the hours worked for each employee. Hours worked and net pay are stored in *WEEKLY*. After all the data is input, a payroll report is generated using data from both files. If *EMPLOY* is filled, the program should sense that this file has data in it and the user should not be prompted for that data. Instead, the user will just enter the *WEEKLY* data, overwriting the *WEEKLY* file, and get a payroll report. Save the program as *PAY* for use later.

Suggested Variables

```
emp, week  File description pointers
name       Employee name
wage
ret        Retirement
tax        Tax rate
hours
net        Net pay   (hours × wage − hours × wage × tax − ret)
```

Output

```
Employee name, wage, ret, tax? Jones 3.5 5.5 .16
Employee name, wage, ret, tax? Smith 4.75 6.35 .21
Employee name, wage, ret, tax? Brown 4.25 5.75 .17
Employee name, wage, ret, tax?

Hours worked for Jones? 34.5
Hours worked for Smith? 38
Hours worked for Brown? 45

NAME     WAGE      RET       TAX      NET PAY
Jones    $3.50     $5.50     16%      $ 95.93
Smith    $4.75     $6.35     21%      $136.25
Brown    $4.25     $5.75     17%      $152.99
```

10. Write a program that will allow input and maintenance of the company's employee file (*EMPLOY*) as described in the *PAY* program in the problem above. Your program should allow you to add or delete employees, or change any part of an employee's record.

11. Write a program that keeps track of student grades. It builds a new *GRADE* file by asking for a name for each of three students and three grades for each student. After all the grades are input, a grade report is printed giving the total points and the average.

Variables

Choose appropriate variables

Output

```
Name and grades? Jones 68 97 24
Name and grades? Smith 76 94 78
Name and grades? Brown 91 56 78

NAME    GRD   GRD   GRD   TOT   AVERAGE
Jones   68    97    24    189   63.0
Smith   76    94    78    248   82.7
Brown   91    56    78    225   75.0
```

12. Rewrite ⇨Program 9–3 so that it works with a file containing the full names (not shortened to 10 characters) and the numbers take up only the space needed for them. In other words, the records will not be the same length. Other than printing the full names in the report, the output should be the same.

13. Write a program that counts the number of words and sentences in a text file. Words end at a space or punctuation, and sentences end at periods, exclamation points, and question marks. You can use a text editor or your C environment to type in a sample text file.

Output

```
File to scan: WORDS.TXT
WORDS.TXT has 173 words and 19 sentences.
```

14. The BraneDed Corporation has run out of storage space, so the president, N. O. Smarts, has directed you to implement a new file-compression scheme he has cooked up—it eliminates every other character in the file. Now as long as you don't have to write the program to decompress it . . .

```
File to compress? JUNK
Now is the time for all good men to come to the aid of their party.
After compression is:
Nwi h iefralgo e ocm oteado hi at.
```

Chapter 10

POINTERS

PREVIEW

One of the advantages that C has over other languages is that it allows access to main memory. Any language can access variables by name in main memory, but in C we often access them by referring directly to where they are stored. This is such an important and useful concept in C that it is imperative that it be fully understood. This chapter covers direct memory access as applied to a number of concepts covered in previous chapters, and so is keyed to those chapters. The material in the sections here may be addressed concurrently with, or any time after, coverage of the chapter in parentheses. The sections are:

▼ Addresses and Pointers. (Chapter 3)

▼ Pointers and Functions. (Chapter 6)

▼ Pointers and Arrays. (Chapter 7)

▼ Pointers and Strings. (Chapter 8)

▼ Allocating Memory. (Chapter 8)

Back in Chapter 1 we saw that main memory was made up of thousands or millions of individual storage spaces, or **locations**, each of which has a distinct numeric **address**. In Chapter 8, we were briefly introduced to the concept of a pointer variable—a variable that contains an address, presumably where some data may be stored. In this chapter we will examine pointers and pointer variables in detail, and see how their use adds flexibility and efficiency to the C language.

ADDRESSES AND POINTERS

When we declare a variable, C calls on the operating system to find an available contiguous set of locations large enough to accommodate that data type, and allocates that space to the variable. For example,

```
float grinch;
```

might result in memory allocation like this:

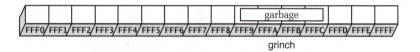

Assuming that *grinch* is a local variable, its value would be garbage.

C allows us to access the variable by name because it keeps track of the address of the first location allocated to the variable. The address of *grinch* is FFF9 (we have used hex notation here as a convenience so that we can identify numbers being used as addresses as opposed to those used as other data values). Unless we demand it, C does not let us know the addresses of variables we declare; it simply uses its own mechanisms to access them.

If we knew where the variable was, instead of referring to the variable's name, we could tell the computer to access the variable that was in the location with the address 7115 or 24236 or FFF9 or whatever. We call this **pointing** to a variable.

The address of a variable, whether we use hex or decimal notation, is just a numeric value, and, like any other numeric value, it can be stored in another variable. As we have seen, a variable that contains an address value, rather than a value we would normally think of as regular data, is a pointer variable, or simply a pointer.

The Pointer Data Type

Every stored value is of one data type or another, and the variables that store these values must accommodate those data types; they must be

declared as the same type. We are familiar with data types such as `short`, `int`, or `double` and know that types are distinguished by the number of bytes allocated for them and the type of notation—straight binary or exponential. A memory address has its own data type. Although ANSI does not give it an official title, we shall refer to it as the pointer data type.

The pointer data type is integral, similar to `int`. Its size, however, depends on your particular implementation of C. In most Cs, the size is the number of bytes in which the target computer stores a memory address. For the sake of discussion, let us assume that a pointer has three bytes. As we said in Chapter 8, it probably doesn't in your C, but since no other common data type has three bytes, it will help us to distinguish pointers from others in our illustrations here.

We have already had some experience with addresses. The `scanf()` function requires addresses rather than variables for its arguments. Remember, the symbol `&` in front of a variable name means "the address of" that variable rather than the value stored in the variable. Using the conversion code `%p` in `printf()`, we can actually print out the address contained in the pointer data type. ⇨Program 10–1 offers an example:

⇨**Program 10–1**

```
#include <stdio.h>

void main(void)
{  long number = 12345;

   printf("Number's value is %li. Its address is %p.\n",
          number, &number);
}
```

Output

```
Number's value is 12345. Its address is FFF4.
```

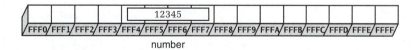

number

The value of the address is printed in hexadecimal notation, and the size of the address is three bytes in our imaginary C. The address is of the location where the variable starts. Here the variable starts at FFF4 (actually, FFFFF4 with a three-byte pointer, but that many characters won't fit on the diagrams!) and spans four bytes, FFF4 through FFF7. Why the specific address FFF4? That address was chosen by C; we had no control

over it. When we declared *number* as a `long`, C found an unallocated four bytes somewhere in memory and allocated it to *number*. In fact, the address could change in subsequent executions of the same program.

Pointer Variables

We can declare a variable as pointer data type, but we must do so in a slightly roundabout fashion. The pointer points to something—it contains the address of something—so in addition to declaring it as a pointer data type, we also state the data type to which it points. An asterisk (*) in front of a variable name in a declaration indicates that it is of type pointer, and the type to which it points is declared in the usual way. In the following declaration *data* is a `float` and *ptr* is a pointer that we usually describe as being "pointer to `float`."

```
float *ptr, data = 100;
```

This declaration allocates four bytes (in a typical C) for *data* and three bytes (in our imaginary C) for *ptr*. Assuming the declaration was internal, *ptr*'s value is garbage. In other words, it points to a memory space somewhere in the system, but we don't know where it is or what value is stored there—garbage pointing to garbage.

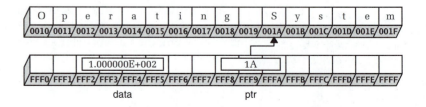

A pointer variable may be assigned and used in the same way that any other variable can, but we must remember that its data type is pointer, and its value is an address, not usual data. Saying

```
ptr = 26;
```

is valid in some non-ANSI Cs (ANSI recognizes that 26 is data type `int`, not pointer), but using the value could be hazardous, because who knows what is stored at memory location 26 (or 1A in hex)? We would have a valid pointer, but it would be pointing to garbage.

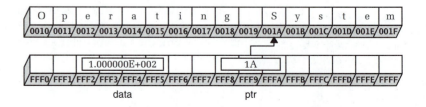

HEADS UP!

The * in a declaration refers only to the variable immediately following it, not to all the variables.

TRAP

Using pointers that do not point to allocated memory.

If, however, we assign a valid address to *ptr*, an address whose contents we know, then we have something useful.

```
void main(void)
{   float *ptr, data = 100;

    ptr = &data;        /* Assign address of data to ptr */
```

Now the value of *ptr* is an allocated address, the address of *data*, and it points to a valid value, 100.

This statement,

```
    printf("%p %p\n", ptr, &data);
```

will produce this output:

FFF2 FFF2   [Actually, FFFFF2 FFFFF2 for a three-byte address.]

The addresses are, of course, the same, but notice that we used the conversion code **%p** for printing **&data**. The variable *data* is type **float**, but **&data** is type pointer.

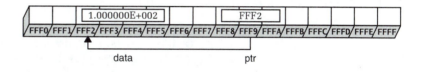

data   ptr

Dereferencing

Often we use pointer variables to access the locations to which they are pointing—a process we refer to as **dereferencing**. The **dereferencing operator**, *, in front of a variable directs the computer to interpret the value of the variable as an address, to go to the location defined by that address, and finally to access the value starting there. Declaring the pointer variable as a pointer to a particular data type is important so that C will know how many bytes beyond the starting address to access, and whether the storage is in straight binary or E notation.

The dereferencing operator (*) looks suspiciously like the symbol we used to declare a variable as a pointer (*). In fact, one might even mistake it for the one we use for multiplication (*). Although the symbols look the same, their functions are totally different depending on where we find them in the program. In a declaration, the * means pointer variable; in any other statement it means to multiply or to dereference—access the contents at the address contained in the variable.

Both the dereferencing operator and the address operator are unary operators. Like the negate (!), unary minus (–), and increment (++)

HEADS UP!

The asterisk has many different meanings.

operators, they have the highest precedence (except for the expression operators such as parentheses), and right-to-left associativity. The multiplication operator is binary; it works with two expressions. In *a, the asterisk means to dereference; in a * b, it means to multiply.

We can access the value 100 in three ways, as shown in ⇨Program 10–2.

⇨**Program 10–2**

```
#include <stdio.h>

void main(void)
{  float *ptr, data = 100;

   ptr = &data;
   printf("%p %p\n", ptr, &data);
   printf("%f %f %f\n", data, *ptr, *&data);
}
```

Output

```
FFF2 FFF2
100.000000 100.000000 100.000000
```

Data types that don't match.

The variable *ptr* is, of course, type pointer, but the notation *ptr is type float because it refers to the value stored at FFF2, the floating point value of *data*. As we saw, &data is type pointer but *&data is float because it refers to the value (*) stored at the location (&) of the variable *data*. To summarize, the value of data is equal to the value of *ptr, which is equal to the value of *&data. All are of type float.

The dereferencing operator can also be used in assignments. If we added these statements to the end of the previous program:

```
*ptr = 200;
printf("%f %f %f\n", data, *ptr, *&data);
```

our output would become

```
FFF2 FFF2
100.000000 100.000000 100.000000
200.000000 200.000000 200.000000
```

Our statement told C to assign the value 200 to the memory location pointed to by *ptr*. In other words, C evaluated the variable *ptr*, found that its value was FFF2, and wrote the value 200 at the location FFF2.

What if our program began with these two statements?

```
{   float *ptr, data = 100;
    *ptr = 200;
```

Both statements are valid, but *ptr*'s value is garbage—it points to nowhere in particular. Assigning 200 there, wherever that is, could be potentially disastrous!

POINTERS AND FUNCTIONS

HEADS UP!

An address, like any other value, can be passed to a function.

All this makes for a diverting mental exercise, but how can we use it? One valuable way is with functions. Instead of passing data values to functions, we can pass addresses. Once the function knows the address of a variable, the function can change the contents at that location. In other words, without knowing a variable's name, we can change its value.

In ⇨Program 10–3 we pass the address of the variable *cost* to the function *inflate* and allow the function to change the value stored there. That address is assigned on entry to the function to the pointer variable *value*. Within the function, we multiply the contents at the location pointed to by *value*.

⇨**Program 10–3**

```
     #include <stdio.h>

     void inflate(double *value, double inflator);

     void main(void)
 m1  {   double cost, inflation = 1.3;

         printf("Enter the project's cost: ");
 m2      scanf("%lf", &cost);
 m3      inflate(&cost, inflation);
 m4      printf("Cost adjusted for inflation is %.2f\n", cost);
     }

 i1  void inflate(double *value, double inflator)
     {
 i2      *value *= inflator;                          /* *value = *value * inflator */
 i3  }
```

Output

```
     Enter the project's cost: 100
     Cost adjusted for inflation is 130.00
```

EXECUTION CHART

Line	Explanation	cost	inflation	value	inflator
m1	Declare variables in `main()`. *value* and *inflator* don't exist yet.	?	1.3	---	---
m2	Input *cost*.	100	1.3	---	---
m3	Call function, pass FFF0 (address of *cost*) and 1.3.	100	1.3	---	---
i1	Allocate and initialize function variables. Variables in `main()` still exist but are not visible.	(100)	(1.3)	FFF0	1.3
i2	Multiply the value at FFF0 by 1.3, store result at FFF0.	(130)	(1.3)	FFF0	1.3
i3	Transfer execution back to m3.	130	1.3	---	---
m4	Print inflated *cost*.	130	1.3	---	---

Passing a variable address, a pointer, rather than a value is often referred to as a **pass by reference** as opposed to a **pass by value**. This program combined both in one call.

The address of *cost* is used more often in this program than the variable itself—in both the `scanf()` and the `inflate()` calls. Why not just declare the variable *cost* as a pointer in the first place, and rewrite the program this way?

```
void main(void)
{   double *cost, inflation = 1.3;

    printf("Enter the project's cost: ");
    scanf("%lf", cost);                          /* This won't work */
    inflate(cost, inflation);
    printf("Cost adjusted for inflation is %.2f\n", *cost);
}
```

▶TRAP◀

Dereferencing a pointer that points nowhere.

The problem is that although *cost* is allocated, it is never assigned a value—where it points, no one knows. If we write a value at the location pointed to by *cost*, as we would in the `scanf()` function, it might end up in the middle of the operating system, change critical instructions, and crash the computer!

HEADS UP!

Passing pointers can overcome the limitation of a single return value.

Returning More than One Value

You can't!

A function can return only one value, but we can effectively get more than one value back to the calling function by putting addresses in the call, having the called function change the values at those locations, and returning to the calling function.

Let us swap the values of two variables as an example. A swap is a common operation done in sorting data, inserting into lists, and performing many other tasks. In a swap, we want the value that was in *a* to end

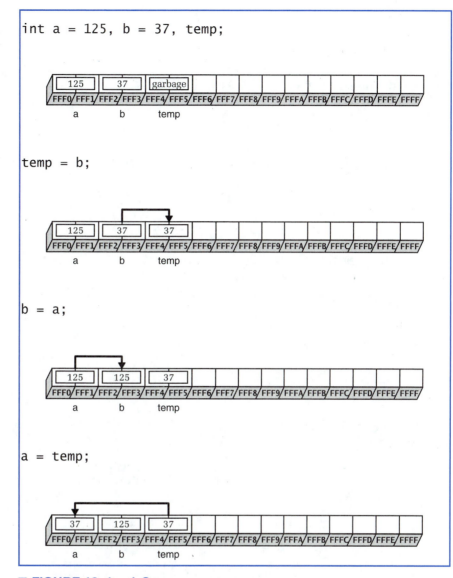

```
int a = 125, b = 37, temp;
```

```
temp = b;
```

```
b = a;
```

```
a = temp;
```

□ **FIGURE 10–1** A Swap

up in *b* and the value that was in *b* to end up in *a*. To do it we will have to use a temporary variable, *temp*, to hold one of the values while we move the other. ❑Figure 10–1 shows the process.

Since we do swaps so frequently, we want a function, *swap()*, that we can call whenever we need it—**swap(a, b)**. We want the values of both *a* and *b* in the calling function to change, but we cannot return two values from the *swap()* function—so let us pass the addresses of *a* and *b* and have *swap()* manipulate the values at those addresses, as in ▷Program 10–4.

⇨Program 10–4

```
#include <stdio.h>

void swap(int *x, int *y);

void main(void)
{  int a = 125, b = 37;

   printf("Before swap   a: %3i    b: %3i\n", a, b);
   swap(&a, &b);
   printf("After swap    a: %3i    b: %3i\n", a, b);
}

void swap(int *x, int *y)
{  int temp;

   temp = *y;
   *y = *x;
   *x = temp;
}
```

Output

```
Before swap   a: 125   b:  37
After swap    a:  37   b: 125
```

❑Figure 10–2 examines *swap()* graphically.

Using Returns and Pointers

The Mobile Mud Concrete Company, as part of its sales-invoice program (⇨Program 10–5), calculates how many trucks it will take to fill an order and figures the price of the order in the function `price()`. The `main()` function then prints out the results. The price is figured at $75 per cubic yard plus $50 per truck, and a truck can carry a maximum of 4 cubic yards. The `main()` function needs both the price and the number of trucks from the `price()` function. One value, in this case the price, can be returned by the function. The other value, the number of trucks, is calculated in the function and assigned at the address contained in the pointer variable *vehicles*. The value of *vehicles* (the address stored there) was initialized in the function call to the address of *trucks*, a variable visible in the `main()` function. Assigning a value at the location pointed to by *vehicles*, then, assigns a value to *trucks*.

```
void swap(int *x, int *y)
{   int temp;
```

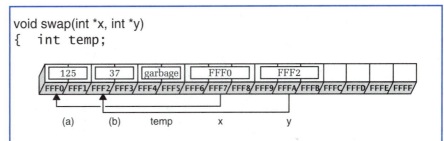

The first line of the definition allocates the variables *x* and *y* and initializes them with the addresses passed from the `main()` function. The variables *a* and *b* still exist, but they are not visible at this time. The local variable *temp* is allocated but has no value yet.

```
temp = *y;
```

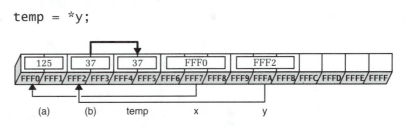

We follow the address stored in *y*, FFF2, to find the value 37. This value is assigned to *temp*. The data type of *temp* is `int`, as is the data type of **y*.

```
*y = *x;
```

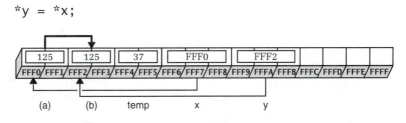

Following the address stored in *x*, FFF0, we find the value 125. This is assigned to the location whose address is stored in *y*, FFF2. The data types of both **x* and **y* are `int`.

```
*x = temp;
```

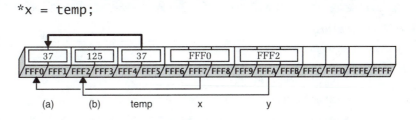

The value of *temp* (37) is assigned to the location whose address is stored in *x*, FFF0.

When the function returns, *x*, *y*, and *temp* disappear, and *a* and *b* are once again visible—but with their values swapped.

❏ **FIGURE 10–2**   The Swap Function

```
#include <stdio.h>

float price(float yds, int *vehicles);

void main(void)
{  float yards;
   int trucks;

       printf("How many yards? ");
m1     scanf("%f", &yards);
m2     printf("   Price:  %.2f  \n", price(yards, &trucks));
m3     printf("   Trucks: %i\n", trucks);
}


p1 float price(float yds, int *vehicles)
   {
p2     *vehicles = (yds - .001) / 4 + 1;      /* .001 adjusts for any possible */
p3     return yds * 75 + *vehicles * 50;                /* approximation error */
   }
```

Output

```
How many yards? 4
   Price:  350.00
   Trucks: 1
```

Output

```
How many yards? 8.2
   Price:  765.00
   Trucks: 3
```

EXECUTION CHART

Line	Explanation	yards	trucks	yds	vehicles
m1	Assign value at address of *yards*.	4	garbage	----	----
m2	Evaluate `printf()` argument, call `price()`, pass value of *yards* (4) and address of *trucks* (FFF2).	4	garbage	----	----
p1	Allocate *yds* and initialize as 4. Allocate *vehicles* and initialize as FFF2.	(4)	(garbage)	4	FFF2
p2	Evaluate expression, assign result at location pointed to by *vehicles*. Since *yds* is `float`, if it was 4, it might approximate to 4.0001 . . . . Subtracting the insignificant .001 will adjust for any such possibility.	(4)	(1)	4	FFF2
p3	Evaluate return expression (350) and pass back to calling point.	(4)	(1)	4	FFF2
m2	Pass return value of `price()` to `printf()` and execute `printf()`.	4	1	----	----
m3	Print value of *trucks*.	4	1	----	----

1. What is a memory location and what is its address?

2. What is a pointer variable?

3. Is there a pointer data type?

4. Define dereferencing.

5. Show two pointer-related uses for the asterisk.

6. Why is it important to declare a variable as a pointer to something?

7. What is the difference between a pass by value and a pass by reference?

8. Can you return more than one value from a function?

PUTTING IT TOGETHER

Reconciling a bank statement is always a tedious task. Let us have our computer help us.

TASK

Write a program that will take our current checking account information plus outstanding transactions during the current period and perform a reconciliation, telling us if we are in balance or not.

ANALYSIS

To perform a manual reconciliation, to the account balance according to our records, we add the value of all outstanding checks (those that we have written but the bank has not yet received) and subtract the outstanding deposits. This should equal the balance according to our bank statement.

In our program we should enter the bank-statement balance and the balance according to the checkbook, as well as each outstanding check and deposit; then have the program print out a summary of the number of outstanding checks and their total, as well as the number of outstanding deposits and their total. Finally, the program should tell us whether we are in balance or, if not, how far off we are.

A sample run might look like this:

```
Bank statement balance: 465.78
Checkbook balance: 284.22
Enter outstanding checks
   ('q' to quit)
   Amount: 182.56
   Amount: 80.35
   Amount: q
Enter outstanding deposits
   ('q' to quit)
   Amount: 50
   Amount: 31.34
   Amount: q
Outstanding: Number   Amount
     Checks:      2    262.91
   Deposits:      2     81.34
You think you have $0.01 more
than the bank thinks you have.
```

We will have to keep track of both balances, the number and accumulated total of the outstanding checks, and the number and total of the outstanding deposits.

DESIGN

Following the sample run, the overall process is:

Input bank and book balances
Input uncleared checks
Input uncleared deposits
Calculate balance
Print summary and balance

If we expand the Input uncleared checks and Input uncleared deposits modules, we would have

Input bank and book balances
While more checks   [Input uncleared checks]
   Input check amount
   Accumulate amount in reconciliation balance
   Count check
While more deposits   [Input uncleared deposits]
   Input deposit amount
   Accumulate amount in reconciliation balance
   Count deposit
Calculate balance
Print summary and balance

The two modules we just expanded are almost alike. The process is the same, but one works with deposits and the other with checks. Since the process is the same, let us have a function—*InData()*—that performs the process and gives the results to the main program. We can return the balance produced in the function and assign it to either a check amount (*ChecksOut*) or deposit amount (*DepositsOut*). To count the checks or the deposits, we will pass the function the address of either the check counter (*NoOfChecks*) or deposit counter (*NoOfDeposits*), and have the function modify the contents at those addresses.

IMPLEMENTATION

⇨Program 10–6 contains the resulting code.

There could be any number of ways of handling this input while accumulating numbers and balances. The *InData()* function, however, encapsulates the operation and allows it to be used in any application requiring that type of task. We don't have to worry about the variables in the application conflicting with those in the function or, indeed, how the function actually operates once it is tested and debugged.

Before we move on, let us examine the way in which we exit the `while` loop in the *InData()* function. When we type an inappropriate character for the `float` variable *Amount*, the `scanf()` stops, returning the value zero, indicating that no assignments were made. It works fine as long as we do not access the input stream again, because the inappropriate character, *q* or whatever we type in, is left in the stream. Whatever accesses the stream next, the next call to the `scanf()`, will be faced with the same character, again inappropriate for a `float`, stopping the next input loop before we even have a chance to type anything.

⇨**Program 10–6**

```
#include <stdio.h>

double InData(short *Number);      /* Input, accumulate checks or deposits */

void main(void)
{   short NoOfChecks = 0, NoOfDeposits = 0;                    /* Counters */
    double BankBalance, BookBalance;        /* Bank statement & checkbook */
    double Balance;             /* Checkbook balance after reconciliation */
    double ChecksOut, DepositsOut;              /* Amounts outstanding */

    /*************************************** Input bank and book balances */
    printf("Bank statement balance: ");
1   scanf("%lf", &BankBalance);
    printf("Checkbook balance: ");
2   scanf("%lf", &BookBalance);
```

(continued)

```
    /********************************************** Input uncleared checks */
    printf("Enter outstanding checks\n");
3   ChecksOut = InData(&NoOfChecks);


    /********************************************** Input uncleared deposits */
    printf("Enter outstanding deposits\n");
4   DepositsOut = InData(&NoOfDeposits);


    /*************************************************** Calculate balance */
5   Balance = BookBalance + ChecksOut - DepositsOut;


    /******************************************************* Print summary */
    printf("Outstanding: Number    Amount\n");
6   printf("       Checks: %6i%9.2f\n", NoOfChecks, ChecksOut);
7   printf("     Deposits: %6i%9.2f\n", NoOfDeposits, DepositsOut);
8   if (Balance == BankBalance)
9       printf("You are in balance.\n");
10  else if (Balance > BankBalance)
11      printf("You think you have $%.2f more\n"
                "than the bank thinks you have.\n",
                Balance - BankBalance);
    else
12      printf("The bank thinks you have $%.2f\n"
                "more than you think you have.\n",
                BankBalance - Balance);
    }


    /***************************** Enter data for either checks or deposits */
    double InData(short *Number)
                                /* Return total amount of checks or deposits */
                                /* Number is count of checks or deposits */
    {   double Amount, Balance = 0;

        printf("  ('q' to quit)\n");
        printf("  Amount: ");
i1      while (scanf("%lf", &Amount) != 0)
i2      {   Balance += Amount;
i3          ++*Number;
            printf("  Amount: ");
        }
i4      while (getchar() != '\n');
i5      return Balance;
    }
```

Output

Output

```
Bank statement balance: 842.39
Checkbook balance: 377.12
Enter outstanding checks
   ('q' to quit)
   Amount: 149
   Amount: 23.87
   Amount: 106.33
   Amount: 305.44
   Amount: q
Enter outstanding deposits
   ('q' to quit)
   Amount: 119.37
   Amount: q
Outstanding: Number    Amount
      Checks:    4     584.64
    Deposits:    1     119.37
You are in balance.
```

```
Bank statement balance: 465.78
Checkbook balance: 284.22
Enter outstanding checks
   ('q' to quit)
   Amount: 182.56
   Amount: 80.35
   Amount: q
Enter outstanding deposits
   ('q' to quit)
   Amount: 50
   Amount: 31.34
   Amount: q
Outstanding: Number    Amount
      Checks:    2     262.91
    Deposits:    2      81.34
You think you have $0.01 more
than the bank thinks you have.
```

EXECUTION CHART

Line	Explanation	NoOf Checks (FFF0)	NoOf Deposits (FFF2)	Number (InData)	Amount (InData)	Balance (InData)
1	Enter bank balance (842.39).	0	0			
2	Enter book balance (377.12).	0	0			
3	Call *InData*, pass address of *NoOfChecks*.	0	0			
i1	Enter *Amount*. It is valid, so go into loop.	(0)	(0)	FFF0	149	0
i2	Accumulate *Amount* into *Balance*.	(0)	(0)	FFF0	149	149
i3	Add 1 to location pointed to by *Number*.	(1)	(0)	FFF0	149	149
i1–i3	Continue entering *Amounts*, accumulating in *Balance*, and incrementing *Number*, until invalid input *q* makes scanf() return value zero.	(4)	(0)	FFF0	305.44	584.64
i4	Flush input stream.	(4)	(0)	FFF0	305.44	584.64
i5	Return *Balance*.	(4)	(0)	FFF0	305.44	584.64
3	Assign return to *ChecksOut*.	4	0			
4	Call *InData*, pass address of *NoOfDeposits*.	4	0			
i1	Enter *Amount*. It is valid, so go into loop.	(4)	(0)	FFF2	119.37	0
i2	Accumulate *Amount* into *Balance*.	(4)	(0)	FFF2	119.37	119.37
i3	Add 1 to location pointed to by *Number*.	(4)	(1)	FFF2	119.37	119.37
i1	Invalid input *y* makes scanf() return value zero.	(4)	(1)	FFF2	119.37	119.37
i4	Flush input stream.	(4)	(1)	FFF2	119.37	119.37
i5	Return *Balance*.	(4)	(1)	FFF2	119.37	119.37
4	Assign return to *DepositsOut*.	4	1			
5–12	Complete program.	4	1			

The `while (getchar() != '\n')` statement at the end of the *InData()* function empties the input stream, leaving it ready for the next input. The next call to `scanf()` will find an empty stream and wait for us to type something.

As usual, we must test for a number of possible conditions. Among them would be no checks or no deposits, in balance, and out of balance either way.

POINTERS AND ARRAYS

Like any other declaration, an array declaration allocates memory space for the variables. For array variables, this memory space is guaranteed to be contiguous—one variable follows the next. For our declaration of the *sales* array we used in Chapter 7, C would have to find 14 bytes of free memory, say at address FFF0, and allocate them to the variables *sales[0]* through *sales[6]*. The variable *sales[0]*, then, would occupy FFF0 and FFF1; *sales[1]*, FFF2 and FFF3, and *sales[6]*, FFFC and FFFD.

```
short sales[] = {3806, 28, 4522, 476, 1183, 47, 12};
```

3806	28	4522	476	1183	47	12		
FFF0/FFF1	FFF2/FFF3	FFF4/FFF5	FFF6/FFF7	FFF8/FFF9	FFFA/FFFB	FFFC/FFFD	FFFE/FFFF	
sales[0]	sales[1]	sales[2]	sales[3]	sales[4]	sales[5]	sales[6]		

You could easily find the address of the beginning of the array, the **base address**, thus:

```
printf("The sales array starts at %p\n", &sales[0]);
```

and the statement would print out FFF0. In C, however, the array name, without any index, is also the base address of the array. It can be used as type pointer, or more specifically, since we declared *sales* as an array of `short`s, as a pointer to `short`. The following,

```
printf("The sales array starts at %p\n", sales);
```

would do exactly the same thing.

The prefix *sales*, however, is not a variable but a constant. Once declared, it cannot be changed. This makes a certain amount of sense. Changing the base address of the array would make all the variable names

HEADS UP!

An array name is a constant.

refer to some other locations. Unfortunately, their values would remain at the old addresses! We can assign values, then, to the variable *sales[0]*, but not to the constant prefix *sales*.

Offsets from the Base Address

HEADS UP!

The value in brackets is an offset from the base address.

We humans can think of *sales[0]*, *sales[1]*, and *sales[2]* as different variables with different names. The concept holds true in C, but C's way of implementing the concept is both simple and elegant. The variables *sales[0]*, *sales[1]*, and *sales[2]* are still different variables with different values, but to C the only identifier is the variable's prefix or base address, *sales*. The index, the number in brackets, is an **offset** from that base address. C interprets *sales[3]* as an offset of 3 from the base address *sales*, FFF0.

But three what? Certainly not bytes, because *sales[3]* does not begin at FFF3. The offset is the number of variables from the base address. In bytes it is the index times the size of an individual variable. The variable *sales[3]* begins at FFF0 + (3 × 2) or FFF6. The variable *sales[0]* begins at FFF0 (FFF0 + (0 × 2)).

TRAP

Working outside of allocated memory.

C keeps track of the base address of an array, but it does not keep track of the highest declared index. We could actually assign a value to *sales[7]* and C would put that value at memory locations FFFE and FFFF (FFF0 + (7 × 2)). This may well be a location that C has allocated for some other purpose, so our assignment will mess things up. Again, it is up to us to see that we do not go out of the bounds of our array.

Pointer Notation

We saw that the prefix for an array is really the base address of the array. Using pointer notation we could refer to the variable *sales[0]*, the first variable of the array, by `*sales`, the contents of the location at the address *sales*. The statement

```
printf("%hi\n", *sales);
```

would print the number 3806, the value of *sales[0]*.

To print out all the values in the array, as above, could we simply add 2 to *sales* at each step, having it point to a different location each time? No, because *sales* is not a variable; it is constant. We could, however, use *sales* in an expression such as *sales* + 4 and use dereferencing to access the contents at other addresses. The statement,

```
printf("%hi\n", *(sales + 4));
```

would print out the number 1183, the value of *sales[4]*.

We have illustrated this pointer notation for accessing array variables and it is certainly valid, but in most cases, it is not considered good form

to mix notations. If you have declared an array using index notation, stick with index notation unless there is some overriding reason to use pointer notation.

Pointer Arithmetic

If *sales* is FFF0, doesn't *sales* + 4 evaluate to FFF4? And why should *sales* + 4 refer to *sales[4]*, whose address is FFF8? It does indeed refer to the address FFF8 because of **pointer arithmetic**. We declared *sales* as an array of `shorts`, which means we can use *sales* as a pointer to `short`. Anytime we do arithmetic with pointers, the values refer to the number of variables, not the number of bytes. We saw this same phenomenon in calculating offsets from base addresses using bracket (`[]`) notation. The expression *sales* + 4, since *sales* is a pointer to `short`, is evaluated as *sales* + (4 × 2) or FFF8. If *x* was declared as a `long double` array and allocated the address 7000 (decimal), then *x* + 3 would be interpreted as *x* + (3 × 10) (assuming 10 bytes for a `long double`) or 7030 (decimal).

The parentheses in the expression *(sales + 4) are important. The dereferencing operator (*) is higher in precedence than the addition operator. Given the values stored in the *sales* array, look at the difference in evaluation with and without parentheses:

3806	28	4522	476	1183	47	12		
FFF0/FFF1	FFF2/FFF3	FFF4/FFF5	FFF6/FFF7	FFF8/FFF9	FFFA/FFFB	FFFC/FFFD	FFFE/FFFF	
sales[0]	sales[1]	sales[2]	sales[3]	sales[4]	sales[5]	sales[6]		

```
*(sales + 4)        *sales + 4
     │                  │
   FFF0               FFF0
        │              3806
     FFF8                  │
        │              3810
     1183
```

Without the parentheses, the dereferencing operator is applied to *sales*. The address there is FFF0 and the value at that location is 3806. To this we add the 4, not 4 × 2, because we are not dealing with pointers any more, yielding the result 3810, hardly what we were looking for.

The notation `*(sales + 4)`, then, is equivalent to `sales[4]`. Both are offsets from the same address. The `for` loop in the program above could be rewritten

```
for (count = 0; count < 7; ++count)
    printf("Variable sales[%hi] =%5hi\n", count, *(sales + count));
```

Since *sales* is a pointer, could we not just increment *sales* and rewrite the `for` loop this way?

```
short *end;

end = sales + 6;
for (; sales <= end; ++sales)
    printf("Variable sales[%hi] =%5hi\n", count, *sales);
```

The new variable *end* keeps track of the address of the end of the array. Its value would be *sales* + (6 × 2) or FFFC. The only problem with this approach is that *sales* is constant, and therefore it cannot be changed. The expression `++sales` would cause the compiler grief.

We could, however use a pointer variable and increment it:

```
short *ptr;

ptr = sales;
for (; ptr <= sales + 6; ++ptr)
    printf("Variable sales[%hi] =%5hi\n", count, *ptr);
```

The increment operator (++), which normally adds 1 to the value of a variable, is being applied to a pointer to `short`; therefore it adds 2 each time, bringing us to the next variable.

YOUR TURN 10–2

1. What is the significance of the prefix of an array?

2. If *var* is declared as `float var[10];`, what is the difference between the expressions `var[4]` and `*(var + 4)`?

3. Given the declaration `float  var[10];`, if var was F000, would `var + 2` be F002?

4. Why can't we put `float  var[10];` and `++var;` statements in the same function?

PUTTING IT TOGETHER

Professor Seligman grades on a curve . . . sort of. He gives hard tests, so no one gets near 100 percent. To make up for that, he takes the difference between the highest score and 100, and adds that to everyone's score. Since his speciality is domestic animal grooming and not computer programming, he has called on us for help.

Create a function that the professor can add to his grading program to adjust all the grades according to his "curve."

ANALYSIS

The function should take an existing list of grades, analyze them to figure the amount to be added, and then adjust the grades in their places in memory. To each grade will be added the difference between the highest grade and 100, so that the highest grade will become 100 and the rest will move up.

The data required by the function is the list of grades and the number of grades in the list.

DESIGN

The function should follow the following process:

    Accept the scores and number of scores
    Determine the high grade
    Determine the amount to add
    Add that amount to each score

To determine the highest grade we can:

    Set up an initial low maximum   [Determine the high grade]
    For each grade
       If grade > maximum
          Set maximum to grade

IMPLEMENTATION

We wrote a function called *curve()* that makes the adjustment to everyone's scores. That function calls another, *high()*, that returns the highest score so the professor can figure his "curve."

⇨Program 10–7 works with the array of student scores using two different notations. The `main()` and *print_scores()* functions use index notation, whereas the *curve()* and *high()* functions take advantage of the fact that an array is a set of contiguously stored variables, and move a pointer from variable to variable.

TEST

The purpose of the `main()` function is simply to test the *curve()* and *high()* functions. By changing the initialization of the *scores* array, we can make a number of tests.

```
#include <stdio.h>

#define MAX_SCORE 100
#define NUM_SCORES 5

void print_scores(int scores[], int students);
void curve(int *scores, int students);
int high(int *scores, int *score);

void main(void)
{  int scores[NUM_SCORES] = {65, 20, 71, 44, 53}; /* Initialize for test */

1      print_scores(scores, NUM_SCORES);
2      curve(scores, NUM_SCORES);
3      print_scores(scores, NUM_SCORES);
}
void print_scores(int scores[], int students) /****** Display the scores */
{  int student;

     printf("Scores: ");
     for (student = 0; student < students; ++student)
        printf(" %3i", scores[student]);
     puts("");
}
c1 void curve(int *grades, int students) /****** Adjust the scores to curve */
{  int *grade;                /* Address of particular score being worked on */
   int add;

c2   add = MAX_SCORE - high(grades, grades + students - 1);
c3   for (grade = grades; grade <= grades + students - 1; ++grade)
c4      *grade += add;
c5                                                        /* End of loop */
}
h1 int high(int *first, int *last) /****************** Determine high value */
h2 {  int max = *first;             /* Set max to first value to be considered */

h3     for (++first ; first <= last ; ++first)            /* Move from second */
                                                          /* element to last */
h4        if (*first > max)                /* If value of element > current max */
h5           max = *first;                                /* Replace max */
h6                                                        /* End of loop */
h7     return max;
}
```

Output

```
Scores:    65  20  71  44  53
Scores:    94  49 100  73  82
```

EXECUTION CHART

Line	Explanation — main():	scores[]	scores		
1	Print array.	65 20 71 44 53	FFF0		
2	Call *curve()*, pass address of *scores* array and number of scores.	65 20 71 44 53	FFF0		

	curve():		**grades**	**grade**	**student**
c1	Initialize *grades* to passed address, and local *students* to passed value.	(65 20 71 44 53)	FFF0	---	5
c2	Call *high()*, pass value of *grades*, which is address of *scores* array, and the address of the last variable in the *scores* array—FFF0 + (*students* × 2) – (1 × 2).	(65 20 71 44 53)	FFF0	???	5

	high():		**first**	**last**	**max**
h1	Initialize *first* and *last* to addresses passed.	(65 20 71 44 53)	FFF0	FFF8	---
h2	Initialize *max* to value at *first*, the first value to be considered.	(65 20 71 44 53)	FFF0	FFF8	65
h3	Increment *first* because we have already used the first value. *first* <= *last*.	(65 20 71 44 53)	FFF2	FFF8	65
h4	Content at *first* (20) not > *max*.	(65 20 71 44 53)	FFF2	FFF8	65
h6	Make *first* point to next element (*scores[2]*).	(65 20 71 44 53)	FFF4	FFF8	65
h3	*first* <= *last*.	(65 20 71 44 53)	FFF4	FFF8	65
h4	Content at *first* (71) > *max*.	(65 20 71 44 53)	FFF4	FFF8	65
h5	Replace *max*.	(65 20 71 44 53)	FFF4	FFF8	71
h6	Make *first* point to next element (*scores[3]*).	(65 20 71 44 53)	FFF6	FFF8	71
h3–h6	Continue until *first* not <= *last*.	(65 20 71 44 53)	FFFA	FFF8	71
h7	Exit function	(65 20 71 44 53)	FFFA	FFF8	71

	curve():		**grades**	**grade**	**student**
c2	Subtract high (71) from *MAX_SCORE* (100). Assign 29 to *add*.	(65 20 71 44 53)	FFF0	???	5
c3	Set *grade* to beginning address of *scores* array. It is <= address of last *scores* variable (FFF8).	(65 20 71 44 53)	FFF0	FFF0	5
c4	Accumulate *add* (29) to content pointed to by *grade*—65, the value of *scores[0]*. It is now 94.	(94 20 71 44 53)	FFF0	FFF0	5
c5	Move *grade* to next *scores* variable.	(94 20 71 44 53)	FFF0	FFF2	5
c3–c5	Continue until *grade* past the address of last *scores* variable, then exit function.	(94 49 100 73 82)	FFF0	FFFA	5

	main():		**scores**		
3	Print scores and quit.	94 49 100 73 82	FFF0		

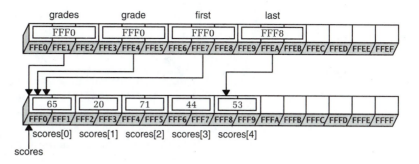

POINTERS AND STRINGS

HEADS UP!

A string value is of data type pointer to char.

A string is nothing more than a character array, and we have seen how we can use pointers with arrays. Let us now apply our new-found pointer skills to strings. In Chapter 8, we mentioned that a string value, "Algonquin" for example, represents the address at which C has chosen to store that set of characters and its terminating null. It is, in fact, a pointer to `char`. The statement

```
printf("%p\n", "Algonquin")
```

prints the address value (00AC in one version of C).

As with any other address value, we can print the contents at a particular address.

```
printf("%c\n", *("Algonquin" + 3))
```

Since "Algonquin" is the address of *Algonquin*, the contents at "Algonquin" + 3 is the letter *o*. ⇨Program 10–8 prints out the characters.

⇨Program 10–8

```
#include <stdio.h>

void main(void)
{  char *letter;

   letter = "Algonquin";
   while (*letter != '\0')
   {  printf ("%c", *letter);
      ++letter;
   }
   printf("\n");
}
```

Algonquin

We declared the variable *letter* as a pointer to `char` and then set its value equal to "Algonquin", which is, of course, the address at which *Algonquin\0* begins in memory—more specifically, the address of the *A*. In the `while` loop, we moved the pointer from character location to character location until the character at the current location was null (\0), C's indicator for the end of the string. As a result, we printed out all the characters in the string.

The initialization of *letter* also could have been done in the declaration:

```
char *letter = "Algonquin"
```

The data types agree—both are type pointer to `char`.

Pointer Versus Array Notation

Let us examine the difference in accessing strings using array notation with indexes and using pointer notation.

We could have two seemingly equivalent declarations as follows:

```
char *pointer = "Algonquin";
char array[] = "Algonquin";
```

In both cases, *Algonquin\0* is stored in memory and *pointer* or *array* points to it. In the first case, C put *Algonquin\0* somewhere in memory, set up a pointer variable *pointer*, and assigned the address of *Algonquin\0* to it. In the second case, C allocated 10 bytes of memory at the address represented by the constant *array*, and copied the characters *Algonquin\0* to that address.

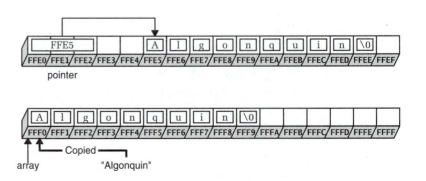

Let us add some additional statements to our declarations.

```
pointer = "Iroquois";                             /* Fine */
array = "Iroquois";                               /* Disaster */
```

In both cases, C chooses a place in memory for *Iroquois\0*. In the first case, C assigns the address to *pointer*, replacing the address of *Algonquin\0*. In the second case, no assignment can be made because *array* is not a variable.

Here are another couple of statements:

```
strcpy(pointer, "Iroquois");                      /* OK */
strcpy(array, "Iroquois");                        /* No problem */
```

Both *pointer* and *array* have sufficient bytes allocated at the addresses to which they point to copy *Iroquois\0* there. In fact, there will be an extra byte at the end—*Iroquois\0\0*. Copying *Canandaigua* in either case would be a disaster because it is longer than the space allocated at either *pointer* or *array*.

Let us rewrite the declarations so that there is no initialization of either variable, and add two different sets of assignments.

```
char *pointer;
char array[10];    /* Had to put something in brackets */

pointer = "Iroquois";                             /* Fine */
array = "Iroquois";                               /* Disaster */
```

or

```
strcpy(pointer, "Iroquois");                      /* Catastrophe */
strcpy(array, "Iroquois");                        /* No problem */
```

In `strcpy(pointer, "Iroquois")`, we could not safely copy *Iroquois\0* to the location being pointed to by *pointer*, because that variable has had no initialization. It does not point to any allocated space, and we might overwrite something important.

Be sure there are allocated bytes where you copy characters.

Ragged Arrays

In Chapter 8 we looked at arrays of strings such as

```
char words[4][6] = {"zero", "one", "two", "three"};
```

We referred to it as an array of arrays with memory organization like this:

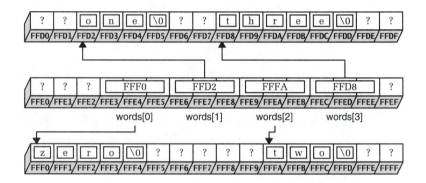

Let us look at another possibility. Instead of storing an array of arrays, we will store an array of pointers to strings—pointers to `char`. Each pointer will point to the base address of a string. In our example, the declaration would change to

```
char *words[4] = {"zero", "one", "two", "three"};
```

or, more simply because of the initialization,

```
char *words[] = {"zero", "one", "two", "three"};
```

If we compare the two arrays in a tabular format, rows and columns, the double-indexed `char` array has the same number of bytes allocated for each string—the same number of columns in each row. The array of pointers has a different number of bytes allocated for each string, giving the right side of the table a ragged look. The first we refer to as a **rectangular array** and the second as a **ragged array**. (We have used the ¤ character to represent null in the diagram.)

Rectangular Array

```
char words[4][6] = {"zero", "one", "two", "three"};
     z  e  r  o  ¤  ¤
     o  n  e  ¤  ¤  ¤
     t  w  o  ¤  ¤  ¤
     t  h  r  e  e  ¤
```

Ragged Array

```
char *words[] = {"zero", "one", "two", "three"};
    z   e   r   o   ¤
    o   n   e   ¤
    t   w   o   ¤
    t   h   r   e   e   ¤
```

There are major differences between the rectangular and the ragged array. The first declares fixed, equal-length strings that reside contiguously in memory. The pointer to the whole group, *words*, and the pointers to each member of the group, *words[0]* and so forth, are constants. The second declares an array of four pointer variables. Were it not for the initialization in the declaration, these pointers would point to garbage.

If the strings are of significantly different lengths, the rectangular array can lead to a great deal of unfilled memory space. It has advantages, however, one of the greatest being its predictability—you always know exactly how large each string is so that your techniques for avoiding overflow can be simpler.

For the ragged array, C has found places in memory to store each of the strings. The allocations for each string are not necessarily contiguous with one another and are just enough to store the string (including the null). The stuff in between the strings is anybody's guess. (Actually, given the initialization, C probably would have stored the strings contiguously, but this is not guaranteed, and given other circumstances and other assignments of the variables in the *words* array, those strings could be all over main memory.)

In Chapter 8, we illustrated arrays of strings, rectangular arrays, with ⇨Program 8–7.

⇨**Program 8–7**

```
#include <stdio.h>

#define STRINGS 4
#define SIZE 6

void main(void)
{   char words[STRINGS][SIZE] = {"zero", "one", "two", "three"};
    int count;

    for (count = 0; count < STRINGS; ++count)
        printf("Digit: %i. Word: %s\n", count, words[count]);
}
```

We could rewrite it using a ragged array as in ⇨Program 10–9.

```
#include <stdio.h>

#define STRINGS 4

void main(void)
{  char *words[STRINGS] = {"zero", "one", "two", "three"};
   int count;

   for (count = 0; count < STRINGS; ++count)
      printf("Digit: %i. Word: %s\n", count, words[count]);
}
```

Output for Both Programs

```
Digit: 0. Word: zero
Digit: 1. Word: one
Digit: 2. Word: two
Digit: 3. Word: three
```

Adding the reassignment of *words[1]* would have an unpredictable and even more disastrous effect in the ragged array example. What would we wipe out by overflowing the memory allocated to *one\0*? The locations allocated to the integer *count*, perhaps?

```
strcpy(words[1], "singular");
for (count = 0; count <= 3; ++count)
   printf("Digit: %i. Word: %s\n", count, words[count]);
```

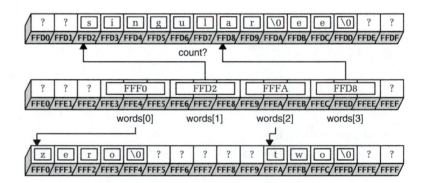

HEADS UP!

Often manipulating a ragged array can be more efficient.

We won't even print out the results; they are apt to be total garbage!

Let us look at an example in which manipulating a ragged array is considerably more efficient than working with a rectangular array. Earlier in this chapter we looked at a swap that switched the values of two variables. Here we will swap strings, first using a rectangular array in ⇨Program 10–10, and then using a ragged array in ⇨Program 10–11. The program swaps the first string with the fourth—*zero* for *three*.

⇨Program 10–10 (Using Rectangular Array)

```c
#include <stdio.h>
#include <string.h>

#define STRINGS 4
#define SIZE 6

void main(void)
{   char words[STRINGS][SIZE] = {"zero", "one", "two", "three"};
    char temp[SIZE];                          /* Temporary string for swap */
    int count;

    /*************************************************** Print out array */
    for (count = 0; count < STRINGS; ++count)
        printf("Digit: %i. Word: %s\n", count, words[count]);

    /************************************* Swap first for fourth string */
    strcpy(temp, words[3]);
    strcpy(words[3], words[0]);
    strcpy(words[0], temp);

    /*************************************************** Print out array */
    printf("\n");
    for (count = 0; count < STRINGS; ++count)
        printf("Digit: %i. Word: %s\n", count, words[count]);
}
```

⇨Program 10–11 (Using Ragged Array)

```c
#include <stdio.h>

#define STRINGS 4

void main(void)
{   char *words[STRINGS] = {"zero", "one", "two", "three"};
    char *temp;                               /* Temporary address for swap */
    int count;

    /*************************************************** Print out array */
    for (count = 0; count < STRINGS; ++count)
        printf("Digit: %i. Word: %s\n", count, words[count]);
```

(continued)

```
/******************************************* Swap first for fourth string */
temp = words[3];
words[3] = words[0];
words[0] = temp;

/*********************************************** Print out array */
printf("\n");
for (count = 0; count < STRINGS; ++count)
    printf("Digit: %i. Word: %s\n", count, words[count]);
}
```

Output for Both Programs

```
Digit: 0. Word: zero
Digit: 1. Word: one
Digit: 2. Word: two
Digit: 3. Word: three

Digit: 0. Word: three
Digit: 1. Word: one
Digit: 2. Word: two
Digit: 3. Word: zero
```

After the swaps, memory will look like ❑Figure 10–3.

Arguments to the `main()` Function

With many operating systems, a program is set in operation by typing its name at the command line—at the keyboard while the operating system is waiting for a command. Using other operating systems, a click on an icon launches a program. Often, in addition to the program name, you can type in various parameters with which the program may work, or add those parameters to the icon's properties. For example, the program *greeting* accepts a name from the person running the program. In the following, `C:>` is the operating system prompt, and the person at the keyboard types the stuff in bold:

C:>**greeting Agnes P. Schreble**

These are known as command-line arguments—data passed from the command line to be used in the program. In C, command-line arguments can be accepted as arguments to the `main()` function. Instead of defining `main()` as having a `void` argument, we will use the following `main()` prototype:

```
void main(int argc, char *argv[])
```

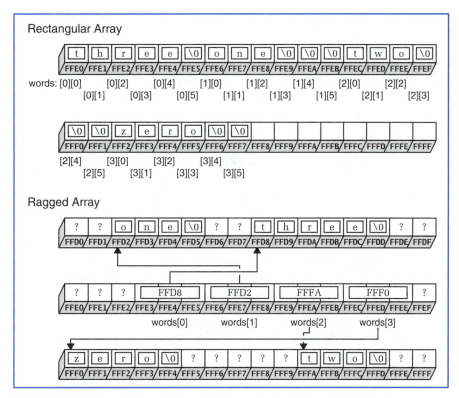

□ **FIGURE 10–3**   Swaps Using Rectangular and Ragged Arrays

In the first swap, using the rectangular array, we needed the strcpy() function and the header file string.h to copy all the characters from one string to another. In the second swap, using the ragged array, we left the strings where they were and moved only pointers. The first required an extra 6-byte string, an extra function, and 17 assignments. The second required only an extra 3-byte pointer and 3 assignments.

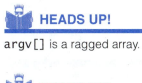

HEADS UP!

argv[] is a ragged array.

HEADS UP!

Whitespace separates command-line arguments.

The variable **argc** and array **argv[]** can actually have any names, but these are the traditional ones used with C that everyone recognizes. They stand for "argument count" and "argument vector" (or "argument value").

Both of these parameters are initialized as a result of the contents of the command line. The int variable *argc* is the number of command-line arguments—the first is always the program name—and the array *argv[ ]* is an array of pointers to char—a ragged array pointing to each individual string in the command line. Whitespace delimits strings in the command line, so our example in ⊃Program 10–12 would have four arguments, with *argc* initialized to 4, and *argv[0]* through *argv[3]* pointing to the strings, with the first, *argv[0]*, pointing to *greeting*.

⇨Program 10–12

```
#include <stdio.h>

void main(int argc, char *argv[])
{  int count;

   printf("The %s program welcomes", argv[0]);
   for (count = 1; count < argc; ++count)
      printf(" %s", argv[count]);
   printf("\n  Hi %s!\n", argv[1]);
}
```

Outputs

```
C:>greeting Agnes P. Schreble
The greeting program welcomes Agnes P. Schreble
   Hi Agnes!

C:>greeting Sheldon Feldermacher
The greeting program welcomes Sheldon Feldermacher
   Hi Sheldon!

C:>greeting Willy F. Q. Lanceford Hogworth, IV
The greeting program welcomes Willy F. Q. Lanceford Hogworth, IV
   Hi Willy!
```

YOUR TURN 10–3

1. Of what data type is "Fred"?
2. Does it make a difference when we declare a string whether we use pointer notation or array notation?
3. What is the difference between a rectangular array and a ragged array?
4. Which type of array takes up less memory space?
5. What are command-line arguments?
6. What separates the strings on the command line?

PUTTING IT TOGETHER

In order to promote its new Krispie Krunchies™ cereal, the marketing crew at Fatuous Foodstuffs, Inc., has decided to offer a Mighty Mutant Power Morphers® Secret Encoder™ ring for 795 boxtops and $119.95 to cover postage and handling. We, being the software gurus, are to write the encoding routine. Once all the kids have their Secret Encoder™ rings, FFI plans to offer a Secret Decoder™ ring for 1,495 boxtops and $219.95 to cover postage and handling. Then, we will have to write the decoding routine.

It should be noted that Fatuous Foodstuffs, Inc., is not entirely devoid of social conscience. Their cereal is made of 64% post-consumer, recycled cardboard (and 36% sugar, of course).

TASK

Create a software routine to take a set of words (a sentence or whatever) and encode it—change its form to be unrecognizable.

ANALYSIS

Our program, to be called *Go*, will be built into a tiny computer contained in the Secret Encoder™ ring. When the program is invoked, the words included after the program name will be encoded and displayed. One of the marketing gang has heard of the ASCII code and cleverly designed an encoding scheme that adds 1 to each character's code in each word. Whitespace is to be left uncoded. A sample execution might be:

Go This message should be encoded.
Go Uijt nfttbhf tipvme cf fodpefe/

Data requirements are simple—just the sentence. It will be encoded in its memory location.

DESIGN

The data is to be received by the program upon the program's invocation, and it consists of words separated by whitespace. This situation literally describes a command-line argument. We can take each string entered on the command line, encode it in place, and print it out with spaces in between.

    Invoke program
    Show unencoded sentence
    Encode words
    Show encoded sentence

We want to encode each word, beginning with the second (the first is the program name).

    Encode words from second to last
        While character not null   [Encode word]
            Add one to character's code
            Move to next character

We will implement the encoding of each word, which is a separate string, in a function, *encode()*, by moving along the pointer sent to it until the content being pointed to is null—the end of the string. ⇨Program 10–13 shows the result.

⇨**Program 10–13**

```
#include <stdio.h>

void encode(char *string);

void main(int argc, char *argv[])
{  int word;

   for (word = 0; word < argc; ++word)
      printf("%s ", argv[word]);
   puts("");

   for (word = 1; word < argc; ++word)  /* Words after prog name encoded */
      encode(argv[word]);

   for (word = 0; word < argc; ++word)
      printf("%s ", argv[word]);
   puts("");
}

void encode(char *string) /********************* Encodes a single string */
{
   while (*string != '\0')
   {  ++*string;                               /* Increment content at string */
      ++string;                                /* Increment address */
   }
}
```

TEST

Fortunately, we can test the algorithm without actually having a Secret Encoder™ ring. For our tests, we have picked a sentence with a variety of characters. The one character that might give us trouble would be the tilde (~), ASCII 126. Incrementing it would make it the ASCII *del* or delete character, which might produce strange results on some displays.

Output

```
C:>Go Hi kids! It's agent Z009.
Go Hi kids! It's agent Z009.
Go Ij ljet" Ju(t bhfou [11:/
```

ALLOCATING MEMORY

Let us look at another method of storing data in which we allocate only the memory we need, and no extra. First we must look at allocating blocks of memory. The **malloc()** function allocates a number of bytes in memory and returns the address of the beginning of that block.

```
void *malloc(size_t bytes)                         <stdlib.h>
```

The return value of `malloc()` is a pointer to `void` because we are not allocating a specific data type here, just a number of *bytes*. The pointer to `void` is ANSI C's generic pointer and it can be converted to any pointer type.

We could use `malloc()` to allocate space for a string, for example, when we have declared only a pointer variable rather than a `char` array.

```
char *string;
string = (char *) malloc(50);
```

After the declaration, the value of *string* is garbage and, of course, it points to garbage. In the assignment, `malloc(50)` allocated 50 bytes in memory and returns the address as a pointer to `void`. We cast that pointer to `void` as a pointer to `char`, and assign it to *string*. Now the value of *string* is changed to point to the beginning of 50 bytes of allocated memory space. (Some Cs will let you get away without casting the pointer to void. To maintain portability, you should cast it.)

If `malloc()` is unable to allocate memory (perhaps you have no free memory left), it returns the NULL pointer. You can test for that after calling the function.

```
string = (char *) malloc(50);
if (string == NULL)
    printf("Outta memory!\n");
```

The **free()** function deallocates a block of memory previously allocated by `malloc()`—returns it to the pool of free memory that C can now allocate for some other purpose.

```
void free(void *address)                           <stdlib.h>
```

If you have finished with the *string* variable, you can make it the *address* argument and release that memory space.

```
free(string);
```

When you use `free()`, be sure that the *address* argument is one that has been allocated by `malloc()`. You could get some bizarre results

HEADS UP!

Cast the pointer.

if this is not the case. Also be sure that you do not access that section of memory using the pointer established by `malloc()` again. Any time after executing `free()`, C is free to allocate the memory for another purpose.

⇨Program 10–14 tests the quality of the random numbers generated by the computer, by generating a set of random numbers in the range 1 through 10. It then adds them up and calculates the average, which should be about 5.5. The size of the set of random numbers is input on the command line when the program is run. We want this program to take up as little memory as possible, so we will allocate the memory for the random numbers after the program is started and we know how much memory we will actually need. Notice that memory is also deallocated, using `free()`, as soon as we are finished with the random numbers.

This program accesses the random numbers using both pointer notation and array notation. Since the variable *rands* is used to keep track of the base address of an array, we might allow ourselves to use array notation in this case. C, of course, does not care.

▶TRAP◀

Accessing deallocated memory.

⇨**Program 10–14**

```
#include <stdio.h>
#include <stdlib.h>
#include <time.h>

#define INT_SIZE 2

void main(int argc, char *argv[])
{   int *rands;                     /* Beginning of the array of random numbers */
    int number, numbers, total = 0;

    srand((unsigned) time(NULL));
    numbers = atoi(argv[1]); /* Number of numbers entered on command line */
                             /* atoi() converts argv[1] string to number */
    rands = (int *) malloc(numbers * INT_SIZE);
    for (number = 0; number < numbers; ++number)        /* Generate numbers */
        *(rands + number) = rand() % 10 + 1;      /* Number between 1 and 10 */
    for (number = 0; number < numbers; ++number)     /* Accumulate numbers */
        total += rands[number];                      /* Array notation instead */
    free(rands);                                      /* Deallocate memory */
    printf("The average of %i random numbers between 1 and 10 is %.2f\n",
           numbers, (float) total / numbers);
}
```

Output (using command line: **prog 2000**)

```
The average of 2000 random numbers between 1 and 10 is 5.54
```

OTHER MEMORY-ALLOCATION FUNCTIONS

There are two other ANSI functions that deal with memory allocation—`calloc()` and `realloc()`. The `calloc()` function allocates a block of memory, initializing it to zero, and returning the address as a pointer to `void`.

```
void *calloc(size_t variables, size_t size)
```

where *variables* is the number of variables in the array, and *size* is the size in bytes of each variable. We could set up an array of 50 `float`s like this:

```
float *array;
array = (float *) calloc(50, FLOAT_SIZE);
```

The `realloc()` function allocates a new block of memory of the desired size, moving the data to the new block. The data will be unchanged except for data at the end of the old block if the size of the new block is smaller. `realloc()`'s return is the address of the new block.

```
void *realloc(void *address, size_t new_size)
```

where *address* is the address of the block to be resized (and probably moved), and *new_size* is its new size in bytes. If the value passed to *address* is NULL, then a new block is allocated, making `realloc()` act just like `malloc()`.

YOUR TURN 10–4

1. What function allocates memory? What function deallocates it?
2. What must be done to the return value of **`malloc()`** to make it useful?
3. What is in the allocated memory after executing the **`free()`** function?

SUMMARY

▲**KEY TERMS** (in order of appearance)

Location	Base address
Address	Offset
Pointing	Pointer arithmetic
Dereferencing	Rectangular array
Dereferencing operator	Ragged array
Pass by reference	Command-line argument
Pass by value	

```
void main(int argc, char *argv[])
```
Purpose: Control function of C program. Puts `argc` strings from command line into `*argv[]`.
Return: None.

```
void *malloc(size_t bytes)                                    <stdlib.h>
```
Purpose: Allocate a block of memory
Return: Success: Address of allocated block. Error: NULL.

```
void free(void *address)                                      <stdlib.h>
```
Purpose: Deallocate a block of memory allocated by `malloc()`, `calloc()`, or `realloc()`.
Return: None.

▲CONCEPT REVIEW

▼ Main memory is made of millions of **locations**, each of which has a unique **address**.

▼ Variables can be accessed not only by name but also by address— **pointing** to the variable.

▼ A pointer is a data type, but it is important that we also state to what data type the pointer points. A declaration of a pointer is accomplished by putting an asterisk in front of the variable name in the declaration.

▼ Like a local variable of any other data type, a pointer's initial value is garbage; it does not point to a valid location.

▼ Accessing data through pointers is called **dereferencing**, which we indicate using the **dereferencing operator**, the asterisk, in a statement other than a declaration.

▼ Pointers are often used in conjunction with functions. A **pass by reference** rather than a **pass by value** passes the address of a variable (or array) to a function, which allows the function to access the location of the variable directly. This can overcome the limitation of allowing only one return value for a function.

▼ An array index is merely an **offset** from the **base address** of the array. The offset is in variables, not bytes. The offset in bytes is the offset value times the number of bytes in the data type.

▼ Arrays can also be accessed using pointer notation and **pointer arithmetic**. Array elements can be accessed using calculated offsets from a base address or, if the pointer is a variable rather than the constant prefix to an array, by changing the value of the pointer.

▼ Strings are arrays and can be accessed in the same ways. Whether to use array or pointer notation depends on consistency, whether a variable pointer is needed, whether space must be initially allocated, and other needs of a particular situation.

▼ An array of arrays is a **rectangular array**. A **ragged array** is an array of pointers to other arrays. Often, memory space may be conserved using ragged arrays.

▼ **Command-line arguments**—arguments to the `main()` function—utilize ragged arrays. The `argc` parameter is the number of arguments, and the `argv[]` array is an array of pointers to those arguments. Whitespace separates the arguments on the command line.

▼ Memory space can be allocated during program execution using the `malloc()` function, which returns a pointer to the allocated space, and deallocated by `free()`.

▲HEADS UP: POINTS OF SPECIAL INTEREST

▼ A pointer is a data type.

▼ An address of stored data is always where the data starts.

▼ The * in a declaration refers only to the variable immediately following it, not to all the variables.

▼ The asterisk has many different meanings.

▼ An address, like any other value, can be passed to a function.

▼ Passing pointers can overcome the limitation of only a single return value.

▼ An array name is a constant.

▼ The value in brackets is an offset from the base address. *The array name, before the brackets represents the base address.*

▼ Avoid mixing pointer and index notation.

▼ Pointer arithmetic is by variables, not bytes. *Adding 1 to a pointer to a 2-byte data type adds 2 to the pointer.*

▼ A string value is of data type pointer to `char`. *The quoted value is treated as a pointer to where C has stored the value.*

▼ Often manipulating a ragged array can be more efficient. *Ragged arrays usually take up less space in memory, and often pointers can be changed rather than copying strings.*

▼ `argv[]` is a ragged array.

▼ Whitespace separates command-line arguments.

▼ Cast the pointer. *The `malloc()` function returns a pointer to `void`. Typically, it must be cast as a pointer to the desired data type.*

▲TRAPS: COMMON PROGRAMMING ERRORS

▼ Using pointers that do not point to allocated memory.

▼ Data types that don't match.

▼ Dereferencing a pointer that points nowhere.

▼ Working outside of allocated memory.

▼ Forgetting the parentheses using pointer notation. *Since the dereferencing operator is higher in precedence than the arithmetic operators, parentheses must be used to force pointer arithmetic.*

▼ Be sure there are allocated bytes where you copy characters.

▼ Accessing deallocated memory. *Once memory has been deallocated by* `free()`, *it can be reused by C for other purposes.*

▲YOUR TURN ANSWERS

▼10–1

1. A memory location is a physical place in memory capable of storing a byte of data. Its address is a specific numeric identifier for each location.

2. A variable used to store an address rather than a typical piece of data.

3. Unofficially, yes. A pointer has all the characteristics of a data type—a specific number of bytes and form of storage, integral in the pointer's case.

4. Accessing the location to which a pointer is pointing.

5. In a declaration, the asterisk means that the variable following is a pointer. In any other statement, the asterisk means dereferencing—following the address to where it is pointing and accessing there.

6. C must know how to treat the data in the location to which the pointer points.

7. Passing a value to a function means that the function will work with a copy of the value in the calling function. Passing by pointer means that the calling function tells the called function where a value is, allowing the called function to access the value directly.

8. No, but you can pass addresses to a function and have the function put values there.

▼10–2

1. The prefix is a constant pointer to the beginning of an array—its base address.

2. Nothing.

3. No. This calculation would be done using pointer arithmetic, adding two variables to the address. If this C had a four-byte `float`, the address would be F008.

4. Because var is a constant, it cannot be assigned. If the declaration was `float *var;`, the other statement would be acceptable.

▼10–3

1. It is pointer to `char`—the address of where C stored *Fred\0* in memory.

2. Yes. Using array notation, the prefix is not variable and we always allocate a certain number of bytes for the string. Using pointer notation, the pointer is variable, but, depending on the initialization, there might be no allocated bytes for the string.

3. A rectangular array is an array of arrays—an array with two indexes. A ragged array is an array of pointers to `char`.

4. Typically, the ragged array.

5. Values passed to the program when it is first started.

6. The delimiter on the command line is whitespace.

▼10–4

1. The `malloc()` function allocates memory and `free()` deallocates it.

2. It must be cast as a pointer to the desired data type.

3. Who knows? Accessing there using the pointer set up by `malloc()` is dangerous.

EXERCISES

1. Given the declarations and statements below, what are the data types (if it's pointer, don't forget *pointer to what*) and values of the expressions. Mention any problems that might arise.

```
char *c, *b, a = 'A';      Expressions:
float d, *e;                   &a  _____
                               *c  _____
*c = a;                        *b  _____
b = c;                          e  _____
e = &d;                        *e  _____
d = 1.5;                       *&d _____
```

2. If C would allow us to make such an assignment (which it won't), what would be the result of the first assignment below? What about the second, which is a legal assignment?

```
float x = 123.45;
int *y;

y = &x;                        /* First assignment */
*y = x;                        /* Second Assignment */
```

3. Fill in the effects of these statement with values and arrows on the following memory diagram.

```
c = &a;
*b = a;
```

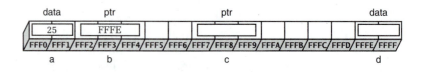

4. Finish the function call and the function that squares both *x* and *y* in the `main()` function.

```
square(___x, ___y);                          /* Function call */

void square(_____a, _____b)          /* Squaring function */
{   ____ *= ____;
    ____ *= ____;
}
```

5. Show an execution chart and the output for the following program.

```c
#include <stdio.h>

float miles_per_gallon(int m, float g, float *c);

void main(void)
{   int miles = 400;
    float mpg, gallons = 20.0, cost = 1.0;

    mpg = miles_per_gallon(miles, gallons, &cost);
    printf("The cost of this trip was %.2f at %.1f mpg.\n", cost, mpg);
}

float miles_per_gallon(int m, float g, float *c)
{
    *c = g * *c;
    return m / g;
}
```

6. Given the following declarations, which statements are invalid and why?

```
double one[10], two[5][5], *ptr, value = 1.0;
```

a. `ptr = &one;`

b. `ptr = one + 3;`

c. `ptr = two[2];`

d. `value = two[3][5];`

e. `printf("%f\n", two[1]);`

f. `one = ptr;`

g. `*ptr = 14.2;`

h. `*one + 2 = 25.1;`

i. `*one = *(one + 3);`

j. `++*two;`

k. `++ptr;`

7. Show the output from this program:

```
#include <stdio.h>

void main(void)
{   short *ptr;
    short array[4] = {1,2,3,4};

    for (ptr = array + 3; ptr >= array; --ptr)
        printf("%hi  ", *ptr);
    printf("\n");
}
```

8. Which are appropriate declarations and initializations for strings?

a. `char a[10] = "Alice";`

b. `char *a = "Alice";`

c. `char *a = {'A', 'l', 'i', 'c', 'e'};`

d. `char *a;`
   `a = "Alice";`

e. `char a[10];`
   `a = "Alice;`

f. `char *a;`
   `strcpy(a, "Alice");`

g. `char a[10];`
   `strcpy(a, "Alice");`

9. What will the following program produce?

```c
#include <stdio.h>
#include <string.h>

void main(void)
{   char *start, *string = "String";

    start = string;
    string = string + strlen(string) - 1;
    while (string >= start)
    {   printf("%c", *string);
        --string;
    }
    puts("");
}
```

10. Rewrite the following program using a ragged array.

Program

```c
#include <stdio.h>
#include <string.h>

void main(void)
{   char string[][10] = {"Strings", "are", "fun.", ""};
    int count = 0;

    while (*string[count] != '\0')
    {   printf("%s ", string[count]);
        ++count;
    }
    puts("");
}
```

Output

```
Strings are fun.
```

11. Correct the following program so it that prints out the data on the command line that follows the program name.

```c
void main(int argc, char argv[])
{   int count;

    for (count = 0; count <= argc; ++count)
        puts(*argv[count]);
}
```

12. What is wrong with the following program segment?
```
char *str, string[] = "Hello";

str = malloc(strlen(string));
strcpy(str, string);
free(str);
puts(str);
```

PROGRAMS

1. Write a program that will figure the average of any number of integer values input into the computer. The value zero should be used to signal the end of input. For the main body of the program use only the three pointer variables given. To ensure that they point to usable places in memory, assign them the addresses of the first three variables below. For example `val = &value;`. Those three statements (and the declarations) are the only times the variables *value*, *counter*, and *total* should appear in the program.

Variables		Output
value		VALUE? **28**
counter		VALUE? **92**
total		VALUE? **-15**
*val	Number to input	VALUE? **0**
*count	Number of values to average	THE AVERAGE IS 35
*tot	Sum of all the values	

2. Write a program that shows the volumes of all rectangular solids with lengths, widths, and heights varying from 1 to 3. For the main body of the program use only the three pointer variables given. To ensure that they point to usable places in memory, assign them the addresses of the first three variables below. Treat these variables the same as those in the last problem.

Variables

```
length
width
height
*len
*wid
*hgt
```

Output

```
LENGTH    WIDTH    HEIGHT   VOLUME
  1         1        1         1
  1         1        2         2
  1         1        3         3
  1         2        1         2
         [And so forth]
```

3. Write a program that generates five random numbers between 25 and 50 and, after generating each random number, keeps track of the smallest, the largest, and the sum of the numbers. A *rnd()* function should generate each random number in the proper range; and a *stats()* function should be used to update the smallest, largest, and sum with each new random number. All printing should be done from `main()`.

Variables and Functions

```
main()                        rnd()  Random number in range
  count
  number   Random number      stats()
  min, max, sum                 num, smallest, biggest
                                total
```

Output

```
Numbers  Minimum  Maximum  Sum
  42       42       42       42
  35       35       42       77
  50       35       50      127
  37       35       50      164
  27       27       50      191
```

4. Write a program to prepare an employee's paycheck stub. You should type in the employee's hours, pay rate, and tax rate. All calculations should be done in the function *PayCheck()* but the resultant information should be printed out in the `main()` function.

Functions and Variables

```
Main()                        PayCheck()
  Hours                         Hrs
  PayRate                       PRate
  TaxRate                       TRate
  GrossPay                      GPay
  Tax                           Tx
  NetPay                        NPay
```

Output

```
Hours, pay rate: 30.5, 12.60
Tax rate (%): 15.2

Gross Pay     $384.30
Taxes           58.41
Net Pay       $325.89
```

5. Design a function that calculates the roots of a quadratic equation. The formula is given below. Since there are two roots, have the function return one, and pass the function an address where it can place the second. Test the function by calling it with *a* set to 1, *b* to 5, and *c* to 4. It should produce the given output.

Quadratic Formula

$$\frac{-b \pm \sqrt{b^2 - 4ac}}{2a}$$

Output

```
The roots are -1 and -4.
```

6. Write a program that accepts keyboard entry of five values and prints out the maximum and minimum. Both the maximum and minimum should be calculated in a separate function and printed out in main().

Functions and Variables

```
main()          min_max()
  values[]        array[]
  smallest        min
  largest         max
  count           count
```

Output

```
Enter 5 values separated by whitespace.
5.74 2.6 18 -3.65 14.2
Minimum: -3.65, Maximum: 18.
```

7. Write a program that accepts three integers from the keyboard, puts them in order, and prints out the ordered set as well as the total. The function *order()* should put the values in order. One way is to compare the first to the second; if it is larger, swap the two. Do the same with the second and third; then with the first and second again. The *swap()* function should perform the swap.

Functions and Variables

```
main()            order()          swap()
  n1, n2, n3        i1, i2, i3       a, b
  total                              temp
```

Outputs

```
Enter three integers: 35 27 52
27, 35, and 52 add up to 114.

Enter three integers: 9 8 7
7, 8, and 9 add up to 24.

Enter three integers: 16 314 72
16, 72, and 314 add up to 402.
```

8. Write a program with a *backward()* function that prints out a string backward. Do not use any string functions.

Functions and Variables

```
main()            backward()
  string[]          string   Address of the string
                    end      Address of the end of string
```

Output

```
Your input? This is a string.
The output: .gnirts a si sihT
Your input? backward?
The output: ?drawkcab
Your input?
```

9. Modify the *backward()* function in the program above so that the function does not print out the string; it actually moves the characters in the string passed from the calling function, so that when the calling function prints out the string, it is backward. You may use a string function to find the end of the string. (*Hint:* Swap characters between the front and back of the string, moving the front and back points toward the center.)

Functions and Variables

```
main()            backward()
  string[]          string   Address of the string
                    temp     Use for swap of chrs from front to back
                    front    Address of current front of string
                    back     Address of current back of string
```

Output

```
Your input? This is a string.
The output: .gnirts a si sihT
Your input? backward?
The output: ?drawkcab
Your input?
```

10. Write a program that inserts line breaks in a string. The resulting lines should be 16 characters or fewer and should break only on whitespace (spaces, tabs, newlines). Assume that you will not encounter more than one whitespace character at a time. (Or to be more robust, *don't* assume that.) The actual line breaks (insertion of newlines) should be done in the function *split()*.

Functions and Variables

```
main()       split()
  string       line
               begin_line   Address of beginning of current line
```

Output

```
Input a string.
Now is the time for all good people to come to the aid
of their party.
Now is the time
for all good
people to come
to the aid of
their party.
```

11. Write a program that takes any number of words from the command line and prints them out sorted. The sort should be done in a separate function, *sort()*, but all printing should be done from `main()`.

12. Write a function *word_analysis()* that receives a string and counts the number of words and sentences in the string, making these available to the calling function. A word ends in a space (or the end of the string), and a sentence ends in a period, question mark, or exclamation point. Test the function by sending it a string such as:

```
"What language?  Why, C of course!"
```

Functions and Variables

```
main()       word_analysis()
  line[]        line
  words         words
  sentences     sentences
```

Output

```
What language?  Why, C of course!
    has 6 words and 2 sentences.
```

13. Write a *dynastring()* function that dynamically allocates a string variable. Each time a string is assigned, the function deallocates any memory that was previously allocated to the string and allocates the exact amount of space needed for the new string, putting its address in the pointer variable sent to it. Use the driver program below to test it. Notice that the first argument passed to *dynastring()* is the address of a pointer—a pointer to a pointer. Be sure to declare it as such in the function and to change the contents at the location rather than the location itself.

Driver Program

```c
#include <stdio.h>
#include <stdlib.h>
#include <string.h>

void dynastring(char **new_string, char *value);

void main(void)
{   char *string1, *string2;

    dynastring(&string1, "Filibuster");
    puts(string1);
    dynastring(&string2, "Flit");
    puts(string2);
    dynastring(&string1, "Flange");
    puts(string1);
    dynastring(&string2, "Fony is not spelled right.");
    puts(string2);
}
```

Output

```
Filibuster
Flit
Flange
Fony is not spelled right.
```

Chapter 11

RECORD-BASED DATA

PREVIEW

When data is manipulated in records that group individual but related values, it is useful to have a mechanism that holds each record together. In this chapter we shall look at such a mechanism. At its conclusion, you should understand:

▼ The characteristics of C's method for accessing records (groups of data).

▼ How these records are defined, declared, initialized, and accessed.

▼ How to use pointers to access the records.

▼ How the records are used with functions.

▼ A typical application of these records in maintaining ordered lists.

▼ How to use these records in conjunction with files.

D ata is often stored and accessed in groups—name, address, and phone number, for example. To work with these groups in our programs, we can set up separate variables for each piece of data and make sure we process them together. Another approach is to set up the data so that it can be accessed as a single unit. We must still be able to get to an individual piece of that unit—the address, for example—but we will also have the option of moving around the entire unit in one operation.

STRUCTURES

HEADS UP!

A structure is a data type made of other data types.

This is the basis of structures in C. A **structure** is a complex data type made up of other data types (including, possibly, other structures). For example, we could combine the three strings (`char` arrays) for name, address, and phone number into one structure, *listing*. Sometimes we will access the entire structure—move it into secondary storage, for example; other times we will access an individual **member** of the structure—change the address, for example.

Definitions and Declarations

The data types we have worked with previously, `float`, `int`, and so forth, have all been defined somewhere else in the language. C knows how many bytes there are in a `float` and its storage format. Structures are data types that we make up ourselves. Their components are existing data types, to be sure, but unless we tell C the makeup of our new data type, C cannot work with it.

Working with a structure, then, will require a step that is already done for us with the standard data types—providing a **structure definition**, where we tell C the makeup of the structure. The definition follows this general format:

```
struct tag {member definitions};
```

For example,

```
struct employee_rec
{   char name[30];
    int dependents;
    float pay_rate;
};
```

HEADS UP!

The tag is the name of the data type.

The *tag*, *employee_rec* in the example, is the name of our new data type. It is the equivalent of `float` or `int` and is used in much the same way—we will declare variables of that data type to be used in the

program. In the **member definitions** we will define each of the individual variables that make up the structure. In our example, we are defining an *employee_rec* data type that is composed of a 30-element `char` array referred to as *name*, an `int` referred to as *dependents* and a `float` referred to as *pay_rate*. Notice the semicolon after the closing brace. It must be there!

Any valid data type can be a member of a structure. Even other structures, if they are defined beforehand, can be members of structures.

It is important to realize that the structure definition only tells C the makeup of the structure. It does not allocate memory. The key word `double`, for example, indicates a data type available for our use; the tag *employee_rec*, once defined, does the same—it indicates a data type available for our use. The member definitions, even though they look like variable declarations, are not. They only inform C of the makeup of the structure.

To use this new data type, we will have to declare variables of that type. Just as we might declare

`double whammy;`

we might also declare

`struct employee_rec full_time;`

allocating memory space for the variable *full_time* of data type *employee_rec*. Assuming an 8-byte `double`, the first declaration allocates 8 contiguous bytes of memory identified by the name *whammy*. Assuming a 2-byte `int` and a 4-byte `float`, the second declaration allocates 36 contiguous bytes identified by the name *full_time*.

Note the key word **struct**. It must be included whenever we refer to a structure data type.

The visibility rules for structure definitions are the same as those for variable declarations. Structure tags defined externally, outside of a function (before `main()`, for example), are visible globally; you can declare structure variables of that type anywhere in your program. Structure tags defined within a program block are visible only locally, within that block. Structure declarations of that type can only be in the same block.

It is often a good idea to define structures externally, where they are visible to all functions. This way you can declare variables of that type locally in any of the functions. It will also allow you to easily pass and return structures (or pointers to structures) because the same definition can be used in the corresponding functions.

C will allow us to both define and declare structures in the same statement. The overall general form is:

`struct` *tag* `{`*member definitions*`}` *names*`;`

For example,

```
struct employee_rec
{   char name[30];
    int dependents;
    float pay_rate;
} full_time, part_time;
```

In fact, the tag is optional:

```
struct
{   char name[30];
    int dependents;
    float pay_rate;
} full_time, part_time;
```

While possibly convenient, such a definition/declaration has some drawbacks. If no tag is stated, we cannot declare variables of that type anywhere else in the program. If the definition/declaration is outside of any function, the definition will be global, but so will be the variables, and, as we pointed out in Chapter 6, global variables reduce modularity. If the definition/declaration is internal, within a function or block, the definition is visible only locally, within the block, not allowing us to declare variables of the same type within other blocks or functions.

Initializations

Default initializations for structures are the same as for other variables— zero for global-lifetime variables and garbage for locals. We may also explicitly initialize structures at the time of their declarations. (Like arrays, some non-ANSI C compilers will not allow initializations of local-lifetime structures.) The important criterion for initializations is that the values are listed in the exact same order as the members in the structure.

In our last example, the structure defined as

```
struct employee_rec
{   char name[30];
    int dependents;
    float pay_rate;
};
```

could have a declaration and initialization as follows:

```
struct employee_rec full_time = {"Beulah Barzoom", 4, 12.63};
```

The entire definition, declaration, and initialization could be contained in one statement.

```
struct employee_rec
{  char name[30];
   int dependents;
   float pay_rate;
} full_time = {"Beulah Barzoom", 4, 12.63};
```

but remember, we said that there are some drawbacks in such a definition/declaration.

▶TRAP◀

Trying to initialize in a definition.

Remember, also, that a definition of a structure allocates no memory space and sets up no variables. Therefore, there can be no initializations made in a definition. The following would not work:

```
struct employee_rec
{  char name[30] = "Beulah Barzoom";        /* These initializations */
   int dependents = 4;                          /* do not */
   float pay_rate = 12.63;                    /* belong here */
} full_time;                    /* Even though there is a declaration here */
```

The sizeof a Structure

C gives us an operator that is useful in a number of instances, but is almost indispensable when dealing with structures. It is **sizeof**, a unary operator on the same precedence level (almost the highest) and with the same associativity (right to left) as other unary operators such as increment and dereferencing. The result of a sizeof operation is the number of bytes in the expression or data-type name following sizeof. If data-type names are used, they must be enclosed in parentheses.

Given the declaration

```
double dip = 47.2;
```

Assuming an 8-byte double,

```
sizeof (double)     /* Parens required for data types */
```

and

```
sizeof dip     /* Parens not required for expressions */
```

would both evaluate to 8.

Parentheses are required for data types, but because of the high precedence of sizeof, they might also be needed for other expressions.

```
sizeof (6 + dip)
```

evaluates to 8 because the expression evaluates to the double value 53.2. On the other hand,

sizeof 6 + dip

evaluates to 49.2 (assuming a 2-byte `int`), because `sizeof 6` is 2 plus the value of *dip*, 47.2, yielding 49.2.

Defining a structure defines a data type, and we can declare variables of that data type. The `sizeof` operator will give us the number of bytes in the structure data type or variable, as ⇨Program 11–1 shows.

⇨Program 11–1

```
#include <stdio.h>

#define NAME_CHRS 30

struct employee_rec
{   char name[NAME_CHRS];
    int dependents;
    float pay_rate;
};

void main(void)
{   struct employee_rec full_time = {"Beulah Barzoom", 4, 12.63};

    printf("Data type's length: %i.\n", sizeof (struct employee_rec));
    printf("Variable's length:  %i.\n", sizeof full_time);
}
```

Output

```
Data type's length: 36.
Variable's length:  36.
```

In the first `printf()` we were careful to enclose the data-type name in parentheses and also refer to the data type as `struct employee_rec`, not just `employee_rec`.

ACCESSING STRUCTURES

Structures are most often accessed—read or assigned—by accessing their individual members. Since we may have many variables of the same structure type and each of these variables will have the same member names, we must tie the member name to the specific structure variable with a **member operator**, a dot (.). The *pay_rate* member of the *full_time* structure is referred to as *full_time.pay_rate*. The second character in the *name* array member of the *part_time* structure is *part_time.name[1]*, while *part_time.name* is the base address of the *name* array in *part_time*. It is, of course, constant.

The member operator is of the highest order of precedence, up there with parentheses and brackets. This high precedence ensures that a member will be associated with its structure before any operations are done on it. Associativity is left to right so that members of structures that are themselves members of other structures will be evaluated correctly. The notation *three.two.one* means that *one* is a member of *two*, which in turn is a member of *three*.

Structure members can be used anyplace we can use any other variables, as shown ⇨Program 11–2.

HEADS UP!

Accessing a member of a structure is just like accessing any other variable.

⇨Program 11–2

```
#include <stdio.h>

#define NAME_CHRS 30

struct employee_rec
{   char name[NAME_CHRS];
    int dependents;
    float pay_rate;
};

void main(void)
{   struct employee_rec full_time = {"Beulah Barzoom", 4, 12.63};

    printf("Employee's name: %s.\n", full_time.name);
    printf("Dependents: %i.\n", full_time.dependents);
    printf("Change pay rate from %.2f to > ", full_time.pay_rate);
    scanf("%f", &full_time.pay_rate);
    printf("Confirm new pay rate: %.2f.\n", full_time.pay_rate);
}
```

Output

```
Employee's name: Beulah Barzoom.
Dependents: 4.
Change pay rate from 12.63 to > 14.25
Confirm new pay rate: 14.25
```

In ⇨Program 11–3, we use our *employee_rec* structure in a program that figures net pay for an employee.

```
#include <stdio.h>

#define TAX_RATE .16                              /* General tax rate */
#define DEP_REDUCTION .02                /* Reduction for each dependent */
#define NAME_CHRS 30

struct employee_rec
{   char name[NAME_CHRS];
    int dependents;
    float pay_rate;
};

void main(void)
{   struct employee_rec employee;
    float hours, gross, tax;
    double net;

    printf("Employee name: ");
    gets(employee.name);
    while (employee.name[0] != '\0')                /* Stop at empty string */
    {   printf("Hours, pay rate, other dependents: ");
        scanf(" %f %f %i",
              &hours, &employee.pay_rate, &employee.dependents);
        gross = hours * employee.pay_rate;
        tax = (TAX_RATE - DEP_REDUCTION * employee.dependents) * gross;
        net = gross - tax;
        printf("   Pay to: %s    $**%.2f**\n", employee.name, net);
        while (getchar() != '\n');                       /* Flush stream */
        printf("Employee name: ");
        gets(employee.name);
    }
}
```

Output

```
Employee name: Maynard Freebisch
Hours, pay rate, other dependents: 36 10.83 2
   Pay to: Maynard Freebisch    $**350.89**
Employee name: Gilda Garfinkle
Hours, pay rate, other dependents: 44 15.25 4
   Pay to: Gilda Garfinkle    $**630.74**
Employee name:
```

In ANSI C an entire structure may be assigned to another structure of the same type. Given the declaration

ASSIGNING STRUCTURES

In many non-ANSI C implementations, you cannot assign a structure all at once. In such cases, the structure would have to be assigned member by member.

```
struct employee_rec full_time, part_time;
```

we may have a statement in our program

```
full_time = part_time;
```

▶TRAP◀

Trying to directly compare two structures.

that copies the contents of all the memory locations in *part_time* to the memory locations in *full_time*. The end result is that the values of all the members of *part_time* have been assigned to the like members of *full_time*. While assigning structures may be possible, directly comparing them is not. You cannot say

```
if (full_time == part_time)
```

You would have to compare the contents of each of the structure's members separately.

YOUR TURN 11–1

1. How are a structure and its members related?
2. How does a structure definition differ from a structure declaration?
3. What is a tag? Is it necessary?
4. How can we tell the number of bytes in a particular data type?
5. When do we use the key word `struct`?
6. Can structure members be initialized as part of the member definitions?
7. How can we access members of a structure variable?

ARRAYS OF STRUCTURES

In our example we have seen an array, *name*, within a structure, but we can also have arrays of structures, for example,

```
struct employee_rec employee[4];
```

which declares an array of four structures. To access the pay rate of the second employee in the array we would refer to *employee[1].pay_rate*. To access the third character of the *name* member of the second employee we would refer to *employee[1].name[2]*.

The array may be initialized by putting a block of values after the declaration. The outer set of braces is required; the inner sets are not but are usually used, as in this case, to separate the values for each of the individual structures. Be sure to follow each closing brace with a comma or, for the last one, a semicolon.

HEADS UP!

Using braces and separate lines makes your initializations easier to read.

```
struct employee_rec employee[4] =  /* Last name first */
    {{"Barzoom Beulah",     5, 12.63},
     {"LaRue LeRoy",        0, 9.50 },
     {"Freebisch Maynard", 3, 10.83},
     {"Garfinkle Gilda",    5, 15.25}};
```

If your C compiler is not ANSI standard, check to make sure this initialization is allowed for local-lifetime variables.

⇨Program 11–4 uses a bubble sort to order by name the employees in the array of structures. It then prints a report alphabetized by last name but with the first name first.

⇨**Program 11–4**

```
#include <stdio.h>
#include <string.h>

#define NAME_CHRS 30
#define TOT_EMPLOYEES 4

struct employee_rec
{   char name[NAME_CHRS];
    int dependents;
    float pay_rate;
};

void main(void)
{   struct employee_rec employee[TOT_EMPLOYEES] =        /* Last name first */
        {{"Barzoom Beulah",     5, 12.63},
         {"LaRue LeRoy",        0, 9.50 },
         {"Freebisch Maynard", 3, 10.83},
         {"Garfinkle Gilda",    5, 15.25}};
```

(continued)

```
/************************************************** Sort structures */
{   struct employee_rec temp;           /* Temporary structure for swap */
    int pos, bottom;                            /* Sort counters */
    int swap = 1;                           /* Goes to 1 if swap made */

    bottom = TOT_EMPLOYEES - 1;
    while (bottom > 0 && swap)
    {   swap = 0;                                   /* No swaps made yet */
        for (pos = 0; pos < bottom; ++pos)
            if (strcmp(employee[pos + 1].name, employee[pos].name) < 0)
            {   temp = employee[pos];
                employee[pos] = employee[bottom];
                employee[bottom] = temp;
                swap = 1;                               /* Swap made */
            }
        --bottom;
    }
}

/************************* Print sorted structures, first name first */
{   char first_first[NAME_CHRS];       /* Stores name, first name first */
    char *space;                            /* Location of space in name */
    int c;                                  /* Counter for employees */

    printf("Name             Dependents  Pay Rate\n");
    for (c = 0; c < TOT_EMPLOYEES; ++c)
    {   /************************** Assign name with first name first */
        space = strstr(employee[c].name, " ");
        strcpy(first_first, space + 1);
        strcat(first_first, " ");
        strncat(first_first, employee[c].name,
                space - employee[c].name);          /* Chars to space */
        printf("%-13.13s        %3i  %8.2f\n",      /* Print record */
            first_first, employee[c].dependents,
            employee[c].pay_rate);
    }
}
}
```

Output

```
Name            Dependents  Pay Rate
Beulah Barzoo           4     12.63
Maynard Freeb           2     10.83
Gilda Garfink           4     15.25
LeRoy LaRue             0      9.50
```

POINTERS TO STRUCTURES

Since a structure is guaranteed to be stored contiguously in memory, pointers to structures are useful. The definition

```
struct employee_rec
{   char name[30];
    int dependents;
    float pay_rate;
};
```

and declaration

```
struct employee_rec *employee;
```

declare *employee* to be a pointer to the structure. In this case, the only memory allocation is the few bytes for the pointer variable *employee*. Where it points, no one knows.

To give it a valid location to which to point, we might have declared an actual structure,

```
struct employee_rec full_time;
```

in which case we can assign the pointer variable to its address:

```
employee = &full_time;
```

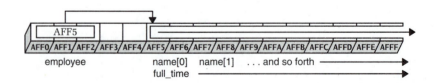

TRAP

Forgetting to cast the pointer.

If we had no need to refer to the structure using the name *full_time*, but only the pointer *employee*, we could allocate memory for the structure using `malloc()` (from Chapter 10):

```
employee = (struct employee_rec *) malloc(sizeof (struct employee_rec));
```

employee   name[0]   name[1]   . . . and so forth ─────────▶

This method also has the advantage of being able to deallocate the memory space using `free()`.

To access an individual member of a structure by its pointer, we would have to refer to the contents at the location of the particular member,

`(*pointer).member`

For example, to access the *dependents* member of the structure pointed to by *employee*, we would use the notation

`(*employee).dependents`

The parentheses are important because the member operator has precedence over the dereferencing operator, and we want *employee* to be evaluated as a pointer first, and then direct us to the *dependents* member.

The operation is common but the notation is somewhat clumsy, so C allows this notation:

`pointer->member`

meaning exactly the same thing. The arrow is made of a dash (-) and a greater-than symbol (>). Our example could be rewritten

`employee->dependents`

meaning the contents of the *dependents* member of the structure pointed to by *employee*, usually referred to as "employee pointer to dependents."

To assign the pay rate we could write the statement

`employee->pay_rate = 14.25;`

A major advantage to using pointers to structures is that when manipulating the structures, it is often not necessary to copy the entire structure from here to there, but only to change pointers—a great saving in the number of operations that the CPU must execute. A perfect example is the sorting of an array of structures with all its required swaps.

Our previous example could be rewritten in ⇨Program 11–5 to swap pointers instead of whole structures, making it execute more efficiently and also work for the non-ANSI Cs that do not allow assignments of entire structures. Notice that the pointer variables in the array *employee* had to be given values of locations that were previously allocated; in this case, to the structure variables in the array *emp*. Even with that extra step, execution will be quicker because there will be far fewer bytes to move.

```
#include <stdio.h>
#include <string.h>

#define NAME_CHRS 30
#define TOT_EMPLOYEES 4

struct employee_rec
{  char name[NAME_CHRS];
   int dependents;
   float pay_rate;
};

void main(void)
{  struct                                  /* Temp array for initialization */
       employee_rec emp[TOT_EMPLOYEES] =
       {{"Barzoom Beulah",     5, 12.63},
        {"LaRue LeRoy",        0, 9.50 },
        {"Freebisch Maynard", 3, 10.83},
        {"Garfinkle Gilda",    5, 15.25}};
   struct employee_rec *employee[TOT_EMPLOYEES];    /* Array of pointers */

   /******************************** Assign pointers to valid locations */
   {  int c;

      for (c = 0; c < TOT_EMPLOYEES; ++c)
         employee[c] = &emp[c];
   }
   /***************************************************** Sort structures */
   {  struct employee_rec *temp;          /* Temporary structure for swap */
      int pos, bottom;                                 /* Sort counters */
      int swap = 1;                          /* Goes to 1 if swap made */

      bottom = TOT_EMPLOYEES - 1;
      while (bottom > 0 && swap)
      {  swap = 0;                                 /* No swaps made yet */
         for (pos = 0; pos < bottom; ++pos)
            if (strcmp(employee[pos + 1]->name, employee[pos]->name) < 0)
            {  temp = employee[pos];
               employee[pos] = employee[bottom];
               employee[bottom] = temp;
               swap = 1;                                 /* Swap made */
            }
         --bottom;
      }
   }
```

(continued)

```
/*************************** Print sorted structures, first name first */
{   char first_first[NAME_CHRS];        /* Stores name first name first */
    char *space;                        /* Location of space in name */
    int c;                              /* Counter for employees */

    printf("Name            Dependents  Pay Rate\n");
    for (c = 0; c < TOT_EMPLOYEES; ++c)
    {   /*************************** Assign name with first name first */
        space = strstr(employee[c]->name, " ");
        strcpy(first_first, space + 1);
        strcat(first_first, " ");
        strncat(first_first, employee[c]->name,
                space - employee[c]->name);         /* Chars to space */
        printf("%-13.13s       %3i  %8.2f\n",       /* Print record */
                first_first, employee[c]->dependents,
                employee[c]->pay_rate);
    }
}
}
```

The execution will be exactly the same as that of ⇨Program 11–4.

STRUCTURES AND FUNCTIONS

A member of a structure can be treated like any other variable. Its value can be passed to a function to initialize a variable of the same data type as the member's. Let us modify ⇨Program 11–3 to calculate the employee's net pay in a function, *pay()*. The new code is in ⇨Program 11–6.

⇨**Program 11–6**

```
#include <stdio.h>

#define TAX_RATE .16                            /* General tax rate */
#define DEP_REDUCTION .02               /* Reduction for each dependent */

struct employee_rec
{   char name[30];
    int dependents;
    float pay_rate;
};

double pay(float hrs, float rt, int dep);       /* Function declaration */
```
(continued)

PASSING STRUCTURES

Many non-ANSI Cs do not allow passing entire structures to functions, nor do they allow a return of the structure from the function. All the values would have to be passed individually with the possibility of only one return value, or you could simplify things by passing a pointer to the structure.

```
void main(void)
{   struct employee_rec employee;
    float hours;
    double net;

    printf("Employee name: ");
    gets(employee.name);
    while (employee.name[0] != '\0')                     /* Empty string */
    {   printf("Hours, pay rate, dependents: ");
        scanf(" %f %f %i",
               &hours, &employee.pay_rate, &employee.dependents);
        net = pay(hours, employee.pay_rate, employee.dependents);
        printf("   Pay to: %s    $**%.2f**\n", employee.name, net);
        while (getchar() != '\n');                       /* Flush stream */
        printf("Employee name: ");
        gets(employee.name);
    }
}

/****************** Calculates net pay given hours, rate, and dependents */
double pay(float hrs, float rt, int dep)             /* Function definition */
{   float gross, tax;

    gross = hrs * rt;
    tax = (TAX_RATE - DEP_REDUCTION * dep) * gross;
    return gross - tax;
}
```

In ANSI C, we can also pass an entire structure to a function. The function will have to have a like structure in its argument declarations, as in ⇨Program 11–7. This is a good reason to make structure definitions externally, so that they will be visible from such functions.

In the call to *pay()*, we pass *hours* and, instead of passing the *pay_rate* and *dependents* members of *employee*, we pass the entire structure. In the function, we declare another *employee_rec* structure, *worker*, which is initialized in the call with the values from *employee*. Notice that the member names in the function have to be exactly as they are described in the structure definition near the beginning of the program.

HEADS UP!

Structure variable names may change, but member names may not.

```
#include <stdio.h>

#define TAX_RATE .16                              /* General tax rate */
#define DEP_REDUCTION .02                /* Reduction for each dependent */

struct employee_rec
{  char name[30];
   int dependents;
   float pay_rate;
};

double pay(float hrs, struct employee_rec worker);

void main(void)
{  struct employee_rec employee;
   float hours;
   double net;

   printf("Employee name: ");
   gets(employee.name);
   while (employee.name[0] != '\0')                    /* Empty string */
   {  printf("Hours, pay rate, dependents: ");
      scanf(" %f %f %i",
            &hours, &employee.pay_rate, &employee.dependents);
      net = pay(hours, employee);
      printf("   Pay to: %s   $**%.2f**\n", employee.name, net);
      while (getchar() != '\n');                        /* Flush stream */
      printf("Employee name: ");
      gets(employee.name);
   }
}
/****************** Calculates net pay given hours, rate, and dependents */
double pay(float hrs, struct employee_rec worker)
{  float gross, tax;

   gross = hrs * worker.pay_rate;
   tax = (TAX_RATE - DEP_REDUCTION * worker.dependents) * gross;
   return gross - tax;
}
```

The function never actually used the *name* member—a bit of inefficiency there. We passed 30 bytes we didn't actually need to.

In ANSI C, a structure may also be returned from a function. Suppose, in ⇨Program 11–8, we add a member, *ytd*, to our example structure to store the accumulated year-to-date pay. The *pay()* function can be modified to add the current net pay to that figure and return the entire structure to the main() function to be assigned to *employee*.

```c
#include <stdio.h>

#define TAX_RATE .16                              /* General tax rate */
#define DEP_REDUCTION .02               /* Reduction for each dependent */

struct employee_rec
{  char name[30];
   int dependents;
   float pay_rate;
   double ytd;                                    /* Accumulated pay */
};

struct employee_rec pay(float hrs, struct employee_rec worker);

void main(void)
{  struct employee_rec employee;
   float hours;
   double old_ytd;

   printf("Employee name: ");
   gets(employee.name);
   while (employee.name[0] != '\0')                      /* Empty string */
   {  printf("Hours, pay rate, dependents: ");
      scanf(" %f %f %i",
            &hours, &employee.pay_rate, &employee.dependents);
      printf("Pay prior to now: ");
      scanf(" %lf", &employee.ytd);
      old_ytd = employee.ytd;
      employee = pay(hours, employee);
      printf("   Pay to: %s    $**%.2f**\n",
            employee.name, employee.ytd - old_ytd);
      printf("   Total to date: $%.2f\n", employee.ytd);
      while (getchar() != '\n');
      printf("Employee name: ");
      gets(employee.name);
   }
}
/****************** Calculates net pay given hours, rate, and dependents */
struct employee_rec pay(float hrs, struct employee_rec worker)
{  float gross, tax;

   gross = hrs * worker.pay_rate;
   tax = (TAX_RATE - DEP_REDUCTION * worker.dependents) * gross;
   worker.ytd += gross - tax;
   return worker;
}
```

Output

```
Employee name: Maynard Freebisch
Hours, pay rate, other dependents: 36 10.83 3
Pay prior to now: 1042.57
    Pay to: Maynard Freebisch    $**350.89**
    Total to date: $1393.46
Employee name: Gilda Garfinkle
Hours, pay rate, other dependents: 44 15.25 5
Pay prior to now: 1467.03
    Pay to: Gilda Garfinkle    $**630.74**
    Total to date: $2097.77
Employee name:
```

Again, there had to be significant changes to the program. Now that the function is returning the structure, it can no longer return a **double** value to assign to *net*. We got around this by storing the previous *ytd* value in *old_ytd*, and calculating the net pay by subtracting the *old_ytd* from the new *employee.ytd*.

In this particular case, there seem to be a number of inefficiencies by passing the entire structure. First, we have had to invent new variables and processes in the **main()** function, and second, passing and returning the entire structure forces C to move a lot of bytes around in main memory.

In Chapter 10, we skirted the problem of needing more than one return value by passing pointers to our function and having the function manipulate the contents directly. Let us again have our function return the **double** value to assign to *net*, but pass it the address of the *employee* structure. In the function, shown in ⇨Program 11–9, we will declare a pointer to an *employee_rec* structure to receive the address.

HEADS UP!

Passing pointers to structures can lead to greater efficiency.

⇨**Program 11–9**

```
#include <stdio.h>

#define TAX_RATE .16                    /* General tax rate */
#define DEP_REDUCTION .02               /* Reduction for each dependent */

struct employee_rec
{  char name[30];
   int dependents;
   float pay_rate;
   double ytd;                          /* Accumulated pay */
};

double pay(float hrs, struct employee_rec *worker);
```

(continued)

```
void main(void)
{   struct employee_rec employee;
    float hours;
    double net;

    printf("Employee name: ");
    gets(employee.name);
    while (employee.name[0] != '\0')                          /* Empty string */
    {   printf("Hours, pay rate, dependents: ");
        scanf(" %f %f %i",
                &hours, &employee.pay_rate, &employee.dependents);
        printf("Pay prior to now: ");
        scanf(" %lf", &employee.ytd);
        net = pay(hours, &employee);               /* Pass address of structure */
        printf("   Pay to: %s     $**%.2f**\n",
                employee.name, net);
        printf("   Total to date: $%.2f\n", employee.ytd);
        while (getchar() != '\n');
        printf("Employee name: ");
        gets(employee.name);
    }
}


/***************** Calculates net pay given hours, rate, and dependents */
double pay(float hrs, struct employee_rec *worker)
{   float gross, tax;

    gross = hrs * worker->pay_rate;
    tax = (TAX_RATE - DEP_REDUCTION * worker->dependents) * gross;
    worker->ytd += gross - tax;
    return gross - tax;
}
```

In the call to the *pay()* function, we passed the address of *employee*, and in the function, we declared *worker* to be a pointer to a structure of type *employee_rec*. Notice that the structure notation within the *pay()* function has changed now that *worker* is a pointer instead of a structure.

YOUR TURN 11–2

1. In an array of structures that includes an array as a member, where does the structure subscript go and where does the member subscript go?

2. How do we initialize an array of structures?

3. In the declaration **struct structure *ptr;** how many bytes are allocated?

4. How can *ptr* above be made to point to allocated memory?

5. How do we access the content at the *mem* member of the structure pointed to by *ptr* above?

6. How can we pass a structure to a function?

7. Can we return a structure from a function?

LINKED LISTS (Optional)

If you have a list of your friends' names and telephone numbers, you could define a structure for the data for a single friend. (We have used the word *pal* in the example instead of *friend* because the latter is a key word in C++, a common extension to the C compiler.)

```
struct pal_rec
{   char name[30];
    char phone[13];
};
```

You could keep the data for all of your friends in an array of structures:

```
struct pal_rec pal[?];
```

How many friends do you have? After making a fool of yourself at the party last weekend, you're not sure. At any rate, you may have to drop a few from the list, but, since a few people laughed, you might pick up some new ones. So how many variables do we include in the array? It will have to accommodate the maximum number of friends that you might ever have, not just the number you have now. After last weekend, that will mean a lot of wasted memory in blank structures.

How do you add a friend? If you keep them in alphabetical order, you will have to insert into the array as we did in Chapter 7—a routine that may, in some cases, be unavoidable, but that will take execution time to move all those structures around. You would have to drop a friend by doing the reverse, again moving a lot of structures. Storing lists in arrays, then, has some major disadvantages: allocating a fixed amount of memory, much of which may be wasted; and having to move a number of structures to add and delete.

Let us look at another method of storing lists in which we allocate only the memory we need, and no extra. We can allocate a specific block of memory using the `malloc()` function, and, when we no longer need it, deallocate it using `free()`. To add a friend, then, we will create a new structure, and to drop one, delete the structure. That, however, will not solve the problem of keeping them in order.

Structures Pointing to Structures

We can keep a set of data in order using a concept called the **linked list**. The list is essentially a chain of structures; the links being created by each structure containing a pointer to the next structure.

HEADS UP!

Any data type, including a pointer to a structure, can be a structure member.

Each structure in memory will have, as one of its members, a pointer to the next structure in the list. To move through the list, we start at the **head** of the list, the address of the first structure; the first structure will contain the address of the second; the second the address of the third; and so forth until the last structure, at the **tail** of the list, has a NULL pointer instead of the address of another structure.

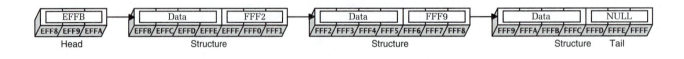

Referring to our example of the list of friends, if we were to set it up as a linked list of structures, we would define the structure as:

```
struct pal_rec
{   char name[30];
    char phone[13];
    struct pal_rec *next;
};
```

The last member of the structure, *next*, is a pointer to the data type *struct pal_rec*. Its value will be the address of the next structure in the list. It makes no difference where these structures are in memory, as long as the previous structure knows where the next structure starts. Assuming that we had allocated space for a number of these structures and properly linked them, our alphabetical list of friends could be as shown:

Friends in Memory			
Address	*name*	*phone*	*next*
CA3A	Deltoid, Bruce	123-456-7890	CB14
CB14	Flowers, May	111-555-1212	NULL
CC0E	Abernathy, Aloysius	111-222-3333	CA3A

We could print them in order using the *print()* function below. For the function to work, it will have to know the head of the list—the address of the first structure. Our call to the function, then, would be

```
                        print(head);

    where head would be CC0E, and the function is:

    /****************************************************** Print out list */
p1  void print(struct pal_rec *pal)
    {                                      /* The first value of pal is the head */
p2     while (pal != NULL)                              /* The tail is not NULL */
p3     { printf("%-30.30s %s\n", pal->name, pal->phone);
p4        pal = pal->next;                             /* Set pal to next address */
       }
    }
```

Output

```
Abernathy, Aloysius                   111-222-3333
Deltoid, Bruce                        123-456-7890
Flowers, May                          111-555-1212
```

EXECUTION CHART

Line	Explanation	pal	pal->name	pal->next
p1	Initialize value of *pal* from pass.	CC0E	Abernathy,	CA3A
p2	*pal* not NULL.	CC0E	Abernathy,	CA3A
p3	Print record.	CC0E	Abernathy,	CA3A
p4	Set *pal* to point to next structure.	CA3A	Deltoid,	CB14
p2	*pal* not NULL.	CA3A	Deltoid,	CB14
p3	Print record.	CA3A	Deltoid,	CB14
p4	Set *pal* to point to next structure.	CB14	Flowers,	NULL
p2	*pal* not NULL.	CB14	Flowers,	NULL
p3	Print record.	CB14	Flowers,	NULL
p4	Set *pal* to point to next structure.	NULL	?	?
p2	*pal* is NULL. Exit loop and return.	NULL	?	?

Inserting into a Linked List

To add to our list, we must first create a new structure. The *newpal()* function, which follows, allocates memory for the structure, and allows input of data for it. We pass nothing to the function, but the function returns the address of the new structure. The *next* member of the structure—the pointer to the next structure—is set to NULL. When the structure is inserted, that will change unless this new one ends up at the end of the list.

```
/********************************************** Set up new record */
struct pal_rec *newpal(void)
{   struct pal_rec *pal;                         /* Address of new record */
                                    /* Create memory space for new record */
    pal = (struct pal_rec *) malloc(sizeof (struct pal_rec));
    if (pal != NULL)                    /* Be sure memory can be allocated */
    {   printf("Name/Phone: ");
        scanf("%[^/]%*c %s", pal->name, pal->phone);
        while (getchar() != '\n');              /* Get rid of \n in stream */
        pal->next = NULL;
    }
    else
        puts("Not enough memory!");
    return pal;
}
```

We insert the new structure in the list by starting from the head and examining each structure in the list. When we find the spot to insert—the new name, for example, is less than the name in the current structure we are examining—we change the pointer in the previous structure to point to the new one, and assign the pointer in the new structure to the address of the current one.

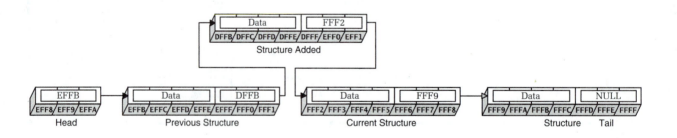

For the friends example, we can write an *insert()* function such as the one following, and call it with

```
insert(&head);    /* Send address in case head changed */
```

Notice that we are passing the function the address of the head rather than the value of the head. It is possible that the new structure we insert will fall at the beginning of the linked list, in which case, the function will have to change the value of the head. Therefore, the function has to know where the head is, not just its value.

The *insert()* function is prototyped with *head* being a pointer to a pointer to a structure. Complicated, but necessary. Remember, *head* is a pointer to a structure. The address of *head* (**&head**), then, is a pointer to a pointer to a structure (****head**). When we access *head* in *insert()*, we use the notation ***head**, meaning follow the address in the *insert() head* (EFF8 in the following diagram) to where it points (EFF8 is the address of the **main()** *head*), and access the value there (EFFB, which is the address of the first structure).

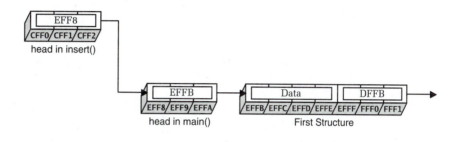

Notice the three other pointers to structure declared in *insert()*. The first, *pal*, is the address of the new record. It is assigned in the **if** statement by a call to the *newpal()* function. If the record is successfully created (the return from *newpal()* is not NULL), the last two pointers are declared. One, *curr*, keeps track of the current record as we move from record to record; the other, *prev*, keeps track of the previous one. When we find the proper location for the new record, the pointer in the previous record is set to the new one (**prev->next = pal**), and the pointer in the new record is set to the current one (**pal->next = curr**).

For the execution example we have chosen the insertion of Ernestine Euforia.

Memory Before Insertion			
Address	*name*	*phone*	*next*
CA3A	Deltoid, Bruce	123-456-7890	CB14
CB14	Flowers, May	111-555-1212	NULL
CC0E	Abernathy, Aloysius	111-222-3333	CA3A

```c
/********************************************* Insert new record into list */
i1  void insert(struct pal_rec **head)
    {   struct pal_rec *pal;                      /* Address of new record */

i2      if ((pal = newpal()) != NULL)              /* New record created */
        {   struct pal_rec *curr,           /* Record being examined for input */
                           *prev = NULL;             /* Record before curr */

i3          curr = *head;
i4          while (curr != NULL                      /* Not at end of list */
                   && strcmp(pal->name, curr->name) > 0)    /* Name > record's */
i5          {   prev = curr;                     /* Save current record address */
i6              curr = curr->next;                      /* Go to next record */
            }
i7          pal->next = curr;                /* Insert in front of current record */
i8          if (prev == NULL)                        /* No previous record */
i9              *head = pal;                             /* First in list */
            else
i10             prev->next = pal;                /* One before points to this */
        }                                         /* New record not created */
        else
i11         printf("Can't create new record.\n");
    }
```

EXECUTION CHART

Line	Explanation	pal	pal-> name	pal-> next	prev	prev-> next	curr	curr-> name	curr-> next
i1	Initialize value of *head* from pass. It points to CC0E								
i2	Call *newpal()*, assign return to *pal*. It is not NULL.	CD21	Euforia	NULL					
i3	Assign *curr* what *head* points to.	CD21	Euforia	NULL	NULL	?	CC0E	Aberna	CA3A
i4	*curr* not NULL, *pal->name* > curr->name.	CD21	Euforia	NULL	NULL	?	CC0E	Aberna	CA3A
i5	Save *curr* in *prev*.	CD21	Euforia	NULL	CC0E	CA3A	CC0E	Aberna	CA3A
i6	Set *curr* to next record.	CD21	Euforia	NULL	CC0E	CA3A	CA3A	Deltoid	CB14
i4	*curr* not NULL, *pal->name* > curr->name.	CD21	Euforia	NULL	CC0E	CA3A	CA3A	Deltoid	CB14
i5	Save *curr* in *prev*.	CD21	Euforia	NULL	CA3A	CB14	CA3A	Deltoid	CB14
i6	Set *curr* to next record.	CD21	Euforia	NULL	CA3A	CB14	CB14	Flower	NULL
i4	*curr* not NULL, *pal->name* not > *curr->name*.	CD21	Euforia	NULL	CA3A	CB14	CB14	Flower	NULL
i7	Set new record pointing to *curr*.	CD21	Euforia	CB14	CA3A	CB14	CB14	Flower	NULL
i8	*prev* not NULL.	CD21	Euforia	CB14	CA3A	CB14	CB14	Flower	NULL
i10	Set *prev* record pointing to new one and return.	CD21	Euforia	CB14	CA3A	CD21	CB14	Flower	NULL

Deleting from a Linked List

A structure is deleted by passing the pointers around it. The pointer in the structure before is changed to point to the structure after the deleted one. The memory space for the deleted structure can then be deallocated.

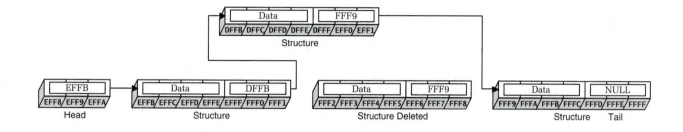

In the friends example, the *dump()* function deletes a record. As in inserting, we pass it a pointer to the head (in case the head must be modified) and examine each record in turn for the one to delete. When we find that one, we assign its pointer to the previous record.

```
prev->next = curr->next;
```

We can then deallocate the current record.

```
free(curr);
```

For our execution example we will delete Aloysius Abernathy.

Memory Before Deletion			
Address	*name*	*phone*	*next*
CA3A	Deltoid, Bruce	123-456-7890	CD21
CB14	Flowers, May	111-555-1212	NULL
CC0E	Abernathy, Aloysius	111-222-3333	CA3A
CD21	Euforia, Ernestine	967-666-7777	CB14

```
                /*************************************** Delete record from list */
d1  void dump(struct pal_rec **head)
    {
d2      if (*head != NULL)                          /* There are names in list */
        {  struct pal_rec *curr,          /* Record being examined for deletion */
                          *prev = NULL;             /* Record before curr */
           char dump_name[30];

           printf("Name to delete: ");
d3         gets(dump_name);
d4         curr = *head;
d5         while (curr != NULL                      /* Not at end of list */
                  && strcmp(dump_name, curr->name)) /* Name != record's */
d6         {  prev = curr;                          /* Save current record address */
d7            curr = curr->next;                    /* Go to next record */
           }
d8         if (curr == NULL)                        /* Didn't find name */
d9            printf("Name not in list.\n");
           else                                     /* Name found */
d10        {  if (prev == NULL)                     /* No previous record */
d11              *head = curr->next;                /* First record dumped */
              else
d12              prev->next = curr->next;  /* Previous rec points to next rec */
d13           free(curr);                           /* Deallocate that memory space */
           }
        }                                           /* List empty */
        else
d14        printf("List empty.\n");
    }
```

EXECUTION CHART

Line	Explanation	*head	dump_name	prev	prev->next	curr	curr->name	curr->next
d1	Initialize value of *head* from pass.	CC0E						
d2	*head* does not point to NULL.	CC0E						
d3	Input name to delete.	CC0E	Aberna	NULL	?	?	?	?
d4	Assign *curr* what *head* points to.	CC0E	Aberna	NULL	?	CC0E	Aberna	CA3A
d5	*curr* not NULL, *dump_name* =curr->name.	CC0E	Aberna	NULL	?	CC0E	Aberna	CA3A
d8	*curr* not NULL	CC0E	Aberna	NULL	?	CC0E	Aberna	CA3A
d10	*prev* is NULL.	CC0E	Aberna	NULL	?	CC0E	Aberna	CA3A
d11	Change *head* to second record.	CA3A	Aberna	NULL	?	CC0E	Aberna	CA3A
d13	Deallocate space at first record and return.	CA3A	Aberna	NULL	?	CC0E	?	?

All the subsidiary functions are shown above; all that remains is to add the main() function, as in ⇨Program 11–10.

⇨Program 11–10

```c
#include <stdio.h>
#include <stdlib.h>
#include <string.h>
#include <ctype.h>

struct pal_rec
{   char name[30];
    char phone[13];
    struct pal_rec *next;
};

void print(struct pal_rec *pal);              /* Print list */
void insert(struct pal_rec **head);           /* Insert new record */
struct pal_rec *newpal(void);                 /* Create new record */
void dump(struct pal_rec **head);             /* Delete record */

void main(void)
{   struct pal_rec *head = NULL;
    int choice;

    printf("(I)nsert, (D)elete, or (P)rint: ");
    while((choice = getchar()) != '\n')       /* Return ends program */
    {   while (getchar() != '\n');            /* Dump end of stream */
        switch (toupper(choice))
        {   case 'I':
                insert(&head);        /* Send address in case head changed */
                break;
            case 'D':
                dump(&head);          /* Send address in case head changed */
                break;
            case 'P':
                print(head);
                break;
        }
        printf("(I)nsert, (D)elete, or (P)rint: ");
    }
}
```

LINKED LISTS (OPTIONAL) **483**

Output

```
(I)nsert, (D)elete, or (P)rint: i
Name/Phone: Deltoid, Bruce/123-456-7890
(I)nsert, (D)elete, or (P)rint: i
Name/Phone: Flowers, May/111-555-1212
(I)nsert, (D)elete, or (P)rint: i
Name/Phone: Abernathy, Aloysius/111-222-3333
(I)nsert, (D)elete, or (P)rint: p
Abernathy, Aloysius          111-222-3333
Deltoid, Bruce               123-456-7890
Flowers, May                 111-555-1212
(I)nsert, (D)elete, or (P)rint: i
Name/Phone: Euforia, Ernestine/967-666-7777
(I)nsert, (D)elete, or (P)rint: p
Abernathy, Aloysius          111-222-3333
Deltoid, Bruce               123-456-7890
Euforia, Ernestine           967-666-7777
Flowers, May                 111-555-1212
(I)nsert, (D)elete, or (P)rint: d
Name to delete: Abernathy, Aloysius
(I)nsert, (D)elete, or (P)rint: p
Deltoid, Bruce               123-456-7890
Euforia, Ernestine           967-666-7777
Flowers, May                 111-555-1212
(I)nsert, (D)elete, or (P)rint:
```

YOUR TURN 11–3

1. How is a linked list linked?

2. What is the head of the linked list? What is the tail?

3. How do we insert a structure into a linked list?

4. How do we delete from a linked list?

FILES AND STRUCTURES

HEADS UP!

A structure easily enforces the fixed-length requirement of certain files.

A structure can be viewed as a fixed-length object stored at an address in memory. This kind of description fits perfectly with the operation of fread() and fwrite(). We can easily move structures to and from files by passing either function the address of the structure, the number of bytes in the structure (which we can get using sizeof), and the number of structures.

In ⇨Program 11–11, we have modified ⇨Program 9–1 from Chapter 9 that accepted employee data and put the data for each employee in a file *EMP.DAT*. In this example, we keep the employee data in a structure, and copy the entire structure into the file. The file, now named

EMPLOYEE.DAT, was opened in mode **"wb"** so that we would start with an empty file, and no special translation of our bytes would be made. Each time we input data for an employee, we write the structure to the file.

⇨**Program 11–11**

```
#include <stdio.h>
#include <stdlib.h>
#define CHRS 30

struct employee_rec
{   char name[CHRS];
    int dependents;
    float pay_rate;
};
void main(void)
{   struct employee_rec employee;
    FILE *employ;

    if ((employ = fopen("EMPLOYEE.DAT", "wb")) == NULL)        /* Open file */
    {   printf("Cannot open file.\n");
        exit(EXIT_FAILURE);
    }
    printf("Employee name: "); /***************** Input and write to file */
    gets(employee.name);
    while (employee.name[0] != '\0')                          /* Empty string */
    {   printf("Pay rate, other dependents: ");
        scanf(" %f %i", &employee.pay_rate, &employee.dependents);
        fwrite(&employee, sizeof employee, 1, employ);
        while (getchar() != '\n');
        printf("Employee name: ");
        gets(employee.name);
    }
    fclose(employ);
}
```

Output

```
Employee name: Maynard Freebisch
Pay rate, other dependents: 10.83 2
Employee name: Gilda Garfinkle
Pay rate, other dependents: 15.25 4
Employee name: Beulah Barzoom
Pay rate, other dependents: 12.63 4
Employee name: LeRoy LaRue
Pay rate, other dependents: 9.50 -1
Employee name:
```

HEADS UP!

Typically, structures written to files make little sense if we look at the file.

Showing the file contents as a result of this program would make little sense. We could see the characters in the strings, but the numbers were written just as they were stored in memory, in binary notation, so those bytes translated as characters would be meaningless.

We could do this week's payroll by reading the employee data from the file, inputting the number of hours for each, and printing the results. In ⇨Program 11–12, both the structure definition and the arguments in the fread() call are exactly the same as in ⇨Program 11–11—except that it was a call to fwrite()—ensuring that the data will be read from the file and written to the structure in exactly the same manner that it was read from the structure and written to the file in the last program.

⇨**Program 11–12**

```c
#include <stdio.h>
#include <stdlib.h>

#define CHRS 30

struct employee_rec
{   char name[CHRS];
    int dependents;
    float pay_rate;
};

void main(void)
{   struct employee_rec employee;
    float hours, gross, tax;
    double net;
    FILE *employ;

    if ((employ = fopen("EMPLOYEE.DAT", "rb")) == NULL)        /* Open file */
    {   printf("Cannot open file.\n");
        exit(EXIT_FAILURE);
    }
    while (fread(&employee, sizeof employee, 1, employ) == 1)        /* Pay */
    {   printf("Hours for %s: ", employee.name);
        scanf(" %f", &hours);
        gross = hours * employee.pay_rate;
        tax = (.16 - .02 * (employee.dependents + 1)) * gross;
        net = gross - tax;
        printf("   Pay to: %s   $**%.2f**\n", employee.name, net);
    }
    fclose(employ);
}
```

Output

```
Hours for Maynard Freebisch: 36
    Pay to: Maynard Freebisch    $**350.89**
Hours for Gilda Garfinkle: 44
    Pay to: Gilda Garfinkle    $**630.74**
Hours for Beulah Barzoom: 39
    Pay to: Beulah Barzoom    $**463.02**
Hours for LeRoy LaRue: 3
    Pay to: LeRoy LaRue    $**23.94**
```

DIRECT ACCESS TO FILES

There are two fundamental types of file access: sequential and direct. In a **sequential access**, you start from the beginning of the file and move toward the end. A novel is accessed sequentially, as is an audio or video tape. In **direct access**, you go directly to a particular point in the file. A phone book can be accessed directly, as can a CD audio disc or video disc. Going to a particular point in a file can be accomplished using the `fseek()` function as long as we know the byte position in the file.

In ⇨Program 11–13 we will change the pay rate of one of the people in the *EMPLOYEE.DAT* file, using both sequential and direct access to the file. We will use sequential access to find the employee in the file. Once we have found the employee's record—matched the name from the file record with the one input from the keyboard—the file position indicator will be beyond that record in the file. We will have to use direct access to return the file position indicator to the byte position of the beginning of the record, so that we may rewrite the record to the file. The record, of course, will be stored in memory as a structure.

⇨Program 11–13

```
#include <stdio.h>
#include <stdlib.h>
#include <string.h>
#define CHRS 30

struct employee_rec
{  char name[CHRS];
   int dependents;                      /* Does not include employee */
   float pay_rate;
};
```

(continued)

```
void main(void)
{   struct employee_rec employee;
    char person[30];
    long record = 0;                               /* long to avoid casting in fseek */
    FILE *employ;

    if ((employ = fopen("EMPLOYEE.DAT", "rb+")) == NULL)        /* Open file */
    {   printf("Cannot open file.\n");
        exit(EXIT_FAILURE);
    }
    printf("Employee's name: ");                    /* Input person to change */
    gets(person);
    while (fread(&employee, sizeof employee, 1, employ) == 1     /* Search */
            && strcmp(person, employee.name) != 0)
        ++record;                                   /* Count record */
    if (feof(employ))                               /* Input name not on file */
    {   printf("%s not on file.\n", person);
    }
    else                                            /* Change pay rate and rewrite */
    {   printf("Pay rate for %s: ", employee.name);
        scanf(" %f", &employee.pay_rate);
        fseek(employ, record * sizeof employee, SEEK_SET);
        fwrite(&employee, sizeof employee, 1, employ);
    }
    rewind(employ);                                 /* Print changed file */
    printf("\nName          Dependents  Pay Rate\n");
    while (fread(&employee, sizeof employee, 1, employ) == 1)
        printf("%-13.13s          %3i  %8.2f\n",
            employee.name, employee.dependents, employee.pay_rate);
    fclose(employ);
}
```

Output

```
Employee's name: LeRoy LaRue
Pay rate for LeRoy LaRue: 4.65

Name         Dependents  Pay Rate
Maynard Freeb        2     10.83
Gilda Garfink        4     15.25
Beulah Barzoo        4     12.63
LeRoy LaRue         -1      4.65
```

Output

```
Employee's name: Ebenezer Bargle
Ebenezer Bargle not on file.

Name         Dependents  Pay Rate
Maynard Freeb        2     10.83
Gilda Garfink        4     15.25
Beulah Barzoo        4     12.63
LeRoy LaRue         -1      4.65
```

We could also have done the search and change without using the variable *record*. Instead of moving the pointer a certain number of bytes from the beginning of the file, we could have moved it backward one record in the file. The changed section of the program would be:

```
while (fread(&employee, sizeof employee, 1, employ) == 1    /* Search */
      && strcmp(person, employee.name) != 0);               /* New ; */
   /* ++record;                                    Don't need this */
if (feof(employ))                                 /* Input name not on file */
{ printf("%s not on file.\n", person);
}else                                             /* Change pay rate and rewrite */
{ printf("Pay rate for %s: ", employee.name);
   scanf(" %f", &employee.pay_rate);
   fseek(employ, -(long)(sizeof employee), SEEK_CUR);        /* Use cast */
   fwrite(&employee, sizeof employee, 1, employ);
}
```

When we moved backward in the file, the offset expression was

`-(long)(sizeof employee)`

The result of the `sizeof` operator is data type `size_t`, a defined data type. It is different in various Cs, but it is often an unsigned integer. The *offset* argument requires a signed long integer value so we must use the cast. Using just `-sizeof employee` would have been a disaster! The value of that expression, instead of being −36, would be some positive garbage number, for example, 65500 in a C where `size_t` was a 2-byte unsigned integer. C would attempt to move the file position indicator and write there, but where is that?

▶TRAP◀

Not casting the offset.

YOUR TURN 11-4

1. Why do structures and fixed-record-length files go together?

2. What is the difference between sequential and direct access?

3. What function allows us direct access to any byte position in a file?

4. What happens if we try to move the file pointer outside the bounds of the file?

PUTTING IT TOGETHER

Esoteric Toys, Inc., sends letters to customers listing only the products Esoteric thinks they might be interested in. Currently, they retype the data by hand—a tiresome process.

TASK

Develop a program to allow Esoteric's people to select specific products from their file and put them in a form that they can merge with their word-processed letters.

In Esoteric's product file are records, each of which consists of the product's name, its cost, and a status—either the character *o* for open, or *l* for listed, meaning that it has been chosen for listing in the file to be merged with the letter. The user should be able to type in the names of products, have the program search for that product, and either say it does not exist or change its status and copy it to the merge file. The process should end when the user hits just the Enter key. At that time, the chosen products and prices should be printed out.

A sample session might look like:

```
Add to list: Ringle
Add to list: Whatzit
Product not on file.
Add to list: Whizzit
Add to list:

Product            Price
Ringle              8.49
Whizzit             4.95
```

Esoteric's product data is stored in a binary file, *PRODUCTS.DAT*, from which Esoteric will choose products. The chosen products will have to be stored in a text file, *PRODUCTS.LST*, for import into the word-processed document. When a product is chosen, its status in the *DAT* file is changed from open to listed. The overall structure of Esoteric's program is:

```
Open files
Choose products
Print list for confirmation
Close files
```

Choosing the products to list is set up as a separate module.

```
[Choose products]
    While more choices
        While not at end of file and no match yet        [Search DAT file]
            Read next record from DAT file
        If at end of file
            Print error message
        Else
            Add to LST file
            Change status in DAT file
```

Esoteric does not want to print a list if nothing has been added to the list, and it wants to delete the *LST* file, so that section of the process combines the printing and closing of the *LST* file.

```
If no listings                          [Print list for confirmation]
    Print error message
    Close LST file
    Delete LST file
Else
    Print listings
    Close LST file
```

Printing the *LST* file is handled in a separate module.

```
[Print listings]
    Set LST file to beginning
    While more listings
        Read listing
        Print listing
```

IMPLEMENTATION

Before ⇨Program 11–14 that follows, we have shown the function used to create a new *DAT* file for testing the program. In this function you can see the data in the *DAT* file as well as how it goes from an array of structures to a file.

```c
/*********************************************** Create file to test program */
void new_file(void)
{   struct product_rec product[4] = {{"Whizzit", 4.95, 'o'},
                                     {"Doowop",  6.50, 'o'},
                                     {"Beedler",  .98, 'o'},
                                     {"Ringle",  8.49, 'o'}};
    FILE *prod;
    int rec;

    if ((prod = fopen("PRODUCT.DAT", "wb")) == NULL)
    {   puts("Can't open file.");
        exit(EXIT_FAILURE);
    }
    for (rec = 0; rec < 4; ++rec)                    /* Put records on file */
        fwrite(&product[rec], 1, sizeof (product[0]), prod);
    fclose(prod);
}
```

⇨Program 11–14

```
#include <stdio.h>
#include <stdlib.h>
#include <string.h>

#define CHRS 20

struct product_rec
{   char name[20];
    float price;
    char status;                                /* "o" for open, "l" for listed */
};

void new_file(void);                            /* Create new file for testing */
int add_to_list(FILE *prod, FILE *list);           /* Transfer to LST file */
void print_list(FILE *list);                            /* Print LST file */

void main(void)
{   FILE *prod, *list;
    int no_of_listings;                         /* Number of records in LST */

    new_file();                                 /* Establish file for testing */

    /******************************************************* Open files */
1   if ((prod = fopen("PRODUCT.DAT", "rb+")) == NULL)
2   {   puts("Can't open file.");
3       exit(EXIT_FAILURE);
    }
4   if ((list = fopen("PRODUCT.LST", "w+")) == NULL)
5   {   puts("Can't open file.");
6       exit(EXIT_FAILURE);
    }
    /************************************** Transfer listings to LST file */
7   no_of_listings = add_to_list(prod, list);

    /***************************************************** Print listings */
8   if (no_of_listings)
9   {   print_list(list);
10      fclose(list);
    }else
11  {   puts("No listings on file.");
12      fclose(list);
13      remove("PRODUCTS.LST");
    }
14  fclose(prod);
}
```

Line	Explanation	no_of_listings	*prod	*list
1	Open *PRODUCT.DAT* file for read and write.	?	*DAT* file description	?
4	Create *PRODUCT.LST* file for read and write.	?	*DAT* file description	LST file description
7	Call *add_to_list()*.	?	DAT	LST
7	Assign return to *no_of_listings*.	2	DAT	LST
8	*no_of_listings* nonzero.	2	DAT	LST
9	Call *print_list()* to print *LST* file.	2	DAT	LST
10	Close *LST* file.	2	DAT	?
14	Close *DAT* file.	2	?	?

```
       /********************************* Add records from DAT file to LST file */
       int add_to_list(FILE *prod, FILE *list)
       {  struct product_rec product;
          char search[20];
          int listings = 0;                      /* Number of records added to LST */

          printf("Add to list: ");
a1        while (gets(search), *search != '\0')          /* No entry stops loop */
          {
             /************** Search through DAT file until end of file or match */
a2           rewind(prod);                   /* Make sure at beginning of DAT file */
                                             /* and EOF error reset */
a3           while (fread(&product, 1, sizeof product, prod) == sizeof product
                   && strcmp(search, product.name));

a4           if (feof(prod)) /******************** Last read was at end of file */
a5              puts("Product not on file.");
             else /***************************************** Put on LST file */
a6           { fprintf(list, "%-20.20s %5.2f\n", product.name, product.price);
a7              ++listings;
a8              fseek(prod, -1L, SEEK_CUR);       /* Set file ptr back to status */
a9              fwrite("l", 1, 1, prod);              /* Change status to "l" */
             }

             printf("Add to list: ");
          }
a10       return listings;
       }
```

Line	Explanation	DAT ptr at	search[]	product. name[]	listings
a1	Input search string. It is not blank.	Whizzit …	Ringle	?	0
a2	Call to `rewind()` also clears any EOF error condition.	Whizzit …	Ringle	?	0
a3	Read first record. It is not equal to *search[]*.	Doowop …	Ringle	Whizzit	0
a3	Read second record. It is not equal to *search[]*.	Beedler …	Ringle	Doowop	0
a3	Read third record. It is not equal to *search[]*.	Ringle …	Ringle	Beedler	0
a3	Read fourth record. It is equal to *search[]*.	End of file	Ringle	Ringle	0
a4	End-of-file error not set because no read attempted there.	End of file	Ringle	Ringle	0
a6	Write name and price on LST file in characters.	End of file	Ringle	Ringle	0
a7	Add 1 to listings.	End of file	Ringle	Ringle	1
a8	Move file position indicator back one byte.	oEnd of file	Ringle	Ringle	1
a9	Write an l there.	End of file	Ringle	Ringle	1
a1	Input search string. It is not blank.	End of file	Whatzit	Ringle	1
a2–a3	Search entire file. Last read is at end of file. Error condition set.	End of file	Whatzit	Ringle	1
a4	`feof()` true.	End of file	Whatzit	Ringle	1
a5	Print error message.	End of file	Whatzit	Ringle	1
a1	Input search string. It is not blank.	End of file	Whizzit	Ringle	1
a2	Call to `rewind()` clears the EOF error condition.	End of file	Whizzit	Ringle	1
a3	Read first record. It is not equal to *search[]*.	Doowop …	Whizzit	Whizzit	1
a4	No end of file error.	Doowop …	Whizzit	Whizzit	1
a6	Write name and price on LST file in characters.	Doowop …	Whizzit	Whizzit	1
a7	Add 1 to listings.	Doowop …	Whizzit	Whizzit	2
a8	Move file position indicator back one byte.	oDoowop…	Whizzit	Whizzit	2
a9	Write an l there.	Doowop …	Whizzit	Whizzit	2
a1	Input search string. It is blank.	Doowop …		Whizzit	2
a10	Return value of listings.	Doowop …		Whizzit	2

```
#define LIST_LEN 27

/*********************************************** Print listings from LST file */
void print_list(FILE *list)
{   char listing[LIST_LEN];              /* Complete listing from LST file */

p1      rewind(list);
p2      puts("\nProduct                  Price");
p3      while (fgets(listing, LIST_LEN, list) != NULL)
p4          printf("%s", listing);
}
```

EXECUTION CHART—*print_list()*

Line	Explanation	listing[]
p1	Set *LST* file back to beginning. Prepare for read.	?
p2	Print headings.	?
p3	Read to first \n in *LST* file.	Ringle ...
p4	Print listing.	Ringle ...
p3	Read to second \n in *LST* file.	Whizzit ...
p4	Print listing.	Ringle ...
p3	Attempt to read in *LST* file. At end of file. Return.	Whizzit ...

TEST

The test should include products from both the beginning and the end of the file, as well as products that are not on the file.

Output

```
Add to list: Ringle
Add to list: Whatzit
Product not on file.
Add to list: Whizzit
Add to list:

Product          Price
Ringle           8.49
Whizzit          4.95
```

SUMMARY

▲**KEY TERMS** (in order of appearance)

Structure	Member operator
Member	Linked list
Structure definition	Head
Tag	Tail
Member definition	Sequential access
`struct`	Direct access
`sizeof`	

▲CONCEPT REVIEW

▼ **Structures** are complex data types made up of individual **members**, which can be simple or other complex data types.

▼ We state the makeup of a structure in a **structure definition** and allocate variables of that structure type in a structure declaration. The key word **struct** begins either a structure declaration or definition, or a statement combining both.

▼ A structure **tag** is the name given to the new structure data type. Declaration statements using the tag can allocate structures of that type.

▼ Structure **member definitions** determine the data types of the individual members of the structure.

▼ Structures may be initialized by putting values in braces in the declaration.

▼ The **sizeof** operator will give us the number of bytes in the entire structure if we refer to the structure variable's name, or to the structure's tag in parentheses.

▼ We can access individual members of a structure by using the structure variable's name followed by a **member operator** (a dot) and the member's name. This notation can be used anyplace we can use an ordinary variable.

▼ In ANSI C, we can assign one entire structure to a like one by simply using structure variables' names.

▼ Arrays of structures are valid in C. They can be initialized using nested braces. In structure/member notation the structure subscript follows the structure name (before the dot) and the member subscript (if any) follows the member name.

▼ In using pointers to structures, we can access an individual member by using the (*pointer).member notation or pointer->member.

▼ Values of members of structures may be passed to functions just like values of simple data types. In ANSI C, we can pass an entire structure, or return one. More often, however, we pass a pointer to the structure and use pointer notation in the function.

▼ A **linked list** is a common application of structures in which order is maintained by having a pointer in each record point to the next record. Using linked lists, we can easily insert into and delete from an ordered list, and the list need not occupy any unused memory.

▼ Memory for individual records of a linked list is allocated as needed by the **malloc()** function, and deallocated by **free()**.

▼ A linked list starts with a **head**, a pointer to the first structure in the list, and ends with a **tail**, the pointer in the last structure in the list which points to NULL.

▼ We can insert records into a linked list by putting the address of the new record in the pointer in the record before the insertion spot, and making the pointer in the new record equal to what the previous one used to be. We can delete a record by making the previous record point directly to the subsequent one. Once a record has been excluded from the list, it may be deallocated.

▼ Structures are often used with fixed-record-length files to contain the record while it is in main memory. The structure may be moved to and from the file using `fwrite()` and `fread()`.

▼ Using structures we can either use **sequential access** to a file, starting from the beginning and moving toward the end, or **direct access**, moving to a specific position in a file with `fseek()`.

▲HEADS UP: POINTS OF SPECIAL INTEREST

▼ A structure is a data type made of other data types.

▼ The tag is the name of the data type.

▼ Structure definitions do not allocate memory.

▼ The declaration of a variable of the structure data type allocates memory.

▼ Accessing a member of a structure is just like accessing any other variable.

▼ Using braces and separate lines makes your initializations easier to read. *Structures can become complicated, but they can be made more readable with whitespace.*

▼ Most C programmers use the arrow notation. *The structure->member notation is more common than the (*structure).member notation.*

▼ Since structures are typically large, using pointers can increase efficiency. *Often a pointer can be manipulated instead of all the bytes in a structure.*

▼ Structure variable names may change, but member names may not.

▼ Passing pointers to structures can lead to greater efficiency. *Only the few bytes of the pointer have to be sent to the function instead of all the bytes of the structure.*

▼ Any data type, including a pointer to a structure, can be a structure member.

▼ The head may change. *In a linked list, if an inserted item becomes the first item, the head of the list changes.*

▼ Don't forget to deallocate memory for deleted structures.

▼ A structure easily enforces the fixed-length requirement of certain files.

▼ Typically, structures written to files make little sense if we look at the file as text.

▲TRAPS: COMMON PROGRAMMING ERRORS

▼ Leaving the semicolon off the end of a structure declaration.

▼ Leaving the `struct` key word out of a structure declaration.

▼ Trying to initialize in a definition.

▼ Forgetting needed parentheses with `sizeof`. *The `sizeof` operator requires parentheses around a data type.*

▼ Trying to directly compare two structures. *Structures must be compared member by member.*

▼ Forgetting to cast the pointer. *The pointer to `void` returned by `malloc()` must be cast as a pointer to the appropriate structure.*

▼ Forgetting the parentheses. *The (*structure).member notation requires the parentheses.*

▼ Not casting the offset. *The offset argument in the `fseek()` function typically must be cast to a `long` integer to work correctly.*

▲YOUR TURN ANSWERS

▼11–1

1. The structure is the overall data type, but it is composed of a number of members of other data types.

2. The definition tells C the makeup of the data type. The declaration sets up variables of that data type and allocates memory.

3. The tag is the name of the data type. It is not necessary if variables are declared in the same statement as the definition. However, without a tag, no variables of that type can be declared later.

4. The `sizeof` operator works with structure data types and variables just as it does with any other data types and variables.

5. Whenever we refer to the structure's tag rather than a structure variable.

6. No. No variables are set up nor is any memory allocated in the definition.

7. By using the member operator between the structure variable name and the member name, we can access the member just like any other variable.

▼11–2

1. Each index immediately follows the corresponding name—*structure[structure index].member[member index]*.

2. As with any other array, the initializations go in braces after the equal sign in the declaration.

3. Only enough bytes to store the pointer—3 in our imaginary C. At declaration, the pointer points nowhere in particular.

4. By assigning it the address of an allocated structure or by allocating memory using `malloc()`.

5. By using either `(*ptr).mem` or `ptr->mem`.

6. In three ways: by passing the individual members to like data types in the function, by passing the entire structure, or by passing a pointer to the structure.

7. Yes, in ANSI C.

▼**11–3**

1. By having, as a part of each structure in the list, a pointer to the next structure in the list.

2. The head is the address of the first structure in the list. The tail is the pointer member of the last structure in the list. It is always `NULL`.

3. By moving through the list until we find the structure in front of which we want to insert. Then we set the pointer in the previous structure to point to the new one, and the pointer in the new one to point to the next.

4. By finding the record we wish to delete, setting the pointer in the previous structure to point to the following structure, and deallocating the space for the deleted structure.

▼**11–4**

1. A structure is a fixed-length object. It can be used to store the record in main memory, and, using `fread()` and `fwrite()`, can be moved to and from files in single blocks.

2. Sequential access starts at the beginning and moves toward the end. Direct access jumps directly to a particular point in the data.

3. The `fseek()` function.

4. Who knows? But probably nothing good. It is up to us to keep within the bounds of the file. C will give us no error message.

EXERCISES

1. Which of the following is invalid and why?

```
a. struct                  b. new_rec
   {  int a, b;               {  int a, b;
      float c;                   float c;
   };                        }struct rec1, rec2;
```

c. ```
struct
{ int first[2];
   char second;
}thing = {{3, 5}, 'S'};
```
d. ```
struct rec
{  int first[2] = {3, 5};
   char second = 'S';
}
```

2. Given this definition, which declarations are invalid and why?

```
struct this
{  float one;
   long two;
};
```

a. `this that, *other;`
b. `struct this those[10];`
c. `struct this it = 25.2, 6;`
d. `struct this them[];`

3. Given this definition and declaration, what notation would you use to access the following:

```
struct rec
{  char name[20];
   float salary;
}item, recs[10], *temp;
```

a. The *name* in the *item* structure.

b. The *salary* in the structure pointed to by *temp*.

c. The address of *salary* in *item*.

d. The fifth character in the *name* of the fourth *recs* structure.

4. Referring to the structure in the previous exercise, which of the following assignments are valid?

a. `recs[4].name[2] = 'd';`

b. `temp.salary = 1234.56;`

c. `item.name = "Schemp";`

d. `item.salary = 1234.56;`

e. `temp->name[4] = 's';`

f. `recs.salary[2] = 1234.56;`

5. Referring to the structure definition in the Exercise 3, declare and initialize (with any values) a two-structure array *arr*.

6. Given the declaration `struct rec record;` (referring to the *rec* structure above), show how you would pass its address to the function *func()* and tell what you would declare in the function to receive it using the identifier *recs*.

7. Referring to the situation above, how would you assign 4256.38 to the salary member of the structure in the function?

8. Change the declaration of the *rec* structure so that you could have a linked list of records. What other variable would you need?

9. Show the statement that would allocate space for a new record in the linked list above.

10. In the situation above, if you were adding this record to the middle of the list, what would you add to the end of the new record, and what would you change in the previous record?

11. How would you change the previous record in the situation above if you were dropping a record in the middle of the list?

12. Show the proper statement to write the following structure on the file pointed to by *file*.

```
struct
{  float yes[14];
   char words[50];
}goods;
```

13. Show the proper statement to move the pointer in the file pointed to by *file* to the beginning of the sixth record if the records are each *length* bytes long.

14. Show the `while` statement that will read 20-byte records from *file* to memory beginning at *loc* until the end of the file is reached.

PROGRAMS

1. Write a program that will accept an employee's name, wage rate, hours, and tax rate from the keyboard and print out the gross and net pay. The employee data, including gross and net pay, should be stored in a structure and the gross and net pay should be figured in a separate function. Overtime (over 40 hours) should be paid at 1.5 times the normal rate.

Suggested Variables

```
employee structure:
  name
  wage_rate
  hours
  tax_rate
  gross_pay
  net_pay
```

Output

```
Enter name, wage rate, hours, tax rate: Jones 8.25 42 .18
Gross pay for Jones is $354.75. Net is $290.90.
```

2. Rewrite the card-dealing program from *Putting It Together* in Chapter 6 to store the deck in a structure array. Each structure variable should have a *value* member for the number on the card and a *suit* member, an array to hold the name of the suit.

Outputs

```
Your hand: King-Hearts Queen-Clubs Ace-Spades Queen-Hearts Ace-Clubs

Your hand: 8-Clubs 9-Hearts 2-Diamonds Ace-Hearts 4-Spades
```

3. Declare a structure tagged *month_data* to store the name of a month and its number of days (don't worry about leap year). Write it in a program that stores data for all the months and allows you to access them by number.

Variables

month_data	Structure tag
name	
days	
months[]	Array of structures
month	Month number input

Outputs

```
Which month? 2
February, or Feb has 28 days.

Which month? 10
October, or Oct has 31 days.
```

4. Rewrite the program above so that you can input the three-character abbreviation for the month and the computer will print out the data for that month. Use the same variables.

Outputs

```
Which month? Feb
Month 2, February, has 28 days.

Which month? Nuv
No such month.

Which month? Nov
Month 11, November, has 30 days.
```

5. Set up a structure tagged *emp_rec* with name and Social Security number. The name member is a structure tagged *name_rec* with members for the first, middle, and last names. Put these in a program that uses a function, *emp_in()*, to input values into the entire structure. Use the `main()` function to print out the information.

Functions, Structures, and Variables

```
main()                              emp_in()
  employee   emp_rec structure         emp    Pointer to emp_rec
    name
    s_s_no
  name       name_rec structure
    first
    middle
    last
```

Output

```
First name: Barnaby
Middle name: Lance
Last name: Gildenstern
Social security number: 123-45-6789
Barnaby L. Gildenstern, 123-45-6789.
```

6. Set up a structure tagged *person_rec* and use an array of three of these to hold data for three persons. Initialize the array with the data as shown below. Your program should accept a portion of a name input at the keyboard, find that person in the array, and print out the person's data as shown.

Data

Name	Age	Height
Bilbao Arlo	28	5.92
Dalrymple Herfy	62	6.02
Greezle Eulalia	35	5.4

Structures and Variables

```
person[]    Array of person_rec structures
  name[]
  age
  height
name_in[]   Name to search for
space       Marks space between first and last names
count       Loop counter
```

Outputs

```
Enter characters for name: Dal
H. Dalrymple is 62 years old and 6.02 feet tall.

Enter characters for name: Zerch
No such name.
```

7. Set up a structure tagged *student_rec* and an array of variables of that type initialized with the data below. Your program should print out a report from that data as shown.

Data

Name	Grade 1	Grade 2	Grade 3
Bilbao Arlo	76	92	88
Dalrymple Herfy	62	79	85
Greezle Eulalia	95	98	93

Structures and Variables

student[]	Array of *student_rec*s
name[]	
grade[]	Three grades
stu	Counter for *student* array
grd	Counter for *grade* array
total	To figure average

Output

Name	1	2	3	Average
Bilbao Arlo	76	92	88	85.33
Dalrymple Herfy	62	79	85	75.33
Greezle Eulalia	95	98	93	95.33

8. Rewrite the previous program so that the main() function, for each student, calls the function *average()*, which returns the average for that student.

9. Rewrite the previous program so that the structure array is initialized in the main() function, but everything else is done in the function *report()*.

10. To keep track of your ever-changing collection of CD albums, you have decided to set up a linked list. Write the program that will add to the list, delete from it, and print it out. Save the program as *ALBUMS* for future use.

Variables, Structures, and Functions

album_rec	Tag for album structure	add()	Add to list
title	Album title	head	
next	Pointer to next record	album	
main()		curr	
head		prev	
option	Add, delete, or print	delete_album()	
print()	Print out list	head	
album		curr	
new_album()	Establish new record	prev	
album		del_title	

11. Write a program to store the entire linked list referred to in the *ALBUMS* program in the previous program in the file *ALBUMS.DAT*.

12. Write a program to take the data from *ALBUMS.DAT* created in the preceding program and reform a linked list.

Chapter 12

THE PREPROCESSOR

AND OTHER FEATURES

PREVIEW

The C language has a number of facilities that make the programming process easier. We have collected some of them together in a self-contained unit here, but everything in this chapter can be addressed at some earlier time. After each module, we have listed a chapter number. That particular module may be addressed concurrently with, or any time after, that chapter. The modules are:

- ▼ The Preprocessor. (Chapter 3)

- ▼ The Preprocessor—File Inclusion. (Chapter 3)

- ▼ The Preprocessor—Macro Replacement. (Chapter 3)

- ▼ The Preprocessor—Conditional Compilation. (Chapter 3)

- ▼ The Preprocessor—Error Messages. (Chapter 3)

- ▼ Renaming Data Types. (Chapter 2)

- ▼ The Enumeration Data Type. (Chapter 4)

- ▼ Conditional Expressions. (Chapter 4)

- ▼ Combining Expressions. (Chapter 5)

- ▼ Nonstructured Program Flow. (Chapter 5)

C and its various implementations have so many features, it would be impossible to cover them all in one book. Even the ANSI standard features are extensive. Here we will show some of the capabilities of the standard language that you may or may not be required to use at present, but that eventually you should know about.

THE PREPROCESSOR

We introduced compiler directives and the preprocessor in Chapter 3. In this section, we will discuss them much more fully. When you compile a program, the first part of the compiler to execute is a segment called the *precompiler* or **preprocessor**. (With some compilers, especially in the UNIX realm, this is actually a separate program, cpp, run first.) This part of the process operates on the source code, making changes in it, but the end result is still source code. The changes, of course, are not made in your source file; they only affect the source code that is passed on to the rest of the compiler.

We will look at a number of preprocessor or compiler **directives**, but no matter what is in the middle, they all start and end in the same way. The beginning of a directive is the # symbol. It must be the first non-whitespace character on the line. (In some non-ANSI compilers, it must be the first character of any kind on the line.) The end of the directive is the first newline character—in other words, the end of the line:

```
#compiler directive
```

An exception to the ending rule is that we are permitted to continue a directive on the next line (after the newline) by putting a backslash (\) at the end of the line:

```
#compiler directive    \
    more directive      \
    more directive      \
    last of directive
```

The preprocessor will strip out the backslash and the newline that follows. The backslash must be the last thing on the line, including comments. Most compilers will choke on this:

```
#compiler directive    \    /* Beginning of directive */
    more directive
```

but will have no problem with this:

```
#compiler directive    /* Beginning of directive */    \
    more directive
```

FILE INCLUSION

We looked at file inclusion and the **#include** directive in Chapter 3. Throughout the text we have used the #include directive to embed the header files provided by C into our source code. This freed us from having to define standard constants (EOF, for example) and having to declare standard functions (printf(), for example).

The form of the #include directive can be either

#include *<fileid>*

as we have used it to this point, or

#include "*fileid*"

The *fileid* is the identification of the file to be placed in the source code. In an MS-DOS system it might be something like *D:\\SYSTEM\\GOODIES.COD* (remember, a double backslash represents a single backslash in a string), which includes not only the filename and extension but also the search path through disks and directories to find the file. For a UNIX system, make the double backslashes (\\) into single slashes (/) and delete the reference to the disk drive (*D:*), */SYSTEM/GOODIES.COD*. Be sure to consult your system's reference manual for the correct format.

This difference in the two forms, < > versus " ", is the way in which the C compiler searches for the file to include. Both forms are system dependent, so you must find out the particulars of your system. The main difference, though, is that the first form, using the < >, searches a specific directory defined by the compiler (or in some cases, the operating system). This is typically the directory in which certain standard files, such as stdio.h, are stored. The other form uses the operating system's default search pattern, typically starting with the directory in which you are currently working. If it doesn't find the file there, it searches as if the *fileid* was enclosed in < >.

What can an include file include? Anything, really—the Declaration of Independence, for example. But to be reasonable, it should make some sense to the C compiler because the compiler will try to compile it. In other words, it should be C source code. The Declaration of Independence made sense to the Founding Fathers, but it won't to the C compiler.

#includes may be nested, typically to about five levels. In other words, we may embed an include file that has an #include directive in it. The second include file will be embedded in position in the first include file, which is embedded in position in the original source code. For example, our include file might contain #include <stdio.h>.

You may have written source code—entire functions, for example—that you want to put in a number of programs. Rather than typing or copying it into each program, you can put it in a file, for example,

▶TRAP◀

Using a single backslash in strings.

HEADS UP!

Include files can contain commonly used program segments.

STRING FUNCTIONS?

Many of the things we have been presenting as string functions are not. They are really macros instead. For example, getchar(), a function that only works with the stdin stream, is usually defined in stdio.h as

```
#define getchar() getc(stdin)
```

The getc() function does the same thing as getchar(), but will work with any stream, including data files (you saw this function in Chapter 9), so rather than defining a new function for getchar(), most Cs just use a getc() that specifically works with stdin.

MYSTUFF.INC in an *INCLUDE* directory, and include it at the appropriate place in each program with the directive

```
#include "\\INCLUDE\\MYSTUFF.INC"
```

HEADS UP!

Thoroughly debug code before putting it in an #include file.

Code should be thoroughly tested and debugged before being put in an include file. Remember, the include file is not part of the source code that is visible to us, only to the compiler. The inclusion is performed by the preprocessor and used only during the compile process. To fix problems in this section of code, you would have to go back to the include file itself. If you change the include file and then recompile your program, it will compile using the new code in the include file.

MACRO REPLACEMENT

We also looked at the #define directive in Chapter 3, but only briefly and only to establish defined constants. Here we will examine its many capabilities. Basically, the **#define** directive tells the preprocessor to replace one set of characters with another. We refer to this replacement as a **macro**. The macro is established in a #define directive:

```
#define macro_name replacement
```

Whitespace is used to divide the keyword from the *macro_name*, and that from the *replacement*.

HEADS UP!

Defined constants in quoted strings will not be replaced.

The macro is used by putting the *macro_name* in some subsequent spot in the program. Almost any spot will do, except that the *macro_name* in a quoted string value or a comment will not be replaced. In Chapter 3, we set up the defined constant *PI*,

```
#define PI 3.14
```

If the statement

```
printf("Area (PI * r * r) = %f\n", PI * r * r);    /* PI defined earlier */
```

appeared later in the program, it would be compiled as

```
printf("Area (PI * r * r) = %f\n", 3.14 * r * r);  /* PI defined earlier */
```

The *replacement* need not be just a single word; it can be anything after the whitespace following the *macro_name*. For example,

```
#define PI 3.14              /* See Nuts 'n Bolts about */
#define AREA PI * r * r              /* Rescanning Macros */

a = AREA;
```

At compile time, the statement would become

```
a = 3.14 * r * r;
```

Remember also that C concatenates quoted strings that are separated only by whitespace. The code

```
"this " "and " "that."
```

would be compiled as

```
"this and that."
```

By using that feature, we can replace strings using macros. For example,

```
#define COMPANY "Ajax Corp"

printf("The earnings for " COMPANY " are %f.\n", earnings);
```

would compile the statement as

```
printf("The earnings for Ajax Corp are %f.\n", earnings);
```

Parameterized Macros

We can define macros with parameters in them that will take on the values of similar parameters in the code when the replacement is made. **Parameterized macros** have one or more parameters in parentheses immediately following the *macro_name*:

```
#define macro_name(parameter_list) replacement
```

RESCANNING MACROS

When a macro is replaced, the compiler rescans the replacement text to see if there are any more macros. If there are, it replaces them and rescans again. For example, we might have these definitions at the beginning of our program:

```
#define FOUR 2 * TWO
#define TWO 2
```

At first glance, it would appear that the TWO in the first line would not be replaced, because TWO was defined after FOUR. This is actually true of the text in the #define directive. If we put the macro FOUR in a statement later on, however, such as

```
printf("%i\n", FOUR);
```

the preprocessor will first translate it to

```
printf("%i\n", 2 * TWO);
```

and then to

```
printf("%i\n", 2 * 2);
```

This is useful when using a number of macros from various sources—different include files, perhaps—and the order of the #defines is not evident.

The *parameter_list* is any number of identifiers separated by commas. The open parenthesis must immediately follow the *macro_name*, with no space in between. The *replacement* should reference those parameters in their desired positions within the *replacement*. For example, given the following:

```
#define area(r) PI * r * r
```

```
surface = area(radius);
```

the macro would have substitute radius for r and the statement would be compiled as:

```
surface = PI * radius * radius;
```

When using macros, we must be sure we understand the order in which things are done. The substitution is made before the program is run. If our statement was:

```
surface = area(radius + 3);
```

we would get some surprising results because, after translation, our statement would be:

```
surface = PI * radius + 3 * radius + 3
```

Because of operator precedence, the order of evaluation would be

```
(PI * radius) + (3 * radius) + 3
```

instead of

```
PI * (radius + 3) * (radius + 3)
```

TRAP

Not putting arguments in parentheses.

A common way to eliminate that problem is to always put the parameters in the macro definition in parentheses, so that whatever is substituted for them will always be in parentheses:

```
#define area(r) (PI * (r) * (r))
```

when substituted in the statement becomes:

```
surface = (PI * (radius + 3) * (radius + 3))
```

HEADS UP!

Be aware of the final substitution when using macros.

Other problems may confront the haphazard macro user. For example, if you set up variable names (other than the macro's parameters), will they conflict with local variables in the code? Will braces, brackets, or other symbols conflict with the control structures in the code? Be sure you are aware of what the final substitution will be with each use of a macro.

One major advantage of macros is that they can usually be considered as typeless. Data of any type can be substituted in the previous macro and it will still work. That carries its own disadvantage. The compiler cannot type-check macro code. In addition, such code usually does not find its way into the elements used by various external debuggers, making debugging difficult.

HEADS UP!

Macro code is typeless, but also cannot be type-checked.

We can use any number of parameters in a macro as long as we separate them with commas:

```
#define avg(x, y, z) (((x) + (y) + (z)) / 3.0) /* Parentheses to be safe */

average = avg(first, second, third);
```

The macro call in the statement would have `first` substituted for `x`, `second` for `y`, and `third` for `z`, making the statement (discarding the unneeded parentheses):

```
average = (first + second + third) / 3.0;
```

Both of our example parameterized macros look very much like functions. In fact, they are often used like functions. Many of the things that we introduced as functions were really macros. The `printf()` "function" is typically a macro defined in `stdio.h` like this:

```
#define printf(  fprintf(stdout
```

The string classification "functions" in `ctype.h` are usually macros. We might define `isupper()` this way:

```
#define isupper(c) ((c) >= 'A' && (c) <= 'Z')
```

By tradition, C programmers use uppercase names for unparameterized macros (symbolic constants, such as *PI*), but for parameterized macros, they use lowercase identifiers to make them look just like functions.

Stringizing and Token Pasting

Let us set up a macro, *print*, that will print the value of a variable of whatever data type, as well as the name of the variable. To use `printf()`, we must have the correct conversion code character or characters, so we will have to call the macro with both the value and the code characters:

```
print(value, code);
```

For example,

```
print(weight, f);
```

If we **#define** our macro like this:

```
#define print(v, c) printf("v: %c\n", v)
```

when the replacement was made, the statement would end up like this:

```
printf("v: %c\n", weight)
```

The *weight* and *f* were never substituted for the *v* and the *c* in the control string because the control string was in quotes and not subject to replacement.

We can solve this problem by stringizing—turning into a quoted string—the replacement, and using C's string concatenation to assemble the control string. The stringizing operator is # and it belongs just before the symbol we want stringized. We will rewrite the **#define**, show the call, and show the replacement in two steps:

```
                         #define print(v, c) printf(#v ": %" #c "\n", v)
Call                     print(weight, f);/* Call */
Replacement, step 1      printf("weight" ": %" "f" "\n", weight);
Replacement, final       printf("weight: %f\n", weight);
```

MACRO OR FUNCTION?

Should you define your routine as a macro or a function? If it's long, it will probably be a function. But if it's short, you may have a choice. Macros have some advantages. When you call a function, passed values must be copied to the function, return addresses kept, execution moved to another part of memory, return values passed back, execution moved again, and so forth. None of this really accomplishes the task of the routine. It is all *overhead*. A macro, on the other hand, is placed directly in line in the code at compile time, so that at run time this overhead is avoided. As a result, macros execute more quickly.

Another advantage of macros is that values passed to functions must be of specific data types. Those used in macros don't; the data type is determined in the substitution or the calculations that follow. For example, with

```
#define square(x) ((x) * (x))
```

the value substituted for *x* could be 4 or 78.2874 or a char or long double variable. The mathematics will accommodate the data type. If *square()* were a function, a value of a specific data type would have to be passed to it. Different data types would require different functions, as exist with the abs(), labs(), and fabs() functions.

A disadvantage of macros is that if they are used repeatedly in a program, they are copied into the code many times. Function code exists only once. Macros, then, could make the executable program longer and take up much more memory.

The **token-pasting** operator, ##, allows us to put together two *tokens* or sets of characters. For example, if in some part of our code we wanted to refer to the variable *factor_min*, or *factor_max*, or *factor_avg*, depending on the situation at that point in the program, we could

```
#define factor(x) factor_ ## x
```

and call it like this:

```
result = 0.2762 * factor(max);
```

The replacement would be:

```
result = 0.2762 * factor_max;
```

Stringizing and token pasting are in the ANSI standard, but non-ANSI Cs may not support these features.

A Macro's Lifetime

Since a macro is replaced before the program is actually compiled, a macro does not have a lifetime during the program execution. It does, however, have an effective range within the source code. Macros are

Macros are essentially global.

effective from the point at which they are defined in the source code to the end of the source code, or to the line where they are undefined using the **#undef** directive:

#undef *macro_name*

For example,

#undef area

Macros may not be redefined unless the redefinition of the macro is the same as the existing definition. This allows, for instance, a macro such as NULL or EOF to be defined in more than one header file without conflict. To change a macro's definition, we would have to #undef (undefine) it and #define it again.

```
#define PI 3.14
. . .                        /* PI is 3.14 in this section of the program */
#undef PI
#define PI 3.14159              /* PI changes to 3.14159 at this point */
```

YOUR TURN 12–1

1. What is the function of the preprocessor and when does this function take place?
2. What is the general form of a preprocessor directive and how does it differ from a statement?
3. What does the #include directive do?
4. How can you see what is inserted by the #include directive?
5. In what parts of a program will a macro replacement be made?
6. Why are parentheses important in parameterized macros?
7. Can we use existing variable names as macro parameters?
8. How can we perform a macro replacement in the middle of a string?
9. How can we put two strings together during a macro replacement?
10. What defines a macro's effective range?

CONDITIONAL COMPILATION

HEADS UP!

Conditional compilation is handy for debugging.

The compiler doesn't necessarily have to consider all the code that you have written. You can direct the preprocessor to skip some. *Skip some?!* After all the time you spent typing the code, why would you want some skipped? There are a number of valid reasons. Often when debugging a program we put in extra statements to see what is happening at a certain point—some printf() functions, perhaps. We do not want these executing after the debugging, so we erase them. And then find a bug or two

more, so we retype them. Instead, let's just leave them in the code, and tell the compiler to ignore them when we are not debugging.

We might be writing a program that will eventually run on more than one type of computer, or be destined for a number of slightly different users. A few lines of code will have to be different for each application. We could leave all the code in the source file, but tell the preprocessor that if this is the Acme Company, compile these lines; if it's Baker, compile those; and so forth.

To accomplish this we use directives that work much like the `if` and `else` statements—the `#if` and `#else` directives. Since the preprocessor does not use the C block structure, we end the `#if` structure with an `#endif`:

```
#if condition

    Compile these statements

#else

    Compile these statements

#endif
```

The `#if`, `#else`, and `#endif` directives work only with the preprocessor, so the *condition* can only react to those things that are active in the preprocessing stage—the results of other preprocessor directives such as `#define`. For example, we may want to declare a variable differently depending on how many records the program might process:

```
#define MAX_RECORDS 45000
. . .
#if MAX_RECORDS <= 32767
    int records;
#else
    long records;
#endif
```

We do not need parentheses around the condition here as we do in the `if` statement. They are, of course, acceptable.

An `#else` branch is not required. We might need an extra variable if we have a lot of records, so we could write

```
#define MAX_RECORDS 45000

. . .
int records;
#if MAX_RECORDS > 32767
    int record_set;
#endif
```

We might use a multibranch structure as we saw in Chapter 4. An #if structure may be nested within another #if structure branch, or, more commonly, we use the multibranch structure in which we combined the if on the same line as the else to make a kind of else if statement. For the preprocessor, we don't have to make up one; there is one—#elif, meaning *else if*. If we had three possibilities for the maximum number of records, we might write

```
#define MAX_RECORDS 45000
. . .
#if MAX_RECORDS <= 127
    char records;
#elif MAX_RECORDS <= 32767
    short records;
#else
    long records;
#endif
```

We can, of course, use as many #elifs as we need.

The keyword **defined** can be used in a *condition* to test to see whether a symbolic constant has been defined. It is always followed by the constant name being tested.

```
if defined name    often written    if defined(name)
```

The value of the constant is immaterial. All that counts is whether it has been used in a #define directive.

For example, let us say that we are testing a program and have inserted debugging statements throughout. Near the beginning of the program we can have the directive

```
#define DEBUG
```

The value of *DEBUG* is nonexistent, empty, but as far as the proprocessor is concerned, it has been defined. Later in the program, we can put

```
#if defined DEBUG
    [debugging statements]
#endif
```

The **#ifdef** directive combines #if and defined(). We could write the first line of the previous segment as

```
#ifdef DEBUG
```

The only advantage of the long form is in cases where you need a *condition* with two or more tests, such as

COMMENT OUT OR CONDITIONALLY COMPILE?

One popular method of not compiling code segments that exist in the source is to comment them out—enclose the code in /* */:

```
/*
    printf("Test value at step 4 is %f\n", test);
    printf("At iteration %i\n", count);
*/
```

This works fine unless one of the statements also has a comment. Most Cs do not support nesting of comments (although some are starting to), so in the following, the second statement would be compiled.

```
/*
    printf("Test value at step 4 is %f\n", test);/* Increase */
    printf("At iteration %i\n", count);
*/
```

Conditional compilation avoids such problems. In addition, using conditional compilation, many sections of code can be turned off or on with a single #define, whereas each commented-out section will have to be dealt with separately.

```
#if defined(DEBUG) and MAX_RECORDS > 500
```

We can test for a constant not having been defined using either the logical not or the **#ifndef** directive.

```
#if !defined(DEBUG)   or   #ifndef DEBUG
```

PREPROCESSOR ERROR MESSAGES

Errors may be introduced just as easily in the preprocessor code as in the rest of the program. You can set up debugging aids in the rest of the program by putting in `printf()` or `puts()` functions at critical points to print out values, error messages, or whatever. You can do a limited amount of that in the preprocessor code with the **#error** directive:

```
#error message
```

where the *message* is any quoted string. The #error directive stops the compile process and prints the *message*. Since the directive stops the compile if it is encountered, it is typically within an #if structure as a "we shouldn't be here" type of thing. For the error directive to be useful, you must anticipate possible errors and place the directives appropriately. For example,

```
#if PARSNIP = 1
    #define TURNIP 3
#elif PARSNIP = 2
    #define TURNIP 0
#else
    #ifndef PARSNIP
        #error "PARSNIP undefined."
    #else
        #error "PARSNIP must be 1 or 2."
    #endif
#endif
```

RENAMING DATA TYPES

Using **typedef** we can change the name of an existing data type to something else,

```
typedef old_name new_name;
```

where the *old_name* is the name of an existing data type—long double, int, a structure tag that we had defined earlier, or even a *new_name* defined earlier. The *new_name* can be used anywhere a data-type name is valid—declaring variables and functions, casts, sizeof operations, and so forth. For example,

```
typedef int INTEGER;
typedef float REAL;
typedef char STRING[MAX_CHRS];
```

establishes three new names for data types, the third being a char array of *MAX_CHRS* length. *MAX_CHRS*, of course, must have been #defined previously. Later in the program we may declare variables using these new names:

```
INTEGER x, y, z = 45;
REAL ity;
STRING names[10];
```

In the third statement, we declared an array of 10 *STRINGS* of *MAX_CHRS* each. The declaration without the typedef would have been

```
char names[10][MAX_CHRS];
```

A convenient way of viewing the **typedef** process is to substitute the declared variable or array for the *new_name* in the **typedef**. In our last example, substituting `names[10]` for STRING in

```
typedef char STRING[MAX_CHRS];
```

yields

```
char names[10][MAX_CHRS];
```

Notice the semicolons after **typedef**. It is a statement and so must have them. Traditionally, new names for data types are in capitals, like defined constants, to make them easily recognizable. A **typedef**ed name must be a complete data type; it cannot be modified by things like **signed** or **unsigned**. Given the previous **typedef**, this is illegal:

```
unsigned INTEGER q;                          /* Illegal */
```

HEADS UP!

Defining data types can enhance portability.

Now that we know how to rename a data type, why do it? One reason is for portability. We know that data types can have different sizes in different implementations of C. Let us say that we are working with a Midget computer as well as a SuperMax. On the Midget, an **int** has 16 bits; a **long**, 32; a **float**, 32; and a **double**, 64. The SuperMax has a 32-bit **int** and a 64-bit **float**. If we want our program to work with 32-bit integers and 64-bit real numbers, no matter which implementation of C we use, we can set up the following near the beginning of our code:

```
#define MACHINE 0          /* 0 = Midget, 1 = SuperMax */

#if MACHINE = 0
   typedef long INTEGER;
   typedef double REAL;
#else
   typedef int INTEGER;
   typedef float REAL;
#endif
. . .
REAL function(INTEGER this, REAL that);
. . .
INTEGER i, j, k;
REAL x, y, z;
```

By changing the **#define** near the beginning of the code, we can compile the program for either computer.

Another reason to use **typedef** is for readability and consistency. Suppose that we are working with various arrays of pointers to a specific structure:

HEADS UP!

typedefs can improve clarity.

```
struct specific
{  char name[40];
   int age;
};
. . .
struct specific *array1[20], *array2[20];/*Similar declarations elsewhere*/
```

We could **typedef** the data type to make the declarations both more clear and more consistent.

```
typedef struct specific *SPEC_PTR[20]
. . .
SPEC_PTR array1, array2;                    /*Similar declarations elsewhere*/
```

Notice that when you **typedef** a **struct** data type as above, you need not use the **struct** key word in future declarations or references.

1. Show the pattern, along with the key words, for a three-branch conditional compilation.
2. How is the key word **defined** used in a conditional compilation?
3. How can we test for a constant definition in a conditional compilation without using the **defined** key word?
4. What preprocessor directive do we use to send an error message?
5. Can we create a new data type using **typedef**?
6. Can we use modifiers such as **long** or **unsigned** with the **typedef** directive?

PUTTING IT TOGETHER (THE PREPROCESSOR AND typedef)

Senator Jack S. Bloehardt, of the Great State of Confusion, would like a quick way of estimating the amount of federal funds needed to cover financial losses from natural disasters—earthquakes in California, volcanic eruptions in the Northwest, blizzards in the Rockies, tornadoes in the Midwest, hurricanes in the East, laryngitis in Washington, D.C.—name your disaster.

TASK

Design a program that will provide the senator and his staff a quick way of estimating federal funds needed.

The calculations are quite complicated and the process is huge, but we will concentrate on the final formula:

$$loss = devastation \times population \times percapita \times case$$

where *loss* is the dollar amount of the losses, *devastation* is the percentage of complete loss in the area, *population* is the number of people in the area adjusted by a factor calculated by dividing the number of people registered in the senator's party by the number registered in the other party, *percapita* is the average loss per person if the devastation was total, and *case* is a factor based on whether the disaster is in the senator's home state (worst case, highest losses) or someone else's state (best case, lowest losses).

IMPLEMENTATION

We want to make the program as flexible as possible, so the important parameters are defined in the beginning of the program. The senator wanted the program to work for estimating the need for funds not only in the senator's home state but also in some other state. Naturally, the calculations would be different. We couldn't remember whether the senator was a Republican or a Democrat, so we allowed for stating a party affiliation prior to compiling.

Only a few of the actual statements are shown in ⇨Program 12–1, but let us examine the preprocessor manipulations.

TEST

Testing the program would, of course, require that the rest of the program be filled in. The tests should include all possible combinations of factors referred to in the preprocessor directives.

⇨**Program 12–1**

```
1 #include <stdio.h>              /* Standard input/output header file */

2 #define DEMOCRAT                     /* If Republican, leave this out */
3 #define PER_CAPITA 25000     /* Loss per person if total devastation */
4 #define DETAIL                     /* Print details, not just result */
5 #define HOMESTATE             /* Change to OTHERSTATE if appropriate */
6 #define BEST_CASE 0.65               /* Least possible amount of loss */
7 #define WORST_CASE 1.35           /* Greatest possible amount of loss */
```
(continued)

```
 8  #ifdef OTHERSTATE
 9    #define STATE "your"
10    #define CASE BEST_CASE                        /* Apply least loss factor */
11  #elif defined HOMESTATE
12    #define STATE "my"
13    #define CASE WORST_CASE                       /* Apply greatest loss factor */
    #else
14    #error "Must define either HOMESTATE or OTHERSTATE."
    #endif

15  #ifdef DEMOCRAT              /* Adjust by percent of population in party */
16    #define population(total, demo, repub) ((total) * (demo) / (repub))
    #else
17    #define population(total, demo, repub) ((total) * (repub) / (demo))
    #endif

18  #if PER_CAPITA > 20000
19    typedef long double LOSSES;        /* Larger data type for high losses */
20    #define CODE "Lf"                      /* Conversion code for data type */
    #else
21    typedef double LOSSES;
22    #define CODE "f"
23  #endif

    void main(void)
24  {  LOSSES loss, devastation;    /* Force final calculation to LOSSES type */
       . . .
25    #ifdef DETAIL
26       printf("Case factor: %g\n", CASE);
27       printf("Adjusted population: %g\n", population(pop, dem, gop));
    #endif
28    loss = devastation * population(pop, dem, gop) * PER_CAPITA * CASE;
29    printf("Funds needed in " STATE " state are %.2" CODE "\n", loss);
    }
```

THE ENUMERATION DATA TYPE

HEADS UP!

C does not enforce **enum**
values.

The enumeration data type (**enum**) sets up a different use of the int data type. The **enum** definition establishes a data type that can hold one integer value from a defined set of possible integer values. A group of constants is established in this definition that are used to represent these values. Variables declared to be of this data type should hold only those values, although C does not actually enforce this. The general form of an **enum** definition is:

enum *tag* {*constant* [= *value*], *constant* [= *value*], . . .};

Line	Explanation
1	Insert source file *stdio.h*.
2–7	Initial defines.
8	*OTHERSTATE* was not defined.
11	*HOMESTATE* was defined in line 5.
12	Define *STATE* as "my".
13	Define *CASE* as *WORST_CASE*, which was defined in line 7 as 1.35.
15	*DEMOCRAT* was defined in line 2.
16	Define *population* macro.
18	*PER_CAPITA*, defined in line 3, is greater than 20000.
19	Set up data type *LOSSES* as `long double`.
20	Define conversion code `Lf` to handle `long doubles`.
24	Declare 2 variables of type *LOSSES* (`long double`) as defined in line 19.
25	*DETAIL* was defined in line 4.
26	Print case factor *CASE*, defined in line 13.
27	Print result of *population* macro, defined in line 16.
28	Calculate *loss* using *population*, defined in line 16, *PER_CAPITA*, line 3, and *CASE*, line 13.

29	Substitute "my" for STATE and "Lf" for CODE, giving:
	`"Funds needed in " "my" " state are %.2" "Lf" "\n"`
	and finally:
	`"Funds needed in my state are %.2Lf\n".`

where the *tag* is the new data type and `constant` is the name of an allowed constant. If a *value* is not stated, the first value is zero and each value is 1 greater than the previous one. For example,

```
enum boolean {false, true, off = 0, on, no = 0, yes};
```

defines the data type *boolean* and its possible values: *false*, *off*, and *no* are zero, and *true*, *on*, and *yes* are 1.

A declaration of variables of an **enum** data type are made following this form:

```
enum tag variable [= value], variable [= value], . . .;
```

For example,

```
enum boolean status, indicator = false;
```

Definitions and declarations can be made in the same statement; for example:

```
enum
    {sun = 1, mon, tue, wed, thu, fri, sat}
    day, first_work_day = mon;
```

TRAP

Defining more than one **enum** value with the same name.

In this example of the combination statement, however, no *tag* is defined. We could not set up another variable, *start_week_end*, using the same defined values, because we cannot define more than one value with the same name:

```
enum {hot, cold} temp;
enum {hot, cold} degrees;        /* This causes an error */
```

will not be accepted by the compiler, but

```
enum warmth {hot, cold} temp;
enum warmth degrees;                        /* No problem */
```

will be accepted.

⇨Program 12–2 sets up enumeration values for the names of the months, and uses them to determine the quarter the month is in.

⇨**Program 12–2**

```
#include <stdio.h>

enum months {JAN = 1, FEB, MAR, APR, MAY, JUN,
             JUL, AUG, SEP, OCT, NOV, DEC};

void main(void)
{   enum months month;

    printf("Enter number for month: ");
    scanf("%i", &month);
    if (month < JAN || month > DEC)   /* C doesn't prevent improper values */
        printf("Invalid Month.\n");
    else
    {   printf("That is in the ");
        if (month <= MAR)
            printf("first");
        else if (month <= JUN)
            printf("second");
        else if (month <= SEP)
            printf("third");
        else
            printf("fourth");
        printf(" quarter of the year.\n");
    }
}
```

enum VALUES

An ANSI C standard compiler actually does not require that an enum variable hold only one of the declared values. The variable may hold any value as long as it is consistent with the `int` data type. Newer offshoots of C, particularly C++, however, do enforce the rule. Since the enum was designed to hold only specified values, and to enhance the portability of the code, most programmers follow the rule.

Outputs

```
Enter number for month: 4
That is in the second quarter of the year.

Enter number for month: 20
Invalid Month.

Enter number for month: 10
That is in the fourth quarter of the year.
```

THE CONDITIONAL EXPRESSION

We have been examining ways of forming two-branch or multibranch structures using sets of statements. C also gives us the **conditional expression**, using the operators ? and :, which allows us to set up a two-branch situation within an expression. The general form of a conditional expression is

condition ? *true_expression* : *false_expression*

C first evaluates the *condition* to true or false. If the condition is true, then C will evaluate the *true_expression*, which becomes the value of the entire conditional expression. Otherwise C will evaluate the *false_expression*. For example, if the value of *x* is 150, then the value of this expression,

```
x > 100 ? x * 1.1 : x * .9
```

is 165, the value of the *true_expression*.

This is not like an `if` statement where the value of the condition allows the program to go to one set of statements or another. A conditional expression, like any other expression, reduces to a single value. As an example, let us say that salespeople are paid their salary plus a commission of 10% on all sales if they sell up to and including $1,000, but 12% on all sales plus a bonus of $100 if they sell over $1,000.

```
pay = salary + (sales > 1000 ? sales *.12 + 100 : sales * .1);
```

If *sales* was $2,000 then the value of the entire conditional expression, everything within the parentheses, would be $340—*sales* * .12 + 100—which would be added to *salary* and the result stored in *pay*.

The parentheses are important in the example above because the precedence of the conditional operator is very low, just above the assignment operators. Its associativity is right to left. Again, refer to Appendix B.

The data type of the entire conditional expression is determined by both of the expressions contained within it, not by which one is eventually chosen. The usual promotion rules apply. If the true expression evaluates to `int` and the false to `float`, then the type of the whole expression is `float` even if the condition is true.

⇨Program 12–3 and ⇨Program 12–4 will produce the same results. Both calculate a salesperson's pay by adding salary to commission. Normal commission is 10% of sales, but if sales is greater than $1,000, the commission is 12% of sales plus a $100 bonus. ⇨Program 12–3 uses a conventional selection structure; ⇨Program 12–4 uses a conditional expression in the final `printf()`.

⇨Program 12–3

```
#include <stdio.h>

void main(void)
{  float comm, salary, sales;

   printf("Input salary and sales> ");
   scanf("%f %f", &salary, &sales);
   if (sales > 1000)
      comm = sales * .12 + 100;
   else
      comm = sales * .1;
   printf("Pay is: %.2f.\n", salary + comm);
}
```

⇨Program 12–4

```
#include <stdio.h>

void main(void)
{  float salary, sales;

   printf("Input salary and sales> ");
   scanf("%f %f", &salary, &sales);
   printf("Pay is: %.2f.\n",
           salary + (sales > 1000 ? sales * .12 + 100 : sales * .1));
}
```

```
Input salary and sales> 200 800
Pay is: 280.00.

Input salary and sales> 200 1500
Pay is: 480.00.
```

COMBINING EXPRESSIONS

We can combine two or more expressions into a single one to make programs more compact or, as we shall see here, to allow us to execute and evaluate a number of expressions where a language element allows only one.

If, for example, we were assigning three different but related variables,

```
length = 14;
width = 6;
height = 2;
```

we could use the **comma operator** to combine the three expressions into one:

```
length = 14, width = 6, height = 2;
```

The comma operator is absolutely last in precedence, has left-to-right associativity, and discards the result of the expression to the left of it. In an expression such as the one above, the value of the entire expression will be the value of the last assignment, 2. Notice that the comma operator does not prevent the execution of all the component expressions. All the assignments in the example above are made, but remember from Chapter 2 that the value of an assignment expression is the value of the assignment. It is these values that are discarded.

If we wanted *height* and *depth* assigned the same value, we could write a single expression as follows:

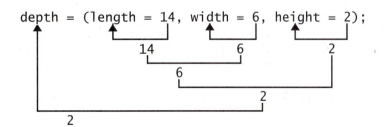

We have used the above expression for illustrative purposes only. Although the expression is correct, we do not advocate such an expression—it's a bit complicated. But let us see how we can apply the comma operator to a sentinel-value-controlled loop. In ⇨Program 12–5, the printf() and scanf() functions have to be repeated because the loop needs something new to test each time through. We can avoid repeating those statements if we include them as expressions in the while loop condition, as shown in ⇨Program 12–6. Both programs produce identical output.

⇨**Program 12–5**

```
#include <stdio.h>

void main(void)
{   float price;
    short quantity;

    printf("Enter 0 0 to quit.\n");
    printf("Enter 'price quantity': ");                              /* Prompt */
    scanf("%f %hi", &price, &quantity);                              /* Input */
    while (price != 0)                                               /* Test */
    {   printf("The total for this item is $%6.2f.\n", price * quantity);
        printf("Enter 'price quantity': ");                          /* Prompt */
        scanf("%f %hi", &price, &quantity);                          /* Input */
    }
    printf("Thank you for your patronage.\n");
}
```

⇨**Program 12–6**

```
#include <stdio.h>

void main(void)
{   float price;
    short quantity;

    printf("Enter 0 0 to quit.\n");
    while (printf("Enter 'price quantity': "),                       /* Prompt */
           scanf("%f %hi", &price, &quantity),                       /* Input */
           price != 0)                                               /* Test */
    {   printf("The total for this item is $%6.2f.\n", price * quantity);
    }
    printf("Thank you for your patronage.\n");
}
```

```
Enter 0 0 to quit.
Enter 'price quantity': 6.29 5
The total for this item is $ 31.45.
Enter 'price quantity': 0 0
Thank you for your patronage.
```

The prompt, input, and test expressions are all contained within the parentheses following `while`. Each time the program gets to the `while` statement, whether from above or being sent back from the end of the loop, the condition expression, with all its component parts, is executed. Here, the `printf()` is executed first and, since it is followed by a comma, its return value (24 because it printed 24 characters) is discarded. Then the `scanf()` is executed, assigning the values to *price* and *quantity*. It is followed by a comma, so its return value, 2, is also discarded. Finally, the test expression is evaluated. It will be either 0 or 1 (false or true) depending on the value of *price* just assigned. That value is not discarded, and becomes the value of the entire expression within the `while` parentheses. In other words, it is that last value that determines whether to stay in the loop or exit it.

This use of the comma operator is not universally accepted in structured environments because of its propensity toward abuse. Can you imagine a `while` condition with 47 statements separated by commas? If you use it, *use it carefully*. Do not make it too long (three expressions is almost too long), and use it only to avoid writing a statement twice in a loop situation.

HEADS UP!

Use the comma operator sparingly, if at all.

YOUR TURN 12–3

1. Why do we use an enumeration data type?
2. Does C check to see that values of `enum` variables are in the list of declared constants?
3. Can a conditional expression alone be a statement?
4. What determines the data type of a conditional expression?
5. What does the comma operator do with the value of the expression immediately preceding it?

NONSTRUCTURED PROGRAM FLOW

The C language offers the programmer a number of ways to approach programming tasks. C is designed to be an all-purpose language and therefore is applicable to the programming style of almost anyone. Structured programming is a style that has been adopted by a number of programmers, but it is neither universally accepted nor universally followed. C makes allowances for this by permitting program flow control that does

not demand structure. The following concepts are not strictly part of structured programming, but are part of the language. Be aware, however, that none of these concepts is absolutely necessary to C programming. There are structured solutions that will replace all of them.

Labels

A **label** identifies a specific place in a program. The identifier is a set of characters following the same naming rules as variables. In fact, label names may even duplicate variable names without interference, but it is considered bad form to have the same name for both a label and a variable. The following are legal label names:

```
Here            NewProcedure
instance1       analysis_section
```

The label should always be the first thing on a line and is followed by a colon. For example:

```
    printf("Preliminary analysis completed.\n");
FinalAnalysis:                              /* Entry point for final analysis */
    Result += SecondSample;
    Adjust = Result / (1 - FudgeFactor);
```

or

```
    x = y * y * 4.7;
action: q = x + 9;
    printf("Percentage: %5.2%%\n", q / 100);
```

Unconditional Transfers

The **goto** statement causes a computer to transfer execution of the program to some specific location, marked by a label. Presumably, this spot in the program is someplace other than the next one in line. In other words, using **goto** you can jump around from place to place in a program. This kind of jumping about makes structured programmers shudder because it allows you to jump out of the middle of one section into the middle of another, severely affecting the program's structure. You will *not* find **goto** statements in structured programs, but they are part of the language, so we will address them here:

```
goto label;
```

When a **goto** statement is encountered in a program, the next statement to execute will be the one immediately following the *label*. The following program segment shows **goto**s in use:

```
{
        . . .
    if (total == 0)
    {   printf("Error, no total.\n");
        goto end;
    }
    if (total < 0)
    {   printf("Error, negative total.\n");
        goto end;
    }
        . . .
end:
    printf("The program has been terminated because of this error\n");
}
```

When the *label* is used as a reference in the goto statement (as opposed to the label marking a location in the program), there is no colon following the label. The semicolon, of course, denotes the end of the statement.

The goto statement must have a place to go to; in fact, the label has to be in the same function as the goto statement.

Trying to goto a place in another function.

Jumping to the End of a Loop

There are two C statements that will disrupt the normal flow of a loop. *Disrupt* is a significant word here because the normal structure of the loop is not maintained. Neither of these statements would be found in a strictly structured program, but, sparingly used and well commented, they are often accepted as part of a well-formed C program.

The **break** statement was introduced in Chapter 4. It causes execution to jump beyond the end of a switch structure. In this instance, it is an indispensable part of the structured C language. But the break statement may also be used in loops—either while, do, or for—for exactly the same purpose. The program segment below would never execute statements 3 or 4; nor would it go through the loop a second time no matter what the value of *x* was:

```
while (x > 9)
{   statement 1;
    statement 2;
    break;
    statement 3;
    statement 4;
}
```

It would be reasonable to ask, "Why even write the program with the **break** and statements 3 and 4 in it?" You probably wouldn't. However, the break statement can be used rather productively in an if statement within a loop, as shown in ⇨Program 12–7. Remember, the break only jumps out of loops and switches, not ifs, so when the if is within a loop, the break will jump beyond the end of the loop.

⇨**Program 12–7**

```c
#include <stdio.h>

void main(void)
{   float price;
    float total = 0;
    short quantity;

    printf("Enter 0 0 to quit.\n");
    while (1)                          /* Always true, loop exit at break below */
    {   printf("Enter 'price quantity': ");
        scanf("%f %hi", &price, &quantity);
        if (price == 0) break;                  /* Exit point for the loop */
        printf("The total for this item is $%6.2f.\n", price * quantity);
        total += price * quantity;
    }
    printf("Your total is $%6.2f.\n", total);
}
```

Output

```
Enter 0 0 to quit.
Enter 'price,quantity': 6.35 8
The total for this item is $ 50.80.
Enter 'price,quantity': 2.50 10
The total for this item is $ 25.00.
Enter 'price,quantity': 0 0
Your total is $ 75.80.
```

⇨Program 12–7 is a nonstructured version of the sentinel-value controlled loop in ⇨Program 5–5 from Chapter 5. The statements used to input the *price* and *quantity* did not have to be repeated, but neither the exit point of the loop nor the conditions for the loop are at the beginning or end of the loop. Instead, the loop conditions are stated in the if and the loop is made to continue by setting the while condition to 1, which is always true. When a price of 0 is input, the if condition is true and execution jumps to the statement following the closing brace.

If the while statement had a condition that might be false, such as while (quantity > 0), the loop would have two possible exit points, the while statement and the break statement. Remember that in Chapter 1, we stated that in structured programming, any structure should have only one entry point and one exit point.

The **continue** statement is similar to **break** except that **continue** does not work with **switch** and it jumps to the end of the loop, not beyond it. In other words, the loop will continue given that the condition is still true:

```
while (x > 9)
{   statement 1;
    statement 2;
    continue;
    statement 3;
    statement 4;
}
```

This will execute differently from the last example with the **break** statement. Statements 3 and 4 will still be skipped, but **continue** will send the execution to the end of the loop, from which point it will go back to the test in **while** and perhaps back through the loop again.

Remember that in a **for** loop, the counting operation is at the end of the loop. The **continue**, then, would send execution to the counting operation and then back to the test at the top of the loop.

In ⇨Program 12–8 we have modified the ⇨Program 12–7 to warn the user if the total is getting too high.

⇨**Program 12–8**

```
    #include <stdio.h>

    void main(void)
    {   float price;
        float total = 0;
        short quantity;

        printf("Enter 0 0 to quit.\n");
1       while (1)                                   /* Loop exit at break below */
        {   printf("Enter 'price quantity': ");
2           scanf("%f %hi", &price, &quantity);
3           if (price == 0) break;                  /* Exit point for the loop */
4           printf("The total for this item is $%6.2f.\n", price * quantity);
5           total += price * quantity;
6           if (total < 100) continue;              /* Goes to end of loop */
7           printf("Your total is getting high.\n");
            printf("It now stands at $%.2f.\n", total);
8       }
9       printf("Your total is $%6.2f.\n", total);
    }
```

EXECUTION CHART

Line	Explanation	price	quantity	total
1	Sets up infinite loop. The value 1 is always true.	?	?	0
2	Input *price* and *quantity*.	14.25	6	0
3	See if *price* is sentinel value. It isn't.	14.25	6	0
4	Display total for the item.	14.25	6	0
5	Accumulate item total in *total*.	14.25	6	85.50
6	The *total* is less than 100, so jump to end of loop at 8.	14.25	6	85.50
8	Go back to `while` at 1.	14.25	6	85.50
1	Still true, of course.	14.25	6	85.50
2	Input *price* and *quantity*.	9.98	3	85.50
3	See if *price* is sentinel value. It isn't.	9.98	3	85.50
4	Display total for the item.	9.98	3	85.50
5	Accumulate item total in *total*.	9.98	3	115.44
6	The *total* is not less than 100. Don't `continue`.	9.98	3	115.44
7	Display the warning message.	9.98	3	115.44
8	Go back to `while` at 1.	9.98	3	115.44
1	Still true, of course.	9.98	3	115.44
2	Input *price* and *quantity*.	0	0	115.44
3	See if *price* is sentinel value. It is, so `break` to beyond loop at 9.	0	0	115.44
9	Display *total* and quit.	0	0	115.44

Output

```
Enter 0 0 to quit.
Enter 'price,quantity': 14.25 6
The total for this item is $ 85.50.
Enter 'price,quantity': 9.98 3
The total for this item is $ 29.94.
Your total is getting high.
It now stands at $115.44.
Enter 'price,quantity': 0 0
Your total is $115.44.
```

YOUR TURN 12–4

1. How do `goto` and labels work together?

2. Why is `goto` not considered entirely proper in a structured program?

3. If a `break` statement is executed from within a loop, where does execution go?

4. If a `continue` statement is executed from within a loop, where does execution go?

5. Why are `break` and `continue` not considered entirely proper in a structured program?

UNIONS

You cannot put two things in the same place at the same time! True, but you can put one thing in that place, and call it by two different names. This is the principal behind **unions**—using different identifiers to access the data in one set of memory locations. The definition of a union looks exactly like the definition of a structure, except for the key word **union** instead of `struct`. The result of the definition, however, is significantly different. A structure defines an aggregate data type, and states the accessible member variables for it. The union defines a data type, but it is one that accommodates a number of variable names of various data types accessing the same space in memory.

For example, let us say that we sell two different types of products; one in bulk (by the pound or fraction thereof), and one packaged (by the package). The units of the bulk product we would want to keep in a `float` variable, packaged units in an `int`. To conserve memory space, we could store either of them at a single memory address by defining a `union` data type like this:

```
union units
{  float pounds;                      /* For bulk products */
   int packs;                         /* For packaged products */
};
```

We could declare a variable (or variables) of that type by putting the name after the definition, or in a separate declaration as in ⇨Program 12–9. C will allocate enough space to accommodate the largest data type in the union, in this case the `float`.

We refer to members of the union just as we refer to members of a structure—with the member operator (`.`). It is important that we use the member of the union with the data type that matches the data stored in the union. In ⇨Program 12–9, `item.pounds` is of data type `float` and `item.packs` is of data type `int`.

```
#include <stdio.h>

union units                                  /* Define the union type */
{  float pounds;                                  /* For bulk products */
   int packs;                                 /* For packaged products */
};

void main(void)
{  union units item;                       /* Declare the union variable */
   char bulk[10];

   printf("Bulk Product (y/n)? ");
   if (*gets(bulk) == 'y')               /* First character of input string */
   {  printf("Pounds? ");
      scanf("%f", &item.pounds);
   }
   else
   {  printf("Packages? ");
      scanf("%i", &item.packs);
   }
   printf("Pounds: %f, Packages: %i\n", item.pounds, item.packs);
}
```

Output

```
Bulk Product (y/n)? y
Pounds? 12.34
Pounds: 12.340000, Packages: 28836
```

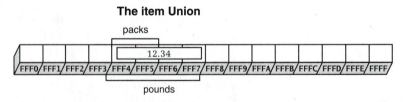

The item Union

The last line of the output bears some examination. The `printf()` function is syntactically correct, and therefore runs without complaint from the compiler. But the output, at least the packages part, is nonsense! We stored 12.34 as a `float` value (4 bytes in this C) in the *item* union. The second part of the `printf()` asked C to get a 2-byte `int` from that

▶TRAP◀

Accessing a union member using the wrong data type.

space. It did, making no sense, of course. You can see that keeping track of the data types currently stored in unions is up to us. C will not do it.

Unions are often used in conjunction with structures. We might have a union of structures, or a union might be part of a structure. Let us expand our previous example to include more information about the product. If it is bulk, we want to know the product ID (a six-digit code), its form (liquid, solid, powder, and so forth), its density (pounds per cubic foot), and the number of pounds. For packaged products we want to know the brand name, type of package (box, blister, bag, and so forth), the package weight (in pounds), and the number of packages. We can declare structures for each of the types of product.

To access one member of the union, we use the *union.member* notation. To access a member of a structure that is a member of a union, we will extend the member notation one more level—*union.structure.member*—or, in ⇨Program 12–10, item.bulk.pounds.

⇨**Program 12–10**

```
#include <stdio.h>
#include <ctype.h>

struct bulk_prods
{   char id[7];
    char form[10];
    float density;
    float pounds;
};

struct packaged
{   char brand[20];
    char pack_type[10];
    float weight;
    int packs;
};

union units                                /* Define union type */
{   struct bulk_prods bulk;            /* Define structure members */
    struct packaged pack;
};

void main(void)
{   char type;
    union units item;                      /* Declare union variable */
```

(continued)

```
        printf("Is this a [b]ulk or [p]ackaged item? ");
        type = toupper(getchar());
        while (getchar() != '\n');                          /*Flush input stream */
        if (type == 'B')                                    /* Use bulk member */
        {   printf("Enter id> ");
            gets(item.bulk.id);
            printf("Enter form> ");
            gets(item.bulk.form);
            printf("Enter density> ");
            scanf("%f", &item.bulk.density);
            printf("Enter weight> ");
            scanf("%f", &item.bulk.pounds);
            printf("You have entered %s, a %s, weighing %g pounds\n",
                    item.bulk.id, item.bulk.form, item.bulk.pounds);
            printf("at a density of %g pounds per cubic foot\n",
                    item.bulk.density);
            printf("giving a volume of %g cubic feet.\n",
                    item.bulk.pounds / item.bulk.density);
        }
        else                                                /* Use pack member */
        {   printf("Enter brand> ");
            gets(item.pack.brand);
            printf("Enter package type> ");
            gets(item.pack.pack_type);
            printf("Enter weight of each package> ");
            scanf("%f", &item.pack.weight);
            printf("Enter number of packages> ");
            scanf("%i", &item.pack.packs);
            printf("You have entered %i %s packages of %s\n",
                    item.pack.packs, item.pack.pack_type, item.pack.brand);
            printf("for a total weight of %g pounds.\n",
                    item.pack.packs * item.pack.weight);
        }
    }
```

Outputs

```
Is this a [b]ulk or [p]ackaged item? b
Enter id> C1684f
Enter form> powder
Enter density> 45.3
Enter weight> 255.8
You have entered C1684f, a powder, weighing 255.8 pounds
at a density of 45.3 pounds per cubic foot
giving a volume of 5.6468 cubic feet.
```

(continued)

```
Is this a [b]ulk or [p]ackaged item? p
Enter brand> Acme
Enter package type> blister
Enter weight of each package> .88
Enter number of packages> 25
You have entered 25 blister packages of Acme
for a total weight of 22 pounds.
```

YOUR TURN 12–5

1. How is a union similar to a structure?

2. How is a union different from a structure?

SUMMARY

▲KEY TERMS (in order of appearance)

Preprocessor	#elif
Directive	defined
#include	#ifdef
#define	#ifndef
Macro	#error
Parameterized macro	typedef
Stringizing	enum
Token-pasting	Conditional expression
#undef	Comma operator
#if	Label
#else	Union
#endif	union

▲NEW STATEMENTS (in order of appearance)

```
goto label;
break;
continue;
```

▲CONCEPT REVIEW

▼ The precompiler or **preprocessor** segment of the compiler makes changes in the source code.

▼ Preprocessor **directives** start with a # symbol and end at the end of a line (or set of lines if each is continued with a backslash).

▼ The `#include` directive temporarily inserts a file of source code lines at that point in the source code.

▼ The `#define` directive tells the preprocessor to replace one set of characters with another. The replacement is called a **macro**. The replacement can be any set of characters—single words, quoted string, formulas, or whatever. Quoted strings are often used to concatenate a set of characters into another quoted string.

▼ We can also use **parameterized macros**—sets of characters, typically expressions, into which other parameters will be substituted at run time. These macros can act just like functions. In fact, many of those things that were previously presented as functions are actually macros.

▼ In macro replacement, the **stringizing** operator, `#`, turns the replacement value into a quoted string, typically so that it can be concatenated into another quoted string. The **token-pasting** operator, `##`, tells the preprocessor to attach the sets of characters on each side of the operator directly together. This is typically used to create a single word, such as a variable name, out of a combination of tokens.

▼ Macros exist from the point in the source code in which they are defined to the end of the code, or until they are `#undef`ined. A macro must be undefined before it can be defined again unless the new definition is exactly the same as the old.

▼ Not all of the source code need be compiled. We often write statements in our programs that we only use for special purposes such as debugging or compiling for different implementations. Using the `#if`, `#elif`, `#else`, and `#endif` directives, we can test for certain conditions, and only those statements in the indicated branches will be compiled.

▼ The condition often includes a test to see whether a constant has been defined. For this purpose, we can use the key word `defined` after the `#if`, or the key word `#ifdef`. To test if a constant has not been defined, we can use the key word `#ifndef`.

▼ We can direct the preprocessor to stop the compile process and print an error message by directing the process to a branch with an `#error` directive.

▼ Using the `typedef` statement, we can change the name of an existing data type to a name of our own choosing. This is often done to make a program listing clearer, to enhance portability, or to simplify the description of complex data types.

▼ The `enum` key word establishes a data type that can hold any one of a number of predefined integer values.

▼ A **conditional expression** evaluates to the value of one of two expressions depending on whether its test is true or false. The condition is followed by a **?** followed by the true expression, a **:**, and the false expression.

▼ Expressions can be combined using the **comma operator**, which discards the value of the previous expression and goes on to the next.

▼ A number of statements in C allow program flow that does not strictly follow the rules of structure, but, given the proper situation, can be handy in programming.

▼ The **goto** statement directs the computer to jump the processing to a place in the program identified by a **label**.

▼ Two unstructured but valid statements can be used with loops. The **break** statement sends execution beyond the end of the loop; and the **continue** statement sends execution to the end of the loop but keeps the execution within the loop.

▼ A **union** allows a single place in memory to be accessed by different identifiers with different data types. It is defined and declared using the **union** key word.

▲ HEADS UP: POINTS OF SPECIAL INTEREST

▼ The preprocessor affects source code.

▼ Include files can contain commonly used program segments.

▼ Thoroughly debug code before putting it in an **#include** file.

▼ Defined constants in quoted strings will not be replaced.

▼ Be aware of the final substitution when using macros.

▼ Macro code is typeless, but also cannot be type-checked.

▼ Macros are essentially global.

▼ Conditional compilation is handy for debugging.

▼ Conditional compilation is handy for development for different platforms.

▼ **#error** directives stop the compiling process.

▼ Defining data types can enhance portability.

▼ **typedef**s can improve clarity.

▼ C does not enforce **enum** values.

▼ Use the comma operator sparingly, if at all.

▼ C will allow breaking the rules of structure in many cases.

▼ Use **goto** with care, if at all.

▼ **break** does not jump out of **if** structures.

▼ **continue** jumps to the end of a loop; **break** jumps beyond it.

▲TRAPS: COMMON PROGRAMMING ERRORS

▼ Putting a comment before a directive.

▼ Putting comments after the backslash. *A comment after the backslash line-continuation character in a* #define *will probably cause the compiler to lose track of the entire directive.*

▼ Using a single backslash in strings. *Since backslash begins special characters, we must use two to indicate a backslash.*

▼ Not putting arguments in parentheses. *In parameterized macros, single parameters may be replaced by expressions, so parentheses must be used in the macro to ensure that the resulting expression executes in the desired order.*

▼ Using something other than preprocessor elements with #if. *The* condition *can only react to those things that are active in the preprocessing stage.*

▼ Defining more than one **enum** value with the same name.

▼ Trying to **goto** a place in another function.

▼ Accessing a union member using the wrong data type.

▲YOUR TURN ANSWERS

▼12–1

1. The preprocessor makes modifications in source code, in response to directives, just prior to the actual compilation of the program.

2. A preprocessor directive begins with any amount of whitespace, a # and the directive key word, and the arguments for the directive. It ends at the end of the physical line or can be continued to the next (and the next) physical line by ending the current physical line with a backslash.

3. The #include directive inserts a file of source code into the program just prior to compilation.

4. You can't in your program. You must access the included file with a text editor.

5. After the directive, anyplace but inside quotes.

6. To isolate the replacement expressions when the substitution is actually performed.

7. No. After the replacement, the names will conflict, causing the compiler problems.

8. We can't.

9. With stringizing and C's normal string concatenation.

10. Its effective range begins where it is defined and ends at the end of the program or at teh line where it is specifically undefined.

▼12–2

1. ```
   #if . . .
       . . .
   #elif . . .
       . . .
   #else
       . . .
   #endif
   ```

2. It tests to see whether a symbolic constant has been set in a `#define` directive.

3. Using `#ifdef` or `#ifndef`.

4. The `#error` directive.

5. No. We can only rename an existing one.

6. No. The data type must be fully defined in the `typedef` statement, including any modifiers.

▼12–3

1. When we want to use a variable that should take on only certain values, such as true or false; red, green, blue, and purple; off or on; and so forth.

2. C does not check.

3. It could, but since the conditional expression evaluates, reduces to a single value, presumably something should be done with that value, such as assigning it to a variable, sending it to a function, and so forth.

4. It is determined by the highest data type of either component expression, whether that expression was chosen or not.

5. The preceding value is discarded.

▼12–4

1. The `goto` statement sends execution to the location of the label in the program.

2. It allows the programmer to go into and out of structures at other than the designated entry and exit points.

3. Beyond the end of a loop.

4. To the end of the loop, but remaining in the loop.

5. For the same reason as the `goto`; it allows the programmer to go into and out of structures at other than the designated entry and exit points.

▼12–5

1. A union is similar to a structure because it defines a data type, in the form of its definition and declaration, and because it uses the member operator to address different members.
   ```

2. A union is different from a structure because it defines a memory space that can be accessed using different names and data types.

EXERCISES

1. What will the output be from the program below?

```
#include <stdio.h>

#define SQUARE(x) ((x) * (x))

int square(int x)
{
    return x * x;
}

void main(void)
{   int a = 2, b = 2;
    printf("SQUARE %i, square %i\n", SQUARE(a++), square(b++));
}
```

2. Why won't this program give the expected results?

```
#include <stdio.h>
#define volume(length, height, width) length * height * width

void main(void)
{   float a = 1, b = 2, c = 3;

    printf("The volume is %f\n", volume(a + 1, b - 1, c - 2));
}
```

3. Show the statements after substitution using the following defined macro:
   ```
   #define cost(a, b) (a + (b) / 6 * 100)
   ```
   a. result = cost(z + 25, 100)
   b. result = cost(f, b * 5)

4. Given the following macro definitions, show the substitutions made for the following macro calls:
   ```
   #define output(a) printf("At " # a ": %s\n", a)
   #define string(a) str ## a
   ```
   a. output(46);
   b. string(ing);

5. Take a previously written program (or several) and rewrite it (them) so that if *DEBUG* is defined, the program prints out the name and value of each variable as soon as it is assigned or reassigned.

6. Define the data type *four_byte* as a 4-byte, unsigned integral data type in your C.

7. Using `typedef`, define a single data type, *info*, that is a structure consisting of an array of three product names, each with an array of sales for the last four quarters. Information for each product should be `typedef`ed as *product*, and sales for each product should be `typedef`ed as *sales*.

8. Show the definition of an enumeration data type tagged *size* with constants *small*, *medium*, and *large* having values of 1, 2, and 3, and *unsized* having the value 9. Declare variables *shirt* and *pants* of this type.

9. Replace the following program segment with one statement using a conditional expression.

```
if (x > 10)
    x = x + y + 150;
else
    x = x + y + 50;
```

10. Replace the following program segment with a `while` statement that performs both the input and the test.

```
printf("Gimme a number ");
scanf("%f", &number);
while (number > 0)
{    [process the number]
    printf("Gimme a number ");
    scanf("%f", &number);
}
```

11. Rewrite ⇨Program 5–1 in Chapter 5, using the `break` and/or `continue` statements.

12. Show the declaration of a union *stuff* that consists of a *rec* structure (below) and an array of 30 characters. Choose your own member names. Define a variable *things* of that type.

```
struct rec
{   char name[20];
    float salary;
};
```

13. Write the statement that assigns "Calabash" to the *name* member of the union in the previous problem.

PROGRAMS

1. Referring to Chapter 3, Program 4 in the "Programs" section, the Ajax Company plans to use the defined constants in other programs as well. Write an include file, *PAYCONST.INC*, that contains those constants, properly commented. Test the include file by using it in the program.

2. Write a macro that will swap the values of two variables of a specified type. The call should be similar to `swap(a, b, float)`. Your macro will have to declare a temporary variable of the appropriate type. Put it in a program that initializes two variables and displays their values before and after the swap.

Output

```
Before: a=5.3. b=3.6.
After:  a=3.6. b=5.3.
```

3. Write a macro, *abso()*, that will return the absolute value of any value given the value and its data type. Test it in a short program.

4. Write a macro the gives the smallest of three values. Test it in a short program.

5. Write a *trace* macro that will allow you to print out the name and the value of a variable or expression during the debugging of your program. It should work with any data type—remember casts! Validate it with the following program.

```
#include <stdio.h>
                                           /* Your macro */

void main(void)
{   int a = 15;
    float b = -3.123;
    trace(a);
    trace(b);
    trace(a + b);
}
```

Output

```
a: 15
b: -3.123
a + b: 11.877
```

6. Depending on certain conditions, a calculation in your program might use one of a number of different variables (*var0a*, *var0b*, *var1a*, and so forth with the number and the last letter varying independently). Write a VAR macro with two parameters that specify the number and letter. Validate it in the following program.

```
#include <stdio.h>
                                            /* Your macro */
void main(void)
{  float x1a = 1.1, x2d = 2.4;
   printf("x1a: %g, x2d: %g\n", VAR(1, a), VAR(2, d));
}
```

Output

```
x1a: 1.1, x2d: 2.4
```

7. Write a macro, *concat(string, number)*, that will concatenate a given number of strings (in a ragged array) at the address of the first string.

8. Set up a partial program that conditionally compiles according to the defined constant *DEBUG*. It should show the following outputs with various values of this constant:

Output

```
DEBUG on.
DEBUG level 1, a=1

DEBUG on.
DEBUG level 2, a=1, b=2

DEBUG on.
DEBUG level>2, a=1, b=2, c=3
```

9. Rewrite Program 2 in the "Programs" section of Chapter 4 so that it uses a conditional expression rather than an `if` statement.

10. Rewrite Program 5 (or 6) in the "Programs" section of Chapter 5 so that the loop is controlled by a set of statements including prompt, input, and test.

11. Rewrite Program 4 in the "Programs" section of Chapter 5 that plays the game Totals, using `break` and/or `continue`.

12. Using `break` and/or `continue`, rewrite Program 5 (or 6) in the "Programs" section of Chapter 5 that translates numeric scores into letter grades.

13. A firm uses two types of containers, boxes and cans. A box's dimensions are its height, width, and length; its volume is the product of the three. A can's dimensions are its diameter and height; its volume is

$$\pi \times radius^2 \times height$$

where the *radius* is half the diameter. Write a program that uses the *in_pack()* function to input the type of container and *out_pack()* to display the type of container and its volume.

To store the container data, set up two structures, one for each type of container. Put these two structures in a *container* union and define a *package* of that type in `main()`. Notice that the *type* is identified first in each structure. It should then be accessible at the beginning of the union, no matter which member you access. Be sure to allocate the same number of characters for *type* in each structure.

Variables and Functions

`box_t`	A structure for box data
`type`	Type of container ("Box")
`height, width, length`	
`can_t`	A structure for can data
`type`	Type of container ("Can")
`diameter, height`	
`container`	A union
`box`	Structure of type *box_t*
`can`	Structure of type *can_t*
`package`	Union of type *container*
`in_pack()`	
`pack`	Pointer to a *container*
`type`	'b' for box or 'c' for can
`out_pack()`	
`pack`	Pointer to a *container*
`volume`	

Output

```
(b)ox or (c)an? c
Diameter height: 2 2
Can: 6.283200 cu.in.
(b)ox or (c)an? b
Height width length: 2 2 2
Box: 8.000000 cu.in.
```

Appendix A

ASCII TABLE

Dec	Hex	Ctrl	Code
0	00	^@	NUL
1	01	^A	SOH
2	02	^B	STX
3	03	^C	ETX
4	04	^D	EOT
5	05	^E	ENQ
6	06	^F	ACK
7	07	^G	BEL
8	08	^H	BS
9	09	^I	HT
10	0A	^J	LF
11	0B	^K	VT
12	0C	^L	FF
13	0D	^M	CR
14	0E	^N	SO
15	0F	^O	SI
16	10	^P	SLE
17	11	^Q	CS1
18	12	^R	DC2
19	13	^S	DC3
20	14	^T	DC4
21	15	^U	NAK
22	16	^V	SYN
23	17	^W	ETB
24	18	^X	CAN
25	19	^Y	EM
26	1A	^Z	SIB
27	1B	^[	ESC
28	1C	^\	FS
29	1D	^]	GS
30	1E	^^	RS
31	1F	^_	US

Dec	Hex	Char
32	20	sp
33	21	!
34	22	"
35	23	#
36	24	$
37	25	%
38	26	&
39	27	'
40	28	(
41	29	)
42	2A	*
43	2B	+
44	2C	,
45	2D	-
46	2E	.
47	2F	/
48	30	0
49	31	1
50	32	2
51	33	3
52	34	4
53	35	5
54	36	6
55	37	7
56	38	8
57	39	9
58	3A	:
59	3B	;
60	3C	<
61	3D	=
62	3E	>
63	3F	?

Dec	Hex	Char
64	40	@
65	41	A
66	42	B
67	43	C
68	44	D
69	45	E
70	46	F
71	47	G
72	48	H
73	49	I
74	4A	J
75	4B	K
76	4C	L
77	4D	M
78	4E	N
79	4F	O
80	50	P
81	51	Q
82	52	R
83	53	S
84	54	T
85	55	U
86	56	V
87	57	W
88	58	X
89	59	Y
90	5A	Z
91	5B	[
92	5C	\
93	5D	]
94	5E	^
95	5F	_

Dec	Hex	Char
96	60	`
97	61	a
98	62	b
99	63	c
100	64	d
101	65	e
102	66	f
103	67	g
104	68	h
105	69	i
106	6A	j
107	6B	k
108	6C	l
109	6D	m
110	6E	n
111	6F	o
112	70	p
113	71	q
114	72	r
115	73	s
116	74	t
117	75	u
118	76	v
119	77	w
120	78	x
121	79	y
122	7A	z
123	7B	{
124	7C		
125	7D	}
126	7E	~
127	7F	DEL

Appendix B

OPERATORS IN PRECEDENCE

Operator	Symbol	Explanation	Example
Expression — Left-to-right associativity			
Parens	( )	To change the order of evaluation.	4 * (6 + 2)
Subscript	[ ]	Subscript of array. Offset in variables from base address.	array[4]
Member	.	Identifies member of structure.	structure.member
Member pointer	–>	Content at location of member of a pointer to a structure.	ptr_to_str->member
Unary — Right-to-left associativity			
Negate	–	Reverse the sign of an expression.	–4
Add	+	Specify a positive value. (This is the default, anyway.)	+4
Increment	++	Add 1 to variable in expression.	++var or var++
Decrement	––	Subtract 1 from variable in expression.	––var or var––
Complement	~	Change 1 bits to 0 and 0 to 1.	~var
Logical NOT	!	Make false expression (0) true (1); make true (nonzero) false (0).	!(time > present)
Dereferencing	*	Contents of location in expression.	*(array + 3)
Address	&	Address of variable.	&var
Size	sizeof	Size of expression or (data type) in bytes	sizeof var
Cast — Right-to-left associativity			
	(*type*)	Convert to data type.	(int)4.2
Multiplicative — Left-to-right associativity			
Multiply	*	Multiply expressions on either side.	6 * 4
Divide	/	Divide expressions on either side.	6 / 4
Remainder	%	Remainder of first divided by second.	6 % 4
Additive — Left-to-right associativity			
Add	+	Add expressions on either side.	6 + 4
Subtract	–	Subtract expressions on either side.	6 – 4
Relational — Left-to-right associativity			
Greater	>	First greater than second?	x + y > z – 19
Less	<	First less than second?	cost < maximum – 100
Greater or equal	>=	First greater than or equal to second?	load >= limit
Less or equal	<=	First less than or equal to second?	TestValue <= Norm
Equality — Left-to-right associativity			
Equal	==	First equals second?	Count + 1 == EndCount
Not equal	!=	First not equal to second?	CheckSum != NewSum
Logical AND — Left-to-right associativity			
	&&	First and second true?	val1 && val2
Logical OR — Left-to-right associativity			
	||	First or second or both true?	val1 || val2
Conditional — Right-to-left associativity			
	? :	If test true, perform first expression, otherwise second.	x > 4 ? p + 9 : p – 14
Assignment — Right-to-left associativity			
Simple	=	Assign value of expression on right to variable on left.	x = y * 22.4
Accumulation	*= /= %= += –=	Perform arithmetic operation on variable to left and value of expression on right. Assign result to variable on left.	a *= x
Sequential Evaluation — Left-to-right associativity			
Comma	,	Dump value of previous operation, perform next.	while(gets(x), *x!=0)

CHARACTER CLASSIFICATIONS

`int isalnum(int character)`   `<ctype.h>`
    Purpose: Test if *character* is alphanumeric: 0–9, A–Z, or a–z.
    Return: True: Nonzero. False: Zero.

`int isalpha(int character)`   `<ctype.h>`
    Purpose: Test if *character* is alphabetic: A–Z or a–z.
    Return: True: Nonzero. False: Zero.

`int iscntrl(int character)`   `<ctype.h>`
    Purpose: Test if *character* is a control code: ASCII 1–31.
    Return: True: Nonzero. False: Zero.

`int isdigit(int character)`   `<ctype.h>`
    Purpose: Test if *character* is a decimal digit: 0–9.
    Return: True: Nonzero. False: Zero.

`int isgraph(int character)`   `<ctype.h>`
    Purpose: Test if *character* is printable, not including space.
    Return: True: Nonzero. False: Zero.

`int islower(int character)`   `<ctype.h>`
    Purpose: Test if *character* is lowercase: a–z.
    Return: True: Nonzero. False: Zero.

`int isprint(int character)`   `<ctype.h>`
    Purpose: Test if *character* is printable, including space.
    Return: True: Nonzero. False: Zero.

`int ispunct(int character)`   `<ctype.h>`
    Purpose: Test if *character* is punctuation.
    Return: True: Nonzero. False: Zero.

`int isspace(int character)`   `<ctype.h>`
    Purpose: Test if *character* is whitespace: space, \f, \n, \r, \t, or \v.
    Return: True: Nonzero. False: Zero.

```
int isupper(int character)                                              <ctype.h>
    Purpose:  Test if character is uppercase: A–Z.
    Return:   True: Nonzero. False: Zero.

int isxdigit(int character)                                             <ctype.h>
    Purpose:  Test if character is a hexadecimal digit: 0–9, A–F.
    Return:   True: Nonzero. False: Zero.
```

CHARACTER CONVERSIONS

```
int tolower(int character)                                              <ctype.h>
    Purpose:  Convert uppercase character to lower.
    Return:   If character uppercase letter, lowercase equivalent, otherwise no change.

int toupper(int character)                                              <ctype.h>
    Purpose:  Convert lowercase character to upper.
    Return:   If character lowercase letter, uppercase equivalent, otherwise no change.
```

DATA CONVERSIONS

```
double atof(char *string)                                               <stdlib.h>
    Purpose:  Convert string to double.
    Return:   Success: Converted number. Error: Meaningless assignment.

int atoi(char *string)                                                  <stdlib.h>
    Purpose:  Convert string to int.
    Return:   Success: Converted number. Error: Meaningless assignment.

long atol(char *string)                                                 <stdlib.h>
    Purpose:  Convert string to long.
    Return:   Success: Converted number. Error: Meaningless assignment.
```

FILES

```
int fclose(FILE *file)                                                  <stdio.h>
    Purpose:  Flush file stream (if open for write) and deallocate file description.
    Return:   Success: Zero. Error: EOF.

int feof(FILE *file)                                                    <stdio.h>
    Purpose:  Determine whether end-of-file indicator for file is set.
    Return:   Nonzero if end-of-file indicator set.

int fflush(FILE *file)                                                  <stdio.h>
    Purpose:  Empty file stream and return data to storage if necessary.
    Return:   Success: Zero. Error: EOF.
```

`char *fgets(char *string, int max, FILE *file)`   <stdio.h>
> **Purpose:** Read a line (up to $max - 1$ characters) from the *file* into the *string*.
> **Return:** Success: *string*. Error: NULL.

`FILE *fopen(char *file_id, char *mode)`   <stdio.h>
> **Purpose:** Open a *file_id* file for *mode*, and establish a description and stream for it.
> **Return:** Success: Pointer to *file* description. Error: NULL.

`int fprintf(FILE *file, char *control_string, arguments)`   <stdio.h>
> **Purpose:** Write on *file* values of arguments in format specified in *control_string*.
> **Return:** Success: number of characters written. Error: negative value.

`int fputs(char *string, FILE *file)`   <stdio.h>
> **Purpose:** Write the *string* onto the *file*.
> **Return:** Success: Nonnegative. Error: EOF.

`size_t fread(void *loc, size_t bytes, size_t items, FILE *file)`   <stdio.h>
> **Purpose:** Read *bytes* * *items* bytes from *file* to *loc*ation.
> **Return:** Success: *items*. Error: Something other than *items*.

`int fscanf(FILE *file, char *control_string, arguments)`   <stdio.h>
> **Purpose:** Assign values from *file* to argument variables according to *control_string*.
> **Return:** Success: number of assignments made. Error: EOF if end of file.

`int fseek(FILE *file, long offset, int origin)`   <stdio.h>
> **Purpose:** Set the *file* pointer at *offset* bytes from *origin*.
> **Return:** Success: Zero. Error: Nonzero.

`long ftell(FILE *file)`   <stdio.h>
> **Purpose:** Obtain current position of *file* pointer.
> **Return:** Success: Bytes from beginning of *file*. Error: –1L.

`size_t fwrite(void *loc, size_t bytes, size_t items, FILE *file)` <stdio.h>
> **Purpose:** Write *bytes* * *items* bytes from *loc*ation to *file*.
> **Return:** Success: *items*. Error: Something other than *items*.

`int getc(FILE *file)`   <stdio.h>
> **Purpose:** Read single character from the *file*.
> **Return:** Success: ASCII (or EBCDIC) value of character read. Error: EOF.

`int putc(int character, FILE *file)`   <stdio.h>
> **Purpose:** Write the *character* on the *file*.
> **Return:** Success: ASCII (or EBCDIC) value of *character* written. Error: EOF.

`int remove(char *filename)`   <stdio.h>
> **Purpose:** Delete the file *filename* from secondary storage.
> **Return:** Success: Zero. Error: Nonzero.

`int rename(char *oldname, char *newname)`   <stdio.h>
> **Purpose:** Change the name of the file *oldname* in secondary storage to *newname*.
> **Return:** Success: Zero. Error: Nonzero.

`void rewind(FILE *file)`   <stdio.h>
> **Purpose:** Return the pointer to the beginning of *file*.
> **Return:** None.

MATH

    int abs(int *expression*)   <stdlib.h>
        Purpose: Obtain absolute value of int *expression*.
        Return: Absolute value of int *expression*.

    double fabs(double *expression*)   <math.h>
        Purpose: Obtain absolute value of double *expression*.
        Return: Absolute value of double *expression*.

    long labs(long *expression*)   <stdlib.h>
        Purpose: Obtain absolute value of long *expression*.
        Return: Absolute value of long *expression*.

    double pow(double *expression*, double *exponent*)   <math.h>
        Purpose: Raise *expression* to the power of *exponent*.
        Return: Result of the exponentiation.

    int rand(void)   <stdlib.h>
        Purpose: Obtain next in a series of random numbers.
        Return: Value between zero and RAND_MAX.

    double sin(double *angle*)   <math.h>
        Purpose: Obtain sine of *angle* stated in radians.
        Return: Sine of *angle*.

    double sqrt(double *expression*)   <math.h>
        Purpose: Obtain the square root of the *expression*.
        Return: Square root of the *expression*.

    void srand(unsigned *seed*)   <stdlib.h>
        Purpose: Set the *seed* for generation of random numbers.
        Return: None.

    time_t time(NULL)   <time.h>
        Purpose: Used as shown to give a different seed for random-number generation.
        Return: Random-number seed.

MEMORY ALLOCATION

    void free(void *address*)   <stdlib.h>
        Purpose: Deallocate a block of memory allocated by malloc(), calloc(), or realloc().
        Return: None.

    void *malloc(size_t *bytes*)   <stdlib.h>
        Purpose: Allocate a block of memory
        Return: Success: Address of allocated block. Error: NULL.

PROGRAM CONTROL

`void exit(int `*`status`*`)`   `<stdlib.h>`
    Purpose: Terminate program in orderly fashion, indicating *status* of termination.
    Return: None.

`void main(int argc, char *argv[])`
    Purpose: Control function of C program. Puts `argc` strings from command line into `*argv[]`.
    Return: None.

STRINGS

`int sprintf(char *`*`string`*`, char *`*`control_string`*`,  arguments)`   `<stdio.h>`
    Purpose: Store at *string* the values of arguments in format specified in *control_string*.
    Return: Success: Number of characters printed. Error: negative value.

`int sscanf(char *`*`string`*`, char *`*`control_string`*`,  arguments)`   `<stdio.h>`
    Purpose: Assign values from *string* to argument variables according to *control_string*.
    Return: Success: Number of assignments made. Error: EOF if end of string.

`char *strcat(char *`*`string`*`, char *`*`add`*`)`   `<string.h>`
    Purpose: Put *add* string at the end of *string*.
    Return: *string*.

`char *strchr(char *`*`reference`*`, int `*`character`*`)`   `<string.h>`
    Purpose: Find the first occurrence of a *character* in a *reference* string.
    Return: Success: Address of the *character* in the *reference* string. Error: NULL.

`int strcmp(char *`*`string1`*`, char *`*`string2`*`)`   `<string.h>`
    Purpose: Compare two strings.
    Return: Positive value if *string1* greater, negative if *string2*, zero if equal.

`char *strcpy(char *`*`destination`*`, char *`*`source`*`)`   `<string.h>`
    Purpose: Copy *source* string to *destination*.
    Return: *destination*.

`size_t strlen(char *`*`string`*`)`   `<string.h>`
    Purpose: Find number of characters at *string*.
    Return: Number of characters at *string*.

`char *strncat(char *`*`string`*`, char *`*`add`*`, size_t `*`max`*`)`   `<string.h>`
    Purpose: Put up to *max* characters of *add* string at the end of *string*.
    Return: *string*.

`int strncmp(char *`*`string1`*`, char *`*`string2`*`, size_t `*`max`*`)`   `<string.h>`
    Purpose: Compare up to *max* characters of two strings.
    Return: Positive value if *string1* greater, negative if *string2*, zero if equal.

```
char *strncpy(char *destination, char *source, size_t max)                    <string.h>
    Purpose: Copy up to max characters of source string to destination.
    Return:   destination.

char *strpbrk(char *reference, char *characters)                              <string.h>
    Purpose: Find first occurrence of any of characters in reference.
    Return:   Success: Address of occurrence. Error: NULL.

char *strrchr(char *reference, int character)                                 <string.h>
    Purpose: Find the last occurrence of a character in a reference string.
    Return:   Success: Address of the character in the reference string. Error: NULL.

char *strstr(char *reference, char *search)                                   <string.h>
    Purpose: Find a search string in a reference string.
    Return:   Success: Address of beginning of search string in reference string. Error: NULL.

char *strtok(char *reference, char *delimiters)                               <string.h>
    Purpose: Extract and mark end of tokens in reference string.
    Return:   Success: Address of beginning of reference string. Error: NULL.
```

TERMINAL INPUT/OUTPUT

```
int printf(char *control_string, arguments)                                   <stdio.h>
    Purpose: Print values of arguments in format specified in control_string.
    Return:   Success: number of characters printed. Error: negative value.

int scanf(char *control_string, arguments)                                    <stdio.h>
    Purpose: Assign values from input stream to argument variables according to control_string.
    Return:   Success: number of assignments made. Error: EOF if end of file.

int getchar(void)                                                             <stdio.h>
    Purpose: Read one character form keyboard.
    Return:   Success: ASCII (or EBCDIC) value of character read. Error: EOF.

char *gets(char *string)                                                      <stdio.h>
    Purpose: Read a line from the the keyboard into the string.
    Return:   Success: string. Error: NULL.

int putchar(int character)                                                    <stdio.h>
    Purpose: Display the character on the screen.
    Return:   Success: ASCII (or EBCDIC) value of character displayed. Error: EOF.

int puts(char *string)                                                        <stdio.h>
    Purpose: Display the string on the screen.
    Return:   Success: Nonnegative. Error: EOF.
```

Appendix D

printf() AND scanf() PARAMETERS

DATA TYPE SPECIFIERS FOR printf()

Specifier	Data Type	Explanation	Sample	Output
c	char	A single character.	"%c",65	A
d	int	PreANSI version of i. Still valid in most ANSI implementations.	"%d",-4725 "%d",4725	-4725 4725
E or e	float or double	Signed E notation With uppercase or lowercase E	"%E",462.58 "%e",462.58	4.625800E+02 4.625800e+02
f	float or double	Standard signed decimal notation with six digits after the decimal point. Negative signs print, positive signs don't.	"%f",462.58 "%f",-1.7225	462.580000 -1.722500
G or g	float or double	Outputs in the numeric format that requires the fewest characters. Trailing zeros or trailing decimal points are not printed.	"%g",1.25 "%G",4.0 "%g",.0000047	1.25 4 4.7e-06
i	int	Signed integer with negative but not positive signs printing.	"%i",-4725 "%i",4725	-4725 4725
n	Pointer to int	Does not print, but adds to character count.	"%n",ptr	
o	unsigned	Prints octal digits.	"%o",327	507 [octal]
p	Pointer	Prints address in hex.	"%p",ptr	D45C
s	String	Prints bytes from address to null.	"%s","Hi Sam"	Hi Sam
u	unsigned	Decimal digits.	"%u",123 "%u",-23456	123 42080 [garbage]
X or x	unsigned	Hex digits with ABCDEF or abcdef.	"%x",735	2df

DATA TYPE SPECIFIERS FOR scanf()

Specifier	Data Type	Explanation	Code	Sample Input	Assignment
c	char	A single character. Whitespace characters (space, tab, or newline) will be assigned, not skipped.	%c	ABC	'A' [65]
d	int	Pre-ANSI version of i. Still valid in most ANSI implementations.	%d	21 pieces	21
e, f, or g	float	Decimal value in either standard or E notation. double requires lf.	%f	···62.15· [· is a space]	62.15
i	int	Integer value in decimal, octal, or hex notation.	%i	21 pieces	21
n	int	Assigns number of characters read so far.	%n	12 34 56	8
o	unsigned	Octal digits.	%o	42	34 [decimal]
p	Pointer	Integer value in decimal, octal, or hex notation.	%p	D45C	D45C
s	String	Assigns characters to first whitespace.	"%s"	Hi Sam	Hi
u	unsigned	Decimal digits.	%u	3740	3740
x	unsigned	Hex digits.	%x	CAB	3243
[ ]	String	Allows specifying of delimiters.	%[^;,]	Smith,John	Smith

INDEX

A

Abacus 3
abs() **210**
Absolute value 210
Access 8
Access, random **10**
Accumulation **158**
Accumulation operator **159**
acos 211
Address, base **420**
Address, memory **10**, 91, 247, 315, **404**
Algorithm **28**
American National Standards Institute (ANSI) **42**
American Standard Code for Information Interchange (ASCII) **20**
Analysis **27**
Analytical Engine 4
And operator **118**
ANSI **42**
ANSI C standard 42, 45, 47, 51, 53, 55, 84, 199, 205, 349, 462, 470, 471
Append 351
Application software **13**
argc **435**
Argument **46**, 84
Argument value 435
Argument vector 435
Arithmetic operation, CPU function **9**
Arithmetic operator **58**
Arithmometer 3
Array **238**
    And pointer 420

Ragged **430**
Rectangular **430**
String 307
Structure 463
ASCII **20**, 22, 48, 53, 292
asin 211
Assembly language **23**
Assignment 45, **62**
Assignment operator 117
Associativity **58**
atan 211
Atanasoff, John 5
Atanasoff-Berry machine 5
atof() **311**
atoi() **311**
atol() **311**

B

Babbage, Charles 3
Base address **420**
Base address offset **421**
Basic 23
Basic Combined Programming Language (BCPL) 42
BCPL 42
Berry, Clifford 6
Binary digit (bit) **21**
Binary file **352**
Binary number system **16**
Binary search **254**
Bit **21**
Block 11, 78, **120**
Body, of loop **162**
Branch **114**
break 130, **533**
Bubble sort **260**, 464

Buffer **349**
Byron, Augusta Ada 4
Byte **22**
Byte access **353**

C

C++ 199
Call **46**, **191**
case **130**
Cast **213**
Cast operator **213**
Central processing unit (CPU) **8**
char 53
Character coding scheme **20**
Character value 48, 54
Close, file 352
Cobol 23
Coding scheme, character **20**
Comma operator **529**
Command-line argument **434**
Comment **44**, 80
Compiler **24**, 44, 81, 508
Computer **2**
Computer generations 6
Concatenate **57**, 511, 514
Condition 114, **117**, 150
Conditional expression **527**
Conditional operator 527
Constant 206, 509
continue **535**
Control function of CPU **9**
Control string **85**, 90
Control structure **112**
    Iteration 112
    Selection 112, **114**
    Sequence 112, **113**

Conversion code 85, **85**, 90
cos 211
cosh 211
Counter, in counter-controlled loop **162**
Counter-controlled loop **162**
Counting **161**
cpp 508
CPU **8**
CPU function
    Arithmetic operation **9**
    Control **9**
    Logical operation **9**
ctype.h 312

D
Data register **12**
Data type **52**
    char **53**
    Declaration **52**
    Definition **52**
    double **55**
    Enumeration 524
    float **55**, 122
    Floating point **55**, 164
    int **54**
    Integral **53**
    long double **55**
    Pointer **315**, 405
    Structure **456**
    void **369**
de Colmar, Thomas 3
Debug 25, 513, 518
Debugability 203
Decimal number system **15**
Declaration **47**
    Array 238
    Constant 81
    Function 81, **192**
    Pointer 317
    String 293
    Structure 457
    Value **52**
    Variable 47, **52**
Decrement operator **165**
default **131**
#define **82**, **510**
defined **518**
Defined constant **82**, 83
Definition 81
    Function 46, **190**
    Structure **456**

Structure member **457**
    Value **52**
    Variable **52**
Delimiter **94**
Dereference **407**
Dereferencing operator **407**
Design **28**
Difference Engine 4
Direct access **487**
Directive **44**, **81**, **508**
Directory 349
Disk 11
Do 151
do **155**
Documentation **79**
DOS 348, 351, 364, 509
double **55**

E
E notation **55**, 87, 164
EBCDIC **20**, 22, 48
Element **238**
#elif **518**
#else **517**
Else 115
else **124**
else if **128**
End, of counter-controlled loop **162**
#endif **517**
End-of-file indicator **367**
ENIAC 6
enum **524**
Enumeration data type 524
EOF 206
Equal operator 117
Equality operator **117**
#error **519**
Executable code **24**
exit() **209**, 352
EXIT_FAILURE 209
EXIT_SUCCESS 209
Exponent (floating-point notation) **55**
Exponentiation 210
Expression **58**, 86
Extended binary-coded-decimal interchange code (EBCDIC) **20**
Extension **348**
External **204**

F
fabs() **210**

Factorial 215
fclose() **352**
feof() **367**
fflush() 351
fgets() **357**
FILE **350**
File **348**
    And structure 484
    Description **350**
    Direct access **487**
    Identifier 348
    Name **348**
    Pointer 350
    Position indicator **350**, 360
    Sequential access **487**
Flag **263**, **301**
float **55**, 122
Floating-point data type **55**, 164
Flush **96**, 298
Folder 349
fopen() **350**
for **162**
Formatted printing 84
fprintf() **353**
fputs() **357**
fread() **369**
free() **439**, 467
fscanf() **355**
fseek() 351, **361**
fsetpos() 351
ftell() **362**
Function **45**, **81**
    And array 247
    Call **191**
    Declaration **192**
    Definition **190**
fwrite() **369**

G
Garbage 52
getc() **357**
getchar() **297**
gets() **299**
Global **204**
goto **532**

H
Hardware **7**, 83
Head **476**
Header file **47**, **81**, **205**
Hex numbers 18
Hexadecimal number system **18**

High-level language **24**
Hollerith, Herman 5

I

IDE **25**
Identifier
    File 348
      Variable 50
IEEE 55
IEEE floating-point notation 55
If 114
`if` **120**
`#if` **517**
`#ifdef` **518**
`#ifndef` **519**
Implementation **28**
`#include` **81**, **509**, 45
Increment operator **165**
Indent 31, 153
Index **238**
Index notation 422
Initialization
    Accumulator **158**
    Array 239
    Counter-controlled loop 162
    Multi-indexed array 267
    String 293
    Structure 458
Initialize **52**
Insert **258**, 475
    Linked list 477
Institute of Electrical and Electronics Engineers (IEEE) 55
Instruction register **12**
`int` 53, **54**
Integer arithmetic 60
Integral data type **53**
Integral number **48**
Integrated development environment (IDE) **25**
Internal **203**
`isalnum()` **313**
`isalpha()` **313**
`iscntrl()` **313**
`isdigit()` **313**
`isgraph()` **313**
`islower()` **314**
`isprint()` **314**
`ispunct()` **314**
`isspace()` **314**
`isupper()` **314**
`isxdigit()` **314**

J

Jacquard, Joseph Marie 3

K

K&R C **42**, 78
Kernighan, Brian W. 42, 78

L

Label **532**
`labs()` **210**
Language
    Assembly **23**
    High-level **24**
    Machine **23**
Library **206**
Lifetime **194**, 204, 515
Line feed 351
Linear search 252
Link **24**
Linked list **476**
Linker 24
Local **194**, 203
Location, memory **10**, 50, 90, 239, **404**
Logarithmic function 210
Logical error 25
Logical operation, CPU function **9**
Logical operator **118**
Logical plan 28
`long` **54**
`long double` **55**
Loop **150**, 533
Lovelace, Countess of 4

M

Machine language **23**
Macintosh 14
Macro **510**
Macro, parameterized **511**
Main memory **10**, 348, 404
`main()` 44
`malloc()` **439**, 466
Mantissa (floating-point notation) **55**
`math.h` 210
Member **456**
Member definition **457**
Member operator **460**
Memory address **10**, 91, 247, 315, **404**

Memory allocation **439**
Memory location **10**, 50, 90, 239, **404**
Mixed arithmetic 61
Mode, file 350
Modifiable lvalue 63
Modular design **25**, 31, 46, 78, 114, 150, 188, 203, 205
Module **25**, 188
Modulo operator 60
MS-DOS 14, 348, 351, 364, 509

N

Name
    File **348**
    Variable **50**
Nest **116**
Nested loop **168**
Newline **46**, 85, 90
Not operator **119**
NULL 213, **299**, 350
Number system
    Binary **16**
    Decimal **15**
    Hexadecimal **18**
Numeric value 48

O

Object code **24**
Offset **421**
Operating system **14**, 83, 348, 404
Operator
    Accumulation **159**
    And **118**
    Arithmetic **58**
    Assignment 117
    Cast **213**
    Comma **529**
    Conditional 527
    Decrement **165**
    Dereferencing **407**
    Equal 117
    Equality **117**
    Increment **165**
    Logical **118**
    Member **460**
    Modulo 60
    Not **119**
    Or **118**
    Relational **117**
    Remainder **60**
Or operator **118**

OS/2 14
OS/400 14
Outline form **30**, 44, 78, 112

P

Parallel array **256**, 271
Parameter declaration **198**
Parameterized macro **511**
Parse **319**
Pascal 23
Pascal, Blaise 3
Pascaline 3
Pass **198**
Pass by reference **410**
Pass by value **410**
Path 349
Physical record 11
Pointer **315**, 404
    Arithmetic **422**
    Data type 405
    Declaration 317
    Notation 421
    To pointer 479
    To structure 466
    To `void` **369**
Pointing **404**
Portability **14**, 54, 439, 521
Positional notation 15, 17
Posttest loop **151**
`pow()` **210**
Precedence **58**
Precision **88**
Precompiler 508
Preprocessor 45, **81**, **508**
Pretest loop **151**
`printf()` 46, 49, **84**, 206, 300
Program **2**
Programmable computer 5
Programming Stages 27
Prompt **92**
Prototype **198**, 205
Pseudocode **30**, **112**
Pseudorandom number 211
Punched card 3, 4, 5
`putc()` **357**
`putchar()` **301**
`puts()` **301**

R

Ragged array **430**
`rand()` **211**
RAND_MAX 212

Random access **10**
Random number 211
Read **8**, 351
Readability 43, 51, 59, 63, **80**, 83,
    133, 153, 203, 521
Real number **48**, 122
Record, physical 11
Rectangular array **430**
Recursion **215**
Register **12**
    Data **12**
    Instruction **12**
Relational operator **117**
Remainder **60**
`remove()` **364**
`rename()` 365
Repeatability 203
Reserved word **51**
Return **193**
`return` **196**
Return character 351
Return value **193**
Reusability 203
`rewind()` 351, **360**
Ritchie, Dennis M. 42, 78
Row-major order 267

S

`scanf()` 90, 207, 295
Scheutz, George and Edward 4
Scope 195
Search, binary **254**
Search, sequential **252**
Secondary storage **11**, 348
Sector 11
Seed **211**
SEEK_CUR **361**
SEEK_END **361**
SEEK_SET **361**
Selection structure 112, **114**
Sentinel value **156**, 530, 534
Sequence structure 112, **113**
Sequential access **487**
Sequential search **252**
`short` **54**
`signed` **53**
`sin` 211
`sinh` 211
Size modifier **87**, 93
`size_t` 302
`sizeof` **459**
Software **7**

Application **13**
    System **13**
Sort **260**, 464, 467
Sorting characters 21
Source code **24**, 45, 81
Special character **48**, 85
`sprintf()` **309**
`sqrt()` **210**
Square root 210
`srand()` **212**
`sscanf()` **310**
Statement **45**
`stderr` **84**
`stdin` **84**, 90
`stdio.h` 45, 47, 81, 205
`stdlib.h` 209
`stdout` **84**, 84
Stepwise refinement **25**
`strcat()` **304**
`strchr()` **320**
`strcmp()` **305**
`strcpy()` **302**
Stream **84**
String 56, 84, 292
String array 307
String, and pointers 427
`string.h` 302
Stringizing **514**
`strlen()` **302**
`strncat()` **305**
`strncmp()` **306**
`strncpy()` **303**
`strpbrk()` **321**
`strrchr()` **321**
`strstr()` **319**
`strtok()` **321**
`struct` **457**
Structure **456**, 539
    And file 484
    Control **112**
    Declaration 457
    Definition **456**
    Initialization 458
    Iteration 112, **150**
    Member **456**
    Member operator **460**
    Pointer to 466
    Selection **112**, **114**
    Sequence 112, **113**
    Tag **456**
Structured programming **112**, 150,
    193, 196, 531

Subdirectory 349
Subscripted variable 238
Swap **261**, 410, 433, 467
`switch` **129**
System software **13**
System, computer 7

T
Tabulating machine 5
Tag **456**, 525
Tail **476**
`tan` 211
`tanh` 211
Task **27**
Termination, program 208
Test **28**
Test plan **28**
Test, in counter-controlled loop **162**
Text file **351**
`time()` **213**
`time.h` 213
Token **321**
Token pasting **515**
`tolower()` **314**
Top-down design **25**, 78, 113, 150, 188
`toupper()` **314**
Transparent 350
Trigonometric function 211
Type specifier **85**
`typedef` **520**

U
`#undef` **516**
Union **537**
`union` **537**
UNIX 14, 348, 351, 364, 508, 509
`unlink()` 364
`unsigned` **53**

V
Value
    Declaration **52**
    Definition **52**
Variable **50**, 62, 83
    Declaration **52**
    Definition **52**
    Identifier 50
    Name **50**
Variable declaration 47
Visibility **195**, 204
VMS 14

`void` **194**, **369**

W
While 151
`while` **153**
Whitespace **43**, 91, 94
Width **88**, 297
Windows 14, 348, 351
Word **22**, 54
Working storage 10
Write **8**, 351

X
XENIX 14

Z
Z3 6
Zuse, Konrad 6

IMPORTANT: PLEASE READ BEFORE OPENING THIS PACKAGE
THIS PACKAGE IS NOT RETURNABLE IF SEAL IS BROKEN.

West Publishing Corporation
620 Opperman Drive
P.O. Box 64779
St. Paul, Minnesota 55164-0779

Source Code Disk for The Art of Programming
LIMITED USE LICENSE